Emotions: A Cultural Studies Reader

Emotions: A Cultural Studies Reader brings together the best examples of recent and cutting-edge work on emotions in cultural studies and related disciplines. The book differentiates between theoretical traditions and ways of understanding emotion in relation to culture, subjectivity and power, thus mapping a new academic territory and providing a succinct overview of cultural studies as well as studies of emotion.

The Reader is divided into two parts.

Part 1 contains key essays from the fields of cultural studies, anthropology, sociology and history. These essays provide insights into how emotions are sociocultural phenomena, how they are culturally and historically specific, how they change over time, across cultures and within societies, and how they participate in the production of power relations.

Part 2 contains essays which illustrate core aspects of cultural emotion studies. They adopt diverse perspectives, topics and methodologies on emotions, offering new understandings of key themes taken up by cultural studies such as nation, the public sphere, popular culture, subjectivity, social identity, discourse and power relations. Together, they demonstrate what emotions 'do' and how they contribute to knowledge production.

Emotions: A Cultural Studies Reader provides students with an essential overview of contemporary academic debate within the humanities and social sciences on the place of emotions in culture, as part of everyday individual, cultural and political life.

Jennifer Harding is Principal Lecturer in Media and Communications at London Metropolitan University. Previous publications include *Sex Acts: Practices of Femininity and Masculinity* (1998) and numerous articles on the body, sexuality, gender, emotions and life history research.

E. Deidre Pribram is Associate Professor and Chairperson of the Communication Arts and Sciences Department at Molloy College, Long Island, New York. She is the author of *Cinema and Culture: Independent Film in the United States, 1980–2001* (2002), and various chapters and articles on film, television, gender and culture.

Emotions: A Cultural Studies Reader

Edited by
Jennifer Harding
and E. Deidre Pribram

Routledge
Taylor & Francis Group

LONDON AND NEW YORK

First published 2009
by Routledge
2 Park Square, Milton Park, Abingdon, Oxon, OX14 4RN

Simultaneously published in the USA and Canada
by Routledge
270 Madison Avenue, New York, NY 10016

Routledge is an imprint of the Taylor & Francis Group, an informa business

Editorial Selection and Material © 2009 Jennifer Harding and E. Deidre Pribram
Chapters © The Contributors

Typeset in Perpetua by
RefineCatch Limited, Bungay, Suffolk
Printed and bound in Great Britain by
CPI Antony Rowe, Chippenham, Wiltshire

British Library Cataloguing in Publication Data
A catalogue record for this book is available from the British Library

Library of Congress Cataloging-in-Publication Data
   Emotions : a cultural studies reader / edited by Jennifer Harding and E. Deidre Pribam. — 1st ed.
     p. cm.
   Includes bibliographical references
   1. Emotions–Cross-cultural studies.   I. Harding, Jennifer.   II. Pribram, E. Deidre.
   BF511.E45 2009
   152.4–dc22

                                                                       2008054232

ISBN 10: 0–415–46929–5 (hbk)
ISBN 10: 0–415–46930–9 (pbk)

ISBN 13: 978–0–415–46929–6 (hbk)
ISBN 13: 978–0–415–46930–2 (pbk)

Contents

Contributors

Lila Abu-Lughod is Professor of Anthropology and Women's and Gender Studies at Columbia University. She is the author of *Veiled Sentiments: Honor and Poetry in a Bedouin Society* (1986) and *Writing Women's Worlds: Bedouin Stories* (1993).

Sara Ahmed is Professor in Race and Cultural Studies at Goldsmiths University in London. Her books include *Differences that Matter: Feminist Theory and Postmodernism* (1998) and *Strange Encounters: Embodied Others in Post-Coloniality* (2000).

Arjun Appadurai is John Dewey Professor in Social Sciences and Senior Advisor for Global Initiatives at The New School in New York City. A specialist on globalisation, he is the author of *Modernity at Large* (1996) and *Disjuncture and Difference in the Global Cultural Economy* (2001).

Lauren Berlant is Professor of English at the University of Chicago. Her books include *The Anatomy of National Fantasy* (1991) and *The Queen of America Goes to Washington City: Essays on Sex and Citizenship* (1997).

Jennifer Biddle is Senior Lecturer in Anthropology in the Division of Society, Culture, Media and Philosophy, Macquarie University. She has written *breasts, bodies, canvas: Central Desert Art as Experience* (2007) and *The Imperative to Feel: Aboriginal Art as Experience* (2006).

Debora Bone is Stroke Center Director at Cabrillo College, California. She has published articles on emotion work by nurses in the context of market-driven health care.

Ian Burkitt is Reader in Social Science at the University of Bradford. He is author of *Social Selves: Theories of Self and Society* (2008) and *Bodies of Thought: Embodiment, Identity and Modernity* (1999).

Judith Butler is the Maxine Elliot Professor in the Departments of Rhetoric and Comparative Literature at the University of California, Berkeley. She is author of numerous publications, including *Gender Trouble: Feminism and the Subversion of Identity* (1990) and *Excitable Speech: A Politics of the Performative* (1997).

Michael Eric Dyson is Professor of Sociology at Georgetown University. His books include *Race Rules: Navigating the Color Line* (1996) and *The Michael Eric Dyson Reader* (2002).

R. Darren Gobert is an associate professor in the Department of English at York University, Toronto. He is currently working on a book about the problems in the philosophy of emotion since Descartes' *Les Passions de l'âme*, and how they have been enacted in the history of spectacle.

Lawrence Grossberg is the Morris Davis Professor of Communication Studies at the University of North Carolina at Chapel Hill. He is author of numerous publications, including *It's a Sin: Essays in Postmodernism, Politics and Culture* (1988) and *Dancing in Spite of Myself: Essays on Popular Culture* (1997).

Jennifer Harding is Principal Lecturer in Media and Communications at London Metropolitan University. She is author of *Sex Acts: Practices of Femininity and Masculinity* (1998) and other articles on the body, sexuality and gender, cultural theory and emotions, and life history research.

Alison M. Jaggar is Professor of Philosophy and Women's Studies at the University of Colorado at Boulder. Her publications include *Feminist Politics and Human Nature* (1983) and *Living with Contradictions: Controversies in Feminist Social Ethics* (1994). She is co-editor of *Gender/Body/Knowledge: Feminist Reconstructions of Being and Knowing* (1989).

Catherine A. Lutz holds a joint appointment at Brown University as Professor of Anthropology and Research Professor with the Watson Institute for International Studies. She is the author of *Unnatural Emotions: Everyday Sentiments on a Micronesian Atoll and Their Challenge to Western Theory* (1988) and *Homefront: A Military City and the American 20th Century* (2001).

Fatima Mernissi is a feminist writer and sociologist. She is currently a lecturer at the Mohammed V University of Rabat. Her books include *Beyond the Veil* (1985), *The Veil and the Male Elite: A Feminist Interpretation of Islam, Doing Daily Battle: Interviews with Moroccan Women* (1991) and *Dreams of Trespass: Tales of a Harem Girlhood* (1995).

Virginia Olesen is Professor of Sociology (Emerita) in the Department of Social and Behavioural Sciences, School of Nursing, University of California, San Francisco. She is author of articles on feminist qualitative research and emotions in health care contexts.

E. Deidre Pribram is Associate Professor in the Communication Arts and Sciences Department at Molloy College in Long Island, New York. She is author of *Cinema and Culture: Independent Film in the United States, 1980–2001* (2002), editor of *Female Spectators: Looking at Film and Television* (1988), and has written numerous articles on film, television, gender and culture.

Elspeth Probyn is Professor of Gender Studies at the University of Sydney. She is author of *Sexing the Self* (1993), and has written chapters for anthologies such as *Feminism and Cultural Studies* (1999) and *The Handbook of Cultural Geography* (2003).

Denise Riley teaches literature and philosophy in the School of English and American Studies at the University of East Anglia. She is author of *'Am I That Name?': Feminism and the Category of 'Women' in History* (1988) and *Impersonal Passion: Language as Affect* (2005).

Michelle Z. Rosaldo (1944–1981) taught at Stanford University, co-founded the Program in Feminist Studies there and is celebrated for her pioneering work in the anthropology of gender. She is author of *Knowledge and Passion: Ilongot Notions of Self and Social Life* (1980).

Nancy Schnog teaches in the English Faculty at McLean School of Maryland. She is co-editor of *Inventing the Psychological: Toward a Cultural History of Emotional Life in America* (1997).

Carol Z. Stearns has an M.D. in psychiatry and a Ph.D. in history. She is the co-author of *Anger: The Struggle for Emotional Control in America's History* (1986), and the co-editor of *Emotion and Social Change: Toward a New Psychohistory* (1988).

Carolyn Kay Steedman is Professor of History at the University of Warwick. She has authored a number of influential works on the history of gender, childhood and class. Her books include *Landscape for a Good Woman: A Story of Two Lives* (first published in 1986, then as a paperback in 1987), *Strange Dislocations: Childhood and the Idea of Human Interiority, 1780–1930* (1995), and *Dust* (2001).

Linda Williams is a professor in the Departments of Film Studies and Rhetoric at the University of California, Berkeley. She is the author of *'Playing the Race Card': Melodramas of Black and White from Uncle Tom to O.J. Simpson* (2001), *Viewing Positions: Ways of Seeing Film* (1994) and *Hardcore: Power, Pleasure and the Frenzy of the Visible* (1989).

Raymond Williams (1921–1988) was a professor of literature at Cambridge, a noted Marxist theorist and a prolific cultural analyst. His books include *Culture and Society, 1780–1950* (first published in 1959, then again in 1963) and *Keywords: A Vocabulary of Culture and Society* (1976).

Simon J. Williams is Professor of Sociology at the University of Warwick. He is author of *Emotions and Social Theory* (2001) and co-editor of *Emotions in Social Life* (1998).

Acknowledgements

We both wish to thank Natalie Foster, Charlotte Wood, and Andrew Watts at Taylor & Francis for guiding us through this project with such smooth professionalism.

Jennifer Harding: I would like to thank Gabriel and Ruth for their love, support and encouragement. I am also grateful for the support of colleagues at London Metropolitan University.

E. Deidre Pribram: I would like to thank the Molloy College community, especially the staff of the James E. Tobin Library and the members of the Communication Arts and Sciences Department. My thanks also to Christine Gledhill for the generous manner in which she has shared both her insights and her friendship. I want to express my appreciation to my family – to my sisters Viv and Inge, to Riley, Ivory, and Sierra, and to my mother-in-law Mabel – for always keeping things emotionally exciting. Above all, my heart-felt gratitude to Cliff Jernigan for the depth of his understanding of oh so many things.

The following were reproduced with kind permission. Whilst every effort has been made to trace copyright holders and obtain permission, this has not been possible in all cases. Any omissions brought to our attention will be remedied in future editions.

"On Structure of Feeling." From *The Long Revolution* by Raymond Williams, published by Chatto & Windus. Reprinted by permission of The Random House Group.

Raymond Williams, *Politics and Letters: Interviews with New Left Review*. London: NLB, 1979. Reprinted with permission of Verso.

Alison M. Jaggar, "Love and Knowledge: Emotion in Feminist Epistemology," in *Gender/Body/Knowledge: Feminist Reconstructions of Being and Knowing,"* eds. Alison M. Jaggar and Susan R. Bordo. New Brunswick, NJ: Rutgers University Press, 1989. Originally published in Inquiry: an Interdisciplinary Journal of Psychology Vol.32: 2 (1989) pp. 151–176. Taylor & Francis Ltd, http://www.informaworld.com, reprinted by permission of the publisher and author.

Lawrence Grossberg, "Postmodernity and Affect: All Dressed Up with No Place to Go." *Communication*, vol. 10, nos. 3–4, 1988. pp. 271–293. Taylor & Francis Ltd, http://www.informaworld.com, reprinted by permission of the publisher and author.

Michelle Z. Rosaldo, "Toward an Anthropology of Self and Feeling," in *Culture Theory: Essays on Mind, Self, and Emotion*, eds. Richard A. Shweder and Robert A. LeVine, 1984. Copyright © Cambridge University Press 1984, reprinted with permission.

Lila Abu-Lughod and Catherine A. Lutz, "Emotion, Discourse, and the Politics of Everyday Life," in *Language and the Politics of Emotion*, eds. Catherine A. Lutz and Lila Abu-Lughod, 1990. Cambridge University Press, reprinted with permission.

Jennifer Biddle, "Shame." *Australian Feminist Studies*, vol. 12, no. 26, 1997. pp. 227–239. Taylor & Francis Ltd, http://www.informaworld.com, reprinted by permission of the publisher and author

Virginia Oelsen and Deborah Bone, "Emotions in Rationalizing Organizations: Conceptual Notes from Professional Nursing in the USA," from *Emotions in Social Life: Critical Themes and Contemporary Issues*, eds. Gillian Bendelow and Simon J. Williams. Copyright © 1998 Routledge. Reproduced by permission of Taylor & Francis Books UK and Gillian Bendelow.

Simon J. Williams, "Modernity and the Emotions: Corporeal Reflections on the (Ir)Rational." Reproduced with permission from *Sociology*, Vol. 32, No. 4, 747–769, November 1998, Sage Journals. By permission of Sage Publications Ltd and the author.

Ian Burkitt, "Powerful Emotions: Power, Government and Opposition in the 'War on Terror.'" Reproduced with permission from *Sociology*, Vol. 39, No. 4, 679–695, 2005, Sage Journals. By permission of Sage Publications Ltd and the author. Sociology, Vol. 39, No. 4, 679–695 (2005)

Carol Z. Stearns, "'Lord Help Me Walk Humbly': Anger and Sadness in England and America, 1570–1750," in *Emotion and Social Change: Toward a New Psychohistory*, eds. Carol Z. Stearns and Peter N. Stearns. New York: Holmes & Meier, 1988, pp. 39–68. Reprinted with permission.

Nancy Schnog, "Changing Emotions: Moods and the Nineteenth-Century American Woman Writer," in *Inventing the Psychological: Toward a Cultural History of Emotional Life in America*, eds. Joel Pfister and Nancy Schnog. New Haven, CT: Yale University Press, 1997. Reproduced with permission.

Carolyn Kay Steedman, "Stories." *Landscape for a Good Woman: A Story of Two Lives.* Little, Brown Book Group, 1986.

Steedman, Carolyn Kay, *Landscape for a Good Woman: A Story of Two Lives.* Copyright © 1986 by Carolyn Kay Steedman. Reprinted by permission of Rutgers University Press.

Michael Eric Dyson, "Does George W. Bush Care about Black People?" *Come Hell or High Water: Hurricane Katrina and the Color of Disaster.* New York: Basic Civitas/Perseus, 2006. © 2006 by Michael Eric Dyson. Published by Basic Civitas, a Member of Perseus Books Group. Reproduced with permission.

Sara Ahmed, "The Organisation of Hate." *The Cultural Politics of Emotion* by Sara Ahmed. Copyright 2004 by Taylor & Francis Group LLC – Books. Reproduced with permission of the author and Taylor & Francis Group LLC – Books in the format Textbook via Copyright Clearance Center.

Arjun Appadurai, "Fear of Small Numbers" in *Fear of Small Numbers: An Essay on the Geography of Anger*, pp.49–85; 139–141. Copyright 2006 Duke University Press. All rights reserved. Used by permission of the publisher.

Lauren Berlant, "Introduction: The Intimate Public Sphere," in *The Queen of America Goes to*

Washington City: Essays on Sex and Citizenship, pp.1–21, 261–266, 289–302. Copyright, 1997, Duke University Press. All rights reserved. Used by permission of the publisher.

Elspeth Probyn, "Shaming Theory, Thinking Dis-Connections: Feminism and Reconciliation," from *Transformations: Thinking Through Feminism,* eds. Sara Ahmed, Jane Kilby, Celia Lury, Maureen McNeil, and Beverley Skeggs. Copyright © 2000 Routledge. Reproduced by permission of Taylor & Francis Books UK and the author. Includes 25 lines from Paula Gunn Allen "Some Like Indians Endure" (in W. Roscoe ed. *Living the spirit: a gay American Indian anthology*, St Martin's Press). Reprinted with the permission of the Estate of Paula Gunn Allen.

Linda Williams, "Melodrama Revised," in *Refiguring American Film Genres: History and Theory,* ed. Nick Browne. Berkeley, CA: University of California Press, 1998. Reproduced with kind permission of the author.

R. Darren Gobert, "Historicizing Emotion: The Case of Freudian Hysteria and Aristotelian 'Purgation'" in *Feeling Our Way,* eds. Laura Cameron et al. Ashgate: 2008. Reproduced with permission.

Fatima Mernissi, "Scheherazade Goes West: Different Cultures, Different Harems." *Scheherazade Goes West: Different Cultures, Different Harems.* New York: Washington Square Press, 2001.

Fatima Mernissi, "Scheherazade Goes West: Different Cultures, Different Harems." From SCHEHERAZADE GOES WEST by Fatema Mernissi. Copyright © 2001 by Fatema Mernissi. Abridged with the permission of Washington Square Press, a Division of Simon & Schuster, Inc. By permission of Edite Kroll Literary Agency Inc.

Denise Riley, "Malediction." *Impersonal Passion: Language as Affect.* Durham, NC: Duke University Press, 2005. Originally published as 'Bad Words'. *Diacritics* 31:4 (2001), 53. © The Johns Hopkins University Press. Reprinted with permission of The Johns Hopkins University Press.

Judith Butler, "Violence, Mourning, Politics." *Precarious Life: The Powers of Mourning and Violence.* London: Verso, 2004. Reprinted with permission.

Introduction: the case for a cultural emotion studies

> To say that two people belong to the same culture is to say that they interpret the world in roughly the same ways and can express themselves, their thoughts and feelings about the world, in ways which will be understood by each other. . . . [C]ulture is about feelings, attachments and emotions as well as concepts and ideas.
>
> Stuart Hall 1997, 2

HALL DESCRIBES EMOTIONS, along with other social practices, as constitutive of culture. As such, emotions are integral to the processes of meaning production. Despite this acknowledgement from Hall and a number of other cultural theorists, cultural studies has been slow to take up systematic, detailed analyses of emotion.

Recent decades have witnessed an enormous amount of work focused on concepts of rationality. Poststructuralist theorists, among others, have thoroughly examined and critiqued Western models of Reason, for instance, calling to account the disproportionate reliance on rationality in Western knowledge-building. Similar 'overhauls' in understandings of the body have been led by feminist and queer theorists, in which the body, historically the sign or possession of the discrete individual, is viewed in many significant and complex ways as a cultural construct. It is our contention that a commensurate exploration of emotions is well overdue.

Certain factors have contributed to a deferral in the development of emotion studies. First, emotions have been understood as a particularly difficult epistemological category, too imbued with 'the personal' and too affiliated with troubling concepts, such as experience, to be amenable to rigorous methods of exploration. Second, emotions have been diminished by their long-standing association with women and other purportedly non-rational social groups, leading to the marginalisation of emotion in knowledge production and, too often, to its entrenchment as irrationality, the antithesis of reason. Third, the study of emotions has been undertaken principally within biology, cognitive psychology and psychoanalysis, which locate emotions predominantly in the bodies and psyches of individuals. For the most part, these disciplines have been less concerned with the social, cultural and historical variability of emotional existence.

Even so, a 'cultural turn' in emotion studies has been developing in different disciplines but without the recognition we believe it deserves. Emotions have become a subject of investigation in cultural anthropology, sociology and history as well as cultural studies. In this move, emotions have come to be seen as not simply individual and inner phenomena, but as collective cultural and historical experiences, potentially eroding dichotomies such as inside/outside, individual/ collective and private/public. The implications of this scholarship are far-reaching; for instance, in challenging traditional relations between emotions and knowledge production, these studies dispute the epistemic, and hence political, authority of dominant groups (Jaggar 1989).

In gathering together the essays for this reader, our aim is, first, to give the culturalist turn in emotion studies the attention it merits and, second, to outline some of the parameters and potentialities of a distinct field of emotion studies within the larger landscape of cultural studies. Appropriately for a cultural studies endeavour, the work in this collection is inter-disciplinary, drawn together from numerous academic fields. As Lauren Berlant notes, in this volume, the interdisciplinary demands of the subject matter push us to work rigorously beyond our expertise 'in ways that feel at once risky and absolutely necessary' (chapter 16: 292). In what follows in this Introduction, we cover the central tenets of cultural studies and apply them to our conceptualisation of a culturalist approach to emotions.

Cultural studies

Cultural studies is a diverse and open-ended intellectual and political project. It does not offer a single theory or compact set of theories. Perhaps it can most usefully be identified in terms of the ground it covers, the methodologies it organises, and in its commitment to investigating power and cultural politics. Indeed, cultural studies practitioners understand the production of theoretical knowledge as a political practice (Barker 2008: 37).

Most famously, culture has been described 'as the study of relationships between elements in a whole way of life', in which cultural analysis attempts 'to discover the nature of the organization which is the complex of these relationships' (R. Williams, chapter 1: 35). From Raymond Williams' perspective, the task facing cultural studies is to make apparent the relationships among the many elements in the social formation that, together, create any particular culture's whole way of life.

Extrapolating from Williams' definition, culture has come to be broadly understood 'both as a way of life — encompassing ideas, attitudes, languages, practices, institutions and struc-tures of power — and a whole range of cultural practices: artistic forms, texts, canons, archi-tecture, mass-produced commodities, and so forth' (Nelson, Treichler and Grossberg 1992: 5). In other words, culture refers to all forms of cultural production and communicative practice, and cultural studies investigates these in relation to other cultural practices and to social and historical structures (Nelson, Treichler and Grossberg 1992: 4).

Defining the project more explicitly, Hall describes culture as a set of historically specific practices, representations, languages and customs, 'concerned with the production and exchange of meanings' (Hall 1997: 2). This has led to cultural studies investigations of signify-ing practices, ideology, discourse, power, knowledge production, popular culture, consumption, subjectivity and social identity. Such work on meaning production explores how the world is socially constructed and represented to us, in meaningful ways, in specific historical contexts (Barker 2008).

As noted earlier, cultural studies is interdisciplinary, drawing from bodies of theory prominent in the last decades, including Marxism, feminism, psychoanalysis, poststructuralism, postmodernism, queer theory and postcolonial theory. No one methodology is adopted by practitioners; rather, cultural studies methodologies are 'pragmatic, strategic and self-reflexive', depending on the questions being asked and the context of asking, as well as the political aims of the project, which are always historically situated (Nelson, Treichler and Grossberg 1992). Contributing to its diversity, cultural studies has developed within different national and political contexts. This reader, with certain exceptions, is focused within the Anglo-American tradition of cultural studies.

Grossberg has suggested three key concerns or guiding principles for cultural studies: radical contextuality; strategic political intervention; and relationality (1997: 235–237).

Radical contextuality refers to the way that cultural studies investigations work across historical and political contexts rather than taking up a fixed theoretical position. In these terms, 'context is not merely the background but the very conditions of possibility of something' (Grossberg 1997: 255). Meaghan Morris suggests that cultural studies works to understand 'how contexts are "made, unmade, and remade", and how contexts change the meaning and the *value* of cultural practices' (Morris 1997: 45; italics in original). The concept of contextuality rejects the absolutist, universalising tendencies of some academic inquiry. Instead, it operates in terms of historical specifics and located analyses, always acknowledging the constantly changing, contested nature of cultural forms and practices.

The principle of strategic political intervention pinpoints cultural studies' involvement in issues of power, dominance and resistance. Concerned with the centrality and productivity of power, cultural studies views it as pervading every level of social interaction, working to both constrain and enable subjectivities and social hierarchies. This has led to an emphasis on subordinated groups based on social identities such as class, race/ethnicity, gender, sexuality and nationality. The theoretical adequacy or productivity of cultural studies is judged by the creation of possibilities for strategic interventions in the everyday practices of individuals and social formations.

Relationality refers to the ways culture, context and power operate interactively. It speaks to the conjunction of cultural practices with other parts of the social formation: material, governmental, institutional, technological and so on. Relationality demands that all aspects of the social formation that affect a phenomenon be taken into account. Without this concept, the danger exists of abandoning 'the commitment to complexity, contingency, contestation, and multiplicity that is a hallmark of cultural studies' (Grossberg 2006: 4). Relationality revisits Raymond Williams' understanding of culture as a whole way of life in which the task of cultural analysis is to make apparent the relationships among the many elements in that way of life.

Cultural studies has been contentious and, for some time, has been dogged by notions of crisis and questions about its contemporary pertinence. Recently, Grossberg has reasserted the political purpose of cultural studies in radically contextualising relations between knowledge and power (2006). He argues that it must remain focused on this goal in order to avoid the universalising and essentialising characteristics of dominant practices of knowledge production that contribute to 'making the very relations of domination, inequality and suffering that cultural studies desires to change' (Grossberg 2006: 2). In order to achieve this goal, cultural studies must continue to make visible and take into account the 'positionality' of all knowledge, including its own (Barker 2008: 38).

We now turn to the application of the key concepts outlined above in developing a culturalist approach to emotions. We believe the advent of emotion studies as a significant new field within cultural studies is both timely and significant.

A culturalist approach to emotions

Applying cultural studies concepts to the emotions leads us to outline certain foundations for our project. First, emotions do not operate in a universally definable way across time and space. They cannot be considered outside of the specificity of their historical contexts. Second, it is necessary to examine how emotions work in social and cultural terms as part of the everyday production and reproduction of social identities and unequal power relations. Third, the ways emotions exist in, interact with, and affect the everyday lives of individuals as part of larger social formations – that is, how they operate relationally – must be explored.

Much of the attention thus far devoted to emotions has focused disproportionately on what they are and where they are located – for instance, as properties of the individual, are they functions of body or mind? The history of thinking about emotion is underpinned by 'debate about relations between emotion, bodily sensation and cognition', in which theories can be divided according to whether they bind emotion to bodily sensation or cognition (Ahmed 2004: 5). Ahmed provides a way out of this dilemma by shifting her focus from emotions as 'things' that people 'have' to thinking about what emotions 'do' (2004: 4). Significantly, this involves thinking about emotions as not solely properties of/in the individual. Following Ahmed, our primary concern in developing a culturalist approach is not to concentrate on debating what emotions *are* but, rather, to explore how they function as social practices in continually changing circumstances – that is, what emotions *do*. We are concerned with the following questions: To what uses are emotions put? What meanings have they accrued that make possible those uses? How do they circulate in the social formation? To this end, we understand emotions as cultural practices which help to give various social formations their meanings and power. We conceptualise emotions as both cultural practice and as constitutive of the possibilities for cultural practice.

There are a number of reasons why a cultural studies way of speaking about emotions has become especially pertinent. To start, emotion studies helps to undermine canonical forms of knowledge production, seeking to broaden notions of what epistemology might include. Second, a culturalist investigation of emotions involves challenging essentialism and deep-rooted dichotomies in Western thought through a commitment to historicising and contextualising the complexity of emotional practices. Third, culturalist interrogations of emotions can contribute significantly to an understanding of power relations in the development of social identities and in the production and exchange of meaning. Fourth, individual processes, whether biological or psychological, have received a great deal more theoretical attention than cultural ones. Finally, emotions matter for cultural politics. We examine each of these pertinences below.

Knowledge production

Considerable impetus for rethinking emotions, and their implications for knowledge and power, has derived from recent challenges to the dominant view of modern Western thought and practice as disembodied, dispassionate and wholly rational. The advent of the modern philosophy of science and the dominant methodology of positivism, emerging and crystallising from the seventeenth century onwards, has resulted in reason being regarded as the faculty most essential to the production of objective, reliable and universal understandings of reality.[1] Over much of the same time period, emotion became accepted as the antithesis of reason and very likely to subvert inquiry.

Reason was thought to exist 'independently of the self's contingent existence', meaning that 'bodily, historical, and social experiences do not affect reason's structure or its capacity to produce atemporal knowledge' (Flax 1990: 41). Scientists were charged with investigating the natural world, using reason to penetrate surface impressions in order to establish true facts and underlying explanations about phenomena and, in so doing, exerting control over nature. The logic of this approach to scientific inquiry rested squarely on a series of conceptual dichotomies: culture/nature, mind/body, reason/emotion, objectivity/subjectivity – in which the former, systematically associated with the masculine, dominate the latter, linked with the feminine (S. Harding 1986: 23).

This model of inquiry and epistemology has come under fierce attack from feminist philo sophers and critics of science on the grounds that neutrality and objectivity are impossible and that the myth of 'the dispassionate investigator' works to reproduce and secure hegemonic relations central to Western societies (Keller 1983a, 1984; Bordo 1987; S. Harding 1986; Jaggar, chapter 2; Flax 1990; H. Rose 1994). Further, rational inquiry does not discover but, rather, creates the phenomena it describes. For example, historians of sex have demonstrated that sex has been differently conceptualised by investigating scientists at different historical moments and that their conceptualisations have reflected the contemporary social organiza- tion of gender (Schiebinger 1986; Martin 1989; Jacobus et al. 1990; Laqueur 1990; Poovey 1990; Oudshoorn 1994; J. Harding 1998).

While thought, including academic inquiry, has been understood as necessarily rational, disembodied and masculine, emotions have been associated with the feminine, nature, the body and the private. Women have been perceived as bearers of emotions – the main group expected to or allowed to feel emotion – and so, inevitably, 'more "subjective", biased and irrational' (Jaggar, chapter 2: 60). Jaggar argues, therefore, that the ideal of the dispassionate investigator functions ideologically to 'bolster the epistemic authority' of dominant groups, traditionally composed of white men, and to discredit the observations and claims of others, mainly women and people of colour. Moreover, 'the alleged epistemic authority of the dominant groups then justifies their political authority', as part of the reproduction of hegemonic power (59).

Medical historian Fay Bound Alberti describes how 'men of science' sought to master 'their own emotions in order to convey an image of detached investigation in the scientific process', because it was believed, from the eighteenth century on, that medical practice required being unemotional 'as a necessary precondition for an objective diagnosis' (Alberti 2006: xxi, xiii). Instead, she argues for the 'culturally situated nature of medical diagnoses', in which the emotions of the investigator are key to understanding how diagnoses are 'socially and politically generated' (xiv).[2] Such a process leads to a revised view of historically diag- nosed illnesses, such as hysteria, hypochondria and neurasthenia, 'revealing more about the operation of gender and class relations' on the part of practitioners than about the emotional lives of those being diagnosed (Alberti: xiv).

Additional critiques of disembodied rationality have derived from critical studies of masculinities (Seidler 1994; Connell 1995), poststructuralist critiques of modernity's grand master narratives (Lyotard 1984; Baudrillard 1983, 1988; Foucault 1980, 1986), and queer theory (Butler 1990; Fuss 1991; Sedgwick 1991; De Lauretis 1991; J. Harding 1998). For instance, the poststructuralist critique of reason has focused on the denial of 'deep structures of meaning' and absolute truths (Baudrillard 1988: 164). In contrast, knowledge is always partial, provisional and contingent; there is no hidden real to be excavated (Pribram 1993).

We concur with Jaggar and other feminist philosophers and critics of science who have argued that reason and emotion are integral to each other (Jaggar, chapter 2; Keller 1983b; H. Rose 1987). However, we do not consider emotion as a more 'authentic' or truthful form of knowledge than reason, as it has sometimes been positioned historically, for instance, in Romantic configurations. As Elspeth Probyn points out, given that we all live within hegemonic structures, emotions may work just as well to obscure as to reveal social relations through, for example, 'common sense' feelings (Probyn 1993: 21).

In their critique of Western concepts of reason, contemporary theorists challenge the intrinsic essentialism of scientific inquiry – in seeking to discover the essence or 'reality' that lies behind the appearance of a phenomenon – and its application in understandings of social organisation.[3] Essentialism is usually understood as a belief in the 'real, true essence of things, the invariable and fixed properties which define the "whatness" of a given entity' (Fuss 1989: xi–xii). Feminists have critiqued essentialism applied to women to denote given and universal characteristics and functions, residing in nature/biology or psychology, shared in common by all women at all times, 'which limit the possibilities of change and thus of social organisation' (Grosz 1990: 334). Similarly, theorists have critiqued essentialist concepts of race, class and sexuality as natural, biologically based and, therefore, unchangeable (Hall 1990; Mercer 1992; Weeks 1994).

One response to the limitations of essentialism has been the emergence of social constructionist approaches to knowledge production, particularly in understanding categories of experience such as gender, race/ethnicity and sexuality. In social construction accounts, identities are no longer viewed as the result of innate essences lodged in the biological individual and, thereafter, giving rise to social differences. Instead, variations among individuals and groups are identified as the historically located effects of political, social and cultural relations. However, as we discuss in the next sections of this introduction, social constructionism is differently practised by theorists within different disciplines, and it does not always provide the only, or a sufficient, alternative to essentialism. Indeed, essentialism and constructionism sometimes share assumptions when it comes to investigating emotions.

Critiques of rationalism and essentialism clearly undermine assumptions about the oppositional and hierarchical relations between reason and emotion. They also potentially disrupt other dualisms: body/mind, individual/collective, inner/outer. Next, we examine these dichotomies and their impact in developing a culturalist understanding of emotions.

Body/mind

In the West, one of the dominant debates concerning the emotions has focused on the body/mind dilemma. Are emotions physiological functions or mental processes? A focus on the corporeal dimensions of emotion has its roots in the modern bio-history of the human body and the consolidation of rationalism.

Since the seventeenth century, the emergence of the Cartesian subject and disciplining of the human body in Western societies has entailed a sharp differentiation between mind and body, in which 'the experience of self has been disembodied and the body cast into a shadowy and troublesome existence' (Burkitt 1999: 45). This distinction has been coextensive with divisions between self and other, inner and outer, and directly related to the historical configuration of modern power relations.

The modern body, emerging with rationalism, was closed, concealed and disciplined.[4] It was developed as 'an "object" and as such a target of knowledge and discipline imposed by self or by the state' (Burkitt 1999: 67). The modern body became more private and individual. Divisions between mind and body, and self and other – that is, 'thought and active, sensate, emotive being which is associated with the body' – are spatialised as the seemingly disembodied self 'watches from a distance and the embodied person who is surveyed', is now 'viewed as a material object' (Burkitt 1999: 66).

Traditionally, emotions have been studied as universal embodied sensations. Writing in 1872, Charles Darwin outlined an early organismic theory of emotions, emphasising their instinctual nature, archaic heritage and functions in human survival (Lupton 1998: 11; S. Williams 2001: 39–41). For those who have prioritised a corporeal perspective, emotions typically are viewed as individual, internal and inherent. All humans are born with a basic set of emotions and, despite variations in expression between societies, such emotions are always pre existing, located within the individual, physiologically based, genetically inscribed, and so 'inherited rather than learnt' (Lupton 1998: 11). Research from this perspective is usually directed at seeking to identify anatomical or genetic bases for emotions, 'showing how emotions are linked to bodily changes' (Lupton 1998: 11). Within this approach, emotions may be seen as 'physiological responses to a given set of stimuli' and/or 'part of an animalistic legacy in human development, subject less to thought and reason than to impulse' (Lupton 1998: 11). Here, emphasis is placed on the assumed individuality and interiority of emotion located in bodily changes.

While biological and physiological explanations of emotion weighed more heavily than mind in earlier eras, and continue to frame inquiry, the difference in the last century and a half is due to the development of the psy disciplines: psychology, psychiatry, psychoanalysis and various psychotherapies. Nikolas Rose describes psychology as a discipline that was constituted in the West between 1875 and 1925 (N. Rose 1985: 3). It brought into existence a new human subject – the psychological self – in which psychic interiority became the frame for understanding the actions and behaviours of ourselves and others (N. Rose 1997: 234, 225–226). The psy subject is characterised by a complex personality which is partly hidden and partly overt.

Concurring that the era Rose identifies marks a change in the way people understood themselves, Carolyn Steedman accounts for it as a new interiority or 'a sense of the self *within*' (Steedman 1995: 4; italics in original). Emblematic of this change was Freudian psychoanalysis's articulation of psychic identity as an individual's 'own lost past, or childhood' formulated as the unconscious mind (Steedman 1995: 4). Nancy Schnog pinpoints the 1920s as the period in which psychoanalysis began to achieve general popularity as middle-class Americans came to understand themselves in terms of psyches, 'shaped by mainstream concepts of psychoanalytical thought' (Schnog 1997: 4). The development of various psy disciplines fuelled the mind/body debate, further polarising discussion by providing scientific and scholarly substance to the psychic spectrum of the dichotomy.

The link between emotions and mind was further solidified, from the mid-twentieth century on, with the rise of cognitive psychology. Proponents of cognitive psychology argue that not only are emotions largely cognitive processes but they are also integral to the functioning of reason. Gobert summarises philosopher Martha Nussbaum's position on emotion as cognition which includes the following precepts: emotions are 'directed by an agent toward an object'; they are rational or 'predicated upon beliefs'; and they involve ethical judgments (Gobert 2006: 17).

More recently, researchers have worked to integrate emotional bodies with their social circumstances, and to restore history to the psychological. Deborah Lupton argues that focusing attention on the role of the body in expressing emotions does not mean viewing emotions as inherent, instinctive and universal responses to stimuli, since bodies are not themselves 'natural' products (Lupton 1998: 32). Rather, experiences of embodiment are always in the process of being constructed through and mediated by sociocultural circumstances and the historical contexts in which we live (Lupton 1998: 32).

For Lupton, discourse plays a crucial role in constructing emotional experience because it is through discourse that 'a constellation of bodily feelings' is interpreted and named as a particular emotion (Lupton 1998: 32). The important point here is that there is a lack of equivalence and, indeed, a gulf of difference, between bodily sensation and emotion: not all bodily sensations come to be articulated as emotion and not all emotions have observable or perceptible bodily sensations, as in the examples of love or pride. Lupton quotes Daniel Miller who makes this point in relation to the emotion of disgust: 'Disgust is a feeling *about* something and in response to something, not just raw unattached feeling. That's what the stomach flu is. Part of disgust is the very awareness of being disgusted, the consciousness of itself' (Miller cited in Lupton 1998: 33; italics in original). The failure of equivalence between bodily sensation and emotion works against a tendency towards reductionism and essentialism.

At the same time, bodily states are vital to producing emotional states – smells, tastes, sounds, touching, sight – conveying without words a variety of emotions, meanings and relationships (Lupton 1998: 34). Touch, depending on the texture of an object or whether the other is a loved one or a stranger, can evoke intense pleasure or disgust, joy or discomfort (Lupton 1998: 35). In this sense, embodied feeling can be a basis and motivation for action, in which 'gut feelings' can be acute, painful and productive. Still, the imperative to interpret and name bodily sensation as emotion must be learned and is bound up with socio-cultural meanings and social relationships. A move in this direction is significant because it articulates a social constructionist approach and works against reductionism, essentialism, and traditional dualisms between mind and body, biology and society. However, social constructionism, generally referring to a critical response to essentialism in the humanities and social sciences, is variously practised and has a number of limitations.

Key branches of the psy disciplines have also attempted to incorporate elements of the social into their understandings of affect. For example, Freudian psychoanalysis posits affect in the early, unconscious and forgotten memory of the recipient (Gobert, chapter 19: 325). Incidents of troubling suppressed memory manifest as physical ailments which the analyst seeks to bring into the conscious and thereby 'cure' (326). Although Gobert acknowledges that Freud allowed for the possibility of inherited emotions that precede an individual's birth, Schnog notes that most developmental theorists working in the Freudian tradition conceive of the child as building 'his or her distinct personality through psychodynamic processes of (mainly) parent–child interaction' (325; Schnog 1997: 6).[5] The latter is a social construction view in that the emotional individual is the outcome of familial and other primary relationships rather than the product of inherited and inherent biology. Such an account provides the possibility for, and an explanation of, differences among individuals. It also allows 'correction' of an individual's affective personality because s/he has been constructed through experienced relationships, that is, primary social interactions. As such, affective experience can be accessed from deep memory and reconstituted.

However, 'psy social construction' approaches also pose several limitations, in common with 'essentialist corporeal' approaches to understanding emotion. First, they tend toward universality rather than being historically and culturally contextualised. Second, they represent dominantly individual rather than collective understandings of emotion formation.

Individual/collective

Historical and cultural differences are ignored in universalising psy social construction theories. For example, in the Freudian model the individual psyche – the subject – materialises as consistent, once gender identification through familial relations in infancy and early childhood occurs, despite differences of class, race, ethnicity or nationality. Psychoanalytic theory generalises subject formation, regardless of variations across people, cultures and eras. Although there are differences between individuals, those variations are the sole result of particularised primary relations. Otherwise, the same pattern of subject formation occurs transculturally and transhistorically – that is, it applies to all individuals across space and time.

Tim Newton calls psychology and social psychology 'studiously ahistorical' when they ignore the 'rich, historically formed social world' into which all children are born and that constitutes the familial, sexual and other relations that inform any person's development (Newton 1998: 66–67). Schnog argues that although 'today's therapeutic common sense tells us that the "psychological" is the deepest part of ourselves – the most intricate and individual aspect of our personhood', historical processes and cultural traditions shape emotions, through 'political systems, economic practices, social rituals, and family structures' (Schnog 1997: 8).

The universalising characteristics of the psydisciplines understand emotions as individually located or embedded. As a result, any attempt to theorise the emotions seemingly must account for their organisation and operation at the level of the individual. In such accounts, individuality is foregrounded while the collective recedes. As Donna Haraway has noted, this is hardly a characteristic of singular disciplines but a deeply rooted tendency in Western thought. Referencing sociobiology, she speaks of the 'unit of selection', the entity such as the organism, the cell or the gene that has been longed for as the defining, originating, essential category of being which 'can unify all the narratives of biological meaning' (Haraway 1989: 353). This sought-after unit of life has full explanatory power and, so, can serve as the foundation for all sociobiological meaning. Historically, numerous approaches to the emotions have taken the individual as their unit of selection or, in Michel Foucault's words, the 'fictitious atom' which defines, explains and determines what the emotions 'are' (Foucault 1995: 194).

In focusing on the individual as the central unit of analysis, because that is the level at which emotions are felt or experienced, researchers confound the experiential with both the origin and meanings of emotion. Gouk and Hills argue that while 'the reading of emotions has tended to concentrate on individual feeling subjects, whose external features are assumed to disclose or disguise personal interior states', emotions are subject to historicity and social currents 'and therefore must be analysed in relation to them' (Gouk and Hills 2005: 21). Similarly, historians Paster, Rowe and Floyd-Wilson object to the 'privileging of emotions as inward rather than social phenomena', pointing out that the 'passionate *individual*' is a recent development that contradicts the early modern understanding of emotions as markers of social status or functions of communal bonds (Paster et al. 2004: 12–13; italics in original).

Using terms parallel to Haraway's, sociologist Zygmunt Bauman locates the appearance of the word 'individual' to mean 'indivisibility' in Western society in the seventeenth century.

> It referred solely to the rather trivial fact that if you go on dividing the entirety of the human population into ever smaller constitutive parts, you won't be able to go further than to a single human person: a single human is the smallest unit to which the quality of 'humanity' can be ascribed, just as the atom of oxygen is the smallest unit to which the qualities of that chemical element can be ascribed.
>
> (Bauman 2005: 19)

Bauman argues that in a society of individuals we listen 'especially attentively to the inner stirrings of our emotions and sentiments' because they are personal, in contrast to the impersonality of reason which is purportedly 'detached, impartial and universally shared'. In contrast, emotions appear to be the 'natural habitat of everything truly private and individual' (Bauman 2005: 17). Yet, Bauman cautions, 'individuality is the end product of *societal* transformation disguised as *personal* discovery' (Bauman 2005: 19; italics in original).

In accounts of emotions that are rooted in the individual, the essence of emotion is what we feel inside. These emotional sensations or experiences are then taken to be the authentic essence of both emotion and self. In an interview-based study, Lupton found that her subjects shared the belief that emotions form 'the most penetrating . . . judgment' about other people as well as about one's self (Lupton 1998: 90). Analysing people's emotional behaviour provides the most accurate 'truth' about who they are; genuinely coming to know one's self depends most on a thorough recognition of one's feelings. Current conceptualisations of emotion are integral to the notion of the individual as central unit of analysis, reassuring us that we are, each, 'real' and 'distinct'. In an ideologically reinforcing practice, emotions verify the authenticity of the individual and the individual validates the authenticity of emotion.

Inner/outer

Social constructionists in history, sociology and anthropology have been keen to disengage emotions from an association with body, biology and nature and to locate them in the external world of culture and society, viewing them as socially and culturally constructed rather than biologically given. However, this does not necessarily mean moving beyond the individual or the inner/outer distinction.

For example, Clarke, Hoggett and Thomson explore 'the intersection between power, politics, and the emotions by arguing that emotions are central to our understanding of the social and political world' (Clarke et al. 2006a: 4). They take up Ahmed's distinction between psychological and sociological interpretations of emotions. The former pursues an 'inside-out' approach in which emotions 'belong' to the individual but get outside to the social. The latter is an 'outside-in' model in which 'emotions are seen essentially as properties of social and cultural practices which somehow then "get inside" individuals' (Clarke et al. 2006b: 171).

While acknowledging that Ahmed's argument finds both accounts lacking, in that emotions are simultaneously constitutive of both the subject and the social, they ultimately determine that her analysis exists at too high a level of abstraction (Clarke et al. 2006b: 173). Instead, they turn to psychoanalyst R. D. Hinshelwood who positions emotions as individual properties but in a system in which they can be exchanged with or relayed to others (ibid., 173–174). The difficulty is that this still locates emotions as belonging to or within the individual and, only subsequently, informing social structures and relations. It fails to dismantle the inside-out problematic of psychological approaches.

To argue that emotions have social uses and effects fails to repudiate a perspective in which emotionally embedded individuals exist a priori to social formations. In such a scenario, individual agents deploy emotions in social spaces as they interact with other individual agents and, thereby, affect social formations and relations. This overlooks Ahmed's crucial point that the problem lies in maintaining a clear distinction between inside and outside, individual and collective. Instead, she suggests, emotions 'produce the very surfaces and boundaries that allow the individual and the social to be delineated as if they were objects' (Ahmed 2004: 10). Emotions are a crucial means by which individuals and social formations are reciprocally constituted.

Researchers have attempted to develop social constructionist accounts of emotions by demonstrating how they may be shaped by social structures, institutions and power relations, and how they may change over time. However, elements of essentialism continue to plague even these understandings. For example, social researchers commonly analyse emotions in terms of feeling rules, discourses, behaviours, displays and standards. They search for ways in which emotions manifest in material forms available to intellectual inquiry, often interpreting these manifestations as the *effects* of an authentic, underlying emotional essence or experience.

When theorists conceive of authentic emotion, it is usually assumed to be located in the experiences of individuals. For instance, Peter Stearns, a strong proponent of understanding emotions as historically changing, has developed studies of the histories of specific feelings (anger, jealousy), based on analysing 'emotional standards'.[6] Stearns defines emotional standards as 'the recommended norms by which people are supposed to shape their emotional expressions and react to the expressions of others' (1994: 2). The advantage to studying emotional standards is that they 'can be established, their changes explored and explained' through such material as advice manuals (1989: 9). At the same time, he contrasts emotional standards against 'emotional experience', in which the latter term is also referred to as 'actual emotions' or ' "real" emotional life' (1994: 3). Stearns locates emotional experience in the individual as 'basic', 'biological' and 'natural impulse', in contrast to the 'social requirements and cultural norms' of emotional standards (1994: 3). However, as a social constructionist, his account allows for the possibility of emotional standards affecting and altering emotional experience because the latter 'has a distinct cognitive component heavily influenced by prevailing rules of feeling' (1989: 9).

A similar stance is adopted by sociologist, Arlie Hochschild, whose early concepts of 'emotion labour' and 'feeling rules', formulated in her pioneering study of flight attendants and the commercialisation of feeling, put emotions on the sociological agenda and beyond. Her work has been foundational for many subsequent theorists in the development of constructionist and culturalist perspectives, including the work of Olesen and Bone in this volume. Hochschild argues that emotions are a commodity that can be bought (as wage labour), sold (as customer service) and managed (by corporate concerns or other entities). Despite the ground-breaking aspects of her work, Hochschild sees the commodification of emotion as a form of capitalist *acting* in contrast with a private, authentic self. The demands of corporately mandated emotion management result in 'an estrangement between self and feeling and between self and display' (Hochschild 1983: 131). In distinguishing between the demands of public jobs and the private emotional self, Hochschild concludes that 'emotional labor poses a challenge to a person's sense of self', in which 'authentic' feeling resides or originates in the latter (136).

Simon Williams suggests that Hochschild's perspective on emotional management is disappointing 'from a comparative historical perspective' because its narrow focus on commercialisation of feeling in the twentieth century and reliance on the questionable certainty of a private/public divide, ignore the fact that 'emotional management has been going on for millennia' and that feeling rules were never only privately negotiated (S. Williams 2001: 69). Also problematic are the ideas that emotions, even managed ones, are complete and finished objects, rather than always in process (Barbalet cited in S. Williams 2001: 69) and that authentic feelings can be fully accessed. Further, the notion that emotions are produced by feeling rules cannot explain why emotions may arise in specific contexts, quite spontaneously, which contradict cultural rules (Burkitt 1999: 123–124). In retaining a notion of authentic emotional experience embedded in the individual, such accounts, which otherwise understand emotions as culturally learned and transmitted, may continue to essentialise.

In other words, some social construction theorists continue to exhibit a desire for essential emotion as a knowable object, possession or state – in Ahmed's terms, 'things' we 'have'. In contrast, it is our contention that emotions, though intangible, are the accumulation of what we apprehend when they are practised or played out in specific circumstances through language, gestures, expressions, bodily sensations and so forth. Following poststructuralist and feminist critiques of master narratives, particularly the narrative of a rationally accessible, unqualified reality, there is no 'essence' of emotion as an absolute, potentially knowable truth.

The culturalist approach we are advocating borrows from social constructionist perspectives but is more specific. Like social construction theories, a culturalist formulation does not focus on the biological individual. Unlike some social construction standpoints, however, a culturalist practice does not limit itself to the realm of the social *individual*. The form of culturalism we develop towards emotions is necessarily engaged with examining how emotion, culture and social formations, as configurations of unequal power relations, are articulated in contextualised and historicised ways to produce boundaries that shape and position individuals and collectives simultaneously.

Some critics express concern that a single-minded culturalist focus subsumes notions of self, emotion and social world under the umbrella of culture (Lyon 1998: 43). Margot Lyon, for instance, criticises the 'narrowness' of a culturalist approach, which she identifies as deriving from cultural anthropology, and concerned primarily with how culture shapes innerness in a process whereby emotion is culturally created and impressed on the individual (Lyon 1998: 41–42). We share some of Lyon's concerns; the schema we are outlining demands an understanding of emotion in terms of various aspects of the social formation – including social structures, patterns of organisation and power relations. This returns to the principle of relationality, which is central to our understanding of a cultural emotion studies. Our outline also works to conceptualise emotion as 'simultaneously of the individual and the group in a way that is both dynamic and capable of clarifying the relationship between the two' (Lyon 1998: 46), in that we hold emotions as constitutive of individuals *and* of cultural communities, practices and beliefs. Indeed, contemporary explorations of notions of subjectivity and personhood as constructed entities demand a more thorough culturalist understanding of emotions.

Yet, we would also like to emphasise that critiques of the 'narrowness' of culturalist approaches, especially with regard to emotion studies, may well be premature. In terms of the cultural emotion studies we delineate here, relatively little work has been undertaken to date. We view the pieces assembled in this reader as an emerging area of scholarship and pursue a culturalist approach to emotions not because it has been 'done' but, precisely, for the reason that it is has barely begun.

We adopt an approach to studying emotion which is both constructionist and culturalist. We reject those aspects of social constructionism which focus on the interiority, depth and individuality of emotion. We investigate emotions in the contexts of more widely felt, commonly shared collective spheres rather than in a realm in which only individual identities are produced.

Social identity and meaning production

Emotions, because they have been perceived as occurring predominantly at the level of individual experience, have been dismissed as a disturbance: irrational and unreliable. Individualism reaffirms commonly evoked models in which emotions emanate from within and potentially leak out or impinge, more or less dramatically, upon the outside social world. They overtake the individual, 'rather as a storm sweeps over the land' (Jaggar, chapter 2: 51), posing a threat to both the feeling individual and the social world s/he occupies.

This conceptualisation of emotion fits with and supports another entrenched dichotomy – the private/public – which locates emotions firmly in a private sphere, their restraint positioned as each individual's responsibility, while reason is public, understood and shared collectively, as part of civil society. However, recent scrutiny reveals the weaknesses of the private/public divide as an analytical category, undermining claims of emotions as internal, individuated and private (Harding and Pribram 2004). Simply because emotions, most conspicuously, are enacted or experienced at the level of the individual does not exclude them from being operative, concurrently, in larger cultural structures and processes. Discourses of the body also chiefly function experientially and at the level of the individual body but, as recent theory has shown, such discourses are intimately connected to larger social operations. Indeed, they are the means by which social institutions and cultural discourses are embodied. We argue a similar set of conditions for emotions: they are the means by which social and cultural formations affect us, that is, render us as feeling beings in a series of complex, intricate ways.

How subjects act emotionally – that is, how they are positioned as well as participate in the positioning of others as *emotional* – is part and parcel of the reproduction of specific categories of subjecthood and the power relations that constitute them. The produced subject, whose production is ongoing and never complete, acts within horizons that comprise the very potential for acting (Butler 1992). We use the term 'subjectivity' to refer to the incomplete and continuing construction of the individual subject within culture, history and discourse, which together bring into view and position, within relations of power, specific sorts of subjects with particular capacities to act. Potential recruits may take up, refuse or refashion the subject positions to which they are directed. Kathryn Woodward suggests that 'the positions we take up and identify with constitute our identities' (Woodward 1997: 39).

A subject is produced who not only acts emotionally but who is also positioned in terms of gender, class, sexuality, race and other modes of identity. Emotion and identity operate relationally. For example, gendered subjects are constructed through particular emotion events in which they express or suppress specific emotions. Gendered subjects must live and *feel* the specificities of such emotional occurrences or events, and they must constantly re-enact – relive and refeel – those specificities as part of the ongoing performance and maintenance of their identities.

A cultural emotion studies examines specific structures of feeling – that is, the emotions different categories of subjects are permitted to experience and express at any historical juncture, and how both individuals and collectives are brought into being through specific articulations of emotion.[7] One of the tasks of a culturalist approach is to chart how emotional subjectivities and social identities are reciprocally constituted, work that currently is being undertaken in richly productive and divergent ways.

In *Landscape for a Good Woman*, Steedman examines envy as an emotion that provides recognition of social exclusion and 'the impossible unfairness of things' (Steedman 1987: 111). For those living in circumstances of poverty and deprivation, envy is a response to experienced material and political differences, a sign of 'the felt injuries of a social system' which neglects the existences and desires of certain groups (114). Yet, envy is almost universally understood as a subjective emotion, either too base or too trivial to be productive and, therefore, ignored as a potential force for social or political change (111).

Steedman uses the example of Freud who interprets his servant's dream, in which she replaces Freud's wife, as an expression of sexual attraction for the master of the house – himself. Calling this 'extraordinary and transparent political paternalism', Steedman argues that, instead, 'the figures of fantasy who replace the reality are actually the possessors of material goods in the material world' (112). Rather than an expression of psychosexual desires, the dreamer recognises the 'felt injuries' and discriminations of the social, political and economic relations in which she exists in the privileged Freud household. Envy, in these terms, is a structure of feeling imbricated with class consciousness, locating an awareness of one's social position in relation to other social subjects (123). As such, it represents a potentially useful political position from which one can express the 'proper envy of those who possess what one has been denied' (123).

Cultural anthropologist Jennifer Biddle explores what she describes as 'the very identity *making* aspect of shame' – an emotion she believes is critical to notions of the self (Biddle, chapter 6: 116; italics in original). Biddle clarifies that the form of shame she takes up is an 'Anglo middle class Western' version – that is, a culturally specific model and, therefore, a Western conception of identity as self and other (124). Members of Western cultures feel a social emotion – 'the other-directed, communicating and performing aspects of shame' – in that another person is required to serve as witness to one's shaming (115).

A shaming event is a 'direct mimetic introversion' of another's negation or rejection; in the act of being severed or differentiated from the other, one is constituted as self (115). Shame, then, is productive in that it shapes and defines self-identity and pinpoints the 'very boundary between self and other' (117, 122). In its capacity to locate the boundary between self and other, Biddle finds shame necessary to certain forms of Western knowledge production, including her own discipline. Cultural anthropology relies on a distinction between self and other at the level of cultural difference (118–119). The maintenance of distinction between investigative self and cultural other is a necessary corollary of professional objectivity and credibility (120).

Judith Butler is also concerned with the boundary between self and other which she refers to as the 'I' and the 'you' (chapter 24). However, in her consideration of grief, she finds that it obscures as much as it delineates such a boundary: 'I have lost "you" only to discover that "I" have gone missing as well' (chapter 24: 388). What has been lost in the death of another, and made evident in the process of grieving, 'is a relationality that is composed neither exclusively of myself nor you, but is to be conceived as *the tie* by which those terms [I and you] are differentiated and related' (388; italics in original). Grief reveals our ties to others and, in doing so, exposes the extent to which we are constituted by those ties. Subjectivity, as evidenced through grief and mourning, is the relationality and inseparability of self and other.

Butler conceives of grief as the condition of possibility for a more equitable global politics. She argues that certain lives are more grievable than others and some are not grievable at all (393). In this 'hierarchy of grief', those for whom no public act of grieving is possible are not constituted as human subjects (393–394). The task is 'to ask about the conditions under which a grievable life is established and maintained', and what processes of exclusion and effacement make other lives impossible for or invisible to grief (396).

All of the above are instances in which a particular emotion is analysed in terms of the ways it informs a specific social identity or an understanding of subjectivity. In the relationality of emotions and identities, meanings are forged, changed and exchanged. Many of those meanings are struggled over and contested. Such contestation occurs, in part, through the realignment of emotional meanings and, therefore, altered conceptions of self and social identity. The struggle over contested emotional meanings works to produce different subject positions that overlap with and reformulate identity categories such as gender, race and ethnicity, sexuality and national identity.

Elsewhere, in connection with the public mourning of Princess Diana's death, we have argued that emotions can intersect with a series of political positionings – for and against the monarchy or as a means to argue issues of class and gender (Harding and Pribram 2002).

Such political positionings are both expressed and constituted through emotions. Although public display of grief in Britain in response to Diana's death did not produce a political crisis, it fuelled debate about appropriate and inappropriate expressions of emotion, framed as a mourning populace in contrast to an unfeeling, out-of-touch monarchy. Additionally, the extent of grief displayed raised questions about the source of the attachment so many felt for Diana. She was frequently discussed in terms of her status as a single mother and divorced wife, a connection some people felt between her circumstances and theirs, despite obvious economic discrepancies (410). As a result, significant conversation took place on issues such as the state of the family unit, the impact of divorce and adultery on women's and children's lives, and the behaviours and attitudes of husbands towards wives.

Such a cultural event can work to position subjects as emotional in relation to other social formations, like the monarchy, the nuclear family or single parenthood, reaffirming existing forms of emotional subjectivity or constituting new ones. The relationality of political positionings with ongoing processes of emotional subjectivity, in turn, operates to alter social identities such as gender or class. Rather than perceiving cultural events or public figures as 'tapping into' the already existing emotions of a potentially wide range of social individuals, it may be more useful to understand cultural events or figures as the means by which social groups express shifting emotional sensibilities and revise the meanings of various social identities. It is the interactivity of emotions with subjectivity, identity and meaning production that renders a culturalist approach to emotions significant for cultural politics.

Cultural politics

Social constructionism provides some tools for challenging essentialisms and the unequal power relations they have supported. However, as we have indicated, social constructionism has limited scope for intervening in cultural politics when it seeks to downplay the biological, thus failing to fully engage with the social *and* the individual. More recently, some sociologists and cultural theorists have challenged constructionists' persistent distinction between society and biology, culture and body, in thinking about emotion.

Simon Williams suggests the body and emotions are potentially the 'most autonomous and recalcitrant' aspect of contemporary human social life (S. Williams, chapter 8: 146). He takes the view that bodies are fundamentally excessive, and emotions lie at the heart of bodily excess. Bodies and passions, while amenable to rational management and control, are fluid and volatile and always 'threaten to "overspill" or "transgress" the socio-cultural boundaries which currently seek to "contain" them' (146). The excessiveness of body and feelings, which cannot quite be contained or explained by social rules and language, reminds us of the intangibility of emotions and sidesteps debate over which contributes more to their genesis and comprehension: society or biology. Instead, we might view emotions as irreducible to 'any one domain or discourse', not biology nor social relations nor discourse (141).

Williams argues that emotions can be seen as 'communicative, intercorporeal and intersubjective, constituted as physical and cultural dispositions through techniques of the body, forged within a particular social habitus' (142). These body techniques, in turn, must be contextualised within culture, history and power relations. Emotions, he argues, are *emergent* properties, located at the intersection of physiological *dispositions*, material *circumstances*, and socio-cultural *elaboration*' (142; italics in original). If embodied emotional experience is understood as interactive and relational, then we can move beyond analyses which focus only on the individual, internal and subjective and make links with broader structures and institutions (S. Williams, chapter 8).

In other words, the challenge is to understand emotion as having both a 'social *and* biological ontology' and to ascertain what the interrelations of the social and biological are (Lyon 1998: 55). That is, to look at how biological and social/cultural understandings might 'mutually inflect and extend what we know' and how the biological and social continually charge each other (Probyn 2005: xiv, 24).

Another consequence of concern about the limits of social constructionism and continued opposition between society and biology is the recent turn in cultural theory to a reconsideration of 'affect', whether physiological or psychological, in contrast to 'emotion'. Some theorists (Gibbs, Probyn) advocate the reintroduction of affect as a way to counter the dismissal of the biological which, they feel, maintains a false distinction between body and society – the continuation of a division between biology and society entails ignoring recent extensive rethinking of the body in cultural and historical terms thus, once again, rendering the body invisible and subordinate to mind/culture. Others (Grossberg, Massumi) have turned to affect to counter what they believe is an overemphasis on meaning, representation and ideology in cultural theory to the exclusion of other key aspects.

Anna Gibbs argues that cultural studies in particular and the humanities in general have neglected affect in its biological sense (Gibbs 2002: 335). On the one hand, this is the result of recent theoretical conceptions that describe the corporeal 'largely as a body of words, the sum of discourses about it' (336). On the other hand, the dominance of cognitive psychology has contributed to the current neglect (336). Relying on the work of Silvan Tomkins, Gibbs postulates affect as inherent in the body, in contrast to 'emotions' and 'feelings' which are culturally constructed (337). Affect operates 'outside of awareness' but '*organizes*, both intra- and inter-corporeally', providing an 'experiential matrix' which is the source of our interactions in and with the world (337; italics in original).

Elspeth Probyn borrows from Gibbs the notion that culturally constructed 'feelings' and 'emotions' 'cannot be substantially divorced from the materiality of the body', and she also turns to Tomkins in order to understand affect as amplifying 'at a physiological level the stimuli of everyday life' (Probyn 2004: 329). Describing affect as 'both intensely individual and social', Probyn indicates that her principal concern is to comprehend 'the physicality of the body' while those interested in emotion 'privilege cognition' and 'sometimes disparage what the feeling body does' (329, 330). Instead, Probyn suggests thinking in terms of two planes: affect as biology and emotion as biography, in which we feel physiologically but also respond emotionally based on our individual histories and social experiences (342).

Although they understand affect as deeply social, both Gibbs and Probyn take the individual as their unit of selection, in Haraway's terms, locating affect with an individuated subject who, then, enters a social world. Such an approach runs the risk of further prolonging the body/mind dilemma as well as limiting the possibility for future discussion that moves beyond the inner/outer problematic.

Further, we argue that individual processes, whether biological or psychological, have received more theoretical attention than cultural ones. It is the further development of a cultural emotion studies with which we are concerned in this reader. Our intention is not to deny either category – body or mind – but neither to fall into the arguments between them. Our interest lies in dealing with emotions as a separate category – a third term – operating alongside but simultaneously and inseparably from the mind/body dilemma. From a cultural perspective, then, it is not a question of biology versus society or nature versus nurture, but nature, nurture and culture as well as body, mind and *emotion*.

Brian Massumi recognises emotion as the quality or content of an experience achieved by passing through semantic or semiotic processes. Emotion functions in the realms of meaning and ideology through 'the sociolinguistic fixing of the quality of an experience which is from that point onward defined as personal' (Massumi 2002: 28). In contrast, affect is equated with intensity and is 'irreducibly bodily and autonomic' in nature, manifesting primarily in the skin, 'at the surface of the body, at its interface with things' (28, 25). Affect is a nonconscious and 'already-felt' state that registers the intensity of experience, in the sense of strength and duration, for a being who is not yet a subject, although 'it may well be the conditions of emergence of a subject' (25, 14). Additionally, affect or intensity is qualifiable, that is, potentially able to transform into an emotional state (26). However, Massumi cautions, there is no direct correspondence between quality and intensity or emotion and affect; they 'follow different logics and pertain to different orders' (27).

Massumi's concern, in trying to develop a theory of affect as intensity, existing apart from processes of signification, is to recover a sense of movement and change in cultural theory. He believes that cultural theories based on concepts of ideology and subject positionings tend to arrest movement, conceiving of subject formation as if it occurs on a grid of potential but limited positions in which there is 'displacement' but not transformation, 'as if the body simply leaps from one definition to the next' (3). Inserting the model of affect as intensity reverses the grounds so that positionality 'is secondary to movement and derived from it' (7). Thus, process, passage and indeterminacy 'have ontological privilege in the sense that they constitute the field of the emergence, while positionings are what emerge' (8).

Massumi's work is indebted to that of Larry Grossberg, who has made the case for the necessity of a theory of affect in cultural studies since the 1980s (Grossberg, chapter 3). Grossberg understands the social formation to be composed of multiple economies of which the affective is one (1997: 241). Cultural studies has tended to narrow the pertinent range of economies to meaning and representation, in which other economies such as the affective are reduced to sub-functions of ideology rather than being considered in terms of their own distinct operations, organisations and effects (1997: 397, 251).

Grossberg defines affect as a form of energy, a motivating force or intensity that identifies 'the strength of the investment' people have in their experiences, practices, identities and meanings (Grossberg 1992: 82). Affect, then, becomes one of the means by which power is constituted, mobilised, circulated and performed. As asignifying, affect is no longer positioned as a sub-function of meaning or ideology; instead, it operates directly in the circuit of power relations. Grossberg's purpose is political: he wishes to identify the strategies and sites where affective empowerment might become possible. 'Those differences which do matter [affectively] can become the site of ideological struggle' (Grossberg 1992: 105).[8]

Affect is detached from ideology or meaning by differentiating it from emotion. Emotions then become 'the product of the articulation of two planes: signification . . . and affect' (Grossberg 1992: 79). While acknowledging the important work currently taking place around theories of affect, this reader is concerned with *emotion*, in Grossberg's sense of incorporating both affect and signification. We understand emotions as signifying practices already imbricated with or articulated through meaning effects and power relations. To return to Massumi's contention that affect and emotion 'follow different logics and pertain to different orders', we are interested in pursuing the logic and order of emotions. To this end, although some of this reader's contributors utilise the term 'affect' in their chapters (Grossberg, Probyn, Riley), and others employ both terms (Ahmed, Rosaldo), we refer consistently to 'emotions'.

Massumi's concern about the stasis of concepts of positionality, given a social ground of movement, change and indeterminacy, reflects limitations in current theorisation regarding the processes by which it is possible for identities to shift, alter or transform. His arguments also speak to existing constraints in tracing the operations that enable or permit subjects to take up certain positions available to them rather than others. We believe that a cultural emotion studies can contribute to an understanding of how such processes of modification and transformation occur.

Discussing his later work on care of the self in a 1984 interview, Foucault describes an interchange between two people:

> For example, the fact that I may be older than you, and that you may initially have been intimidated, may be turned around during the course of our conversation, and I may end up being intimidated before someone precisely because he is younger than I am. (Foucault 1997: 292)

Foucault uses this instance in the micro-relations of power to indicate power's productivity and mutability, pointing out that such relations are 'mobile, reversible, and unstable' (292). His illustration is, precisely, an *interchange* in which something has been transferred, negotiated, altered. This rather simple example has two significant aspects. First, although Foucault does not specify this, the interchange has occurred through the dynamics of emotion relations, here, intimidation whether through fear or awe. Second, the emotional shift takes place on the basis of a category of social identity, in this instance, age. The meaning of 'age' modulates over the course of the conversation; initially, the power to intimidate through age belongs to the older individual. However, during the course of the conversation alternate meanings are negotiated or produced and the advantage of age – in the sense of being able to intimidate – shifts to the younger participant.

In Foucault's imagined scenario, what makes change through interchange possible is that age is saturated with emotional meanings. We can imagine a number of ways in which age is reconstructed in the course of the conversation to affect a shift or reversal in the meanings deployed by the two conversationalists – one younger, one older. Initially, perhaps, age is associated with wisdom and the older party is treated with, and expects, the intimidation that attaches to respect or veneration. Then, in the process or mobilisation of interaction, alternative implications of age are taken up. Age may emerge as the sign of generational change in which the parties either wish to or are forced to acknowledge the passing of expertise from one generation to the next. Intimidation by a younger other is invoked through the awareness of one's own dwindling intellectual powers and social influence. Emotions have fluctuated, meanings have altered, and power differentials, however slight, have shifted. What enables such transactions to occur is the interrelationality among emotions, power and meanings.

It is in their capacity to circulate meanings, to transmit social relations and to constitute subjectivity, that emotions are significant for cultural politics. They are forces that produce human relations, energies and activities, operating in complex circuits of social, cultural and individual relations. Emotions circulate: that is what they *do*, bringing into being relations among individuals, and between individuals and social structures. They comprise an integral part of the constitution, organisation and application of aspects of the social formation. For instance, the family is not only an economic, social and discursive system, but is also produced through feelings of love, a sense of duty and the desire for security. While discourses of nationalism and patriotism can be understood to produce loyalty and pride, equally, loyalty and pride are operative in the construction of nationalism and patriotism.

In the context of his 1984 interview, Foucault defines power relations as the means by which 'one person tries to control the conduct' of another, whether through 'amorous, institutional, or economic relationships' (1997: 291–292). A society cannot exist without power relations but the ethical goal, in Foucault's terms, is to 'play these games of power with as little domination as possible' (1997: 298). Emotion relations do not exist between people in some kind of equivalency or equilibrium. They are utilised in the exerting and reaffirming of power differentials. In this sense, emotions may be viewed as a terrain upon and through which unequal power relations are constructed, and social identities and subject positions become fixed.

However, to view emotions as simply subordinating is to duplicate concepts of emotions as negative forces, as burdens we are forced to endure and against which we must be constantly vigilant. It is to deny that emotion relations, like power relations, are productive: they not only subordinate, they create. Graham Richards argues that psychologising emotions has resulted in, first, rendering them pathological and, second, focusing on a handful of extraordinary emotions such as fear or anger, which then become representative of the entirety of emotional experience (Richards 2005: 51–52). Instead, extreme emotions 'are quite untypical of our quotidian emotional lives' which oscillate around 'irritation, boredom, impatience, mild amusement, transient frustration, resignation, apprehension, nostalgia, chagrin, contentment, affection, slight feelings of envy and vague dissatisfaction' (51).

Richards points to the sheer *ordinariness* of emotions, their perpetual presence in our day-to-day lives as well as during exceptional events. It is in terms of their ordinariness, we argue, that emotions need far greater study. It is in their everyday, always-present qualities – the way they infuse all social spaces and interactions – that we may come to understand how emotions circulate, activate and transform relations and how, in doing so, they work to constitute both subjects and social formations.

How emotions circulate, create and subordinate as they are relayed throughout the social formation is complex, fluid and insufficiently understood. The essays in this reader all work to clarify and extend our grasp of the many intricate ways that emotion matters. Following Grossberg, the task facing cultural studies, in addition to pinpointing the locations and terms within which emotions constrain, is to identify the strategies and sites where emotional investments make contestation and transformation possible.

Emotions: A Cultural Studies Reader brings together a wide-ranging collection of essays by accomplished scholars engaged in the academic study of emotions. Collectively, they provide a strong foundation for the overdue establishment of emotion studies within cultural studies. The reader is divided into two parts. Each part is preceded by an introduction that describes the rationale for the sections included and briefly outlines the essays that follow.

Part 1, 'Disciplinary developments', includes contributions which we consider vital to the development of a cultural emotion studies, gathered from the fields of cultural studies, cultural anthropology, sociology and history. The essays in Part 1 were written over a period of 44 years (1961–2005) and evidence the gradual, significant emergence of interest in emotions across these disciplines. In different ways, each chapter outlines key elements of a culturalist approach to emotions and signals directions for further investigation within each discipline and beyond. All the essays provide understandings of emotions as sociocultural phenomena that are culturally and historically specific, and that function as part of the production of unequal power relations.

Part 2, 'Considering culture', draws together essays that illustrate core aspects of a culturalist approach to emotions. Each chapter contributes to the historicisation and contextualisation of emotions, indicates ways the development of a cultural emotion studies furthers strategic political intervention and works to relate emotions to other aspects of the social formation. Although the chapters in 'Considering culture' interact with other essays in this collection in multiple ways, we have grouped them according to whether they primarily consider emotions at the level of national identity, public life, popular arts or subjectivity. Together, they represent existing productive explorations of emotions within cultural studies as well as indicate the way forward to future investigations.

Notes

1   Jaggar argues that, while a distinction between reason and emotion has a very long history in Western thought, an extreme polarisation of the two developed with the rise of modern science in the seventeenth century and a redefinition of reason as 'a purely instrumental faculty' (Jaggar, chapter 2: 50).

2   For more on the emotions of scientific and medical investigators see Dror (2005).

3   Prevailing forms of knowledge-building are essentialist because of their assertion, first, that it is possible to establish the definitive truth of a scientific claim and, second, that scientists and rational thinkers can arrive at complete explanations of a phenomenon by discovering the essence or 'reality' that lies behind it (Popper 2002 [19]).

4   This is in contrast to a 'medieval "grotesque" body', which was more open to the world (Burkitt 1999: 45).

5   On Freud and his retention of evolutionary and, therefore, pre-existing, instinctual emotions see also Steedman (1995: 84).

6   Peter Stearns has undertaken much of this work in partnership with Carol Stearns. Here, we cite only from his single-authored work.

7   Harding and Pribram (2004) includes a more detailed discussion of our use of the term 'structures of feeling'.

8   A more detailed analysis of Grossberg's views on affect is provided in Harding and Pribram (2004).

Bibliography

Ahmed, S. (2004) *The Cultural Politics of Emotion*. Edinburgh: Edinburgh University Press.

Alberti, F. B. (2006) 'Introduction: Medical History and Emotion Theory', in F. B. Alberti (ed.) *Medicine, Emotion, and Disease, 1700–1950*. Basingstoke: Palgrave Macmillan.

Barker, C. (2008) *Cultural Studies. Theory and Practice*. 3rd edition. London: Sage.

Baudrillard, J. (1983) 'The Ecstasy of Communication', in H. Foster (ed.) *The Anti-Aesthetic: Essays on Postmodern Culture*. Port Townsend, WA: Bay Press.

—— (1988) *Jean Baudrillard: Selected Writings*. M. Poster (ed.). Stanford, CA: Stanford University Press.

Bauman, Z. (2005) *Liquid Life*. Cambridge: Polity Press.

Bordo, S. (1987) *The Flight to Objectivity: Essays on Cartesianism and Culture*. Albany, NY: State University of New York Press.

Burkitt, I. (1999) *Bodies of Thought: Embodiment, Identity and Modernity*. London: Sage.

Butler, J. (1990) *Gender Trouble: Feminism and the Subversion of Identity*. New York and London: Routledge.

—— (1992) 'Contingent Foundations: Feminism and the Question of "Postmodernism" ', in J. Butler and J. Scott (eds) *Feminists Theorize the Political*. New York and London: Routledge.

—— (1993) *Bodies That Matter: On the Discursive Limits of 'Sex'*. New York and London: Routledge.

Clarke, S., Hoggett, P. and Thompson, S. (2006a) 'The Study of Emotion: An Introduction', in S. Clarke, P. Hoggett, and S. Thompson (eds) *Emotion, Politics and Society*. Basingstoke: Palgrave Macmillan.

—— (2006b) 'Moving Forward in the Study of Emotions: Some Conclusions', in S. Clarke, P. Hoggett and S. Thompson (eds) *Emotion, Politics and Society*. Basingstoke: Palgrave Macmillan.

Connell, R. W. (1995) *Masculinities*. Cambridge: Polity Press.

De Lauretis, T. (1991) 'Queer Theory: Lesbian and Gay Sexualities, An Introduction', *differences*, 5:3, iii–xviii.

Dror, O. (2005) 'Dangerous Liaisons: Science, Amusement and the Civilizing Process', in P. Gouk and H. Hills (eds) *Representing Emotions: New Connections in the Histories of Art, Music and Medicine*. Aldershot: Ashgate.

Flax, J. (1990) 'Postmodernism and Gender Relations in Feminist Theory', in L. Nicholson (ed.) *Feminism/Postmodernism*. New York: Routledge.

Foucault, M. (1980) *The Order of Things*. London: Tavistock Publications.

—— (1986) *The Archaeology of Knowledge*. Trans. A. M. Sheridan Smith. London: Tavistock Publications.

—— (1995 [1975]) *Discipline and Punish: The Birth of the Prison*. New York: Vintage.

—— (1997 [1984]) 'The Ethics of the Concern of the Self as a Practice of Freedom', in Paul Rabinow (ed.) *Ethics: Subjectivity and Truth*. New York: New Press.

Fuss, D. (1989) *Essentially Speaking: Feminism, Nature and Difference*. New York: Routledge.

—— (1991) *Inside/Out: Lesbian Theories, Gay Theories*. New York: Routledge.

Gibbs, A. (2002) 'Disaffected', *Continuum: Journal of Media & Cultural Studies*, 16:3, 335–341.

Gobert, R. D. (2006) 'Cognitive Catharsis in *The Caucasian Chalk Circle*', *Modern Drama*, 49:1 (Spring), 12–40.

Gouk, P. and Hills, H. (2005) 'Towards Histories of Emotions', in P. Gouk and H. Hills (eds) *Representing Emotions: New Connections in the Histories of Art, Music and Medicine*. Aldershot: Ashgate.

Grossberg, L. (1992) *We Gotta Get Out of This Place: Popular Conservatism and Postmodern Culture*. New York: Routledge.

—— (1997) *Bringing It All Back Home: Essays on Cultural Studies*. Durham, NC: Duke University Press.

—— (2006) 'Does Cultural Studies Have Futures? Should It? (Or What's the Matter with New York?)', *Cultural Studies*, 20:1, 1–32.

Grossberg, L., Nelson, C. and P. Treichler (eds) (1992) *Cultural Studies*. New York and London: Routledge.

Grosz, E. (1990) 'Conclusion: A Note on Essentialism and Difference', in S. Gunew (ed.) *Feminist Knowledge: Critique and Construct*. London and New York: Routledge.

Hall, S. (1990) 'Cultural Identity and Diaspora', in J. Rutherford (ed.) *Identity: Community, Culture, Difference*. London: Lawrence and Wishart.

—— (1997) 'Introduction', in S. Hall (ed.) *Representation: Cultural Representations and Signifying Practices*. London: Sage/Open University.

Haraway, D. (1989) *Primate Visions: Gender, Race, and Nature in the World of Modern Science*. New York: Routledge.

Harding, J. (1998) *Sex Acts: Practices of Femininity and Masculinity*. London: Sage.

Harding J. and Pribram, E. D. (2002) 'The Power of Feeling: Locating Emotions in Culture', *European Journal of Cultural Studies*, 5:4, 407–426.

—— (2004) 'Losing Our Cool? Following Williams and Grossberg on Emotions', *Cultural Studies*, 18:6, 863–883.

Harding, S. (1986) *The Science Question in Feminism*. Milton Keynes: Open University Press.

Hochschild, A. R. (1983) *The Managed Heart: Commercialization of Human Feeling*. Berkeley: University of California Press.

Jacobus, M., Keller, E. F. and Shuttleworth, S. (eds) (1990) *Body/Politics: Women and the Discourses of Science*. London and New York: Routledge.

Keller, E. F. (1983a) 'Gender and Science', in S. Harding and M. B. Hintikka (eds) *Discovering Reality. Feminist Perspectives on Epistemology, Metaphysics, Methodology, and Philosophy of Science*. Dordrecht, Holland: D. Reidel Publishing Company.

—— (1983b) *A Feeling for the Organism: The Life and Work of Barbara McClintock*. New York: W. H. Freeman.

—— (1984) *Reflections on Gender and Science*. New Haven, CT: Yale University Press.

Laqueur, T. (1990) *Making Sex: Body and Gender from the Greeks to Freud*. Cambridge, MA, and London: Harvard University Press.

Lupton, D. (1998) *The Emotional Self: A Sociocultural Exploration*. London: Sage.

Lyon, M. L. (1998) 'The Limitations of Cultural Constructionism in the Study of Emotion', in G. Bendelow and S. J. Williams (eds) *Emotions in Social Life: Critical Themes and Contemporary Issues*. London and New York: Routledge.

Lyotard, J. (1984) *The Postmodern Condition: A Report on Knowledge*. Minneapolis: University of Minnesota Press.

Martin, E. (1989) *The Woman in the Body: A Cultural Analysis of Reproduction*. Milton Keynes: Open University Press.

Massumi, B. (2002) *Parables for the Virtual: Movement, Affect, Sensation*. Durham, NC: Duke University Press.

Mercer, K. (1992) ' "1968" Periodising Postmodern Politics and Identity', in L. Grossberg, C. Nelson and P. Treichler (eds) *Cultural Studies*. New York and London: Routledge.

Morris, M. (1997) 'A Question of Cultural Studies', in A. McRobbie (ed.) *Back to Reality? Social Experience and Cultural Studies*. Manchester: Manchester University Press.

Nelson, C., Treicheler, P. and Grossberg, L. (1992) 'Introduction', in L. Grossberg, C. Nelson and P. Treichler (eds) *Cultural Studies*. New York and London: Routledge.

Newton, T. (1998) 'The Sociogenesis of Emotion: A Historical Sociology?, in G. Bendelow and S. J. Williams (eds) *Emotions in Social Life: Critical Themes and Contemporary Issues*. London: Routledge.

Oudshoorn, N. (1994) *Beyond the Natural Body: An Archaeology of Sex Hormones*. London and New York: Routledge.

Paster, G. K., Rowe, K. and Floyd-Wilson, M. (2004) 'Introduction: Reading the Early Modern Passions', in G. K. Paster, K. Rowe and M. Floyd-Wilson (eds) *Reading the Early Modern Passions: Essays in the Cultural History of Emotion*. Philadelphia: University of Pennsylvania Press.

Poovey, M. (1990). 'Speaking of the Body: Mid Victorian Constructions of Female Desire', in Jacobus, Keller and Shuttleworth (eds) *Body/Politics: Women and the Discourses of Science*. London and New York: Routledge.

Popper, K. (2002 [1963]) *Conjectures and Refutations. The Growth of Scientific Knowledge*. London: Routledge.

Pribram, E. D. (1993) 'Seduction, Control, and the Search for Authenticity: Madonna's *Truth or Dare*', in C. Schwichtenberg (ed.) *The Madonna Connection: Representational Politics, Subcultural Identities, and Cultural Theory*. Boulder, CO: Westview Press.

Probyn, E. (1993) *Sexing the Self: Gendered Positions in Cultural Studies*. London: Routledge.

—— (2004) 'Everyday Shame', *Cultural Studies*. 18:2/3 (March/May), 328–349.

—— (2005) *Blush: Faces of Shame*. Minneapolis: University of Minnesota Press.

Richards, G. (2005) 'Emotions into Words – Or Words into Emotions?', in P. Gouk and H. Hills (eds) *Representing Emotions: New Connections in the Histories of Art, Music and Medicine*. Aldershot: Ashgate.

Rose, H. (1987) 'Hand, Brain and Heart: A Feminist Epistemology for the Natural Sciences', in S. Harding and J. F. O'Barr (eds) *Sex and Scientific Inquiry*. Chicago, IL: The University of Chicago Press.

—— (1994) *Love, Power and Knowledge. Towards a Feminist Transformation of the Sciences*. Cambridge: Polity Press.

Rose, N. (1985) *The Psychological Complex: Psychology, Politics and Society in England, 1869–1939*. London: Routledge & Kegan Paul.

—— (1997) 'Assembling the Modern Self', in Roy Porter (ed.) *Rewriting the Self: Histories from the Renaissance to the Present*. London: Routledge.

Schiebinger, L. (1986) 'Skeletons in the Closet: The First Illustrations of the Female Skeleton in Nineteenth Century Anatomy', *Representations*, 14, 42–83.

Schnog, N. (1997) 'On Inventing the Psychological', in J. Pfister and N. Schnog (eds) *Inventing the Psychological: Toward a Cultural History of Emotional Life in America*. New Haven, CT: Yale University Press.

Sedgwick, E.K. (1991) *The Epistemology of the Closet*. Hemel Hempstead: Harvester Wheatsheaf.

Seidler, V. J. (1994) *Unreasonable Men: Masculinity and Social Theory*. London and New York: Routledge.

Stearns, P. (1989) *Jealousy: The Evolution of an Emotion in American History*. New York: New York University Press.

—— (1994) *American Cool: Constructing a Twentieth-Century Emotional Style*. New York: New York University Press.

Steedman, C. K. (1987) *Landscape for a Good Woman: A Story of Two Lives*. New Brunswick, NJ: Rutgers University Press.

—— (1995) *Strange Dislocations: Childhood and the Idea of Human Interiority, 1780–1930*. Cambridge, MA: Harvard University Press.

Weeks, J. (1994) *The Lesser Evil and the Greater Good: The Theory and Practice of Social Diversity*. London: Rivers Oram Press.

Williams, R. (1975 [1961]) *The Long Revolution*. Westport, CT: Greenwood.

Williams, S.J. (2000) 'Reason, Emotion and Embodiment: Is "Mental" Health a Contradiction in Terms?', *Sociology of Health and Illness*, 22:5, 559–581.

—— (2001) *Emotion and Social Theory*. London: Sage.

Woodward, K. (1997) 'Concepts of Identity and Difference', in K. Woodward (ed.) *Identity and Difference*. Thousand Oaks, CA, and London: Sage/Open University Press.

PART 1

Disciplinary developments

Introduction

PART 1 OF THE READER comprises key contributions from the fields of cultural studies, anthropology, sociology and history, each discipline represented by its own section. Collectively, we believe, they provide a firm foundation for developing a cultural emotion studies. In very different ways, they outline significant aspects of a culturalist perspective on emotion. They provide insights into how emotions are sociocultural phenomena, how they are culturally and historically specific, how they change over time, across cultures and within societies, and how they participate in the production of unequal power relations. In other words, each chapter contributes to an understanding of what emotions do.

Culturalist foundations

Although unsustained across the discipline, within cultural studies there have been specific important investigations of emotions as part of everyday personal, cultural and political life. Such foundational work addresses the ways in which emotions might contribute to knowledge production, and how they operate in the reproduction of subjectivity, culture and power relations. The first section, 'Culturalist foundations', comprises three chapters representing early, influential work in the field. Each of the contributions elaborates concepts that we consider vital for a cultural emotion studies. Raymond Williams paved a prescient, landmark way in the 1960s with his conceptualisation of 'structure of feeling' and, two decades later, Lawrence Grossberg added another important dimension with the development of 'economy of affect'. Alison Jaggar, a feminist philosopher rather than a cultural theorist, impacted cultural studies and many other disciplines with her key work on 'emotional hegemony'. She helped to forge a fundamental rethinking of relations between emotion, epistemology and power. Although each of these authors uses different words — feeling, affect or emotion — to describe their object of inquiry, all three share in common a concern with the political possibilities of inserting emotion into culture and epistemology.

The two excerpts of Raymond Williams' work included in Chapter 1, 'On structure of feeling', represent Williams' major writings on the concept of structure of feeling, first appearing in, respectively, 1961 and 1979. A ground-breaking effort in identifying and analysing emotions as collective, historical and cultural phenomena, structure of feeling is an important starting place in building a cultural studies framework.

Williams described structure of feeling as 'the felt sense of the quality of life at a particular place and time' (chapter 1: 36). The emphasis on 'felt' is important; Williams was describing something 'of feeling much more than of thought – a pattern of impulses, restraints, tones' (44). He draws a distinction between the knowledge which can be derived from an era's institutions and social structures versus an understanding of its emotional relations – that is, something that exists beyond or in addition to the articulated beliefs and values of a specific society or social group.

Williams uses structure of feeling as a class-linked concept, analysing what he believes are the principal structures of feeling for each class in a particular era. He also utilises it as a periodising concept, arguing that every generation develops its own, specific structure of feeling. Williams argues that the structure of feeling of any given time or place is extremely difficult to recapture. This is so because the historical past, 'the period culture, consciously studied, is necessarily different from the culture as lived' (1975: 59). Precisely what is missing from historical investigation, what is omitted from documentation and records, is an epoch's lived sense, its structure(s) of feeling.

The concept of structure of feeling opens up significant theoretical possibilities. First, it allows the emotions to have specific, ascertainable and important effects without rendering them irrational. Second, structure of feeling incorporates the idea that emotions are culturally constituted and culturally shared. While feelings remain largely intangible, their structures of organisation and behaviour become available to investigation, considerations largely absent from theoretical formulations prior to or contemporary with Williams. He outlines emotions as rich, complex sociocultural practices; as such, emotions produce culture.

Alison Jaggar's chapter, 'Love and knowledge: emotion in feminist epistemology', provides an important basis for both historicising and politicising emotion. In this essay originally published in 1989, she challenges the primacy accorded rationality in modern Western thought and the associated subordination of emotion as the opposite of reason and, thereby, subversive of knowledge. She argues that emotions are socially constructed and perform a hegemonic function through the subordination and marginalisation of subjects considered 'emotional'.

Jaggar argues that the ideological function of discourses on the emotions works to align dominant political, social and cultural groups with reason and to subordinate those groups linked with emotion. Consequently, women and people of colour are viewed as more subjective, biased and irrational. Such an 'assignment of reason and emotion', Jaggar argues, bolsters the authority of dominant groups and discredits subordinate groups, constituting a process of 'emotional hegemony' (chapter 2: 60).

Jaggar understands emotions as working to position individuals within structures of dominance or relations of power – emotional hegemony. However, when contradictory emotions are felt by a sufficient number of people, they form the basis for the constitution of subcultural experiences and groups. She moves on to consider how 'outlaw' emotions might be politically and epistemologically productive.

Lawrence Grossberg has consistently argued for the investigation and politicisation of affect within cultural studies. In his chapter, 'Postmodernity and affect: all dressed up with no place to go', an argument begun in 1988 and further developed in later work, he conceptualises an 'economy of affect' as a significant dimension of the social formation. He attempts to link the individual to larger cultural processes through the activities and energies of affect and, significantly, to explore how power operates through affect.

This work is a response to a tendency, which he identifies within the British tradition of cultural studies, to equate meaning and representation with culture and, so, to reduce the affective to a sub-function of ideology. Through his conceptualisation of 'affective economies', he attempts to prevent affect from being subsumed under the ideological in cultural studies or the libidinal in psychoanalytic theory.

He proposes adding affect into 'the already crowded relations' of signification (meaning, representation, language), economy (material production, distribution, consumption) and libido (desire, sexuality) (chapter 3: 76). Everyday life is the articulation of all of these planes of effects operating together, along with potential others. Defining affect as one form of 'psychic energy', he attributes to it the authority of 'investment': it determines or constitutes what matters to people (77, 78). Affect is one means by which power is constituted, mobilised, circulated and performed. Affect becomes an important form of energy or intensity that motivates relations of power among individuals as well as between individuals and the social forces working to govern their conduct.

In his chapter, Grossberg specifically analyses postmodernity as a change in the culture of affect and, more generally, works to locate affect as a foundation for a progressive politics. Things that matter affectively can be taken up as sites of ideological assertion or contestation. Further, the analysis of affect can help to explain why certain ideologies take hold and not others, or how, through affective investments, ideologies are internalised and naturalised.

Contributions from cultural anthropology

As a discipline, cultural anthropology has provided an early, ongoing and profound contribution to a cultural emotion studies. Through its cross-cultural comparisons of emotional concepts and behaviours, cultural anthropology has demonstrated that emotions are not universal, inherent or pre-cultural. In relativising emotions between cultures, cultural anthropologists have documented specific ways in which emotions are culturally constructed, variable and non-equivalent (an emotion in one culture does not neatly translate as an equivalent emotion in another culture, distinguished solely in being named by a different word).

Significant early contributors to an ethnographic culturalist perspective include Clifford Geertz (1973, 1987), Fred Myers (1979, 1986), Michelle Rosaldo (1980, 1983, chapter 4), Lila Abu-Lughod (1986) and Catherine Lutz (1986, 1988). In their chapter, 'Emotion, discourse, and the politics of everyday life', Abu-Lughod and Lutz point out that, for the most part, anthropological work prior to 1980 followed the accepted dominance of psychological models. 'But only recently has the *doxa* itself – that emotions are things internal, irrational, and natural – been exposed and questioned' (chapter 5: 101). Their essay provides an overview of the study of emotion in cultural anthropology (100–102).

The three chapters in 'Contributions from cultural anthropology' share in common not only a concern with the cultural constructedness of emotions but also a focus on the role of emotions in subject formation. Each of the essays examines how an individual culture's notions of emotionality are intertwined with a culture-specific understanding of subjecthood.

In 'Toward an anthropology of self and feeling', Rosaldo compares Western concepts of emotion with those of the Ilongot, a Filipino community. In Ilongot accounts, the emotional actions of individuals 'refer almost exclusively to public and political concerns' and not, as in the West, to individuated personal or psychological motivations (91). Exemplifying the kind of work cultural anthropology has offered up, Rosaldo uses these differences to outline a culturalist account of emotions which 'insists upon the sociocultural bases for experiences once assigned to a subjective and unknowable preserve of psychic privacy' (85). Further, cultural differences indicate that the Western notion of universal emotions is suspect.

Instead, Rosaldo argues in terms of emotions as 'embodied thoughts', meaning that they 'are structured by our forms of understanding' of cultural practices, symbols and ideas (89). Emotions, then, reflect the ways in which we are actively involved in a social world.

Not only are emotions felt differently by various communities of people, Rosaldo argues, but those ways of feeling are dependent on a culture's notion of subjectivity which is also culturally specific. The way groups constitute themselves *as* selves brings into being distinct emotions and distinctive relations towards emotion. Forms of subjectivity are culturally constituted and emotions are intricately involved in that process. 'Lives of feeling' are linked to 'conceptions of the self' and 'both of these are aspects of particular forms of polities and social relations' (94). Culture provides the framework within which our subjectivities and emotional existences are socially ordered and constrained.

Summarising the history of emotion studies in cultural anthropology, Abu-Lughod and Lutz argue there are three dominant strategies to be pursued: making cultural comparisons; tracking historical changes; or analysing discourse. In 'Emotion, discourse, and the politics of everyday life', they are primarily concerned with the last approach, exploring the parameters and relevancy of discourse.

Defining discourse in the Foucauldian sense, such an approach entails 'careful analysis of the richness of specific social situations', paying attention to 'the many ways emotion gets its meaning and force from its location and performance in the public realm of discourse' (104). In these terms, emotional discourses are 'pragmatic acts and communicative performances' that constitute and affect the social arena, including a potentially wide array of social issues and relations (106). Emotional discourses are forms of social action bound up with power relations that create effects in the world, both constructing as well as contesting realities and subjectivities.

'Attention to discourse also leads us to a more complex view of the multiple, shifting, and contested meanings possible in emotional utterances and interchanges', moving away from understandings of emotion as biological or psychological functions and, simultaneously, expanding our understanding of the complex things emotions do, rather than viewing them as simplistically monolithic (106). Abu-Lughod and Lutz also note that emotion as discourse need not be limited to linguistic models but may also incorporate bodily techniques and postures. By viewing emotion as discourse, attention is focused on the cultural-historical specificity of emotion and the transmission of power; that is, the many, changing ways emotions both establish and alter unequal social relations.

In 'Shame', Jennifer Biddle examines the identity-delineating functions of that particular emotion, and its centrality to certain forms of Western knowledge production. She argues that shame holds significance in Western cultures due to its role in producing 'self' and 'other'. A similar configuration of shame is not present in Walpiri Aboriginal society because it is not structured on the basis of a private/public distinction (119). For Westerners, shame can occur only in the presence of another person and so is necessarily social. 'We make objects of ourselves, objects of others, and are made objects by others. . . . In shame, the self expresses itself where it finds itself virtually, negatively differentiated, severed as it is, from the other' (114). Shame works to create identity through the emotional distinctions made between self and other: 'logically, if the other is disgusted, the self must be repugnant' (115). Through these feelings, the boundary of self-difference is determined.

Biddle goes on to argue how the shaming qualities which establish self and other are integral to the discipline of cultural anthropology and its modes of knowledge production. There can be no investigation without the delineation of cultural difference. Further, an ethnographer who fails to maintain sufficient distinction between one's 'own' culture and an 'other' culture loses the professional credibility of objectivity by 'going native' (120). But, Biddle argues, in this structuration it is ultimately the anthropologist who becomes foreign or other because it is shameful to overtly acknowledge another's difference and to deny him, her, or them recognition. To deny recognition is to replicate a history which failed to recognise the mistreatment of Australian Aboriginal peoples.

Sociological perspectives

Sociologists of emotions have provided useful insights into ways in which emotions are socially constructed. Adopting a variety of perspectives, they have investigated how emotions might be shaped by social structures, institutions and power relations, and how individual subjects are affected by 'feeling rules' and emotional management.

While it might be argued that emotions feature implicitly or explicitly in the classical sociological writings of Marx, Durkheim, Weber and Simmel, it is only in the last two and a half decades that a distinctive body of work on the sociology of the emotions has begun to emerge (Williams and Bendelow 1998: xv). Arlie Hochschild's *The Managed Heart* (1983) and Norman Denzin's *On Understanding Emotion* (1984) were landmark texts, signalling the beginnings of more intensive sociological interest in the emotions. Hochschild made a highly significant contribution to culturalist understandings of emotion through her study of 'emotional labour' and the 'commercialisation of feeling' among flight attendants, arguing that emotions are not natural but produced through 'feeling rules' which shape how emotion is expressed and managed according to social norms in specific social contexts. Denzin provided a phenomenological understanding of the social construction of emotions as cognitive assessments and moral judgements of the individual's place in the world – that is, part of the 'interpretive', everyday practices of the person.

Critics have raised concerns about the over-determinism of Hochschild's structuralist approach to emotion and the lack of analysis of the role of power and social institutions in a phenomenological approach. Deborah Lupton, among others, has advocated a poststructuralist understanding of emotions with an emphasis on the discursive production of emotion and the emotional subject (1998). Sociologists such as Simon Williams, Ian Burkitt and Lupton have been concerned with the role of the biological in sociological explanations and of the body in the sociology of emotion. In the last decade, a number of sociologists have made the case for the development of a distinctive sociology of emotions, producing collections of essays and monographs aimed at defining the scope of investigation (Barbalet 1998, 2002; S. Williams and Bendelow 1998; S. Williams 2001).

While critics have raised concerns about certain aspects of Hochschild's work, the concept of 'emotional labour' and consideration of the effects of social structures in producing emotions have continued to be relevant to subsequent researchers – for instance, Oleson and Bone, whose essay is included in this volume. Their understanding of 'emotional labour' is relevant to a culturalist approach to emotions because it does not assume the existence of a true self and underlying authentic emotion. Rather, it takes account of changing multiple subjectivities and cultural contexts, focusing on the complex and dynamic interplay between individual emotional expression and structural constraints.

In 'Emotions in rationalizing organizations: conceptual notes from professional nursing in the USA', Oleson and Bone consider the impact of changes in organisational structures – in particular, financially driven pressures to rationalise and become more efficient – on emotions and emotional behaviours for the nursing profession in the United States of America. Since 'emotional work' and the expression of emotion are central to health care and to nurses' professional identity, there is a potential tension between that emotion work and the structural demands for efficiency which includes early dismissal of patients, larger workloads and substitution of other personnel for nurses. For instance, in the 1990s, organisational efficiency and cost containment measures led to a decrease in the number of nurses involved in direct patient care and, simultaneously, to an increase in the level of responsibility for patient outcome. The result was a reduction in the amount of time available for all aspects of work, including emotional labour while, at the same time, a new 'patient focus' approach was developing, building on hospitality models of customer relations. Nurses were caught between competing models with contradictory emotional demands.

Emotional labour is understood by the authors to involve interplay between 'individual expression, normative and structural constraints, and the dynamics of change' (128). Most work on emotional labour has been conducted in management studies and has looked at the theme of fitting workers' emotions to company goals. Oleson and Bone argue for a more complex understanding that is capable of capturing the complexities of performing emotional labour within commodifying service economies while being sensitive to multiple subjectivities and the changing dynamics of workplace culture.

Simon Williams' essay, 'Modernity and the emotions: corporeal reflections on the (ir)rational', focuses on emotions and modernity, discussing the latter's problematic distinction between reason and emotion, and the contradictory features of modernity as both order and chaos. His concern is to search for ways of being and knowing which overturn dualistic thought and practice.

Williams argues against seeing reason and emotion as fundamentally opposed and towards a view of rationality as a passionately held belief, which is in part 'irrational' or 'unreasonable'. He argues for moving beyond the historical dichotomisation of reason and emotion and its broader set of accompanying distinctions: mind/body, nature/culture, public/private (141). He considers arguments that emotions are central to reason and epistemology. Williams outlines his own view that emotions are multi-faceted phenomena which cannot be reduced to any one domain or discourse. He understands emotions as essentially 'communicative, intercorporeal and intersubjective, constituted as physical and cultural dispositions through techniques of the body, forged within a particular social habitus' (141–142). Emotions provide the basis for social reciprocity and exchange, as well as a link between the individual and the broader social structure. This view of emotions as interactive and relational is a way of moving beyond emotions as internal and individualistic, and towards an approach which indicates how they construct institutions as well as individuals.

Ian Burkitt's essay, 'Powerful emotions: power, government and opposition in the "War on Terror" ', provides an analysis of emotion and power relations, adopting some of Foucault's insights on power. He argues that sociologists should view emotions relationally, that is, as part of the relations between people rather than as individual or internal phenomena. Burkitt examines how emotions are integral to power and government through consideration of the 'War on Terror' declared by many Western governments in the aftermath of 9/11, and which is widely couched in terms of fear and hope. He analyses two selected events: a peace demonstration in London on 15 February 2003, which was part of global protests against the Iraq war; and the effects of the train bombings in Madrid on 11 March 2004. His intention is to show how governments use emotion to direct conduct, yet how this has unpredictable and unintended consequences for all involved, opening up, in Jaggar's terms, both hegemonic and potentially subversive moments.

Burkitt analyses newspaper coverage of the two events, which were both reactions against attempts to direct the public's conduct through the manipulation of emotion and, in both instances, involved mass protests and the clear public performance of emotion. He argues that emotion is integral to attempts to incite, induce and seduce and, hence, is integral to government, opposition and resistance and power relations. Any analysis of power, government and politics that does not consider emotion, he argues, misses an essential element.

Historical approaches

Historians have contributed to the development of a culturalist approach to emotions by historicising them – that is, undertaking the detailed, specific analyses required to indicate the ways emotions have changed over time and how such changes are connected to contemporaneous social, political, economic and ideological events. In doing so, historians of emotions have added significantly to an understanding of the relational aspects of emotions as part of larger social formations.

Still, some historians express concern that the study of emotions is relatively new to the discipline and not yet sufficiently embraced. Gouk and Hills, for example, note that 'the scarcity of historically contextualised studies is striking' (2005: 16). Although individual historians have undertaken studies since the nineteenth century, when the notion originated that emotions had histories, 'professional historians have only turned towards the subject comparatively recently' (2005: 16).

Predecessors influencing contemporary culturalist approaches include Norbert Elias whose 1939, *The Civilizing Process*, argued that, beginning in the sixteenth century, members of the elite and middle classes began to repress anger and other emotions. In his view, the development of more 'refined' manners and self-control was a necessary part of the transformation to modernity (Rosenwein 1998: 237). Also significant is the work of Lucien Febvre who argued, as early as 1943, for the establishment of emotions as an object of historical inquiry (Ulbricht 2008). Similarly influential is the work of a number of social historians (Stone 1977; Shorter 1975; Ariès 1962) who explored the history of the family, particularly in terms of the development of love or affectionate relationships between spouses and between parents and children (Ulbricht 2008; Gillis 1988: 87).

Although Elias postulated a view of emotions as both learned and subject to cultural change, and he, Febvre, and the social historians all tie the emotional changes they describe to various aspects of modernity, they share in common similar limitations. Their accounts have a teleological aspect in which Western society progresses from the 'primitive' to the 'civilized' in terms of social behaviour, from the more dangerous, evolutionary emotions to the rise of Enlightenment reason, or from cold and remote relationships to the discovery of warmer expressions of romantic or maternal love (Rosenwein 1998: 238; Ulbricht 2008; Gillis 1988: 88). More recently, Peter Stearns and Carol Stearns have made important contributions to the field through their studies of specific emotions as they existed and altered in different periods (1985, 1986, 1988, 1989, 1994).

The three chapters represented in 'Historical approaches', in their respective studies of specific emotions (anger and sadness, moodiness, envy), provide the careful, thorough work required to historicise emotions. Further, each chapter relates its study of specific emotions in, respectively, the early modern period, the nineteenth century and the twentieth century, to other factors in the social formation, primarily class and gender. To that end, all three investigations help to account for the development or perpetuation of social inequities.

In ' "Lord help me walk humbly": anger and sadness in England and America, 1570–1750', Carol Stearns analyses personal diary accounts of anger and sadness in England and the USA. During the late seventeenth century and early eighteenth century, a new understanding of emotion emerged concerning the relative appropriateness of feeling and acting upon anger versus sadness. Prior to the late seventeenth century, most diarists had difficulty thinking of themselves as angry; indeed, it represented the sin of pride and was meant to be expressed by God, not mortals. Instead, those writing described themselves as 'aggrieved' which, in the definition of the time, denoted 'saddened by an affront' (178). Yet, by the eighteenth century, it became possible to express anger much more frequently and more comfortably.

Stearns attributes the change to the development of the belief that human beings are able to control their emotions. This new conceptualisation made it safer to feel anger because it could now be restrained. However, she points out that this development applied primarily to middle- and upper-class men who, fitted with a new sense of control and self-assertiveness, were better able to meet the demands of an emerging modernity. Meanwhile, women and members of the lower classes 'remained in the older mold' of sadness, which continued to require 'submissive-ness and passivity' (184). The effect was to increase the differences and distance between privileged men and other social groups, thereby exacerbating social inequities.

Stearns' chapter indicates the enormous potential and productivity in careful, detailed historical analyses of the emotions. But she also outlines some of the methodological problems in undertaking such studies. Recalling Raymond Williams' concern about the difficulties in recapturing the structures of feeling of earlier times, Stearns acknowledges that while diaries and autobiographies are some of the best sources available to historians, they pose certain limitations. For instance, one can draw conclusions about the larger population from the accounts of diarists only 'with caution', many aspects of emotional life are left out of the accounts made by individuals, and studying diaries tends to 'exaggerate the importance of the cognitive aspect of emotions' over other forms of emotional practices and experience (171).

Nancy Schnog, in 'Changing emotions: moods and the nineteenth-century American woman writer', engages with the nineteenth-century definition of mood as '[f]its of variable or unaccountable temper; especially melancholy, gloomy, or bad-tempered fits' (191). She exam-ines this notion of mood, akin to contemporary uses of 'moodiness', in connection with two nineteenth-century social movements: the cult of domesticity; and the Romantic ideal of art-istic genius. Looking at literature by American women writers such as Louisa May Alcott's 1864 novel *Moods*, and Kate Chopin's 1899 *Awakenings*, Schnog explores how such writers used the concept of mood to either affirm or challenge prevailing notions of female character and women's social roles.

In the sentimental literature that peaked in popularity in the 1850s, moodiness was viewed as a major flaw in women. Married middle-class women were instructed to banish 'anxiousness, sadness, nervousness, irritability . . . self-absorption, sulkiness, standoffishness, and coldness' (193). Instead, they were expected to take up habitual cheerfulness as the domestic ideal. Reacting against the limitations of cheerfulness, some women writers of the post-Civil War era borrowed concepts from the male Romantic movement that linked tem-pestuous moods to 'individualism, creativity, and emotional depth' (193). These women writers began to depict moody female characters in terms that rendered them as admirable or com-plex as male characters, rather than flawed.

In turning to romanticism, an important understanding of emotion that had sustained male writers for some time, these writers reworked the meaning of mood for women. In a two-step process, they moved their characters beyond the confinement of the domestic politics of cheerfulness while also arguing for the potential in women's lives of more public and creative roles. By negotiating the contradictions in domestic versus romantic emotion, Schnog argues, women writers revised the 'historically and politically constituted category of moods' (192). They countered the politics of cheerfulness with a cultural politics that deployed emotion in an attempt to expand women's lives.

Carolyn Steedman's chapter, 'Stories', is an excerpt from her highly influential 1987 book, *Landscape for a Good Woman: A Story of Two Lives*. In it, Steedman relates a double biography, that of her own 1950s childhood in South London and her mother's 1920s working-class existence in Northern England. *Landscape for a Good Woman* was a significant work in the move to more autobiographical and personal forms of analysis, a methodology that grew out of feminism. However, Steedman's use of personal stories in order to insert emotion into political, economic and social theory has been less noted. 'Stories' strategises ways to include emotions in historical analyses.

Her concern is to investigate envy not simply as an individual or psychological phenomenon but as political and material. Envy, Steedman argues, is about longing and wanting in response to *material* lack, to the things which are socially and culturally withheld. She calls this the 'politics of envy', a potentially potent political tool that is largely overlooked (211). Steedman links the politics of envy to working-class culture and, especially, to working-class women and children. Arguing that the emotional lives of working-class cultures have been virtually ignored or reduced to a romanticised sameness, she points out that people, like her mother, who live such lives are aware of the resulting emotional effects just as they are aware of other repercussions. Her mother's life stories were 'designed to show me the terrible unfairness of things, the subterranean culture of longing for that which one can never have' (211).

Steedman attempts to redress the omission of categories like envy from historical analysis and, therefore, from politics. She argues against 'the structures of political thought that have labelled this wanting as wrong', or dismissed envy as personal pettiness and insignificant (219). In doing so, Steedman poses the question of what precisely is the relationship between 'stories' – personal, emotional – and 'history'?

Bibliography

Abu-Lughod, Lila (1986) *Veiled Sentiments: Honor and Poetry in a Bedouin Society*. Berkeley: University of California Press.

Ariès, P. (1962) *Centuries of Childhood: A Social History of Family Life*. London: Jonathan Cape.

Barbalet, J. (1998) *Emotion, Social Theory and Social Structure*. Cambridge: Cambridge University Press.

—— (2002) *Emotions and Sociology*. Oxford: Blackwell Publishing.

Denzin, N. (1984) *On Understanding Emotion*. San Francisco: Jossey Bass.

Elias, N. (1978/[1939]) *The Civilising Process. Vol. I: The History of Manners*. Oxford: Basil Blackwell.

—— (1982/[1939]) *The Civilising Process. Vol. II: State Formations and Civilisation*. Oxford: Basil Blackwell.

Febvre, L. (1973) *A New Kind of History: From the Writings of Febvre*. London: Routledge & Kegan Paul.

Geertz, C. (1973) *The Interpretation of Cultures*. New York: Basic Books.

—— (1987) *Works and Lives*. Stanford, CA: Stanford University Press.

Gillis, J. R. (1988) 'From Ritual to Romance: Toward an Alternative History of Love', in C. Z. Stearns and P. Stearns (eds) *Emotion and Social Change: Toward a New Psychohistory*. New York: Holmes & Meier.

Gouk, P. and Hills, H. (2005) 'Towards Histories of Emotions', in P. Gouk and H. Hills (eds) *Representing Emotions: New Connections in the Histories of Art, Music and Medicine*. Aldershot: Ashgate.

Hochschild, A. R. (1983) *The Managed Heart: Commercialization of Human Feeling*. Berkeley: University of California Press.

Lupton, D. (1998) *The Emotional Self: A Sociocultural Exploration*. London: Sage.

Lutz, C. (1986) 'Emotion, Thought, and Estrangement: Emotion as a Cultural Category', *Cultural Anthropology* 1, 405–436.

—— (1988) *Unnatural Emotions: Everyday Sentiments on a Micronesian Atoll and Their Challenge to Western Theory*. Chicago: University of Chicago Press.

Myers, F. (1979) 'Emotions and the Self: A Theory of Personhood and Political Order Among Pintupi Aborigines', *Ethos* 7, 343–370.

—— (1986) *Pintupi Country, Pintupi Self: Sentiment, Place, and Politics Among Western Desert Aborigines*. Washington, DC: Smithsonian Institution Press.

Rosaldo, M. Z. (1980) *Knowledge and Passion: Ilongot Notions of Self and Social Life*. Cambridge: Cambridge University Press.

—— (1983) 'The Shame of Headhunters and the Autonomy of Self', *Ethos* 11, 135–151.

—— (1984 [chapter 4]) 'Toward an Anthropology of Self and Feeling', in R. Shweder and R. LeVine (eds) *Culture Theory: Essays on Mind, Self, and Emotion*. Cambridge: Cambridge University Press.

Rosenwein, B. H. (1998) 'Controlling Paradigms', in B. H. Rosenwein (ed.) *Anger's Past: The Social Uses of Emotion in the Middle Ages*. Ithaca, NY: Cornell University Press.

Shorter, E. (1975) *The Making of the Modern Family*. New York: Basic Books.

Stearns, C. Z. and Stearns, P. (1986) *Anger: The Struggle for Emotional Control in America's History*. Chicago: University of Chicago Press.

—— (1988) *Emotion and Social Change*. New York: Holmes & Meier.

Stearns, P. (1989) *Jealousy: The Evolution of an Emotion in American History*. New York: New York University Press.

—— (1994) *American Cool: Constructing a Twentieth-Century Emotional Style*. New York: New York University Press.

Stearns, P. and Stearns, C. Z. (1985) 'Emotionology: Clarifying the History of Emotions and Emotional Standards', *American Historical Review* 90: 4 (October), 813–836.

Stone, L. (1977) *The Family, Sex and Marriage in England, 1500–1800*. New York: Harper & Row.

Ulbricht, O. (2008) 'Historians Coping with Emotion: From Lucien Febvre to William Reddy', paper presented on The History of Emotions panel at the European Social Science History Conference, Lisbon, Portugal, 26 February–1 March.

Williams, R. (1975 [1961]) *The Long Revolution*. Westport, CT: Greenwood.

Williams, S. and Bendelow, G. (1998) *Emotions in Social Life. Critical Themes and Contemporary Issues*. London and New York: Routledge.

I CULTURALIST FOUNDATIONS

Chapter 1

Raymond Williams

ON STRUCTURE OF FEELING

THE ANALYSIS OF CULTURE, in the documentary sense, is of great importance because it can yield specific evidence about the whole organization within which it was expressed. We cannot say that we know a particular form or period of society, and that we will see how its art and theory relate to it, for until we know these, we cannot really claim to know the society. This is a problem of method, and is mentioned here because a good deal of history has in fact been written on the assumption that the bases of the society, its political, economic, and 'social' arrangements, form the central core of facts, after which the art and theory can be adduced, for marginal illustration or 'correlation'. There has been a neat reversal of this procedure in the histories of literature, art, science, and philosophy, when these are described as developing by their own laws, and then something called the 'background' (what in general history was the central core) is sketched in. Obviously it is necessary, in exposition, to select certain activities for emphasis, and it is entirely reasonable to trace particular lines of development in temporary isolation. But the history of a culture, slowly built up from such particular work, can only be written when the active relations are restored, and the activities seen in a genuine parity. Cultural history must be more than the sum of the particular histories, for it is with the relations between them, the particular forms of the whole organization, that it is especially concerned. I would then define the theory of culture as the study of relationships between elements in a whole way of life. The analysis of culture is the attempt to discover the nature of the organization which is the complex of these relationships. Analysis of particular works or institutions is, in this context, analysis of their essential kind of organization, the relationships which works or institutions embody as parts of the organization as a whole. A key-word, in such analysis, is pattern: it is with the discovery of patterns of a characteristic kind that any useful cultural analysis begins, and it is with the relationships between these patterns, which sometimes reveal unexpected identities and correspondences in hitherto separately considered activities, sometimes again reveal discontinuities of an unexpected kind, that general cultural analysis is concerned.

It is only in our own time and place that we can expect to know, in any substantial way, the general organization. We can learn a great deal of the life of other places and times, but certain elements, it seems to me, will always be irrecoverable. Even those that can be recovered are recovered in abstraction, and this is of crucial importance. We learn each element as a precipitate, but in the living experience of the time every element was in solution, an inseparable part of a complex whole. The most difficult thing to get hold of, in studying any past period, is this felt sense of the quality of life at a particular place and time: a sense of the ways in which the particular activities combined into a way of thinking and living. We can go some way in restoring the outlines of a particular organization of life; we can even recover what Fromm calls the 'social character' or Benedict the 'pattern of culture'. The social character—a valued system of behaviour and attitudes—is taught, formally and informally; it is both an ideal and a mode. The 'pattern of culture' is a selection and configuration of interests and activities, and a particular valuation of them, producing a distinct organization, a 'way of life'. Yet even these, as we recover them, are usually abstract. Possibly, however, we can gain the sense of a further common element, which is neither the character nor the pattern, but as it were the actual experience through which these were lived. This is potentially of very great importance, and I think the fact is that we are most conscious of such contact in the arts of a period. It can happen that when we have measured these against the external characteristics of the period, and then allowed for individual variations, there is still some important common element that we cannot easily place. I think we can best understand this if we think of any similar analysis of a way of life that we ourselves share. For we find here a particular sense of life, a particular community of experience hardly needing expression, through which the characteristics of our way of life that an external analyst could describe are in some way passed, giving them a particular and characteristic colour. We are usually most aware of this when we notice the contrasts between generations, who never talk quite 'the same language', or when we read an account of our lives by someone from outside the community, or watch the small differences in style, of speech or behaviour, in someone who has learned our ways yet was not bred in them. Almost any formal description would be too crude to express this nevertheless quite distinct sense of a particular and native style. And if this is so, in a way of life we know intimately, it will surely be so when we ourselves are in the position of the visitor, the learner, the guest from a different generation: the position, in fact, that we are all in, when we study any past period. Though it can be turned to trivial account, the fact of such a characteristic is neither trivial nor marginal; it feels quite central.

The term I would suggest to describe it is *structure of feeling*: it is as firm and definite as 'structure' suggests, yet it operates in the most delicate and least tangible parts of our activity. In one sense, this structure of feeling is the culture of a period: it is the particular living result of all the elements in the general organization. And it is in this respect that the arts of a period, taking these to include characteristic approaches and tones in argument, are of major importance. For here, if anywhere, this characteristic is likely to be expressed; often not consciously, but by the fact that here, in the only examples we have of recorded communication that outlives its bearers, the actual living sense, the deep community that makes the communication possible, is naturally drawn upon. I do not mean that the structure of feeling, any more than the social character, is possessed in the same way by the many individuals in the community. But I think it is a very deep and very wide possession, in all actual communities, precisely because it is on it that communication depends. And what is particularly interesting is that it does not seem to be, in any formal sense, learned. One generation may train its successor, with reasonable success, in the social character or the general cultural pattern, but the new generation will have its own structure of feeling, which will not appear to have come 'from' anywhere. For here, most distinctly, the changing organization is enacted in the organism: the new generation responds in its own ways to the unique world it is inheriting, taking up many continuities, that can be traced, and repro-ducing many aspects of the organization, which can be separately described, yet feeling its whole life in certain ways differently, and shaping its creative response into a new structure of feeling.

Once the carriers of such a structure die, the nearest we can get to this vital element is in the documentary culture, from poems to buildings and dress-fashions, and it is this relation that gives significance to the definition of culture in documentary terms. This in no way means that the documents are autonomous. It is simply that, as previously argued, the significance of an activity must be sought in terms of the whole organization, which is more than the sum of its separable parts. What we are looking for, always, is the actual life that the whole organization is there to express. The significance of documentary culture is that, more clearly than anything else, it expresses that life to us in direct terms, when the living witnesses are silent. At the same time, if we reflect on the nature of a structure of feeling, and see how it can fail to be fully understood even by living people in close contact with it, with ample material at their disposal, including the contemporary arts, we shall not suppose that we can ever do more than make an approach, an approximation, using any channels.

We need to distinguish three levels of culture, even in its most general definition. There is the lived culture of a particular time and place, only fully accessible to those living in that time and place. There is the recorded culture, of every kind, from art to the most everyday facts: the culture of a period. There is also, as the factor connecting lived culture and period cultures, the culture of the selective tradition.

When it is no longer being lived, but in a narrower way survives in its records, the culture of a period can be very carefully studied, until we feel that we have reasonably clear ideas of its cultural work, its social character, its general patterns of activity and value, and in part of its structure of feeling. Yet the survival is governed, not by the period itself, but by new periods, which gradually compose a tradition. Even most specialists in a period know only a part of even its records. One can say with confidence, for example, that nobody really knows the nineteenth-century novel; nobody has read, or could have read, all its examples, over the whole range from printed volumes to penny serials. The real specialist may know some hundreds; the ordinary specialist somewhat less; educated readers a decreasing number: though all will have clear ideas on the subject. A selective process, of a quite drastic kind, is at once evident, and this is true of every field of activity. Equally, of course, no nineteenth-century reader would have read all the novels; no individual in the society would have known more than a selection of its facts. But everyone living in the period would have had something which, I have argued, no later individual can wholly recover: that sense of the life within which the novels were written, and which we now approach through our selection. Theoretically, a period is recorded; in practice, this record is absorbed into a selective tradition; and both are different from the culture as lived. [. . .]

The further area of relations, that we must now examine [in the 1840s], is that described and interpreted by such concepts as the social character and the structure of feeling. The dominant social character of the period can be briefly outlined. There is the belief in the value of work, and this is seen in relation to individual effort, with a strong attachment to success gained in these terms. A class society is assumed, but social position is increasingly defined by actual status rather than by birth. The poor are seen as the victims of their own failings, and it is strongly held that the best among them will climb out of their class. A punitive Poor Law is necessary in order to stimulate effort; if a man could fall back on relief, without grave hardship in the form of separation from his family, minimum sustenance, and such work as stone-breaking or oakum-picking, he would not make the necessary effort to provide for himself. In this and a wider field, suffering is in one sense ennobling, in that it teaches humility and courage, and leads to the hard dedication to duty. Thrift, sobriety, and piety are the principal virtues, and the family is their central institution. The sanctity of marriage is absolute, and adultery and fornication are unpardonable. Duty includes helping the weak provided that the help is not of such a kind as to confirm the weakness: condoning sexual error, and comforting the poor, are weaknesses by this definition. Training to the prevailing virtues must be necessarily severe, but there is an obligation to see that the institutions for such training are strengthened.

This can be fairly called the dominant social character of the period, if we look at its characteristic legislation, the terms in which this was argued, the majority content of public writing and speaking, and the characters of the men most admired. Yet, of course, as a social character, it varied considerably in success of transmission, and was subject to many personal variations. The more serious difficulty arises as we look more closely at the period and realize that alternative social characters were in fact active, and that these affected, in important ways, the whole life of the time. A social character is the abstract of a dominant group, and there can be no doubt that the character described—a developed form of the morality of the industrial and commercial middle class—was at this time the most powerful. At the same time, there were other social characters with substantial bases in the society. The aristocratic character was visibly weakening, but its variations—that birth mattered more than money; that work was not the sole social value and that civilization involved play; that sobriety and chastity, at least in young men, were not cardinal virtues but might even be a sign of meanness or dullness—are still alive in the period, all in practice, some in theory. In attitudes to the poor, this character is ambiguous: it includes a stress on charity, as part of one's station, very different from punitive rehabilitation, but also a brutality, a willingness to cut down troublemakers, a natural habit of repression, which again differ from the middle-class attitude. The 1840s are very interesting in this respect, for they show the interaction of different social characters: Tory charity against Whig rehabilitation; brutality and repression against positive civilization through institution. Some of the best criticism of the Whig Poor Law came from Tories with a conscious aristocratic ideal, as most notably in Young England. Brutality and repression are ready, in crisis, but as compared with the twenties and thirties, are being steadily abandoned in favour of positive legislation. Play may be frowned on by the social character, but the decade shows a large increase in light entertainment, from cheap novels to the music-halls. Not only is the dominant social character different, in many ways, from the life lived in its shadow, but alternative social characters lead to the real conflicts of the time. This is a central difficulty of the social character concept, for in stressing a dominant abstraction it seriously underestimates the historical process of change and conflict, which are found even when, as in the 1840s, such a social character is very strong. For we must add another alternative, of major importance: the developing social character of the working class, different in important respects from its competitors. As the victims of repression and punitive rehabilitation, of the gospel of success and the pride of birth, of the real nature of work and the exposure to suffering, working-class people were beginning to formulate alternative ideals. They had important allies from the interaction of the other systems, and could be a major force either in the Corn Laws repeal or in the Factory legislation, when these were sponsored by different sections of the ruling class. But the 1840s show an important development of independent aims, though these are to be realized, mainly, through alliance with other groups. Thus Chartism is an ideal beyond the terms of any dominant group in the society, and is more than an expression of democratic aspirations; is also an assertion of an individual dignity transcending class. The Ten Hours Bill, in working-class minds, was more than a good piece of paternal legislation on work; it was also the claim to leisure, and hence again to a wider life. At the same time, in their own developing organizations, the most radical criticism of all was being made: the refusal of a society based either on birth or on individual success, the conception of a society based on mutual aid and co-operation.

We can then distinguish three social characters operative in the period, and it is with the study of relations between them that we enter the reality of the whole life. All contribute to the growth of the society: the aristocratic ideals tempering the harshness of middle-class ideals at their worst; working-class ideals entering into a fruitful and decisive combination with middle-class ideals at their best. The middle-class social character remains dominant, and both aristocrats and working people, in many respects, come to terms with it. But equally, the middle-class social character as it entered the forties is in many respects modified as the forties end. The values of work and self-help, of social position by status rather than birth, of the sanctity of marriage and the emphasis on thrift, sobriety and charity, are still dominant. But punitive rehabilitation, and the attitudes to weakness and suffering on which it rests, have been, while not rejected, joined by a major ideal of public service, in which the effort towards civilization is actively promoted by a genuine altruism and the making of positive institutions.

This is one level of change, and such analysis is necessary if we are to explore the reality of the social character. In some respects, the structure of feeling corresponds to the dominant social character, but it is also an expression of the interaction described. Again, however, the structure of feeling is not uniform throughout the society; it is primarily evident in the dominant productive group. At this level, however, it is different from any of the distinguishable social characters, for it has to deal not only with the public ideals but with their omissions and consequences, as lived. If we look at the fiction of the forties, we shall see this clearly.

The popular fiction of the periodicals, so carefully studied by Dalziel, is very interesting in this context. At first sight we find what we expect: the unshakeable assumptions of a class society, but with the stress on wealth rather than birth (aristocrats, indeed, being often personally vicious); the conviction that the poor are so by their own faults—their stupidity and depravity stressed, their mutual help ignored; the absolute sanctity of marriage, the manipulation of plot to bring sexual offenders to actual suffering; the fight against weakness, however terrible, as one of the main creators of humble virtue. All this, often consciously didactic, is the direct expression of the dominant social character, and the assumptions tend to be shared by the pious 'improving' fiction (cf. Mrs Tonna's *Helen Fleetwood*) and by the sensational fiction which the improvers condemned. But then we are reminded of the extent to which popular fiction retains older systems of value, often through stereotyped conventions of character. The 'fashionable novel' of high life only became unfashionable late in the decade. The typical hero is sometimes the successful exponent of self-help, but often he is an older type, the cultivated gentleman, the soldier governed by a code of honour, even the man who finds pleasure a blessing and work a curse. To the earlier hero, loss of income and the need to work were misfortunes to be endured; to have a safe fortune was undoubtedly best. The new attitude to work came in only slowly, for understandable reasons. (Ordinary middle-class life was still thought too plain and dull for a really interesting novel.) Further, heroes of either kind are capable of strong overt emotion; they can burst into public tears, or even swoon, as strong men used to do but were soon to do no more. Heroines have more continuity: they are weak, dependent, and shown as glad to be so, and of course they are beautiful and chaste. One interesting factor, obviously related to a continuing general attitude in the period, is that schools, almost without exception, are shown as terrible: not only are they places of temptation and wickedness, mean, cruel and educationally ridiculous, but also they are inferior to the home and family, as a way of bringing up children. This is perhaps the last period in which a majority of English public opinion believed that home education was the ideal. From the sixteenth century, this belief had been gaining ground, and its complete reversal, with the new public-school ethos after Arnold, is of considerable general importance. But the new attitude does not appear in fiction until *Tom Brown's Schooldays* in 1857.

In the popular fiction of the forties, then, we find many marks of older ways of feeling, as well as faithful reproduction of certain standard feelings of the approved social character. We find also, in an interesting way, the interaction between these and actual experience. The crucial point, in this period, is in the field of success and money. The confident assertions of the social character, that success followed effort, and that wealth was the mark of respect, had to contend, if only unconsciously, with a practical world in which things were not so simple. The confidence of this fiction is often only superficial. What comes through with great force is a pervasive atmosphere of instability and debt. A normal element, in these stories, is the loss of fortune, and this is hardly ever presented in terms consistent with the social character: that success or failure corresponded to personal quality. Debt and ruin haunt this apparently confident world, and in a majority of cases simply happen to the characters, as a result of a process outside them. At one level, the assumptions of the social character are maintained: if you lose your fortune, you get out of the way—you cannot embarrass yourself or your friends by staying. But this ruthless code is ordinarily confined to subsidiary characters: the parents of hero or heroine. For the people who matter, some other expedient is necessary. It is found, over the whole range of fiction, by two devices: the unexpected legacy, and the Empire. These devices are extremely interesting, both at the level of magic and at the level of developing attitudes necessary to the society.

Magic is indeed necessary, to postpone the conflict between the ethic and the experience. It is widely used in sexual situations, where hero or heroine is tied to an unloved wife or husband, while the true lover waits in the wings. Solutions involving infidelity or breaking the marriage are normally unthinkable, and so a formula is evolved, for standard use: the unsuitable partner is not merely unloved, but alcoholic or insane; at a given point, and after the required amount of resigned suffering, there is a convenient, often spectacular death, in which the unloving partner shows great qualities of care, duty, and piety; and then, of course, the real love can be consummated. In money, the process is similar: legacies, at the crucial moment, turn up from almost anywhere, and fortunes are restored. Nobody has to go against the principle that money is central to success, but equally very few have to be bound by the ethic preached to the poor: that the deserving prosper by effort. This element of cheating marks one crucial point of difference between the social character and the actual structure of feeling.

The use of the Empire is similar but more complex. Of course there were actual legacies, and these eventually changed the self-help ethic, in its simplest form: the magic, at this stage, lay in their timing. But the Empire was a more universally available escape-route: black sheep could be lost in it; ruined or misunderstood heroes could go out and return with fortunes; the weak of every kind could be transferred to it, to make a new life. Often indeed, the Empire is the source of the unexpected legacy, and the two devices are joined. It is clear that the use of the Empire relates to real factors in the society. At a simple level, going out to the new lands could be seen as self-help and enterprise of the purest kinds. Also, in the new lands, there was a great need for labourers, and emigration as a solution to working-class problems was being widely urged, often by the most humane critics of the existing system. In 1840, 90,000 people a year were emigrating, and in 1850 three times as many. In a different way, in terms of capital and trade, the Empire had been one of the levers of industrialization, and was to prove one major way of keeping the capitalist system viable. These factors are reflected in fiction, though not to the same extent as later in the century, when Imperialism had become a conscious policy. Meanwhile, alongside this reflection of real factors, there was the use as magic: characters whose destinies could not be worked out within the system as given were simply put on the boat, a simpler way of resolving the conflict between ethic and experience than any radical questioning of the ethic. This method had the additional advantage that it was consonant with another main element of the structure of feeling: that there could be no general solution to the social problems of the time; there could be only individual solutions, the rescue by legacy or emigration, the resolution by some timely change of heart.

Now the fascinating thing about the structure of feeling as described is that it is present in almost all the novels we now read as literature, as well as in the now disregarded popular fiction. This is true of the reflections and of the magic. Disraeli seems daring in dramatizing the two-nation problem in the love of an aristocrat and a Chartist girl, but Sybil, following the pattern of almost all poor heroines in such situations in the periodicals, is discovered in the end to be 'really' a dispossessed aristocrat. (The uniting of the two nations is in fact, in Disraeli, the combination of agricultural and industrial property, a very sanguine political forecast, and the same pattern is followed in *Coningsby*, where the young aristocrat marries the Lancashire manufacturer's daughter, and is elected for an industrial constituency.) Mrs Gaskell, though refusing the popular fiction that the poor suffered by their own faults, succeeds in *Mary Barton* in compromising working-class organization with murder, and steers all her loved characters to Canada. Kingsley, in *Alton Locke*, sends his Chartist hero to America. And these are the humane critics, in many ways dissenting from the social character, but remaining bound by the structure of feeling.

The same correspondence is evident in novels less concerned with the problems of the society. The novels of Charlotte and Anne Brontë are, in terms of plot and structure of feeling, virtually identical with many stories in the periodicals: the governess-heroine, the insane wife or alcoholic husband, the resolution through resignation, duty, and magic. Dickens, similarly, uses the situations, the feelings, and the magic of periodical fiction again and again.

This connection between the popular structure of feeling and that used in the literature of the time is of major importance in the analysis of culture. It is here, at a level even more important than that of institutions, that the real relations within the whole culture are made clear: relations that can easily be neglected when only the best writing survives, or when this is studied outside its social context. Yet the connection must be carefully defined. Often it is simply that in the good novel the ordinary situations and feelings are worked through to their maximum intensity. In other cases, though the framework is retained, one element of the experience floods through the work, in such a way as to make it relevant in its own right, outside the conventional terms. This is true of Elizabeth Gaskell, in the early parts of *Mary Barton*; of Charlotte Brontë, taking lonely personal desire to an intensity that really questions the conventions by which it is opposed; of Dickens, certainly, in that the conventional figure of the orphan, or the child exposed by loss of fortune, comes to transcend the system to which he refers, and to embody many of the deepest feelings in the real experience of the time. These are the creative elements, though the connection with the ordinary structure of feeling is still clear. The orphan, the exposed child, the lonely governess, the girl from a poor family: these are the figures which express the deepest response to the reality of the way of life. In the ordinary fiction, they were conventional figures; in the literature they emerge carrying an irresistible authenticity, not merely as exemplars of the accidents of the social system, but as expressions of a *general* judgement of the human quality of the whole way of life. Here, in the 1840s, is the first body of fiction (apart from occasional earlier examples, in Godwin and perhaps Richardson) expressing, even through the conventional forms, a radical human dissent. At the level of social character, the society might be confident of its assumptions and its future, but these lonely exposed figures seem to us, at least, the personal and social reality of the system which in part the social character rationalized. Man alone, afraid, a victim: this is the enduring experience. The magic solutions will be grasped at, in many cases, in the end, but the intensity of the central experience is on record and survives them. And it is at this point that we find the link with a novel like *Wuthering Heights*, which rejects so much more of the conventional structure. Here, at a peak of intensity, the complicated barriers of a system of relationships are broken through, finally, by an absolute human commitment. The commitment is realized through death, and the essential tragedy, embodied elsewhere in individual figures who may, by magic, be rescued from it, becomes the form of the whole work. The creative elements in the other fiction are raised to a wholeness which takes the work right outside the ordinary structure of feeling, and teaches a new feeling.

Art reflects its society and works a social character through to its reality in experience. But also, art creates, by new perceptions and responses, elements which the society, as such, is not able to realize. If we compare art with its society, we find a series of real relationships showing its deep and central connections with the rest of the general life. We find description, discussion, exposition through plot and experience of the social character. We find also, in certain characteristic forms and devices, evidence of the deadlocks and unsolved problems of the society: often admitted to consciousness for the first time in this way. Part of this evidence will show a false consciousness, designed to prevent any substantial recognition; part again a deep desire, as yet uncharted, to move beyond this. As George Eliot wrote, recording this latter feeling, in 1848:

> The day will come when there will be a temple of white marble, where sweet incense and anthems shall rise to the memory of every man and woman who has had a deep *Ahnung*, a presentiment, a yearning, or a clear vision of the time when this miserable reign of Mammon shall end—when men shall be no longer 'like the fishes of the sea'—society no more like a face one half of which—the side of profession, of lip-faith—is fair and God-like, the other half—the side of deeds and institutions—with a hard old wrinkled skin puckered into the sneer of a Mephistopheles.

Much of the art, much of the magic, of the 1840s, expressed this desire. And at this point we find ourselves moving into a process which cannot be the simple comparison of art and society, but which must start from the recognition that all the acts of men compose a general reality within which both art and what we ordinarily call society are comprised. We do not now compare the art with the society; we compare both with the whole complex of human actions and feelings.

Q: *The concept of 'structure of feeling' is one of the most notable theoretical innovations of* The Long Revolution *and is one which you have consistently used and developed in the long span of time from that book right up to the present, with* Marxism and Literature. *At the outset, you define the structure of feeling as follows in* The Long Revolution: *'The term I would suggest is* structure of feeling: *it is as firm and definite as "structure" suggests, yet it operates in the most delicate and least tangible parts of our activity. In one sense, this structure of feeling is the culture of a period: it is the particular living result of all the elements in the general organization.'*[1] *You then go on: 'I do not mean that the structure of feeling, any more than the social character, is possessed in the same way by the many individuals in the community. But I think it is a very deep and wide possession, in all actual communities. . . . One generation may train its successor, with reasonable success, in the social character or the general cultural pattern, but the new generation will have its own structure of feeling, which will not appear to have come "from" anywhere.'*[2] *The essential point of reference for the notion of structure of feeling here appears to be not so much a class, or a society, as a generation. Although it is never brought out explicitly, the same emphasis recurs in your treatment of the 1840s and again much later in* Marxism and Literature. *The passage just quoted continues: 'The new generation responds in its own ways to the unique world it is inheriting, taking up many continuities, that can be traced, and reproducing many aspects of the organization, which can be separately described, yet feeling its whole life in certain ways differently, and shaping its creative response into a new structure of feeling.*[3] *The whole problematic of generations is, of course, also very important in your novels and other work. The first critical query we would like to pose about your definition of a structure of feeling is this: any given historical period will always contain at least three adult generations who are active and producing meanings within a single time-span — that is, setting aside the problem of plurality of classes. How can one speak of 'the structure of feeling' of a period, as you do in your account of the 1840s, when at least three structures of feeling would appear to be definitionally present in so far as there would be at least three active generations?*

RW: The general reason is the close connection in my account between the notion of the structure of feeling as accessible for analysis and what appears to be new cultural work. For rightly or wrongly, I think on the whole rightly, we do usually identify the point at which a cultural generation seems to form with what is often, in terms of the actual lives of the people who compose that group, just a decade of their activity. If one takes for example the 1930s, one can trace the emergence of a particular structure of feeling there, in a set of young writers with whom that decade is then retrospectively identified, although most of them in fact continued to write until the sixties, some even into the seventies. The way in which I have tended to apply the term in analysis is to the generation that is doing the new cultural work, which normally means a group which would have a median age of around thirty, when it is beginning to articulate its structure of feeling. It follows that one would then identify the structure of feeling of the middle-aged and the elderly with earlier decades. It was in that sense that I spoke of the structure of feeling of the 1840s. But I did not sufficiently clarify my procedure there.

Q: *The second question, then, is how the concept can be articulated to a plurality of classes. For in Victorian England, to pursue the example, there were at least three major social classes — landed aristocracy, industrial bourgeoisie and urban proletariat, not to speak of agricultural labourers, rural small-holders, as well as a heterogeneous petty-bourgeoisie. Paradoxically, you do directly refer to these classes when you discuss the notion of 'social character', but not when you analyse the 'structure of feeling'. The impression is left that a structure of feeling could be common to all classes in a society, once its only referent is generational. What was your view of this problem?*

RW: It has exercised me greatly. The concept was initially developed from the accessible evidence of actual articulations in texts and works that I could read. The result was that in societies in which class contributions to that kind of writing were highly differential, it was all too possible to overlook the existence of alternative structures. There is certainly not enough stress on these in *The Long Revolution*, where the notion is presented in essentially temporal and general terms. I would now want to use the concept much more differentially between classes. But it is also important to note that this diversity is itself historically variable. For example, during the 1660s and 1670s two contemporary structures of feeling of absolutely contrasted character existed even among the limited social class that was actively contributing to cultural work. There are other periods, however, in which one structure seems to be more widespread. The 1840s was just such an example. For although the structure of feeling I was analysing in those novels, written mainly by middle-class or lower-middle-class writers, was a class possession — if one pushes the analysis its many class elements are quite clear — it was to a surprising extent shared by the working-class writers who were beginning to contribute at that time. The problem in a case like this, of course, is that the evidence for the concept is only going to be articulate and available in fully expressed work. Yet it can be objected that the notion illegitimately infers from this range of evidence the existence of a structure which is much wider and is unexpressed. I feel the force of this criticism.

Q: *How exactly did you come to develop the concept?*

RW: The first time I used it was actually in *Preface to Film*. The passage reads: 'In the study of a period, we may be able to reconstruct, with more or less accuracy, the material life, the social organization, and, to a large extent, the dominant ideas. It is not necessary to discuss here which, if any, of these aspects is, in the whole complex, determining; an important institution like the drama will, in all probability, take its colour in varying degrees from them all. . . . To relate a work of art to any part of that observed totality may, in varying degrees, be useful, but it is a common experience, in analysis, to realize that when one has measured the work against the separable parts, there yet remains some element for which there is no external counterpart. This element, I believe, is what I have named the *structure of feeling* of a period and it is only realizable through experience of the work of art itself, as a whole.'[4] In other words, the key to the notion, both to all it can do and to all the difficulties it still leaves, is that it was developed as an analytic procedure for actual written works, with a very strong stress on their forms and conventions. It is a much more straightforward notion when it is confined to that. Yet the pressure of the 'general argument was continually leading me to say, and I think correctly, that such works were the articulate record of something which was a much more general possession. This was the area of inter-action between the official consciousness of an epoch – codified in its doctrines and legislation – and the whole process of actually living its consequences. I could see that here might very often be one of the social sources of art. The example I then worked on was the contrast between the formal ideology of the early Victorian middle class and the fiction its writers produced. The point of the deliberately contradictory phrase, with which I have never been happy, is that it was a structure in the sense that you could perceive it operating in one work after another which weren't otherwise connected – people weren't learning it from each other; yet it was one of feeling much more than of thought – a pattern of impulses, restraints, tones, for which the best evidence was often the actual conventions of literary or dramatic writing. To this day I find that I keep coming back to this notion from the actual experience of literary analysis rather than from any theoretical satisfaction with the concept itself.

Q: *Keeping to literary documentation for the moment, then, there still seems to be some uncertainty in your chronological application of the term. You've explained very clearly that the structure of feeling of any given period relates primarily to the creative work done by the active younger generation. You've written in* Marxism and Literature *that while 'the effective formations of most actual art relate to already manifest social formations, dominant or residual', 'it is primarily to an emergent formation that the structure of feeling, as solution, relates'. In other words, other artistic formation represents structures of feeling as precipitate rather than as solution. That seems quite consistent. But on the same page you also say: 'At times the emergence of a new structure of feeling is best related to a rise of a class: England 1700–1760.'[5] That is a long time: 1700 to 1760. It is the better part of a century. Some three generations would have been active in that period at the median age of thirty. Again, in your work on drama you very tellingly use the concept of structure of feeling to trace the liberal deadlock between individual and society: yet this structure spans the whole epoch from Ibsen to Brecht or beyond. Again, a multi-generational process seems to be at work. Did you mean that there were successive structures of feeling which were generationally distinct but cognate in other ways, each representing a modulation of the last?*

RW: I have no simple answer, but perhaps some clarification. The epoch from 1700 to 1760 is a very complex one, because it includes two radically opposed structures of feeling that are related to the rise of the same class – Augustan classicism and bourgeois realism. I keep trying to work on this, because it's theoretically so important. Of course it can be partly clarified by distinguishing fractions of the class, within a key variable in university education. Moreover it is a time of conscious cultural composition of the new class; I mean to write about Johnson in this sense. Certainly within one generation there was a dominant classicism and an emergent realism, but it is one of the extraordinary facts about the period from 1760 on that a very vigorous realism is eventually contained and displaced, for a further generation and even beyond. One way of tracking that down would be in the limits of each earlier structure of feeling. The methodological problem is similar to that in other fields. You isolate, by analysis, a particular structure, but when it is truly dominant, influencing or even determining later periods, you move almost without noticing it from a seized moment of structural analysis to what is of course, all the time, also a historical movement and development. But then, while acknowledging that there are also other movements, there is great value in tracing, as you put it, successive modulations in a structure of feeling, until you reach the point where there is a qualitative break – the 1790s in England for example – and then you postulate a period and try to analyse a newly emerging structure of feeling.

Q: *Another problem posed by your unit of analysis, so to speak, is how one delimits a particular generation in any given society. For it is a delicate methodological question where you actually draw the lines between age-groups. To take your criterion, at any one moment there are those with a median age of thirty: but what about those with a median age of twenty-five or forty? Where do they fit? This is a problem that occurs quite frequently in everyday speech. What solution would you adopt for it?*

RW: This is a very difficult question. There are periods like the 1840s, which reveal a generation of writers – in this case novelists – who were not merely physically of the same age, but who were fully contemporary with each other in the sense that they manifestly share certain perceptions, preoccupations and styles of work. Then there are other periods in which a range of coeval writers do not seem to compose a generation in that sense at all: different figures are there and are doing different kinds of work. A further complication can occur if biological contemporaries compose or publish their work at a major temporal distance from each other, yet with close internal connections. An example which illustrates this problem is the fact that Hobbes was in age a contemporary of Jacobean dramatists like Webster or Tourneur. But the Jacobean playwrights were young men who published their plays in their twenties. Hobbes, because of all sorts of vicissitudes but also the nature of his work, did not publish until his middle or old age. So one might ask how a play like *The White Devil* or *The Atheist's Tragedy* could be described as contemporary with *Leviathan*. But I think if you read *Leviathan* beside them, you get a mutual illumination on both. They share a very precise structure of feeling in common, including the absolutely basic premise, contradicting so much of the official consciousness of the time, of an initial condition of war of all against all. The Jacobean dramatists produced this structure very suddenly, as a set of formal conventions; the action of a drama becomes a virtually endless series of struggles between mutually destructive individuals, from which there is no release. This very sharply contrasts with plays that had been written only ten years before, in which maximum havoc may be let loose but there is always the concept of an authority which will resolve it, at whatever level of loss. Hobbes takes the assumptions of Webster or Tourneur as his starting-point, but he works through them to a kind of resolution with a new definition of authority. That is the later, historical effect.

So the problem of generations is certainly a very tricky one: perhaps we need another term distinct from the biological category. I have been particularly conscious of this myself, since I have not since 1945 worked contemporarily with my own generation and I think these asymmetries always happen. Should one speak in this sort of cultural analysis of a generation of work rather than a generation of birth? I'm trying to resolve this now, with some new methodology of cultural formations.

Q: *Your discussion of structures of feeling frequently employs a contrast between past and present, in* The Long Revolution. *You write, for example: 'It is only in our own time and place that we can expect to know, in any substantial way, the general organization. We can learn a great deal of the life of other places and times, but certain elements, it seems to me, will always be irrevocable. Even those that can be recovered are recovered in abstraction, and this is of crucial importance. We learn each element as a precipitate, but in the living experience of the time every element was in solution, an inseparable part of a complex whole. The most difficult thing to get hold of, in studying any past period, is this felt sense of the quality of life at a particular place and time: a sense of the ways in which the particular activities combined into a way of thinking and living.'*[6] *You go on to speak of living witnesses being 'silent' once we approach the past. The general suggestion is that it is much more difficult to seize or interpret a structure of feeling in the past than in the present, where an experience of it is immediately available. Yet surely your argument, if anything, should work in the opposite direction. In the present, the immensity of unselected cultural activity before us should make it very difficult to grasp, from within, the nature of the contemporary structures of feeling — particularly given the uncertainty as to what direction much of this activity will take. Whereas the past is typically characterized by a certain crystallization of historical judgment as to what works or documents were most central to it: its materials are more fixed. The fluidity and indeterminacy of the present surely render it at least as, if not more, difficult to interpret than the past? At times you seem close to conceding this — once when you say that not all those who experience or bear the structure of feeling of any given period may have any awareness of it at all, which must mean that it is no simple matter to discern at any one point. In another passage, in your chapter on dramatic forms, you say: 'It is never easy, in one's own generation, to see whether the [present] situation is that of 1630 or 1735, with plenty of activity, but on no lasting basis, or 1530 or 1890, at the beginning of a major movement.'*[7] *This seems a much more plausible position. But how can you reconcile it with your earlier assertion?*

RW: I think that I quite simply confused the quality of *presence*, which distinguishes a structure of feeling from an explicit or codified doctrine, with the historical present — which is another matter altogether. What I would now wish to say is that while a structure of feeling always exists in the present tense, so to speak grammatically, I do not now think it more recoverable or more accessible in the temporal present than in the past. I did feel, when I re-read *The Long Revolution* ten or fifteen years later, that the part which had stood up best was the concluding analysis of the structure of feeling at the time it was written — because it grasped the facts of widespread dissent, yet, situating them within the structure of feeling, saw the dissent as a largely negative reaction, out of which a new constructive period was rather unlikely to come. Of course, there was plenty of evidence for this in the actual conventions and styles of the period. So one might by lucky chance locate a structure of feeling in the present, but theoretically I would not say that it is easier to do so. For the structure is precisely something which can only be grasped as such by going beyond the indiscriminate flux of experiences that are contemporary with one. On the other hand I think the reason that the confusion arose was that I did want to insist very sharply on the true presence of a structure of feeling, as distinct from the official or received thought of a time, which always succeeds it.

Q: *The phrase you have just used has a ring of* Scrutiny *to it. To what extent did the notion of structure of feeling represent a way of retaining Leavis's emphasis on experience, but giving it an objective and historical form?*

RW: Yes, 'experience' was a term I took over from *Scrutiny*. But you must remember that I was all the time working on historical changes in literary conventions and forms. Leavis's strength was in reproducing and interpreting what he called 'the living content of a work'. By contrast, the whole *Scrutiny* tradition was very weak in all consideration of formal questions, particularly when it was a question of deep formal structures which had undergone historical change. I was very conscious of this when writing on drama. On the other hand, most ordinary kinds of English Marxist analysis I knew passed so quickly from the literary products to what they represented that it jumped over the works themselves in finding their social affiliations. The notion of a structure of feeling was designed to focus a mode of historical and social relations which was yet quite internal to the work, rather than deducible from it or supplied by some external placing or classification.

Q: *You've stressed the literary origins of the notion of 'structure of feeling' – its aid to your critical work on texts. Isn't there, however, a danger in* The Long Revolution *of a kind of silent elision from the texts of a period as privileged evidence of the structures of feeling to the structures of feeling as privileged evidence of the social structure or historical epoch as such? The concept then tends to become an epistemology for gaining a comprehension of a whole society. That movement, from text to structure of feeling to history, seems much less defensible.*

RW: I now feel very strongly the need to define the limits of the term. There are cases where the structure of feeling which is tangible in a particular set of works is undoubtedly an articulation of an area of experience which lies beyond them. This is especially evident at those specific and historically definable moments when very new work produces a sudden shock of *recognition*. What must be happening on these occasions is that an experience which is really very wide suddenly finds a semantic figure which articulates it. Such an experience I would now call pre-emergent. On the other hand, a dominant set of forms or conventions – and in that sense structures of feeling – can represent a profound blockage for subordinated groups in a society, above all an oppressed class. In these cases, it is very dangerous to presume that an articulate structure of feeling is necessarily equivalent to inarticulate experience. For example, it seems probable that the English working class was struggling to express an experience in the 1790s and 1830s which in a sense, because of the subordination of the class, its lack of access to means of cultural production, but also the dominance of certain modes, conventions of expression, was never fully articulated. If you look at their actual affiliations, what is striking is a great grasping at other writings. Working people used Shelley; they used Byron, of all people; they responded very strongly to Mrs Gaskell. Should they or should they not have? These works could only have been approximations or substitutes for their own structure of feeling. Then there are historical experiences which never do find their semantic figures at all. I felt this very much in writing *The Country and City*. Even though there is much more literary expression than is usually allowed, there are still vast areas of silence. One cannot fill that silence with other people's structures of feeling.

Q: *That delimits the notion of social experience from articulated structure of feeling. But there is still the problem of the epistemological privilege of experience itself in your work. In* The Long Revolution *you say a number of times that the key to any description is the particular experience that is its starting-point. This idea, that experience is epistemologically determinant, finds a very central formulation in your introduction, where you write: 'I do not confine myself to British society because of any lack of interest in what is happening elsewhere, but because the kind of evidence I am interested in is only really available where one lives.'[8] This assumption leads to consequences that are quite unwarranted historically. For example, when you discuss the 1840s, you list seven decisive influences on the structure of feeling of the decade. Not one of them has anything to do with foreign or overseas developments. Yet if you look at Elizabeth Gaskell's*

Mary Barton, *a novel you discuss, you find a direct warning to her readers of the dangers of a repetition in England of the Parisian insurrections of 1848. In fact, English contemporaries were keenly aware of the seismic upheaval of 1848 in Europe — only a few years earlier Peel was actually fortifying his country house against the dangers of possible armed attack on it. Yet because 1848 was not a national experience in the direct sense, it is not even mentioned in your account.*

RW: The list of main features of the 1840s I gave was actually meant to mark off the way in which its history was conventionally assumed to be reflected in literature. The purpose of the analysis of literature was then to try to show all the pressures which were overlooked by it. Thus *Mary Barton* was composed within a structure of feeling which made it peculiarly apposite to the conjuncture of 1848, when the European explosion occurred — that was the point of her introductory note. For one of the determining characteristics of so much of the English writing of the late 1840s was an anxious oscillation between sympathy for the oppressed and fear of their violence. That tension is one of the deep processes of composition of *Mary Barton*. You can also find it in George Eliot, who wrote a letter responding warmly to the French revolution of 1848, and wishing a similar event would occur here — but then typically saying that it could not, since the English poor lacked the necessary ideas and intelligence. That combination of movement of sympathy and fear of violence is very important to the structure of feeling I was describing. I would certainly stress it more today.

Q: *Your reply still remains within the terms of the lived experience you were reconstructing, however. The point is that the composition of your book appears to join these limits, by appealing in its turn to the privilege of national experience. There is a connection between your initial statement of method and the particular lack of the stress you have just noted.*

RW: I concede this. But I should explain that the sentences you've quoted from my introduction were really referring much more to Part III of *The Long Revolution*, where I actually was surveying the contemporary situation in England, and even attempting in outline the total analysis, whose absence you've pointed out in Part II. The claim about evidence where one lives wasn't related as such to the 1840s. However, I am not using this to evade the theoretical point, which I think is correct. If the mode of analysis is viable, it must be applicable anywhere. Some elements of a structure of feeling are, of course, only traceable through a rather close analysis of language, which will always be a national one. But the most normal evidence for such a structure is conventions, which are often international. My own view, as a matter of fact, is that the most interesting use I have been able to make of it is, much more than the essay on the 1840s, my accounts of Ibsen and Brecht — of whose contexts of experience I knew very little.

Q: *That is a very helpful clarification. But the wider problem of the category of experience remains perplexing. It must be the only word you use recurrently that is not given an entry in* Keywords. *In Leavis's writing it is a subjectivist notion of value — of 'life'. Despite the fact that you have transformed its* Scrutiny *usage, the term does continue to carry something of its intellectual heritage. For your most recent discussion of a structure of feeling defines it as the field of contradiction between a consciously held ideology and emergent experience. The idea of an emergent experience beyond ideology seems to presuppose a kind of pristine contact between the subject and the reality in which this subject is immersed. Doesn't that leave the door sufficiently ajar for a Leavisian notion of 'life' or 'experience' to return?*

RW: No. That should be very clear. For after all the basic argument of the first chapter of *The Long Revolution* is precisely that there is no natural seeing and therefore there cannot be a direct and unmediated contact with reality. On the other hand, in much linguistic theory and a certain kind of semiotics, we are in danger of reaching the opposite point in which the epistemological wholly absorbs the ontological: it is only in the ways of knowing that we exist at all. To formalist friends, of whom I have many, who affect to doubt the very possibility of an 'external' referent, it is necessary to recall an absolutely founding presumption of materialism: namely that the natural world exists whether anyone signifies it or not. The fact is that we have been passing through a phase of rabid idealism on the left in the sixties and seventies. It is a positive relief to read Timpanaro's reminder that physical organisms exist in an undeniably material world whether or not they have ever been signified.

That said, I think the relation between signification and referent in one's own situation differs from that in any other. This is very difficult to formulate. But in the case of other situations, one learns only through recorded articulations; all that one has is necessarily, as it were, texts or documents. Certainly in one's own time one gathers far more than most people realize from just these versions of an endless documentation. By contrast in the whole process of consciousness – here I would put a lot of stress on phenomena for which there is no easy knowing because there is too easy a name, the too easy name is 'the unconscious' – all sorts of occurrences cut across the established or offered relations between a signification and a reference. The formalist position that there is no signified without a signifier amounts to saying that it is only in articulation that we live at all. Now maybe this is just a generalization from my own history, but I have found that areas which I would call structures of feeling as often as not initially form as a certain kind of disturbance or unease, a particular type of tension, for which when you stand back or recall them you can sometimes find a referent. To put it another way, the peculiar location of a structure of feeling is the endless comparison that must occur in the process of consciousness between the articulated and the lived. The lived is only another word, if you like, for experience: but we have to find a word for that level. For all that is not fully articulated, all that comes through as disturbance, tension, blockage, emotional trouble seems to me precisely a source of major changes in the relation between the signifier and the signified, whether in literary language or conventions. We have to postulate at least the possibility of comparison in this process and if it is a comparison, then with what? If one immediately fills the gap with one of these great blockbuster words like experience, it can have very unfortunate effects over the rest of the argument. For it can suggest that this is always a superior instance, or make a god out of an unexamined subjectivity. But since I believe that the process of comparison occurs often in not particularly articulate ways, yet is a source of much of the change that is eventually evident in our articulation, one has to seek a term for that which is not fully articulated or not fully comfortable in various silences, although it is usually not very silent. I just don't know what the term should be.

Notes

1   *The Long Revolution* (hereafter LR), 1975/[1961], Greenwood Press, Westport, Connecticut, p. 64.
2   LR, p. 65.
3   LR, p. 65.
4   *Preface to Film*, pp. 21–2.
5   *Marxism and Literature*, p. 134.
6   LR, p. 63.
7   LR, p. 297.
8   LR, p. 14.

Chapter 2

Alison M. Jaggar

LOVE AND KNOWLEDGE: EMOTION IN FEMINIST EPISTEMOLOGY

WITHIN THE WESTERN PHILOSOPHICAL tradition, emotions usually have been considered as potentially or actually subversive of knowledge.[1] From Plato until the present, with a few notable exceptions, reason rather than emotion has been regarded as the indispensable faculty for acquiring knowledge.[2]

Typically, although again not invariably, the rational has been contrasted with the emotional, and this contrasted pair then has often been linked with other dichotomies. Not only has reason been contrasted with emotion, but it has also been associated with the mental, the cultural, the universal, the public, and the male, whereas emotion has been associated with the irrational, the physical, the natural, the particular, the private, and, of course, the female.

Although western epistemology has tended to give pride of place to reason rather than emotion, it has not always excluded emotion completely from the realm of reason. In the *Phaedrus*, Plato portrayed emotions, such as anger or curiosity, as irrational urges (horses) that must always be controlled by reason (the charioteer). On this model, the emotions were not seen as needing to be totally suppressed but rather as needing direction by reason: for example, in a genuinely threatening situation, it was thought not only irrational but fool-hardy not to be afraid.[3] The split between reason and emotion was not absolute, therefore, for the Greeks. Instead, the emotions were thought of as providing indispensable motive power that needed to be channeled appropriately. Without horses, after all, the skill of the charioteer would be worthless.

The contrast between reason and emotion was sharpened in the seventeenth century by redefining reason as a purely instrumental faculty. For both the Greeks and the medieval philosophers, reason had been linked with value insofar as reason provided access to the objective structure or order of reality, seen as simultaneously natural and morally justified. With the rise of modern science, however, the realms of nature and value were separated: nature was stripped of value and reconceptualized as an inanimate mechanism of no intrinsic worth. Values were relocated in human beings, rooted in their preferences and emotional responses. The separation of supposedly natural fact from human value meant that reason, if it were to provide trustworthy insight into reality, had to be uncontaminated by or abstracted from value. Increasingly, therefore, though never universally,[4] reason was reconceptualized as the ability to make valid inferences from premises established elsewhere, the ability to calculate means but not to determine ends. The validity of logical inferences was thought independent of human attitudes and preferences; this was now the sense in which reason was taken to be objective and universal.[5]

The modern redefinition of rationality required a corresponding reconceptualization of emotion. This was achieved by portraying emotions as nonrational and often irrational urges that regularly swept the body, rather as a storm sweeps over the land. The common way of referring to the emotions as the "passions" emphasized that emotions happened to or were imposed upon an individual, something she suffered rather than something she did.

The epistemology associated with this new ontology rehabilitated sensory perception that, like emotion, typically had been suspected or even discounted by the western tradition as a reliable source of knowledge. British empiricism, succeeded in the nineteenth century by positivism, took its epistemological task to be the formulation of rules of inference that would guarantee the derivation of certain knowledge from the "raw data" supposedly given directly to the senses. Empirical testability became accepted as the hallmark of natural science; this, in turn, was viewed as the paradigm of genuine knowledge. Epistemology was often equated with the philosophy of science, and the dominant methodology of positivism prescribed that truly scientific knowledge must be capable of intersubjective verification. Because values and emotions had been defined as variable and idiosyncratic, positivism stipulated that trustworthy knowledge could be established only by methods that neutralized the values and emotions of individual scientists.

Recent approaches to epistemology have challenged some fundamental assumptions of the positivist epistemological model. Contemporary theorists of knowledge have undermined once rigid distinctions between analytic and synthetic statements, between theories and observations, and even between facts and values. However, few challenges have thus far been raised to the purported gap between emotion and knowledge. In this essay, I wish to begin bridging this gap through the suggestion that emotions may be helpful and even necessary rather than inimical to the construction of knowledge. My account is exploratory in nature and leaves many questions unanswered. It is not supported by irrefutable arguments or conclusive proofs; instead, it should be viewed as a preliminary sketch for an epistemological model that will require much further development before its workability can be established.

Emotion

1 What are emotions?

The philosophical question: What are emotions? requires both explicating the ways in which people ordinarily speak about emotion and evaluating the adequacy of those ways for expressing and illuminating experience and activity. Several problems confront someone trying to answer this deceptively simple question. One set of difficulties results from the variety, complexity, and even inconsistency of the ways in which emotions are viewed, in both daily life and scientific contexts. It is, in part, this variety that makes emotions into a "question" at the same time that it precludes answering that question by simple appeal to ordinary usage. A second set of difficulties is the wide range of phenomena covered by the term "emotion": these extend from apparently instantaneous "knee-jerk" responses of fright to lifelong dedication to an individual or a cause; from highly civilized aesthetic responses to undifferentiated feelings of hunger and thirst,[6] from background moods such as contentment or depression to intense and focused involvement in an immediate situation. It may well be impossible to construct a manageable account of emotion to cover such apparently diverse phenomena.

A further problem concerns the criteria for preferring one account of emotion to another. The more one learns about the ways in which other cultures conceptualize human faculties, the less plausible it becomes that emotions constitute what philosophers call a "natural kind." Not only do some cultures identify emotions unrecognized in the West, but there is reason to believe that the concept of emotion itself is a historical invention, like the concept of intelligence (Lewontin 1982) or even the concept of mind (Rorty 1979). For instance, anthropologist Catherine Lutz argues that the "dichotomous categories of 'cognition' and 'affect' are themselves Euroamerican cultural constructions, master symbols that participate in the fundamental organization of our ways of looking at ourselves and others (Lutz 1985, 1986), both in and outside of social science" (Lutz 1987:308). If this is true, then we have even more reason to wonder about the adequacy of ordinary western ways of talking about emotion. Yet we have no access either to our emotions or to those of others, independent of or unmediated by the discourse of our culture.

In the face of these difficulties, I shall sketch an account of emotion with the following limitations. First, it will operate within the context of western discussions of emotion: I shall not question, for instance, whether it would be possible or desirable to dispense entirely with anything resembling our concept of emotion. Second, although this account attempts to be consistent with as much as possible of western understandings of emotion, it is intended to cover only a limited domain, not every phenomenon that may be called an emotion. On the contrary, it excludes as genuine emotions both automatic physical responses and non-intentional sensations, such as hunger pangs. Third, I do not pretend to offer a complete theory of emotion; instead, I focus on a few specific aspects of emotion that I take to have been neglected or misrepresented, especially in positivist and neopositivist accounts. Finally, I would defend my approach not only on the ground that it illuminates aspects of our experience and activity that are obscured by positivist and neopositivist construals but also on the ground that it is less open than these to ideological abuse. In particular, I believe that recognizing certain neglected aspects of emotion makes possible a better and less ideologically biased account of how knowledge is, and so ought to be, constructed.

2 Emotions as intentional

Early positivist approaches to understanding emotion assumed that an adequate account required analytically separating emotion from other human faculties. Just as positivist accounts of sense perception attempted to distinguish the supposedly raw data of sensation from their cognitive interpretations, so positivist accounts of emotion tried to separate emotion conceptually from both reason and sense perception. As part of their sharpening of these distinctions, positivist construals of emotion tended to identify emotions with the physical feelings or involuntary bodily movements that typically accompany them, such as pangs or qualms, flushes or tremors; emotions were also assimilated to the subduing of physiological function or movement, as in the case of sadness, depression, or boredom. The continuing influence of such supposedly scientific conceptions of emotion can be seen in the fact that "feeling" is often used colloquially as a synonym for emotion, even though the more central meaning of "feeling" is physiological sensation. On such accounts, emotions were not seen as being *about* anything: instead, they were contrasted with and seen as potential disruptions of other phenomena that *are* about some thing, phenomena, such as rational judgments, thoughts, and observations. The positivist approach to understanding emotion has been called the Dumb View (Spelman 1982).

The Dumb View of emotion is quite untenable. For one thing, the same feeling or physiological response is likely to be interpreted as various emotions, depending on the context of its experience. This point is often illustrated by reference to the famous Schachter and Singer experiment; excited feelings were induced in research subjects by the injection of adrenalin, and the subjects then attributed to themselves appropriate emotions depending on their context (Schachter and Singer 1969). Another problem with the Dumb View is that identifying emotions with feelings would make it impossible to postulate that a person might not be aware of her emotional state because feelings by definition are a matter of conscious awareness. Finally, emotions differ from feelings, sensations, or physiological responses in that they are dispositional rather than episodic. For instance, we may assert truthfully that we are outraged by, proud of, or saddened by certain events, even if at that moment we are neither agitated nor tearful.

In recent years, contemporary philosophers have tended to reject the Dumb View of emotion and have substituted more intentional or cognitivist understandings. These newer conceptions emphasize that intentional judgments as well as physiological disturbances are integral elements in emotion.[7] They define or identify emotions not by the quality or character of the physiological sensation that may be associated with them but rather by their intentional aspect, the associated judgment. Thus, it is the content of my associated thought or judgment that determines whether my physical agitation and restlessness are defined as "anxiety about my daughter's lateness" or "anticipation of tonight's performance."

Cognitivist accounts of emotion have been criticized as overly rationalist, inapplicable to allegedly spontaneous, automatic, or global emotions, such as general feelings of nervousness, contentedness, angst, ecstasy, or terror. Certainly, these accounts entail that infants and animals experience emotions, if at all, in only a primitive, rudimentary form. Far from being unacceptable, however, this entailment is desirable because it suggests that humans develop and mature in emotions as well as in other dimensions; they increase the range, variety, and subtlety of their emotional responses in accordance with their life experiences and their reflections on these.

Cognitivist accounts of emotion are not without their own problems. A serious difficulty with many is that they end up replicating within the structure of emotion the very problem they are trying to solve—namely, that of an artificial split between emotion and thought—because most cognitivist accounts explain emotion as having two "components": an affective or feeling component and a cognition that supposedly interprets or identifies the feelings. These accounts, therefore, unwittingly perpetuate the positivist distinction between the shared, public, objective world of verifiable calculations, observations, and facts and the individual, private, subjective world of idiosyncratic feelings and sensations. This sharp distinction breaks any conceptual links between our feelings and the "external" world: if feelings are still conceived as blind or raw or undifferentiated, then we can give no sense of the notion of feelings fitting or failing to fit our perceptual judgments, that is, being appropriate or inappropriate. When intentionality is viewed as intellectual cognition and moved to the center of our picture of emotion, the affective elements are pushed to the periphery and become shadowy conceptual danglers whose relevance to emotion is obscure or even negligible. An adequate cognitive account of emotion must overcome this problem.

Most cognitivist accounts of emotion thus remain problematic insofar as they fail to explain the relation between the cognitive and the affective aspects of emotion. Moreover, insofar as they prioritize the intellectual over the feeling aspects, they reinforce the traditional western preference for mind over body.[8] Nevertheless, they do identify a vital feature of emotion overlooked by the Dumb View, namely, its intentionality.

3 Emotions as social constructs

We tend to experience our emotions as involuntary individual responses to situations, responses that are often (though, significantly, not always) private in the sense that they are not perceived as directly and immediately by other people as they are by the subject of the experience. The apparently individual and involuntary character of our emotional experience is often taken as evidence that emotions are presocial, instinctive responses, determined by our biological constitution. This inference, however, is quite mistaken. Although it is probably true that the physiological disturbances characterizing emotions—facial grimaces, changes in the metabolic rate, sweating, trembling, tears, and so on—are continuous with the instinctive responses of our pre-human ancestors and also that the ontogeny of emotions to some extent recapitulates their phylogeny, mature human emotions can be seen as neither instinctive nor biologically determined. Instead, they are socially constructed on several levels.

Emotions are most obviously socially constructed in that children are taught deliberately what their culture defines as appropriate responses to certain situations: to fear strangers, to enjoy spicy food, or to like swimming in cold water. On a less conscious level, children also learn what their culture defines as the appropriate ways to express the emotions that it recognizes. Although there may be crosscultural similarities in the expression of some apparently universal emotions, there are also wide divergences in what are recognized as expressions of grief, respect, contempt, or anger. On an even deeper level, cultures construct divergent understandings of what emotions are. For instance, English metaphors and metonymies are said to reveal a "folk" theory of anger as a hot fluid, contained in a private space within an individual and liable to dangerous public explosion (Lakoff and Kovecses 1987). By contrast, the Ilongot, a people of the Philippines, apparently do not understand the self in terms of a public/private distinction and consequently do not experience anger as an explosive internal force: for them, rather, it is an interpersonal phenomenon for which an individual may, for instance, be paid (Rosaldo 1984).

Further aspects of the social construction of emotion are revealed through reflection on emotion's intentional structure. If emotions necessarily involve judgments, then obviously they require concepts, which may be seen as socially constructed ways of organizing and making sense of the world. For this reason, emotions are simultaneously made possible and limited by the conceptual and linguistic resources of a society. This philosophical claim is borne out by empirical observation of the cultural variability of emotion. Although there is considerable overlap in the emotions identified by many cultures (Wierzbicka 1986), at least some emotions are historically or culturally specific, including perhaps *ennui, angst*, the Japanese *amai* (in which one clings to another, affiliative love) and the response of "being a wild pig," which occurs among the Gururumba, a horticultural people living in the New Guinea Highlands (Averell 1980:158). Even apparently universal emotions, such as anger or love may vary crossculturally. We have just seen that the Ilongot experience of anger apparently is quite different from the modern western experience. Romantic love was invented in the Middle Ages in Europe and since that time has been modified considerably; for instance, it is no longer confined to the nobility, and it no longer needs to be extramarital or unconsummated. In some cultures, romantic love does not exist at all.[9]

Thus, there are complex linguistic and other social preconditions for the experience, that is, for the existence of human emotions. The emotions that we experience reflect prevailing forms of social life. For instance, one could not feel or even be betrayed in the absence of social norms about fidelity: it is inconceivable that betrayal or indeed any

distinctively human emotion could be experienced by a solitary individual in some hypothetical presocial state of nature. There is a sense in which any individual's guilt or anger, joy
or triumph, presupposes the existence of a social group capable of feeling guilt, anger, joy,
or triumph. This is not to say that group emotions historically precede or are logically prior
to the emotions of individuals; it is to say that individual experience is simultaneously social
experience.[10] In later sections, I shall explore the epistemological and political implications
of this social rather than individual understanding of emotion.

4 Emotions as active engagements

We often interpret our emotions as experiences that overwhelm us rather than as responses
we consciously choose: that emotions are to some extent involuntary is part of the ordinary
meaning of the term "emotion." Even in daily life, however, we recognize that emotions are
not entirely involuntary, and we try to gain control over them in various ways, ranging from
mechanistic behavior modification techniques designed to sensitize or desensitize our feeling
responses to various situations to cognitive techniques designed to help us to think differently about situations. For instance, we might try to change our response to an upsetting
situation by thinking about it in a way that will either divert our attention from its more
painful aspects or present it as necessary for some larger good.

Some psychological theories interpret emotions as chosen on an even deeper level—as
actions for which the agent disclaims responsibility. For instance, the psychologist Averell
likens the experience of emotion to playing a culturally recognized role: we ordinarily
perform so smoothly and automatically that we do not realize we are giving a performance.
He provides many examples demonstrating that even extreme and apparently totally involving displays of emotion in fact are functional for the individual and/or the society.[11] For
example, students requested to record their experiences of anger or annoyance over a two-
week period came to realize that their anger was not as uncontrollable and irrational as they
had assumed previously, and they noted the usefulness and effectiveness of anger in achieving various social goods. Averell, notes, however, that emotions are often useful in attaining
their goals only if they are interpreted as passions rather than as actions, and he cites the case
of one subject led to reflect on her anger who later wrote that it was less useful as a defence
mechanism when she became conscious of its function.

The action/passion dichotomy is too simple for understanding emotion, as it is for
other aspects of our lives. Perhaps it is more helpful to think of emotions as habitual
responses that we may have more or less difficulty in breaking. We claim or disclaim
responsibility for these responses depending on our purposes in a particular context. We
could never experience our emotions entirely as deliberate actions, for then they would
appear nongenuine and inauthentic, but neither should emotions be seen as nonintentional,
primal, or physical forces with which our rational selves are forever at war. As they have
been socially constructed, so may they be reconstructed, although describing how this might
happen would require a long and complicated story.

Emotions, then, are wrongly seen as necessarily passive or involuntary responses to the
world. Rather, they are ways in which we engage actively and even construct the world.
They have both mental and physical aspects, each of which conditions the other. In some
respects, they are chosen, but in others they are involuntary; they presuppose language and
a social order. Thus, they can be attributed only to what are sometimes called "whole
persons," engaged in the on-going activity of social life.

5 Emotion, evaluation, and observation

Emotions and values are closely related. The relation is so close, indeed, that some philosophical accounts of what it is to hold or express certain values reduce these phenomena to nothing more than holding or expressing certain emotional attitudes. When the relevant conception of emotion is the Dumb View, then simple emotivism certainly is too crude an account of what it is to hold a value; on this account, the intentionality of value judgments vanishes, and value judgments become nothing more than sophisticated grunts and groans. Nevertheless, the grain of important truth in emotivism is its recognition that values presuppose emotions to the extent that emotions provide the experiential basis for values. If we had no emotional responses to the world, it is inconceivable that we should ever come to value one state of affairs more highly than another.

Just as values presuppose emotions, so emotions presuppose values. The object of an emotion—that is, the object of fear, grief, pride, and so on—is a complex state of affairs that is appraised or evaluated by the individual. For instance, my pride in a friend's achievement necessarily incorporates the value judgment that my friend has done something worthy of admiration.

Emotions and evaluations, then, are logically or conceptually connected. Indeed, many evaluative terms derive directly from words for emotions: "desirable," "admirable," "contemptible," "despicable," "respectable," and so on. Certainly it is true (pace J. S. Mill) that the evaluation of a situation as desirable or dangerous does not entail that it is universally desired or feared but it does entail that desire or fear is viewed generally as an appropriate response to the situation. If someone is unafraid in a situation generally perceived as dangerous, her lack of fear requires further explanation; conversely, if someone is afraid without evident danger, then her fear demands explanation; and, if no danger can be identified, her fear is denounced as irrational or pathological. Thus, every emotion presupposes an evaluation of some aspect of the environment while, conversely, every evaluation or appraisal of the situation implies that those who share that evaluation will share, *ceteris paribus*, a predictable emotional response to the situation.

The rejection of the Dumb View and the recognition of intentional elements in emotion already incorporate a realization that observation influences and indeed partially constitutes emotion. We have seen already that distinctively human emotions are not simple instinctive responses to situations or events; instead, they depend essentially on the ways that we perceive those situations and events, as well on the ways that we have learned or decided to respond to them. Without characteristically human perceptions of and engagements in the world, there would be no characteristically human emotions.

Just as observation directs, shapes, and partially defines emotion, so too emotion directs, shapes, and even partially defines observation. Observation is not simply a passive process of absorbing impressions or recording stimuli; instead, it is an activity of selection and interpretation. What is selected and how it is interpreted are influenced by emotional attitudes. On the level of individual observation, this influence has always been apparent to common sense, noting that we remark on very different features of the world when we are happy or depressed, fearful or confident. This influence of emotion on perception is now being explored by social scientists. One example is the so-called Honi phenomenon, named after a subject called Honi who, under identical experimental conditions, perceived strangers' heads as changing in size but saw her husband's head as remaining the same.[12]

The most obvious significance of this sort of example is illustrating how the individual experience of emotion focuses our attention selectively, directing, shaping, and even partially defining our observations, just as our observations direct, shape, and partially define our emotions. In addition, the example has been taken further in an argument for the social construction of what are taken in any situation to be undisputed facts, showing how these rest on intersubjective agreements that consist partly in shared assumptions about "normal" or appropriate emotional responses to situations (McLaughlin 1985). Thus, these examples suggest that certain emotional attitudes are involved on a deep level in all observation, in the intersubjectively verified and so supposedly dispassionate observations of science as well as in the common perceptions of daily life. In the next section, I shall elaborate this claim.

Epistemology

6 The myth of dispassionate investigation

As we have already seen, western epistemology has tended to view emotion with suspicion and even hostility.[13] This derogatory western attitude toward emotion, like the earlier western contempt for sensory observation, fails to recognize that emotion, like sensory perception, is necessary to human survival. Emotions prompt us to act appropriately, to approach some people and situations and to avoid others, to caress or cuddle, fight or flee. Without emotion, human life would be unthinkable. Moreover, emotions have an intrinsic as well as an instrumental value. Although not all emotions are enjoyable or even justifiable, as we shall see, life without any emotion would be life without any meaning.

Within the context of western culture, however, people have often been encouraged to control or even suppress their emotions. Consequently, it is not unusual for people to be unaware of their emotional state or to deny it to themselves and others. This lack of awareness, especially combined with a neopositivist understanding of emotion that construes it just as a feeling of which one is aware, lends plausibility to the myth of dispassionate investigation. But lack of awareness of emotions certainly does not mean that emotions are not present subconsciously or unconsciously or that subterranean emotions do not exert a continuing influence on people's articulated values and observations, thoughts and actions.[14]

Within the positivist tradition, the influence of emotion is usually seen only as distorting or impeding observation or knowledge. Certainly it is true that contempt, disgust, shame, revulsion, or fear may inhibit investigation of certain situations or phenomena. Furiously angry or extremely sad people often seem quite unaware of their surroundings or even their own conditions; they may fail to hear or may systematically misinterpret what other people say. People in love are notoriously oblivious to many aspects of the situation around them.

In spite of these examples, however, positivist epistemology recognizes that the role of emotion in the construction of knowledge is not invariably deleterious and that emotions may make a valuable contribution to knowledge. But the positivist tradition will allow emotion to play only the role of suggesting hypotheses for investigation. Emotions are allowed this because the so-called logic of discovery sets no limits on the idiosyncratic methods that investigators may use for generating hypotheses.

When hypotheses are to be tested, however, positivist epistemology imposes the much stricter logic of justification. The core of this logic is replicability, a criterion believed capable of eliminating or canceling out what are conceptualized as emotional as well as evaluative biases on the part of individual investigators. The conclusions of western science thus are presumed "objective," precisely in the sense that they are uncontaminated by the supposedly "subjective" values and emotions that might bias individual investigators (Nagel 1968:33–34).

But if, as has been argued, the positivist distinction between discovery and justification is not viable, then such a distinction is incapable of filtering out values in science. For example, although such a split, when built into the western scientific method, is generally successful in neutralizing the idiosyncratic or unconventional values of individual investigators, it has been argued that it does not, indeed cannot, eliminate generally accepted social values. These values are implicit in the identification of the problems considered worthy of investigation, in the selection of the hypotheses considered worthy of testing, and in the solutions to the problems considered worthy of acceptance. The science of past centuries provides sample evidence of the influence of prevailing social values, whether seventeenth-century atomistic physics (Merchant 1980) or, competitive interpretations of natural selection (Young 1985).

Of course, only hindsight allows us to identify clearly the values that shaped the science of the past and thus to reveal the formative influence on science of pervasive emotional attitudes, attitudes that typically went unremarked at the time because they were shared so generally. For instance, it is now glaringly evident that contempt for (and perhaps fear of) people of color is implicit in nineteenth-century anthropology's interpretation and even construction of anthropological facts. Because we are closer to them, however, it is harder for us to see how certain emotions, such as sexual possessiveness or the need to dominate others, currently are accepted as guiding principles in twentieth-century sociobiology or even defined as part of reason within political theory and economics (Quinby 1986).

Values and emotions enter into the science of the past and the present, not only on the level of scientific practice but also on the metascientific level, as answers to various questions: What is science? How should it be practiced? and What is the status of scientific investigation versus nonscientific modes of enquiry? For instance, it is claimed with increasing frequency that the modern western conception of science, which identifies knowledge with power and views it as a weapon for dominating nature, reflects the imperialism, racism, and misogyny of the societies that created it. Several feminist theorists have argued that modern epistemology itself may be viewed as an expression of certain emotions alleged to be especially characteristic of males in certain periods, such as separation anxiety and paranoia (Flax 1983; Bordo 1987) or an obsession with control and fear of contamination (Scheman 1985; Schott 1988).

Positivism views values and emotions as alien invaders that must be repelled by a stricter application of the scientific method. If the foregoing claims are correct, however, the scientific method and even its positivist construals themselves incorporate values and emotions. Moreover, such an incorporation seems a necessary feature of all knowledge and conceptions of knowledge. Therefore, rather than repressing emotion in epistemology it is necessary to rethink the relation between knowledge and emotion and construct conceptual models that demonstrate the mutually constitutive rather than oppositional relation between reason and emotion. Far from precluding the possibility of reliable knowledge, emotion as well as value must be shown as necessary to such knowledge. Despite its classical antecedents and like the ideal of disinterested enquiry, the ideal of dispassionate enquiry is an impossible dream but a dream nonetheless or perhaps a myth that has exerted enormous influence on western epistemology. Like all myths, it is a form of ideology that fulfils certain social and political functions.

7   The ideological function of the myth

So far, I have spoken very generally of people and their emotions, as though everyone experienced similar emotions and dealt with them in similar ways. It is an axiom of feminist theory, however, that all generalizations about "people" are suspect. The divisions in our society are so deep, particularly the divisions of race, class, and gender, that many feminist theorists would claim that talk about people in general is ideologically dangerous because such talk obscures the fact that no one is simply a person but instead is constituted fundamentally by race, class, and gender. Race, class, and gender shape every aspect of our lives, and our emotional constitution is not excluded. Recognizing this helps us to see more clearly the political functions of the myth of the dispassionate investigator.

Feminist theorists have pointed out that the western tradition has not seen everyone as equally emotional. Instead, reason has been associated with members of dominant political, social, and cultural groups and emotion with members of subordinate groups. Prominent among those subordinate groups in our society are people of color, except for supposedly "inscrutable orientals," and women.[15]

Although the emotionality of women is a familiar cultural stereotype, its grounding is quite shaky. Women appear more emotional than men because they, along with some groups of people of color, are permitted and even required to express emotion more openly. In contemporary western culture, emotionally inexpressive women are suspect as not being real women,[16] whereas men who express their emotions freely are suspected of being homosexual or in some other way deviant from the masculine ideal. Modern western men, in contrast with Shakespeare's heroes, for instance, are required to present a facade of coolness, lack of excitement, even boredom, to express emotion only rarely and then for relatively trivial events, such as sporting occasions, where expressed emotions are acknowledged to be dramatized and so are not taken entirely seriously. Thus, women in our society form the main group allowed or even expected to feel emotion. A woman may cry in the face of disaster, and a man of color may gesticulate, but a white man merely sets his jaw.[17]

White men's control of their emotional expression may go to the extremes of repressing their emotions, failing to develop emotionally, or even losing the capacity to experience many emotions. Not uncommonly these men are unable to identify what they are feeling, and even they may be surprised, on occasion, by their own apparent lack of emotional response to a situation, such as death, where emotional reaction is perceived appropriate. In some married couples, the wife implicitly is assigned the job of feeling emotion for both of them. White, college-educated men increasingly enter therapy in order to learn how to "get in touch with" their emotions, a project other men may ridicule as weakness. In therapeutic situations, men may learn that they are just as emotional as women but less adept at identifying their own or others' emotions. In consequence, their emotional development may be relatively rudimentary; this may lead to moral rigidity or insensitivity. Paradoxically, men's lacking awareness of their own emotional responses frequently results in their being more influenced by emotion rather than less.

Although there is no reason to suppose that the thoughts and actions of women are any more influenced by emotion than the thoughts and actions of men, the stereotypes of cool men and emotional women continue to flourish because they are confirmed by an uncritical daily experience. In these circumstances, where there is a differential assignment of reason and emotion, it is easy to see the ideological function of the myth of the dispassionate investigator. It functions, obviously, to bolster the epistemic authority of the currently dominant groups, composed largely of white men, and to discredit the observations and claims of the currently subordinate groups including, of course, the observations and claims of many people of color and women. The more forcefully and vehemently the latter groups express their observations and claims, the more emotional they appear and so the more easily they are discredited. The alleged epistemic authority of the dominant groups then justifies their political authority.

The previous section of this chapter argued that dispassionate enquiry was a myth. This section has shown that the myth promotes a conception of epistemological justification vindicating the silencing of those, especially women, who are defined culturally as the bearers of emotion and so are perceived as more "subjective," biased, and irrational. In our present social context, therefore, the ideal of the dispassionate investigator is a classist, racist, and especially masculinist myth.[18]

8 Emotional hegemony and emotional subversion

As we have seen already, mature human emotions are neither instinctive nor biologically determined, although they may have developed out of presocial, instinctive responses. Like everything else that is human, emotions in part are socially constructed; like all social constructs, they are historical products, bearing the marks of the society that constructed them. Within the very language of emotion, in our basic definitions and explanations of what it is to feel pride or embarrassment, resentment or contempt, cultural norms and expectations are embedded. Simply describing ourselves as angry, for instance, presupposes that we view ourselves as having been wronged, victimized by the violation of some social norm. Thus, we absorb the standards and values of our society in the very process of learning the language of emotion, and those standards and values are built into the foundation of our emotional constitution.

Within a hierarchical society, the norms and values that predominate tend to serve the interest of the dominant group. Within a capitalist, white supremacist, and male-dominant society, the predominant values will tend to serve the interests of rich white men. Consequently, we are all likely to develop an emotional constitution quite inappropriate for feminism. Whatever our color, we are likely to feel what Irving Thalberg has called "visceral racism"; whatever our sexual orientation, we are likely to be homophobic; whatever our class, we are likely to be at least somewhat ambitious and competitive; whatever our sex, we are likely to feel contempt for women. The emotional responses may be so deeply rooted in us that they are relatively impervious to intellectual argument and may recur even when we pay lip service to changed intellectual convictions.[19]

By forming our emotional constitution in particular ways, our society helps to ensure its own perpetuation. The dominant values are implicit in responses taken to be precultural or acultural, our so-called gut responses. Not only do these conservative responses hamper and disrupt our attempts to live in or prefigure alternative social forms, but also, and insofar as we take them to be natural responses, they blinker us theoretically. For instance, they limit our capacity for outrage; they either prevent us from despising or encourage us to despise; they lend plausibility to the belief that greed and domination are inevitable universal human motivations; in sum, they blind us to the possibility of alternative ways of living.

This picture may seem at first to support the positivist claim that the intrusion of emotion only disrupts the process of seeking knowledge and distorts the results of that process. The picture, however, is not complete; it ignores the fact that people do not always experience the conventionally acceptable emotions. They may feel satisfaction rather than embarrassment when their leaders make fools of themselves. They may feel resentment rather than gratitude for welfare payments and hand-me-downs. They may be attracted to forbidden modes of sexual expression. They may feel revulsion for socially sanctioned ways of treating children or animals. In other words, the hegemony that our society exercises over people's emotional constitution is not total.

People who experience conventionally unacceptable, or what I call "outlaw," emotions often are subordinated individuals who pay a disproportionately high price for maintaining the status quo. The social situation of such people makes them unable to experience the conventionally prescribed emotions: for instance, people of color are more likely to experience anger than amusement when a racist joke is recounted, and women subjected to male sexual banter are less likely to be flattered than uncomfortable or even afraid.

When unconventional emotional responses are experienced by isolated individuals, those concerned may be confused, unable to name their experience; they may even doubt their own sanity. Women may come to believe that they are "emotionally disturbed" and that the embarrassment or fear aroused in them by male sexual innuendo is prudery or paranoia. When certain emotions are shared or validated by others, however, the basis exists for forming a subculture defined by perceptions, norms, and values that systematically oppose the prevailing perceptions, norms, and values. By constituting the basis for such a subculture, outlaw emotions may be politically because epistemologically subversive.

Outlaw emotions are distinguished by their incompatibility with the dominant perceptions and values, and some, though certainly not all, of these outlaw emotions are potentially or actually feminist emotions. Emotions become feminist when they incorporate feminist perceptions and values, just as emotions are sexist or racist when they incorporate sexist or racist perceptions and values. For example, anger becomes feminist anger when it involves the perception that the persistent importuning endured by one woman is a single instance of a widespread pattern of sexual harassment, and pride becomes feminist pride when it is evoked by realizing that a certain person's achievement was possible only because that individual overcame specifically gendered obstacles to success.[20]

Outlaw emotions stand in a dialectical relation to critical social theory: at least some are necessary to develop a critical perspective on the world, but they also presuppose at least the beginnings of such a perspective. Feminists need to be aware of how we can draw on some of our outlaw emotions in constructing feminist theory and also of how the increasing sophistication of feminist theory can contribute to the reeducation, refinement, and eventual reconstruction of our emotional constitution.

9 Outlaw emotions and feminist theory

The most obvious way in which feminist and other outlaw emotions can help in developing alternatives to prevailing conceptions of reality is by motivating new investigations. This is possible because, as we saw earlier, emotions may be long-term as well as momentary; it makes sense to say that someone continues to be shocked or saddened by a situation, even if she is at the moment laughing heartily. As we have seen already, theoretical investigation is always purposeful, and observation is always selective. Feminist emotions provide a political motivation for investigation and so help to determine the selection of problems as well as the method by which they are investigated. Susan Griffin makes the same point when she characterizes feminist theory as following "a direction determined by pain, and trauma, and compassion and outrage" (Griffin 1979:31).

As well as motivating critical research, outlaw emotions may also enable us to perceive the world differently from its portrayal in conventional descriptions. They may provide the first indications that something is wrong with the way alleged facts have been constructed, with accepted understandings of how things are. Conventionally unexpected or inappropriate emotions may precede our conscious recognition that accepted descriptions and justifications often conceal as much as reveal the prevailing state of affairs. Only when we reflect on our initially puzzling irritability, revulsion, anger, or fear may we bring to consciousness our "gut-level" awareness that we are in a situation of coercion, cruelty, injustice, or danger. Thus, conventionally inexplicable emotions, particularly, though not exclusively, those experienced by women, may lead us to make subversive observations that challenge dominant conceptions of the status quo. They may help us to realize that what are taken generally to be facts have been constructed in a way that obscures the reality of subordinated people, especially women's reality.

But why should we trust the emotional responses of women and other subordinated groups? How can we determine which outlaw emotions are to be endorsed or encouraged and which rejected? In what sense can we say that some emotional responses are more appropriate than others? What reason is there for supposing that certain alternative perceptions of the world, perceptions informed by outlaw emotions, are to be preferred to perceptions informed by conventional emotions? Here I can indicate only the general direction of an answer, whose full elaboration must await another occasion.[21]

I suggest that emotions are appropriate if they are characteristic of a society in which all humans (and perhaps some nonhuman life, too) thrive, or if they are conducive to establishing such a society. For instance, it is appropriate to feel joy when we are developing or exercising our creative powers, and it is appropriate to feel anger and perhaps disgust in those situations where humans are denied their full creativity or freedom. Similarly, it is appropriate to feel fear if those capacities are threatened in us.

This suggestion obviously is extremely vague, verging on the tautologous. How can we apply it in situations where there is disagreement over what is or is not disgusting or exhilarating or unjust? Here I appeal to a claim for which I have argued elsewhere: the perspective on reality available from the standpoint of the oppressed, which in part at least is the standpoint of women, is a perspective that offers a less partial and distorted and therefore more reliable view (Jaggar 1983:chap. 11). Oppressed people have a kind of epistemological privilege insofar as they have easier access to this standpoint and therefore a better chance of ascertaining the possible beginnings of a society in which all could thrive. For this reason, I would claim that the emotional responses of oppressed people in general, and often of women in particular, are more likely to be appropriate than the emotional responses of the dominant class. That is, they are more likely to incorporate reliable appraisals of situations.

Even in contemporary science, where the ideology of dispassionate enquiry is almost overwhelming, it is possible to discover a few examples that seem to support the claim that certain emotions are more appropriate than others in both a moral and epistemological sense. For instance, Hilary Rose claims that women's practice of caring, even though warped by its containment in the alienated context of a coercive sexual division of labor, nevertheless has generated more accurate and less oppressive understandings of women's bodily functions, such as menstruation (Rose 1983). Certain emotions may be both morally appropriate and epistemologically advantageous in approaching the nonhuman and even the inanimate world. Jane Goodall's scientific contribution to our understanding of chimpanzee behavior seems to have been made possible only by her amazing empathy with or even love for these animals (Goodall 1987). In her study of Barbara McClintock, Evelyn Fox Keller describes McClintock's relation to the objects of her research—grains of maize and their genetic properties—as a relation of affection, empathy, and "the highest form of love: love that allows for intimacy without the annihilation of difference." She notes that McClintock's "vocabulary is consistently a vocabulary of affection, of kinship, of empathy" (Keller 1984:164). Examples like these prompt Hilary Rose to assert that a feminist science of nature needs to draw on heart as well as hand and brain.

10   Some implications of recognizing the epistemic potential of emotion

Accepting that appropriate emotions are indispensable to reliable knowledge does not mean, of course, that uncritical feeling may be substituted for supposedly dispassionate investigation. Nor does it mean that the emotional responses of women and other members of the underclass are to be trusted without question. Although our emotions are epistemologically indispensable, they are not epistemologically indisputable. Like all our faculties, they may be misleading, and their data, like all data, are always subject to reinterpretation and revision. Because emotions are not presocial, physiological responses to unequivocal situations, they are open to challenge on various grounds. They may be dishonest or self-deceptive, they may incorporate inaccurate or partial perceptions, or they may be constituted by oppressive values. Accepting the indispensability of appropriate emotions to knowledge means no more (and no less) than that discordant emotions should be attended to seriously and respectfully rather than condemned, ignored, discounted, or suppressed.

Just as appropriate emotions may contribute to the development of knowledge, so the growth of knowledge may contribute to the development of appropriate emotions. For instance, the powerful insights of feminist theory often stimulate new emotional responses to past and present situations. Inevitably, our emotions are affected by the knowledge that the women on our faculty are paid systematically less than the men, that one girl in four is subjected to sexual abuse from heterosexual men in her own family, and that few women reach orgasm in heterosexual intercourse. We are likely to feel different emotions toward older women or people of color as we reevaluate our standards of sexual attractiveness or acknowledge that black is beautiful. The new emotions evoked by feminist insights are likely in turn to stimulate further feminist observations and insights, and these may generate new directions in both theory and political practice. The feedback loop between our emotional constitution and our theorizing is continuous; each continually modifies the other, in principle inseparable from it.

The ease and speed with which we can reeducate our emotions unfortunately is not great. Emotions are only partially within our control as individuals. Although affected by new information, these habitual responses are not quickly unlearned. Even when we come to believe consciously that our fear or shame or revulsion is unwarranted, we may still continue to experience emotions inconsistent with our conscious politics. We may still continue to be anxious for male approval, competitive with our comrades and sisters, and possessive with our lovers. These unwelcome, because apparently inappropriate emotions, should not be suppressed or denied; instead, they should be acknowledged and subjected to critical scrutiny. The persistence of such recalcitrant emotions probably demonstrates how fundamentally we have been constituted by the dominant world view, but it may also indicate superficiality or other inadequacy in our emerging theory and politics.[22] We can only start from where we are—beings who have been created in a cruelly racist, capitalist, and male-dominated society that has shaped our bodies and our minds, our perceptions, our values and our emotions, our language and our systems of knowledge.

The alternative epistemological models that I would suggest display the continuous interaction between how we understand the world and who we are as people. They would show how our emotional responses to the world change as we conceptualize it differently and how our changing emotional responses then stimulate us to new insights. They would demonstrate the need for theory to be self-reflexive, to focus not only on the outer world but also on ourselves and our relation to that world, to examine critically our social location, our actions, our values, our perceptions, and our emotions. The models also show how feminist and other critical social theories are indispensable psychotherapeutic tools because they provide some insights necessary to a full understanding of our emotional constitution. Thus, the models would explain how the reconstruction of knowledge is inseparable from the reconstruction of ourselves.

A corollary of the reflexivity of feminist and other critical theory is that it requires a much broader construal than positivism accepts of the process of theoretical investigation. In particular, it requires acknowledging that a necessary part of theoretical process is critical self-examination. Time spent in analyzing emotions and uncovering their sources should be viewed, therefore, neither as irrelevant to theoretical investigation nor even as a prerequisite for it; it is not a kind of clearing of the emotional decks, "dealing with" our emotions so that they not influence our thinking. Instead, we must recognize that our efforts to reinterpret and refine our emotions are necessary to our theoretical investigation, just as our efforts to reeducate our emotions are necessary to our political activity. Critical reflection on emotion is not a self-indulgent substitute for political analysis and political action. It is itself a kind of political theory and political practice, indispensable for an adequate social theory and social transformation.

Finally, the recognition that emotions play a vital part in developing knowledge enlarges our understanding of women's claimed epistemic advantage. We can now see that women's subversive insights owe much to women's outlaw emotions, themselves appropriate responses to the situations of women's subordination. In addition to their propensity to experience outlaw emotions, at least on some level, women are relatively adept at identifying such emotions, in themselves and others, in part because of their social responsibility for caretaking, including emotional nurturance. It is true that women, like all subordinated peoples, especially those who must live in close proximity with their masters, often engage in emotional deception and even self-deception as the price of their survival. Even so, women may be less likely than other subordinated groups to engage in denial or suppression of outlaw emotions. Women's work of emotional nurturance has required them to develop a special acuity in recognizing hidden emotions and in understanding the genesis of those emotions. This emotional acumen can now be recognized as a skill in political analysis and validated as giving women a special advantage in both understanding the mechanisms of domination and envisioning freer ways to live.

Conclusion

The claim that emotion is vital to systematic knowledge is only the most obvious contrast between the conception of theoretical investigation that I have sketched here and the conception provided by positivism. For instance, the alternative approach emphasizes that what we identify as emotion is a conceptual abstraction from a complex process of human activity that also involves acting, sensing, and evaluating. This proposed account of theoretical construction demonstrates the simultaneous necessity for and interdependence of faculties that our culture has abstracted and separated from each other: emotion and reason, evaluation and perception, observation and action. The model of knowing suggested here is nonhierarchical and antifoundationalist; instead, it is appropriately symbolized by the radical feminist metaphor of the upward spiral. Emotions are neither more basic than observation, reason, or action in building theory, nor are they secondary to them. Each of these human faculties reflects an aspect of human knowing inseparable from the other aspects. Thus, to borrow a famous phrase from a Marxian context, the development of each of these faculties is a necessary condition for the development of all.

In conclusion, it is interesting to note that acknowledging the importance of emotion for knowledge is not an entirely novel suggestion within the western epistemological tradition. The archrationalist Plato himself came to accept that in the end knowledge required a (very purified form of) love. It may be no accident that in the *Symposium* Socrates learns this lesson from Diotima, the wise woman!

Notes

I wish to thank the following individuals who commented helpfully on earlier drafts of this chapter or made me aware of further resources: Lynne Arnault, Susan Bordo, Martha Bolton, Cheshire Calhoun, Randy Cornelius, Shelagh Crooks, Ronald De Sousa, Tim Diamond, Dick Foley, Ann Garry, Judy Gerson, Mary Gibson, Sherry Gorelick, Marcia Lind, Helen Longino, Andy McLaughlin, Uma Narayan, Linda Nicholson, Bob Richardson, Sally Ruddick, Laurie Shrage, Alan Soble, Vicky Spelman, Karsten Struhl, Joan Tronto, Daisy Quarm, Naomi Quinn, and Alison Wylie. I am also grateful to my colleagues in the fall 1985 Women's Studies Chair Seminar at Douglass College, Rutgers University, and to audiences at Duke University, Georgia University Centre, Hobart and William Smith Colleges, Northeastern University, the University of North Carolina at Chapel Hill, and Princeton University, for their responses to earlier versions of this chapter. In addition, I received many helpful comments from members of the Canadian Society for Women in Philosophy and from students in Lisa Heldke's classes in feminist epistemology at Carleton College and Northwestern University. Thanks, too, to Delia Cushway, who provided a comfortable environment in which I wrote the first draft.

A similar version of this essay appeared in *Inquiry: An Interdisciplinary Journal of Philosophy* (June 1989). Reprinted by permission of Norwegian University Press.

1   Philosophers who do not conform to this generalization and constitute part of what Susan Bordo calls a "recessive" tradition in western philosophy include Hume and Nietzsche, Dewey and James (Bordo 1987:114–118).

2   The western tradition as a whole has been profoundly rationalist, and much of its history may be viewed as a continuous redrawing of the boundaries of the rational. For a survey of this history from a feminist perspective, see Lloyd 1984.

3   Thus, fear or other emotions were seen as rational in some circumstances. To illustrate this point, Vicky Spelman quotes Aristotle as saying (in the *Nichomachean Ethics*, Bk. IV, ch. 5): "[Anyone] who does not get angry when there is reason to be angry, or who does not get angry in the right way at the right time and with the right people, is a dolt" (Spelman 1982:1).

4   Descartes, Leibnitz, and Kant are among the prominent philosophers who did not endorse a wholly stripped-down, instrumentalist conception of reason.

5   The relocation of values in human attitudes and preferences in itself was not grounds for denying their universality because they could have been conceived as grounded in a common or universal human nature. In fact, however, the variability, rather than the commonality, of human preferences and responses was emphasized; values gradually came to be viewed as individual, particular, and even idiosyncratic rather than as universal and objective. The only exception to the variability of human desires was the supposedly universal urge to egoism and the motive to maximize one's own utility, whatever that consisted in. The value of autonomy and liberty, consequently, was seen as perhaps the only value capable of being justified objectively because it was a precondition for satisfying other desires.

6   For instance, Julius Moravcsik has characterized as emotions what I would call "plain" hunger and thirst, appetites that are not desires for any particular food or drink (Moravcsik 1982:207–224). I myself think that such states, which Moravcsik also calls instincts or appetites, are understood better as sensations than emotions. In other words, I would view so-called instinctive, nonintentional feelings as the biological raw material from which full-fledged human emotions develop.

7   Even adherents of the Dumb View recognize, of course, that emotions are not entirely random or unrelated to an individual's judgments and beliefs; in other words, they note that people are angry or excited *about* something, afraid or proud *of* something. On the Dumb View, however, the judgments or beliefs associated with an emotion are seen as its causes and thus as related to it only externally.

8   Cheshire Calhoun pointed this out to me in private correspondence.

9   Recognition of the many levels on which emotions are socially constructed raises the question whether it makes sense even to speak of the possibility of universal emotions. Although a full answer to this question is methodologically problematic, one might speculate that many of what we westerners identify as emotions have functional analogues in other cultures. In other words, it may be that people in every culture might behave in ways that fulfil at least some social functions of our angry or fearful behavior.

10   The relationship between the emotional experience of an individual and the emotional experience of the group to which the individual belongs may perhaps be clarified by analogy with the relation

between a word and the language of which it is a part. That the word has meaning presupposes it's a part of a linguistic system without which it has no meaning; yet the language itself has no meaning over and above the meaning of the words of which it is composed together with their grammatical ordering. Words and language presuppose and mutually constitute each other. Similarly, both individual and group emotion presuppose and mutually constitute each other.

11   Averell cites dissociative reactions by military personnel at Wright Paterson Air Force Base and shows how these were effective in mustering help to deal with difficult situations while simultaneously relieving the individual of responsibility or blame (Averell 1980:157).

12   These and similar experiments are described in Kilpatrick 1961:ch. 10, cited by McLaughlin 1985:296.

13   The positivist attitude toward emotion, which requires that ideal investigators be both disinterested and dispassionate, may be a modern variant of older traditions in western philosophy that recommended people seek to minimize their emotional responses to the world and develop instead their powers of rationality and pure contemplation.

14   It is now widely accepted that the suppression and repression of emotion has damaging if not explosive consequences. There is general acknowledgment that no one can avoid at some time experiencing emotions she or he finds unpleasant, and there is also increasing recognition that the denial of such emotions is likely to result in hysterical disorders of thought and behavior, in projecting one's own emotions on to others, in displacing them to inappropriate situations, or in psychosomatic ailments. Psychotherapy, which purports to help individuals recognize and "deal with" their emotions, has become an enormous industry, especially in the United States. In much conventional psychotherapy, however, emotions still are conceived as feelings or passions, "subjective" disturbances that afflict individuals or interfere with their capacity for rational thought and action. Different therapies, therefore, have developed a wide variety of techniques for encouraging people to "discharge" or "vent" their emotions, just as they would drain an abscess. Once emotions have been discharged or vented, they are supposed to be experienced less intensely, or even to vanish entirely, and consequently to exert less influence on individuals' thoughts and actions. This approach to psychotherapy clearly demonstrates its kinship with the "folk" theory of anger mentioned earlier, and it equally clearly retains the traditional western assumption that emotion is inimical to rational thought and action. Thus, such approaches fail to challenge and indeed provide covert support for the view that "objective" knowers are not only disinterested but also dispassionate.

15   E. V. Spelman (1982) illustrates this point with a quotation from the well-known contemporary philosopher, R. S. Peters, who wrote "we speak of emotional outbursts, reactions, upheavals and women" (*Proceedings of the Aristotelian Society*, New Series, vol. 62).

16   It seems likely that the conspicuous absence of emotion shown by Mrs. Thatcher is a deliberate strategy she finds necessary to counter the public perception of women as too emotional for political leadership. The strategy results in her being perceived as a formidable leader, but an Iron Lady rather than a real woman. Ironically, Neil Kinnock, leader of the British Labour Party and Thatcher's main opponent in the 1987 General Election, was able to muster considerable public support through television commercials portraying him in the stereotypically feminine role of caring about the unfortunate victims of Thatcher economics. Ultimately, however, this support was not sufficient to destroy public confidence in Mrs. Thatcher's "masculine" competence and gain Kinnock the election.

17   On the rare occasions when a white man cries, he is embarrassed and feels constrained to apologize. The one exception to the rule that men should be emotionless is that they are allowed and often even expected to experience anger. Spelman (1982) points out that men's cultural permission to be angry bolsters their claim to authority.

18   Someone might argue that the viciousness of this myth was not a logical necessity. In the egalitarian society, where the concepts of reason and emotion were not gender-bound in the way they still are today, it might be argued that the ideal of the dispassionate investigator could be epistemologically beneficial. Is it possible that, in such socially and conceptually egalitarian circumstances, the myth of the dispassionate investigator could serve as a heuristic device, an ideal never to be realized in practice but nevertheless helping to minimize "subjectivity" and bias? My own view is that counterfactual myths rarely bring the benefits advertised and that this one is no exception. This myth fosters an equally mythical conception of pure truth and objectivity, quite independent of human interests or desires, and in this way it functions to disguise the inseparability of theory and practice, science and politics. Thus, it is part of an antidemocratic world view that mystifies the political dimension of knowledge and unwarrantedly circumscribes the arena of political debate.

19   Of course, the similarities in our emotional constitutions should not blind us to systematic differences. For instance, girls rather than boys are taught fear and disgust for spiders and snakes, affection for fluffy animals, and shame for their naked bodies. It is primarily, though not exclusively, men rather than women whose sexual responses are shaped by exposure to visual and sometimes violent pornography. Girls and women are taught to cultivate sympathy for others: boys and men are taught to separate themselves emotionally from others. As I have noted already, more emotional expression is permitted for lower-class and some nonwhite men than for ruling-class men, perhaps because the expression of emotion is thought to expose vulnerability. Men of the upper classes learn to cultivate an attitude of condescension, boredom, or detached amusement. As we shall see shortly, differences in the emotional constitution of various groups may be epistemologically significant in so far as they both presuppose and facilitate different ways of perceiving the world.

20   A necessary condition for experiencing feminist emotions is that one already be a feminist in some sense, even if one does not consciously wear that label. But many women and some men, even those who would deny that they are feminist, still experience emotions compatible with feminist values. For instance, they may be angered by the perception that someone is being mistreated just because she is a woman, or they may take special pride in the achievement of a woman. If those who experience such emotions are unwilling to recognize them as feminist, their emotions are probably described better as potentially feminist or prefeminist emotions.

21   I owe this suggestion to Marcia Lind.

22   Within a feminist context, Berenice Fisher suggests that we focus particular attention on our emotions of guilt and shame as part of a critical reevaluation of our political ideals and our political practice (Fisher 1984).

References

Averell, James R. 1980. "The Emotions." In *Personality: Basic Aspects and Current Research*, ed. Ervin Staub. Englewood Cliffs, N.J.: Prentice-Hall.

Bordo, W. R. 1987. *The Flight to Objectivity: Essays on Cartesianism and Culture*. Albany, N.Y.: SUNY Press.

Fisher, Berenice. 1984. "Guilt and Shame in the Women's Movement: The Radical Ideal of Action and its Meaning for Feminist Intellectuals." *Feminist Studies* 10:185–212.

Flax, Jane. 1983. "Political Philosophy and the Patriarchal Unconscious: A Psychoanalytic Perspective on Epistemology and Metaphysics." In *Discovering Reality: Feminist Perspectives on Epistemology, Metaphysics, Methodology and Philosophy of Science*, ed. Sandra Harding and Merrill Hintikka. Dordrecht, Holland: D. Reidel Publishing.

Goodall, Jane. 1986. *The Chimpanzees of Bombe: Patterns of Behavior*. Cambridge, Mass.: Harvard University Press.

Griffin, Susan. 1979. *Rape: The Power of Consciousness*. San Francisco: Harper & Row.

Hinman, Lawrence. 1986. "Emotion, Morality and Understanding." Paper presented at Annual Meeting of Central Division of the American Philosophical Association, St. Louis, Missouri, May 1986.

Jaggar, Alison M. 1983. *Feminist Politics and Human Nature*. Totowa, N.J.: Rowman and Allanheld.

Keller, E. F. 1984. *Gender and Science*. New Haven, Conn.: Yale University Press.

Kilpatrick, Franklin P., ed. 1961. *Explorations in Transactional Psychology*. New York: New York University Press.

Lakoff, George, and Zoltan Kovecses. 1987. "The Cognitive Model of Anger Inherent in American English." In *Cultural Models in Language and Thought*, ed. N. Quinn and D. Holland. New York: Cambridge University Press.

Lewontin, R. C. 1982. "Letter to the editor." *New York Review of Books*, 4 February:40–41. This letter was drawn to my attention by Alan Soble.

Lloyd, Genevieve. 1984. *The Man of Reason: 'Male' and 'Female' in Western Philosophy*. Minneapolis: University of Minnesota Press.

Lutz, Catherine. 1985. "Depression and the Translation of Emotional Worlds." In *Culture and Depression: Studies in the Anthropology and Cross-cultural Psychiatry of Affect and Disorder*, ed. A. Kleinman and B. Good. Berkeley: University of California Press, 63–100.

——. 1986. "Emotion, Thought and Estrangement: Emotion as a Cultural Category." *Cultural Anthropology* 1:287–309.

——— . 1987. "Goals, Events and Understanding in Ifaluck and Emotion Theory." In *Cultural Models in Language and Thought*, ed. N. Quinn and D. Holland. New York: Cambridge University Press.

McLaughlin, Andrew. 1985. "Images and Ethics of Nature." *Environmental Ethics* 7:293–319.

Merchant, Carolyn M. 1980. *The Death of Nature: Women, Ecology and the Scientific Revolution*. New York: Harper & Row.

Moravcsik, J. M. E. 1982. "Understanding and the Emotions." *Dialectica* 36, 2–3: 207–224.

Nagel, E. 1968. "The Subjective Nature of Social Subject Matter." In *Readings in the Philosophy of the Social Sciences*, ed. May Brodbeck. New York: Macmillan.

Quinby, Lee. 1986. Discussion following talk at Hobart and William Smith colleges, April 1986.

Rorty, Richard. 1979. *Philosophy and the Mirror of Nature*. Princeton, N.J.: Princeton University Press.

Rosaldo, Michelle Z. 1984. "Toward an Anthropology of Self and Feeling." In *Culture Theory*, ed. Richard A. Shweder and Robert A. Levine. New York: Cambridge University Press.

Rose, Hilary. 1983. "Hand, Brain, and Heart: A Feminist Epistemology for the Natural Sciences." *Signs: Journal of Women in Culture and Society* 9, 1:73–90.

Schachter, Stanley, and Jerome B. Singer. 1969. "Cognitive, Social and Psychological Determinants of Emotional State." *Psychological Review* 69:379–399.

Scheman, Naomi. 1985. "Women in the Philosophy Curriculum." Paper presented at the Annual Meeting of Central Division of the American Philosophical Association, Chicago, April 1985.

Schott, Robin M. 1988. *Cognition and Eros: A Critique of the Kantian Paradigm*. Boston, Mass.: Beacon Press.

Spelman, E. V. 1982. "Anger and Insubordination." Manuscript; early version read to midwestern chapter of the Society for Women in Philosophy, spring 1982.

Wierzbicka, Anna. 1986. "Human Emotions: Universal or Culture-Specific?" *American Anthropologist* 88:584–594.

Young, R. M. 1985. *Darwin's Metaphor: Nature's Place in Victorian Culture*. Cambridge: Cambridge University Press.

Chapter 3

Lawrence Grossberg

POSTMODERNITY AND AFFECT: ALL DRESSED UP WITH NO PLACE TO GO[1]

Introduction: a modest proposal

THE DISCOURSES OF postmodernism are undoubtedly both too anxious and too immodest. Simply amassing historical events (atomic warfare, televisualization, computerization, etc.) or texts (whether in galleries, streets, cinemas or televisions) does not justify the fascinating and ultrarapid leap into such highly charged abstractions as the "disappearance of the real" or the appearance of the schizophrenic subject. In the attempt to control our anxiety, we might inscribe above our desks Nietzsche's admonition that when studying monsters, one must take care not to become one oneself. Similarly, in an effort to be more modest, we might add his observation that what is important is not the news that god is dead, but the time this news takes to have its effects. The first reminds us that differences which are politically as well as theoretically significant continue to exist; a narrative which makes the impossibility of narrative into an apocalypse is still a narrative. The second reminds us that history is complex; it is produced as events move through it, along different vectors, with different speeds.

Yet while I am critical of the various attempts to talk *about* the postmodern, I do not want to abandon the effort to understand contemporary cultural practices in the light of the question of historical difference and specificity. To put it in this way is, I hope, to offer a more modest way of locating the postmodern within contemporary political and intellectual work. Correlatively, I want to suggest a more modest strategy of theorizing around concrete events and effects without fetishing them and without abandoning the gains that have been made by theoretical critiques of essentialism. Anti-essentialism should not be confused with a fetishism of the particular. I want to distinguish anti-essentialist arguments from anti-theoretical arguments. While we must begin by approaching contemporary practices and events as statements to be, as Donna Haraway (1987) has phrased it, "taken literally," we must not abandon the "detour through theory" which Marx (1973) thought necessary to transform the empirically available into the concretely understood. We must attempt to move, slowly and carefully, between different levels of abstraction, from specific events (any description of which is always an abstraction) to the most decontextualized categories and concepts, and back again. This is a way of recognizing, first, the complexity of social realities and second, one's own socially determined position within the history one describes and yet, not abandoning the possibility of realistic and value-laden political intervention. Will Straw (1987) recently characterized the "style" of many of those who write about the postmodern as "a discourse of cumulative anecdote . . . signifying the epic/epoch." This leap, which confuses accumulation as the construction of a text with its interpretation, constitutes a powerful ideological moment in which any (politically) demystifying impulse is abandoned. The accumulation of fact, even when framed within a narrative may offer some semantic sense but it constitutes neither an account nor a theory.

Still, there is something extremely compelling about such anecdotal logics, so let me begin by simply recalling a few examples of postmodern statements, drawn from a very narrow range of discourses: the recent emergence of a style of television ads that can be described as cynical, if not nihilistic, and super-realistic (by which I mean that they offer the grainy and gritty details of everyday life with no sense of transcendence, not even that of the grandeur of meaninglessness): Jordache's *film noir* scenarios of despair and the imminent collapse of our lives, constructed through images of a girl running away from home, a boy trying to make sense of his parents' divorce; Honda's many fragmented scenes of urban life and decay, or more powerfully, an ad which offers a series of graffiti-scrawled questions—from the existential to the mundane—and then says, "If it's not an answer, at least it's not another question"; Converse's image of a couple breaking up in which the assertion that they can and will remain friends is greeted with an ice cream cone in the face, followed by the order to "take a walk"; the self-conscious irony of Nike's commercial using "Revolution"; Levi's commercials predicated on the assumption that after everyone and everything one has loved has left, you still have your jeans; a Volkswagen commercial in which the young driver readily admits to his mother that "it's not supposed to be a nice car. (After all) it's the eighties." These are successful advertising campaigns but what are they selling: depression? reality?

Such statements are of course to be found all across contemporary cultural production: on television—consider USA Network's moment in which director Terry Gilliam describes how he likes the idea of thinking he can change the world and of fighting as hard as he can to do it but knowing all along that it's a lot of nonsense; or MTV's self-promos; post-holocaust films like *River's Edge* (where the holocaust has already happened) and *Mad Max* (where the hitech utopian future resembles the contemporary image of a war zone); in fiction—for example, however classist the yuppie culture of *Less Than Zero* (Ellis, 1985:189–90), statements resonate beyond their class: "But you don't need anything. You have everything./No I don't./What don't you have?/I don't have anything to lose." Or in slogans and humor: a recent Tufts University newspaper which offered the following two statements as the "best philosophy of life": "Don't sweat the small stuff. It's all small stuff."

But if we are to understand such statements, it is not a matter of looking for the formal practices that mark their textual difference. If anything, the various postmodern texts often betray themselves as "modernism with a vengeance," magnifying and multiplying many of the formal practices constitutive of various modernist movements. This is, of course, not to deny a significant difference between them: what was a crisis for the modernists has become common sense, if not the occasion of celebration. If one makes an effort to construct such a postmodern aesthetics, the generic diversity is overwhelming. One would have to include, or at least justify excluding, a wide range of texts: not only the hyperfragmented, the hyperrealistic and the neohistorical (in which the real history of the audience provides the codes: e.g., Keith Haring's Jetsons-inspired graffiti or Stanley Kubrick's use of "The Mickey Mouse Club Theme" in the closing to *Full Metal Jacket*) but also the neofantastic; one would have to include not only the self-consciously ironic and deconstructive (Max Headroom, Pee Wee Herman) statements, but neonostalgic ones (*Rambo, Top Gun, Back to the Future, E.T.*) and cynical ones (*Blue Velvet, The Lives and Times of Molly Dodd*). One would have to include not only the new horror and gore movies, but the various 'New Age' texts as well.[2] And of course, part of the very structure of the assemblage of "postmodern texts" is precisely that a text need not appear postmodern to be appreciated as such (e.g., the appropriation of various reruns and styles, and in some cases, the instant appropriation of a text as "intentionally doublecoded": *Dragnet*, superhero comics).

The point is that neither such individual statements, nor the formal categories we construct, can be separated from the context within which their particular effects are articulated. They are not texts to be interpreted, nor merely embodiments of, nor microcosmic representations of, a postmodern world. They are, as Deleuze and Guattari (1977) would have it, point-signs always imbricated in contradictory, complex and changing rhizomatic contexts. They take great pains to differentiate such a "linguistics of flows" from the "linguistics of the signifier", even from one in which the transcendence of the signifier is established only by its withdrawal. Point-signs have no identity, no difference; they are merely the intersections and fissures of flows and breaks along vectors of effectivity.

One response to the impossibility of finding meaning intrinsic to a particular text has been to suggest that our understanding of cultural statements must depend crucially on how they are decoded, used and even enjoyed by particular audiences. For example, what makes the above examples of advertisements so striking is that probably the most common response is "of course. So what?" What seems obviously "commonsensical" and at the same time ironic today, would have been considered, within the terms of modernism, only thirty years ago, to be the mark of either insanity or poetic genius. But once again, we must tread cautiously, for while the practices of appropriation, interpretation and consumption are significant aspects of the concrete effects and articulations of these statements, these practices are no less problematic than the statements themselves. Again, while they have to be taken literally, that only defines the beginning of our work, not its conclusion. They are, in fact, part of the context which we are constructing which is then in need of some accounting. The surfaces of everyday life—whether in practices and relations of production or consumption—may be the site of important struggles, but they are not the totality of the social formation nor of the determinations of everyday life.

Neither appeals to encoding nor to decoding can define the answer or even the language of the answer. Whether we begin with observations of, for example, the increasing formal and self-conscious fragmentation of cultural texts, or of the tone of certain texts as they seemingly speak the ultrarapid languages of obsolescence and fascination, we have only begun to define the problem. Similarly, to take account of the ways in which people appropriate, decode and enjoy these texts only continues the necessary work of constructing the complicated space within which the question of interpretation has to be asked. One can only begin to understand how these postmodern statements are functioning, to move beyond the fact of their existence, if we look at both their trajectory and their mode of existence (i.e., their plane of effectivity). We have to examine their movement into the center of popular culture and everyday life and their emergence along, and construction by, multiple vectors or codes constituting the social and cultural space of our advanced capitalist formation. Thus, one can only speak of an emergent assemblage of statements, a complex array of cultural formations and intersecting codes which exist within the larger contradictory terrain of contemporary history, economics, ideology, pleasure, etc.—in fact, the terrain that is articulated as everyday life.

The very postmodernity of these formations is marked by contradictory semiotic and political tendencies and effects. It is not enough to collect "postmodern statements"— although it is fun to do so; rather the increasing presence and power of such statements must be taken seriously, not only in the worlds of art and media, but in everyday life as well, as an emergent aspect of the popular. There is something anxious, even terrifying, about such statements, just as there is something pleasurable (and even funny) about them. We may laugh at statements like "Life is hard and then you die" even as we are horrified and condemned by them. It is only if we begin to look at the complex ways in which these statements are inserted into and function within the social formation that we can offer effective political responses to the contemporary demands of history.

I want to begin with a rather simple observation: that much of what is talked about as "the postmodern" is predicated on the perception that something "feels" different, not only about particular aesthetic practices, but about a wide variety of life-experiences and historical events. Yet it is not clear what the status of this "feeling" or experience is, in what planes of our existence it is anchored. Moreover, there are two inseparable but different perspectives one can take here, two different questions one can ask, two different ways of entering onto the same terrain: first, what are the complex determinations or conditions of possibility of this "feeling" and second, what are the effects that we are trying to describe as an emergent historical "feeling," what conditions does it make possible. My main concern here is the latter and my argument is that we should not too quickly recuperate it into either a phenomenological transcendentalism or into a deconstructive theory of the ideological production of experience. That is, there is no reason to assume that it is necessarily and primarily operating within either a signifying or representational economy. While not denying that it is partly ideological and always articulated to ideological positions, one need not assume that its most significant effects are located on such planes. There is even less justification in assuming that descriptions of its ideological effects provide a sufficient account.

The specificity of the postmodern

I want to speculate on the popularity of these postmodern statements for, in fact, they are not only increasingly obvious but also increasingly popular; there is, in fact, nothing weirder than mainstream television today. What is the effectivity of these postmodern statements? What is it that one "hears" in them as we place them into the context of contemporary life? What do they evoke or invoke? It is not a "structure of feeling"—as a phenomenological description of the lived—but rather a particular attitude or mood—"empowering nihilism" or an "indifference to indifference"—embodied and enacted, in part, in a particular set of discursive strategies—"authentic inauthenticity" or "realistic irony." I will return to these concepts later in the argument. This discursive maneuvre is neither wholly ideological nor simply semiotic. It is "communicated" through a different mode, in a different plane of effects—the "affective."

The affective is one plane of everyday life, one form of communicative economy. If we recognize the diversity of communicative economies, then we can recognize the truth in Baudrillard's (1985:13) description of the postmodern as "a virus" that leaps across social organs and domains, and my own claim (Grossberg, 1987) that it functions like billboards providing the imaginary unity and continuity of America:

> The pleasure of fashion is certainly cultural, but doesn't it owe more to that immediate consensus, shining through the game of signs? The styles also go out like epidemics, when they have ravaged the imagination, and when the virus gets tired, the price to pay, in terms of wasted signs, is exactly that of the epidemics in terms of lives: exorbitant. But everyone agrees to it. Our social marvel is that ultrarapid surface of the circulation of signs (and not the

ultraslow one of the circulation of meaning). We love to be immediately con-
taminated, without thinking about it. . . . Fashion, like many other processes, is
an irreducible phenomenon because it takes part in exactly the sort of senseless,
viral and in some way asocial mode of communication, which only circulates so
fast because it sidesteps the mediation of reason. The logic of difference, of
distinction, could not alone explain that: it is too slow.

However, unlike Baudrillard, I do not want to give up the possibility of struggle and the
reality of contradiction. Nor do I want, in the name of anti-essentialism, to establish a new
essentialism which would isolate this affective communication from, or substitute it for, the
complex processes of the determination and articulation of the social formation. The social
formation is characterizable only in its historically specific complexity. And although that
complexity (or difference) is always structured in historically specific ways, its structuration
is never completed and secure. The contradictions are never finally "stitched up" into a
singularly coherent structure. Moreover, the history of such struggles to disarticulate and
rearticulate social, cultural and political relations is precisely the history of the continuing
establishment and reshaping of multiple regimes of power. It is within such struggles that the
concrete effects of any practice are determined. Although such regimes are themselves not
reducible to a single plane of determination, their autonomy is always limited by the ways
they themselves are linked together into specific relations. For example, although systems of
power organized around gender and sexual difference cannot be explained in terms of
economic and class relations, their specific historical forms cannot be understood apart from
the ways they are articulated into specific economic and class relations.

There are two implications of this conception of the social formation worth pointing to:
first, there are no guarantees in history. Practices, relations and social positions are not
inherently identified with each other, nor are their politics, meanings and effects determined
outside of the real social context within which people can and do struggle—not necessarily
in ways that are intentional or resistant—to "make history in conditions not of their own
making." As Hall (1985) puts it, although such correspondences are always real, they are
never necessary. Second, there is no secure knowledge, no position outside of the social
formation from which anyone, including critics and intellectuals, can survey the entire
terrain. Consequently, critics cannot assume the validity of their own interpretations, nor of
their political agendas. More importantly, people are not cultural dopes who are totally
unaware of their own interests and needs and subordinations. One cannot tell people where
or how to struggle, but that does not mean one cannot intervene, in intelligent and effective
ways, into the space of everyday life. It does mean that such interventions depend, not upon
judgements critics bring from their own social position, but upon a real effort to map out
some of the complex and contradictory vectors operating at specific sites in the social
formation. But I also want to emphasize the limits of both the lack of guarantees and antielitism. On the one hand, no social practice, no cultural text determines its own effects, or
speaks its own truth. On the other hand, not every effect or articulation involves real
struggle, not every struggle is won, not every victory is resistant, and not all resistance is
progressive.

As Stuart Hall wrote in 1960, "The task of socialism is to meet people where they are—
where they are touched, bitten, moved, frustrated, nauseated—to develop discontent and at
the same time, to give the socialist movement some direct sense of the times and the ways in
which we live." The terms of Hall's description echo Williams' structure of *feeling* although,
to a certain extent, both authors failed to theorize the added depth that the notion of
"feeling" brings, as well as the historically specific forms of this socialist project. Still, Hall's
statement offers us rich advice, for it makes three demands upon us: first, that we enter onto

the terrain of the popular in order to make intelligible when, where and how people live. This is not the phenomenological task of discovering the forms of consciousness that people have of their existence (although that is certainly a part). The second demand is that we recognize the complexity and multiple determinations of such positions. Finally, it demands that socialism's task be understood, not as defining the place, time and form of revolution and change but rather, of prising open already existing contradictions and "thereby renovating and making critical an already existing activity" (Gramsci, 1971:331).

Thus we neither celebrate nor panic in the face of contemporary developments and tendencies, nor do we merely stitch them (and history along with them) into our already defined theoretical and political positions. The task of understanding the postmodern, to return to my beginning, can only proceed by theorizing from and around the concrete and can only proceed toward opening up a more explicit "politics of the possible" (Chambers, 1985) and "finding another way of imagining the future" (Hall, 1987). Such a position establishes a sharp difference between Marxist efforts to come to grips with the postmodern and what Guattari (1986:40) describes as "the deplorable conclusion to which many intellectual and artistic groups have come, especially those who claim the banner of postmodernism . . . that [it is] inevitable that we remain passive in the face of the rising wave of cruelty and cynicism that is in the process of flooding the planet and that seems determined to last." But even Guattari here takes too much for granted: namely that it is obvious that there is a link between contemporary forms of cynicism and of cruelty, and that these are "flooding" the planet.

Strategies of the left

Let me briefly turn to the question of how the Left has responded to the challenge of the postmodern, and the dominant interpretations and frameworks it has put forth. The first and most influential Marxist response to the emergence of the postmodern—derived from literary theory—reads it as a new ideological formation in which postmodern statements are ideological texts. For example, Jameson (1984) assumes that the structures of various discourses are direct expressions of the structures of our experiences which are, in turn, directly determined by our insertion into the economic relations of late capitalism. It is as if ideology's determination of experience were immediate and causal. Apart from the theoretical objections which can be raised to challenge this view, it ignores that there is something different, something "postmodern," about the way in which ideology works today.

Let me explain by turning to the question of mystification: how do we hold on to such a critical notion if we renounce theories of false consciousness? Part of the radical solution which both Gramsci (1971) and Althusser (1970) offered was to argue that ideology is a matter of practices rather than beliefs or, if you prefer, that belief is a matter of practice. As Slavoj Zizek (1987) recently argued, the best description of the working of ideology is "they don't know it but they are doing it." That is, ideological activities are always characterized by the fact that illusion structures real social activities. When Marx claimed that the ideology of capitalism was Hegelian idealism—the belief that particular entities (commodities) were the expression of universal abstract value—he was not claiming that people hold such a belief. Common sense is not Hegelian; it is on the contrary nominalist. People believe in the reality of the concrete particular. But people act as if an ideal universal value existed. People know how things really are but they act as if they had mystical beliefs. This distance—between belief and action—is crucial for it allows both the reality of mystification and the possibility of a space for critical work and struggle. But Zizek goes on to argue that this critical space has disappeared in the operation of what one might call a postmodern ideological formation. There is, instead, a cynical irony operating in the realm of ideology. People know what they are doing but they continue doing it anyway. They are aware of ideological mystification but enter into it anyway. Thus, contemporary ideological practice already assumes the distance toward the dominant ideology which had defined the possibility of critically responding to it. Thus the very need, if not the possibility, of a critical relation to the dominant ideology is apparently undermined. This cynicism, the collapse of distance, is also ironic—it operates by refusing to take its own ideological positions—or anything for that matter—too seriously. In fact, within this cynical reason, the real evil is taking any ideological belief too seriously, regardless of whether it is dominant or oppositional. But this analysis, however accurate, leaves the crucial question unanswered: why has this cynical irony, which has certainly had a long history, suddenly become part of the popular attitude?

The second strategy of the Left—derived from art criticism—argues that in the contemporary context, all of culture—including the production of meaning and consciousness—has been incorporated into capitalist commodity relations. For example, Frith and Horne (1987) talk about the "equation" of art and commerce, as a result of which the "aesthetic effect" of texts cannot be separated from their market effects. Further, they argue that the desires they address cannot be separated from their market effects; increasingly, art situates the viewer as spectator *cum* consumer. While I do not want to disagree entirely with this position, I do want to raise two objections to too strong an interpretation of it. The first is historical: after all, art (and culture in general) was incorporated into the capitalist economy long before the contemporary era, both in terms of its mode of production and distribution. Its location within the market economy is not new. What is new is the mass availability of cultural commodities. The second objection is conceptual: if the difference between art and commerce has, in some significant way, collapsed in recent times, it is important that we try to identify the specific dimension in which this indifference (the apparent irrelevance of the difference) is manifested. It does not follow, necessarily, that art can be reduced to a commodity if we situate it in people's lives. That it is a commodity does not deny that it still may be other things as well. Moreover, the concrete complexity of the practices of consumption suggests that such artistic practices, even if they situate the audience as consumer, may also situate them in other contradictory subject positions.

Another way of saying this is that there is a tendency to treat the commodity as a simple and transparent, ahistorical concept, forgetting that, for Marx, it operates on a very general level of abstraction. On the one hand, the concept of the commodity implies a relation between use value and exchange value; on the other hand, it implies a contradiction between the forces and relations of production. These two equations are not only mapped onto each other in historically specific ways but are also each articulated in historically specific ways. It is only as we begin to examine the complex nature of the relation between sign and commodity, and recognize the multiplicity of communicative economies within which various texts operate, that we can begin to unravel the outlines of everyday life.

The third strategy is the most complex and amorphous: the "politics of transgression and pleasure." Such a strategy views pleasure as a second dimension of the effectivity of particular textual practices and, following Chambers (1985:211), assumes that pleasure operates "on the immediate surfaces of everyday life." It "transforms the seeming 'obviousness' of popular culture into an imaginative conquest of everyday life," and serves as "an affirmation of your right to inhabit the present." Such views are often deconstructive in that they assume that structure and the singularity of meaning are always repressive; it is only through the explosion of the signified, and the ascension of the signifier, that the threatening possibilities of anarchic libidinal gratification are liberated. They often celebrate such deconstructive orgasms as the positive face of the postmodern, ignoring the fact that, in the popular media, even the most fragmented texts and images often offer new forms of identity and coherence; fragmented identities are still identities although they incorporate new forms of fragmentation into identity (e.g., cyborgs like Max Headroom and Robocop). I do not mean to equate all such views of pleasure and transgression. There are significant differences among left views of pleasure, ranging from an ultrapositive, elitist view (e.g., Barthes' [1975] distinction between *plaisir* and *jouissance*) to Jameson's (1983) negative vision of pleasure as "the consent of life in the body" to Baudrillard's (1986) image of fascination as an indifference "at least as great" as that of the simulacrum.

Let me briefly identify three problems with the attempt to locate the politics of the postmodern in the regime of pleasure. First, such theories ignore the complexity of "pleasure" itself: they fail to distinguish between desire, emotion, satisfaction, need and enjoyment. They also fail to note the ambiguity which arises from the different discursive economies within which pleasure has been theorized: as the satisfaction of need, the avoidance of pain, the dissipation of tension, and pure positivity. They often end up ignoring the complex relations that exist between forms of pleasure and ideological formations. As a result, pleasure is often reduced to an ideological process (despite their protestations to the contrary—e.g., Jameson [1983] and Mercer [1986]) or to the ideological determinations of libidinal displacements (as in *Screen* theory). Neither of these positions adequately analyzes the complex and often contradictory relations that exist between ideological and libidinal economies, as different planes of effects.

Second, such theories often ignore the fact that pleasure is never inherently, essentially, or necessarily a form of resistance, not even of empowerment. Pleasure is only empowering within specific contextual determinations. That the very assertion of pleasure may be, at a particular moment, a political statement, does not guarantee the political effectivity of pleasure in any social conjuncture. As Judith Williamson (1986) has argued, after we acknowledge and even describe the pleasures of popular culture, we have still to return to the question of its concrete political articulation. Finally, like theories of the postmodern as ideology, such theories fail to notice the postmodern ambiguity of pleasure, an ambiguity captured in such statements as "Seek small pleasures; big ones are too risky," or sex is "nothing but thirty seconds of squelching noises" (Johnny Rotten).

Affective communication

I want to turn to the question of Baudrillard's "other mode of communication" in order to make some brief suggestions about the modality of its communicative economy. Then I shall turn to the question of its historically specific place within the social formation, i.e., the question of its determinations and determinants within a postmodern formation. Again, we might begin by taking a lesson from Guattari (1986:41) in order simply to acknowledge effectivities other than those we are used to dealing with: "concrete social formation . . . stem from something more than a linguistic performance: there are ethnological dimensions and ecological ones, semiotic and economic factors, aesthetic, corporeal and fantasmatic ones . . . a multitude of universes of reference." Guattari's last phrase is particularly significant: we are not in the (post) structuralist's refusal of referentiality (in the name of the primacy of the signifier) but rather are in the realm of the multiple planes of effectivity and referentiality.

I want to introduce a fourth term into the already crowded relations of signification, economy and libido: "affect" or "corporeal attitude". In order to begin to explain this notion, let me turn to two figures who have made important efforts to theorize what I take to be similar (but not identical) concepts. Such discussions make clear the need to constantly return to the problem of historical specificity and determination. In the context of debates around postmodernity, no figure is more important than Nietzsche, and his theory of the "will to power" (as read by Deleuze [1977]) provides important insights into what I am calling "affect." For Nietzsche, the notion of force (or power) always assumes, not only a multiplicity of specific forces but also, a principle which "brings forces into synthesis." Such a "genealogical principle" is, at once, differential and genetic; it produces, simultaneously, the *quantitative* difference between forces and the *qualitative* identity of each force. This quantitative difference is the measure of power; in Nietszche's terms, it constitutes the difference between dominating and dominated forces. The qualitative difference defines the directionality of the vector of each force as either active or reactive. It is, according to Deleuze, only in this complex economy of relations, that the "will to power," as the source of value, can be either affirmative or negative. One final point needs to be made lest we falsely assume that this genealogical principle—the Will to Power—is universal. It is always contextually specific; it is, echoing both Althusser and Foucault, determined by what it determines. It is itself always the concrete product of the *field of forces on which it operates.*

The second figure I want to introduce here is Freud (as interpreted by Laplanche and Pontalis [1973]) from whom I have taken the term "affect," where it was used to refer to psychic energy. Psychic energy could be either bound to a specific idea or unbound; hence, there is the possibility of affect without an idea and ideas without affect. Since Freud, the notion of affect has been lost, either in the psychoanalytic substitution of sexual energy—libido—for affect, or in the nonpsychoanalytic reduction of affect to universal principles (as in Jung and Reich). (It is, after all, important to remember that one of Freud's attacks on Jung was that he had collapsed the difference, desexualizing libido into every "tendency towards.") Nevertheless, if we are to understand the notion of psychic energy, we have to ask how it has been erased and where it has been lost. Freud's metapsychology depends upon the necessity of holding together three perspectives that are, in a sense, contradictory, but are not, as is sometimes assumed, mutually exclusive: the topographical, the dynamic, and the economic. The topographical perspective constructs a structural model of elements as relations: usually ego-id-superego. The dynamic perspective constructs a battleground of conflicting forces: the conscious versus the unconscious. And the economic perspective, finally, constructs a machine or space defined by the circulation and distribution of energy: an economy of cathexis.

One can read the history of psychoanalysis, although this is obviously an oversimplification, as progressively making each of these perspectives less important than the preceding one (e.g., in ego psychology, the conflict is defined topographically; on the other hand, Lacan's return to Freud was, in part, a recovery of the dynamic model, with its dynamism now defined by the semiotics of the unconscious). But for Freud, psychic conflict is also located, albeit in transformed terms, within the economic model—for there is always an other to libidinal energy. The libido is never the only form or organization of psychic energy. More importantly, it is never originary; it arises anaclitically, leaning upon other instincts or drives. Libido, the energy of the sexual instincts, is always located in a larger economy of difference. Of course, the project of describing the terrain of this larger economy occupied Freud all of his life, as he increasingly recognized its complexity and contradictions. Thus, on the one hand, the sexual instincts are opposed to the ego instincts (the instincts of self-preservation); this difference is closely related to that between the pleasure principle and the reality principle. On the other hand, both of these instinct-sets are part of a larger apparatus—Eros or the Life Instincts—which is in turn connected and opposed to another apparatus—Thanatos or the Death Instincts. As one moves to this even higher level of abstraction, the proliferation of psychic "principles" becomes increasingly difficult to unravel. But it is here that we discover at least one of the major ambiguities of "pleasure" in psychoanalytic theory: pleasure is located in both the constancy principle which seeks homeostasis, and the Nirvana principle which seeks to reduce all tension to zero. Pleasure is thus describable, on the one hand, as the total absence of tension and, on the other hand, as the discharge of excess tension and the maintenance of a state of balance.

It is interesting that both Lacanians (e.g., Laplanche and Pontalis) and anti-Lacanians (e.g., Deleuze and Guattari) agree that one cannot define this energy except in its effects and transformations without falling into various metaphysical ideologies. Both sides seem to recognize its connection with notions of life-force, will, preconstitutive life-world, and Heideggerian mood, but are unwilling to follow these traditions because they conceptualize and recast the problem as one of origins. Affect or psychic energy is the very existence of tension, of a relationship which is always a difference, marked upon larger contradictory fields. Moreover, affect is not a homogeneous category: one need only think of Deleuze and Guattari's (1977) distinction between three kinds of psychic energy: Libido (as the connective synthesis of production); Numen (as the disjunctive synthesis of recording); and Voluptas (as the conjunctive synthesis of consumption). Finally, affect is both qualitative and quantitative. It can be characterized quantitatively—as a measurable "quota" (in Freudian terminology)—and qualitatively—as a state of mood (or what is often expressed as an emotional attitude).

By citing Nietzsche and Freud, I do not mean to equate my use of "affect" with either the will to power or psychic energy. I merely intend to demonstrate that there is a history of attempts to theorize economies other than those of value, ideology and libido. In fact, I want to distinguish between libidinal economies of desire and affective economies of mood as two different planes on which psychic energy is organized. If desire is always focused (as the notion of cathexis suggests), mood is always dispersed. While both may be experienced in terms of needs, only libidinal needs can be, however incompletely, satisfied. Moods are never satisfied, only realized. If desire assumes an economy of depth (e.g., in the notion of repression), mood is always on the surface (which is not to be equated with consciousness). It is the coloration or passion within which one's investments in, and commitments to, the world are made possible. Finally, affective economies empower difference while libidinal economies do not. Pleasure and desire operate within a structure in which it is their own satisfactions—however infinitely deferred—that define the operation of the system. They are systems replete with content. Affect is contentless; it is precisely aimed, on the contrary, at constituting not only the possibility of difference, but the terms within which such differences are possible in a particular affective economy. Consider, for example, the affective need for security and intimacy, both psychically and materially, in home and relations. Such a need is never satisfied by particular relationships but only by a more general attitude or mood within which any particular relationship has its effects.

In concluding this discussion of affect, let me draw four conclusions. First, affect produces systems of *difference* that are *asignifying*. Affect constructs a difference, both quantitatively (as a measure of the degree of energizing) and qualitatively (as a particular mood, within which other differences function). The very form of affective difference—not only the "conditions of its possibility" but the very ways in which such differences are mapped—are not necessarily the same as those which construct other more typically discussed systems. Only if we recognize the different economies operating in everyday life can we come to terms with both the specificity of various social practices and the contradictory terrain of everyday life. Thus, for example, if the unconscious is like a language, it is also not like a language; the specificity of its effects depends in part on the differences between libidinal and semiotic economies. This does not deny that affect, and affective difference, may themselves be implicated directly in systems of power. Nor does it deny that such affective differences can be and are articulated ideologically and libidinally into other structures and forms of social difference and power.

Second, affect describes historically specific modes and organizations of *material* attitude or orientation. Although it always involves vectors into the materiality of the social world, affect is neither the intentionality of consciousness nor of the lived body (understood phenomenologically). Third, affect describes, not a subjective property, but the historically specific processes in which the subject is defined by the intensive qualities (the affective states) through which it passes. That is, the subject is constituted nomadically, by its movements across the fields of affective difference. The affective subject is always transitory, defined by its qualitative and quantitative trajectories. And finally, the form of *empowerment* operating at the affective level involves something other than control, direction or meaning. The very possibility of struggle depends upon an affective empowerment, what Gramsci (1971) referred to as an "optimism of the will." Benjamin (1968) recognized that the strongest ideological position would entail an organization of pessimism in which a sense of the lack of power to change the world operates, not only in our maps of intelligibility but also in the most basic sites of our impassioned relation to the world. This of course does not answer the question of the politics of such affective economies; it is open to struggle and articulation. Affect defines, then, a condition of possibility for any political intervention; it is, however, ideologically, economically and libidinally neutral except as it is articulated into these systems under specific historical conditions.

Postmodernity and affect

To bring these remarks to a close, let me return to the question of the nature or status of the "event" of postmodernity or at least, to the nature or status of the sorts of postmodern statements with which I opened this paper. If we are to understand their real effects and significance, we have to locate them within the changing historical relations in the social field of forces. When Gramsci (1971) talked about the "war of positions," he had in mind something other than my model of the complexities and contradictions between and within the historically specific formations and economies of affect, libido, semiosis and value. Yet I think it is not unfair to appropriate this image to describe the way in which particular cultural statements are positioned within the social formation, and their political effects determined. In this context, I want to talk about the affective force of such statements in terms of a "crisis" of the historical form of our dialectical or dialogical (in Bakhtin's [1981] sense) relation to the social world (which includes words as well as things).

It is possible to identify two vectors in this crisis. The first was already operating—both historically and semiotically—in a great deal of modernist cultural practices. It involves an increasingly problematic relation between affect and ideology, in our very ability to invest in the meanings—and meaningfulness—of the world, to locate any meaning as a possible and appropriate source of an impassioned commitment (in whatever qualitative state). We could describe this as the dissolution of what Foucault (1970) has called the "epistemological doublet." It is an increasing inability to live on the border of subjectivity and objectivity. This becomes semiotically coded, in many modernist texts, as the reduction of subjectivity to objectivity, and of objectivity to subjectivity. It is lived as an increasing sense of horror or terror, not only in the fact of objectivity but also in the fact of subjectivity as well. Thus, if we consider contemporary experience, we can suggest that the affective poles of boredom and terror are organized in a nonlinear way around the possibilities of the absence (in pure objectivity) and uncontrollable excess (in pure subjectivity) of affectivity. This becomes, in recent history, an even more powerful determinant when language and meaning are themselves rendered objective through theoretical work and when such theoretical positions begin to enter into "common sense." But even in this "crisis", there remains an investment, not only in libidinal relations, but also in an ideology of libidinal gratification (e.g., in the counterculture of the 60s).

The second vector of this restructuring of the field of forces that I am referring to as the crisis of the postmodern is defined precisely by the increasingly problematic nature of the relations between affect and libido. To put it crudely, structures of pleasure are themselves, increasingly, only problematically cathected. There are, no doubt, many events that can partially explain how pleasure itself came to be mistrusted if not itself seen as threatening: e.g., the apparent failures of the counterculture of the sixties and of its obvious attempt to create and invest itself in an ideology of libidal pleasure; the important successes of feminism in pointing out that libidinal, as well as gender relations, are overcoded by relations of power; the major redistribution—sometimes involuntarily enforced—of the relations between labor and leisure. It has become increasingly obvious that leisure—both as a space within everyday life, as the site of our "private" and privileged identities, and as specific forms of activities, is intimately implicated in broader relations of power.

To live in the space of this growing gap between affective and libidinal economies—or perhaps more accurately, of these mobile and growing gaps—is to be suspicious of any object of desire, as well as of desire itself. "This is the generation that inherited the cry, 'I can't get no satisfaction.' And they live its contradictions, grabbing at satisfaction while rejecting the possibility itself" (Aufderheide, 1986:14). Contrary to popular wisdom, this is not a cultural space in which people seek risks or seek to live on the edge. It is rather a space in which people seek to feel the thrill without the reality—because the reality of the edge threatens to make the thrill itself too real and too dangerous. As Glenn O'Brien (1987) has recently suggested, it is enough to know someone, who is only a phone call away, who lives life on the edge. Libido has become the enemy—not only for the neoconservatives who seek to attack such pleasures but for those who are drawn to those pleasures as well: "Sex is now a conceptual act; it's probably only in terms of the perversions that we can make contact with each other at all. The perversions are completely neutral, cut off from any suggestion of psychopathology—in fact most of the ones I've tried are out of date" (Ballard, 1972:63). One need only consider the viral, ultrarapid proliferation of sexually transmitted diseases: sex *has* become a terminal illness. The current campaign by the Right against pleasure is not simply manipulative; it does connect into real changes in the affective economy of contemporary life.

The postmodern signals a shift in the complex economy of everyday life; as a crisis, it points to significant changes in what one might call the "anchoring effects" through which different communicative economies are related to one another. The contemporary formations of the ideological and libidinal economies, however specifically and historically defined, continue to anchor themselves within the affective in terms of the commitment to difference: all that matters, in terms of their conditions, is that something specific and different matters. Affective difference, then, must always be anchored in the differences constituted by other economies. On the other hand, within the conditions of affectivity, it doesn't matter what matters. What does matter is precisely the quality and quantity of the mattering (the mood, the passion) itself. But if the very possibility of anchoring affect in nonaffective differences is problematic, then, literally, nothing matters. Affect becomes, temporarily and locally, free-floating. Affect can only construct difference from indifference; its difference must be defined without an economy of difference. The crisis can be described in terms of the need to make something matter (to care—in whatever form, to make a commitment) without the possibility of connecting the various economies (of difference). Affect (or mood) itself, in those circumstances becomes increasingly suspect, available to the articulations of the same structures of power: caring about anything, if not impossible, is always either too easy (to be significant) or too difficult (to be possible). But moods, like ideologies, are unavoidable and so, like the cynical irony of postmodern ideology, there is a cynical logic of moods as well (what I have called "authentic inauthenticity"[3]) in which only the quantity of affect becomes relevant. What matters is how much you care, not how you care ("I'd rather feel bad than not feel anything at all"), or in what you care. Our postmodern heroes—most recently, Oliver North—are those who are different only because of the quantity of affect, only because they are able to care so much about something (whether we agree with it or not) that they make themselves different (even though they don't make a difference) and, not coincidentally, achieve some victory. That they become our "heroes," if only for a brief moment, depends on the fact that their only difference is affective. In all other respects they are like us: their transformation depends upon their impassioned relations to goals and/or ordinary skills.[4]

In a recent Bloom County cartoon depicting "the premature arrival of the future" (Toffler, 1977), Binkley finds himself "all dressed up with no place to go." Binkley, whose narratives often involve his being visited by his nightmares coming out of his closet, is confronted with his worst nightmare yet—he is visited by his future self and shown his future:

> (Young Binkley) We married Lizzie "The Lizard" Blackhead??
> (Old Binkley) We call her "Queen Elizabeth." Now come . . . follow me into your future world, younger self . . . This ugly little dwelling is our house. We call it "Binkley Manor." We moved here in 1998. That's our '93 Volkswagon. We call it our "Little Lamborghini." It's all a way of somehow dealing with the mediocrity of our adult life . . . And the failed dreams of our youth. *Your* youth.
> (Young Binkley) Hey . . . There's a gopher wetting on my foot . . .
> (Old Binkley) *Bad dog, Rambo . . . Bad dog!*

There is, in this, like the ads that I cited earlier, something that rings depressingly true. Binkley will have to face the next morning and, despite the terror and pessimism, find a way of affectively negotiating his way through everyday life. The commonplace has, after all, become dangerous (e.g., driving to work in Los Angeles). Whatever the historical facticity, everyday life feels threatening, and we are all worried that Freddy or Jason is, in fact, our next door neighbor.

If there is a political crisis implicit in this situation, it is a crisis, not of a particular politics (the rise of neoconservativism), nor of anomie (as alienation), nor of apathy (as disinterest). It is a crisis of the very possibility of politics, not in a form which negates the very real and continuing construction of ideological, economic, state and libidinal regimes of power. It is rather a problematization of the very ability to articulate these structures (which we increasingly recognize and acknowledge) to the site of our own sense of how and where we can be empowered and our sense of difference constituted. However, the point is not merely to accede to the crisis but to articulate new forms of affective empowerment by which people are able to construct and invest in difference. But even that is perhaps misleading, for it seems to suggest that there is a kind of totalized affective disempowerment or nihilism. The increasingly rapid move of a postmodern cultural formation into the center of the field of popularity suggests that its statements serve, in part, to offer strategies for affective empowerment in the face of the postmodern crisis.

Thus, the postmodern cultural formation is not, as Baudrillard might have it, the celebration of nihilism and indifference. It is not the production of nihilism as the site of empowerment but the production of forms of empowerment in the face of the possibilities of, and to a certain extent the reality of, nihilism. There is a truth to the notion that the only certainty today is ambiguity because it is less constraining: reality is, after all, "too constraining as a lifestyle." Postmodern statements are not empowering because they are nihilistic (nor merely in spite of it); they are both nihilistic and empowering.[5] Thus, the interpretive task facing us is to identify the strategies and sites of affective empowerment made available in the contemporary cultural forms of popular mood or attitude. If the Left fails to recognize the reality of affective empowerment, and fails to identify the particular sites that are currently and widely available, then it will not be able to recognize that a space for struggle can be, and is already being, fashioned. Nor will it be able to identify the sites of empowerment which have to be rearticulated to different political and ideological projects. That means that the response of the Left to this crisis cannot be to define new goals or new moralities but rather, in a historically specific way, to enter the contradictory terrain of everyday life on which this postmodern formation is only one vector, to re-articulate it, to reconnect it, to the real concerns, needs and struggles of people.

Notes

1   I am greatly in debt to my graduate students for the many hours of fruitful exchange which have contributed to whatever strengths this paper may have. I wish to especially thank Jon Crane, Charles Acland and Anne Balsamo for their invaluable comments on an earlier draft. This paper is offered as a tentative move into the terrain of postmodern culture and contemporary politics. See also Grossberg (1986, 1987, forthcoming b).

2   Only if we recognize this diversity can we understand the changes and movements within the terrain of popular culture. Thus, for example, Springsteen's success has always depended on a certain neonostalgia but his more recent "superstardom" has depended upon a shift in the form of his songs from mythic-fantasy to pop neorealism.

3   Authentic inauthenticity refers to a communicative logic in which the only truth is that there is no truth (and that is, in fact, true). In social terms, it refers to not faking the fact that one is faking it. It might be thought of as a set of codes of simulation which does not function in the name of either the real or the hyperreal. See Grossberg (forthcoming a).

4   The question of contemporary popular heroes provides a good example of the need for recognizing historical complexity and the diversity of communicative economies if we are to note both the similarities and differences between various cultural and historical formations. For example, I would challenge Beniger's (forthcoming) identification of the popularity of Kate Smith in the famous war-bond campaign (as reported by Merton [1946]) with more contemporary forms. Merton's explanation depends upon the audience's "acute need to believe" and their response to Smith's "perceived sincerity." He further points to their perception that they "could've been like Kate." Beniger equates this to a *USA Today* poll (Dec. 3, 1986, p. 8C) of "the most believable sports figure endorsing products" which suggests that their believability depends upon their ordinariness, upon how much they are like us. But he fails to see that these two identifications depend upon significantly different economies: the relation to Smith has "a social basis . . . [she belongs] to the ingroup. She is kinfolk." The relation to "stars" like John Madden or Bob Uecker takes for granted that their ordinariness, like their sincerity, is obviously inauthentic. It is for just this reason that a fan of Madden's is unlikely to make a statement like the following, by a "devotee" of Smith: "I trust *her*. If *she* were a fake, I'd feel terrible." We, on the other hand, expect our heroes to be fakes, not only as images (Rambo) but as realities (Reagan). We know that sincerity is just another pose, but so what . . .? Beniger is unable to recognize the difference, partly because he fails to place the forms of heroes into larger cultural formations and historical contexts. But more importantly, he attempts to understand the communicative economy within which such popular heroes operate in terms of a redrawn line between interpersonal and mass communication—the result is that the question becomes one of the audience's interpretation of the size of the intended audience—instead of in terms of the historically articulated relations between different communicative economies and planes of effects.

5   In another paper (Grossberg, forthcoming a), I have begun to describe some of the forms of empowering nihilism; that is, some of the ways in which affect is articulated into a logic of authentic inauthenticity as strategies of empowerment: ironic authenticity (e.g., Pee Wee Herman, Madonna); sentimental authenticity (e.g., Rambo, Springsteen): hyperreal authenticity (e.g., *Bladerunner*).

References

Althusser, Louis (1979). *For Marx*. Ben Brewster, trans. New York: Vintage.

Aufderheide, Pat (1986). "Sid and Nancy: Just Say No." *In These Times*. 11 (November 19–25): 14.

Bakhtin, Mikhail (1981). *The Dialogic Imagination*. C. Emerson and M. Holquist, trans. Austin: University of Texas Press.

Ballard, J. G. (1985) *The Atrocity Exhibition*. London: Triad/Panther.

Barthes, Roland (1975). *The Pleasure of the Text*. Richard Miller, trans. New York: Hill and Wang.

Baudrillard, Jean (1985). "The Child in the Bubble." *Impulse*. 11: 12–13.

Baudrillard, Jean (1986). "Interview." *FlashArt*. 130 (October/November).

Beniger, James R. (forthcoming). "Personalisation of Mass Media and the Growth of Pseudo-Community."

Benjamin, Walter (1968). *Illuminations*. Hannah Arendt, ed. New York: Harcourt, Brace and World.

Chambers, Iain (1985). *Urban Rhythms: Pop Music and Popular Culture*. New York: St. Martin's Press.

Deleuze, Gilles (1977). "Active and Reactive." *The New Nietzsche: Contemporary Styles of Interpretation*. David B. Allison, ed. New York: Delta. 80–106.

Deleuze, Gilles and Guattari, Felix (1977). *Anti-Oedipus: Capitalism and Schizophrenia*. Robert Hurley, et al., trans. New York: Viking Press.

Ellis, Brett Easton (1985). *Less Than Zero*. New York: Simon and Schuster.

Foucault, Michel (1970). *The Order of Things: An Archaeology of the Human Sciences*. New York: Pantheon.

Frith, Simon and Horne, Howard (1987). *Art into Pop*. London: Methuen.

Gramsci, Antonio (1971). *Selections from the Prison Notebooks*. Q. Hoare and G. Nowell-Smith, trans. New York: International Publishers.

Grossberg, Lawrence (1986). "History, Politics and Postmodernism." *Journal of Communication Inquiry*. 10: 61–77.

Grossberg, Lawrence (1987). "The In-difference of Television." *Screen*. 28 (Spring): 28–45.

Grossberg, Lawrence (forthcoming a). "Youth, Television and the Democratisation of Difference." *Popular Music*.

Grossberg, Lawrence (forthcoming b). "Putting the Pop Back into Postmodernism." *Universal Abandon?* A. Ross, ed. Minneapolis: University of Minnesota Press.

Guattari, Felix (1986). "The Postmodern Dead End." *FlashArt*. 128 (May): 40–41.

Hall, Stuart (1960). "Editorial." *New Left Review*. 1:1.

Hall, Stuart (1985). "Signification, Representation, Ideology: Althusser and the Post-Structuralist Debates." *Critical Studies in Mass Communication*. 2 (June): 91–114.

Hall, Stuart (1987). "Gramsci and Us." *Marxism Today* (June): 16–21.

Haraway, Donna (1987). "Apes, Aliens, Cyborgs and Women: Feminist Theory, Colonial Discourse, and the Contest for Science." Lecture delivered at the University of Illinois, Urbana (April 22).

Jameson, Fredric (1983). "Pleasure: A Political Issue." *Formations of Pleasure*. London: Routledge and Kegan Paul. 1–13.

Jameson, Fredric (1984). "Postmodernism, or the Cultural Logic of Late Capitalism." *New Left Review*. 146 (July/August): 53–92.

Laplanche, J. and Pontalis, J.-B. (1973). *The Language of Psychoanalysis*. D. Nicholson-Smith, trans. New York: W. W. Norton.

Marx, Karl (1973). *Grundrisse*. M. Nicolaus, trans. New York: Vintage.

Mercer, Colin (1986). "Complicit pleasures." *Popular Culture and Social Relations*. T. Bennett, et al., eds. Milton Keynes: Open University Press. 50–68.

Merton, Robert K. (1946). *Mass Persuasion: The Social Psychology of a War Bond Drive*. New York: Harper.

O'Brien, Glenn (1987). "What is Hip?" *Interview*. 27 (July): 42–3.

Straw, Will (1987). "Intersections and Directions in Cultural Studies" Panel Discussion at Carleton University, Centre for Communication, Culture and Society, Ottawa, March 4.

Toffler, Alvin (1971). *Future Shock*. New York: Bantam.

Williamson, Judith (1986). "The Problems of Being Popular." *New Socialist*. (September): 14–16.

Zizek, Slavoj (1987). "The Subject Supposed to . . . (Know, Believe, Enjoy, Desire)." Lecture delivered at the Symposium on "Wars of Persuasion: Gramsci, Intellectuals and Mass Culture." University of Massachusetts, Amherst. April 24.

II CONTRIBUTIONS FROM CULTURAL ANTHROPOLOGY

Chapter 4

Michelle Z. Rosaldo

TOWARD AN ANTHROPOLOGY OF SELF AND FEELING

FOR PURPOSES OF ARGUMENT, my past is mythic. Once upon a time (it sometimes helps to think), the world was simple. People knew that thought was not the same as feeling. Cognition could be readily opposed to affect, explicit to implicit, "discursive" to "presentational" forms of symbols, outer "mask" to inner "essence," mere facts of "custom" to less malleable dispositions and personalities.

For comparatists, these oppositions merged with the contrast between the variable and the universal, the relatively cultural and the relatively biological. For sociologists, the opposition between the social and the individual was evoked. And for psychologists, these contrasts paired with processes that were conventionally assigned to either "shallow" or "deep" aspects of the mind. Finally, to anthropologists, such oppositions made good sense because we recognized that, however strange the customs of the people that we studied in the field, we all could speak of individuals who, in personality, recalled our enemies, friends, or mothers: There was, it would appear, a gap between the personality and its culture. Moreover – although in an almost contradictory vein – we knew that learning any culture's rules (like how to bow or to ask for a drink) was not the same as feeling that *their* ways of doing things could satisfy *our* impulses and needs: Affective habits, even when culturally shaped, appeared autonomous from the sorts of facts that cluttered our ethnographies.[1]

Has there been progress? Although it strikes me that in some ways the dichotomies mentioned here are inevitable, as they appear unduly wedded to a bifurcating and Western cast of mind, I want to argue that the development, in recent years, of an "interpretive" concept of culture provides for changes in the way we think about such things as selves, affects, and personalities. The unconscious remains with us. Bursts of feeling will continue to be opposed to careful thought. But recognition of the fact that thought is always culturally patterned and infused with feelings, which themselves reflect a culturally ordered past, suggests that just as thought does not exist in isolation from affective life, so affect is culturally ordered and does not exist apart from thought. Instead of seeing culture as an "arbitrary" source of "contents" that are processed by our universal minds, it becomes necessary to ask how "contents" may themselves affect the "form" of mental process. And then, instead of seeing feeling as a private (often animal, presocial) realm that is – ironically enough – most universal and at the same time most particular to the self, it will make sense to see emotions not as things opposed to thought but as cognitions implicating the immediate, carnal "me" – as thoughts embodied.

In what follows, I will begin by speaking first about the power and limitations of the contrasts just evoked, discussing a set of intellectual developments that suggest a need for revised models. I then sketch some sorts of evidence likely to support a different, and more culturalist, account of how our feelings work – one that insists upon the sociocultural bases for experiences once assigned to a subjective and unknowable preserve of psychic privacy.

Signs of the times

To begin, it is quite clear that a discomfort with "our" opposed terms is not original to myself. One can trace something of the movement with which I am concerned in developments in the last twenty or so years in psychology, anthropology, and philosophy.

Thus, years ago structuralists abolished affect, posited an identity between "mind" and the world, and then recovered "energy" through notions like "anomaly" and "liminality."[2] "Cognitive dissonance" placed feeling *inside* cognitive discourse.[3] Social psychologists and anthropologists argued that "personalities" are the illusory product of reflections that abstract from social life.[4] And psychoanalysts, in a different but related vein, retreated from instinctual, unreflective, and mechanical conceptions of the self in elaborating such terms as "ego" and "object."[5] More recently, Foucault (1978) has argued that "repression" is itself the product of a world where we "confess." A stress on "narcissism" has made concern with "face" (rather than with tabooed drives) a central motive for the psyche,[6] and "action language" has attempted to displace "unconscious structures" in psychoanalytic accounts of mental process.[7] That all of this has happened at a time when terms like *action* and *intention* have become the problematic foci of much philosophical discourse,[8] when literary theorists have attempted to "deconstruct" our views of selves and actors,[9] and, finally, when anthropologists, like myself (Rosaldo 1980),[10] have shown renewed concern for how selves, affects, and persons are constructed in a particular cultural milieu – all this suggests that something deeper is at stake than hackneyed cultural relativism or youthful distrust of received categories.

An advocate may not be the best person to name the substance of a trend. Nor is the "trend" of which I speak sufficiently delimited or well formed for me to claim that an enriched concept of culture is the key to recent arguments in fields as different as anthropology and psychoanalysis. What I would argue, however, is that central to the developments evoked here is an attempt to understand how human beings understand themselves and to see their actions and behaviors as in some ways the creations of those understandings. Ultimately, the trend suggests, we must appreciate the ways in which such understandings grow, not from an "inner" essence relatively independent of the social world, but from experience in a world of meanings, images, and social bonds, in which all persons are inevitably involved.

Perhaps one of the deepest and most probing instances of this contemporary turn of thought is P. Ricoeur's masterful *Freud and Philosophy* (1970). In it, Ricoeur contrasts two interdependent and yet – he suggests – irreconcilable perspectives in the writings of the founder of psychoanalysis. First and most critically, Freud's texts make use of what Ricoeur sees as an hermeneutic, or interpretivist, approach, wherein our symptoms and the images in our dreams reflect experiences, things heard and seen, as these are linked to one another through associative chains and established in the course of living in the world. But, at the same time, Ricoeur makes clear that in the Freudian account our psychic images have force, our symptoms depth, because they interact with biologically based energies and histories of repressed desires. Surely, the subsequent history of psychoanalysis can be traced through theorists concerned with universally given instincts and those who stress the ego – or the patient, whose development is shaped by understanding, intelligence, social relationships, and self-knowledge. The "energetics" and "hermeneutics" that Ricoeur discerns in Freud have thus, in fact, become mutually dependent yet uneasy bedfellows in most academic psychoanalysis. Ricoeur's contribution was, at once, to emphasize the central place of meaning, language, and interpretation in psychoanalytic discourse and then to show the tensions that accompany a seemingly insoluble split between the poles of meaning and desire.

Desire and meaning are not, of course, identical to such opposed terms as affect and cognition, feeling and thought, or, for that matter, personality and culture/society. And yet, much of the interest of the formulations developed by Ricoeur is that one apprehends a commonality between his terms and more pervasive analytic themes. In anthropology, as in psychology, the cultural/ideational and individual/affective have been construed as theoretically, and empirically, at odds. And, furthermore, in both one finds the second set of terms described as basic, brute, precultural fact – and therefore granted analytical primacy. Thus, among most early writers in the culture, and personality school, the organization of culture was that of the culturally typical personality writ large; just as, for later thinkers, culture answered to the typical actor's typical problems.[11] Subsequently, such theories of "reflection" were abjured, but psychological anthropologists tended continually to see in culture a set of symbols answering to (or perhaps channeling) unconscious needs,[12] whereas social anthropologists like Victor Turner (1967) readily proclaimed that symbols work at opposed poles, serving as tokens of society's rules while making an immediate appeal to semen, feces, blood, and the desires fixed within our universal bodies. Durkheim's (1915) insistence on the dual nature of "mankind" (and his assumption that our social worlds are made to organize, or transcend, a selfish, biologically given individuality) was thus reiterated in a tradition that construed the individual's inner world in terms of processes that could be channeled by, but were in essence separate from, the culturally variable facts of social life.

Although the "dual" nature Durkheim saw may prove a legacy – or truth – impossible to avoid, it seems to me that cultural analysis in recent years has (much like the "hermeneutics" highlighted by Ricoeur) led to a reordering of priorities. Loathe to deny desire or the inner life, the recent trend has been to stress the ways that innerness is shaped by culturally laden sociality. Instead of emphasizing the psychological cast of cultural forms, this recent turn – elaborated perhaps most tellingly in the works of Clifford Geertz (1973a)[13] – insists that meaning is a public fact, that personal life takes shape in cultural terms, or better yet, perhaps, that individuals are necessarily and continually involved in the interpretive apprehension (and transformation) of received symbolic models.

For present purposes, what is important here is, first, the claim that meaning is a fact of public life and, second, the view that cultural patterns – social facts – provide a template for all human action, growth, and understanding. Cultural models thus derive from, as they describe, the world in which we live, and at the same time provide a basis for the organization of activities, responses, perceptions, and experiences by the conscious self. Culture so construed is, furthermore, a matter less of artifacts and propositions, rules, schematic programs, or beliefs than of associative chains and images that suggest what can reasonably be linked up with what: We come to know it through collective stories that suggest the nature of coherence, probability, and sense within the actor's world. Culture is, then, always richer than the traits recorded in ethnographers' accounts because its truth resides not in explicit formulations of the rituals of daily life but in the practices of persons who in acting take for granted an account of who they are and how to understand their fellows' moves. Thus, for ethnographers in the field, a set of rules that tells them what the natives do can never show them how and why a people's deeds make psychological sense because the sense of action ultimately depends upon one's embeddedness within a particular sociocultural milieu.

What then of affect? One implication of this recent "culturalist" style of thought is that our feeling that something much deeper than "mere" cultural fact informs the choices actors make may itself be the product of a too narrow view of culture. If culturally organized views of possibility and sense must figure centrally in the acquisition of a sense of self – providing images in terms of which we unselfconsciously connect ideas and actions – then culture makes a difference that concerns not simply *what* we think but how we feel about and live our lives. Affects, then, are no less cultural and no more private than beliefs. They are instead, cognitions – or more aptly, perhaps, interpretations – always culturally informed, in which the actor finds that body, self, and identity are immediately involved.[14]

It thus becomes, in principle, no more difficult to say of people that they "feel" than that they "think." Nor is it necessary to assume that affect is inherently more individual than belief or that individuality is itself something other than the apprehension, by a person over time, of public symbols and ideas. One recognizes that it makes no sense to see in culture personality writ large. But neither, from the "interpretivist" point of view, does it make sense to claim that individuals – with their different histories, different bodies, and different ways of being more or less emotionally involved – are cultural systems cast in miniature. Through "interpretation," cultural meanings are transformed. And through "embodiment," collective symbols acquire the power, tension, relevance, and sense emerging from our individuated histories. It may well be that we require psychologies – or physiologies – or "energy" to fully grasp the ways in which symbolic forms are shaped, and given sense, through application to "embodied" lives. But then (as Ricoeur saw) it seems that insofar as they are culture-bound, psychologies lose their energetic force; whereas, when culture-free, accounts of psychic energies are, at best, provisional.

"Hot" mindless passion and its opposite, "cold" de-contexted thought, may have their use as ideal types. But danger lies in blindness, on the one hand, to the fact that histories of experience, and so of affect, are essential to all thought, and, on the other, that we could perhaps respond with fear but not with love or hate, desire, shame, resentment, or joy were not emotion schooled by public cultural discourse. A grasp of individuality requires a grasp of cultural form; analyses of thought must figure centrally in analyses of feeling. Or stated otherwise, I would insist that we will never learn why people feel or act the way they do until, suspending everyday assumptions about the human psyche, we fix our analytic gaze upon the symbols actors use in understanding human life – symbols that make our minds the minds of social beings.

Toward ethnographies

To some of you, these claims may seem ridiculous; to others, careless; to others, common sense. In what follows I want to ground my somewhat sweeping stance with reference to a set of concrete observations. The ethnographic materials to follow are presented with a goal of showing how my abstract claims may have empirical implications: They make a difference for the things we look at and the ways we understand. The first example argues that emotions are not things but processes that are best understood with reference to the cultural scenarios and associations they evoke. The second seeks to challenge a prevailing view that tells us to distinguish private "selves" and social "persons." And in my third example I discuss comparative findings, which suggest that selves and feelings, shaped by culture, may be understood in turn as the creation of particular sorts of polities.

What are emotions?

I gather that among psychologists in recent years it has become fashionable to note that affect enters into thought and to suggest that "selves" and "personalities" are not enduring inner things but congeries of ways of acting and understanding that derive from social life. But at the same time most recent writers appear to be impressed by evidence claiming that "hot" cognitions, "preferences," and our "basic" and apparently "unthinking" styles of emotional response are relatively independent of the stuff of culture, thought, and reason. Experimental data – some have argued – are thus challenging unduly cognitive and rational conceptions of the self. Emotions are, it seems, neither as conscious nor as controllable as certain Philistines might like. Thus Freud is vindicated.[15]

The difficulty with such formulations, I suggest, is that they make things sound too simple. Freud's unconscious, Ricoeur makes clear, is far from lacking in such things as cultural experience, knowledge, or thought. Nor does the fact that some emotions (and, of course, some thoughts!) appear to have no reasoned cause mean that our lives are ordinarily split into "hot" feelings somehow wired in and "cold" and variable styles of reason.[16] Surely, experience argues forcefully that thoughts and feelings are not the same. And it seems easier to insist that people elsewhere think differently about their agriculture or gods than to insist (as it was at one time fashionable to say) that primitives are unrepressed or then again (to parody myself) that there is nothing universal about such things as happiness and anger. But that the Balinese no more feel "guilt" than we feel *lek*, the Balinese emotion closest to our "shame" – and that these differences relate to how we think about the world – is, to me, equally clear.[17]

My point is not to argue that contemporary academic psychology, located, as it is, within our oppositional terms, is but "our" folk belief disguised in weighty tomes[18] – by observing, for example, that the Ilongots (the Philippine people I studied in the field) do not conceptualize an autonomous inner life in opposition to life-in-the-world. I could, for instance, demonstrate that most Ilongots tend to see in feelings hidden facts no more disturbing or long-lasting than feelings expressed and that they speak of hearts that think and feel without distinguishing thought and affect. But, then again, I would remark that Ilongot concepts, even though they do not match our own, make implicit contrasts closely parallel to ours in that they speak at times of *nemnem* (thought, to think, reflect), at times of *ramak* (want, to want, desire), at times of *rinawa* (heart, desire, to will, feel, think of moving/doing). Thought and feeling are not distinguished, but Ilongot discourse comprehends a gap between passive reflection and thought fueled with affect, or acts of desiring, in a way that parallels our dichotomies. Ilongots are, in short, both like and unlike us. What is at stake is not so simple as the abandonment of "our" constructs in confrontation with a people who appear to challenge our discourse but rather a reflection on the limits of the ways in which the problem has hitherto been posed.

Or stated otherwise, rather than argue that the stuff of feeling is – in some essential and "brute" sense – either "the same" or "different" from the stuff of thought, it seems to me that what an anthropologist should do is point to ways in which, where psychological issues are concerned, the public and symbolic stuff of culture makes a difference. Thus, for me, the crucial point – and one much more profound than it initially appears – is recognition of the fact that feeling is forever given shape through thought and that thought is laden with emotional meaning. I can then argue – much as proposed earlier – that what distinguishes thought and affect, differentiating a "cold" cognition from a "hot," is fundamentally a sense of the engagement of the actor's self. Emotions are thoughts somehow "felt" in flushes, pulses, "movements" of our livers, minds, hearts, stomachs, skin. They are *embodied* thoughts, thoughts seeped with the apprehension that "I am involved." Thought/affect thus bespeaks the difference between a mere hearing of a child's cry and a hearing *felt* – as when one realizes that danger is involved or that the child is one's own.[19]

What processes account for such involvement of the self – what sorts of histories, capacities, desires, frustrations, plans – may well belong to the psychologist's domain. Among other things, they will include propensities for physical response and the awareness that enduring images of who one is are intimately at stake: Emotions are about the ways in which the social world is one in which *we* are involved. But this aside, the stakes, solutions, threats, and possibilities for response are apt, in every case, to take their shape from what one's world and one's conceptions of such things as body, affect, and self are like. Feelings are not substances to be discovered in our blood but social practices organized by stories that we both enact and tell. They are structured by our forms of understanding.[20]

Thus stated, a view that feelings can be classified into a set of universal kinds becomes no more acceptable than the view that one can speak of a generality of personalities. One *can*, of course. And partial clarity is obtained – but only because our words for kinds of people, kinds of feelings, and so on evoke a background of assumptions that then guide the way to see and thus may keep us from attending to what in fact is going on. Somebody slights me. I respond with tension, anger, rage. But what I feel depends on how I understand what happened and construe my options in response.

For example, it is common knowledge within our world that events like slights make people angry. Anger felt can be expressed, but if denied or – even worse – repressed, it is "turned inward" in a manner that can lead to everything from melancholy to explosion. We can "vent" anger, arbitrarily, on unfortunate innocents within our view. We can "deny" true feelings and, in consequence, be damned to inner turmoil. But what we cannot do are two things common among the Philippine Ilongots I knew: We cannot be "paid" for "anger," which, so satisfied, then dissolves, and we cannot "forget" an "anger" whose expression would prove undesirable. The Ilongots understood that feelings could be hidden. But they did not think of hidden or forgotten affects as disturbing energies repressed; nor did they see in violent actions the expression of a history of frustrations buried in a fertile but unconscious mind.

I recall an incident in which a man who I had thought to have been frustrated by his "brother's" carelessness in making plans, got drunk and fought with the offender. To me, the deed stood as a clear expression of disruptive feelings hitherto repressed. To the Ilongots, however, the fight was seen as nothing more than an unfortunate consequence of drink, which "dissolved" consciousness and in so doing led the fighter to forget bonds with his brother. By my account, one would expect to see in subsequent actions further symptoms of a conflict that to me seemed real and deep. If seething anger *was* an inner truth revealed in drink, I should have found its symptoms lingering in sobriety. But what in fact ensued were simply signs of "shame" – an affect dictated by the brawler's restored knowledge of significant, though forgotten, kinship ties. Ilongots who – to my observer's eye – had failed to recognize the psychological bases for the brawl proved right in that their understanding was the one that guided both men in the days that followed.

It would be possible, of course, to translate this event into the terms of Western psychological discourse and argue that a need for solidarity in this case had led the relevant actors to deny their true emotions. But what is difficult to understand, as long as Ilongot "anger" is construed within our analytic frame, is how and why the Illongots concerned could be content with what to me appeared the sort of outcome that could only lead to renewed conflict. Certainly, the event bore some relation to a history of tensions that my friends saw no cause to address. But the failure of my vision – of how "anger" grows and is resolved – to comprehend their very real success in keeping "anger" from disrupting bonds of kin suggests that in important ways their feelings and the ways their feelings work must differ from our own.

Further probing into how Ilongots think that "anger" works – the fact that Christianity was seen as an alternative to killing in response to death of kin because "God does away with grief and anger"; their reasons for surprise in learning that American soldiers had not received compensatory payments from their former enemy, the Japanese; their sense that I was wrong when I desired to talk a feeling through instead of treating a prestation as an "answer" to my "anger" at a friend; their claim that since "I couldn't kill my wife, I just decided to forget my anger" – would of course be necessary to a satisfying understanding of the Ilongot account. How and why *we* think of "anger" as a thing to be expressed, whereas Ilongots tend to think of "anger" less in terms of volatility repressed and more in terms of how and if it can be answered, cannot be explicated here.

And yet I hope this anecdote suggests the viability of what strikes me as its theoretical counterpart: That affects, whatever their similarities, are no more similar than the societies in which we live; that ways of life and images of the self (the absence, in the Ilongot case, of an interior space in which the self might nurture an unconscious rage) decide what our emotions can be like in shaping stories of their likely cause and consequence. Ilongot discourse about "anger" overlaps with, yet is different from, our own. The same thing can be said about the things Ilongots feel. Or stated otherwise, the life of feeling is an aspect of the social world in which its terms are found.

Person and self

People everywhere – as Irving Hallowell[21] proposed – are apt to have some notion of personal identity over time and of the boundaries between themselves and others. Whatever the connections we may feel with fellow men, we recognize (and grant significance to) some of our differences as well – and in this limited sense a concept of the self is apt to be a cultural universal.

Less certain are the questions of what self-constructs may be like, how vulnerable they are to facts of context and of sociocultural milieu, and how and if they contrast with ideas concerning other aspects of what people are about.

Anthropologists, following such diverse thinkers as the Frenchman Marcel Mauss and the American G. H. Mead,[22] have held to a distinction between the "me" and "I" – between the social person characterized by ideas about the body, soul, or role and a more intimate and private self. Thus, Meyer Fortes[23] has taken pains to show that African peoples typically enjoy vocabularies for talking first about "the person" as described for kinsmen, courts, or cures and, then again, about the "individual" who enjoys a "destiny" that is hers or his alone. Similarly, Ilongots have ways of talking about kinds of kin, of workers and the like, and ways to speak of what is *talagatu* (really hers or his) – those actions that can only be explained with reference to an individual's way of being in the world. Thus, Ilongots see the *rinawa* (or heart) as something that responds and acts within the world, but also claim that actions of the "heart" are often hidden, inexplicable, opaque, autonomous. The Ilongot notion of the "heart" would then – to Fortes – be a token of the individuated self that is but masked, presented, staged in public life.

In challenging this standard view, I would not claim that Ilongot individuals do not exist. Rather, I want to argue that an analytic framework that equates "self/individual" with such things as spontaneity, genuine feeling, privacy, uniqueness, constancy, the "inner" life, and then opposes these to the "persons" or "personae" shaped by mask, role, rule, or context, is a reflection of dichotomies that constitute the modern Western self. And in this case "our" distinctions prove misleading as a frame on which to hang Ilongot constructs.

A number of points seem relevant. First, Ilongot hearts are not fixed entities that stand behind or underneath a public world where personhood is both affirmed and challenged. As numerous ethnographies suggest, our notions of a constant "I" – alluded to by the experiences that make a lengthy dossier[24] – are not found in tribal cultures in which kinship *and* identity are forever things to be negotiated in diverse contexts. The Ilongot who today confronts me as an affine may well tomorrow be my son, a difference that describes not only how we speak but how we act and feel in daily life. Personal names may change when one contracts disease, moves to a new locale, makes friends, or marries. And character is seen less as a product of one's nature or experience in life than of the situations in which the actor currently is found. Success in headhunting, Christian conversion, birth of children, illness, age, the loss of kin or confrontation with a slight – are all things that can "go to" the heart and make *it* "different." Yesterday's "energy" and "anger" can – through marriage or conversion – turn to utter calm.

Correspondingly, among Ilongots, personality descriptions are extremely rare, as are strategic reckonings of motivation. Accounts of why particular persons acted as they did refer almost exclusively to public and political concerns – surprising actions giving rise to the despairing claim that "one can never know the hidden reaches of another's heart." In general, Ilongots do not discern intentions, trace responsibility, or reckon blame by asking if offenders "knew" that they wronged others through their actions. Nor do they promise or hold fellows to account for failure to fulfill the expectations of their kin and friends. People can, of course, be duplicitous – "hide the wishes of their hearts" and "lend their tongues" to parties whom they only formally support in public meetings. But what they do not do is receive gifts in "payment" for the "anger in their hearts" and then insist that a mere ritual is inadequate to resolve emotions that continue to be strong. Most of the time there is no gap between the inner heart and what one does or says: Hearts move and in so doing make for human life and talk.

For Ilongots, in short, there is no necessary gap between "the presentation" and "the self."[25] What is most true of individuals, their deepest sense of who they are, is located in a set of actions – hunting, headhunting, growing rice – that displays the "energy" or "anger" that gives shape and focus to all healthy human hearts. What is more, these deeds do not achieve the separation of the individual from the group. Lack of focus makes one "different," but the Ilongot ideal is best described as one of "sameness," parity, or equality. Deviance, illness, madness, and failure to perform are typically attributed to things outside the self: Spiritual forces may cause crops to fail or make a person wild or weak by taking the heart out of one's body. But no one sees in deviant acts the telling symptoms of a person's character or worth. Nor do Ilongots in their self-reflections speak of personal histories or distinctive psychic drives to account for the peculiarities of deeds or dreams. For Ilongot men, the act of taking heads is probably the occasion for their most intense, most magical, and most focused sense of self. And yet the irony, from our point of view, is that self-realization in this form is what makes adult men "the same" as equal fellows. The act of killing does not prove the individual's inner volatility or worth; it is a social fact, permitting equal adult men to engage in the cooperation appropriate to adults. In short, it seems misleading to identify individuality with the Ilongot sense of self, first, because Ilongots do not assume a gap between the private self and public person and, second, because the very terms they use in their accounts of how and why they act place emphasis not on the individual who remains outside a social whole but rather on the ways in which all adults are simultaneously autonomous and equal members of a group.

A last point follows from those just discussed. In thinking about personhood and selves, the analyst distinguishes between a public discourse and a less accessible inner life, the first described by role and rule, the second by a less articulate discourse of gesture, tone, and hidden truth. I proposed earlier that what individuals *can* think and feel is overwhelmingly a product of socially organized modes of action and of talk, and that society itself, as in the Ilongot case, provides its actors images that combine such things as action, thought, emotion, and health, connecting "anger" in the self to public life in which one wants to be "the same" as equal fellows. It would seem to follow that what we call "real feelings" or the inner self are simply silences discerned, given *our* analytical discourse, silences that do not necessarily help us to grasp the ways that culture shapes and is shaped by human experience.

For us, the attributes of individuals describe the core of what we really are. Ritual actions, things we do "because of" roles and norms, become mere artifice and play; the "masks" that mundane rules provide do not describe subjective life. But our concern with the individuals and with their hidden inner selves may well be features of *our* world of action and belief – itself to be explained and not assumed as the foundation for cross-cultural study.

Comparisons

Self and person, I have argued, need not be conceptually opposed, although it strikes me as perfectly reasonable to insist that, given variations in experience-in-the-world, all individuals will differ. The distinction can be challenged first of all with reference to ethnographic materials like those just sketched. But second, it can be questioned on the basis of comparative accounts that show how notions of the person, affective processes, and forms of society itself are interlinked. My hunch, in very general terms, is that there is a good deal of cross-cultural variability in the ways that people think about the opposition between private and public, inner life, and outer deed, and that these differences prove related, on the one hand, to conceptions of such things as bodies, souls, relationships, and roles and, on the other, to the life of feeling.

Perhaps the area in which anthropologists have come closest to exploring linkages of this sort is that described by the classic opposition between the affects "guilt" and "shame."[26] Assuming people everywhere to have destructive impulses requiring their society's control, several theorists have suggested that affective sanctions – "shame" or "guilt," the eye of social expectation, or the voice of inner principle and rule – will operate (either together or apart) in checking the asocial strivings of the self. Thus, "guilt" and "shame" have been proposed as guardians of social norms and the foundations of a moral order in a world where individuals would not readily pursue unselfish goals. "Guilt" as a sanction is then associated with our individualistic and rapidly changing social form, and "shame" with those societies that subordinate the person to a hierarchical whole, displaying more concern for continuity than for change.

The contrast has been criticized, of course, and I would not defend it here. The "shameful" Japanese have "guilt," and we, it seems, have "shame." And yet the contrast speaks to something many of us find true: That there are correspondences between emotions, social forms, and culturally shaped beliefs. The difficulty with "guilt and shame" is that it sorts just "us" from "them," asking how "they" achieve adherence to their norms and rules in lieu of mechanisms we use to an equivalent sort of end. What is not recognized is the possibility that the very problem – how society controls an inner self – may well be limited to those social forms in which a hierarchy of unequal power, privilege, and control in fact creates a world in which the individual *experiences* constraint.

For Ilongots – and, I suggest, for many of the relatively egalitarian peoples in the world – there is no social basis for a problematic that assumes need for controls, nor do individuals experience themselves as having boundaries to protect or as holding drives and lusts that must be held in check if they are to maintain their status or engage in everyday cooperation. In reading recently about the hierarchical Javanese,[27] I was impressed that "shame" for them is something of a constant sentinel, protecting the (male) self from a distressing mundane sphere; whereas, for Ilongots – and people like them, I would think – "shame" operates only with reference to occasional sorts of contexts and relationships. Rather than (as seems the case, e.g., with Mediterranean peasants or with Benedict's Japanese)[28] needing to guard a public presence and restrain such forces as might undermine the status of their families and homes, Ilongots are concerned primarily not to protect but rather to assert the potency of equal, "angry" hearts in everyday affairs. Thus, Ilongot "shame" is not a constant socializer of inherently asocial souls, but an emotion felt when "sameness" and sociality are undermined by confrontations that involve such things as inequality and strangeness. For Ilongots, such inequalities breed feelings of "anger" and the shows of force through which imbalances are overcome. But "shame" emerges when – because of weakness, age, or the relationships involved – inferiors accept their place and then withdraw in "shamed" acceptance of subordination.[29]

My point, in short, is that the error of the classic "guilt and shame" account is that it tends to universalize our culture's view of a desiring inner self without realizing that such selves – and so, the things they feel – are, in important ways, social creations. "Shames" differ as much cross-culturally as our notions of "shame" and "guilt." Further investigation would, I am convinced, make clear that "shame" in the Ilongot world differs from that experienced by participants in somewhat more inegalitarian African tribal groups and that these differ in turn from that experienced in societies organized as states. Symbolic bonds of "shame" and sex; the question as to whether "shame" requires that men or women be restrained; the sense of boundaries to defend; issues of who feels "shame" and when, and of relationships between the sense of "having shame" and "being shamed" by fellows – all are, I would imagine, cultural variables dependent on the nature of encompassing social formations. Thus, whereas the affect "shame" may everywhere concern investments of the individual in a particular image of the self, the ways that this emotion works depends on socially dictated ways of reckoning the claims of selves and the demands of situations.

Once it is recognized that affects and conceptions of the self assume a shape that corresponds – at least in part – with the societies and polities within which actors live their lives, the kinds of claims that they defend, the conflicts they are apt to know, and their experiences of social relations, it becomes possible furthermore to suggest that the ethnocentric error of exporting "our" view is closely linked to the distinctions criticized in this chapter. In brief: Because we think of a subjective self whose operations are distinct from those of persons-in-the-world, we tend to think of human selves and their emotions as everywhere the same. Taking a somewhat opposed view, I am led – as it should now be clear – to note significant ways that people vary. Not only does "shame" appear to differ, given differences in sociopolitical milieu, but tentative observations argue that much the same thing can be said of the emotions called by names like "envy," "happiness," "love," and "rage."

Thus, for instance, in my recent work, I have been struck by what appears a constancy in the ways that "anger" works in what I call "brideservice" – loosely, hunter-gatherer – groups, in which people appear to think of "anger" as a thing, that, if expressed, will necessarily destroy social relations.[30] The Ilongots – whose social relationships are of this sort – respond to conflict with immediate fear of violent death; they say they must forget things lest expression make men kill; and, as suggested in the anecdote described earlier, they seem quite capable of "forgetting anger" in those contexts where a show of violence has no place. The notion, common in more complex, tribal – in my terms, "bridewealth" – groups, that "anger" can and should be publicly revealed in words and, correspondingly, that "anger" held within may work to other people's harm in hidden, witchlike ways[31] appears as foreign to them as it does to foraging brideservice groups around the world for whom disputing persons either separate or fight — and the expression of violent feelings is seen as always dangerous.

More detail than is possible here would be necessary to clarify and explain the forms of "anger" in these groups. The shapes of witchcraft, the contrast between the use of ordeals in bridewealth groups and duels in the brideservice case, the fact that peoples like Ilongots "pay" for "anger" rather than loss suffered in the case of marriage or the murder of one's kin — all would figure in such an explanation. But what I hope is clear is that my earlier claims — that Ilongot "anger" differs from our own and that Ilongots do not generally differentiate self and person — are not the simple arguments of a relativist who fears that use of our terms will blind us to the subtle ways that Ilongots construe their situation. So much is obvious. More significant is the theoretical point that relates lives of feeling to conceptions of the self, as both of these are aspects of particular forms of polities and social relations. Cultural idioms provide the images in terms of which our subjectivities are formed, and, furthermore, these idioms themselves are socially ordered and constrained.

Conclusion

Society — I have argued — shapes the self through the medium of cultural terms, which shape the understandings of reflective actors. It follows that insofar as our psychology is wedded to our culture's terms in its accounts of people elsewhere in the world, it is unlikely to appreciate their deeds. Previous attempts to show the cultural specificity of such things as personality and affective life have suffered from failure to comprehend that culture, far more than a mere catalogue of rituals and beliefs, is instead the very stuff of which our subjectivities are created. To say this is, of course, to raise more questions than I can pretend to solve — old questions about the nature of both mind and culture. But it strikes me that considerations like the ones evoked here are valuable as correctives to those classically employed in helping us to go beyond a set of classic answers that repeatedly blind our sight to the deep ways in which we are not individuals first but social persons.

Notes

This chapter has grown out of reflections following completion of my monograph *Knowledge and Passion* (1980); in particular, I have been reading and thinking about the sense in which cultural analyses may also be accounts of affect. Much of the relevant reading was completed while I was a fellow at the Center for Advanced Study in the Behavioral Sciences, partially supported by a grant from the National Endowment for the Humanities. The paper was first presented at the SSRC conference on Concepts of Culture and Its Acquisition organized by Richard A. Shweder and Robert A. LeVine. I am particularly grateful to Clifford Geertz, Sherry Ortner, Renato Rosaldo, David Schneider, Mari Slack, and Mark Snyder for their comments.

1   The notion that experiences such as these might testify to a divide between affect and cognition, psychology and culture was occasioned by a reading of the early chapters of Robert A. LeVine's useful book, *Culture, Behavior and Personality* (1973). My conclusions, however, differ from LeVine's, as the chapter should make clear.

2   Here I have in mind, first of all, Claude Levi-Strauss, who, of course, abolishes "affect" as something other than a consequence of cognitive processes in, e.g., *Totemism* (1963b) and "The Effectiveness of Symbols" (1963a). Furthermore, it seems to me that "mediation" in Levi-Strauss, like "anomaly" in Douglas (1966) or "liminality" in Turner (1967, 1969), can be seen as a concept designed to "recover" energy and affect within the context of a structuralist perspective.

3   For classic sources on cognitive dissonance, see Festinger (1964).

4   D'Andrade's (1965) classic study in this regard has been followed by the research and theoretical writings of Shweder (1979a, 1979b, 1980). Among psychologists, the works of Daryl Bem (1974) and Walter Mischel (1973) are relevant.

5   Here I am pointing to a commonality (noted also, I believe, by Roy Shaefer) in impulse shared by ego psychologists like Erikson (e.g., 1963) and object relations theorists like Winnicott (1953) and Fairbairn (1954). See Chodorow (1978) for an extremely useful discussion of the significance of object relations theory.

6   In reading Kohut (1971), I was struck by the sense in which his work seemed a psychodynamic counterpart to the masterful sociology of "face" developed by Erving Goffman (1959). Hochschild's (1979) suggestion that we see "emotion work" and "emotion rules" as the "deep" counterpart to Goffman's "face work" (1967) provides the missing link. Interestingly, in all of these writers, there is an ambiguity as to whether their analytic constructs are intended to be universal (and thus the product of strictly analytical concerns) or more local reflections of self-constructs and problems peculiar to the modern West. My hunch is that both factors are operative; this is a piece of intellectual history that remains to be told.

7   Shaefer (1976) is quite explicit as to the continuities between his efforts and those of "self," "ego," and "object" psychologists, although he claims that they sought to accomplish through "structure" and "mechanism" analytical ends that require an emphasis, instead, on agency, consciousness, or intention.

8   I have in mind here the work of linguistically oriented philosophers like Searle (1969), and Grice (1975), on the one hand, and of philosophers interested in conceptions of self, person, and affect (e.g., Perry 1975; 1976, 1980; Williams 1973), on the other. For many of these people, one important context for their reflections is the rise of the notion of a "cognitive science" and a desire to clarify the kind of analysis appropriate to "thought" itself.

9   The key name here, of course, is Derrida (1976), but his continuity with structuralism's attack on "the subject" (see, e.g., Donato 1977) and the challenge to conventional "humanism" posed by other "post-structuralists" such as Foucault (1972) also deserve to be noted.

10   The concern has a history, but key recent texts include: Crapanzano (1973), Dieterlen (1973), C. Geertz (1973b), H. Geertz (1959), Levy (1973), Myers (1979), Paul (1976), and Turner (1970). One could, in addition, list a host of dissertations and unpublished papers and several symposia at recent anthropology meetings.

11   Among those who see cultural organization as essentially that of personality, I would cite (whatever their differences), Benedict (1959), Kardiner (1939), Kardiner et al. (1945), and Mead (1935). Whiting (e.g., 1964) and his collaborators tend more to the view that culture-formation processes resemble those of symbol-formation in Freud; in this view, personality (or, more narrowly, child development) is seen as something that *explains* (rather than paralleling, or being reflected in) culture.

12   Key exemplars are Spiro (1967) and Obeyesekere (1974).

13   To his name should be added, minimally, those of David Schneider (1968) and Dell Hymes and J. Gumperz (1972), who have stressed the need for a properly cultural understanding of the apparently "natural" or "functional" domains of kinship and language, respectively. The culturalist turn also is reflected, of course, in a host of monographs by younger scholars: e.g., Ortner (1978), M. Rosaldo (1980), R. Rosaldo (1980), and Schieffelin (1976). See also the work of such historians as N. Davis (1975) and W. Sewell (1980).

14   Although I would reject his formulation of emotions as "judgments," R. Solomon's somewhat uneven attempts to reconceptualize *The Passions* (1976) have influenced my own. One contribution of his that deserves particular note is his attempt to describe differences among emotions in terms of differences in situations and inclinations toward action rather than differences in internal feeling states (Solomon 1984); on this, contrast Davitz (1969).

15   I cannot begin to cite the relevant psychological literature, which ranges from Schachter and Singer's classic study (1962) of the impact of thought on affect to Ekman's materials (e.g., 1974) on universals in the expression of emotion to more recent formulations of the relation between "hot," or "energized," emotional states and "cooler" modes of thought (e.g., Mandler 1975). For a provocative – though ultimately, I think, unsatisfactory – overview, see Zajonc (1980). For a dissident – although, to me, more promising – view, see Smith (1981).

16   Of course, one can find *both* variability and relative universality in *both* domains. A complement, perhaps, to Ekman's work on universals in emotional experience/expression is that of Berlin (1972)

and Berlin and Kay (1969) on universals in the categorization of plants and colors. But my argument in this chapter (in particular, my discussion here of "anger") is that in neither case do universals begin to tell the whole story. The observation that some kinds of feelings or perceptions may be relatively "given" in the nature of the world, of human society, or of the human "processing" apparatus will prove misleading if taken as "bedrock" for an account of the ways that thought and feeling work in human minds. What is most deeply felt or known, what is felt first, perceived most clearly, or experienced as a standard base or core need not be the "common denominator" Western analysts perceive among such diverse things as Ilongot and American styles of anger. And I would argue that we are most likely to understand the force of "anger, passion" in Ilongot hearts by starting not with isolated experiences we share, but with those Ilongot lives and stories in which *their* "anger" is described.

17   See Geertz 1973b.

18   These remarks owe a good deal to an unpublished paper by Catherine Lutz, "Talking About 'Our Insides': Ifaluk Conceptions of the Self."

19   To cast the matter in linguistic terms, it is the difference between a statement cast in universal terms – "John's rug is green" – and deixis, a statement anchored in the speaking self – "I know John"; "I see the rug"; "I hate the color green." Deixis, of course, has proved problematic for propositionally oriented linguistics (see, e.g., Silverstein 1976), and, from conversations with John Perry, I gather that the "I" in sentences like those just presented gives metaphysical headaches to philosophers. My suggestion is that the "problem" of emotions is in some ways *the same* as the problem of deixis – a parallel suggesting that reflections in one domain might prove illuminating to the other.

20   Hochschild's (1979) work on "emotion rules" is probably the most explicit formulation in this regard. Given my problems with the notion of culture-as-rule, I find more useful a comparable but more flexible formulation by Schieffelin in which he talks about "cultural scenarios" (1976).

21   See Hallowell 1955.

22   Mauss's distinctions (1938) are between "person," "self," and "individual" and are understood in terms of a developmental cultural sequence, with "the individual" a modern construct. But the opposition between "person" and "self/individual" parallels Mead's (1934) analytical formulation of a split between the interdependent constructs "me" and "I."

23   See Fortes 1959. Unfortunately, Fortes is more concerned to document the presence in African thought of notions of individual uniqueness than to develop the Meadian concern with an interaction between social typifications ascribed to persons and their sense of individual identity.

24   I owe the point about the dossier to a paper by Jean Jackson, "Bara Concepts of Self and Other" (1980).

25   There *is* in Ilongot a gap between the things I say, reveal, and those I hide, but the latter are not associated with such things as self and essence. As indicated in note 6, it is not clear to me if Goffman's classic formulation is intended to describe universal or more local processes of self-definition.

26   In fact, I would suggest that of all themes in the literature on culture and personality, the opposition between guilt and shame has proven most resilient (e.g., Benedict 1946; Dodds 1951; Doi 1973; Levy 1973; Lynd 1958; Piers & Singer 1953), at least in part because guilt and shame are affects concerned at once with psychological state and social context (thus providing a significant terrain for culturally oriented social scientists) and in part because the opposition is consistent with numerous others in our psychological and sociological vocabularies (inner/outer, Oedipal/pre-Oedipal, male/female, The West/The Rest, modern/primitive, egalitarian/hierarchical, change-oriented/traditional, and so on).

27   The reference is to Ward Keeler's doctoral dissertation on Javanese *wayong wang* theater "Father Puppeteer," and his article, "Shame and Stage Fright in Java" (1983).

28   For classic cases in which shame seems to operate as a "fence," protecting, in particular, such things as personal or family honor, see Benedict 1946 for Japan; Campbell 1964 for Greek shepherds; Pitt-Rivers 1954 for Spanish peasants. In reading about shame in hierarchical Southeast Asia (e.g., Java, Bali), one senses that something slightly different is going on (see C. Geertz 1973b; H. Geertz 1959; Keeler 1982, 1983).

29   See my paper "The Shame of Headhunters and the Autonomy of the Self" (1983) for a fuller formulation.

30   The brideservice/bridewealth division is developed in Collier and Rosaldo (1981). This typological cut – like its predecessors band/tribe, hunting/agriculture – is, needless to say, vulnerable

to challenge. It is proposed here primarily as an illustration of the *kinds* of ways in which differences in social formation might interact with differences in self/affect constructs. One needs some notion of the kinds of differences that make a difference if interactions of any kind are to be grasped.

31   Examples abound. See, e.g., Harris 1978 and Strathern 1975 for the dangers of hidden anger. See, e.g., Briggs 1970, Robarchek 1977, and Rosaldo 1980 for the danger of anger expressed.

References

Bem, D., & Allen, A. 1974. On predicting some of the people some of the time: the search for cross-situational consistencies in behavior. *Psychological Review* 81(6):506–20.

Benedict, R. 1946. *The Chrysanthemum and the Sword*. Boston: Houghton Mifflin.

—— 1959. *Patterns of Culture*. Boston: Houghton Mifflin.

Berlin, B. 1972. Speculations on the growth of ethnobotanical nomenclature. *Language in Society* 1:51–86.

Berlin, B., & Kay, P. 1969. *Basic Color Terms: Their Universality and Evolution*. Berkeley: University of California Press.

Briggs, J. 1970. *Never in Anger*. Cambridge, Mass.: Harvard University Press.

Campbell, J. 1964. *Honour, Family and Patronage*. Oxford: Clarendon Press.

Chodorow, N. 1978. *The Reproduction of Mothering*. Berkeley: University of California Press.

Collier, J., & Rosaldo, M. 1981. Sex and politics in simple societies. In S. Ortner & H. Whitehead, eds., *Sexual Meanings*. Cambridge: Cambridge University Press.

Crapanzano, V. 1973. *The Hamadsha*. Berkeley: University of California Press.

D'Andrade, R. 1965. Trait psychology and componential analysis. *American Anthropologist* 67:215–28.

Davis, N. 1975. *Society and Culture in Early Modern France*. Stanford, Calif.: Stanford University Press.

Davitz, J. 1969. *The Language of Emotion*. New York: Academic Press.

Derrida, J. 1976. *Of Grammatology*. Gayatri C. Spivak, trans. Baltimore: Johns Hopkins University Press.

Dieterlen, G. 1973. *La Notion de la Personne en Afrique Noire*. Paris: CNRS.

Dodds, E. 1951. *The Greeks and the Irrational*. Berkeley: University of California Press.

Doi, T. 1973. *The Anatomy of Dependence*. Tokyo: Kodansha International.

Donato, E. 1977. *The Structuralist Controversy: The Languages of Criticism and the Sciences of Man*. Baltimore: Johns Hopkins University Press.

Douglas, M. 1966. *Purity and Danger*. New York: Praeger.

Durkheim, E. 1915. *The Elementary Forms of the Religious Life*. New York: Macmillan.

Ekman, P. 1974. Universal facial expressions of emotion. In R. LeVine, ed., *Culture and Personality*. Chicago: Aldine.

Erikson, E. 1963. *Childhood and Society*. New York: Norton.

Fairbairn, W. 1954. *An Object-Relations Theory of the Personality*. New York: Basic Books.

Festinger, L. 1964. *Conflict, Decision and Dissonance*. Stanford, Calif.: Stanford University Press.

Fortes, M. 1959. *Oedipus and Job in West African Religion*. Cambridge: Cambridge University Press.

Foucault, M. 1972. *The Archeology of Knowledge*. A. M. Sheridan Smith, trans. London: Tavistock.

—— 1978. *The History of Sexuality*. Robert Hurley, trans. New York: Pantheon Books.

Geertz, C. 1973a. *The Interpretation of Cultures*. New York: Basic Books.

—— 1973b. Person, time and conduct in Bali. In C. Geertz, *The Interpretation of Cultures*. New York: Basic Books.

Geertz, H. 1959. The vocabulary of emotions: a study of Javanese socialization process. *Psychiatry* 22:225–37.

Goffman, E. 1959. *The Presentation of Self in Everyday Life*. Garden City, N.Y.: Doubleday.

—— 1967. On face work. In E. Goffman, ed., *Interaction Ritual*. New York: Pantheon Books.

Grice, P. 1975. Logic and conversation. In P. Cole & J. C. Morgan, eds., *Syntax and Semantics*, vol. 3: *Speech Acts*. New York: Academic Press.

Hallowell, A. I. 1955. The self and its behavioral environment. In A. I. Hallowell, ed., *Culture and Experience*. Philadelphia: University of Pennsylvania Press.

Harris, G. 1978. *Casting Out Anger*. Cambridge: Cambridge University Press.

Hochschild, A. 1979. Emotion work, feeling rules, and social structure. *American Journal of Sociology* 85:551–75.

Hymes, D. & Gumperz, J. eds. 1972. *Directions in Sociolinguistics*. New York: Holt, Rinehart, and Winston.

Jackson, J. 1980. *Bara concepts of self and other*. Paper presented at the 1980 Meetings of the American Anthropological Association. December.

Kardiner, A. 1939. *The Individual and His Society*. New York: Columbia University Press.

Kardiner, A., Linton, R., DuBois, C., and West, J. 1945. *The Psychological Frontiers of Society*. New York: Columbia University Press.

Keeler, W. 1982. *Father puppeteer*. Unpublished doctoral dissertation, University of Chicago. *Comprehensive Dissertation Index*. 1982 Supplement 5:227.

—— 1983. Shame and stage fright in Java. *Ethos* 11:152–65.

Kohut, H. 1971. *The Analysis of the Self*. New York: International Universities Press.

LeVine, R. 1973. *Culture, Behavior and Personality*. Chicago: Aldine.

Levi-Strauss, C. 1963a. The effectiveness of symbols. In C. Levi-Strauss, ed., *Structural Anthropology*. New York: Basic Books.

—— 1963b. *Totemism*. Boston: Beacon Press.

Levy, R. 1973. *The Tahitians*. Chicago: University of Chicago Press.

Lutz, C. N.d. *Talking about "our insides": Ifaluk conceptions of the self*. Unpublished manuscript, State University of New York (Binghamton).

Lynd, H. 1958. *On Shame and the Search for Identity*. New York: Harcourt, Brace.

Mandler, G. 1975. *Mind and Emotion*. New York: Wiley.

Mauss, M. 1938. Une Catégorie de l'Espirit Humaine: La Notion de Personne Celle de "Moi." *Journal of the Royal Anthropological Institute* 68:263–82.

Mead, G. H. 1934. *Mind, Self and Society*. Chicago: University of Chicago Press.

Mead, M. 1935. *Sex and Temperament in Three Primitive Societies*. New York: Morrow.

Mischel, W. 1973. Toward a cognitive social learning reconceptualization of personality. *Psychological Review* 80(4):252–83.

Myers, G. 1979. Emotions and the self: a theory of personhood and political order among Pintupi aborigines. *Ethos* 7(4):343–70.

Obeyesekere, G. 1974. Pregnancy cravings (dola-duka) in relation to social structure and personality in a Sinhalese village. In R. LeVine, ed., *Culture and Personality*, pp. 202–21. Chicago: Aldine.

Ortner, S. 1978. *Sherpas Through Their Rituals*. Cambridge: Cambridge University Press.

Paul, R. 1976. The Sherpa temple as a model of the psyche. *American Ethnologist* 3(1):131–46.

Perry, J., ed. 1975. *Personal Identity*. Berkeley: University of California Press.

Piers, G., & Singer, M. 1971. *Shame and Guilt*. New York: Norton.

Pitt-Rivers, J. 1954. *The People of the Sierra*. New York: Criterion Books.

Ricoeur, P. 1970. *Freud and Philosophy*. New Haven, Conn.: Yale University Press.

Robarchek, C. 1977. Frustration, aggression, and the nonviolent Semai. *American Ethnologist* 4(4):762–79.

Rorty, A. 1976. *The Identities of Persons*. Berkeley: University of California Press.

—— 1980. *Explaining Emotions*. Berkeley: University of California Press.

Rosaldo, M. 1980. *Knowledge and Passion: Ilongot Notions of Self and Social Life*. Cambridge: Cambridge University Press.

—— 1983. The shame of headhunters and the autonomy of the self. *Ethos* 11:135–51.

Rosaldo, R. 1980. *Ilongot Headhunting 1883–1974*. Stanford, Calif.: Stanford University Press.

Schachter, S., & Singer, J. 1962. Cognitive, social and psychological determinants of emotional state. *Psychological Review* 65:379–99.

Schieffelin, E. 1976. *The Sorrow of the Lonely and the Burning of the Dancers*. New York: St. Martin's Press.

Schneider, D. 1968. *American Kinship: A Cultural Account*. Englewood Cliffs, N.J.: Prentice-Hall.

Searle, J. 1969. *Speech Acts*. Cambridge: Cambridge University Press.

Sewell, W. 1980. *Work and Revolution in France: The Language of Labor from the Old Regime to 1848*. Cambridge: Cambridge University Press.

Shaefer, R. 1976. *A New Language for Psychoanalysis*. New Haven, Conn.: Yale University Press.

Shweder, R. 1979a. Rethinking culture and personality theory part I: a critical examination of two classical postulates. *Ethos* 7:255–78.

—— 1979b. Rethinking culture and personality theory part II: a critical examination of two more classical postulates. *Ethos* 7:279–311.

—— 1980. Rethinking culture and personality theory part III: from genesis and typology to hermeneutics and dynamics. *Ethos* 8:60–95.

Silverstein, M. 1976. Shifters, linguistic categories, and cultural description. In K. Basso & H. Selby, eds., *Meaning in Anthropology*, pp. 11–55. Albuquerque: University of New Mexico Press.

Smith, M. Brewster, 1981. *The metaphorical basis of selfhood*. Paper presented to a symposium on Culture and Self, University of Hawaii.

Solomon, R. 1976. *The Passions: The Myth and Nature of Human Emotion*. New York: Anchor/Doubleday.

—— 1984. Getting angry: the Jamesian theory of emotion in anthropology. In R. A. Schweder and R. A. LeVine, eds., *Culture Theory: Essays on Mind, Self and Emotions*. Cambridge: Cambridge University Press.

Spiro, M. 1967. *Burmese Supernaturalism*. Englewood Cliffs, N.J.: Prentice-Hall.

Strathern, A. 1975. Why is shame on the skin? *Ethnology* 14(4):347–56.

Turner, T. 1970. Oedipus: time and structure in narrative form. In R. Spencer, ed., *Forms of Symbolic Action*, pp. 26–68. Seattle: University of Washington Press.

Turner, V. 1967. *The Forest of Symbols*. Ithaca, N.Y.: Cornell University Press.

—— 1969. *The Ritual Process: Structure and Anti-Structure*. Chicago: Aldine.

Whiting, J. 1964. Effects of climate on certain cultural practices. In Ward Goodenough, ed., *Explorations in Cultural Anthropology*, pp. 511–44. New York: McGraw-Hill.

Williams, B. 1973. *Problems of the Self*. Cambridge: Cambridge University Press.

Winnicott, D. W. 1953. Transitional objects and transitional phenomena. *International Journal of Psycho-Analysis* 34:89–97.

Zajonc, R. B. 1980. Feeling and thinking: preferences need no inferences. *American Psychologist* 35(2):151–75.

Chapter 5

Lila Abu-Lughod and Catherine A. Lutz

EMOTION, DISCOURSE, AND THE POLITICS OF EVERYDAY LIFE

EMOTIONS ARE ONE of those taken-for-granted objects of both specialized knowledge and everyday discourse now becoming part of the domain of anthropological inquiry. Although still primarily the preserve of philosophy and psychology within the academic disciplines, emotions are also ordinary concerns of a popular American cultural discourse whose relationship to such professional discourses is complex and only partially charted. Tied to tropes of interiority and granted ultimate facticity by being located in the natural body, emotions stubbornly retain their place, even in all but the most recent anthropological discussions, as the aspect of human experience least subject to control, least constructed or learned (hence most universal), least public, and therefore least amenable to sociocultural analysis. [. . .] On the contrary, the sociocultural analysis of emotion is both feasible and important. [. . .]

We begin by setting out four strategies that have been or could be used to develop the anthropology of emotion: essentializing, relativizing, historicizing, and contextualizing emotion discourse. We then consider the field of meanings and diverse deployments of the key term "discourse," without which, we argue, "emotion" cannot properly be understood. Paying special attention to the theoretical terms "discourse" is meant to replace, we argue that the most productive analytical approach to the cross-cultural study of emotion is to examine discourses on emotion and emotional discourses as social practices within diverse ethnographic contexts. [. . .] [This] approach [is] distinguished by its focus on the constitution of emotion, and even the domain of emotion itself, in discourse or situated speech practices, by its construal of emotion as about social life rather than internal states, and its exploration of the close involvement of emotion talk with issues of sociability and power – in short, with the politics of everyday life.

This [chapter] enters a dynamic and growing field of debate on questions about the relationship between the emotions, society, and cultural meaning.[1] Most anthropological works in this field prior to 1980 simply accepted psychological orthodoxy on emotions: Emotions are psychobiological processes that respond to cross-cultural environmental differences but retain a robust essence untouched by the social or cultural. The diverse approaches within the anthropology of emotions may have reflected the heterodoxies of psychology, insofar as there developed various Freudian approaches (e.g., Hiatt 1984), analyses based on learning theory (e.g., Robarchek 1979), and ethological and attachment perspectives (e.g., Lindholm 1982). But only recently has the *doxa* itself – that emotions are things internal, irrational, and natural – been exposed and questioned.

Much work done in the fields of psychiatric and psychological anthropology can be characterized as essentialist in its approach to emotion (even when other aspects of the person are viewed as more fundamentally social in origin or character). From early culture and personality work between World Wars I and II through much contemporary work in psychological anthropology, the amount and kinds of emotion that people experience are assumed to be predictable outcomes of universal psychobiological processes. A particular experience is assumed to stimulate identical emotions in all nonpathological humans, as when mothers are assumed to become attached to their newborns naturally and independently of social context (Scheper-Hughes 1985). In some of this work, for example, it is taken for granted that individuals have a limited and/or necessary amount of affection or love to distribute across persons to whom they become attached; hence the not infrequent concern with the effect on a child of having multiple caretakers, and the question of whether such children have less intense feelings for the mother and/or for other adults. In a related vein, Lindholm (1982) has argued that Swat Pukhtun (Pakistan) social organization promotes fragmented and agonistic social relations, thwarting the need for love in most contexts, but particularly in adult males. The result is that the institution of friendship must bear, virtually alone, the heavy burden of fulfilling that need; because love cannot be expressed in other arenas, friendships become intense and voracious.

Elsewhere (e.g., Hiatt 1984; Scheff 1977), emotions are viewed as "things" with which social systems must "deal" in a functional sense. Ritual frequently has been seen as a device that allows for the expression of preexisting emotions that would create problems if not expressed. Adolescent initiation ceremonies, for example, are presented as means for containing the affective turbulence of young boys. In a somewhat different vein, emotions are sometimes treated as psychic "energies" implicitly marshaled in the service of constructing a social order. Spiro (1965) presents a version of this view when he argues that the emotional conflicts of Burmese men, which include, in his view, their homosexual feelings, are channeled into and defused by entrance into the monkhood.

The strategy of essentializing emotions has several unfortunate consequences. First, if feelings are considered the essence of emotion, then the most reliable way to explore emotions would be through introspective reports. This approach deflects attention from social life and its possible implication in the very language of emotion. It also prevents us from looking at the role of emotional discourses in social interactions. Second, it reinforces the assumption of universality in the forms of distinct emotions (e.g., shame and guilt are each central and separate feelings), in their meaning (e.g., anger in one culture feels/means the same as anger in another), and in emotional processes (e.g., emotions are primarily intrapsychic and subject to masking, repression, and channeling). Finally, hand in hand with essentialism goes a strange invisibility of emotion itself as a problem, since positing emotion universals allows us more easily to take emotion for granted.

For those both committed to some sort of cross-cultural analysis and suspicious of the certainties and unexamined cultural assumptions about that which we most take for granted, three alternative strategies of questioning appear to be fruitful. The first strategy is to do what anthropologists have always to some extent done: to bring into question the certainty and universality of ways we think about and talk about things such as emotions by investigating whether it is so elsewhere.[2] A good deal of (often implicitly) comparative work exists, from the fertile early work by H. Geertz (1959) on the vocabulary of emotion in Java, by C. Geertz (1973) on the person in Bali, and by Briggs (1970) on Utku emotion expression, to Levy's (1973) explication of Tahitian ideas and silences on the subject of emotion.

The most important recent examples of the relativizing strategy are found in the seminal work of Myers (1979, 1986) and Rosaldo (1980). Unlike much of the earlier ethnopsychological work on emotion, their interpretive approach to emotions stresses not what culturally variable ideas about emotion can tell us about other "deeper" psychological processes, but rather what implications these ideas have for social behavior and social relations. These analysts helped place emotions squarely in the realm of culture by pointing to the ways local cultural concepts of emotion such as the Ilongot *liget* (anger) and the Pintupi *ngaltu* (compassion) borrow from broader cultural themes and reflect, in their ideological shape, the forms of indigenous social relationships. If these works did not always or consistently deessentialize emotions, they certainly began the important process of suspending concern with the psychological paradigm. For both, furthermore, differences observed in talk about emotion had to be traced to social structure rather than to a pure realm of autonomous ideology.

While some of the work of relativizing has been done by examining specific concepts of emotion used in different cultures, many studies of emotion even show how fragile the category itself is. For example, Howell (1981) argues that for the Chewong (Malaysia), what we call "affect" is seen as a minor phenomenon; talk about emotion is replaced by talk about normative rules that provide, she argues, "an idiom for . . . organizing the individual's relationship to himself, to his fellow[s] . . ., and to nature and supernature" (142). Obeyesekere (1985) shows that in Sri Lanka emotion is likely to be taken as a sign of Buddhist religious prescription achieved or unachieved. For the Ifaluk (Micronesia), emotion is often construed as moral judgment and has a similar pragmatic force (Lutz 1988).

In Riesman's work on the Fulani of West Africa, a subtle transition from the analysis of particular emotion concepts and their role in social relations to the questioning of the very cultural meaning and social structural effects of emotionality itself illustrates the direction we think the anthropology of emotion ought to take. In his earlier work, Riesman (1977) was especially concerned to lay out the dimensions of Fulani notions of *pulaaku* (translated as 'Fulaniness' but something others might have called 'honor') and *semteende*, or 'shame'. In his later work (1983), he began to make a suggestive argument linking social hierarchy to emotionality itself, arguing that self-control or relative lack of emotional expressiveness is simultaneously taken as a badge of, justification for, and realization of the social superiority of nobles over their ex-slaves. If the meaning of emotionality differs cross-culturally and the applications to social organization of emotional practice are variable, then any certainties about universals are undermined.

A second strategy for those interested in emotions as sociocultural phenomena is to historicize them. That means subjecting discourses on emotion, subjectivity, and the self to scrutiny over time, looking at them in particular social locations and historical moments, and seeing whether and how they have changed. Although a host of potential studies remain to be done, a few works have attempted this sort of investigation. Some have been concerned with the history of formal and informal theories of emotions in the West, and others have examined the fate of particular emotions (Cancian 1987; Gardiner, Metcalf, and Beebe-Center 1970; MacFarlane 1987; Stearns and Stearns 1986). Norbert Elias (1978) has argued, mostly from a reading of etiquette manuals, that vast transformations of affective life in Europe took place concomitant with the development of the absolutist state. Among these he includes an expansion of the contexts in which disgust occurs and a diminution of aggressive affect or behavior. That he calls this the "civilizing process" is symptomatic of his uncritical interpretation of these changes as involving a refinement of a somehow preexisting affectivity, a position that many anthropologists would regard with skepticism. Still, his work opens up an argument about the kinds of changes that have taken place in one geographical, historical setting.

Other scholars have examined these changes in terms of the disappearance of or shift in the social locus of various emotions, as well as the manipulation of emotional discourses for state purposes. The problem of sadness has received an impressive number of historical treatments. Jackson (1985), like Harré and Finlay-Jones (1986), takes on the focused task of tracing the extinction of an emotion called "accidie" and the significance of the obsolescence of "melancholy," both so important during medieval times, in the contemporary period. Sontag (1977) argues that the nineteenth-century Romantic movement came to celebrate individuality in part by viewing sadness as a mark of refinement, as a quality that made the person suffering from it "interesting." The rise of individualism brought with it the celebration of difference; one of the routes by which the new individuals could distinguish themselves was through a focus on feelings defined as aspects of unique personalities. Radden (1987) takes these views further by noting that melancholy was primarily a male complaint, one that was at least in part socially valorized. She argues that the related modern discourse on depression differs in pinpointing women as its bearers and in portraying the syndrome as more unequivocally deviant, deficient, and medical in nature.[3] In a different vein and in a non-Western setting, Good and Good (1988) explore the ways in which the Islamic Republic of Iran now organizes, to an unprecedented degree, both public and private emotional discourses. It has transformed the public discourse of sadness and grief, which before the revolution was central to religious ritual, self-definition, and social understanding, into a sign of political loyalty to the state.

What might be most productive, however, would be to begin by tracing the genealogy of "emotion" itself so that, in an enterprise analogous to Foucault's (1978) critical investigation of the production of "sexuality" in the modern age, we might consider how emotions came to be constituted in their current form, as physiological forces, located within individuals, that bolster our sense of uniqueness and are taken to provide access to some kind of inner truth about the self (Abu-Lughod, 1990; Lutz 1986). One promising line of questioning might be to build on Foucault's insights about the growing importance of confession (to which a discourse of emotion is often bound both inside and outside psychotherapy) as a locus of social control and discourse production in the eighteenth and nineteenth centuries.

Foucault's description of his own project suggests more directly how emotion discourse might represent a privileged site of the production of the modern self. He writes, in the second volume of The History of Sexuality, that he wishes "to analyze the practices by which individuals were led to focus their attention on themselves, to decipher, recognize, and acknowledge themselves as subjects of desire, bringing into play between themselves and themselves a certain relationship that allows them to discover, in desire, the truth of their being" (Foucault 1985:5–6).[4] He also notes that in each historical period it is "not always the same part of ourselves, or of our behavior, [that] is relevant for ethical judgment," but in contemporary Western society, "the main field of morality, the part of ourselves which is most relevant for morality, is our feelings" (1983:238). Feelings can play this role because they are currently constituted as the core of the self, the seat of our individuality.[5]

The third strategy is to focus on social discourse, building less on anthropology's comparative bent or the broad historical framing of the problem than on a commitment to careful analysis of the richness of specific social situations, whether here or there, as Geertz (1987) puts it. It is a strategy [that] explore[s], through close attention to ethnographic cases, the many ways emotion gets its meaning and force from its location and performance in the public realm of discourse. [It] also ask[s] how social life is affected by emotion discourse. To assess the nature and value of this strategy first requires attention to the term at its center: the word "discourse."

"Discourse" has become, in recent years, one of the most popular and least defined terms in the vocabulary of Anglo-American academics. It pervades the humanities and now haunts many of the social sciences. Rather than being alarmed by its spread, however, it might be better to ask why so many have adopted it. The best way to pursue that question is to consider what theoretical work they want the term to do.

As everyone readily admits, defining discourse precisely is impossible because of the wide variety of ways it is used. To get a sense of why people use it, and why we have found it useful in thinking about emotion, it might be helpful to consider what terms it replaces. What is discourse not? To what is discourse counterposed? This varies by discipline, but we will be concerned only with anthropology because its peculiar appropriation of the term from the French poststructuralist vocabulary is inflected by the prior and concurrent usage of the term by anthropological linguists.

First, particularly for those whose concerns are linguistic, the term discourse marks an approach to language as spoken and used rather than as a static code analyzable apart from social practice. In Saussure's *langue/parole* distinction, discourse would fall on the side of *parole*. What those who invoke discourse in this context might want to add, however, is that *langue* either does not exist (e.g., Hopper 1987) or at least is always embodied in particular utterances by particular individuals. In privileging speech, those who use the term discourse generally also want to assert the importance of pragmatics versus semantics. The "code," whether it be grammar, structure, model, or, in this case, some purported underlying presocial emotional matrix, is taken as emergent in a social context, even if it is not analyzed as a peculiar Western cultural construct.

Although in some senses associated with speech, discourse is also commonly used instead to suggest a concern with verbal productions more formal, elaborate, or artistic than everyday conversation. Examples of classic forms of discourse in this sense are poems, songs, laments, prayers, myths, and verbal dueling forms such as sounding (Labov 1972). Discourse is also used by some who identify with postmodernism in its literary incarnation to stress the spoken quality of language (Tedlock 1983, 1987a and b) and to evoke its dialogic aspect, allegedly ignored by those of us who live in literate societies. Yet others use the term discourse as a way of including even the nonverbal, like music, crying, or the "unsaid" of past utterances and present unarticulated imagination (Tyler 1978) in our consideration of the meanings humans make.

Sherzer's (1987) recent article advocating a discourse-centered approach to language and culture demonstrates the wide range of uses and resulting ambiguity of the term. Blending many of these senses of discourse together in his "purposely vague" definition, he writes that discourse is

> a level or component of language use . . . [which] can be oral or written and can be approached in textual or sociocultural and social-interactional terms. And it can be brief like a greeting and thus smaller than a single sentence or lengthy like a novel or narration of personal experience and thus larger than a sentence and constructed out of sentences or sentence-like utterances . . . Discourse is an elusive area, an imprecise and constantly emerging and emergent interface between language and culture, created by actual instances of language in use. (296)

The unfortunate vagueness of this definition is the product of a failure to grasp that terms are used to signal perspectives and to carve out academic domains, not just to refer to definable entities. The kinds of usages we have described thus far for the increasingly employed term discourse could be characterized as largely sociolinguistic or literary. All that is being keyed is an interest in language in context, texts, and the public and social character of what we study. [. . .]

[. . .][A]nother way of using discourse [has] more ambitious theoretical goals and different disciplinary roots. Discourse in this other sense is a word that has been taken up by those who find the critique of social theory associated with French poststructuralists like Michel Foucault persuasive, or at least those who have begun to borrow its vocabulary. With this move, the semantic field and pragmatic deployment of the term have begun to shift.

Although only beginning to find its way into anthropological writing, discourse in this much wider Foucaultian sense is being adopted to do the theoretical work of refiguring two terms that it replaces: culture and ideology. For many, the no less definable term "culture" has become problematic for several reasons. First, built into it is a distinction between a realm of ideas, even if public rather than in people's heads, and material realities and social practices, a distinction some users of discourse would like to problematize. Second, the term seems to connote a certain coherence, uniformity, and timelessness in the meaning systems of a given group, and to operate rather like the earlier concept of "race" in identifying fundamentally different, essentialized, and homogeneous social units (as when we speak about "a culture"). Because of these associations, invoking culture tends to divert us from looking for contests for meaning and at rhetoric and power, contradictions, and multiple discourses, or what some now refer to as "heteroglossia."[6] It also falsely fixes the boundaries between groups in an absolute and artificial way.[7]

"Ideology" too has come to carry with it meanings that some social theorists want to shed. The Marxist alternative to culture, it has the virtues of seeming less unifying than culture. It can be pluralized even within one society, and is always linked to historically specific social groups assumed from the start to be engaged in struggles of domination and resistance. However, it retains, perhaps even more strongly than the notion of culture, the radical distinction between a realm of ideas and a material or social reality because of its historical association with a distinction between base and superstructure.[8] And even more problematically, it sets up an implicit opposition between itself, denoting a mystifying or at least motivated and interested vision of the world, and some sort of uninterested, unmotivated, and objective truth available either to a class or, perhaps more commonly, to the critical social scientist. Foucault uses discourse to suggest his rejection of these dualisms that are easily and sometimes unconsciously evoked by the notion of ideology.[9]

[. . .]"[D]iscourses . . . [are] . . . practices that systematically form the objects of which they speak" (Foucault 1972:49). For the final work discourse is meant to do, as social theory, is to suggest a concern not so much with meaning as with a kind of large-scale pragmatics. Taking texts and talk and all sorts of other social practices as productive of experience and constitutive of the realities in which we live and the truths with which we work, this approach also considers how power might produce discourses as well.[10] In suggesting that we attend to the efficacy of discourse, this newer and wider usage still resembles the more limited sociolinguistic uses outlined earlier. Yet it goes further by looking at more than speech, by recognizing the local, contradictory, and fragmented character of discourses, and by insisting that discourses be understood in relation not just to social life but to power.

Thus, the term [discourse], resonating with its many current uses, stands as a token of our common wariness of mentalist models, our refusal to treat language as simply reflecting thought or experience, and our insistence that all those productions in a community that could be considered cultural or ideological be analyzed as social practices, tied to relations of power as well as to sociability.

[D]iscourse, often as the situated social practices of people speaking, singing, orating, or writing to and about each other, [is] a point of entry for the study of emotion. [It] address[es] one or both of two issues: the discourse *on* emotions – scientific or everyday, Western or non-Western – and emotional discourses, that is, discourses that seem to have some affective content or effect. [. . .]

The turn here to discourse is a turn to detailed, empirical studies of conversation, poetics, rhetoric, and argument about and with emotional content. Building on the work of others who have explored facets of emotion in performance and language (Basso 1985; Brenneis 1987; Crapanzano 1989; Feld 1983; Good, Good, and Fischer 1988; Irvine 1982; Ochs and Schieffelin 1989; Sabini and Silver 1987 and 1988; B. Schieffelin and Ochs 1986; E. Schieffelin 1976; Urban 1988; White and Kirkpatrick 1985), we argue for a view of emotion as discursive practice. What advantages does this have for our understanding of emotion? What can those interested in emotion learn from considering its relation to discourse?

In contrast to other approaches, the emphasis on discourse in studying emotion keeps us fixed on the fact that emotions are phenomena that can be seen in social interaction, much of which is verbal. As the sociolinguist Gumperz has also said of discourse studies, "mere talk to produce sentences . . . does not by itself constitute communication. Only when a move has elicited a response can we say communication is taking place" (1982:1). Attention to discourse leads us therefore to study new problems, such as how an audience's response to emotional performances can be unpredictable given the former's ability to attend to only some parts of the performance and to make idiosyncratic sense of those parts. Attention to discourse also leads us to a more complex view of the multiple, shifting, and contested meanings possible in emotional utterances and interchanges, and from there to a less mono-lithic concept of emotion. The focus on discourse allows not only for insight into how emotion, like the discourse in which it participates, is informed by cultural themes and values, but also how it serves as an operator in a contentious field of social activity, how it affects a social field, and how it can serve as an idiom for communicating, not even necessar-ily about feelings but about such diverse matters as social conflict (White 1990), gender roles (Lutz 1990), or the nature of the ideal or deviant person (Fajans 1985).

The study of emotion as discourse allows us to explore how speech provides the means by which local views of emotion have their effects and take their significance. If earlier scholars who rejected the notion that emotion was sensation preferred the notion of emotion as judgment (Solomon 1976), their view has since been supplemented by the insight that judgments might better be viewed as socially contested evaluations of the world phrased in an emotional idiom and evident in everyday speech behavior. Rather than seeing them as expres-sive vehicles, we must understand emotional discourses as pragmatic acts and communicative performances. The more general interest in the social sciences in how language implements social reality coincides with the interest in how emotions are sociocultural facts. If emotions are social phenomena, discourse is crucial to understanding how they are so constituted.

[E]motion and discourse should not be treated as separate variables, the one pertaining to the private world of individual consciousness and the other to the public social world. Taking seriously Wittgenstein's (1966) insights about the relationship between emotion and language, articulated first in his description of what kind of "language-game" talk of joy and anger is, we argue that emotion talk must be interpreted as *in* and *about* social life rather than as veridically referential to some internal state.

Emotion should not be viewed, as our quotidian perspective might suggest, as a substance carried by the vehicle of discourse, expressed by means of discourse, or "squeezed through," and thereby perhaps distorted in, the shapes of language or speech. Rather, we should view emotional discourse as a form of social action that creates effects in the world, effects that are read in a culturally informed way by the audience for emotion talk. Emotion can be said to be *created in*, rather than shaped by, speech in the sense that it is postulated as an entity in language where its meaning to social actors is also elaborated. To say this is not to reduce the concept of emotion to the concept of speech, even though a discourse-centered approach might be construed as a rejection or obscuring of the body.

Although we focus on emotion as discourse, working to pry emotion loose from psychobiology, that does not mean that we do not recognize the possibility that emotions are also framed in most contexts as experiences that involve the whole person, including the body. Here Bourdieu's thoughts on "body hexis" are suggestive, providing ways of thinking about the fact that emotion is embodied without being forced to concede that it must be "natural" and not shaped by social interaction. He defines body hexis as a set of body techniques or postures that are learned habits or deeply ingrained dispositions that both reflect and reproduce the social relations that surround and constitute them. The child, for instance, learns these habits by reading, via the body rather than the mind's eye, the cultural texts of spaces and of other bodies (Bourdieu 1977:90).

Extending this definition to the emotions enables us to grasp how they, as cultural products, are reproduced in individuals in the form of embodied experience. To learn how, when, where, and by whom emotions ought to be enacted is to learn a set of body techniques including facial expressions, postures, and gestures. For example, rather than thinking or speaking the respect (*gabarog*) that helps reproduce a gender hierarchy on Ifaluk atoll in Micronesia, girls follow the curve of their mothers' backs in embodying the bent-over posture of respect. Similarly, emotions such as love or friendship that are thought to emanate from ineffable positive feelings between two people might be cued, Bourdieu notes (1977:82), by a sensed similarity of body hexis produced by being reared under similar physical and social conditions. We might eventually develop an analysis of the kinds of bodily discourse on emotion that includes emotional postures that are simultaneously (1) phenom-enologically experienced, (2) vehicles for symbolizing and affecting social relations (e.g., when angry glaring represents the imposition of moral obligation), and (3) practices that reveal the effects of power (as in gestures of respect and shame in many cultures).[11]

The move to ensure that emotions remain embodied, however, should be seen as more than an attempt to position them in the human body. Embodying the emotions also involves theoretically situating them in the social body such that one can examine how emotional discourses are formed by and in the shapes of the ecologies and political economies in which they arise.

Emotion can be studied as embodied discourse only after its social and cultural – its discursive – character has been fully accepted. To take language as more than a transparent medium for the communication of inner thoughts or experience, and to view speech as something essentially bound up with local power relations that is capable of socially con-structing and contesting realities, even subjectivity, is not to deny nonlinguistic "realities." It is simply to assert that things that are social, political, historically contingent, emergent, or constructed are both real and can have force in the world.

[T]he pragmatic force of emotion discourse and the social character of emotion [is shown] by how centrally bound up discourses on emotion (local theories about emotions) and emotional discourses (situated deployments of emotional linguistic forms) tend to be with social issues. Because we think that it will be more theoretically productive, we have made central questions about the ways emotion discourse can be related to the social. [. . .]

Two aspects of social relations emerge as crucially tied to emotion discourse: sociability and power relations. The links to sociability can be seen in the salience of emotion language in settings where solidarity is being encouraged, challenged, or negotiated, or in the essentially interactional nature of discourse as it engages performers or speakers and audiences or interlocutors. Fajans (1985) had earlier shown that the core of Baining (New Britain) emotional discourse was concerned with threats to social cohesion; a central emotion term, translated as "hunger," was used to talk about the importance of ties to others and their mediation through food exchange. [. . .]

Recent work has begun to show that power seems even more thoroughly bound up with such discourses. We look particularly for the ways power relations determine what can, cannot, or must be said about self and emotion, what is taken to be true or false about them, and what only some individuals can say about them. The real innovation is in showing how emotion discourses establish, assert, challenge, or reinforce power or status differences. Discourses on fear have been singled out in a number of studies of colonial violence as crucial aspects of the discursive practices of dominant groups (Stoler 1985; Taussig 1987). Talk of fear of the dominated other in colonial contexts can be interpreted as a means by which powerful groups accomplish several purposes. They justify their suppression of those their rhetoric of fear implicitly paints as powerful and threatening to erupt, as Taussig (1987) argues occurred among rubber collectors in Columbia in the early part of this century. As Stoler (1985) demonstrates in the case of Dutch planters in Indonesia, they also thereby bargain with other elites for the resources and support needed to face down the purported threat.[12]

Scheper-Hughes's fieldwork in a Brazilian underclass community traces the relationship between emotional discourse and political economy. In one analysis (1985), she shows how a purportedly universal mother love is replaced by an emotional rhetoric of detached waiting regarding young infants because of the high infant mortality rate. In another (1988), she discusses how the syndrome *nervios* is part of discursive practice that transforms the symptoms of hunger into the less politically charged terms of emotional anxiety and "nerves" and of individual pathology, whose therapy is tranquilizers rather than a redistribution of food, wealth, and power.[13]

[. . .] In suggesting that we consider not emotions but the discourses of emotion, [we] do not deny the force of emotion and subjective experience. [We] do advocate a shift in focus that may be illuminating. Arguing that the reality of emotion is social, cultural, political, and historical, just as is its current location in the psyche or the natural body, discourses on emotion and emotional discourses are commentaries on the practices essential to social relations. As part of the politics of everyday life, these discourses are not, therefore, just the stuff of psychological anthropology but of sociocultural and linguistic theory as well. [This is] both a nonindividualized and a nonreductionist approach to emotion and a more dynamic socially and politically grounded analysis of all discursive practice.

Notes

1   For recent reviews, see Heelas (1986), Levy and Wellenkamp (1987), and Lutz and White (1986).
2   For a recent consideration of anthropology's (with the exception of feminist anthropology's) role in developing cultural critiques, see Marcus and Fischer (1986).
3   This shift may have corresponded to the general process of medicalization and normalization that, for Foucault (1978), characterize the modern age.
4   See also Foucault (1983) for a clear discussion of his views on the relationship between subjectivity and subjection or the creation of the individual through disciplinary power.

5   Foucault's assertion, of course, calls for ethnographic evidence, the beginnings of which Lutz (1988:53–80) provides. It would be worth speculating further whether the proliferation of emotion discourse in American life, combined with the construal of emotion as a private and subjective state, might not both confirm a sense of self as separate (in giving the individual "experiences" of his or her own – as Lutz (1986:299), Riesman (1983:123), and Foucault (1985:5) have argued in linking the construction of "experience" and the sense of individuality) – and provide an idiom for asserting the existence of bonds between people in the face of the actual attenuation of such bonds by mobility, distance, and the social fragmentation of class, gender, and race.

6   Heteroglossia is a term that seems to have filtered into anthropology, both in the narrow linguistic sense of many languages and in the larger sense of many discourses, through Bakhtin (1981). For a critical discussion of the absence of social theory in and the conservative implications of most of the work on culture done under the rubric of cognitive anthropology, see Keesing (1987). The notion of culture promoted by interpretive anthropology has many critics, but Asad's (1983) consideration of the problems as related to the study of religion is particularly intelligent.

7   See Appadurai (1988) for a persuasive argument that "natives," people from certain faraway places who belong to those places and are somehow incarcerated in those places and especially in their "mode of thought," are "creatures of the anthropological imagination" – that is, produced by anthropological discourse. For a discussion of the similarity of the concepts of culture and race, see Mitchell (1988:105).

8   See Williams (1973, 1977) and Comaroff (1985) for attempts to mediate this divide.

9   For an elaboration of the problems with ideology, see Foucault (1980:117–18).

10   Foucault himself substituted the term 'apparatus' (*dispositif*) for discourse in some of his later work on sexuality in order to emphasize that he was concerned with "a thoroughly heterogeneous ensemble" of nondiscursive elements – statements, writings, architectural forms, rules, institutions, etc. – that are related to one another in varying ways and have, as a formation, "a dominant strategic function" (1980:194–5).

11   See Scheper-Hughes and Lock (1987) for a view of the "three bodies" that can be applied to the three bodies of emotion just described.

12   She also shows the power of the denial of fear by those same planters. Denial or negation both posits a fear and a threat and claims to have conquered them (cf. Kress and Hodge 1978).

13   See also Hochschild (1983) on the relationship between power and the emotional practices of service workers, such as stewardesses, in the United States.

References

Abu-Lughod, Lila. 1986. *Veiled Sentiments: Honor and Poetry in a Bedouin Society*. Berkeley: University of California Press.

—— 1990. Shifting Politics in Bedouin Love Poetry. In L. Abu-Lughod and C. Lutz, eds., *Language and the Politics of Emotion*. Cambridge: Cambridge University Press, pp. 24–45.

Appadurai, Arjun. 1988. Putting Hierarchy in Its Place. *Cultural Anthropology* 3:36–49.

Asad, Talal. 1983. Anthropological Conceptions of Religion: Reflections on Geertz. *Man* (n.s.) 18:237–59.

Bakhtin, Mikhail M. 1981. *The Dialogic Imagination*. M. Holquist, ed. Austin: University of Texas Press.

Basso, Ellen. 1985. *A Musical View of the Universe*. Philadelphia: University of Pennsylvania Press.

Bourdieu, Pierre. 1977. *Outline of a Theory of Practice*. Cambridge: Cambridge University Press.

Brenneis, Donald. 1987. Performing Passions: Aesthetics and Politics in an Occasionally Egalitarian Community. *American Ethnologist* 14:236–50.

Briggs, Jean. 1970. *Never in Anger*. Cambridge, MA: Harvard University Press.

Cancian, Francesca. 1987. *Love in America: Gender and Self-Development*. Cambridge: Cambridge University Press.

Comaroff, Jean. 1985. *Body of Power, Spirit of Resistance: The Culture and History of a South African People*. Chicago: University of Chicago Press.

Crapanzano, Vincent. 1989. Preliminary Notes on the Glossing of Emotions. *Kroeber Anthropological Society Papers* Nos. 69–70:78–85.

Elias, Norbert. 1978 (1939). *The History of Manners*, trans. E. Jephcott. New York: Pantheon Books.

Fajans, Jane. 1985. The Person in Social Context: The Social Character of Baining "Psychology." In

G. White and J. Kirkpatrick, eds., *Person, Self, and Experience: Exploring Pacific Ethnopsychologies.* Berkeley: University of California Press, pp. 367–97.

Feld, Steven. 1983. *Sound and Sentiment; Birds, Weeping, Poetics and Song in Kaluli Expression.* Philadelphia: University of Pennsylvania Press.

Foucault, Michel. 1972. *The Archaeology of Knowledge and the Discourse on Language.* New York: Pantheon.

—— 1978. *The History of Sexuality*, Vol. 1. New York: Pantheon.

—— 1980. *Power/Knowledge.* Colin Gordon, ed. New York: Pantheon.

—— 1983. On the Genealogy of Ethics: An Overview of Work in Progress. In H. Dreyfus and P. Rabinow, *Beyond Structuralism and Hermeneutics*, 2nd ed. Chicago: University of Chicago Press, pp. 229–52.

—— 1985. *The Use of Pleasure.* Vol. 2 of *The History of Sexuality.* New York: Random House.

Gardiner, H. M., Ruth C. Metcalf, and John Beebe-Center. 1970 (1937). *Feeling and Emotion: A History of Theories.* Westport, CT: Greenwood Press.

Geertz, Clifford. 1973. Person, Time, and Conduct in Bali. In *The Interpretation of Cultures.* New York: Basic Books, pp. 360–411.

—— 1987. *Works and Lives.* Stanford: Stanford University Press.

Geertz, Hildred. 1959. The Vocabulary of Emotion: A Study of Javanese Socialization Processes. *Psychiatry* 22:225–37.

Good, Mary-Jo Delvecchio, and Byron Good. 1988. Ritual, the State, and the Transformation of Emotional Discourse in Iranian Society. *Culture, Medicine, and Psychiatry* 12(1):43–63.

Good, Mary-Jo Delvecchio, Byron Good, and Michael M. J. Fischer. 1988. *Emotion, Illness and Healing in Middle Eastern Societies* (Special Issue). *Culture, Medicine and Psychiatry* 12(1).

Gumperz, John. 1982. *Discourse Strategies.* Cambridge: Cambridge University Press.

Harré, Rom, and Robert Finlay-Jones. 1986. Emotion Talk Across Times. In Rom Harré, ed., *The Social Construction of Emotions.* Oxford: Basil Blackwell, pp. 220–33.

Heelas, Paul. 1986. Emotion Talk Across Cultures. In Rom Harré, ed., *The Social Construction of Emotions.* Oxford: Basil Blackwell, pp. 234–66.

Hiatt, L. R. 1984. Your Mother-in-Law Is Poison. *Man* 19:183–98.

Hill, Jane. 1987. Weeping and Coherence in Narrative and Selfhood: The Sorrows of Dona Maria. Paper presented at the annual meetings of the American Anthropological Association, Chicago.

Hochschild, Arlie. 1983. *The Managed Heart.* Berkeley: University of California Press.

Hopper, Paul. 1987. Emergent Grammar. *Proceedings of the 13th Annual Meeting of the Berkeley Linguistics Society.* Berkeley, CA: Berkeley Linguistics Society, pp. 139–57.

Howell, Signe. 1981. Rules Not Words. In P. Heelas and A. Lock, eds., *Indigenous Psychologies.* London: Academic Press, pp. 133–43.

Irvine, Judith. 1982. Language and Affect: Some Cross-Cultural Issues. In H. Byrnes, ed., *Contemporary Perceptions of Language: Interdisciplinary Dimensions.* Washington, DC: Georgetown University Press, pp. 31–47.

Jackson, S. W. 1985. Acedia the Sin and Its Relationship to Sorrow and Melancholia. In A. Kleinman and B. Good, eds., *Culture and Depression: Studies in the Anthropology and Cross-Cultural Psychiatry of Affect and Disorder.* Berkeley: University of California Press, pp. 43–62.

Keesing, Roger. 1987. Models, "Folk" and "Cultural": Paradigms Regained? In D. Holland and N. Quinn, eds., *Cultural Models in Language and Thought.* Cambridge: Cambridge University Press, pp. 369–93.

Kress, Gunther, and Robert Hodge. 1979. *Language as Ideology.* London: Routledge & Kegan Paul.

Labov, William. 1972. Rules for Ritual Insults. In *Language in the Inner City.* Philadelphia: University of Pennsylvania Press.

Levy, Robert. 1973. *Tahitians: Mind and Experience in the Society Islands.* Chicago: University of Chicago Press.

Levy, Robert, and Jane Wellenkamp. 1987. Methodology in the Anthropological Study of Emotion. In R. Plutchik and H. Kellerman, eds., *The Measurement of Emotions.* New York: Academic Press.

Lindholm, Charles. 1982. *Generosity and Jealousy: The Swat Pukhtun of Northern Pakistan.* New York: Columbia University Press.

Lutz, Catherine. 1986. Emotion, Thought, and Estrangement: Emotion as a Cultural Category. *Cultural Anthropology* 1:405–36.

—— 1988. *Unnatural Emotions: Everyday Sentiments on a Micronesian Atoll and Their Challenge to Western Theory.* Chicago: University of Chicago Press.

—— 1990. Engendered Emotion: Gender, Power, and, the Rhetoric of Emotional Control in American Discourse. In L. Abu-Lughod and C. Lutz, eds., *Language and the Politics of Emotion*. Cambridge: Cambridge University Press, pp. 69–91.

Lutz, Catherine, and Geoffrey White. 1986. The Anthropology of Emotions. *Annual Review of Anthropology* 15:405–36.

MacFarlane, Alan. 1987. *The Culture of Capitalism*. Oxford: Basil Blackwell.

Marcus, George, and Michael M. J. Fischer. 1986. *Anthropology as Cultural Critique*. Chicago: University of Chicago Press.

Mitchell, Timothy. 1988. *Colonising Egypt*. Cambridge: Cambridge University Press.

Myers, Fred. 1979. Emotions and the Self: A Theory of Personhood and Political Order Among Pintupi Aborigines. *Ethos* 7:343–70.

—— 1986. *Pintupi Country, Pintupi Self: Sentiment, Place, and Politics Among Western Desert Aborigines*. Washington, DC: Smithsonian Institution Press.

Obeyesekere, Gananath. 1985. Depression, Buddhism and the Work of Culture in Sri Lanka. In A. Kleinman and B. Good, eds., *Culture and Depression: Studies in the Anthropology and Cross-Cultural Psychiatry of Affect and Disorder*. Berkeley: University of California Press, pp. 134–52.

Ochs, Elinor, and Bambi Schieffelin. 1989. Language Has a Heart. *Text* 9:7–25.

Radden, Jennifer. 1987. Melancholy and Melancholia. In David Levin, ed., *Pathologies of the Modern Self*. New York: New York University Press, pp. 231–50.

Riesman, Paul. 1977. *Freedom in Fulani Social Life*. Chicago: University of Chicago Press.

—— 1983. On the Irrelevance of Child Rearing Practices for the Formation of Personality. *Culture, Medicine and Psychiatry* 7:103–29.

Robarchek, Clayton. 1979. Learning to Fear: A Case Study of Emotional Conditioning. *American Ethnologist* 6:555–67.

Rosaldo, Michelle Z. 1980. *Knowledge and Passion: Ilongot Notions of Self and Social Life*. Cambridge: Cambridge University Press.

—— 1983. The Shame of Headhunters and the Autonomy of Self. *Ethos* 11:135–51.

—— 1984. Toward an Anthropology of Self and Feeling. In R. Shweder and R. LeVine, eds., *Culture Theory: Essays on Mind, Self, and Emotion*. Cambridge: Cambridge University Press, pp. 137–57.

Sabini, John, and Maury Silver. 1987. Character: The Moral and the Aesthetic. *International Journal of Moral and Social Studies* 2:189–201.

—— 1988. Emotion, Character, and Responsibility. In F. Schoemann, ed., *Responsibility, Character, and the Emotions*. New York: Cambridge University Press.

Saussure, Ferdinand de. 1966. *Course in General Linguistics*. New York: McGraw-Hill.

Scheff, Thomas. 1977. The Distancing of Emotion in Ritual. *Current Anthropology* 18:483–505.

Scheper-Hughes, Nancy. 1985. Culture, Scarcity and Maternal Thinking: Maternal Detachment and Infant Survival in a Brazilian Shantytown. *Ethos* 13:291–317.

—— 1987. The Madness of Hunger: Sickness, Delirium and Human Needs. Paper presented at the annual meetings of the American Anthropological Association, Chicago.

Scheper-Hughes, Nancy, and Margaret Lock. 1987. The Mindful Body: A Prolegomenon to Future Work in Medical Anthropology. *Medical Anthropology Quarterly* 1:6–41.

Schieffelin, Bambi, and Elinor Ochs, eds. 1986. *Language Socialization Across Cultures*. Cambridge: Cambridge University Press.

Schieffelin, Edward L. 1976. *The Sorrow of the Lonely and the Burning of the Dancers*. New York: St. Martin's Press.

Sherzer, Joel. 1987. A Discourse-Centered Approach to Language and Culture. *American Anthropologist* 89:295–309.

Solomon, Robert. 1976. *The Passions*. New York: Anchor Press/Doubleday.

Sontag, Susan. 1977. *Illness as Metaphor*. New York: Farrar, Straus.

Spiro, Melford. 1965. Religious Systems as Culturally Constituted Defense Mechanisms. In M. Spiro, ed., *Context and Meaning in Cultural Anthropology*. New York: Free Press, pp. 100–13.

Stearns, Carol, and Peter Stearns. 1986. *Anger: The Struggle for Emotional Control in America's History*. Chicago: University of Chicago Press.

Stoler, Ann. 1985. *Capitalism and Confrontation in Sumatra's Plantation Belt, 1870–1979*. New Haven, CT: Yale University Press.

Taussig, Michael. 1987. *Shamanism, Colonialism, and the Wild Man: A Study in Terror and Healing*. Chicago: University of Chicago Press.

Tedlock, Dennis. 1983. *The Spoken Word and the Work of Interpretation*. Philadelphia: University of Pennsylvania Press.

—— 1987a. Questions Concerning Dialogical Anthropology. *Journal of Anthropological Research* 43(4):325–37.

—— 1987b. On the Representation of Discourse in Discourse. *Journal of Anthropological Research* 43(4):343–4.

Tyler, Steven. 1978. *The Said and the Unsaid*. New York: Academic Press.

Urban, Greg. 1988. Ritual Wailing in Amerindian Brazil. *American Anthropologist* 90:385–400.

White, Geoffrey, and John Kirkpatrick, eds. 1985. *Person, Self and Experience: Exploring Pacific Ethnopsychologies*. Berkeley: University of California Press.

White, Geoffrey. 1990. Moral Discourse and the Rhetoric of Emotions. In Lila Abu-Lughod and Catherine Lutz, eds., *Language and the Politics of Emotion*. Cambridge: Cambridge University Press, pp. 46–68.

Williams, Raymond. 1973. Base and Superstructure in Marxist Cultural Theory. *New Left Review* 82:3–16.

—— 1977. *Marxism and Literature*. Oxford: Oxford University Press.

Wittgenstein, Ludwig. 1966. *Zettel*. G. Anscombe, trans. London: Basil Blackwell.

Chapter 6

Jennifer Biddle

SHAME

The sun is getting dim. Will I pay for who I've been?[1]

IN MANY WAYS, I didn't want to write this paper. Reproducing it here is no easier. It is risky. Painful. Like the itch to pull the scab from the still healing wound, I resist doing damage here to what needs protecting most. Shame is powerful stuff, contagious and self-propagating. To discuss it is likely to invoke it, for so ashamed are we in Eurocentric cultures—so shame bound am *I*—that it is shameful, shame-making, even to speak of shame.[2] Which explains why in part there is comparatively little material available on the subject. And why, in part, I have felt compelled to write about it. The models available do not provide the meaning(s) I seek.[3] I also want to begin this paper as it will end, in evoking a certain impossible and compelling ambivalence—the very hallmark of shame.

As much as shame seeks to avert itself—there is no feeling more painful—shame seeks to confess. To be heard, to be borne by another, to find a witness—shame seeks to be allowed the very conditions denied it in its rupture—recognition by another. For shame arises from a failure to be recognised. 'Rape by looking' is how Sartre[4] describes the violence of its force, for in shame we are reduced to being an object only for the other's jurisdiction. Sentenced without trial, shame judges, ridicules, terrorises whatever pretence we might hold of being autonomous, successful, self-determining subjects. Eternally caught with our hands where they shouldn't be, in an instant shame reminds us of the state of dependency in which our lives began, and how vulnerable we remain to an approving, an allowing other. Shame is an acknowledgment which the body volunteers virtually to the other. Hot blush on the skin, dropping of the eyes, drooping of the eyelids, withdrawing to avoid the naked, exposed, alienated feelings of shame—these are effects tangible, evident, witnessable. A most social emotion, shame communicates, or as Eve Kosofsky Sedgwick puts it, shame *performs*, dependent as it is upon 'interpellation by a witness'.[5]

The very performative nature of shame's expression is nowhere more evident than in 'man's best friend'. Mimetic beasts *extraordinaire*: dogs perform shame. Slinking away 'tail between the legs', skulking around or hiding under the couch—dogs at least appear to know when they have transgressed the expectation of their masters; when they've been caught out. As Silvan Tomkins notes, dogs display the self-consciousness, the self-doubt, the human condition, that we recognise as shame.[6] But never of course where it matters most. That is, in the realm of what 'We' consider the 'private'—matters of toiletry, of the sexual, of the genitals. A sense of the private is to shame as virtue is to sin literally; the gift Eve gave to Adam in the apple. The story of creation, the genesis of social life as we know it, is a story of shame.[7] Adam and Eve 'were both naked and were not ashamed' prior to the eating from the tree of life.[8] To know good from evil, right from wrong, private from public, is to know shame. And it is clearly this that dogs *do not* know. As Freud remarks in a footnote to *Civilization and Its Discontents*, dogs are found contemptible because they are 'not ashamed' of their 'sexual functions' and have 'no horror of excrement'.[9] Dogs do the very things every human society disallows—fuck indiscriminately, that is, continuously and publicly disregard the incest taboo, and literally, 'eat shit'. And it is this very vacillation, the capacity to display shame but not to be constrained by it, that makes dogs so privileged in European society. Dogs are 'man's best friends' because they do these things so shamelessly, *despite* knowing—performing—shame.[10] And I wonder, in turn, if this is not more what Warlpiri people mean in calling persons who do not heed the proper constraints and prohibitions on sexual relations *jarntu-piya*, dog-like. Really, dogs ought to know better. As should people. Not surprising, it is us *kardiya*—European, Whitefellas—whom I most often heard referred to in that way, *jarntu-piya, dog-like*, as we behave and outside 'proper' human standards and expectations *like dogs* as we are seen to be.[11]

These performative aspects of shame deal something of a cruel blow, however, to the human sufferer. The emotion that makes us most want to disappear makes us appear all the more vividly. Fire hydrant red, the surface of the skin blushes and betrays the desire for self-effacement in shame, lighting up a certain beacon, as it were, to the very wish that the floor, the ground, the world, something, anything, will swallow up the mortified indignant self. The physiological responses of the body which act to reduce communication when the self feels distressed and frightened—avoiding eye contact, shoulders slumping, head bowing—are actions which ironically, even cruelly perhaps, communicate most clearly.[12] Even at its most dejected, or perhaps precisely then, the self beckons to the other. Both warning and appeal, shame like the hot sweat terror of the nightmare or the reddening flush of fever seeks the cool, reassuring hand of the other's re-embrace. But is, of course, the very register of its denial.

That it is the skin which registers shame is not arbitrary. The skin, the epidermis, is understood in more traditional figurings of the body as the outer covering of the material body; the limit, as it were, to the bounded individual self. According to Merleau-Ponty, it is the skin, flesh that unites and dis-unites us with others ultimately. He privileges 'haptic sensibility' because our own corporeality is called into being each and every time we observe another, through the extension, project or retraction of our 'intentional arc' or 'corporeal schema'.[13] As Alphonso Lingis succinctly puts it, 'to recognise another . . . is to be touched by a body'.[14] We make objects of ourselves, object of others, and are made objects by others through our fleshly inhabitations. And through touching again such distinctions reverse and exchange and dissolve altogether in the 'intertwining', as Merleau Ponty calls it, the mimetic interchangeability of ourselves with others as subject *and* object. In shame, the self expresses itself where it finds itself virtually, negatively differentiated, severed as it is, from the other; naked, exposed, and replete in its vulnerability; worn, like the very fig leaves that Adam and Eve first adorned to cover their shame, on the skin.

In stressing here as I do the register of the skin in the painful self differentiation that shame evokes, I have cause to hesitate. For the blush has been seen as a sign of no small importance in evolutionary theorising. Darwin found the blush to be 'the most peculiar and human of all expressions', a capacity animals, despite dogs' appearance to the contrary, are not deemed to possess.[15] The blush distinguishes man from animal. And in the tendency of evolutionary theory, as predictable as it is pernicious, what distinguishes man from animal separates man from man, or more precisely, white man from black man. For black people according to other writers in the nineteenth century did not blush, or rather, could not be *seen* to blush, and thus were closer 'to the beasts who feel no shame'.[16] Moreover, black persons were seen to live in hordes, tribes and in contexts where clearly questionable moral standards were displayed, and therefore were understood as lacking the proper displays of privacy that civilisation commands. Which adds another dimension altogether to Kosofsky Sedgwick's figuration of shame as dependent upon 'interpellation by a witness'.[17] For the witness here not only has the jurisdiction to confer shame, but also ultimately to deny it.

All these other-directed, communicating and performing aspects of shame are not, of course, how shame is experienced. There is no emotion that individuates, that isolates, that differentiates the self, more. As Tomkins says, shame is 'an experience of the self by the self'.[18] In the hot sleepless nights that ensue when the *how could I be so stupid* scenario replays itself, runs and re-runs again like a B-grade matinee, relentless, predictable and compelling; in the narcissistic retreat to bed and Family Blocks of Cadbury Chocolate; in the acute self condemnation and punitive redress—there is no reasoning with, nor quieting of shame's torment. Scud-missile-accurate, shame is not so much an affect of self failure, as it is a punishment for self failure.[19] Shame is experienced less as about what the self has done but what the self *is*. And hence the desire to 'self efface' as Kosofsky Sedgwick puts it. To desist, literally. Or, the next best thing, to withdraw into the comforts of symbolic thumb sucking, the return to the womb, with the likely slippage into the self-denigration of depression where the diminution in self regard and high degree of self reproach conjoin with the inhibition of the self. The overwhelming nature of shame's interruptive force has been closely tied to the paralysis and inactivity likely in melancholia and depression.[20]

The self-failure feeling of shame is, of course, like all forms of social response, learned. Shame can arise from any number of sources where parental disapproval frustrates, bewilders or wounds the symbiotic bond of mirroring and mutuality that initially constitutes the infant's experience. The so-called 'disgust/contempt response' has been identified as a major source of shame; a surprisingly punitive response often denied by parents.[21] Socialisation is anything but benign. The brief flash of the 'contempt/disgust' face—accompanied or not by the verb 'yuck' or other equally non-appreciative noises—nostrils flared, nose squished up, lips sneering, eyes widened or the turning away of the face altogether. The infant perceives by this that logically, if the other is disgusted, the self must be repugnant, that the self, in short, has failed. Shame is a direct mimetic introversion of the other's negation; self failure is an internalisation of the other's abject rejection. The disgust/ contempt response occurs at a time when the infant's dependency on the other—on their presence, their care and thus, on their love—is total. Any withdrawal of the love of the other is not only perceived as life threatening, it actually may be life threatening to the infant.[22] What is experienced in shame is a virtual loss, the abrupt withdrawal of the other, the absence of love, an interruption so acute precisely because it runs counter to infantile expectation. That shame remains an experience which manifests as an interruption through-out adult life and demonstrates the ongoing dependent expectation the self has on the other's benevolent witness.

In short, shame itself is a major source of shame,[23] which serves to explain the contagious nature of shame in adult life. Of course, all emotions are somewhat 'catchy'. Anger is likely to produce anger as a defensive response; happiness and effervescence particularly are likely to be infectious, what we called at school *contact high*, the feeling you'd get of being *high* around others who were, even though you weren't, an effect Quentin Tarantino perfects in *Pulp Fiction* in the remarkable 'feel good' scene where, after shooting up, John Travolta drives, cruises, flies, his convertible and so do we.[24] But shame is even more contagious. No one writing on shame fails to mention its inordinately contingent and contiguous effects. Witnessing someone else being shamed and/or the converse, witnessing when someone ought to be ashamed and they aren't, is likely to induce shame in response. 'Contact' shame may be just as painfully experienced, and equally identity delineating, as a direct shame response. Indeed, that the two are so closely related (it seems to me, confused as they are from childhood on), is what makes shame so powerful and so social an emotion. For it is also the parents' inability to see themselves as separate from the infant, and not only the infant's transitivism, that gives rise to shame. Like dogs, infants take pleasure in their own bodies and excrement. This pleasure may produce in the 'properly' socialised adult, an 'ashamed' response: at once ashamed on behalf of the child (as witness) and on behalf of themselves (as a parent, they can never be simply a witness, both introjecting and projecting themselves in and on the body and activities of the child). In turn, parental shame is mimicked, introjected and displayed again by the child who may re-infest the parent. A certain identity–identificatory cycle of symbiosis and mimesis is engendered even as it is broken in shame.

It is the very identity *making* aspect of shame that most interests me here. The rejection by the other in a direct shame event makes for a most distinct self boundary, for what differentiates the self from the other constitutes self, dependent as identity necessarily is on difference. But self differentiation is necessarily provisional. The complex recognition of the self in another which 'contact' shame evokes demonstrates the ongoing debt to the other, for, and in, self recognition. This double movement of shame, it seems to me, is critical, at once producing the very possibility of self identity and destabilising it in the process. A sign-post of sociability, shame is the very 'threshold between introversion and extroversion';[25] the differential between immersion in the other and self distinction; the dilemma and danger of being both one of the crowd and the star performer.

Contrary to expectation, it may be *because* shame does not attribute specific cause that it plays a crucial role in the development of what we know as the self. Shame may be a particularly demonstrative 'lived contestation' of the law in the kind of terms United States feminist philosopher, Judith Butler, describes,[26] for the terms of the law are not only exposed, but reiterated through the very act of shame's expression. It is the un-named, unspoken aspects of self-identity—bodily bits and functions, physical appearance, sexual practices and preferences—which shame articulates. Bodily and sexualised aspects of the self are considered to be private experiences and expressions, belonging to 'me' alone. The self is acutely identified in the issues and experiences concomitant with shame in part because these self-identifying aspects and affiliations are not consciously or discursively formulated, even if they are socially coded and normatively regulated. Kosofsky Sedgwick calls shame 'a kind of free radical' because it can and does attach itself to a variety of contexts and things which, as a general rule, are not knowable or predictable in advance.[27]

It is this that appears ultimately to distinguish shame from the closely related negative affect of guilt. As the work of Helen Lewis suggests, guilt is an affect associated more with formalised rules and norms.[28] One is guilty of doing or not doing some *thing*. Reparation and retribution belong to the structure of guilt because of its activity oriented causation, and activity oriented potential resolution.[29] Doing something in relation to the other whom we have failed assuages us from feeling guilty (if temporarily).[30] In guilt, it is another who we feel has suffered, and the self who is to blame. And thus, guilt is other-focussed in the self's attempt to resolve the negative affect. But shame shares little of this activity-based cause and resolve structuring. It cannot make amends or ask forgiveness, for who is at fault ultimately? The other for catching out the unsuspecting self? Or is the bad, offensive, ultimately abject self who is to blame? Shame results in inactivity and paralysis because the transgression is given no specific attribute, even if, childishly (which is precisely the point) it is at once *both* the other *and* the self who is to blame. In short, shame seems far less to be about normative prohibitions and repression than guilt does. It is less identified with specific rules and more generally concerned with the very boundary between self and other.

Shame also differs from guilt developmentally. Some recent work indicates that infant-ile shame develops earlier than the self conscious, ego-dependent affect of guilt—between three and seven months, as opposed to two to three years of age.[31] That shame-responses emerge in the primary state of narcissism before cognitive notions of prohibitions or indeed an independent self emerges which knows it has transgressed, may help to explain why shame is perhaps more acutely experienced, more painfully felt, as being about the self in totality, than guilt is.

Shame is not only inherently ambivalent, but it serves to structure identity ambiva-lently. For the self is positioned impossibly between, on the one hand, the desire to be loved by, and to be like, the parent/other whose identity it depends on for its own. And, on the other hand, its own desires and impulses, including the desire for self-definition through differentiation, that is, the desire to reject—or indeed create—a shaming-response. Self identity, in fact, comes into being precisely at this moment, for the self in shame does not completely renounce or give up the interest in the interrupted act. 'Temptations are merely increased by constant frustration' we know from Freud.[32] Identity is most manifest when it fails—either to meet the approval of the other or to fulfil self-pleasure in the activity interrupted. And shame ensures the failure of both simultaneously. Indeed, it is the failure to meet either the demands of the self or the other that seems to me to make shame so potent, so productive and so painful an emotion. The virtual vexation of unsatisfied desire; the material bearing of the unbearable; a loss that cannot be incorporated on either side of a preposterous equation—shame arises as an impossible and yet necessary imperative of the continuously emergent self, bound to the very other it is equally bound to fail in order for its very identity.

To imagine that somehow one might be freed from the force of shame, liberated from its repressive and normative coercions, is rendered problematic in this kind of account which locates self-identity as bound by and to shame. Further, it is a kind of psychic-suicide. For to try and do away with shame in its entirety is literally to throw the baby out with the bath water. But the movement to embrace shame—therefore to see its positive role in self development—is often uncritically made. Schneider's account, for one recent example, positions shame as a properly humanising and socially respectful emotion.[33] The properly socialised self should accept the restraint imposed by the other—what he calls 'discretion shame'—in order to avoid degradation and disapproval, or what he calls 'disgrace-shame'. In other words, if one has a properly developed sense of shame, it ought to keep one from feeling ashamed. And while I may agree with his formulation here, the problem is *how do you know what that 'proper sense of shame' is?* For a 'proper sense of shame' has not been equal in its distribution nor magnanimous in its effects. It is, after all, the prostitute who is shameless, but the gentleman, let us not forget, who is discreet. Sexual difference is not one factor among others in shame.[34]

According to Georges Bataille it is women's position alone to signify shame, that is, to acknowledge the taboo broken in the sexual act.[35] For Bataille, following Freud, all sexual acts must be perceived to be illicit. It is the presence of taboo, that is, the presence of the sacred, of religion, and thus of eroticism in social life, that separates man from animal and, in turn, ensures the reproduction of human society. In Bataille's formulation, put crudely, human reproduction is dependent upon eroticism, eroticism dependent on shame, and shame, in turn, dependent upon woman.

'Accepting the taboo', or rather, the failure to accept the taboo, has been nothing less than the defining characteristic of feminine subjectivity, and Bataille is not alone here in his figurations. For what, if not shame, did Madame Bovary die of? And was it not shame ultimately that caused Anna Karenina to throw herself under the train after Vronsky's departure? And as for Hester Prynne, was she not made to wear the scarlet letter A in place of her very lack of shame, the badge literally serving to substitute for her lack of discretion—red lantern hanging in the window of the brothel, rouge to the courtesan's cheek?[36]

Lest all of this sound very nineteenth-century and no longer relevant, it should perhaps be remembered that it was just last year that Hawthorne's novel was made into a major Hollywood film.[37] And I am Hester as all women are Hester (maybe despite Demi Moore) and so my father reminded me. The first time I wore makeup was in the fashion of the mid-1970s—all purple eye shadow and frosted pink lip balm my cousin taught me to apply with the tip of my little finger and green nail polish after Liza Minelli in *Cabaret* and, no doubt, mine was a piebald and nasty effect. But it did not feel that way. At least not until my father called me a *painted lady* and commanded that I was not to leave the house until I *scrubbed my face*. The blush I had so carefully applied high on my cheekbones like the lady at Sears and Roebuck had said, was nothing compared to the literal blush that flooded my face then, and now again, as I tell this story.

But shame is not only a most telling affect in the development of the self. It is also a telling affect in the anthropological endeavour. And not telling, for shame also works to silence. *Truth or Dare?*—anthropology, like the adolescent party game, is structured by both the limits of shame, and breaking with its restraints.

Of course, that anthropology shares affective affinity with shame is no great revelation. What else is an anthropologist if not someone who is by definition fearless, unabashed, audacious—the inveterate adventurer; the insatiable traveller? But here again, the working of shame and its gendering is evident. The best known anthropological practitioner is a woman. The marked term, as it were, making for notoriety. Infamous indeed is Margaret Mead, with all the sexual and sexist undertones implied; conjoined, as she and her work have become, where the travel, the exotic places, her various husbands and lovers and sex itself, metonymically all unite. The slide from the bold to the hussy is inevitable. As it recently figured in the weekend magazine, the name Margaret Mead has become 'an immediate and enduring metaphor for steamy things that happened in torrid, languid jungles and gave her a reputation'.[38] In short, it is *shamelessness* which Margaret Mead is best known for. As is the practice of anthropology itself.[39]

Anthropologists intentionally put themselves in the out-of-place, in the wrong place, and thus, the place occupied by shame. Even if it is never taught in undergraduate courses, this is the first principle of the ethnographer's sensibility—to enhance awareness through being out of place *oneself*. Field work, like shame, exalts self-difference. In the classic ethnographic tradition, it may be Azande, Mountain Arapesh or Warlpiri culture which is written about. But that understanding, that demarcation of cultural difference, can only come into being through self-delineation, self-differentiation. It is the ethnographer's virtual experience that provides the basis for understanding similarity and difference. Their very bodies, their own selves stand representatively, but also literally for, and as, their culture in the field. Not quite the sacrificial lamb or the rat in the laboratory maze, nevertheless the anthropologist's corporeality provides a certain testing site. The mirror that the other holds up to the anthropologist at once heightens, delineates and disarms the certainty of self-definition. It is not the other who is the foreigner in field work—it is the self. 'In the mirror one always sees oneself looking', Adam Phillips notes, 'the foreigner allows you to be yourself by making a foreigner out of you'.[40]

Being a foreigner—that is, being selfconscious of one's difference—is the terrain of shame. The vulnerability apparent in the child's need to identify—a vulnerability which makes children extremely prone to shame[41]—is no less apparent in anthropologists, dependent as they are on recognition by, and of, the other. A recognition likely, at best, to be fraught. Or at least it was in my field experience. Mostly I tried to make myself disappear, walking as I did each morning to the school, in the early days of what they call in the literature 'the first and most uncomfortable stage of field work'.[42] You know, like you do when you walk down a city street and see construction workers ahead and draw your breasts in and tighten your buttocks and try to keep your hips from swaying and hold your breath as if all this holding and sucking and tucking might literally reduce your size so you will not be noticed. Will not be—but of course you will be—hassled and wolf-whistled at and made to feel that it is your difference, *you*, who has caused the rupture. Shame. Warlpiri are worse than construction workers in this respect. They feign an indifference you can see: eyes to the ground, fascinated by their feet, very, very still they stand. Their attempts to self-nullify under your gaze make you want to annul yourself even more. It is left to the dogs to do the more overt shaming. Scabied, scabrous, rhinoceros-skinned beasts—these are not animals for petting or preening. 'Watch-dog' is far too prim a term for their vigilante-like defence. It was the dogs I mostly tried to disappear from. The dogs whom I first had to encounter from the piles of rubble, the heaped blankets, and mattresses and bodies I would later know as Nungarrayi's camp; my Uncle's home; my own. My untrained eye was unable to differentiate the persons who stirred and looked and turned to tend the smouldering fire in one movement. And it was in the same movement that they would yell at the by now barking, chasing, biting dogs. Throw sticks, rocks, *kardaku* (billy can), anything that was available. At the dogs that is, not at me, although it always felt by implication that I was the target. My difference was a threat that the dogs knew about for sure. Later, these same dogs will cease to bark and attack me. Was it because I was by then always accompanied by the *wurlkurmanu*, the old women, my own dog, the kids? Because I smelt different—my diet of sugar, damper and tinned meat, did that make the difference? Or was it because I had learned to walk 'properly' as my mother-in-law teased me about later, individuating, as she always did, what seemed my cultural idiosyncrasies. *Lungkarda-piya* she says I walked then, 'Blue Tongue Lizard-like', furtive, fast and straight for home.

It isn't only that you *feel* watched and judged in the field—in shame—you are. Even more perhaps in a society like Warlpiri not structured by the distinction between public and private, where the exposed, vulnerable feelings of constantly being under the gaze border upon, and incite the sharp delineational effects of shame.

It would be too simple to say that what I speak of here is the taboo on looking, and yet this is the issue.[43] For anthropologists break the most stringent taboo of all—staring at strangers. Tomkins argues that the taboo on looking is stronger even than the (varying) taboos on sexual relations.[44] His account of the child's acquisition of the 'proper' way to (not) look serves to figure the kind of compelling impossibility of the anthropologist's task I aim to describe here.[45] Tomkins writes of the child, who in infantile characteristic shame, hides behind parents' backs when a stranger comes to visit. The parent is ashamed because the child overtly signifies the other's strangeness. The form the shaming takes is to coerce the child to come out and greet the stranger, at which point the child may, in equally characteristic infantile behaviour, fix their gaze on the eyes of the stranger. This in turn also shames the parent, because in staring the child also overtly signifies the stranger's difference. The child, in short, is in a no-win situation where, as Tomkins puts it, 'they are caught between the shame of looking and the shame of being ashamed to do so'.[46]

The child's dilemma is not, of course, solved in later life. As Adam Phillips reminds us, 'there is no solution for unconscious desire';[47] no way out of the contradictory structures and ambivalences which shape and determine what it means to be human. And perhaps anthropology is in this sense particularly human, embracing, as it does, the very taboo on looking which it is compelled to keep breaking. The dilemma for the modern anthropologist is, to put it simply: how to look without staring. Without being seen to look.[48] How to keep looking without turning the other into an inert, cauterised spectacle. Or to put it in the form of a question, for ultimately it is irresolution which drives my argumentation—is it possible to posit difference without denying recognition, that is, without causing shame?

This is not a rhetorical question. Whatever knowledge, whatever experience, whatever sense of *Warlpiri-ness* I may have, is based on recognition. That is, it is predicated and mediated by the very profound and complicated machinations of mutual recognition. It is on the basis of my being recognised, and recognising, that the thing called my field work proceeded. That is, it was and is through being understood *as the same as*: through the terms of what Myers calls from his work with Pintupi 'relatedness',[49] be that an idiom expressed through the overt structures kinship provided, or through the commonalities made by sharing the everyday existence of camp, food and experience, or what Samson calls 'consociate' relationship,[50] or generally, the relationships established and behaviour expected in being part of a particular 'mob'; or the more precise forms of recognition based on more individuated identifications (just as my field work was not conducted with 'the' Warlpiri, nor was I always or only 'the' European—even if these terms also never ceased their currency). In short, it was mutuality and similarity that was manifest, expressed, offered, not irreconcilable or irreducible difference. And it is precisely this recognition which is put at risk, breached, each and every time by the generic, categorical, seemingly innocuous presence of a third person. A crime I am guilty of, shamed by, countless times in my work each and every time I write—or speak—the words 'the' Warlpiri, 'Aborigines' or *Yapa*[51]—I violate, despite my best intentions to do otherwise, a most important principle of Aboriginal sociability, as von Sturmer puts it, '*not* to speak about others in their absence'.[52]

Again, I state the obvious. It is shameful—shame making—to overtly acknowledge another's difference. To deny recognition. To fail to recognise 'relations'. And yet this is precisely what my discipline demands. I am reminded here of the (shameful) stories that circulated when I was an undergraduate of certain anthropologists who, by staying 'too long' in the field, marrying 'informants' or any number of forms of 'going native', lost their objectivity. And in turn, lost their credibility. The disciplinary terms of the discipline are here exposed in the process of the airing of its own laundry. For what else if not normative goads were these stories? Epitaphs read aloud in advance—warnings—to the fledgeling field worker? As if to say: *sympathise and fraternise and understand the other, yes. But do not fail to keep their difference—your distance—resolute. Recognition found must ultimately be denied.* This is taken for granted in the discipline, this is the unspoken contract, the real rite of passage, the impossible imperative of the anthropologist. Like the child, the anthropologist is ambivalently caught, unable ultimately to recognise the very thing most revered—the difference of another.

This impossibility is compounded in the Australian context. Field work is difficult in Australia—painful, shameful—because of witnessing how badly Aboriginal people are treated. Not only in the gross negligence(s), the slap-in-the-face disparity of the Third World conditions, but in ongoing, day to day, interactions. It is a dense and varied palette, the colours and forms shame can take. From the more 'mild' shamings like mispronouncing or calling aloud a taboo name, or speaking too loudly, as if language difference were a hearing deficit or *Yapa*, Warlpiri were deaf, which you might think, given how often *Kardiya*, Europeans, speak with other *Kardiya* while *Yapa* are present, usually about topics which concern *Yapa* most; or the paternalistic public scolding when someone is late for work or has not fulfilled duties (and the power differential itself is always uni-directional boss to worker, European to Aboriginal, parent to child); to the more serious shamings, in the perpetually changing governmental policy on Aboriginal Land Rights, indigenous health policies, bilingual education, community employment projects . . . and the equally perpetual flow of experts, anthropologists, linguists, land councillors, educational advisers in and out of Aboriginal communities who in asking what amounts to the same questions year after year after year demonstrate their inability ultimately to recognise. This failure to recognise is nothing less than a refusal, von Sturmer argues; a refusal to recognise difference in the most profound of senses. As he describes it:

> the question of recognition is ultimately about recognising the possibility of being within other forms of sociality. It is this which is being refused. Aboriginal people will be allowed things: property. They will be allowed human rights, as human beings. But there is a refusal nonetheless of their forms of being.[53]

The anthropological project necessarily takes shape within and against these terms. That is, within and against an entire history of a failure to recognise—the shameful treatment—of Aboriginal people.

In other words, the kind of identity—identificatory efficacy of shame I describe above is deeply confounded in Australian field work, or at least it was in my experience. For in these contexts, I identified with *Yapa* sympathetically, painfully, who were being made ashamed. But this was a split experience, confounded by the shame I felt on behalf of Europeans (who should know better). And in identification, for I also am European, and likely to cause shame (and have, do, will), and so am no different ultimately from these persons or from the entirety of Western Colonial history and ashamed because of it. In an instant, all this. Shame floods me and reminds me of the neutral observer I can never simply be. Mimetic modes of knowing, seeing resemblances, recognition—the visceral effects of close contact—take place in a 'flash' Michael Taussig argues.[54]

But in this case, as is always the case with shame, it is a split recognition. The prostitute's prowess, divided loyalty. For which resemblance can I identify as my own? which will not incur renunciation? where can identification be found that will not find me out otherwise?

It is not my intention here to castigate shame for its negative effects alone. On the contrary, what I describe in shame's workings here—its structure and structuring effects *make* for the very possibilities of difference I describe. I took my cue literally from these shaming interactions, learning to identify culturally encoded patterns of behaviour and expectations in response; learning how *not* to behave; learning how to differentiate my behaviour, my expectations from other Europeans; learning (and failing to learn continuously) how *not* to shame *Yapa*. And the register was always—is—my own self, that is, the difference I know through shame.

This identity making—and the contagious confusions of shame—were not, however, confined to my experience alone. Later in my field work I will inadvertently shame *Yapa*, my younger sister to be precise, one day in Katherine, when after a particularly trying drive from Lajamanu with three flat tyres, it is my dirtiness and bare feet which will cause us difficulty getting served in a particular food shop. As my younger sister said to me, *you look too much like Yapa Nampijinpa*, and banished me to the garage toilet to clean up. And I hope this story also illustrates—for the fingers of shame are far reaching—that *Yapa* and *Kardiya* both suffer the shame of those perceived to be out of place. Hanging out with Blackfellas in the Northern Territory if you are a Whitefella engenders shame all around. And the effects disseminate. As my sister said, she'd never experienced difficulty in that shop before.

One of the most distinctive characteristics of Warlpiri society in my experience is its very emphasis on shame; an emphasis which, according to Duncan, is shared throughout Aboriginal Australia.[55] Stanner argues that 'the emotion shame is perhaps the most powerful in Aboriginal life'.[56] But despite the agreement on the central role of shame, there has been little written explicitly concerned with its expression.[57] I do not intend to be so imperious here as to provide an account of Warlpiri notions of shame. Suffice it to say, *kurnta* (shame) or *kurntanga* (the resultant condition) are complex experiences and expressions. Unlike in European society, shame is openly acknowledged and voiced by Warlpiri. Thus, as much as my shameful identifications delineated identity, so too did attention to the terms of shame's verbalisation. Perhaps most profoundly in the simplest of facts: I had not thought about shame before living with Warlpiri. Nor had I experienced so much of it. In this sense, perhaps I mimetically caught shame from Warlpiri in the sense that Franz Boas caught reciprocity from the Kwakiutl or Malinowski function from the Trobriand Islanders. But unlike my forefathers, I cannot say with clarity where my experience ends and the Warlpiri's begin. I cannot locate, circumscribe or halt the circulation of shame's effects, saturating as it has, my pre- and post- and during field experience(s); delineating and producing, as it has, so much of my understanding of Warlpiri identity and my own. And necessarily transforming both.

I find myself here, in reflecting on shame, in the tenuous territory it makes for; vertiginously walking, as seems to be my place, the precipice of its making. So unrelenting is shame's grip, so canker-like is its festering, that its eruptions and likely return are guaranteed. Won't I be accused of being one of *those* anthropologists, one of the shameless ones, who can no longer be objective; who can no longer tell the difference?

Yet it is precisely through shame that I have come to know of difference. I am deeply in shame's debt. As much as it may haunt and stultify, shame also shapes and defines, and makes for the very delineations called self-identity. It structures, necessarily, we come to realise, the difference(s) we call cultural. Indeed, that shame and its visitations are highly individuated—in a sense, contentless and generalised, as I describe—is what makes for its very productivity. The very plethora of divergent positions on how to write 'anthropology' these days, the angst of identity politics as it manifests itself and menaces the ethnographic endeavour, attests, it seems to me, to the very unfinished workings of shame. The original desire has not been renounced. The debt to shame in the anthropological project if anything, is a growing one. Eve Kosofsky Sedgwick argues that shame needs to be refigured outside of the either/or terms in which it has traditionally been found. If it can be reworked outside of terms which see shame either, as she puts it, '*good* because it preserves privacy and decency, *bad* because it colludes with self repression or social repression',[58] then it holds important potentialities for refiguring difference. For the making of identity. It is towards this possible refiguring that this paper gestures.

Notes

This chapter derives from reflections on my field research with Warlpiri Aborigines in the Tanami Desert, conducted between 1989 and 1991. This research was funded by the Australian Institute of Aboriginal and Torres Strait Islander Studies (ALATSIS) and the Carlyle Greenwell Bequest, Department of Anthropology, University of Sydney. The relatives I refer to here are members of my Warlpiri family, whose generosity I gratefully acknowledge. I would also like to thank Jane Sloan particularly, Alan Rumsey and Chris Lyttleton for helpful comments on earlier drafts of this chapter.

1   Tori Amos, 'Happy Phantom', *Little Earthquakes* (WEA International Inc) Germany, 1992, track 6.
2   The model of shame I develop here, it should be stressed, is an intentionally Eurocentric and Euro-specific one; a model necessarily class based, ethnically orientated and genderised by both the figurations of the literature, and my own identifications. This very particular focus is intentional. Rather than developing a universalist or cross-cultural model, my intention instead is to augment the

very productive nature of shame's workings in and through a dominant Eurocentric project of anthropological research and writing.

3   There is less material written on shame than on guilt in the psychoanalytic tradition, although there is a growing contemporary interest in shame, as Nathanson notes. D.L. Nathanson, 'Foreward' (1992) to C.D. Schneider, *Shame, Exposure and Privacy* (W.W. Norton) New York and London, 1977, p. vii.

In the anthropological tradition, this position is reversed. A plethora of studies on shame, particularly in Mediterranean and Melanesian literatures, exists. Compare A.L. Epstein, *The Experience of Shame in Melanesia: An Essay in the Anthropology of Affect*, Royal Anthropological Institute of Great Britain and Ireland, Occasional Paper No. 40, 1984; and A. Strathern, 'Why is Shame on the Skin' in J. Blacking (ed.), *The Anthropology of the Body* (Academic Press) London, 1977. The classic distinction, generally traced back to the work of Ruth Benedict, between 'shame cultures' (cultures typified by external rewards/punishments or 'social control') versus 'guilt cultures' (cultures typified instead by internalised mechanisms to regulate behaviour) is, strictly speaking, no longer utilised. However, a certain differential structuring remains. Ruth Benedict, *The Chrysanthemum and the Sword* (Houghton Mifflin) Boston, 1946.

The emphasis on shame in *other* cultures in anthropology implicitly works to other-orient shame away from 'our' experience and society. Likewise, the focus on guilt in psychoanalysis has implicitly equated modern, Western Judaic/Christian cultures with guilt. The work of Foucault, despite its opposition to psychoanalysis, needs to be included in this tendency because of its emphasis on the technologies of sin and confession in modernity. M. Foucault, *The History of Sexuality: An Introduction*, trans. R. Hurley (Penguin) Harmondsworth, 1978; Foucault, 'Technologies of the Self' in L.M. Martin, H. Gutman and P.H. Hutton (eds), *Technologies of the Self* (University of Massachusetts Press) Amhurst, 1988; Foucault, 'About the Beginning of the Hermeneutics of the Self: Two Lectures at Dartmouth', *Political Theory*, vol. 21, no. 2, 1993.

It is, however, precisely away from these kinds of understandings of shame that this article moves. Shame is instead figured here in terms of its complex mimetic effects in the making of and for self-identity, and thus, in its central role in the anthropological endeavour of other-differentiating.

4   J.P. Sartre, *Being and Nothingness: An Essay on Phenomenological Ontology*, trans. H.E. Barnes (Philosophical Library) New York, 1956, p. 578.

5   Eve Kosofsky Sedgwick, 'Queer Performativity: Henry James "The Art of the Novel" ', *GLQ* vol. 1, no. 1, 1993, p. 4.

6   Silvan Tomkins, 'Affect, Imagery, Consciousness', *The Negative Affects*, vol. 2 (Springer) New York, 1963, p. 121.

7   M. Lewis, *Shame: The Exposed Self* (Free Press) New York, 1992, begins his account of shame by recounting the Genesis myth.

8   Genesis 2:25.

9   S. Freud, *Civilization and Its Discontents*, trans. J. Strachey (W.W. Norton) New York and London, 1961, p. 47.

10   And of course, dogs are 'Our' best friends because we project onto/into them accordingly. Dogs not only do that which 'Us civilised humans' are disallowed from doing, but which 'We' ultimately still want to do, at least according to Freud, *Civilization and Its Discontents*. See also further discussion in Freud, *Totem and Taboo*, trans. J. Strachey (1950) (Routledge & Kegan Paul) London, 1960.

11   See also F.R. Myers' comments on Pintupi who similarly call people who 'copulate indiscriminately' *like dogs*. F.R. Myers, *Pintupi Country, Pintupi Self: Sentiment, Place and Politics among Western Desert Aborigines* (Smithsonian Institution Press and Australian Institute of Aboriginal Studies) Washington and London, 1986, p. 123.

12   cf. Tomkins, 'Affect, Imagery, Consciousness', pp. 119–21; Kosofsky Sedgwick, 'Queer Performativity', p. 45.

13   M. Merleau-Ponty, *The Visible and the Invisible*, ed. C. Lefort, trans. A. Lingis (1964) (Northwestern University Press) Evanston, 1968.

14   Alphonso Lingis, 'Bodies that Touch Us', *Thesis Eleven*, no. 36, 1993, p. 167.

15   cf. Schneider, *Shame, Exposure and Privacy*, p. 3; Tomkins, 'Affect, Imagery, Consciousness', p. 120.

16   Schneider, *Shame, Exposure and Privacy*, p. 4.

17   Kosofsky Sedgwick, 'Queer Performativity', p. 4.

18   Tomkins, 'Affect, Imagery, Consciousness', p. 133.

19   cf. M. Lewis, *Shame*, p. 99.

20   See Kosofsky Sedgwick, 'Queer Performativity'; and M. Lewis, Shame (chapter 7 particularly).

21   cf. M. Lewis, Shame; and Tomkins, 'Affect, Imagery, Consciousness', p. 128. Lewis is here referring to Anglo-American middle-class child rearing practices. He does not, unfortunately, return to the issue of the disgust/shame response in his discussion of cultural variation in shame (see 'Chapter Eleven: Shame Across Time and Place'). My interest in this shame source is, however, precisely what may be culturally specific. For the role of abjection in the disgust/shame response—its acute identity-making effects, as Kristeva figures abjection—may help to explain why shame is such a predominant emotion in Anglo middle-class Western culture, particularly because it is repressed. J. Kristeva, The Powers of Horror: An Essay on Abjection, trans. L.W. Roudiez (Columbia University Press) New York, 1982.

22   cf. Freud, Civilization and Its Discontents, p. 71; Kosofsky Sedgwick, 'Queer Performativity', p. 5.

23   Lewis, Shame, pp. 98f. Tomkins, 'Affect, Imagery, Consciousness', pp. 123–8.

24   Quentin Tarantino (writer and director), Pulp Fiction, a Mirimax presentation of A Band Apart and Jersey Films Production.

25   Kosofsky Sedgwick, 'Queer Performativity', p. 8.

26   J. Butler, Bodies that Matter (Routledge) New York and London, 1993, p. 12.

27   Kosofsky Sedgwick, 'Queer Performativity', p. 12.

28   It is beyond the scope of this chapter to discuss the important ways in which shame and guilt also share certain psychic structurings, the most obvious being, as both M. Lewis, Shame; and H.B. Lewis, Shame and Guilt in Neurosis (International Universities Press) New York, 1971 discuss, the internalisation of rage at the other.

29   Again, it is an explicitly culturally-specific model of shame in self development I posit here intentionally.

30   I differentiate here perhaps too sharply for some of the more subtle appreciations of guilt's modern manifestations. Guilt may also be associated with a more general 'angst' regardless of action or activity. Or as Marianne Faithfull puts it: 'I feel guilt, I feel guilt, though I know I've done no wrong I feel guilt'. M. Faithfull, 'Guilt', Broken English (Island Records) London, 1979. This particularly modern condition might be described, following H.B. Lewis, as the 'insoluble dilemma' where the back and forth thinking about the other, and blaming the self, results in a generalised condition of irresolution and anxiety. This in turn correlates certain obsessive and potentially paranoid ideation with guilt, as opposed to the more likely affinities shame holds with depression, according to Lewis. H.B. Lewis, Shame and Guilt in Neurosis, p. 252.

31   Kosofsky Sedgwick, 'Queer Performativity', p. 5; M. Lewis, Shame, p. 93.

32   Freud, Civilization and Its Discontents, p. 173.

33   Schneider, Shame, Exposure and Privacy.

34   It is beyond the scope of this chapter to take up the issue of sexual difference and shame in a more rigorous form than my gesturing here allows. But see Sarah Kofman, The Enigma of Woman: Woman in Freud's Writing, trans. C. Porter (Cornell University Press) Ithaca and London, 1985, pp. 48–50, in which, she argues that for Freud, the veil of shame 'covers' the moral (conventional) and the genital (natural) lack which woman bears in relation to man. But the very 'trick of nature' that is shame— 'feminine modesty'—is, in her account of Freud, a position enviable and unbearable by man ultimately, for woman thus provides for the very reproduction of human society (and here, Bataille's and Freud's similarities are clear). In short, shame—woman—necessarily shows up man's insufficiency.

35   G. Bataille, Eroticism, trans. M. Dalwood (1962) (Marion Boyars Publishers) London and New York, 1990.

36   See G. Flaubert, Madame Bovary: Provincial Lives, trans. G. Wall (1857) (Penguin) Harmondsworth, 1992; L. Tolstoy, Anna Karenina, trans. C. Garnett (1875–1876) (Reprint Society) Kingswood, 1966; and N. Hawthorne, The Scarlet Letter (1850) (Bloomsbury) London, 1995.

37   Roland Joffe (director and producer) The Scarlet Letter (1995).

38   'Sex, Lies and Anthropology', Good Weekend Magazine, Sydney Morning Herald, 9 March 1996.

39   A correlation played on, it seems to me, in a recent collection by D. Kulick and M. Willson entitled Taboo: Sex, Identity and Erotic Subjectivity in Anthropological Fieldwork (Routledge) London and New York, 1995. For all that anthropologists have 'discovered' taboos in other societies, they have necessarily broken taboos in their own. But that this correlation positions the ethnographer in the affective territory of shame's workings, as my argument suggests, is disappointingly not discussed in this collection.

40   Adam Phillips, Terrors and Experts (Faber & Faber) London, 1995, pp. 6, 15.

41   cf. Tomkins, *Shame*, p. 214.

42   R.H. Wax, 'The First and Most Uncomfortable Stage of Fieldwork', *Doing Fieldwork: Warnings and Advice* (University of Chicago Press) Chicago, 1973, p. 15.

43   *Simple Simon, the half-wit's ignorance, the gesticulations of the mimic*—it isn't only within academic papers where stating the obvious, or being too obvious, is considered shameful.

44   Tomkins, *Shame*, p. 157.

45   Tomkins, *Shame*, p. 171.

46   Tomkins, *Shame*, p. 171.

47   Phillips, *Terrors and Experts*, p. 7.

48   It isn't only the stranger's difference which is overtly signified through the child's looking and not-looking. It is also potentially the child's. For the other side of the imperative implicit in *don't stare* is the equally strong goad *don't make a spectacle of yourself* that is, do not be *seen* by others to be looking or not-looking. The intersubjective nature of shame's reciprocal manifestation, and its dependency on 'witness', on the ocular focus of another, are here demonstrated.

49   Myers, *Pintupi Country, Pintupi Self*.

50   Basil Samson, *The Camp at Wallaby Cross: Aboriginal Fringe Dwellers in Darwin* (Australian Institute of Aboriginal Studies) Canberra, 1980, p. 12.

51   *Yapa* is the term Warlpiri use to refer to themselves, sometimes to refer to other Aboriginal persons, and generally, to differentiate the obverse term *Kardiya*—European, Whitefella, non-Warlpiri, outsider, Other.

52   J. von Sturmer, ' "R Stands for . . ." An Extract from a Mabo Diary', Special Edition of the *Australian Journal of Anthropology (TAJA)*, vol. 6, nos 1/2, 1995, p. 102, emphasis added.

53   von Sturmer, ' "R Stands for . . ." ', p. 103.

54   Michael Taussig, *Mimesis and Alterity: A Particular History of the Senses* (Routledge) New York and London, 1993, p. 39.

55   P. Duncan, 'Shame in Australia', Honours Thesis in Department of Prehistory and Anthropology, Australian National University, Canberra, 1986.

56   W.E.H. Stanner, *White Man Got No Dreaming: Essays 1938–1973* (Australian National University Press) Canberra, 1979, p. 95.

57   L.R. Hiatt, 'A Spear in the Ear', *Oceania*, vol. 37, 1966, pp. 153–4; Hiatt, 'Your Mother-in-Law is Poison', *MAN*, vol. 19, no. 2, 1984, pp. 183–98; Duncan, 'Shame in Australia'; and Myers, *Pintupi Country, Pintupi Self* are exceptions. Von Sturmer's work needs to be included here, dealing as it does, both explicitly and implicitly with the compelling questions of how to recognise, and how to avoid shaming, Aboriginal people(s). See J. von Sturmer, 'Talking with Aborigines', *Institute of Aboriginal Studies Newsletter*, no. 15, 1981; von Sturmer, 'Aborigines, Representation, Necrophilia', *Art & Text*, no. 32, 1989; von Sturmer, ' "R Stands for . . ." '.

58   Kosofsky Sedgwick, 'Queer Performativity', p. 14.

III SOCIOLOGICAL PERSPECTIVES

Chapter 7

Virginia Olesen and Debora Bone

EMOTIONS IN RATIONALIZING ORGANIZATIONS: CONCEPTUAL NOTES FROM PROFESSIONAL NURSING IN THE USA

Introduction

THE HIGHLY DYNAMIC domain of health and healing contains the great human themes of life and death, separation and reconciliation, greed and generosity, hope and despair accompanied by a gamut of emotions: joy, sorrow, rage, grief, pride, embarrassment, all sociologically constituted. These themes and emotional expressions occur in organizations that are already highly bureaucratized or are becoming bureaucratized in varying degrees, as well as in informal settings. Thus, health care organizations present opportunities to analyse the interplay between structures and emotions. As Lutz and White remind us, 'principles of social organization construct size, stability and status characteristics of the audience for performance of emotions' (1986: 420).

The interplay of emotions and structure is an old question in the sociology of organizations, reaching back at least as far as Weber's observation that conflicts emerge when 'substantive justice oriented to the concrete instance and person collide' with the 'formalism and rule-bound and cool "matter of factness" of bureaucratic administration' (Gerth and Mills 1958: 229–31). However, a new dimension in this question emerges out of pressures induced by the fiscal crisis in American health care for organizations to rationalize and become more efficient. This new dimension, changes in organizational structures, poses the issue of how emotions and emotional behaviours fare in altering contexts, an issue in the sociology of emotions which has received relatively little sustained attention.

Here we try to lodge the analysis and understanding of emotions and emotional behaviour in changing organizational contexts as a beginning move to a more dynamic sociology of emotions. To examine this we review the current situation of professional nursing in the United States. Like many other providers in the American health care system, nurses face increasing rationalization of organizational contexts (hospitals, clinics, health maintenance organizations (HMOs), hospices) as the system struggles to become more cost-efficient. Early dismissal of patients, larger workloads, substitution of other personnel for nurses, all figure in the cost-conscious scenario. Because expression of emotions is thought to be significantly embedded in the work of nursing care and nurses' professional orientation, this trend creates the potential for tension between structural demands for efficiency and the expression of emotion. This is particularly intriguing, if one accepts the view of some nurses that emotional work is central to care and the nurse's professional identity.

Our choice of nursing does not imply that other health care professionals, such as physicians, physical therapists, or social workers, who work in these changing organizations are not affected with regard to the emotional components of their work. Along with other observers, we recognize the possibility that many medical and helping professionals may experience tensions between 'the unrealizability of empathetic, personal concern and rational universal detachment' (Weigert and Franks 1989: 210; see also Fox 1989: 100–1). We have limited our discussion to professional nursing (registered nurses and licensed vocational nurses) in order more effectively to focus on and draw out conceptual problems which bear on issues of emotions in changing organizations. To further narrow the analysis and avoid illfounded generalizations we restrict our discussion to nursing in the United States, while recognizing that rationalizing trends under way in other western societies – the UK for example – also impinge on nurses (Strong and Robinson 1990).

Although we recognize the highly gendered nature of this profession, an issue developed extensively in other analyses (Garmarnikov 1978; Davies 1995), here we do not centre gender. To do so risks an essentialist stance, i.e. women are inherently emotional and are the only ones who can do such work, which obviates analysis of changing emotions in changing structures if emotional expression *is* inherent in femaleness.[1] It also overlooks the wide variety of emotional experience and expression in women (and men) and necessitates comparative discussions beyond the scope of this chapter. Thus the chapter does not reveal women's or females' emotional labour in changing organizations, though issues of gender and changes in emotional labour would be of interest in a comparative analysis. Rather, it explores how institutional and economic change interacts with emotional labour in a largely female profession oriented to caring as a way to understand the larger problems of emotions in changing organizational contexts.

To set the stage for this discussion we review, first, major themes around emotions in organizations and then material on nursing in changing social and economic contexts.

Emotions in organizations

The ideal-typical conceptualization of bureaucracy as completely rationalized and free of subjective or emotional elements has given way to more complex views of the interrelationship of emotions and structures (Gibson 1994). A host of studies from organizational theorists recognize that rationality is bounded, hence space emerges for the exercise of subjectivity and emotion. In contrast to the imagery of a perfectly rational organization where emotion is excluded, rationally designed organizations do not and cannot exclude emotionality (Gibson 1994: 21). Organizational structures and the work contexts within them are seen to contain a mix of rational and emotional elements which are reciprocally influential. Jones's study of a rape crisis organization demonstrates this point by showing that work 'routine may include authentic emotions and strategies that help the worker successfully do the work while being true to their self-expression' and argues that 'simultaneous expression of emotion and distance demonstrates the need to realize the role of emotions in occupational settings and the process of work' (1996: 26).

As Shott has argued, structure and norms 'are the framework of human action, rather than its determinant, shaping behaviour without dictating it' (1979: 1321). Individuals seeking solutions to complex organizational problems draw on emotional resources which are influenced by and in turn influence context and structure (Collins 1981: 994). This contemporary formulation of the interrelationship of structure and emotion still permits, indeed facilitates, examination of the central question in this chapter: how emotions are felt, constructed and enacted within the dynamics of organizational change where structure and emotion intertwine. In particular, this framing leaves open the question of the relationship between expressed and felt emotions, a topic to which we shall return in our discussion of American nursing.

At the heart of these issues is Hochschild's influential concept of 'emotional labour' (1983), which empirically demonstrated and theoretically outlined the impact of culture and economic orientation on emotion and the expression or lack thereof of emotions deemed appropriate to realize entrepreneurial economic interests. For our purposes emotional labour lies at the interstices of individual expression, normative and structural constraints, and the dynamics of change.

With a few exceptions to be discussed shortly, most research on emotional labour has been found in management studies where the question of increasing productivity, profit, etc., is central. These studies nevertheless delineate the important theme of fitting workers' emotions to company goals, hence they bear on our discussion of the increasing rationalization of the American health care system, which clearly raises questions of competition, profit and productivity.

Studies of emotional labour in service occupations can be divided into inquiries into occupations where the recipient of service is a customer and those where he or she is a client or patient. This distinction points to the sociological boundary, not always clear, between occupations and professions. Socialization to emotional behaviour can and does occur in both occupations and professions, but professional mandates which carry moral concern for the person *may* impinge more intensively on emotional behaviour; for example, the admonitions for affective neutrality, universalism, detached concern in physicians' behaviour (Lief and Fox 1963). Moreover, in most cases the relationship between the seller and the customer is more bracketed, less ambiguous and briefer than that between professional and client/patient.[2]

However, as we shall detail shortly, the elements of managed care bring into play themes which shift the definition of 'the patient' and, indeed, of the provider as the search for cost containment impinges on emotional behaviour. It is precisely the blurring of the distinction between patient as patient and patient as customer that becomes significant in the shifting managed-care scenarios. Consequently, the literature on emotions in customer service relations becomes relevant in the health care setting.

The literature on emotions in a wide variety of customer service occupations abundantly documents organizations' formal and informal efforts through recruitment, socialization and rewards or punishments to try to ensure that employees display the desired emotions, whether the emotions be positive, negative or neutral (for informative reviews of this literature see Ashforth and Humphrey 1993; Gibson 1994). Jovial employees at Disneyland (Van Maanen and Kunda 1989), neutral or angry bill collectors (Sutton 1991), fast food servers' routinized responses (Leidner 1993), all reflect a display of organizationally mandated emotions which, one could argue, have become the property of the organization, hence rationalized and commodified (Hochschild 1983; Sugrue 1982).

Whereas the literature on consumer service organizations reveals management efforts to commodify workers' emotions, an important theme, mostly ignored in that literature, is explored in material on patient/client settings, namely, how experience and expression of emotion are juxtaposed (Ashforth and Humphrey 1993). A study of case-workers in a public housing office shows that clients' tears led case-workers not only to feel and express sympathy, but to make decisions favourable to the client (Garot 1995), while angry clients were handled neutrally and did not receive favourable decisions. Detectives faced with victims who would dissolve in emotional outbursts had difficulty in expressing emotional support even if they felt empathetic (Stenross and Kleinman 1989). Nurses working with terminally ill patients, troubled by the bureaucratic necessity to undertake neutral, heroic measures when they preferred to give emotionally supportive care, experienced 'outlaw emotions': shame, guilt, dysphoria (Jaggar 1989; Burfoot 1994). In short, the bureaucratic requirement that emotional labour *not* be performed had emotional consequences for these nurses.

A critical factor in the tension between experience of and expression of emotion in care settings is temporality. Bureaucratic strictures in rationalized settings which demand a certain amount of physical work done within specific time-limits create tensions for care-givers who experience certain emotions for patients, but who are restricted from expressing them. Foner's ethnographic study of nurses and nurses' aides in a nursing home documents how this tension constrains the emotional labour of nurses' aides, sometimes to patients' detriment (1994: 73–4). This study and Diamond's ethnography of a nursing home (1992) detail the problems in emotional expression when bureaucratization occurs. A nurses' aide nostalgically recalled a less rule-bound era, 'Everything was nice in those days' (Foner 1994: 73), to capture the shift in rules and emotional expression.

There are, however, some exceptions, which are found in settings where emotional expression is valued as a means of recruiting or retaining patients – not unlike certain commercial enterprises. Studying a dedicated AIDS ward, Kotarba *et al.* found a free range of emotions and emotional involvement which they attribute to the fact that 'a warm environment is useful for attracting patients and ensuring repeat visits in an increasingly competitive market for middle class (privately insured) HIV/AIDS patients' (1996: 12). Thus, there is a range of relationships in the experience and expression of emotion, running from instances where contexts work against expression of emotions which nurses may wish to express, to settings where they must express emotion whether or not they wish to do so.

To understand emotional dynamics in contemporary nursing practice in institutional settings, it is useful to review briefly the history of nursing in the United States, situating the emotional labour of nurses within the structural conditions that shaped the development of the profession.

Nursing history and emotional labour

During colonial times, nursing care in America was provided informally by family members and neighbours. Overseeing nutrition, hygiene, first aid and convalescent care were among the household skills women settlers acquired (Donahue 1985). Modern American nursing traces its origins to the Civil War, in the 1860s, when women served as nurses in field hospitals, tending wounded and sick soldiers (Donahue 1985). Nursing expertise in managing the environment of, and care for, sick patients was kept rigorously distinct from the medical skills of diagnosis and cure. Building on gendered *domestic* divisions of labour, the work of providing nurturance and emotional support fell 'naturally' to the nurse.

By the end of the nineteenth century, nursing became an acceptable vocation for young middle-class women. Hospitals and training schools were established in many of the large eastern cities. Student nurses lived a regimented, semi-military lifestyle, received on-the-job training for two or three years, and provided the majority of nursing care in hospitals (Flood 1981). Graduate nurses moved quickly into the community, working as private duty nurses in the homes of better-off families.

Early nursing texts gave instructions in 'hospital etiquette', indicating the proper manners of the professional nurse. Advice on issues such as greeting doctors, handling difficult patients or how to maintain good relations among the staff was offered (Hampton 1949 [1893]). Nurses were expected to control personal feelings and adhere to ideals of devotion and calling. Their work was motivated by a sense of duty and an obligation to care (Reverby 1987).

By the early twentieth century, the modern health professions were dominated by two masculinist ways of organizing work and setting priorities: the bureaucratic rationalization of hospital administration and the scientific rationality of medicine. The mundane and feminine 'details' of nurses' care-giving work, including emotion work, tended to be devalued and under-recognized (Davies 1995). This presented a dilemma for elite nurses, educators and superintendents, who sought to professionalize nursing by aligning themselves with rationality and efficiency without losing the traditionalists, who emphasized 'maternalist' qualities in nurses (Melosh 1982; Brannon 1994).

After the Second World War, an influx of economic resources, medical and technological innovations, and social policies transformed American health care services into a formidable health care industry, with nurses as its largest single group of employees (Melosh 1983). As nursing care became much more complex, conscious interest in 'nurse–patient interactions' and the 'psycho-social status' of patients reflected both the impact of the social sciences in nursing and attempts to articulate non-technical aspects of clinical care. During the postwar decades, efforts to balance 'high tech' with 'high touch' aspects of nursing took place under conditions of rapid expansion and a relative availability of resources.

Nursing in managed care

The 1990s are a time of massive restructuring and change in the American health care system, characterized by cost containment measures and new managerial strategies, which affect the delivery of nursing care services. Key issues include temporality, as labour speed-ups reduce nursing time with the patient; role adjustments, as nurses move into advanced practice and team management; and customer relations, as patients are reconceptualized as clients. The emotional work of providing support to patients and managing feelings of staff, families and clients often falls to the nurse, who is being asked to adapt quickly to fundamental shifts in the organization of work.

These changes are highly complex, occurring within diverse nursing practices differentiated by speciality, geographical region, type of organization and level of skill. Some trends contradict others. Older models overlap and coexist with newer formats, creating a pastiche or bricolage from which it is difficult to draw specific conclusions. Though hospital managers have designed new work systems, outlining and understanding the implications at the level of patient care is an empirical task for the future and well beyond the scope of this chapter. Nevertheless, it is possible to identify a number of characteristics of managed care and integrated health care systems, driven by economic pressures, that are currently shaping nursing practices both in and out of the hospital.

The impetus to redesign the delivery of health care in the USA began during the 1980s as both privatized and federally subsidized hospital and insurance systems grappled with escalating costs of providing care. Previously, reimbursement for health care was designed as a 'cost-based retrospective system' (DeLew *et al.* 1992: 162), in which insurance plans or government programmes paid some or all of the health care costs of qualified participants to the providers.

In the 1980s, new 'fixed-priced prospective payment systems' (DeLew *et al.* 1992), linked to diagnostic related groups (DRGs), were instituted in part as incentives for hospitals to be efficient. Both the streamlining of public spending and the principles of market competition in the private sector gave financial impetus to a new round of rationalization in the delivery of health care services. Management consultants were recruited from other industries to instruct hospital administrators how to reduce labour costs, streamline mid-level management, shorten hospital stays and render operations 'leaner and meaner' (MacLaren 1994; Riley 1994; Sovie 1995).

Health maintenance organizations developed capitated plans by which insurees' health needs would be met for a flat fee, encouraging decreased use of services. Preferred provider organizations negotiated reduced fees with physician groups, promising increased numbers of clients in exchange for lower rates. Hospital mergers reduced duplication of services, thereby cutting costs while making some services less accessible to clients. Each of these changes has made an impact on the organization of nursing work. Shorter hospitalizations, increases in outpatient services and increases in home health care have been effective in reducing expensive hospital stays. However, with outpatient procedures and home care expanding, only the sickest patients are hospitalized. Nurses are attending to the needs of patients with highly complex medical problems and these sicker patients have more acute emotional needs as well (Himali 1995).

Managed-care plans strive for efficiency by rationalizing the organization of work and streamlining the delivery of services (McLaughlin *et al.* 1995). Since nursing labour costs are expensive, hospitals are redesigning the utilization of nursing staff. Where a decade ago there was much talk about nursing shortages, today hospital managers attempt to use fewer nurses more effectively (Zimmerman 1995). Nurses are expected to move flexibly from one speciality unit to another, or take 'call off' time, according to variations in census. Hospitals have fewer permanent staff and save benefits costs by using part-time and, *per diem* nurses. New information systems, standardized care plans and labour-saving hospital equipment are employed to reduce nursing hours. While working conditions for staff nurses deteriorate, better educated and more experienced nurses are moving away from direct patient care into case manager or supervisory roles (Buerhaus 1994).

Hospitals are also changing the 'skill mix', increasing the numbers of less trained licensed vocational or practical nurses (LVN and LPN), and utilizing unlicensed assistive personnel (UAP). Care is organized by team models in which various tasks are performed by specialized ancillary providers (Fritz and Cheeseman 1994). Registered nurses intervene with technical skills and oversee and document the work performed by others (Campbell 1988). They may be responsible for a greater number of patients, but are no longer provid-ing primary care. In this instance, the emotion work becomes that of managing other personnel more than interacting with patients.

The overall impact of managed care has been to decrease the number of nurses involved in direct patient care while increasing the levels of responsibility for patient outcome. In general, this has reduced the amount of time available for all aspects of work, including emotional labour. Here it is useful to distinguish between the nurse's expression of emotion as part of the service work of caring for patients, and the experience of emotion as she responds both to the organizational changes and to their consequences for patient care. During this time of change, the emotional standards for expression, as well as expectations and feelings about new organizational processes, are in flux. Adapting to change is itself emotionally demanding. Nurses' responses to organizational restructuring have included feelings of uncertainty, impotence, anger, grief, frustration, resentment and insecurity (DeMoro 1996; Droppleman and Thomas 1996).

While hospitals and care-providers have not specifically addressed the emotional dynamics of health care workers, most hospitals have introduced multiple educational and organizational incentives to engage staff, including nurses, in the restructuring process. One such strategy, Total Quality Management (TQM), borrowed from industrial management,[3] is a managerial rationalization strategy in which work processes are monitored and evaluated according to specific outcome criteria. The patient is conceptualized as a client and indicators of customer satisfaction are used to determine quality. Data are collected on an ongoing basis and multidisciplinary teams are rewarded for devising and implementing 'action plans' to improve service delivery (Flarey 1995; Kelly 1995; Zonsius and Murphy 1995). The TQM approach to health care management claims to be 'patient focused' and builds on hospitality models of customer relations. However, the criteria developed for organizational efficiency and cost containment may differ from clinical criteria based on nursing standards of care. Nurses find themselves caught between competing models with contradictory demands.

The emphasis on patient relations creates an interesting paradox of emotion work under managed care. On the one hand, organizational restructuring has reduced the amount of time available for nurse–patient interactions, yet on the other hand, efforts to improve customer satisfaction have drawn attention to the clients' subjective needs. The complexity of the 'psycho-social' dimensions of care makes them an important focus of attention in nursing.

This has not gone unnoticed in nursing. A growing body of advice literature, in-services and continuing-education options for nurses indicates renewed interest in gaining emotional skills for handling the complexity of patient care in the redesigned settings of today's health care system. In wide-ranging articles, attention is focused on clarification of what emotional assessments and interventions might be appropriate in a variety of clinical situations in the managed-care context. Topics include conflict resolution, empathic relationships, caring for the dying, dealing with grief and loss, handling difficult people, reassuring anxious patients and creating a sense of security and trust (Baker 1995; Davidhizar 1992; Davidhizar and Bowen 1993; Ellis 1993; Raudonis 1993; Schaefer and Peterson 1992; Teasdale 1995).

In sum, nurses working in today's rapidly changing health care services face multiple demands in which sophisticated emotional skills and flexibility are needed to handle the increased workloads, high levels of patient acuity and labour speed-ups. Nurses manage their own feelings, those of their patients and those of other workers, each interaction grounded in the shifting contexts of cost containment (see Thoits 1996 for an illuminating discussion of managing others' emotions). Paradoxically, managed care is simultaneously diminishing the structural support for nurses to provide traditional emotional support, and increasing the emphasis on customer relations and patient satisfaction as quality measures of successful outcomes.

Empirical questions about the emotion work of nurses

What these observations about emotional dynamics in the changing work of nurses mean for the conceptualization of emotions in changing structures can be glimpsed in a series of questions which contain themes or implicit concepts that lead to our final discussion. These might also guide empirical research to explore the question of emotions in changing institutions.

Regarding emotions, will the newly redesigned organization of work require new or different emotional competencies? Is the labour-intensive work of providing emotional support during illness being replaced with stylized performances of hospitality and routin-ized niceness? As service workers experience labour speed-ups and are required to do more faster, how might emotions be felt and experienced differently? When individuals confront restructuring of emotional work, do flexible emotionalities emerge, replacing earlier, more uniform emotional standards? What adaptations of expression and communication of feel-ings transpire during the emotional nano-seconds of the brief and efficient encounter between nurse and patient in the managed-care environment? For some nurses, emotional involvement is considered one of the rewards of care-giving work. Does renewed profes-sional interest in caring and empathy represent efforts of nurses to reclaim this role, holding firm to traditional emotional turf?

On a micro level, what political economy of emotion management might emerge? If nurses are not performing some of the emotion work needed to assist patients through illness, how has this work been redistributed among other practitioners such as psycho-therapists, social workers and pastoral care workers? In what ways are families taking on more emotional labour? Are patients assuming greater responsibility for their own emo-tional needs as providers of this care become scarce or are limited in what they do? What, if any, will be the influence of textually mediated emotional labour, that is, the emotional responses set down in in-service educational writing or ward procedures? Will these alter the 'sentimental order' (Strauss *et al.* 1982)? All of these questions, grounded in health care systems, suggest the utility of a theoretical framework that links emotional dynamics, struc-tural contexts and variations of self within rapidly changing organizations. We now discuss a few conceptual approaches with which to interpret the complexities of performing emotional labour within commodifying service economies.

Conceptual and theoretical implications

Where the organization of work in health care organizations was relatively stable and predictable for many decades, recent mergers, downsizing and restructuring have resulted in levels of worker insecurity in health care settings hitherto more familiar in other industries. Economic uncertainties, rapid redesign of services provided, and role redefinitions all con-tribute to a highly labile work climate wherein both workers and work are transformed. Thus, the economic realities of flexible accumulation (Harvey 1989; Jameson 1992) have important implications for contemporary subjectivities, as is well documented elsewhere (Giddens 1991; Flax 1993; Martin 1994). These are not only visible, but palpable for those working in health care contexts; for example, the stress on measuring patient satisfaction as a quality measure of successful outcomes (Fuller and Smith 1991). The economic uncertain-ties and rapid redesign of services and role definitions contribute to a highly fluid work climate wherein workers and work undergo transformation.

This suggests that the conceptual properties of a frame with which to understand emotions in changing structures must include and intertwine self, emotion and structure, a view notably articulated in Lofland's analysis of grief (1985). However, we cannot assume a unified, static self, and particularly not a unified, static professional self in the case of American nurses. What is required is a conceptualization that captures the fluidity of multiple selves.

In organizational contexts – and others as well – individuals bring a multiplicity of selves emergent from and influenced by the multiple realities which characterize their lives (Schutz 1962: 207–29). The work setting is not impermeable; it is but another site on which and in which histories, relationships, trajectories and valences play on and through the interacting individuals. The experiences in that worksite are not merely of the worksite *qua* worksite, but are constructed of these multiple historical moments and dimensions, even as are selves in those contexts (Scott 1991). Thus worksites represent fragmented possibilities that can be shaped and reshaped.

Theoretically, those interacting in shifting, unstable, rationalizing organizations themselves possess shifting, unstable, emergent 'mobile subjectivities' (Ferguson 1993). These move along many trajectories: race, class, gender, age, sexual orientation, familial position, regional origin, to name but a few. In the case of the nurse these are nested within and run through the individual's professional self, which is diversified by type of schooling, specialization, views on issues within nursing, likes or dislikes of certain kinds of patients (Liaschenko 1995). This does not deny that there may be, indeed is, varying agreement among nurses as to what 'good' professional care is. There is a moral core to the profession which is shared in varying degrees. However, those sharing that moral core to whatever degree are not static entities frozen in a timeless mould of 'the nurse' but are constantly emergent and altering as they construct themselves, their work, and their being in the changing care contexts.

This recognizes that those who provide care in shifting, rationalizing organizations both experience and express emotion not only in terms of what the organizations' demands are (and the demands may be fragmentary and diverse), but also because the selves brought to the context and created within it are multiple, hence providing the opportunity for many diverse responses. One has only to read Foner's (1994) or Diamond's (1992) accounts of the care in nursing homes to realize the layered complexities of emotional experience and expression in rationalized contexts.

Further, in understanding the complexities of intersubjectivity, it is helpful to consider that social actors shift adeptly and sometimes concurrently between different experiential modes – physical, cognitive and emotional – as well as between solo and joint levels of interaction (Clark *et al.* 1994). Intensity of feelings and cognitive reflexivity may be high or low (Mills and Kleinman 1988) depending on the situation, making it impossible to suggest any simplistic predictability. However, one consequence of working under conditions of rapid structural change may be 'emotional lag' (Olesen 1990). This refers to one of several possible relationships between a self or selves socialized to experience and express certain emotions and what is demanded or arises in changing structures and contexts. For example, as we have noted earlier, some altering structures pose normative demands for more neutral or even cooler responses than nurses socialized to a more supportive emotional style are comfortable in making (Burfoot 1994; James 1989, 1992).[4] A countering case might be found in the situation where providers, accustomed to relating to clients (formerly patients) in modes which once would have been characterized as 'affectively neutral' (Parsons 1953), now must present much warmer emotional responses. In both cases, the lag occurs between one part of the self, socialized to experience and express certain emotions, and another part emergent from the changed circumstances where expression of emotion differs. In the experience of emotional lag, expression might register along a wide continuum, ranging from authentic to fake, expressed in terms of diverse sets of realities, contexts and work criteria.

Because the self in its many facets continually reflects on multiple emotional encounters, assessing those encounters and the required or created emotional expression, the discrepancy between feeling and expression, past and emergent selves, may well generate another level of emotion. This might take the form of ambivalence, shame, or anger in discrepant situations or perhaps even pride in being able to transcend emotions experienced by an older self and to realize those in a newly emergent self. This second-order emotional reflexivity may lead to resistance to expected norms ranging from outlaw emotions to glazed numbness, alternatively defying local convention, or being unable to assimilate or perform appropriately. What will be of theoretical interest is whether new emotional skills emerge as individuals succeed or fail to develop an agility to adapt to the increased fluidity and ambivalences of emotionality required in contemporary work settings (Martin 1994).

The dynamics of how such new skills, emotional perceptions and expressions emerge are in part grounded in the important context of the workplace. The case of Total Quality Management illustrates this. As the emphasis on interpersonal skills in TQM philosophies suggests, the emotion work of service providers is a priority in managed-care contexts. While there are some efforts to standardize this work, it cannot be totally rationalized. Workers are embedded in workplace cultures which derive from workers' interactions and interpretations of the setting and their own multiple subjectivities (Foner 1994; Kotarba et al. 1996). This means they have the potential to select among numerous possible emotional experiences and expressions at the point of service; this type of emotional decision-making cannot be determined ahead of time. The microdynamics of emotional expression in the shifting scenarios of managed care will enter and play through those scenarios, shaping interactions and framing new levels of emotional definition and competencies which may or may not fit structural imperatives.

Using the case of American nursing in the highly rationalizing climate of contemporary managed care, we have attempted to delineate some elements with which to explore emotional experience and expression in shifting social structures. Such exploration requires that the elements of emotion, self, structure be intertwined in a framework which is sensitive to multiple subjectivities, temporality and the dynamics of workplace culture. It should also attend to second-order emotions emergent from the ruminations of the reflexive self or selves assessing emotional lag or congruence. Further conceptual refinement and empirical exploration of these elements are key tasks to advance the sociology of emotions and to grasp the emotional dynamics of care in contexts where, in spite of the redefinition of the patient as consumer, suffering, one of the key attributes of the patient, still occurs (Stacey 1976).

Notes

1   While it is the case that nursing is predominantly female, the gendered nature of the profession in part can be explained by labour force dynamics which allocate less powerful persons (women, women of colour) to dirty work (physical care) and devalued work such as emotional labour (Navarro 1994; Butter et al. 1987).

2   A district general manager quoted in Strong and Robinson's study of the NHS neatly poses this distinction between professional and commercial service work: 'A professional dealing with a patient has a one to one relationship which transcends organizational concerns . . . in the NHS there's a personal and emotional side. We have to deal with patients who are frightened and worried. This puts huge pressure on us, far greater than customers put on Burton's' (1990: 190). Nevertheless, emotion displays in customer service organizations must convey some sensitivity and concern if they are not to appear synthetic and offensive (Ashforth and Humphrey 1993: 96).

3   This approach to business is built on work done by W. Edward Deming and others in continuous quality improvement (CQI) during the 1950s. In 1987, the quality movement was applied to health care in a demonstration project by the Harvard Community Health Plan and was later incorporated into the accreditation policies of the Joint Commission on Accreditation of Healthcare Organizations (JCAHO) (Zonsius and Murphy 1995).

4   There are also instances where emotions change too rapidly for structural expectations; for instance, the persistent fear, reported among some health care providers and students, of persons with AIDS (Gillon 1987; Gerbert et al. 1988; Bosk and Frader 1990; American Civil Liberties Union 1990; Cooke et al. 1990). Fear has outpaced structural and professional expectations for emotional expression in some health care educational contexts and practice settings. Many places as yet do not well or

readily accommodate the presence and consequences of these fears, although there have been some alterations in structures in schools of nursing regarding how faculty should work with students who express fear of or refuse to care for patients with AIDS and in professional nursing associations which offer train-the-trainer sessions to resocialize providers who fear giving such care.

Bibliography

American Civil Liberties Union (1990) *Epidemic of Fear: A Survey of AIDS Discrimination in the 1980s and Policy Recommendations for the 1990s*. New York: ACLU.

Ashforth, B. E. and Humphrey, R. H. (1993) 'Emotional labour in service roles: the influence of identity', *Academy of Management Review* 1: 88–115.

Baker, K. M. (1995) 'Improving staff nurse conflict resolution skills', *Nursing Economics* 13(5): 295–8.

Bosk, C. L. and Frader, J. E. (1990) 'AIDS and its impact on medical work: the culture and politics of the shopfloor', *Millbank Quarterly Supplement on the Impact of AIDS* 68: 40–60.

Brannon, R. L. (1994) *Intensifying Care, the Hospital Industry, Professionalization, and the Reorganization of the Nursing Labour Process*. Amityville, NY: Baywood Publishing.

Buerhaus, P. I. (1994) 'Economics of managed competition and consequences to nurses, Part I and Part II', *Nursing Economics* 12(1): 10–17 and 12(2): 75–80, 106.

Burfoot, J. H. (1994) 'Outlaw emotions and the sensual dynamics of compassion: the case of emotion as instigator of social change', unpublished paper, Department of Sociology, Middlebury College, Burlington, VT.

Butter, I. H., Carpenter, E. S., Kay, B. J. and Simmons, R. (1987) 'Gender hierarchy in the health labour force', *International Journal of Health Services* 17(1): 133–49.

Campbell, M. (1988) 'Management as "ruling": a class phenomenon in nursing', *Studies in Political Economy* 27 (Fall): 29–51.

Clark, C., Kleinman, S. and Ellis, C. (1994) 'Conflicting reality readings and interactional dilemmas. Part I: The conceptual model', in J. Wentworth (ed.) *Social Perspectives on Emotion*. Greenwich, CT: JAI Press.

Collins, R. (1981) 'On the microfoundations of macrosociology', *American Journal of Sociology* 86: 984–1014.

Cooke, M., Koenig, B., Beery, N. and Folkman, S. (1990) 'Which physicians will provide AIDS care?', unpublished paper presented at the 6th International Conference on AIDS, San Francisco, CA (UCSF Center for AIDS Prevention Studies).

Davidhizar, R. (1992) 'When the nurse encounters crying', *Today's OR Nurse* (March): 28–32.

Davidhizar, R. and Bowen, M. (1993) 'Responding to irritable people in the OR setting', *Today's OR Nurse* (September/October): 43–7.

Davies, C. (1995) *Gender and the Professional Predicament in Nursing*. Milton Keynes, Bucks: Open University Press.

DeLew, N. *et al.* (1992) 'A layman's guide to the US health care system', *Health Care Financing Review* 14(1): 151–69.

DeMoro, R. A. (1996) 'It's the reality that's scary in current health care trends', *California Nurse* 92(1): 3, 10.

Diamond, T. (1992) *Making Grey Gold: Narratives of Nursing Home Care*. Chicago: University of Chicago Press.

Donahue, M. P. (1985) *Nursing, The Finest Art: An Illustrated History*. St Louis, MO: C. V. Mosby.

Droppleman, P. G. and Thomas, S. P. (1996) 'Anger in nurses: don't lose it, use it', *American Journal of Nursing* 96(4): 26–32.

Ellis, C. (1993) 'Incorporating the affective domain into staff development programs', *Journal of Nursing Staff Development* 9(3): 127–30.

Ferguson, K. E. (1993) *The Man Question: Visions of Subjectivity in Feminist Theory*. Berkeley, CA: University of California Press.

Flarey, D. L. (1995) *Redesigning Nursing Care Delivery: Transforming Our Future*. Philadelphia, PA: J. B. Lippincott.

Flax, J. (1993) *Disputed Subjects: Essays on Psychoanalysis, Politics and Philosophy*. New York: Routledge.

Flood, M. E. (1981) 'The troubling expedient: general staff nursing in United States hospitals in the

1930s: a means to institutional, educational, and personal ends', unpublished dissertation, University of California School of Education, Berkeley, CA.

Foner, N. (1994) *The Caregiving Dilemma: Work in an American Nursing Home*. Berkeley, CA: University of California Press.

Fox, R. C. (1989) *The Sociology of Medicine: A Participant Observer's View*. Englewood Cliffs, NJ: Prentice-Hall.

Fritz, D. J. and Cheeseman, S. (1994) 'Blueprint for integrating nurse extenders in critical care', *Nursing Economics* 12(6): 327–31.

Fuller, L. and Smith, V. (1991) 'Consumers' reports: management by customers in a changing economy', *Work, Employment and Society* 5(1): 1–16.

Garmarnikov, E. (1978) 'Sexual divisions of labour: the case of nursing', in A. Kuhn and A. M. Wolpe (eds) *Feminism and Materialism*. London: Routledge & Kegan Paul.

Garot, R. (1995) 'Substantive rationality in a bureaucratic setting', unpublished paper, Department of Sociology, University of California, Los Angeles, CA.

Gerbert, B., Maguire, B., Badner, V., Altman, D. and Stone, G. (1988) 'Why fear persists: health care professionals and AIDS', *Journal of the American Medical Association* 260: 3481–3.

Gerth, H. H. and Mills, C. W. (eds) (1958) *From Max Weber: Essays in Sociology*. New York: Oxford University Press.

Gibson, D. (1994) 'The struggle for reason: the sociology of emotion in organizations', unpublished paper, Anderson Graduate School of Business, University of California, Los Angeles, CA.

Giddens, A. (1991) *Self and Society in the Late Modern Age*. Stanford, CA: Stanford University Press.

Gillon, R. (1987) 'Refusal to treat AIDS and HIV positive patients', *British Medical Journal* 294: 1332–3.

Hampton, I. (ed.) (1949 [1893]) *Nursing of the Sick*. New York: McGraw-Hill.

Harvey, D. (1989) *The Condition of Postmodernity*. Cambridge: MA: Blackwell.

Himali, U. (1995) 'Managed care: does the promise meet the potential?', *The American Nurse* 1: 15–16.

Hochschild, A. R. (1983) *The Managed Heart: The Commercialization of Human Feeling*. Berkeley, CA: University of California Press.

Jaggar, A. M. (1989) 'Love and knowledge: emotion in feminist epistemology', in A. M. Jaggar and S. R. Bordo (eds) *Gender/Body/Knowledge: Feminist Reconstructions of Being and Knowing*. New Brunswick, NJ: Rutgers University Press.

James, N. (1989) 'Emotional labour: skill and work in the social regulation of feelings', *Sociological Review* 37(1): 15–42.

James, N. (1992) 'Care = organisation + physical labour + emotional labour', *Sociology of Health and Illness* 14(4): 488–509.

Jameson, F. (1992) *Postmodernism, or, The Cultural Logic of Late Capitalism*. Durham, NC: Duke University Press.

Jones, L. (1996) 'Rape crisis work and the unpersonal relationship: the delicate balance of intimacy and social distance', unpublished paper, Department of Sociology, University of Arizona, Tucson, AZ.

Kelly, K. (ed.) (1995) *Health Care Work Redesign*. Thousand Oaks, CA: Sage.

Kotarba, J. A., Ragsdale, D. and Morrow, J. R., Jr (1997) 'Everyday culture in a dedicated HIV/AIDS hospital unit', *Sociology of Health and Illness*, forthcoming.

Leidner, R. (1993) *Fast Food, Fast Talk: Service Work and the Routinization of Life*. Berkeley, CA: University of California Press.

Liaschenko, J. (1995) 'Artificial personhood: nursing ethics in a medical world', *Journal of Nursing Ethics* 2(3): 185–96.

Lief, H. I. and Fox, R. C. (1963) 'Training for detached "concern" in medical students', in H. E. Lief *et al.* (eds) *The Psychological Basis of Medical Practice*. New York: Harper & Row.

Lofland, L. H. (1985) 'The social shaping of emotion: the case of grief', *Symbolic Interaction* 8: 171–90.

Lutz, C. and White, G. M. (1986) 'The anthropology of emotions', *Annual Review of Anthropology* 15: 405–36.

MacLaren, E. (1994) 'Basics of managed care', *Nurseweek* (June): 10–11.

McLaughlin, F. E., Thomas, S. and Bates, M. (1995) 'Changes related to care delivery patterns', *JONA* (*Journal of Nursing Administration*), 25(5): 35–46.

Martin, E. (1994) *Flexible Bodies*. Boston, MA: Beacon Press.

Melosh, B. (1982) 'The Physician's Hand', Work, Culture and Conflict in American Nursing. Philadelphia, PA: Temple University Press.

Melosh, B. (1983) 'Doctors, patients, and "big nurse": work and gender in the post-war hospital', in E. C. Lagemann (ed.) *Nursing History: New Perspectives, New Possibilities*. New York: Teachers College Press.

Mills, T. and Kleinman, S. (1988) 'Emotions, reflexivity, and action: an interactionist analysis', *Social Forces* 66(4): 1009–27.

Navarro, V. (1994) *The Politics of Health Policy: The US Reforms, 1980–1994*. Cambridge, MA: Blackwell.

Olesen, V. L. (1990) 'The neglected emotions: a challenge to medical sociology', *Medical Sociology News* 16(1): 11–25.

Parsons, T. (1953) 'Illness and the role of the physician', in C. Kluckhohn and H. A. Murray (eds) *Personality in Nature, Society and Culture*. New York: Knopf.

Raudonis, B. M. (1993) 'The meaning and impact of empathic relationships in hospice nursing', *Cancer Nursing* 16(4): 304–9.

Reverby, S. (1987) *Ordered to Care: The Dilemma of American Nursing, 1850–1945*. Cambridge: Cambridge University Press.

Riley, D. W. (1994) 'Integrated health care systems: emerging models', *Nursing Economics* 12(4): 201–6.

Schaefer, K. M. and Peterson, K. (1992) 'Effectiveness of coping strategies among critical care nurses', *Dimensions of Critical Care Nursing* 11(1): 28–34.

Schutz, A. (1962) 'On multiple realities', in his *Collected Papers: The Problem of Social Reality*, ed. M. Natanson. The Hague: Martinus Nijhoff.

Scott, J. (1991) 'The evidence of experience', *Critical Inquiry* 17: 773–9.

Shott, S. (1979) 'Emotion and social life: a symbolic interactionist analysis', *American Journal of Sociology* 84: 1317–34.

Sovie, M. D. (1995) 'Tailoring hospitals for managed care and integrated health systems', *Nursing Economics* 13(2): 72–83.

Stacey, M. (1976) 'The health services consumer, a sociological misconception' *Sociological Review*, Monograph 22.

Stenross, B. and Kleinman, S. (1989) 'Highs and lows of emotional labour, detectives' encounters with criminals and victims', *Urban Life* 17(4): 435–52.

Strauss, A. L., Fagerhaugh, S., Suczek, B. and Wiener, C. L. (1982) 'Sentimental work in the technological hospital', *Sociology of Health and Illness* 12: 254–78.

Strong, P. M. and Robinson, J. (1990) *The NHS: Under New Management*. Milton Keynes, Bucks: Open University Press.

Sugrue, N. M. (1982) 'Emotions as property and context for negotiation', *Urban Life* 11(3): 280–92.

Sutton, R. I. (1991) 'Maintaining norms about expressed emotions', *Administrative Science Quarterly* 36: 245–68.

Teasdale, K. (1995) 'Theoretical and practical considerations on the use of reassurance in the nursing management of anxious patients', *Journal of Advanced Nursing* 22: 79–86.

Thoits, P. A. (1996) 'Managing the emotions of others', *Symbolic Interaction* 19(2): 85–110.

Van Maanen, J. and Kunda, G. (1989) ' "Real feelings": emotional expression and organizational culture', in M. M. Staw and L. L. Cummings (eds) *Research in Organizational Behaviour* 11: 43–103; Greenwich, CT: JAI Press.

Weigert, A. and Franks, D. D. (1989) 'Ambivalence: a touchstone of the modern temper', in D. D. Franks and E. D. McCarthy (eds) *The Sociology of the Emotions*. Greenwich, CT: JAI Press.

Zimmerman, P. G. (1995) 'Replacement of nurses with unlicensed assistive personnel: the erosion of professional nursing and what we can do', *Journal of Emergency Nursing* 21(3): 208–12.

Zonsius, M. K. and Murphy, M. (1995) 'Use of total quality management sparks staff nurse participation in continuous quality improvement', *Nursing Clinics of North America* 30(1): 1–12.

Chapter 8

Simon J. Williams

MODERNITY AND THE EMOTIONS: CORPOREAL REFLECTIONS ON THE (IR)RATIONAL

> Life as immediately experienced is precisely that unity of being formed and that reaching out beyond form . . . Life is always more life than there is room for . . .
>
> (Simmel 1971:370)

> The history of corporeality is not merely the disciplining of the body and the destruction of sensuality any more than it is the great emancipation of the body's potential: it is the paradoxical combination of the two.
>
> (Falk 1994:66)

WHILST MUCH HAS BEEN written about processes of Western rationalisation and the 'crises' of modernity, few writers have sought to address these issues through the specific lens of the emotions. To be sure, writers such as Marx and Durkheim, Weber and Simmel were not blind to the emotional implications of their analyses, yet these insights remain at best partial and under-developed in comparison with their more explicit theoretical focus on questions of social order and social action, liberty and discipline, autonomy and control. In contrast to these traditional sociological concerns, we now have a rapidly growing body of literature on the emotions in social life: issues which, in turn, connect up with the proliferation of body-oriented discourse and the move to a more 'postmodern' form of theorising.

It therefore seems both timely and instructive to relate these disparate bodies of literature together through a focus on modernity and the emotions. Central issues here include the problematic relationship between reason and emotion, the contradictory features of modernity as both order and chaos, and the search for alternative, more 'authentic', ways of being and knowing; ways which overturn centuries of dualist thought and practice, opening up new possibilities for the 'resensualisation' or 're-enchantment' of Western society.

It is within this intellectual climate and context that the present paper is located. In particular, I wish to argue for a position which, rather than seeing reason and emotion as fundamentally opposed, instead views rationality itself as a 'passionately' held belief or cherished ideal: one which is, in large part, 'irrational' or 'unreasonable'. Western thought, in other words, both traditionally and to the present day, displays an 'irrational passion for dispassionate rationality' (Rieff 1979), the contradictions of which are only now becoming fully apparent.

Seen in this new more sensual light, reason and emotion are not in fact antithetical to one another. Rather, the duality which, analytically speaking, has cast them as two separate 'things' has in fact been turned, over the course of Western history and culture, into a dualism; an ideological position in which the former has been prioritised (if not reified or fetishised) over the latter, for social and political ends. To be sure, 'gains' have undoubtedly occurred through this rationalising process, from the civilising of bodies to the historical decline of infectious diseases, yet the tensions within modernity itself, as both order and chaos, are now becoming increasingly apparent. Modernity, in short, is collapsing under the weight of its own contradictions. Where this leaves us, of course, is a hotly debated issue. What seems clear, however, is that the obituary for modernity should not yet be written: intimations of postmodernity remain just that. Emotions, as we shall see, lie at the heart of these issues, reflecting and reinforcing these dilemmatic features of modernity at one and the same time.

In the first section of this paper, I examine these claims further through a preliminary discussion of what, precisely, emotions are, and how they relate to dominant structures of Western rationality. The aim here is to paint, in broad brush strokes, a more 'integrated' model of being and knowing in which emotion is no longer seen as the embodied enemy of disembodied reason but is in fact its ally. It is reasonable, in short, to re-think reason itself. Having done so, I then proceed to consider, through the lens of the emotions, the contradictory features of modernity as both 'order' and 'chaos'. In particular, following the recent work of writers such as Meštrović and Mellor and Shilling, I argue that what we are currently witnessing, for better or worse, is the rise of new 'effervescent' forms of the 'sacred': developments which are changing the ways in which people 'see' and 'keep in touch' with the world around them. Modernity, I conclude, is, at one and the same time, both the antithesis and confirmation of a more sensually based order; one in which the emotions come to the fore and rationality, as traditionally conceived, fights an increasing 'rearguard action'.

Being and knowing: 're-embodying' reason

Historically and to the present day, emotions have been regarded as the very antithesis of the detached, scientific mind and the quest for objectivity, truth and wisdom. Whilst the split between reason and emotion was never, in fact, absolute for the Greeks,[1] these divisions were greatly sharpened during the seventeenth century when reason became redefined as a purely 'instrumental' faculty 'uncontaminated' by values and emotions. Linked to the rise of modern science, this positivist doctrine stipulated that trustworthy knowledge could only be established by methods which neutralised the values and emotions of its (dis)embodied practitioners. The objective scientific mind could, therefore, enjoy access to the 'facts' of nature, in an unmediated manner, devoid of subjective baggage or the value-laden clutter of human feelings.

This, in turn, relates to a broader set of distinctions which, traditionally speaking, have sought to separate mind from body, nature from culture, the public from the private. As defining characteristics and dominant features of Western thinking, these divisions, together with the broader rationalist view of the world which underpins them, have come under increasing attack from a variety of quarters (Seidler 1994). Recent approaches to epistemology, for example, have served to undermine rigid distinctions such as 'fact' and 'value', 'head' and 'heart', and to question the notion that emotions are simple instinctual responses with no role to play in knowledge acquisition or cognitive reflection (Rose 1994). Similarly, work within cultural anthropology has done much to challenge the rationality/ emotionality divide, including the role of symbols and meanings in the development of mind, self and emotion (Lutz 1988; Rosaldo 1984; Shweder 1984; Shweder and LeVine 1984).[2]

Contra centuries of Western thinking, reflective thought, as Damasio (1994) convincingly demonstrates, requires the 'tagging' of cognition with emotions. Without this capacity, decision-making becomes difficult if not impossible as there is no criterion with which to drive cognition in a given direction. Emotions, in other words, are central to the 'effective deployment' of reason. They are also involved, on a deep level, in all observation, from the supposedly dispassionate observations of science to the common perceptions of everyday life (Jaggar 1989:153–4). This is not, of course, to deny that our feelings can wreak havoc with the processes of logical thought and rational decision-making: they can and do. Yet, the absence of emotion, as recent studies show, is apparently no less damaging or devastating (Damasio 1994).[3]

Seen in this light, emotions and feelings are not in fact 'intruders' into the bastion of male reason, rather they are 'enmeshed within its network, for better or worse' (Damasio 1994:xvi). Rather than repressing emotion in Western epistemology, therefore, it is necessary to fundamentally 'rethink the relation between knowledge and emotion and construct conceptual models that demonstrate the mutually constitutive rather than oppositional relation between reason and emotion. Far from precluding the possibility of reliable knowledge, emotion as well as value must be shown as necessary to such knowledge' (Jaggar 1989:157). Just as 'appropriate' emotions may contribute to the development of knowledge, so too the growth of knowledge may contribute to the development of appropriate emotions. Emotion, in short, is vital to systematic knowledge: a relationship which, at its best, is reciprocal and mutually informing/reinforcing (Jaggar 1989:163).

Underpinning these issues lies a deeper set of questions concerning what, precisely, emotions are, and the role they play in the very constitution of society and the dynamics of everyday life. These are issues I shall elaborate on more fully below. For the moment, however, let me address the specific ontological issues they raise. Whilst debates continue to rage over the relative contribution of biology and society to that intangible human compound, 'the emotions',[4] they are, I suggest, best seen as complex, multi-faceted phenomena which are irreducible to any one domain or discourse. Emotions, in other words, are thinking, moving, feeling 'complexes' which, sociologically speaking, are *relational* in nature and linked to 'circuits of selfhood' (Denzin 1984); comprising both corporeal, embodied aspects, as well as socio-cultural ones.[5]

Whilst basic emotions – rooted, it would seem, in our biological make-up and shared amongst all human beings as embodied agents – are involved, they are endlessly elaborated, like colours on a painter's palette, across time and through culture. As Burkitt (1997:42) states:

> Emotions . . . are multi-dimensional and cannot be reduced to biology, relations, or discourse alone, but belong to all these dimensions as they are constituted in ongoing relational practices. As such, the objects of our study in the sociology of emotions cannot be understood as 'things', but are complexes composed of different dimensions of embodied, interdependent human existence.

Seen in this way, emotions are essentially communicative, intercorporeal and intersubjective, constituted as physical and cultural dispositions through techniques of the body, forged within a particular social habitus. These body techniques, in turn, can only properly be understood within the context of the power relations of particular social and cultural groups, located within historical space and time (Burkitt 1997:42). Emotions, in other words are *emergent* properties, located at the intersection of physiological *dispositions*, material *circumstances*, and socio-cultural *elaboration*.

Not only do emotions underpin the phenomenological experience of our bodies in sickness and health (Bendelow and Williams 1998), they also provide the basis for social reciprocity and exchange – what Wentworth and Yardley (1994) term the 'deep sociality' of emotions – and the 'link' between personal problems and broader public issues of social structure: itself the defining hallmark of the 'sociological imagination' (Mills 1959).

This interactive, relational character of embodied emotional experience and expression, offers us a way of moving 'beyond' microanalytic, subjective, internal or individualistic analyses, towards broader landscapes and wider vistas in which embodied agency can be understood 'not merely as individual but also as institution making' (Csordas 1994:14; Lyon and Barbalet 1994). The emphasis here is on the active, emotionally expressive body as the basis of self and sociality, meaning and order, set within the broader socio-cultural realms of everyday life and the 'ritualised' forms of interaction and exchange they involve (Williams and Bendelow 1998).

How then, do these emotional issues translate into current debates about the future of modernity, and what questions do they raise concerning the relationship between bodily order and corporeal transgression? It is to these specific issues that I now turn.

Modernity and ambivalence: a preliminary sketch

A fundamental point of departure in this paper is that, far from being an inherently stable, rational 'order', modernity, however we describe it, is in fact highly ambiguous and contradictory. Cutting a swathe through the proliferation of current literature and debates on the 'fate' of modernity, it can simply be stated that modernity, ever since its inception, has embraced, in paradoxical fashion, the centrifugal tendency for 'order' and the centripetal tendency for 'chaos'. The history of modernity, in short, involves both liberty and discipline (Wagner 1994), certainty and doubt, the Apollonian (i.e. control) and the Dionysian (i.e. chaos) (Rojek 1994, 1995).

Bauman (1992, 1991) is perhaps the key exponent of this view, noting how the roots of so-called 'postmodernity' are firmly located within the contingent 'project' of modernity itself. Seen in this light, postmodernity, properly interpreted, does not necessarily signify the end of modernity. Rather, it is no more or less than the modern mind (Bauman 1991:272) taking a . . .

> long, attentive and sober look, at its conditions and its past works, not fully liking what it sees and sensing the urge to change. Postmodernity is modernity coming of age: modernity looking at itself at a distance rather than from inside, making a full inventory of its gains and issues, psychoanalysing itself, discovering the intentions it never before spelled out, finding them mutually cancelling and incongruous . . . coming to terms with its own impossibility; a self-monitoring modernity, one that consciously discards what it was once unconsciously doing.

For Bauman, order and chaos are twin features of modernity: two sides of the same coin. The modern project – the elements of which include the legislative ambitions of philosophical reason, gardening ambitions of the state, ordering ambitions of the applied sciences – construed under-determination, ambivalence and contingency as a threat; making their 'elimination into one of the main *foci imaginarii* of social order' (1991:16).

Order, in other words, tied as it is to a rationalist ambition of an inherently controllable world, is continuously engaged in a war for survival: a war in which chaos – i.e. 'the miasma of the indeterminate and unpredictable' – is its only alternative. It is against this chaotic negativity, that the positivity of order construes itself. The negativity of chaos, in other words, is itself a product of order's self-constituted positivity: 'its side-effect, its waste, yet the *sine qua non* of its (reflective) possibility . . . without chaos, no order' (Bauman 1991:7).

From this it follows that raw existence – i.e. existence free of intervention, unordered existence – now becomes allied or associated with *nature*: 'something to be *mastered, subordinated, remade* so as to be readjusted to human needs . . . [a] socially effected order in which artificiality is natural' (Bauman 1991:7). Here, we return again to the earlier discussion concerning the ideological association of the emotional body with nature as opposed to culture, biology as opposed to society, the private as opposed to the public.

This, in turn, raises deeper ontological questions concerning the nature of bodily order and corporeal transgression. As sensual as well as sensory beings, our corporeality is inextricably bound up with '(human) desire as opposed to (animal) need' (Falk 1994): an 'exuberant', 'uncontainable' flow which is centrally organised around the pleasure/pain axis. Eroticism and the emotions lie at the heart of these issues. To be sure, bodies, as the history of Western civilisation shows, are amenable to discipline and control – from the prison to the factory, the school to the asylum – but they are also fundamentally 'excessive': always leaning, through their libidinal flows and corporeal desires, their pleasures and their pains, their agonies and their ecstasies, in the direction of excess and threatening to 'overspill' their culturally constituted boundaries.[6]

As thinkers as diverse as Schopenhauer, Nietzsche and Simmel remind us, the will or passions are stronger than the mind, threatening to overturn the rationally ordered world. Indeed, it [is] from this very 'recalcitrance', including the supposedly 'unruly' nature of bodily emotions and desires, that the need for 'discipline' and control arises (cf. Bakhtin 1968 and Elias 1978 on the (un)civilised body). Bodies, in short, rooted as they are in the problem of human desire and the vicissitudes of the emotions, are sensual rather than ascetic, fluid rather than static, volatile rather than fixed.

From this it follows that questions surrounding modernity and ambivalence, are intimately related to problems of bodily desire and the vicissitudes of human emotions in Western thought, expressing, on the one hand, the rational impulse for order, and on the other hand, the corporeal spectre of chaos and transgression. It is to a fuller account of these dual features of modernity as both 'order' and 'chaos', 'regulation' and 'transgression', together with their emotional consequences for embodied individuals, groups and collectivites, that I now turn.

The Apollonian impulse for rational 'order'

To be sure, 'disciplined' bodies have been around since time immemorial. From religious denunciation of the slimy desires of the flesh in Christian Pauline teaching, to the long historical curve of the civilising process from the Renaissance onwards, the body has been steadily socialised, rationalised and individualised (Shilling 1993). In mediaeval times, as Elias's (1978) work on the history of manners so clearly shows, desires and impulses were freely and directly expressed in conscious thoughts and actions: from warrior nobilities' brutal killings to the grotesque realism of Rabelaisian carnival culture and its parodying of feudal hierarchies. With the subsequent development of 'civilised bodies', however, a growing division occurs between consciousness and drives, as thresholds of shame and embarrassment rise and foresight, forward planning and strategic decision-making increase. As Elias (1978:257) explains:

> The autonomous individual self-controls produced in this way in social life, such as 'rational thought' or 'moral conscience', now interpose themselves more sternly than ever before between spontaneous and emotional impulses, on the one hand, and the skeletal muscles, on the other, preventing the former with greater severity from directly determining the latter (i.e. action) without the permission of these control mechanisms.

These civilising processes, and the psychogenetic transformations they involve, are not without their costs. Rather, as Freud's (1982/[1930]) deliberation on *Civilisation and its Discontents* suggest, the passionate affects struggle no less violently within: the well-spring of discontent, the tragedy of the human condition in civilised times. The civilising process, in short, is never entirely without pain: 'it always leaves scars' (Elias 1982:244).

If this is true of civilised bodies in the past, then it is particularly true of consumer bodies in the present. Within consumer culture our relationship to commodities is predicated less upon real need than upon their inexhaustible ability to 'incite desire'. 'I consume therefore I am' becomes a dominant cultural motif (Falk 1994), as representations (of the 'good' life) are substituted for reality, and settled convictions are overturned in favour of 'flexibility, mobility and an incessant search for the new' (Featherstone 1991). It is against this backdrop that the project of the self becomes translated, to a greater or lesser degree, into the possession of 'desired goods' and the pursuit of 'artificially framed lifestyles'. As Giddens states: 'The consumption of ever-novel goods becomes in some part a substitute for the genuine development of self; appearance replaces essence as the visible signs of successful consumption come actually to out-weigh the use-values of the goods and services in question' (1991:198).

Given these commodifying pressures, there is a tendency for individuals to place ever more importance upon the appearance and presentation of the body as constitutive of self-identity. Here, in a seemingly 'narcissistic' (Lasch 1979) or 'reflexive' age (Giddens 1991), a premium is placed upon corporeal images of youth, beauty, health and fitness. The closer the body approximates to these idealised images, the higher its 'exchange-value' (Featherstone 1991:177). This, together with the 'sexualisation of wants and desires' (Seidman 1991), means that the body itself becomes something of a 'fetishised' commodity; one which has to be attractively 'packaged', 'marketed' and 'sold'. Indeed, it would not be too much of an exaggeration to say that within consumer culture the balance has tilted from bodies producing commodities (i.e. 'externalising objects of labour'), to commodities producing bodies (i.e. 'internalising objects of consumption') (Faurschou 1988).

It is within this context that body maintenance comes to the fore. Whilst in pre-modern times, bodily discipline/asceticism was sought to serve higher spiritual ends and repress the 'temptations' of the flesh, today it is instead concerned with the (aesthetic) cultivation of outer appearance and the (hedonistic) expression of desire. Here, 'inner' concerns with health and the optimal functioning of the body merge imperceptibly with 'outer' concerns with appearance (i.e. 'the look'), movement and control of the body across social time and space (Featherstone 1991). Today, the firm, well-toned and muscled body has become a symbol of 'correct *attitude*'; 'it means that one "cares" about oneself and how one appears to others, suggesting willpower, energy, control over infantile impulse, the ability to "make something" of oneself' (Bordo 1990:94–5).

Even emotions, the last bastion of 'authenticity' in an 'inauthentic' age, have been 'put to work', so to speak, in advanced capitalist society. Hochschild's (1983) *The Managed Heart*, for example, is replete with references to the 'human costs' of emotional labour, from 'burnout' to feeling 'phony', 'cynicism' to 'emotional deadness', 'guilt' to self 'blame': costs which, she suggests, could be reduced if workers felt a greater sense of control over the conditions of their working lives.

In highlighting these emotional dilemmas, particularly amongst the middle classes, Hochschild forces home the more general sociological point, alluded to above, that human feeling, in advanced capitalist society, has itself become increasingly 'commoditization'. As she states (1979:569):

> When deep gestures of exchange enter the market sector and are bought and sold as an aspect of labour power, feelings are commoditized. When the manager gives the company his [sic] enthusiastic faith, when the airline stewardess gives her passengers her psyched-up but quasi-genuine reassuring warmth, what is sold as an aspect of labour power is deep acting.

As Stearns (1994) perceptively argues, twentieth-century cultural styles, particularly those cultivated in contemporary America, stunt and stifle the emotions behind a veneer of '*cool*' – a situation succinctly summarised in the street credible phrase 'chill out'. These issues have recently been taken further by Meštrović (1997), who claims, radically perhaps, that we are now living in what he terms a 'postemotional' age; a 'neo-Orwellian world' of 'mechanised feelings' and 'quasi-emotional responses'. Modernity's diametrically opposed tendencies toward *order* and *chaos* have, according to Meštrović, resulted in a new hybrid world of rationally ordered, McDonaldised emotions (i.e. bite-sized, pre-packaged, rationally manufactured emotions): a 'happy meal' consumed by the masses (cf. Ritzer 1992). Postemotionalism, as Meštrović explains, is a system designed to avoid 'emotional disorder', prevent 'loose ends' in emotional exchange, civilise 'wild' arenas of emotional life, and in general to order emotions so that the social world 'hums as smoothly as a well-maintained machine' (1997:150). The power of the rational mind, enshrined by the Enlightenment, has therefore given way to an 'indolent mindlessness' and kitsch emotional reactions to serious problems and world issues.

Central to these developments has been the emergence of the 'post-other-directed' type who takes his/her cues from peers and the media as to when s/he should rationally choose to exhibit curdled/vicarious indignation, niceness or other pre-packaged emotions. Within such a neo-Marcusean society of 'happy consciousness', feeling becomes increasingly separated from action, and 'compassion fatigue' looms large: a 'viscerated compassion' churned out by the culture industry which is really more like pity. The 'ways of escape' have also, Meštrović claims, been rationalised and McDonaldised, from leisure to pseudo-therapy: leaving little room for a truly 'authentic' or spontaneous emotional response. Even sexuality has lost its more spontaneous connection with eroticism, through the prioritisation of reflexive (i.e. cognitive) control (cf. Giddens 1992) over embodied sensuality and the temporary fusion of selves (cf. Bataille 1985, 1987/[1962]): what Jackson and Scott (1997) have succinctly termed the 'Taylorisation of sex'. The result is the dawning of artificially contrived 'authenticity' – what Meštrović appositely refers to as the 'authenticity industry'. The McDonaldisation of emotions, in short, has been an attempt to make the 'Enlightenment project, therapy, civilisation, and communities all seem predictably "nice" and to create Disneyesque, artificial realms of the authentic' (Meštrović 1997:98).

Seen in this light, postemotionalism, as Meštrović insists, is best viewed as an extension of the 'cult of the machine'. As such, it holds the potential to degenerate further into an entirely new form of totalitarianism: one which is so 'nice', 'tolerant' and 'charming', whatever the event, that it is hard to resist. Within this 'counterfeit' logic, a new form of barbarism is dressed up in refined language and cultural euphemisms (such as 'ethnic cleansing') are used to disguise motives that should never qualify as 'civilised' (i.e. a 'counterfeit civilising process') (Meštrović 1997).

Discussion of these postemotional issues, in turn, simultaneously points us in two temporal directions. On the one hand, looking *back*, it recalls Simmel's (1971) classic essay on the fate of mental life in the metropolis. For Simmel, there is perhaps no psychic phenomenon which is so unconditionally reserved for the city as the blasé outlook and its associated features of reserve, aversion and indifference, both to people and the distinctions between things. On the other hand, looking *forward*, it succinctly captures the cultural contradictions and banal features of what is fast becoming an 'information-overloaded' society – including the advent of so-called cyberspace – in which fact becomes fiction and television reality. (See also Tester (1998) and Williams (1998) for a debate on the relative merits of this case.)

Postemotional or just plain bored and blasé, the tensions and dilemmas of modernity as a rationally ordered, McDonaldised world, are therefore thrown into critical relief through a focus on the vicissitudes of emotions and the problem of 'authenticity' in a seemingly 'inauthentic' age. Yet is this the whole story? Are we simply 'passive dupes' of the system, postemotional or otherwise, or are the 'lines of escape' still open for our 'recalcitrant' bodies and 'unruly' minds? It is to these questions that I now turn through a consideration of modernity's chaotic tendencies and the ever present threat or promise of corporeal 'transgression'.

The corporeal desire for 'transgression': the return to 'Dionysian' values?

> Transgression does not deny the taboo but transcends and completes it.
>
> (Bataille 1987/[1962]:63)

> The gods, their myths and rituals have changed their names, but they are still hard at work in both sociality and the environment.
>
> (Maffesoli 1995:139).

As I have argued, the full story of modernity has never simply been about order and discipline, but also about chaos and disorder, liberty and autonomy, the contingent and the unpredictable. From Schopenhauer to Nietzsche, Bataille to Simmel, the passionate unruly will to life, and the Dionysian quest for the 'authentic', have been constant themes; haunting the ambitions of the modernist 'gardener' and disrupting the vision of a 'perfect', rationally ordered world.[7]

Whilst Meštrović's thesis ends up prioritising rational control and mechanised logic as the order of the (postemotional) day, I wish to hold on, instead, to what for some may be a seen as a more optimistic view of the body and the emotions in contemporary society as the most autonomous and recalcitrant aspect of human social life; feelings and passions which, whilst central to society and amenable to (rational) management and control, always threaten to 'overspill' or 'transgress' the socio-cultural boundaries which currently seek to 'contain' them.

To be sure, Meštrović acknowledges the continuing existence of this more autonomous realm of human feelings, yet the general thrust of his analysis reduces them to the status of mere 'pockets of authenticity' in an 'inauthentic age'; a colonisation, in effect, of that last true bastion of human freedom and spontaneity, the emotions. The arguments contained in this paper, however, suggest that this can never be case: the neo-Orwellian fiction of a fully mechanised world, like the dreams of the modernist 'gardener', remain just that. Rational colonisation of the life-world can, in short, never be absolute. Lines of escape will always be found: our transgressive bodies/recalcitrant minds will see to that. Here we return again to an ontological view of the body as fundamentally excessive/transgressive; something which is related, in *dialectical* fashion, to the broader socio-cultural 'order', constituting both its confirmation and repudiation all at once.

More generally, I wish to pick up on a theme only partially addressed earlier: namely, the emotional underpinnings of reason and the social order, from the Enlightenment onwards. As Shilling (1997) has shown through a close re-reading of the so-called 'underground wing' of Durkheim's sociology, his vision of society, *contra* rationalist interpretations, was of the emergence of a moral order shaped less by cognitive control than the sensual impulses and possibilities of 'effervescent bodies'. For Durkheim, in other words, the rational demands of society are intimately related to the 'irrational "fires" of effervescent sociality': forms of sociality which, through the immanence of powerful passions and emotions associated with the 'sacred', sensually transform people's experiences of their 'fleshy selves and the world around them' (Shilling 1997).[8]

As Durkheim reminds us, the Enlightenment, properly understood, made a 'religion' out of rationality: a veritable 'cult' of reason which, paradoxically, since its inception, has involved an 'irrational overestimation of its powers' (Meštrović 1997:80). Worshipping reason, both inside and outside the academy, has (until quite recently) been the order of the day, a ritual dance of identification if not 'salvation' in a secular age: one which, like all forms of worship, takes on certain 'sacred' qualities which both shape and sustain its fetishised existence. Emotions, in short, *contra* centuries of dominant Western dualistic thinking, are central to reason, even when ideologically denounced as its antithesis.

More generally, in worshipping the Enlightenment, its 'dark side', including the Holocaust, Communism and fascism, has conveniently been left out of the equation: a legacy founded, as Meštrović rightly reminds us, on both 'science and irrationalism, human rights as well as brutal oppression, cosmopolitanism as well as nationalism' (1997:86). Seen in this light, the Enlightenment project, like the civilising process itself, has something of a 'counterfeit' logic or feel to it: a 'one-sided ideological commitment' to the seemingly 'positive' aspects of rationality at the expense of the negative; the 'virtuous' and 'humanitarian' at the expense of the 'violent and destructive' (Meštrović 1997:86). Indeed, even so-called critical social theorists, such as Adorno and Marcuse, Horkheimer and Habermas, paradoxically support the Enlightenment 'project' through the sanctification of seemingly 'rational' solutions to problems of 'over-rationalisation': an 'emotional sanctification' of a truly 'authentic' rationality to counter the worst excesses of capitalism and its pernicious brand of instrumental rationality (Meštrović 1997:80–6).

Against this allegedly 'postemotional backdrop' and 'counterfeit logic', new decivilising trends, waves of informalisation, and manifestations of collective effervescence are, it is claimed, coming to the fore, for better or worse. Taking each of these issues in turn, whilst an overall direction is certainly detectable concerning the development of civilised bodies, it is none the less clear that these civilising processes are uneven and can indeed go 'into reverse'. This is particularly so when groups are threatened with the loss of their existing social position, or when relations between 'established' and 'outsider' groups in society lead to the use of violence as a means of frustrated expression on the part of these latter groups (Shilling 1993:168–70).[9]

Waves of both formalisation and informalisation complicate the picture further: processes in which, during periods such as the 1960s, a highly 'controlled decontrolling of the emotions' took place (see, for example, Wouters 1998, 1987, 1986, and Mennell 1990). As Mennell (1990) notes, civilising processes take centuries to solidify and years to inculcate in the young, yet only moments to break down or transgress. At the very least, arguments such as the 'controlled de-controlling of emotions notwithstanding', these decivilising processes suggest a situation that sits 'uneasily beside the stable internalisation of behavioural codes' and socio/psychogenic restraints and controls (Shilling 1993:173). This, coupled with the fact that individuals may 'selectively apply these civilised standards, depending on the differing social contexts they inhabit', and the situational imperatives embedded within them (Shilling 1993:172), suggests that a focus on 'civilised bodies' may in fact miss a significant part of contemporary 'decivilised' social life: both public and private.

These issues have been taken much further by recent writers such as Maffesoli, for whom waves of informalisation are merely part of a broader picture concerning the resurgence of Dionysian values. Rooted in a Durkheimian concern with 'collective effervescence' and the 'sacred', together with the Bataillean theme of the 'heterogeneous' – i.e. a concern with all those 'excessive' things which stand opposed to the rationalistic, capitalistic, profane world and the instrumental push towards social 'homogeneity – Maffesoli celebrates, in true Nietzschean style, what he claims to be a shift from the Promethean to the Dionysian in Western culture. A shift, that is, from the Weberian Protestant Ethic (i.e. productivist modernity) towards a society, or more precisely a form of *sociality*, governed by the 'empathetic logic of emotional renewal' and the (non-productivist) expressivity of collective effervescence. We are living, Maffesoli claims, at a decisive moment in the history of modernity, one in which the 'rationalization of the world' is being displaced if not replaced by a 're-enchantment of the world': i.e. a period of 'emotional renewal'.

In advancing these arguments, Maffesoli appears, at first sight, to be developing a distinctively different view of social life and social change, one which is more or less opposed to the rationalistic assumptions embedded in notions such as 'modernisation', the cognitively oriented emphasis on issues of 'individualisation' and 'social reflexivity' in late modernity (cf. Giddens and Beck), or the mechanised logic of 'postemotional society' (cf. Meštrović). For Maffesoli, in contrast, we live in an age characterised by a 'decline of individualism' and a 'return of the tribes': a form of 'sociality' based on a new 'culture of sentiment' and multiple forms of 'being together' (what he terms '*proxemics*') (Evans 1997).

The 'sacred canopy' has indeed all but collapsed, only to be replaced by a series of more shifting alliances and sensual solidarities which, taken together, spell a 're-enchantment' of the world in a multitude of disparate, effervescent ways. Signs of this, Maffesoli (1996:72) claims, are all around us:

> even in the most aseptic places, and in the gregarious solitude that the contemporary techno-structure has contrived to construct, we already see a collective reappropriation of space that ploughs its furrows deep. Sporting events, musical or political gatherings, the sounds and hubbub of the streets of our towns, and festive occasions of all kinds forcefully underline the pre-eminence of the whole. What is more, its pre-eminence increasingly tends to result in a fusional reality, or in what is termed 'the return of Dionysiac values', with individual characteristics being replaced by organicity or what Fourier called the '*architectonic*' of the whole.

For Maffesoli the 'underground centrality' of sociality – one which 'bubbles up' in resistance to stifling Promethean instrumental rationality – bestows strength, vitality and effervescence to social life: an emotional rejuvenation of social life and an antidote to the cultural 'crisis' of individualism (Evans 1997). From New Age movements and alternative therapies, to the 'relativization of the work ethic', and from networks of 'amourous camaraderie' to the importance of dress and cosmetics, the emblematic figure of Dionysus gives rise to what Weber termed ' "emotional cults" as opposed to the atomization characteristic of bourgeois or aristocratic dominance' (Maffesoli 1995:156). Sociality, in other words – a 'fusion realm' or 'communalised empathy' – constitutes all those forms of 'being together' which, for the past few decades, have been transforming society. 'Losing one's body' within the 'collective body', in short, either literally or metaphorically, 'seems to be a characteristic feature of the emotional or affective *community* that is beginning to replace our utilitarian "society"' (Maffesoli 1996:154).

This, in turn, as Evans (1997:231) notes, marks a shift from morality as an overarching, universal system of duties and obligations to a system of rules, to a more 'protean, ambivalent, fractal and relativistic' emphasis on local ethics and a 'stylisation of life' more in keeping with Foucault's deliberations on the 'care of the self' in Ancient Greek culture (i.e. an '*ethics of aesthetics*') than with the Kantian tradition of 'legislative' reason.

Certainly, Maffesoli paints a very different picture of contemporary social and emotional life than any other we have so far encountered: a view which, as suggested above, champions the Dionysian over the Promethean, the polymorphously perverse over the orderly and rational, the fusional over the individualistic, and so forth. In this respect, like Latour (1993), he forces us to confront the intriguing question of whether or not we have ever truly been 'moderns', stressing instead important elements of cultural continuity with the past, including the 'traditional world' of clans, bands and 'tribes' (Evans 1997). Seen in this light, Giddens's emphasis on late modernity as a detraditional order based on a reflexively mobilised self, appears, at the very least, problematic (Evans 1997).

Maffesoli's own position, however, is equally problematic. Perhaps the main problem concerns the fact that, in adopting this largely one-sided Dionysian stance, the contradictory features of modernity as *both* 'rationalisation' and 'subjectification' – i.e. the dialectic between the instrumentalisation of the world as embodied in science and technology, and the growth of individualism, expressivity, freedom and democratic rights (cf. Touraine 1995) – are underplayed (Evans 1997). Underpinning this, as I have argued throughout this paper, is a 'modernist' binary view of reason and emotion as somehow distinct or separable. This, coupled with an overly felicitous view of neo-tribes – including the fact that 'neo-tribalism' itself rests on a highly individualised society (Evans 1997) – which fails to acknowledge the dangers of Dionysian orgiastic sociality, means that, like Meštrović, Maffesoli too falls foul of the temptation to overstretch his explanatory frame of reference. To be sure Maffesoli puts his finger on an important trend in contemporary society, yet in doing so the picture he paints remains at best partial: the 'truth', in truth, is somewhere in between. Modernity, as Evans states, 'is not simply identified with a reified totalised system of rationalised oppression and disenchantment, but rather, is a complex network of *mixed possibilities* involving a constant *dialectic* between the subject and reason' (1997:240).

Seen in this light, Mellor and Shilling (1997) present a more promising line of development. In keeping with Maffesoli, Mellor and Shilling point to the rise of a new virulent, effervescent form of the 'sacred', a reconfiguration of embodied sensuality which, they claim, is changing how people 'see' and 'keep in touch' with the world around them. In contrast to Maffesoli, however, they go on to offer what is, perhaps, a more 'balanced' assessment of its legacies, for better or worse.

On the one hand, early forms of Protestant modernity (for example, the disciplined and individualistic) are, they suggest, being extended through 'banal forms of sociality' and the 'individualisation of contracts'. On the other hand, these disciplined bodies are 'slowly but surely giving way to more sensual forms of sociality; forms which echo the seductive sacred corporeality of Counter-Reformation baroque cultures, substituting "tribal fealties" (i.e. 'blood commitments' which reject rationality as a basis for sociality) for individual con-tracts' (1997:173; see also Melucci 1996 and Ruthven 1989). In this respect, information-based society may indeed have become banal, but it has not yet (fully) absorbed 'people's sensualities into its circuitry' (Mellor and Shilling 1997:173).

Seen in these terms, the Janus-faced nature of modernity as both order and chaos, discipline and liberty, is again fully evident. The return of the sacred and the resurgence of more sensual, carnal forms of knowledge and experience is not, in other words, simply the return to prominence, in time-honoured Durkheimian tradition or Maffesolian postmodern theorising, of effervescent forms of *solidarity*, but also the opportunity for new conflicts, dangers and fears to emerge. Indeed, from the bloodshed of the Balkan war to the resurgence of neo-fundamentalism, feelings and passions can run high in ways which prove both troubling and difficult to 'manage' rationally. The sacred, in short, can be 'virulent, violent and unpredictable'. As Mellor and Shilling (1997:201) state: 'The emo-tions that emerge from social relationships and solidarities may enable people to "keep warm together" in a world which too often appears out of control and morally bank-rupt [cf. Maffesoli], but they can also prompt a passionate intensity, hatred and blood revenge.'

Whatever the outcome, one thing remains clear, namely the 'resilience' of human bodies to cognitive control and the enduring significance of more sensual (i.e. emotional and 'sacred') forms of solidarity and 'carnal forms of knowledge'; good or bad, bloody or harmonious, binding or destructive. Postemotional control, in short, can never be absolute. Herein, as ever, lie the corporeal dynamics and emotional underpinnings of modernity as *both* order and chaos, liberty and discipline, transgression and taboo.

Discussion and concluding remarks

Where, then, does all this leave us in terms of current debates on modernity and the emotions at the turn of the century? First, as I have argued, we need to divest ourselves of centuries of former dualistic thinking which has cast emotions as the poor relation, if not the scandal, of reason. Not only do emotions, as embodied, relational modes of being, underpin our most intimate thoughts and actions in the social world, they are also, as we have seen, central to the very process of rational thought itself. Without emotions, social life, including our decision-making capacities and our ability to make informed choices amongst a plurality of options, would be impossible. It is time, therefore, *contra* Enlightenment Utopian/dys-topian visions of a 'pure' (i.e. 'uncontaminated') rationality, to construct epistemological and ontological models of being and knowing which incorporate rather than repress the emotions in Western thought and practice.

Seen in this light, even those who emphasise the so-called 'extra-rational' dimensions of writers such as Durkheim (such as Shilling or Maffesoli), inadvertently perpetuate the very dualisms from which we have been trying to escape, missing something important in the process. Emotions do not have to be, and indeed never should have been, 'extra-rational'. To be sure, like the body to which they are so closely tied, they can prove recalcitrant things, wreaking havoc with processes of logical thought and rational decision-making. Yet their absence, as we have seen, appears no less devastating: loosening our hold on all that we, as thinking, feeling subjects and knowledgeable human beings, hold dear. The 'irrational passion for dispassionate rationality', in short, appears wholly unreasonable: the relic of an outdated, 'counterfeit' Enlightenment model that turned reason into a 'project', and which, throughout the centuries, has served to justify the disadvantage experienced by 'marginalised' groups in society (for example, women, children, ethnic minorities). 'Outlaw' emotions and recalcitrant feelings, therefore, have a legitimate role to play in the questioning of what is, in effect, a highly questionable order: one founded on, and organised around, the 'driving out' of emotions by the steady hand of (male) reason (Jaggar 1989). Even if we accept, for a moment, the analytical distinction between reason and emotion, it is clear, as Weber's deliberations on 'world religions' and the fate of 'charismatic leaders' so clearly testify, that processes of rationalisation do not lead to the disappearance of emotions, but rather to their *redistribution* or reappearance in a variety of different forms (Hervier-Leger 1993). Emotions and reason, in short, are never entirely separable.

This, in turn, leads us on to a broader set of questions concerning the nature of modernity itself. As I have argued, following writers such as Bauman, a defining feature of modernity concerns its *ambivalence*, founded as it is on both order and chaos. Indeed, far from seeing the recent cultural emphasis on the emotions as somehow 'postmodern', I have chosen instead to emphasise the fact that, ever since its inception, modernity has always rested on and wrestled with its emotional foundations, including the passionate sanctification of rationality itself. What we are currently witnessing, therefore, is simply modernity facing up to the 'limitations' of its own over-hyped/disingenuous model of disembodied rationality, including a (grudging) acknowledgement of its emotional foundations and their role in knowledge generation, transmission and acquisition. Rationality and the emotions, in other words, are starting to coalesce in a more 'open' climate of discussion and debate than ever before. To call this 'postmodern' is, however, clearly premature; the rational project is not in fact dead. Rather it is simply undergoing a period of (uncomfortable) readjustment. It is also not difficult, as Meštrović rightly argues, to discern the outlines of an alternative, 'authentic' Enlightenment project: one involving an honest, if somewhat painful, appraisal of its 'mixed legacies' and a 'dialogue with other non-Enlightenment traditions in the spirit of accommodation and common ground, rather than the imposition of yet another ideology based on a dead past' (Meštrović 1997:86).

Certainly, as we have seen, contemporary Western societies are currently undergoing something akin to a 'return of the repressed': one involving a shift to Dionysian values, a resurgence of effervescent bodies and the rise of new forms of sensual solidarity and the 'sacred' (Mellor and Shilling 1997). Seen in these terms, we are not, to answer Agnes Heller's (1989) tantalising question, 'living in a world of emotional impoverishment': quite the reverse!

Underpinning this is a translation of modernity's problems of order and chaos into corporeal questions of conformity and transgression: issues which point us to the broader historical, social and cultural relations within which human corporeality is itself inextricably entwined. Bodies, as I have argued, through their corporeal flows and libidinal desires, their pleasures and their pains, passions and intensities, are fundamentally 'excessive'. To be excessive, however, implies the existence of 'limits' from which these corporeal transgressions take place. According to Falk (1994:61), human corporeality, in other words, as a form of transgression

> demands the existence of limits confining, restricting and defining the human body, just as transgression itself generally demands borders. Corporeality is a cultural and also an historical category. As the orders, as a system of boundaries, change in history (and from culture to culture), so the crossing of boundaries and thus the forms of corporeality also change.

While eroticism, for example, like dirt and pollution, is universal, the transgressions it embraces have their own historicity (cf. Douglas 1970, 1980/[1966]). Similarly, the manner in which corporeal flows are (sexually) coded, and the ritually guarded boundaries they transgress, are also a product of the socio-cultural webs within which human corporeality is de/confined. Human corporeality, in short, is never lived 'in the raw' (Grosz 1994). As Falk (1994:65, my emphasis) states:

> The increase in the density of limits, categories and norms related to corporeality produces a multiplicity and diversification of transgressions as a complementary opposition, though primarily in the *experience* [as opposed to the *expressive*] dimension of corporeality . . . The more articulated and multifarious the restrictions on corporeality, the more sophisticated the forms of transgression become. Lack of restraint emphasising corporeal expression is replaced by a diversification of the scale of sensory pleasures.

Given this view, it is possible, following Falk, to interpret the history of human corporeality across the long historical curve of the civilising process as a paradoxical combination of both discipline and emancipation. As the scale of human corporeal *expression* becomes restricted through the 'shielding' and 'instrumentalising' of the body, the field of *experience* widens, diversifies and becomes more sensitive. An increase in the quantity of restrictions placed on the direct expression of corporeal pleasures, in other words, is accompanied by a diversification and intensification of the quality of human sensual experience. The history of corporeality is not, therefore, merely the 'disciplining' of the body and the 'destruction of sensuality', any more than it is the 'great emancipation of the body's potential'. Rather, it is the 'paradoxical combination of the two' (Falk 1994:66). As a consequence, transgression itself becomes more complex, subtle and sophisticated: including the 'transgression of transgression' itself (Grosz 1994, 1995). Emotions, as I have argued, lie at the heart of these corporeal issues and the sensual dilemmas they embody.

So what, then, of the 'fate' of emotions at the turn of the century? More specifically, how do the issues discussed here translate into questions of 'authenticity' in what is clearly an *ambivalent* or uncertain age? On the one hand, following Meštrović, the neo-Orwellian spectre looks set to continue apace, with further McDonaldisation, and an 'authenticity' industry bent on 'inauthenticating' everything. Here we confront at least two closely interrelated paradoxes. First, that the more we search for the 'authentic', the more 'inauthentic' it becomes. Secondly, the fact that our contemporary obsession with the manufacture of so-called 'real feelings' (cf. Baudrillard's simulacra) ultimately translates into a repressed longing for the 'authentic'; one which, to return to the first point, can never be reached in a culture such as ours (Meštrović 1997:74).

On the other hand, as I have argued throughout the course of this paper, the very nature of human embodiment and corporeal desire as fundamentally excessive/transgressive, together with the positive and negative features of emotions as both 'world-building' and 'world-destroying', 'knowledge-generating' and 'knowledge-disrupting', suggests that what at first sight may seem like 'pockets of authenticity', in fact turn out to be as much vistas of defiance and resistance, sensuality and effervescence. From the loss of self in eroticism to the aggression vented in gang warfare, and from the 'unruly' behaviour of a child to New Age movements, communal festivities, sporting and musical events, spontaneous emotions are 'hard at work' in apparent defiance of social conventions, for better or worse, richer or poorer. In doing so, however troubling their manifestations may be, they none the less express the irrepressible spirit and recalcitrant language of the heart: one which, despite its best efforts, rational modernity will never manage to crush or destroy.

Notes

1   Even Plato, who compared emotions to galloping horses, which had to be 'tamed' by the charioteer of reason, recognised that without the horses the charioteer would be redundant (see Jaggar 1989).

2   See also Crossley (1998) for an emotionally informed reconstruction of the Habermasian project and his theory of communicative action.

3   A classic example of this was the case of Phineas Gage, a nineteenth-century railroad worker whose frontal lobes were damaged when an iron bar shot through them as the result of an accidental explosion. Along with the emotional deficits which followed this damage, Gage had great difficulty in planning his ordinary life: making disastrous social decisions whilst dithering endlessly over inconsequential issues. Damasio (1994) and colleagues have now studied many patients with this kind of damage, and propose that it was this socio-emotional guidance system which was affected in the brain of the original Phineas Gage and many other such cases since his time. Emotions, in short, guide reason and furnish us with priorities amongst multiple goals and options.

4   Broadly speaking, approaches to emotions can be conceptualised on a continuum ranging from the 'organismic' (i.e. biological) at one end [and] the 'social constructionist' (i.e. cultural and dis-cursive) at the other, with 'interactionist' approaches, as the term implies, somewhere in between. For useful recent critiques of the constructionist approach, see Lyon (1998) and Craib (1997, 1995).

5   Whilst, at an analytical level, terms such as 'feeling' may be further subdivided into their component parts – i.e. the split between emotion and sensation, so central to social constructionist accounts (Harré 1986; Armon-Jones 1986) – these distinctions are rarely acknowledged or invoked at the level of lived experience. Rather, embodiment, emotionality and sensuality are thoroughly inter-fused and inextricably intertwined. Only when this taken-for-granted, pre-objective relationship we have to our 'mindful bodies' (Scheper-Hughes and Lock 1987) is disrupted, do such categories come into play (Leder 1990). The point, therefore, is not to abandon these and other analytical distinctions (such as the distinction between emotions and sentiments), nor to blunt our concep-tual tools, but rather to acknowledge their limits at the pre-objective level of lived on-going experience.

6   It is tempting, in fact, to push these claims further through a privileged ontological position: namely that bodies are *first and foremost* excessive. Clearly, as discussed more fully towards the end of the paper, order and transgression exist in a symbiotic relationship to one another, yet recourse to a *process* metaphysic would undoubtedly see bodily order, fixity and stability as secondary to corporeal fluidity and flow: a position strongly endorsed in recent post-structuralist feminist theorising (Battersby 1998).

7   See Jackson and Scott (1997) for an interesting recent discussion of these contradictory themes and conflicting imperatives in relation to modern discourses surrounding (hetero)sexuality – i.e. the tension between the (late) modernist rationalisation or 'Taylorisation' of sex on the one hand, and the shift towards other, more 'post-Fordist' forms of sexuality, permitting greater diversity and flexibility, on the other. See also Crawford (1980, 1984, 1994, 1998), Lowenberg and Davis (1994) and Martin (1994) for related themes surrounding health.

8   Whilst Durkheim's use of the term 'effervescent' may indeed have been a helpful one, Mellor and Shilling's corporeal appropriation of it is, at times, problematic. Can one really, for example, have an 'effervescent' body? A nice analogy perhaps, but not a very accurate descriptor. Seen in this light, efflorescent/efforescence may, perhaps, be more appropriate. I am grateful to one of the anonymous reviewers for drawing this corporeal point to my attention.

9   See, for example, Dunning, Murphy and Williams (1988) on the decivilising surge of violence in Britain, and Elias and Scotson (1994/[1965]) on *The Established and the Outsiders*.

References

Armon-Jones, C. 1986. 'The Thesis of Constructionism', in R. Harré (ed.) *The Social Construction of Emotions*.

Bakhtin, M. 1968. *Rabelais and his World*. Cambridge, Mass.: MIT Press.

Bataille, G. 1987 [1962]. *Eroticism* (transl. by M. Dalwood). London: Boyars.

Bauman, Z. 1991. *Modernity and Ambivalence*. Cambridge: Polity Press.

Bauman, Z. 1992. *Mortality, Immortality and Other Life Strategies*. Cambridge: Polity Press.

Bendelow, G. and Williams, S. J. 1998. 'Emotions, Pain and Gender', in G. Bendelow and S. J. Williams (eds.), *Emotions in Social Life: Critical Themes and Contemporary Issues*. London: Routledge.

Bordo, S. 1990. 'Reading the Slender Body?, in M. Jacobus, E. F. Keller and S. Shuttleworth (eds.) *Body/Politics: Women and the Discourse of Science*. London: Routledge.

Burkitt, I. 1997. 'Social Relationships and Emotions'. *Sociology* 31:37–55.

Craib, I. 1995. 'Some Comments on the Sociology of the Emotions'. *Sociology* 29:151–8.

Craib, I. 1997. 'Social Constructionism as Social Psychosis'. *Sociology* 31:1–15.

Crawford, R. 1980. 'Healthism and the Medicalization of Everyday Life? *International Journal of Health Services* 10:365–88.

Crawford, R. 1984. 'A Cultural Account of "Health": Control, Release and the Social Body', in J. B. McKinlay (ed.) *Issues in the Political Economy of Health Care*. London: Tavistock.

Crawford, R. 1994. 'The Boundaries of Self and the Unhealthy Other: Reflections on Health, Culture and AIDS'. *Social Science and Medicine* 38:1347–66.

Crawford, R. 1998. 'The Ritual of Health Promotion', in S. J. Williams, J. Gabe and M. Calnan. (eds.) *Theorising Health, Medicine and Society*. London: Sage.

Crossley, N. 1998. 'Emotions and Communicative Action', in G. Bendelow and S. J. Williams (eds.) *Emotions in Social Life: Critical Themes and Contemporary Issues*. London: Routledge.

Csordas, T. J. (ed.) 1994. *Embodiment of Experience: The Existential Ground of Culture and Self*. Cambridge: Cambridge University Press.

Damasio A. R. 1994. *Descartes' Error: Emotion, Reason and the Human Brain*. New York: Putnam.

Davis, K. 1995. *Re-Shaping the Female Body: The Dilemma of Cosmetic Surgery*. London: Routledge.

Denzin, N. K. 1984. *On Understanding Emotion*. San Francisco: Jossey Bass.

Douglas, M. 1980/[1966]. *Purity and Danger: An Analysis of the Concepts of Pollution and Taboo*. London: Routledge and Kegan Paul.

Douglas, M. 1970. *Natural Symbols: Explorations in Cosmology*. London: Cresset Press.

Dunning, E., Murphy, P. and Williams, J. 1988. *The Roots of Football Hooliganism*. London: Routledge.

Elias, N. 1978/[1939]. *The Civilizing Process: Vol I: The History of Manners*. Oxford: Basil Blackwell.

Elias, N. 1982/[1939]. *The Civilizing Process, Vol II: State Formations and Civilization*. Oxford: Basil Blackwell.

Elias, N. and Scotson, J. 1994/[1965]. *The Established and the Outsiders*. London: Sage.

Evans, D. 1997. 'Michel Maffesoli's Sociology of Modernity and Postmodernity: An Introduction and Critical Assessment'. *Sociological Review* 45:221–43.

Falk, P. 1994. *The Consuming Body*. London: Sage.

Faurschou, G. 1988. 'Fashion and the Cultural Logic of Postmodernity', in A. Kroker and M. Kroker (eds.) *Body Invaders; Sexuality and the Postmodern Condition*. Basingstoke: Macmillan.

Featherstone, M. 1991. 'The Body in Consumer Culture', in M. Featherstone, M. Hepworth and B. S. Turner (eds.) *The Body: Social Process and Cultural Theory*. London: Sage.

Freud, S. 1982 [1930]. *Civilization and Its Discontents*. London: Hogarth Press.

Giddens, A. 1991. *Modernity and Self-Identity: Self and Society in the Late Modern Age*. Cambridge: Polity Press.

Giddens, A. 1992. *The Transformation of Intimacy: Love, Sexuality and Eroticism in Modern Societies*. Cambridge: Polity Press.

Grosz, E. 1994. *Volatile Bodies: Toward a Corporeal Feminism*. Bloomington and Indianapolis: Indiana University Press.

Grosz, E. 1995. *Space, Time and Perversion*. London: Routledge.

Harré, R. (ed.) 1986. *The Social Construction of Emotions*. Oxford: Basil Blackwell.

Heller, A. 1989. 'Are We Living in a World of Emotional Impoverishment?' *Thesis Eleven 22*.

Hervier-Leger, D. 1993. 'Present-day Emotional Renewals: The End of Secularization or the End of Religion?', in W. H. Swastos *A Future for Religion? New Paradigms for Social Analysis*. London: Sage.

Hochschild, A. R. 1983. *The Managed Heart; The Commercialisation of Human Feeling*. Berkely: University of California Press.

Jackson, S. and Scott, S. 1977. 'Gut Reactions to Matters of the Heart: Reflections on Rationality, Irrationality and Sexuality'. *Sociological Review* 45:551–75.

Jaggar, A. 1989. 'Love and Knowledge: Emotion in Feminist Epistemology', in S. Bordo and A. Jaggar (eds.) *Gender/Body/Knowledge: Feminist Reconstructions of Being and Knowing*. New Brunswick: Rutgers University Press.

Lasch, C. 1979. *The Culture of Narcissism: American Life in an Age of Diminishing Expectations*. New York: Norton.

Latour, B. 1993. *We Have Never Been Modern*. London: Harvester/Wheatsheaf.

Leder, D. 1990. *The Absent Body*. Chicago: University of Chicago Press.

Lowenberg, J. S. and Davis, F. 1994. 'Beyond Medicalisation-Demedicalisation: The Case of Holistic Health'. *Sociology of Health and Illness* 16:579–99.

Lutz, C. 1988. *Unnatural Emotion*. Chicago: University of Chicago Press.

Lyon, M. 1988. 'The Limitations of Cultural Constructionism in the Study of Emotions', in G. Bendelow and S. J. Williams (eds.) *Emotions in Social Life: Critical Themes and Contemporary Issues*. London: Routledge.

Lyon, M. and Barbalet, J. 1994. 'Society's Body: Emotion and the "Somatization of Social Theory" ', in T. Csordas (ed.) *Embodiment of Experience*.

Maffesoli, M. 1995. *The Time of Tribes: The Decline of Individualism in Mass Society*. London: Sage.

Maffesoli, M. 1996. *Ordinary Knowledge*. Cambridge: Polity Press.

Martin, E. 1994. *Flexible Bodies: The Role of Immunology in American Culture from the Age of Polio to the Age of AIDS*. Boston, Mass.: Beacon Press.

Mellor, P. and Shilling, C. 1997. *Re-Forming the Body: Religion, Community and Modernity*. London: Sage.

Melucci, A. 1996. *The Playing Self: Person and Meaning in the Planetary Society*. Cambridge: Cambridge University Press.

Mennell, S. 1990. 'Decivilising Processes: Theoretical Significance and Some Lines of Research'. *International Sociology* 5:205–23.

Meštrović, S. G. 1997. *Postemotional Society*. London: Sage.

Mills, C. W. 1959. *The Sociological Imagination*. New York: Oxford University Press.

Rieff, P. 1979. *Freud; The Mind of a Moralist*. London: Chatto and Windus.

Ritzer, G. 1992. *The McDonaldization of Society*. London: Sage.

Rojek, C. 1994. *Ways of Escape: Modern Transformations in Leisure and Travel*. Lanham, Md: Rowman and Littlefield.

Rojek, C. 1995. *De-Centring Leisure: Rethinking Leisure Theory*. London: Sage.

Rosaldo, M. 1984. 'Toward an Anthropology of Self and Feeling', in R. A. Shweder and R. A. LeVine (eds.) *Culture Theory: Essays on Mind, Self and Emotion*.

Rose, H. 1994. *Love, Power and Knowledge: Towards a Feminist Transformation of the Sciences*. Cambridge: Polity Press.

Ruthven, M. 1989. *The Divine Supermarket*. London: Chatto and Windus.

Scheper-Hughes, N. and Lock, M. 1987. 'The "Mindful" Body: A Prolegomenon to Future Work in Medical Anthropology'. *Medical Anthropology Quarterly* 1:6–41.

Seidler, V. 1994. *Unreasonable Men Masculinity and Social Theory*. London: Routledge.

Seidman, S. 1991. *Romantic Longings: Love in America, 1830–1980*. New York: Routledge.

Shilling, C. 1993. *The Body and Social Theory*. London: Sage.

Shilling, C. 1997. 'Emotions, Embodiment and the Sensation of Society'. *Sociological Review* 45:195–219.

Shweder, R. A. 1984. 'Anthropology's Romantic Rebellion Against the Enlightenment: Or There's More to Thinking Than Reason and Evidence', in R. A. Shweder and R. A. LeVine (eds.) *Culture Theory: Essays on Mind, Self and Emotion*.

Shweder, R. A. and LeVine, R. A. (eds.) 1984. *Culture Theory: Essays on Mind, Self and Emotion*. Cambridge: Cambridge University Press.

Simmel, G. 1971. *On Individuality and Social Forms (Selected Writings)* (edited with an Intro. by D. N. Levine). Chicago/London: University of Chicago Press.

Stearns, P. N. 1994. *American Cool: Constructing a Twentieth-Century Emotional Style*. New York: New York University Press.

Tester, K. 1998. 'Bored and Blasé: Television, the Emotions and Georg Simmel', in G. Bendelow and S. J. Williams (eds.) *Emotions in Social Life: Critical Themes and Contemporary Issues*. London: Routledge.

Touraine, A. 1995. *Critique of Modernity*. Cambridge: Polity Press.

Wagner, P. 1994. *A Sociology of Modernity: Liberty and Discipline*. London: Routledge.

Wentworth, W. M. and Yardley, D. 1994. 'Deep Sociality: A Bioevolutionary Perspective on the Sociology of Emotions', in W. M. Wentworth and J. Ryan (eds.) *Social Perspectives on Emotion*. Greenwich, Conn.: JAI Press Inc.

Williams, S. J. 1998. 'Emotions, Cyberspace and the 'Virtual' Body: A Critical Appraisal', in G. Bendelow and S. J. Williams (eds.) *Emotions in Social Life: Critical Themes and Contemporary Issues*. London: Routledge.

Williams, S. J. and Bendelow, G. 1998. 'Emotions in Social Life: Mapping the Sociological Terrain', in G. Bendelow and S. J. Williams (eds.) *Emotions in Social Life: Critical Themes and Contemporary Issues*. London: Routledge.

Wouters, C. 1986. 'Formalization and Informalization: Changing Tension Balances in Civilizing Processes'. *Theory, Culture and Society* 3(2):1–18.

Wouters, C. 1987. 'Developments in the Behavioural Codes Between the Sexes: The Formalization of Informalization in the Netherlands 1930–85'. *Theory, Culture and Society* 4:405–27.

Wouters, C. 1998. 'Changes in the "Lust Balance" of Love and Sex Since the Sexual Revolution: The Example of the Netherlands', in G. Bendelow and S. J. Williams (eds.) *Emotions in Social Life: Critical Themes and Contemporary Issues*. London: Routledge.

Chapter 9

Ian Burkitt

POWERFUL EMOTIONS: POWER, GOVERNMENT AND OPPOSITION IN THE 'WAR ON TERROR'

IN THE RECENT PAST, I have outlined a relational view of emotions, in which I argue that sociologists should study emotion as part of the relations and interactions between humans rather than as primarily an individual or internal phenomenon (Burkitt, 1997: 2002). Here, I want to extend and elaborate on this position by studying emotion as a factor in relations of power, government and opposition, with particular reference to the current 'war on terror'. It seems to me that this is a prime example of the use of emotion in political relations, because even the name given to the effort to combat international terrorism – bestowed largely by Western governments after the events of 11 September 2001 in the USA – evokes a particular, clearly defined emotion. However, within this I focus on two specific events: the peace demonstration in London on 15 February 2003, which was part of a series of global protests against the impending Iraq war; and the aftermath of the train bombings in Madrid on 11 March 2004. These events have been selected because they sharply illustrate the way governments use emotion to direct conduct, yet they also show how this has unpredictable and unintended consequences for all involved. As I hope to demonstrate, emotion is a necessary if uncontrollable element in emergent power relations and, thereby, is also at the root of political relations.

However, the protests against the Iraq war and the mobilization of large groups of Spanish people following the Madrid bombings alerted us once more to the power and limitation of mass movements in politics, along with the emotional power that works both within and through crowds. It was a sharp reminder that emotion can move people (quite literally) into protest and can enthuse and electrify a crowd. Such mass demonstrations, taken together with the recent upsurge of protest against globalization and also the collective expression of emotion in Britain after the death of Princess Diana, are indicators of the way that sudden emotional shocks or political issues can shake the 'apathy and indifference which seems to characterise the here and now' (Tester, 1997: 147). While I generally agree with Tester on this issue and that '[w]e might be found to be politically guilty in so far as we rarely and scarcely raise a sustained and loud voice against what "our" governments do in "our" name' (1997: 146), I think this makes even more interesting instances when people break this silence. Indeed, I argue here that the millions worldwide who protested against the Iraq war, and those Spanish people who protested at the Madrid bombings and the political aftermath, did care about sounding out a loud and clear voice about what their governments were about to do, or did do, in their name. For a brief spell the protests offered a glimpse of the possibility of a reconstituted public space of political affiliation, with crowds united through their differences. Yet such apparent unity is a complex production and should never be taken at face value, which is something else I want to investigate here. Before that, I want briefly to review some theories that might help us understand emotions as powerful forces in crowds and political gatherings, before moving on to consider how emotions play a crucial role in relations of power.

The sociology of emotions and mass movements

One of the antecedents to the approach known as the sociology of emotions is to be found in the works of Emile Durkheim, who believed that '[c]ollective representations, emotions, and tendencies are caused not by certain states of the consciousness of individuals but by the conditions in which the social group in its totality is placed' (1938: 106). Like others of his generation (Freud, for instance), Durkheim was heavily influenced by Le Bon (1896) and thought that collective emotional forces were irrational and too powerful for individual consciousness to resist. In that sense they were 'social currents', like currents of opinion, which acted as coercive forces upon individual behaviour and consciousness, shaping conduct and thought. However, in his study of religion, Durkheim (1915) developed a more fully rounded view of emotions as forces that act in the constitution and reconstitution of social groups through the heightened emotional intensity of collective religious rituals and performances. The symbols of the group – such as the totem – became emblems in which the emotions of dependence and vitality created in collective rituals were invested. That is because the group is 'too complex a reality to be represented in all its complex unity' (Durkheim, 1915: 220), and so ends up being represented by totems, flags, beliefs or ideas.

However, the emotional 'effervescence' produced in collective rituals serves not only to reproduce the unity of the group, it can also threaten to tear it apart through the irrational emotional forces it unleashes. The morality of the everyday world, which is composed of dispersed activities acted out with mediocre levels of emotional intensity, is threatened with being overturned by ceremonial and ritual gatherings that 'produce such a violent super-excitation of the whole physical and mental life that it cannot be supported very long' (Durkheim, 1915: 216). Although temporary, such effervescent gatherings give the participants an inkling of a possible world beyond the everyday order. Yet Durkheim could also see the role played by powerful effervescent emotions in times of permanent social change, where 'under the influence of some great collective shock, social interactions have become much more frequent and active. Men look for each other and assemble together more than ever. The general effervescence results which is characteristic of revolutionary or creative epochs' (1915: 210–11).

Indeed, Durkheim understands that in Western modernity collective effervescence now takes place mainly around political rather than religious rituals and symbols. For him, the contemporary ideal in which a high level of emotional intensity is invested is 'moral individualism': that is, respect for the dignity, value and rights of each individual (Durkheim, 1957). As Arendt (1973) has pointed out, this may have changed the character of modern revolutions in that, rather than being outpourings of destructive anger, they are more about the exercise of political capacities. In modern revolutions, the aim of collective action is to establish a public space of civic freedom and participation for all people, something I think is evident in the study presented here.

However, while Durkheim's ideas are helpful in beginning to understand the role of powerful effervescent emotions in the configuration and reconfiguration of social groups and mass movements, nevertheless there are some problems with his concepts. Durkheim seems to suggest that collective forces – be they currents of emotion or opinion – are always successful in creating unity amongst groups because of their sui generis power, which is too great for individuals to resist. Perhaps Durkheim created sui generis concepts of society because, just as for the clan, a social group is too complex a reality to be represented clearly in all its complex unity (or should that be diversity?). Furthermore, in terms of emotion, even though his later work identifies a more rational role for the emotions in evaluating beliefs and ideas in political systems – such as moral individualism – Durkheim still holds to the idea of emotions as irrational forces too complex to analyse. Thus, 'when [emotion] has a collective origin it defies critical and rational examination' (Durkheim and Mauss, 1963: 88).

This approach is contradicted by recent work on the emotions, in which they are understood as intelligent responses to perceptions of value and, as such, part of the system of ethical reasoning (Nussbaum, 2001). This does not preclude the possibility that emotions can operate in unpredictable and disorderly ways, because they attach us to people, objects or ideals that we value but which are beyond our own personal control. This leaves us vulnerable to grief, anger and fear should the people or things we love be lost or threatened. Because emotions are necessary to the very act of evaluation, they are bound to play a role in our thinking about the good and the just, and therefore in evaluations of political ideas and ideals. My own standpoint on the emotions differs from Nussbaum's cognitive theory – by which she means that emotions are 'concerned with receiving and processing information' (2001: 23) – for I understand emotions as 'communications of state' through embodied activity and discursive articulation in social relations (Burkitt, 2002). However, this does not rule out accepting the role of emotion in judgement. Indeed, my own view of emotions as discursive articulations of feelings and responses to others with whom we are socially related, also proposes the view that emotions are not necessarily irrational forces but have a pattern to them that follows a relational 'logic'. However, those relations are also power relations, and we cannot, in my view, separate people's emotional responses and judgements of value from the power relations in which they are located.

Power, emotion and the 'war on terror'

It was Max Weber who observed that action in political relations is 'determined by highly robust motives of fear and hope' (Weber, 1970: 79, quoted in Barbalet, 2004). How prescient his comments now seem, because those two emotions have figured largely in political rhetoric and relations post-11 September 2001. Fear has been used by Western governments, especially in Britain and the United States, when they repeatedly warn of threatened and imminent terrorist attacks; and hope is raised that action in the 'war on terror' will remove these threats to peace and security. However, in a recent piece on the emotional responses to 11 September, Kemper (2002) broadens this out to make predictions about six emotions – anger, sadness, fear, joy, shame and guilt – and how they affected different groups in the US depending on their relation to the events of that day. Furthermore, these emotions are linked to power relations because *anger* results from a loss of status; *fear* from the loss of power relative to the other; *sadness* from a loss of status which is irremediable; and *joy* from a gain in status. Likewise, *guilt* is felt when one feels one has used excess power on another; and *shame* when one has acted in a way that belies one's status in the eyes of another. In this relational view, then, the emotions are linked to one's place in the power and status structure of society.

In terms of his definition of power, Kemper takes a Weberian stance, by which he refers to power as 'all those actions designed to obtain compliance with one's own wishes, desires, and interests over the resistance of another' (Kemper, 2002: 54). In this light, power is said to include both threatened and actual physical assault, verbal abuse, deception and manipulation, or threatened and actual deprivation of another's benefits or privileges. By such means one person seems compelled to comply, against their own will, with the wishes and desires of another. We could therefore study the outcomes of social interaction in terms of power by trying to discover whose position in the power structure has increased, decreased, or stayed the same as a result of that interaction.

However, I want to begin here with a different definition of power and a different standpoint on the emotions in power relations. Rather than remain with a definition of power that makes the relation of one individual over and against another central, and which places status as a key element in power relations, I will develop some of Foucault's insights on power. These insights are interesting because they implicitly contain some notion of the emotions that are elements in the weave of power relations and that emerge within – certainly Western – forms of government. Foucault says that power is 'a total structure of actions brought to bear upon possible actions: it incites, it induces, it seduces . . . [it is] a way of acting upon an acting subject or acting subjects' (1982: 220). So power is *not* an action that imposes itself directly on another person by the very force of imposition: it works more subtly through social relations as a structure of actions that aims to *affect* a field of possible actions. Thus, 'power is less a confrontation between two adversaries or the linking of one to the other than a question of government . . . it designate[s] the way in which the conduct of individuals or of groups might be directed' (Foucault, 1982: 221).

We can also see from the above how emotion is integral to the ordering of the emergent relational field of government, because to incite, induce and seduce involve emotion. In order to incite, people must be provoked or stirred in some way, with anger being the usual response to provocation. To induce, people must be persuaded or motivated in a way that calls out a certain type of conduct. As Nussbaum (2001) says, 'any political conception needs to concern itself with citizens' motivations' (p. 401–2), both to ensure that the conception is feasible and to ensure that it has a chance of being stable over time. Finally, the act of seduction must produce a desire or longing for a person, object, goal or ideal. Thus, while status is obviously important in relations of power and is central to the experience of shame and embarrassment, this is not the only factor to be considered in the study of power and emotion.

More than this, emotions are intense, ambivalent, and closely connected with one another. As Freud illustrated, emotion is often ambivalent in the sense of 'the direction towards the same person of contrary – affectionate and hostile – feelings' (Freud, 1981[1963]: 478). Such ambivalent emotions are also interconnected and can alternate with each other, so that: 'hope alternates uneasily with fear, as a single event transforms hope into grief, as grief, looking about for a cause, expresses itself as anger, as all these can be the vehicles for an underlying love' (Nussbaum, 2001: 22). It is the ambivalence and alternation of emotion, which, I suggest, makes emotional responses hard to predict in all relations, including political relations. This means it is difficult for governments, or any other political group, to manipulate emotion in order to govern by directing conduct. Incitement, inducement and seduction cannot be gauged precisely for everyone enmeshed in the networks of power relations, although this does not stop those in government attempting to manipulate emotional currents.

'War on terror' and war on Iraq: incitement, inducement and seduction

The political possibility of a War on Iraq emerged in the wake of the events of 11 September 2001 and was sold mainly to the American, British and Spanish people – whose governments were key players in the coalition forces shaping up for war – as part of a global 'war on terror'. The language used to describe the reaction to 11 September is interesting in itself, because it invokes the fear and hope that Weber observed as the robust motives that determine action in a political community. Fear, because the possibility of being caught in a terrorist attack – of being injured or killed, or of this fate befalling someone we love or value – is something to be dreaded. Hope, because it is desired that the war on terror will solve this problem and remove the threat of terrorism. Yet, as Kemper (2002) predicted, the group he labelled as 'New Yorkers/Most Americans' would also feel anger at the strikes on the World Trade Center and the Pentagon, as these were centres and symbols of US power. Thus, the strikes were perceived as a loss of status that had to be restored. Given this, anger can be predicted as an important emotion in the reaction to 11 September, certainly among many citizens of the US, who saw this as a loss of status. This would exist alongside fear and, eventually, hope.

However, recalling the events of 11 September 2001 as they unfolded on the television news, one can argue that they fitted with Mellencamp's (1990) analysis of shock and trauma and how TV operates during the coverage of catastrophes. This coverage breaks into the normal schedules of television time, emphasizing the shock in 'the time of the now' by disrupting regular, repetitive time. In this disruption there is 'a shift between the safe assurance of successive time and story and the break-in of the discontinuity of the real in which the future hangs in the balance, the intrusion of shock, trauma, disaster, crisis' (Mellencamp, 1990: 244). In this break there is the possibility of a revolutionary moment in the disruption of regularity, and yet television acts to normalize and regularize the catastrophe. It does this by endlessly replaying the film of the catastrophe, just as TV news kept on replaying the footage of the planes crashing into the twin towers, in order to incorporate the event into regular, everyday reality and memory, and to 'acknowledge then alleviate fear and pain . . . achieving mastery over loss' (Mellencamp, 1990: 258). Television news also provides a search for the answer or the explanation for the catastrophe in order to make it safe and reduce audience anxiety. As Mellencamp says, '[t]elevision promises shock and trauma containment over time via narration of the real' (1990: 254).

This happened in the wake of 11 September, as over the following days and weeks a narrative was provided to explain and contain the catastrophe. At first reports were uncertain as to what was happening, but gradually shaped into a story of a possible terrorist atrocity. Then, as the possibility emerged that planes had been used 'like missiles', the story began to evolve of an 'attack' on the centres of US power. A battery of experts, commentators and politicians, plus a slew of interviews with people on the streets, began to draw parallels with the attack on Pearl Harbor in 1941. Out of this, a story was gradually constructed about a provocative attack on the US that was in effect a 'declaration of war', and the conclusion was drawn – sometimes explicitly, sometimes left hanging in the air – that the response would have to be similar to that of 1941. The narrative of incitement to war was being woven by drawing parallels from collective stories of history: from events already familiar to us.

One could argue that, in addition, various governments – certainly in the US and in Britain – have attempted to build on these narratives and incite and seduce the public by manipulating the emotional responses to September 11 in order to direct conduct. The narrative of war was used to construct the very idea of a 'war on terror' and to unify public opinion behind the various strategies designed to wage this war. Support was also elicited by attempting to incite powerful emotions. Anger at what was deemed to be a provocative attack, along with fear and anxiety about possible future catastrophes, was channelled into support for the wars on Afghanistan and Iraq. Hope was raised that the 'war on terror' would be a preventative measure to protect the public and ensure peace and security. The seductive image was held out of a safe and secure world for oneself, one's family, friends, community and nation. However, in the run-up to the war on Iraq, both the US and British governments tried not only to get public support for the war by inciting powerful emotions, they also tried to induce people through persuasion. Both governments claimed to have intelligence to show that Saddam Hussein possessed weapons of mass destruction which could be used against the US and Britain: either in a direct attack against home territory, on overseas interests, or by passing on such weapons to terrorists. The two now infamous dossiers on weapons of mass destruction produced by the British government are examples of the attempts made to induce the British people into supporting the Iraq war.

However, such techniques of government do not always work; nor do the effects of television and media coverage in normalizing and regularizing those shock moments where the future becomes open and indeterminate. As Gauntlett (1995) remarks, 'television does not have predictable, direct effects' (p. 115), and parts of a population may seize the revolutionary chance to effect political change that Mellencamp (1990) sees in the break of regular schedules by catastrophe coverage. I argue here that sections of the Spanish population did precisely this in their mass response to coverage of the Madrid bombings in the media, including their response to the actions of the Spanish government after the catastrophe. But before moving on to study the mass opposition to the Iraq war and the protests over the Madrid incidents, I want to say a word or two about the method of data collection and analysis employed here.

The data for this study

In terms of drawing evidence for this study, I have concentrated on newspaper reports surrounding the highly emotive issue of the 'war on terror'. To limit the scope of the study I have chosen to focus on two main events as reported by three broadsheet newspapers in the UK – *The Times, The Guardian* and *The Observer*, the latter being the Sunday edition of *The Guardian* newspaper group. I have chosen to use broadsheet newspapers because their coverage of the events in question was more extensive and involved detailed reports of demonstrations by journalists, in which protesters were also given direct voice to articulate their own emotions. Furthermore, I have selected these two newspaper groups because, traditionally and historically, one has been seen to broadly represent the right wing of political opinion, the other broadly the centre-left. However, it needs to be said that the war in Iraq did not divide opinion along those old traditional party-political lines, and both newspaper groups published articles that were pro- and anti-war.

The two cases selected for study are reporting of the large peace demonstration in London on 15 February 2003 against the impending war on Iraq, and the Madrid train bombings of 11 March 2004 and subsequent reaction in the Spanish general election of 14 March 2004. The reason I have selected these two events is that both were reactions against attempts to direct conduct through the manipulation of emotion, and both involved mass protests with the clear public performance of emotion. They therefore illustrate how attempts at limiting the field of possible actions through manipulation of emotional currents in power relations can be partially successful and also a dismal failure, producing the opposite effect of that intended. In other words, they illustrate how emotions work both in attempts by government to govern *and* in the opposition to those attempts.

Previous studies have outlined numerous ways in which the enactment of public displays of emotion can be viewed. Two themes, among others, emerged from the study of the mass mobilized mourning following the death of Princess Diana in Britain (Kear and Steinberg, 1999) that seem highly relevant to the data from the study presented here and my initial analysis of it (I was not familiar with this work prior to that). One was the examination of the events as cultural-political phenomena, emphasizing their role in the reconstitution of political affiliation and ideological formations. The other theme was the analysis of the events in terms of the question of shifting boundaries, especially around constructions such as 'the people' and 'the nation' (Kear and Steinberg, 1999: x). The two themes were then applied to the data – along with the theories of Durkheim, Arendt, Nussbaum and Foucault – in order to deepen my original analysis and interpretation of the data, complexifying and enriching my reading of it. Exactly how these theories and themes elucidate the data should become evident as I proceed.

Opposition to the war on Iraq

Although it had been gradually building over previous months, opposition to the impending war on Iraq came to a head on 15 February 2003 with one of the largest political demonstrations ever held in London. Indeed, this was part of a series of huge demonstrations that day in cities all over the world. What is of interest here is the way that the London demonstration was reported in British newspapers with respect to the emotions of the crowd and what various reporters had to say about its unity and diversity: the latter illustrating the theme of shifting boundaries by which the crowd was seen as both unified and divided. While *The Times* of Monday 17 February had a lead article which said that 'more than six million peace demonstrators across the world have failed to sway the United States, which last night vowed to press on this week with plans for war against Iraq' (p. 1), inside was a more detailed report of the London rally. Under a headline which read, 'Middle England packs a picnic and sets off to change the face of politics', the article – written by a reporter present at the demonstration – paints a picture of a typically British protest: a middle-class, polite affair with only a smattering of troublesome and noisy political activists (*The Times*, 17 February 2003: 12–13). On the ground the march is described as a 'restrained affair', evoking the stereotype of the British as emotionally reticent. The following extract from the report gives the general tone.

> At 11.45 am, people started to move. The mood was convivial, the pace tortoise-like. Here and there you could spot the usual suspects, the anarchists who love to snarl and spit violence, but they were completely sidelined by the overwhelming garden-centre ordinariness of the crowd.
>
> (*The Times*, 17 February 2003: 12)

In the above, the reporter attempts to articulate the feeling of the crowd – the mood – which she describes as 'convivial'. The only anger reported is attributed to a group of anarchists, who are summarily dismissed as 'the usual suspects' – a known minority group – contrasted with the safe 'garden-centre ordinariness' of the majority who, it would seem, could never get cross about anything. In this report, the unity of the crowd is constructed through middle-class identity and mildness of temperament, around which a boundary is drawn leaving 'the usual suspects' on the outside to snarl and spit violence. The piece goes on like this throughout, except when the journalist reports the actual sentiments and opinions articulated by the marchers. In contrast, these reveal strong feelings and emotions on the subject of the war, especially in that people feel the British government is not listening to their concerns. The following, the words of a woman demonstrator taken from the same report, is typical of views expressed: ' "I know I am going to get emotional today," she said. "It is becoming more believable now. Tony Blair is not dealing with us. He is not listening. No one is listening" ' (*The Times*, 17 February 2003: 12). The report does conclude that '[t]his was not politics as usual. This was the British people saying, politely but firmly, that they want someone to listen' (*The Times*, 17 February 2003: 13). However, once again, politeness is emphasized against firmness, tempering the strength of feeling of protesters.

On the same page of *The Times* is a report by another journalist who was at the demonstration and spent the day talking to protesters. This report is composed of the views of 10 demonstrators in their own words, without any added journalistic comment. Again, we find the expression of strong emotions in contrast to the feeling conveyed by the main report. Here are a few snippets: 'We feel strongly against the war, but we feel we didn't have an opportunity to express that'; 'It makes you despair of any of them [politicians], but the march has been exhilarating'; 'We feel so strongly about the issue it's got us to our first march' (*The Times*, 17 February 2003: 12). In these brief quotations we can see the strength of feeling articulated by these people, even if this is not always expressed as a clear emotion such as anger. There is despair because of their perceived political impotence, yet at the same time the feeling of exhilaration the march has given people: the collective effervescence felt in a crowd unified in a purpose and sounding out a loud and clear voice of opposition to the government.

In contrast to the report in *The Times*, the main article in *The Observer* written by a reporter at the demonstration stresses the diversity in the crowd rather than its middle-England uniformity. The report notes 'the colourful warmth of feeling in the extraordinary crowds' and that carrying banners there were nuns, Muslims, toddlers, lecturers, hairdressers, and Nottingham County football supporters, in addition to 'the usual suspects' (that phrase again) – 'CND, Socialist Workers' Party, the anarchists' (*The Observer*, 16 February 2003). The report of the feelings of people talked to in the crowd is similar to *The Times*, in that there was a strong feeling of not being listened to and, thus, democracy was not working properly. One person, whose words are quoted directly, says 'No one's being consulted, and its starting to feel worrying – more worrying than the scaremongering we've been getting about the terrorist threat' (*The Observer*, 16 February 2003). Another report in the same edition is more up-front about the negative emotions felt in the crowd, in that 'What unites them is anger against Bush and Blair, but mainly Blair' (*The Observer*, 16 February 2003). So here, solidarity is seen as being created through the emotion of anger, which has been stirred by a government not listening to its people.

However, it could be said that it is more likely to find strong emotions among those involved in street protests and rallies because of the collective effervescence generated by a crowd. What of those who did not take part in such demonstrations? A hint of the complexity and difference of opinion and emotion among a more varied section of the population can perhaps be found in a report by three journalists from *The Observer* newspaper, who spent a day in The Beano Café near Kings Cross, London, talking to customers about their views on the possibility of war against Iraq. In general, they found feelings of concern and worry about the impending war. This was for a variety of reasons: it was felt the war would really be fought over oil; that they did not trust the US government; that George W. Bush only wanted to settle scores for his father – the US President at the time of the first Gulf War; and that the British government was too subservient to the US government. While people were generally sceptical about the official reasons being given for war there was also concern over Saddam Hussein, who was seen as an evil tyrant. But there were also feelings of *indifference* expressed by a large number of people, many of whom did not have any opinions about the war. Both the arguments and the high level of emotion expressed by pro- and anti-war activists had not really moved them. One customer expressed the following view to a journalist:

> 'To be honest it doesn't really affect me', he said nonchalantly, shrugging his shoulders. 'I mean, it's so far away. I'd be worried if they started calling people up to go to war, though. Or if there was a big backlash from the Muslim community in this country.'
>
> (*The Observer*, 19 January 2003: 15)

Thus, it seems that the attempts of the government to incite, induce and seduce public feeling and opinion in the months prior to the Iraq war had a mixed effect, and one could even venture to say they had failed. For the people above, there seemed to be concern and worry about the actual, as opposed to official, reasons given for the build-up to war. And, perhaps, for a still larger number there was simply indifference. Of course, some people would remain strongly in support of government policy on Iraq, but the point I want to make here is this: that how people responded to attempts to incite, induce and seduce were unpredictable in advance. This is because emotions have a complex logic, embedded as they are in the multiple networks of social relations and power relations, affording different positions and possibilities for government, opposition and resistance.

With some sections of the population the effect of attempts to govern, to direct the conduct of individuals or groups through emotion, had the opposite effect of that intended. The feelings stirred by the impending war only caused anger and outrage *expressed toward the UK government*, especially among those opposed to it, who thought the government was not listening to their views. Many of these people would be those who voted for 'New Labour' in their two landslide election victories of 1997 and 2001 and who longed for the actualization of the 'New Labour mantras: of social inclusion, community and a revived sense of socially responsible compassion' (Hey, 1999: 61). It is therefore no accident that in the relational logic of power and politics the anger and outrage of this group of people turned towards the government in the build-up to war on Iraq, rather than to Saddam Hussein or international terrorists. These people turned against a government and its leadership that had promised social inclusion but now was not listening to *them*. In the face of this, the crowds who turned out to protest seized a revolutionary moment – albeit fleeting – in which a tangible space of civic freedom and participation could be celebrated and cemented through a convivial street carnival and protest, one that also gave a sense of exhilaration. Illustrating the second theme of my analysis, new political affiliations were created, if only temporarily, in which diverse individuals formed a crowd united by anger at the existing government and excitement at the power of their collective voice.

The Madrid bombings

The events in Madrid on 11 March 2004 and what happened in the Spanish general election three days afterwards provide a different illustration of the points above. On 11 March, a number of bombs were exploded on commuter trains coming into central Madrid during the morning rush hour. The following day the event was reported in the *Guardian* under the headline 'Massacre in Madrid'. The report begins, 'Spain was in a state of profound shock, mourning and anger last night after the worst terrorist attack in Europe since the Lockerbie bombing . . .' (*Guardian*, 12 March 2004: 1). Similar emotions are reported in *The Times*, which carries an article on page five headlined 'Tide of grief and revulsion sweeps nation'.

While both newspapers report the Spanish nation united through the emotions of shock, grief, and anger, *The Times* is more certain as to who the anger is directed against – the Basque separatist group Eta. In the immediate aftermath of the bombings the Spanish government let it be known through the media that emerging evidence seemed to implicate Eta in the atrocity. The report in *The Times* focuses on the crowds that gathered in Madrid city centre to mourn those who died in the bombings and express their anger, stating that 'the hundreds gathered in Puerto del Sol . . . had no doubts who was to blame. Every slogan they chanted, every banner they waved condemned Eta, the Basque separatists' (*The Times*, 12 March 2004: 5). This contrasts with reports in the *Guardian*, which do not claim that everyone was blaming Eta. So while both newspapers saw the Spanish people as united in their emotional reaction to the bombings, there was uncertainty as to whom their anger and grief was directed against. This was important because the then Spanish government, led by the conservative Popular Party and its Prime Minister, Jose Maria Aznar, had been a partner in the coalition forces in the war against Iraq and tough opponents of Eta. If the bombings were the work of an Islamic group, as some suspected, rather than Eta, this might work against the government in the elections just two days away. In this case, its pro-war stance could cost it votes, as the Spanish people might believe they had paid a heavy price for the government's support for the war, while if Eta were to blame this would justify the government's stance of not negotiating with them. Indeed, Prime Minister Aznar attempted to direct the feelings of the Spanish people when, using highly emotive language, he stated:

> 11 March 2004 has taken its place in the history of infamy . . . There are no negotiations possible or desirable with these assassins that have so often sown death through all of Spain [referring indirectly to Eta]. We will defeat them. We will succeed in finishing off the terrorist band, with the strength of the rule of law and with the unity of all Spaniards. (*Guardian*, 12 March 2004: 1)

Here is a direct appeal for unity among all Spanish people and an attempt to consolidate that unity as support for the Popular Party with their tough stance against Eta.

A headline article in *The Times* the following day about mass demonstrations across Spain, in which an estimated 11.4 million people took to the streets, repeats many of the sentiments found in the *Guardian* report. Under the headline 'Millions march against terror', it says the crowds expressed grief, anger, revulsion and outrage. They also seemed to want to express their unity in a way that Prime Minister Aznar was hoping, with the journalist reporting sections of the crowd chanting, 'A people united will never be defeated' (*The Times*, 13 March 2004: 1). However, at this point *The Times* was still reluctant to report on emerging evidence that a group with links to al-Qaeda may have been behind the bombings. It was also reluctant to mention the possible ambivalence in the emotional mood of the crowds, although it does report that not all the anger was directed at the terrorists. 'One banner in Bilbao drew attention to the Spanish Prime Minister's support for the Iraq war. "No to war, Aznar, look where you got us" it declared' (*The Times*, 13 March 2004: 2).

As stronger evidence emerged towards Election Day that it was a group with links to Islamic extremists who were responsible for the bombings, and not Eta, then feelings quickly began to turn against the existing government. Aznar's Popular Party lost the election to the Socialist Party on 14 March 2004. The reports in the following day's newspapers in Britain are indicative of the way the emotional tide had changed amongst a large number of Spanish people. The *Guardian* reported in its front-page headline, 'Furious voters oust Spanish government', and in the following report it was claimed there had been an 'angry reaction' to the government and that they had also faced 'angry protests' from crowds on Election Day. Joaquin Leguina, a former president of Madrid's regional government said, 'There's a feeling of anguish, sadness, horror'. This was directed at the government as a handful of young protesters screamed at Mariano Rajoy, Aznar's successor as leader of the Popular Party, 'murderer . . . we did not want to go to war' (the *Guardian*, 15 March 2004: 1). This same incident is reported in *The Times* with protesters shouting 'Liar!' and 'Get our troops out of Iraq!' (*The Times*, 15 March 2004: 1). Nevertheless, *The Times* reports the same change in emotion as the *Guardian*, as a sub-headline to the lead article claims 'Socialists sweep in as furious voters exact revenge over Iraq war' (*The Times*, 15 March 2004: 1). An article on the election and the protests surrounding it claims that 'More than 26 million angry, fearful and traumatized Spaniards voted yesterday in an election unlike any held in the West': this was because of its 'sheer drama and emotional intensity' (*The Times*, 15 March 2004: 3). Indeed, *The Times* reports that peace flags were draped outside polling stations and inside white doves cut out of paper decorated the halls. Although this type of emotional outpouring is unusual around elections in the West, it is perhaps only a very dramatic illustration of how emotion underlies the act of voting (Barbalet, 2004).

Nevertheless, what is clear about the extraordinary election in Spain in March 2004 is the way that overt emotion expressed by crowds on the street and voters queuing to vote was reported in the media and amplified. Once again, we find in this the two themes that are key to this analysis. First, the shifting boundaries of constructs like 'the people' and 'the nation', with newspapers claiming everyone in Spain was united through emotion, and some claiming unity against a common enemy. However, this attributed unity begins to splinter over the events of the next three days as more complex groupings of opposition to the government begin to appear. The protests begin to display some of the attributes of the London march against the Iraq war, with the reconstitution of political affiliation achieved in mass protest through collective effervescence: the collective expression of emotion. Again, we see that attempts to direct conduct through emotions aimed at inciting, inducing or seducing are unpredictable because emotion is ambivalent and often conflicting. In this case, it was anger and fury mixed with grief and mourning in a cocktail aimed at the Spanish government that proved lethal for political leaders. Their attempts to direct the emotions of the Spanish people only worked against them, as many felt their grief was being used to manipulate them. This, coupled with people's prior affiliations to certain values as a majority of Spanish people had been against involvement in the Iraq war, served to turn the tide of anger against Aznar's government.

All these ambivalent and alternating emotions are caught by Almudena Grandes, a Madrid novelist and anti-war campaigner, who sums up his own feelings and those of others who turned out to protest against the Aznar government on election night. He reports how the horror felt by Spanish people about the terrorist attacks turned to rage against the government:

> the rage, the indignation, the ferocity and, at the same time, the spontaneity of the strangest, most sorrowful and most emotional demonstrations in which I have taken part during my life . . . For more than two and a half-hours I was at the corner of Genova and Campoamer, with tears in my eyes and immeasurable rage in my throat . . . And we were not afraid. There was no room in us for fear. This was our funeral, our personal and furious homage to the victims. We would have felt pain even if Eta had been guilty; we did not hate Eta any more or less than we hated al-Qaeda. We hated murderers infinitely, all murderers, and this hate motivated us, not fear . . . [But the hate was partly turned against the government because] you do not play with corpses . . . we had said no to the war – this is what we were shouting. (*Guardian*, G2 section, 17 March 2004)

Here, we find a range of ambivalent and alternating emotions – rage, hate, sorrow and grief (in rejection of fear) – being aimed at murderers and at the Spanish government. The protest was not only a revolutionary constitution of a public space of civic freedom and participation, as the London demonstration had been, it was also a funeral: a collective and ritualistic performance of grief that was a response to catastrophe, shock and trauma. The crowds that gathered across Spain could be seen as seizing that revolutionary break in regular time caused by catastrophe to create a space of civic participation and the reconstitution of political affiliation. Also, as Durkheim (1915) pointed out, after a collective shock social interaction becomes more frequent as people look for each other and assemble together in the need for mutual dependence. A collective ritual of grief is not just the vehicle for expressing emotion, but also a way of recreating solidarity among the group when unity is threatened by the loss of one or more members. Ritualized mourning could also be seen, in a Freudian sense, as a way for the group or nation to incorporate the lost members back into its own collective body through public ceremony and performance.

Yet it must not be forgotten that what Almudena Grandes was describing above was also a furious protest: a howl of grief and rage directed at the Spanish government that, in the course of three days, brought it down.

Conclusion

From the two cases studied here, I would argue that it is impossible to fully understand the attempts of governments to govern a population and direct conduct, along with the resistance and opposition to this, without acknowledging the central place of emotions in these power relations. Emotions are powerful collective forces involved in the reconstruction of social groups and, as such, in the maintenance of the status quo. Because of this, governments will always be tempted to stir powerful emotions in their strategies for directing conduct: inciting, inducing and seducing a people. Yet powerful emotions are not only involved in the reproduction of the social order, they also threaten its very existence, especially when they are acted out in collective ritualistic performances. In contemporary societies, such collective performances can express the desire to exercise political capacities in a civic arena and, in so doing, present the possibility of creating new political affiliations in a more active public space. The potential revolutionary power of emotion does not stem from its irrationality, but rather from its 'relational logic' which follows the pattern of people's attachments to others, to symbols and to ideals. Because emotions are ambivalent and alternating they are not predictable in advance, especially when the people and things we value highly are threatened or lost. Then, powerful emotions play a part in political judgements, just as here anger and grief were inextricably linked to the assessment of governments that were deemed to have not listened to a large section of their people and acted irresponsibly. Thus, emotions have a complex relational logic and are embedded in relations of power, affording different positions and possibilities for government, opposition and resistance. Any analysis of power, government and politics that doesn't consider emotion misses its essential element.

References

Arendt, Hannah (1973) *On Revolution*. Harmondsworth: Penguin.
Barbalet, Jack (2004) 'Emotions in Political Practices and Political Analysis', Plenary Presentation, Politics and Emotions Conference, University of the West of England.

Burkitt, Ian (1997) 'Social Relationships and Emotions', *Sociology* 31(1): 37–55.

Burkitt, Ian (2002) 'Complex Emotions: Relations, Feelings and Images in Emotional Experience', in Jack Barbalet (ed.) *Emotions and Sociology*, pp. 151–67. Oxford: Blackwell/The Sociological Review.

Durkheim, Emile (1915) *The Elementary Forms of the Religious Life*. London: George Allen & Unwin.

Durkheim, Emile (1938) *The Rules of Sociological Method*. New York: Free Press.

Durkheim, Emile (1957) *Professional Ethics and Civic Morals*. London: Routledge.

Durkheim, E. and M. Mauss (1963) *Primitive Classification*. London: Cohen & West.

Foucault, Michel (1982) 'The Subject and Power', in H.L. Dreyfus and P. Rabinow *Michel Foucault: Beyond Structuralism and Hermeneutics*, pp. 208–26. Brighton: Harvester.

Freud, Sigmund (1981[1963]) *Introductory Lectures on Psychoanalysis*. Harmondsworth: Pelican.

Gauntlett, David (1995) *Moving Experiences: Understanding Television's Influences and Effects*. London: John Libbey.

Hey, Valerie (1999) 'Be(long)ing: New Labour, New Britain and the "Dianaization" of Politics', in Adrian Kear and Deborah Lynn Steinberg (eds) *Mourning Diana: Nation, Culture and the Performance of Grief*. London: Routledge.

Kear, A. and D.L. Steinberg (eds) (1999) *Mourning Diana: Nation, Culture and the Performance of Grief*. London: Routledge.

Kemper, Theodore D. (2002) 'Predicting Emotions in Groups: Some Lessons from September 11', in Jack Barbalet (ed.) *Emotions and Sociology*, pp. 53–68. Oxford: Blackwell/The Sociological Review.

Le Bon, Gustave (1896) *The Crowd: A Study of the Popular Mind*. London: Fisher Unwin.

Mellencamp, Patricia (1990) 'TV Time and Catastrophe, or "Beyond the Pleasure Principle" of Television', in Patricia Mellencamp (ed.) *Logics of Television: Essays in Cultural Criticism*, pp. 240–66. Bloomington: Indiana University Press.

Nussbaum, Martha C. (2001) *Upheavals of Thought: The Intelligence of Emotions*. Cambridge: Cambridge University Press.

Tester, Keith (1997) *Moral Culture*. London: Sage.

Weber, Max (1970) 'Politics as a Vocation', in H.H. Gerth and C. Wright Mills (eds) *From Max Weber: Essays in Sociology*, pp. 77–128. London: Routledge.

IV HISTORICAL APPROACHES

Chapter 10

Carol Z. Stearns

'LORD HELP ME WALK HUMBLY': ANGER AND SADNESS IN ENGLAND AND AMERICA, 1570–1750

RECENT HISTORICAL WORK on emotion, initially derived from an expanded exploration of family life, has raised questions about changes in personality associated with modernization. The focus, of course, has been on an eighteenth-century watershed. Yet it is love and sexuality, rather than a wider emotional spectrum, that have commanded attention. Recent revisionist work, furthermore, in arguing for continuity rather than change, makes it clear that the watershed itself is far from definitively established. The present essay addresses both the question of change and the problem of the range of emotions involved. It explores the ways in which people handled some negative emotions in the early modern period in England and America. It follows from the clear need to attend to emotions beyond love and sex, and it tries to address the eighteenth-century transformation with a subtlety missing in both the pioneer and the revisionist efforts in this area.

Since the historiography of emotion has thus far concentrated on making temporal rather than national distinctions, this article will take a transatlantic approach. This is not to suggest that there may not have been significant differences between the emotional climates of early modern England and America, but simply that until more basic work is done on delineating early modern emotionality in general, making national distinctions within a Western context is premature. I have limited my attention to English-language sources as a matter of convenience, but again not because I postulate that Anglo-American emotionality in this period was significantly different from say French or Dutch.[1]

This article is based on diaries and autobiographies because these are some of the best sources historians possess for exploring the personal goals and struggles of earlier generations. Although diaries as we know them did not exist before the sixteenth century, by the period we are considering they were becoming voluminous. Certainly, there are problems with these sources. For one thing, diarists probably are never typical of their era, and so one must be careful not to draw conclusions about the larger population based on their products, except with caution. A second problem is that even when typical, diarists, like all of us, have a self-image to preserve, and like all of us cannot be totally honest with themselves even if they wish to be.[2] Thus, even if diarists are conscious of their emotions they may choose not to commit what they know to paper. This distortion, in the service of preservation of self-image, is an advantage as well as a problem, however, because it allows us to glimpse something of the diarist's emotionology as well as his emotions, and to learn a great deal about the struggle to keep the two in harmony.[3]

Finally, and obviously, there is a great deal about emotional life which does not appear in the pages of diaries. To get the full flavor of a culture's emotional life without being there to observe is certainly a formidable, and ultimately impossible, task, but many different sorts of sources, literary sources as well as records of interactions such as those at festivals, law courts, and riots, need to be used. The diaries are some help here, since most writers recorded a great deal of their observations of the behavior of others as well as chronicling their own feelings and thoughts, but certainly it would be good to use records which make such observations in a more systematic fashion, and certainly studying the diaries alone tends to exaggerate the importance of the cognitive aspect of emotions and to underrate the importance of behavior. Thus, the diaries are a good source with which to begin to study early modern emotions, but there is no claim here that from the diaries alone definitive statements can be made.[4]

This article uses, further, only a selection of diaries, and not all those available in print, or certainly in manuscript.[5] It is meant then to be a pilot study which will erect some hypotheses that can be tested in more extensive work on the history of early modern emotions. The writer admits first to historical prejudice. She believes that people's feelings and their experience change over time—that there are modal forms, within a culture, for emotional experience, and that these differ between cultures and chronological periods. These differences, which we all intuit with no difficulty when we experience the "different-ness" of, say, Donne's poetry, a Puritan sermon, or a Jacobean tragedy, are often difficult to formulate precisely. This difficulty has in turn plagued historians of everyday life, and so although the first generation of historians to talk about love and family experience stressed the great gap between the premodern and modern experience, the more recent revisionist wave has essentially argued that there is no historical change in some of the fundamentals of life such as family interaction and emotional experience.[6] It is one purpose of this study, through using the diaries, to see if some testable formulations about change in emotional experience can be generated.[7]

This essay will concentrate on two emotions, anger and sadness, which are of interest to the author since she has worked on one of them, anger, before, and since it is widely believed that the two emotions are very much connected.[8]

Before the end of the seventeenth century, most diarists had difficulty thinking of them-selves as angry. To be sure, many diarists had difficulty thinking of themselves as having emotions which could be named at all, and their records are useful to us only in making us aware of the lack of interest many had in their inner lives. But for the first intro-spective diarists, conscious anger was a rarity. Interactions or situations which were noxious often stimulated arousal, but the arousal would be labeled as sadness rather than as anger.

Roger Lowe, an apprentice during the years he kept his diary, had his most difficult interactions with his master, but experienced their conflicts as arousing grief rather than anger. For instance, "I thought it sad for me to be ingaged 9 years . . . to sell my Master's ware . . . and get no knowledge." When his master insists on commandeering money he has earned as a scribe, apart from his duties as apprentice, Lowe relates what happened "to my great greefe." Later, his Master promises and then refuses to give him a new set of clothes, "soe I would have none and parted with greefe."

Lest one argue that it was only toward social superiors that Lowe had difficulty conceptualizing anger, examples of a similar pattern in other situations will be offered. Lowe is out for the day and someone steals his horse so there is no easy way to go home: "I was highly perplexed, yet bore it very patiently." A woman starts some malicious gossip about him, and he is "in some greefe" about it. A friend steals his love letters and passes them around, which "was matter of much griefe to me and I was very sad upon it."[9]

Ralph Josselin, a Puritan clergyman, had similar disinclination to find himself angry. Conflictual situations would often be noted, a sign they were troubling him, yet he did not label his reaction. When his stepmother cheats him out of inheritance from his father he says only that "wee could not agree . . . I departed from her," and that "frends were not so kinde as I expected." When he is not paid as well as he has been promised in a new ministry, "I confesse I was stumbled at their dealings and some abuses offered mee." He sometimes seems to have a glimmer that something like anger may be bothering him, but he does not label the feeling and instead asks immediately that the feeling turn into something else. Thus, in a dispute about a living, "lord learne me patience and wisdome." In a dispute about doctrine where someone speaks to him "very unkind words, Lord . . . helpe me to walk humbly," and he later asks for help in "patienting my heart under some trialls, the Lord give mee an humble, condescending spirit, weaken my soule. . . ." In a dispute with his wife, he is aware of arousal and discomfort, but wants to skip over labeling his feeling, and get back to equanimity. "I find my heart apt to unquietnes . . . and it troubles mee . . . I thinke I have cause, but I am sure I should bee more patient and counsellable." It is interesting that what is repressed in the daytime emerges in dream material: "They say dreames declare a man's Temperament, this night I dreamd I was wondrous passion with a man that wrongd mee and my child insomuch as I was ashamed of my selfe, god in mercy keepe mee from that evill, in the day, I did that and that in passion for which I was sorry."[10]

Non-Puritans too, in this early period, are not eager to see themselves as angry, and are more likely to present themselves as sad. For instance, John Dee, involved in various disputes, wrote that his economic problems, "do not so much grieve my hart as the rash, lewde, fond and most untrue fables and reports of me."[11] Or Anne Clifford, whose diary covered a long dispute with her husband about his use of her money: "Sometimes I had fair words from him and sometimes foul, but I took all patiently, and did strive to give him . . . assurance of my love," and when he canceled her jointure said, "I am resolved to take all patiently, casting all my care upon GOD." Instead of becoming angry at her husband she became sad so that at Church, "my eyes were so blubbered with weeping that I could scarcely look up."[12] Mrs. Freke, of a less exalted social class, but involved in similar disputes with her spouse, resorted to a standard posture of tears, grief, and drug abuse, but not to anger.[13]

The anger of others made early modern people uncomfortable. Anger in other people was often observed and even labeled, and yet one could not respond in kind. Various solutions to this problem emerged. When a friend is angry, Roger Lowe is sad. One coping mechanism was to avoid angry situations. For instance, Lowe arranged to get someone else to broach his problems to his master. Another solution was to turn to God for support. When another woman is in a "rage" at his girl friend in his presence, "this was matter of great greife of harte unto me . . . my trust is in God who will helpe in trouble. Though the storme be now, yet I have hopes I shall see a calme." When he wrongly blames someone for forging his name and that man is offended with him this is "Great griefe. But God will help." It is intriguing to see that other people when angry are experienced as extremely threatening, perhaps a result of the repression of one's own anger leading to exaggerated projections of the anger of others. In a religious dispute, Lowe is worried that the "contention had like to have beene hott," and that the other man "should doe me some hurt."[14]

Others also found it uncomfortable to be confronted with anger. When Samuel Sewall, of New England, is involved in religious and governance disputes, a man speaks to him with "fierceness" and "I was stricken with this furious expression." When he asks to have a bill paid, and the response is anger, Sewall writes, "I know no reason for this Anger; the Lord sanctify it to me, and help me to seek more his Grace and favor."[15] Anger needs almost to be explained away, and certainly help is needed to bear it. When Ebenezer Parkman catechizes a dying woman, and her brother angrily objects to his questions, Parkman spends paragraphs in his diary defending himself, talks of this as a trial for days, and has difficulty sleeping. Years later he notes with pleasure that the man apologized.[16]

It would be mistaken, though, to conclude, because early modern people had difficulty recognizing their own anger, or feeling comfortable with anger in others, that angry behavior was not a commonplace in their culture. Other historians have commented upon the rough-and-tumble tone of early modern society, the readiness to start physical fights, the institutionalization of duels, the easy cursings and swearing, and violent games, sports, and punishments.[17] Obviously, the very discomfort with anger which has been described by the diarists is evidence that frequent anger did exist.

Fighting was common among people whom we would be surprised to find fighting today. For instance, Anthony Wood made no comment on seeing students pelting a man in the pillory with eggs or a priest fighting in the street. John Oglander was unsurprised to see gentlemen beating each other with sticks, and Oliver Heywood was not startled to see an adult severely beat rowdy boys. Dueling was not remarkable, even in Puritan New England.[18]

Abuse of servants was taken for granted, so that when another minister struck his maid causing her to "bleed much," Ralph Josselin's only comment was that "it might have been my condicion if mercy had not prevented it." Sewall also was unsurprised at a man who fell into an "angry passion with his servant."[19]

Quarrels between neighbors were probably frequent, and resulted in behavior that we might find surprising, but which elicited no particular comment from the diarists, such as an incident in which Elias Ashmole recorded that his neighbor piled garbage against his garden wall. Romantic difficulties might frequently lead to quarrels and even to violence. Ashmole reported one such in which the aggressor was blamed but no one seemed to take any steps regarding his attempt to kill a rival.[20]

Verbiage was often very angry, and on the part of people from whom today we might expect more restraint. For instance, Anthony Wood registered no surprise when the Master of Balliol said one of his books was "not fit to wipe one's arse with." Sewall related that in a dispute over a servant, a General Nicholson spoke with a "roaring voice" and was so "furiously Loud, that the Noise was plainly heard in the Council Chambers." Sewall frequently reported "vehement" fights and "fiery" words in council meetings.[21]

How can it be that so much anger existed in a culture in which people denied anger among themselves? Can it be that diarists were unusually restrained people? It may be that, tending to be more introspective than others, they might also have been less expressive, but it seems doubtful that they were totally different in their emotional styles from all they interacted with. It is notable that Sewall, who has difficulty admitting his own anger, observed high levels of anger in the other Puritan magistrates with whom he worked, men who, we can be certain, were loath to recognize anger in themselves. Oliver Heywood made similar observations of nonconformist ministers in England. The explanation seems to be that men who did not recognize in themselves the feeling of anger could yet act as though they were angry. For instance, Richard Norwood, who never called himself angry, described starting a fight with a quarterstaff when someone spoke to him scornfully. He said nothing about his feelings here.[22] Roger Lowe, always loath to say he was angry, when called a bastard, vowed to be the death of the offender and "buffeted hime very mery."[23] This was not the only time he got into a physical fight and yet recorded no emotion preceding it.[24] Sewall admitted that he and Cotton Mather had substantial public disputes, and refers to Mather's anger, though never admitting to the emotion in himself. Similarly, he admits to a dispute with a neighbor over digging a cellar, and that they "storm" and speak "opprobrious words" but he does not say he is angry.[25] It is as though there were a dissociation between feeling and action. These seventeenth-century people are acting as though they are in a Skinnerian paradigm where there is a stimulus and a response, but no recognized mediating ego or self. In other words, there is little cognition that emotions exist, and therefore little sense that behavior flows from conscious feelings and can be controlled.

It was this lack of cognition and of a sense that through cognition one could control behavior that was soon to change. Emotional styles do not change overnight and it is not being suggested here that a sharp break is discernible, but it is notable that by the late seventeenth century, more diarists began to write as though they had an awareness of feelings, and that from this awareness a sense came that behaviors could be controlled. Certainly, many diarists still maintained the older style, and many who used a newer style at times reverted. What is notable, though, is that a new style, which had hardly existed before, was being developed, and it was a style which was to become predominant by the nineteenth century. This new style suggested that behaviors could be controlled even if feelings were intense. For instance, Sewall, in dispute with another magistrate, noted that the man spoke "vehemently" and he told him he "was in a passion." The man denied this, and Sewall said that therefore "it was so much the worse."[26] In other words, if one is in control of one's feelings one should control one's behavior. A similar belief is seen in John Oglander's discussion of a gentleman who was "by nature very passionate, yet in his wisdome he conquered that passion so much that you would think him to be of a mild disposition."[27]

Henry Newcome was a Puritan minister who at the end of the seventeenth century wrote a book about the necessity for controlling the expression of anger. He said that men should not let themselves be ruled by passion but should protect the soul by erecting walls against passion, much like the walls around a city. He agreed with the old idea that men are born with temperaments, and some more easily angered than others, but his emphasis was on the fact that all could exert self-control.[28] This view was expressed clearly in his auto-biography, in which the angry behavior of others was condemned as a failure, and rather than being simply assumed to result from temperament or passion, required explanation. For instance, "I was exceedingly perplexed about my wife. God knows what I should do. These four years have I now lived with her and do not know how to humor her. When she is angry, I do aggravate her passion by saying anything." He concludes that this must be because women were naturally weak. Dudley Ryder similarly judged angry behavior harshly and thought it could be controlled. He used the word *childish* to describe his sister's angry outbursts, and wrote of his parents:

> At supper father and mother had some little dispute, as they generally have every time they meet at table. I have been thinking which is in fault . . . but indeed they are both very much in fault, my mother for saying everything in a cross way . . . and my father for continuing the matter that gave offense and pushing it on.[29]

At the same time that anger is being condemned as controllable in others, diarists are beginning to be able to label it in themselves. For Roger Lowe, in the early seventeenth century, this was a rarity, though he did at one point admit to a quarrel that made him "very angry" and then to feeling upset about it. Writing in the early eighteenth century, Ebenezer Parkman had similarly allowed the possibility he might be angry in noting a falling-out between other ministers and hoping therefore that he would not "forget myself."[30] Oliver Heywood in 1673 censured himself for a "sharp dispute" in which "I was in some passion . . . my spirit was too warm." By the late seventeenth century Henry Newcome, more often than not, labeled his response to noxious experiences as anger. He mentioned, for example, expressing anger at a messenger who brought him bad news, and then condemned himself for doing it. He noted "peevish folly in my heart, envy and anger" when he was not invited to a fair. On a difficult journey, "I could not but observe the folly of my spirit, that I should be angry at the length and hardness of the way as if the inhabitants were in fault. . . . Should the earth be removed for thee?" In an argument over the repair of his house, "I urged it too far and too hotly . . . passion never does good. I was troubled hereupon." This is not to say that Newcome did not occasionally describe difficult situations as making him "weary" rather than angry, or project his own anger onto others, but for the most part, it is notable that he was able to label his responses as anger, and that this gave him a sense that he could control his behavior that seemed to be lacking in some of the earlier diarists.[31]

Dudley Ryder, writing in the early eighteenth century, had an even more explicit notion of when he was angry. For instance, he commented that when his maid sent his wig to London by mistake, "it put me into a great deal of concern and I never spoke so angrily to a servant before." Spotting and labeling his feelings gave him a sense that he could master them. Continuing with the maid, "I was vexed to find the passion had so much power over me. I began to suspect my own temper more than ever and afraid lest it should betray me hereafter into some unlucky hit." He was developing, in sum, a sense that he was not merely the agent of uncontrolled passions, but that he had a character, a self, and that this afforded him some control: "Was in a very ill humour all this evening, everything . . . disposed me to be angry . . . I cannot but be concerned that I have such a disposition which may grow up in time if not checked to be very ill humour and make me extremely troublesome." And commenting on his mother's bad temper, "I am too apt to be guilty of the same kind of peevishness myself. I have too much of her temper but I am resolved to endevor to quell at its first rise every secret resentment and uneasiness that comes upon me. I know how to do it already pretty well with respect to others by preventing its being discovered to others but this is not enough."[32] Diarists like Newcome and Ryder, then, are developing a new sense that there is a self, what we might call an ego, appearing in the Skinnerian black box, and that the human self is not simply a stimulus-response machine, but an agent of control. Thus, the dissociation between self-perception and behavior, which was characteristic of the earlier diarists, was no longer a prime mechanism for confronting noxious stimuli. The new sense of the self, which was just beginning to emerge in late seventeenth-century diarists' perception of their own anger, was to become the modal form for dealing with the emotion by the nineteenth century. A change was taking place, albeit slowly. Angry emotions, once denied, projected, or acted out without acknowledgment, were now being identified and labeled, and in the process, giving some men a sense that they had more control over their behaviors. Some corollaries of this changing style in anger control will now be explored.

There is a seeming paradox in the fact that although the earlier diarists had difficulty seeing themselves as angry, they were more comfortable than the later ones with the notion of an angry God. Exploring this apparent puzzle leads to deeper understanding of both points of view and to the reasons for change. Certainly, up to the last third of the seventeenth century, God's anger for minor trespasses was held to be a constant fact of life, and many diarists explained the slightest pieces of bad fortune as resulting from punishment by the wrathful Almighty. Lowe, worried about career plans, wrote that "I was in a troubled condition in my mind considering my unsettlednes, and that God was highly offended with me." Josselin frequently noted God's anger at him and at his town. Norwood had similar fears. Charles Lloyd Cohen finds it a commonplace of Puritan psychology that the individual felt subject to God's ire for all infractions, "lying under the wrath," perceiving "nothing but death and wrath . . . terrible expressions of wrath."[33]

Since God could be angry, and the individual could not, it was not surprising to find individuals indirectly expressing rage by counting on the Lord for revenge. For instance, when Lowe's love letters are purloined, he calls the thief a "stinking Raskell . . . a develish, malicious, dissembling, knavish rascall"; admitting to no anger on his own part, he says he feels only grief, but "God will not faile those that trust in him." A more clear-cut example comes when his girl friend's sister spreads malicious gossip about him. He writes this poem:

> Well, I'm content, though fortune on me frowne,
> God will me raise, though the world would cast me downe,
> And I with patience will their Mallice bear. . . .
> But vengeance will att last light on their head, . . .
> In time my quarrelle will revenged be,
> Till then I'll waite and only seeke to God . . .
> And they that are the acters of my greefe
> May they cry out and yet find no releife.[34]

In other words, the anger that Lowe could not feel himself could be projected onto God, and he could count on God to avenge him, for God, and only God, was allowed anger.

But by the late seventeenth century, some people were beginning to question God's wrath, and to postulate a more merciful Lord. Henry Newcome made this argument explicitly in his book against anger, asking men to stop fighting over religious matters, and to imitate God, who as incarnated in Christ, was meek and loving. In his own life, Newcome attempted to act on this. When a minister seized a pulpit cushion Newcome thought belonged to him, he wrote, "I could have taken these passages ill, but I thought it best to take no notice of it . . . for so I think Jesus Christ in such a case, would have done." Dudley Ryder found it common sense that God was forgiving, and wrote "we don't conceive . . . of God to suppose that He would be this inexorable malicious being."[35]

The change in the perception of God paralleled a changing view of the propriety of anger in hierarchy. Earlier, anger was clearly viewed as the prerogative of those on top, and led to no surprise. Anthony Wood displayed no shock in relating how RB, a chaplain, thrust his servant down the stairs and kicked her. Elizabeth Freke had no comment when her daughter-in-law told her maid she had a "good mind to kick her downe staires." Richard Norwood has no comment on the fact that when he tried to abandon his ship, his Captain "fell upon me with his truncheon, giving me three or four blows, and would have me ask him forgiveness." Roger Lowe was constantly expecting his Master to be angry with him, and was surprised whenever he was not.[36]

During the later seventeenth century, however, a new view was being developed that those on top in hierarchies, whether husbands, parents, or masters, should moderate their anger and rule by gentleness. The diarists who thought of God as gentle also had this view of hierarchies. Newcome wrote that inferiors should be spared anger. He was proud that as a minister he did better than in those congregations where "men [were] usually flying off," while he, writing mildly, masters opposition. Anger against children, or servants, when not controlled, was viewed as lower-class: "There is not a more disgusting sight," wrote John Witherspoon in 1797, "than the impotent rage of a parent who has no authority. Among the lower ranks of people, who are under no restraint from decency, you may sometimes see [a parent] . . . running out in the street after a child . . . with looks of fury . . . it fills every beholder with horror."[37]

The earlier view assuming that anger is justifiable when one is on the right side, and that God, always on the right side, may be angry, allowed conversion of anger to zeal. It is best, if one is clearly in the right, to be tough. As John Oglander put it, "Let thy sword, rather than thy tongue, give thy enemy the advantage." Early Puritan religious writers condemned lukewarmness, and argued that zeal for God was good. "Anger in strength and starkness intends the driving away, and despelling of the evill . . . against which it riseth." Zeal combines "love and anger" and "proceeds from love of the Lord."[38]

The new view has been discussed at length in other contexts. In England at least, disgust with the excesses of the Civil War and then the general context of early Enlightenment thought condemned zeal as unwarranted. It was not always clear which was the right and which was the wrong side. Translated into emotional direction, then, anger must be very modulated. The whole point of Newcome's book against anger was that religious differences were almost never so important as to justify ire, or "uncivil expression." He explicitly argued against the older view that those who moderated their anger were "pusillanimous." Dudley Ryder knew he had strong feelings about politics, but said that, just because those feelings worked him "up into a kind of heat . . . [which] . . . makes me speak with too much warmth and eagerness," he must restrain himself. Even if the opponent was a papist, it was distasteful to argue in a "noisy loud voice." Ryder observed explicitly that in his day there was a change in what was considered good manners even in a political argument. In arguing politics with him, his aunt "is extremely violent and cannot tell how to keep her temper. . . . She still keeps to the old way of saying the most absurd and shocking things that silence one at once. . . ."[39]

Another contrast between old and new emerged. While in the old view anger was the prerogative of those on the top of hierarchies, anger on the part of those at the bottom of hierarchies was so unacceptable, even shocking, that it was viewed not as anger but madness in the sense of insanity.[40] Interestingly enough, though, as we have seen, the early diarists almost uniformly did not feel entitled to the emotion. It would seem as though even in earthly relationships, they had a sense of being one down, and of being uncomfortable with self-assertion. Since children, even upper-class children, were socialized to feel that they were on the bottom, they may never have grown up to feel comfortable with assertive postures, or at least with acknowledging them as such even when they did flail out. David Hunt has made this point in his study of the child rearing of Louis XIII of France. He has argued that the whippings the child constantly received were designed, in some way, to suppress his sense of autonomy, and to prepare him for a role of submissiveness.[41] Thus, even those on the top of hierarchies were not to feel comfortable with experiencing themselves as on top, or with emotions that were clearly assertive. An example of such unease appears in the musings of Adam Eyre in 1647:

> This night I whipped Jane [a servant] for her foolishness, as yesterday I had done for her sloathfulness; and hence am induced to bewayle my sinfull life, for my failings in the presence of God Allmighty are questionless greater than hers are to me; wherefore, unless Thou, my most mercifull God, be mercifull unto mee, what shall become of mee?[42]

This is old-fashioned in that the anxiety comes not so much from the view that one should be gentle, as God is gentle, but from the fear that no matter what one's position on earth, one is always in a servile position vis à vis the potentially angry Deity. Many writers have discussed, in Puritan thought, the emphasis placed on creating feelings of submission, and combatting pride. Discomfort with anger would seem to fit in here. Richard Norwood illustrates the connection between anxiety about pride and anger when relating his experience in a falling-out with another man:

> wherein I gave place to passion even unto rage and fury, which . . . was stirred up . . . chiefly by pride. . . . In the heat of which fury I had thoughts and inclinations in my heart of cutting down his house, yea of killing him, and that if I should do so God would yet be merciful and would be reconciled to me again. Behold an example of the stupendous wickedness of the heart.[43]

We see here the notion that if one is certain one is in the right there is some sense that anger is justifiable. But we see also that the idea of asserting oneself so strongly makes people uncomfortable—it is in fact the sin of pride; therefore anger must be repressed and left to God, the only being entitled to that emotion. Thus there is a kind of wavering between the belief that "zealous" anger is justifiable, and the inhibitory notion that to assume one has a right to be zealous in this fashion is to be sinfully prideful. It may well be, because this problem remained unresolved, that when anger did emerge, it so often seemed unmodulated and accompanied by an inner sense of conflict. There are cultures in which the legitimacy of anger is defined, as in early modern Europe and America, by being in the right, but in which the experience of anger is less conflicted. That is because in these cultures, which value self-assertion, it is not necessarily sinful or dangerous to claim that one is indeed in the right.[44]

The new view, beginning to emerge by the late seventeenth century, was more democratic, made greater allowance for the possibility of the individual's reasonable assessment that he was in the right, and developed a new view of God. In eighteenth-century religious thought, God was more like man than he had been earlier. A sharp division between God who was allowed anger and man who was allowed none no longer seemed reasonable. In fact, God's likeness to a good man was the basis of Dudley Ryder's discussion about whether God could be angry.[45] To admit anger now was not so very terrible, because it no longer had the connotation of untoward assertiveness. Contrast William Byrd's cheerful note that "I . . . was angry with my man for not getting up and gave him warning," with the above-mentioned Adam Eyre, who about a century earlier, had been so nervous about berating his servant.[46] By the early eighteenth century, it was all right to admit that one felt angry. Of course, angry behavior must be controlled, but one could look at angry feelings and talk about them without abject shame, as part of the effort to maintain behavior. This is one reason that in the late eighteenth and early nineteenth centuries, spates of books attacking anger became popular. Anger could be recognized, as it infrequently was before, and this raised the whole new problem of what to do about it.[47]

No discussion of early modern anger can be complete without some discussion of sadness in the same period. The word *aggrieved*, which once meant saddened by an affront, before it took on its more modern connotation of "angered," is testimony to a past in which sadness and anger were less clearly differentiated than they are to us. In the early modern period, when anger in oneself could not be easily identified and labeled, sadness was much more acceptable than it was to become. One is struck, in reading the diaries, at how freely and unembarrassedly men burst into tears. Religious sympathies frequently drew tears from Samuel Sewall, but also from the Anglican Oglander.[48] Oglander "could do nothing but sigh and weep for two nights and a day," because of his worries about the fate of King Charles in 1647.[49] Ralph Josselin found himself in tears over money problems. Romantic problems also led grown men to cry. Sewall's son Sam "told me with Tears that these sorrows [arising from discord between him and his wife] would bring him to his Grave." Lowe cried to a woman friend over his failure to win a girl he had courted. Ryder, too, was frequently in tears, both privately and to confidantes, about girl problems. Heywood cried after a dispute with his wife. Norwood, both as a young adolescent and a youth, found it normal to cry over difficulties related to changes of residence.[50]

The early modern period showed a great fascination and sympathy with the idea of melancholy.[51] Newcome wrote of a young Michael Buxton who had fallen "into Melancholy. His condition much to be lamented; but it is far better than sin, which is the condition of too many." Many of the diarists felt it appropriate to portray themselves as doleful, and the sense they convey is that they felt that dolefulness was somehow opposed to sin. Norwood wrote that at one point his image of God was that "he allowed of no joy nor pleasure, but of a kind of melancholy demeanor and austerity." Parkman, after a pleasant visit with relatives, "grievously and sadly reflected upon my Levity this Evening," and had to justify himself by suggesting, "But there was nothing criminal in my conduct when one . . . considers what a time of Joy it was with us. However, I think I might have spent more time with the graver people." It was fashionable, in reflecting back on one's life, to admit to great sorrow and dolefulness.[52]

By the early eighteenth century, tears were still in fashion, but there was beginning to be some sense of the desirability of good cheer, as in Ryder's diary, or John Byrom's statement, in 1728: "it was the best thing one could do to be always cheerful . . . and not suffer any sullenness . . . a cheerful disposition and frame of mind being the best way of showing our thankfulness to God." In several diaries, the hint begins to emerge that it is in fact an obligation to be cheerful.[53] By the mid-nineteenth century, furthermore, male tears were quite out of fashion, and there was a generally felt responsibility even among evangelicals to be optimistic.[54]

The discomfort with identifying anger connected with the readiness to be sad. To be sad was to be passive, submissive, and helpless. Often the remedy was prayer. The sad person did not assert himself but begged for help from the Almighty. One is struck by a certain narcissism in some of these early reactions to other peoples' problems. When misfortune befalls others, the almost universal response is to think that such a thing could happen to oneself and pray God that it does not.[55] These people, presented with difficult situations, had little sense that they could assert themselves to control the situation, and therefore resorted to a supplicant, whiny posture, asking for help from above.[56] They were the exact opposite of the Kaluli of Papua New Guinea, as discussed by Edward L. Schieffelin, who modally value assertiveness, encourage anger rather than sadness, try to transform sadness into anger, and are rarely depressed. In Schieffelin's New Guinea, the connection here discussed between sadness and anger holds, but is simply turned on its head.[57]

Lack of ease with conscious anger and readiness to embrace the position of tearful supplicant seem to have something to do with the early modern sense that emotions assail rather than belong to one. Feelings were experienced often as overwhelming assaults, as when Lowe wrote of his fiancée that "att those times my effections ran out violently after her, so as that I was never contented . . . unles I had seene her." Josselin wrote constantly of the sense that he might be assailed by evil feelings, and that only God protected him. When an acquaintance seduced a widow, he felt that only "god's goodness [kept] . . . I and mine . . . not in the same condiction." Observing a drunkard, "lord thy name be blessed in keeping mee from that sin." Norwood, writing of his lusts, felt he had no self-control, and that only the fact that God would punish him with affliction could raise fear in him and prevent vice. Oliver Heywood, upset with worry about his children, mused, "Oh Lord, How weak and slippery is the soul of man! how easily is the mind put out of order! how hard to be settled and composed! . . . how little power have I over my own thoughts."[58] This sort of experience did not disappear all at once, so that even in the eighteenth century we find William Stout writing similarly of his attraction to a woman, his "affection and passion" as dangerous forces to be resisted.[59]

Richard Norwood, during the years of his spiritual conversion, suffered tremendous guilt over his lusts, and felt that he was being punished by a siege of dreadful nightmares. His nightmares, including visions of his father "greviously angry with me," in his understanding had nothing to do with his own conflicts and were totally out of his control. He explained his dreams of "strange-passions, affections, lusts, and blasphemies" as coming from the outside, the affliction of Satan, who also was "deforming my countenance," and he later attributed the problem to staying in a haunted house. Satan was also felt to be the source of angry dissension among neighbors by Heywood.[60] The unquestioned assumption behind all this, however, is that one does not have control over one's feelings.

While Puritan thought, even in the late seventeenth century, had emphasized submission, and instructed people to rely on God's grace for help with troublesome emotions, in some diarists there emerged now an increasing sense of self-control. Ebenezer Parkman, writing in the early eighteenth century, for example, felt that he could develop systematic self-inspection to the point of self-regulation: "to look into Myself and view the state of my Heart . . . my Thoughts run more free from those confusions and interruptions than in the day," and he resolved to introspect regularly that "I may learn the most suitable regular method of forming my own Thoughts and Action."[61] Emory Elliott has noted the same emphasis on possibilities for assertion of the self and de-emphasis on submission in the preaching of Cotton Mather in the late seventeenth century.[62] That Mather and Parkman were Puritans, like the earlier Josselin, is certainly true; but the earlier Puritan had no such systematic sense of how to go about self-control, and evinced a much more pervasive sense that he was constantly being assailed by waves of inexplicable and uncontrollable emotion than emerges in the diary of the later Parkman. Parkman, in fact, shares more in this sense with the non-Puritan Ryder, his contemporary chronologically, than with Josselin. His passage is not unlike Ryder's, who in starting his diary said he intended "particularly to observe my own temper and state of mind" in order to seek out causes of disturbance and to enable him to "mend" himself. Ryder's stance was to be surprised when assailed by feeling and to endeavor immediately to "check myself" rather than to pray to God. Ryder, in commenting on others, clearly felt that people who fluctuated in their emotions lacked a certain self-control and were curiosities, requiring explanation.[63]

Both the old and new views shared the characteristic Western distinction between emotion, considered dangerous, and reason, considered superior.[64] For both, the picture of a man controlled by passion, and particularly angry passion, was quite stereotyped, deriving from classical descriptions, and was akin to the picture of a madman—thus the double meaning of the word *mad*, connoting both anger and insanity, and Walter Calverley's disdain for an acquaintance who "fell into a great fury, as is usually his way when contradicted. . . . By his behaviour one would have taken him to be a madman."[65]

What was new, then, was not a revision of the standard dichotomy—reason, superior; emotion, inferior—but rather, an increasing sense of the possibility that man did have some ability to control emotion. In fact, in the new view, if anger were under control, it was in some cases legitimate to display it, for anger could be useful, or instrumental. The early writer, Roger Lowe, could conceive of this sort of instrumental anger only in relation to non-humans. In a tussle with a ram, "I looked att [him] . . . with an angry countenance," in order to frighten him. Later writers, though, could picture instrumental anger as legitimate with people. For instance, Newcome wrote "A servant of mine . . . would not be ruled, but oft was overseen in drink, and I found at this time, that anger for this did quicken to duties and bring in comfort, whereas other anger works quite contrary." It feels all right to Newcome to choose to be angry, for he believes that God, in assessing man, will judge "without Passion." William Byrd similarly notes that he beat his servant Joe "for being very saucy, after which he was very sullen and very good." Anger has its purposes. And part of using it wisely came from staying in control. As Byrd wrote of an encounter with another troublesome employee: "found my man late, which made me very angry with him. However, I kept my temper pretty well, thank God."[66] Great emphasis was placed in the latter half of the seventeenth century and after, on the importance of keeping temper, of punishing children "calmly" and without "passion."[67] Thus, the new view, though clearer on the possibility of controlling behavior than of controlling feeling, did allow for the latter as well, and was more optimistic about its possibility than the old view had been. Anger in the earlier view had been legitimized only by being in the service of the right side, that is, God's side, and such anger needed its own word, zeal. The new view implied that man, through the use of reason, could judge when anger was justified; since reason must be paramount in such judgment, then anger could be acceptable only if it was anger without passion. "Zeal," was no longer virtuous.

All these changes added up, in fact, to a twofold shift in emotionology. The larger change was from the view that man had little control over his own feelings and behavior to the view that good men did have control. Secondly, while there was no change in the belief that unrighteous anger was reprehensible, there was a subtle alteration in understanding of what legitimized anger; the earlier view allowing it only to those on the upper level of hierarchical relationships, the new view legitimizing it solely by its reasonableness, which was identified in part by its dissociation from passion and its accompaniment by self-control.

The diaries offer striking evidence that the change in emotionology drastically affected emotional experience. The old emotionology almost never allowed people to acknowledge anger comfortably. In situations, which for modern people might arouse a consciousness that one was angry, the earlier diarists expressed instead a sense of unease or sadness. They evinced angry behavior, but did not conceptualize themselves as angry. When the emotionology began to change, anger was recognized and labeled in the self, and a connectedness between feeling and behavior was experienced, which reinforced a sense of self-control.

Earlier personalities frequently expressed a sense of lack of control, and not surprisingly, their feelings were often experienced as vague somatic complaints afflicting the self rather than as cognized emotions identified as part of the self. Although careful quantification has not been done here, one is certainly struck in reading the earlier diarists at the frequency of their complaints about minor physical difficulties.[68] It is also interesting that similar words were used for feelings and for fevers or diseases and pains, such as "violent," "senseless and raging" and "angry." "Distemper" was used without distinction for an emotion or a somatic condition. Words for good feelings were like words for sensuous experiences such as eating, as when Norwood, feeling happy, called life "savory."[69]

It was more characteristic of later personalities to display an interest in emotion as distinct from soma. To modern eyes, it is striking how many of the earlier diaries are simply recordings of events with no statement of the writer's emotions at all. Although certainly some later diarists did the same, it was more characteristic by the eighteenth century to display an introspective, self-conscious style.[70] It is also characteristic of the later diaries to display an interest in the subject of personality or character that was lacking in the earlier writers, for whom behavior was almost always seen as a vector resulting from the various forces of temper and humor, rather than as resulting from clearly defined personalities differing from man to man.[71] The novel, as a newly developing literary form, may thus be seen in the context of the history of emotions as resulting from a new interest in the personality of the individual. By the eighteenth century, a literary genre that viewed characters as often helpless creatures of fate and passion, assailed by emotion in much the same way they might be assailed by illness, would have been anachronistic. Jacobean plays would have seemed foreign. The novel, with its interest in the individual's personality, and its view that plot was determined by character, gave literary expression to a new emotionology, which held that behavior was determined by self.[72]

Both anthropologists and psychiatrists have displayed a great deal of interest in the question of whether modern, westernized personalities, with their emphasis on the self as a controlling agent, their interest in individual personality, and their highly developed sense of cognized emotions as opposed to somatic experience, are less prone to depression than more traditional personalities. Some writers have argued that it is typical of less developed countries, or lower socioeconomic groups, to have a more limited vocabulary for emotions and to somaticize all complaints. Recently, however, a revisionist view has argued that depression exists in all cultures, merely manifesting itself differently from place to place, and that some cultures, while lacking verbal distinctions for emotional differences that may seem important to us, have vocabularies for variations in emotion important to them but lacking in us.[73]

This study addresses some of these questions. It is striking, in reading the earlier diaries, how often the writers feel sad, although they seem to have no reason.[74] An emotionology which, as we have seen, encouraged people to feel sad rather than angry, often resulted in sad people. Although a recent work on the psychology of Puritanism has argued that the Puritan, through submission, usually found strength and joy, we are struck by how often doubt and moroseness persisted even after conversion.[75] Norwood's musings after his conversion reveal that his sufferings were far from over. He complains that he feels feeble, slow, and timorous, doubting and despairing, and that he seems "in general to have lost much of that youthful heat and vigour in the way of God which before I enjoyed."[76] In fact, it is typical of the earlier diarists to embrace a kind of depressive demeanor, reminiscent of what Robert Levy has noted in his work on Tahitians: "If depression is defined . . . subtly as 'a decrease in self-esteem; a sense of helplessness; the inhibition of ego functions to varying degrees; and a subjective feeling of sadness or loss' . . . then there is a suggestion of 'depressive tone' for most of the informants."[77]

It is hardly surprising, in view of the fact that the earlier diarists viewed feelings, including sad feelings, as coming from outside the self, that cures for their depressions involved external panaceas, like pills to take away anger, or healing rituals controlled by others.[78] There was little sense here, as began to appear later with Newcome and Ryder, that one can cure oneself from emotional disturbance through use of the ego. Clifford Geertz has noted that our view of the self as an agent that controls behavior and emotion is relatively unusual in the world today. This essay suggests that even in the West it is a relatively recent view.[79]

Why did a change take place? In offering causal explanations for a change in personality, both direct causes and functional explanations have some merit. One way to think about changes in personality is to consider changes in child rearing. Early seventeenth-century children were certainly raised in a world that must have appeared capricious. The pervasive sense of uncertainty about attaining even the basic requirements for life characteristic of early modern society has been discussed at length by both Keith Thomas and Robert Muchembled. Unquestionably, some of this uncertainty with which adults lived was experienced by their children. And in the specific case of children, indeed, one is struck by how unprotected they were, with near-fatal accidents a commonplace in the diaries.[80] The recording of these in part simply restated the view that one has no control over the world, but it indicated that the parents involved took little care to structure the environments of children in order to systematically protect them from danger. This certainly was to change somewhere in the middle of the eighteenth century.[81]

But why did parents not provide more protection at an earlier period? Surely, with easy access to manpower this would have been possible. The answer must be that they simply did not see the world as a controllable place and think in terms of controlling it. As Keith

Thomas has discussed at length, this sense of lack of control began during the Englighten-ment period to be replaced by the notion that man could take charge, but there is no one simple explanation for this change. It is hardly surprising that children raised in a world where they felt there was no control even over the basics of preserving life grew up with less of a sense of control than those raised, as was more typical in the middle and upper classes from the eighteenth century on, in carefully regulated environments. Although some historians have derided this sort of approach to a culture, and rightly warned against characterizing whole cultures as neurotic, the diaries themselves offer ample empirical evidence that the writers did experience themselves as lacking control.[82]

But a sense of lack of control was not simply taught by parent to child apart from cultural context. If emotional styles were simply passed on fixedly, they could never change. It can be argued that the older personalities were well-adapted to the requirements of their culture, and that child-rearing styles are maintained or changed according to cultural need. Hierarchical societies benefit from submissive, if slightly depressed participants, and the fact that even those on the upper ends of the hierarchy tended to have conflicts over assertion and to fancy themselves submissive to the greater Authority probably helped to curb extreme abuses of power. The dissociation between feeling and behavior that existed in this sort of society was not a serious problem, for most interactions were between individuals who knew each other, and seldom involved huge numbers of people.[83] If people acted in a rough-and-tumble and physically aggressive manner, their actions would rarely get out of hand or lead to major problems because of community supervision. Enough easily enforce-able outside regulators of behavior existed to make the development of strong internal controls unnecessary. Thus, shame rather than guilt was typically used to punish infractions, and major sins were seen to be sins of self-assertion against higher authority rather than, as later, infractions of behavior by man against man.[84]

In the more complicated society developing in the eighteenth century, the new sort of personality was more adaptive. Economically, the society relied on people to be assertive rather than submissive and passive. But people now frequently interacted in larger groups, often where they were not known to others. In such situations, uncontrolled rough-and-tumble anger could be a serious problem. It was important that people develop inner controls. Thus some sense of the self as possessing control and initiative was useful and adaptive, as might not have been the case before.[85]

Yet while a change from a sad-submissive mode to a more assertive mode can be noted in men, it is vital to recognize that this change did not take place as clearly in women. Even nineteenth-century women were characteristically tearful rather than angry, and used the stance of martyr when aggrieved.[86] Women, in other words, remained in the older mold. Grasping this new differentiation in emotionology for the sexes may prove useful in future explorations of the relationship between modernization and changing gender distinctions. Clearly, although in some sense nineteenth-century women benefited from being placed on pedestals that denied anger to them, in another sense, they were being left behind as men modernized. One wonders, in this context, if there was not a certain hypocrisy in the prevalent emotionology that men offered to nineteenth-century women. Was this, indeed, simply a dressed-up version of what was essentially an outdated stance of self-abnegation? Perhaps, indeed, the older historiography that viewed Victorian women as oppressed saw a certain truth which the feminist/revisionist view, that Victorian women benefited from the moral pedestal, has overlooked.[87]

Reading the diaries, one sees that sadness is associated with helplessness and a with-drawing, pulling in, or even denial of the self. When confronted with difficulties, the diarists' sad responses have a submissive and frightened quality. To acknowledge one's anger in the face of obstacles is to legitimate the self and to retain initiative.[88] Even if for the most part one decides to suppress one's anger, one keeps, in the face of conflict, a sense that one is in charge, if only because one can exercise self-control. If middle- and upper-class men could do this increasingly from the early eighteenth century, while women and the lower classes were still saddled with an emotionology demanding submissiveness and passivity, then the gap between privileged men and their wives or social inferiors could only increase. A new world view created differentiated emotional experiences that reinforced inequalities.

The point is not, of course, that the new personalities were psychologically healthier or superior. The author believes firmly that psychological health can be defined only within a culture. However, the relativist implication that one cannot in any way negatively characterize the emotional tone of another culture seems as mistaken as a tendency to judge prematurely or without awareness of the culture's own standards. An assumption that all cultures have equivalent cognitive solutions to their worries prematurely cuts off the effort to listen attentively to what the culture reveals affectively. The assertion that there is a sad or helpless tone in the early modern diaries discussed is based not on modern prejudice, but on careful reading of the diarist's own statements. Historians who, in their zeal to respect the past, deny even the theoretical possibility that another culture could be more anxious or otherwise affectively troubled than our own, would be the equivalent of the good-natured but mistaken psychotherapist, who rushes to assure the patient that "you're fine" before listening to what the patient wants to say. There were emotional differences between early modern people and ourselves, and it would be unrealistic to imply that their style had no disadvantages. This is different from saying that they were all neurotic.[89]

The fact that, like the Tahitians, early modern people typically displayed a more depressive stance than our own, does not mean that they were depressed in the sense of being mentally ill.[90] While one is struck by the depressive tone of some of the earlier personalities, it is clear that increasing the sense of self-control has also led to a great deal of struggle and guilt in modern personalities. Though the later diarists, when acknowledging anger, demonstrated a certain sense of self-reliance, this was often accompanied by anxiety about self-control. The decline of the obligation to be sad was accompanied by hints of a new, perhaps equally onerous duty to be cheerful. The sense of the self, or ego, was often overwhelmed by the sense of duty, or superego. To be self-conscious, in modern parlance, is, after all, to be slightly uncomfortable. The increasing belief that behavior could be controlled took away an outlet for feeling which had previously been widely used. Now that behavior was so strictly judged, it could hardly be as spontaneous. For the early modern person, who conceptualized problems and controls as coming from outside, there may have been no more anxiety about feeling than for the modern person with his internalized superego.[91] The purpose, again, is certainly not to judge, but rather to depict a change. And thus one must return to the contention of those who deny significant emotional changes over time.

Revisionist historians of emotions, such as Peter Gay, Carl Degler, and Linda Pollock, have emphasized the relative constancy of human nature and stressed the determining aspects of biology in shaping human love or sexuality. A more subtle version of this point of view emerged in Philip Greven's book *The Protestant Temperament*, which stressed continuities in three basic personality types or temperaments from the colonial period through the mid-nineteenth century. Both theoretically and factually, this approach presents problems for historians. Greven seems to suggest that personalities or temperaments are equally distributed historically. If this is so, then modal personalities do not change from time to time, and the study of personality is one for the biologist or psychologist but not for the historian. This certainly seems counterintuitive, since most of us recognize evidence from the past as being foreign in some sense. It also seems to contradict Greven's own belief in the importance of child-rearing practices in the formation of personality, since we know that child-rearing practices do change over time. This is not to say that there are not huge differences and varieties in personalities within any one historical period. It might even be true that the differences within any one period are more significant and far-ranging than the differences between modal personalities from period to period. However, if there is any change in modal personality over time, it would seem to be the job of historians to delineate rather than to obscure this.

In practice, Greven's eagerness to find his three types unchanged through the centuries causes him to make two sorts of errors. Error one is to refuse to see that evangelicals of the seventeenth century differed significantly from those of the nineteenth century. Error two is to exaggerate differences between groups in any one century. An example of the first type of error is the equation of eighteenth-century attempts to suppress conscious anger with the unconscious displacement and projection of anger through witchcraft accusations found in seventeenth-century Salem. A similar mistake is to minimize the significance of the fact that the evangelicals of the earlier period were troubled by a wrathful God, while their nineteenth-century descendants had replaced him with a God of love. In the same vein, it is mistaken to use nineteenth-century evidence of the care with which evangelicals governed their children to argue that child rearing in the seventeenth century was similarly careful, when the evidence indicates how very poorly controlled the early child-rearing efforts were.[92]

The second sort of error Greven makes is to exaggerate distinctions among eighteenth-century people. Although evangelicals and moderates are clearly separated in his treatment, they were not so clearly separated in real life. The efforts of the evangelicals to deal with anger through suppression that Greven cites sound very much like those of his moderates.[93]

My argument, then, is not that there are not profound personality differences within historical periods—this is a truism—but rather that when historians go looking for them, they may obscure changes that do take place over time. My formulation of these changes, which I hope will be tested by more extensive historical research, is as follows: During the course of the seventeenth century, a new emotionology of the relationship between feeling and behavior was evolving, and along with this came new views on the relative appropriateness of sadness and anger. The increasing ability to see the self as angry seems to be connected with a new sense of control and of personal assertiveness, at least on the part of middle- and upper-class men, and this in turn seems associated with the needs of a modernizing society. The new emotionology was far from an academic exercise; it profoundly altered the emotional experience of many ordinary people.

Appendix: Diaries used in this essay

1   Elias Ashmole. *The Diary and Will of Elias Ashmole.* Edited by R. T. Gunther. Oxford, 1927. Ashmole, a royalist scientist, was born in 1617. The diary goes from about 1633 to 1687. There is little recording of emotion.

2   Nicholas Assheton. *Journal.* Edited by Rev. F. R. Raines. Chetham Society, 1848. The journal covers 1617–18 and is remarkable for almost no discussion of emotions.

3   Richard Boyle. *The Lismore Papers. . . . Diaries of Sir Richard Boyle . . . Earl of Cork.* Edited by Alexander B. Grosart. London, 1886, 5 volumes. No significant recorded emotions. Years covered are 1611–37.

4   Robert Bulkeley. "The Diary of Bulkeley of Dronwy, Anglesey 1630–1636." Edited by Hugh Owen, in *Transactions Anglesey Antiquarian Society and Field Club.* Liverpool, 1936. A gentleman farmer and J.P., with little recording of emotions.

5   William Byrd. *William Byrd of Virginia. The London Diary (1717–1721).* Edited by Louis B. Wright and Marion Tinling. New York, 1958. Virginia planter educated as a lawyer.

6   John Byrom. *The Private Journal and Literary Remains of John Byrom*. Edited by Richard Parkinson. Vols. 32, 34, 44. Manchester, 1853–57. The writer was born in 1691. Letters start about 1707.

7   Walter Calverley. "Memorandum Book of Sir Walter Calverley, Bart." *In Yorkshire Diaries and Autobiographies in the Seventeenth and Eighteenth Centuries*. Edited by James Raine. Durham, 1883?. Very little introspection. Years covered are 1663–1748.

8   Anne Clifford. *The Diary of the Lady Anne Clifford*. Edited by Vita Sackville-West. London, 1923. She was born in 1590, the daughter of an earl. The diary goes only to 1619.

9   John Dee. *Autobiographical Tracts*. Edited by James Crosley. Chetham Society, 1851. An astrologer. Dates from the 1570s to the 1590s.

10   Adam Eyre. "A Dyurnall. . . ." In *Yorkshire Diaries and Autobiographies in the Seventeenth and Eighteenth Centuries*. Edited by James Raine. Durham, 1877. Eyre was a yeoman who fought for Parliament in the Civil War. The diary covers 1647–49.

11   Elizabeth Freke. *Mrs. Elizabeth Freke Her Diary 1671 to 1714*. Edited by Mary Carbery. Cork, 1913. Diary of a wealthy English lady.

12   James Fretwell. "A Family History." In *Yorkshire Diaries* (see item 10). Years from end of seventeenth to mid-eighteenth centuries. Few emotions.

13   Oliver Heywood. *The Reverend Oliver Heywood, Autobiography, Diaries*. Edited by J. Horsfall Turner. Brighouse, Eng., 1882–85. Diary of a nonconformist born in 1629. Diary covers 1660s through 1702, but mostly 1660s and 1670s.

14   John Hobson. "The Journal of Mr. J. H." In *Yorkshire Diaries* (see item 10). Years from 1725 to 1726. Writer was a tanner. Doesn't record much on feelings.

15   William Jefferay. *The Journal of William Jefferay, Gentleman*. Edited by John Osborne Austin. Providence, R.I., 1899. Diary of an English gentleman farmer who emigrated to New England but was not a Puritan. Covers years from 1591 to 1623, though not written until about 1650.

16   Ralph Josselin. *The Diary of Ralph Josselin 1616–1683*. Edited by Alan MacFarlane. Cambridge, Eng., 1976. Introspective Puritan.

17   Roger Lowe. *The Diary of Roger Lowe*. Edited by William Sachse. London, 1938. Puritan apprentice. Covers 1663–74.

18   Henry Machyn. *The Diary of Henry Machyn 1550–1553*. Edited by John Gough Nichols. London, 1848. Not much introspection but plenty of observation of the behavior of others.

19   Adam Martindale. *The Life of Adam Martindale*. Edited by Rev. Richard Parkinson. Chetham Society, 1844. Covers through 1684. Written retrospectively. Author, a Puritan minister, born 1623.

20   Henry Newcome. *The Autobiography of Henry Newcome, MA*. Edited by Richard Parkinson. Manchester, 1852. Puritan minister, born 1627, who was nonetheless a loyalist in Civil War. Covers through 1690s. Mostly written retrospectively.

21   Richard Norwood. *The Journal of Richard Norwood*. Edited by Wesley Frank Craven and Walter B. Hayward. New York, 1945. English Puritan who later traveled to Bermuda. Written in 1639 but covers his early life. He was born in 1590.

22   John Oglander. *Sir John Oglander. A Royalist's Notebook*. Edited by Francis Bamford. New York, 1971. Covers 1585–1655.

23   Ebenezer Parkman. *The Diary of Ebenezer Parkman, first part 1719–55*. Edited by Francis G. Walett. Worcester, 1974. New England Puritan minister.

24   John Penry. *The Notebook of John Penry, 1593*. Edited by Albert Peel. London, 1944. A Welsh Congregationalist, born in 1563 and involved with the Marprelate tracts. Not really a diary and little on emotion.

25   Walter Powell. *The Diary of Walter Powell 1603–1654*. Edited by Joseph Alfred Bradney. Bristol, 1907. Steward to the Earl of Worcester. Little on emotions.

26   Dudley Ryder. *The Diary of Dudley Ryder 1715–1716*. Edited by William Mathews. London, 1939. Nonconformist who later became parliamentarian. Diary starts at age twenty-four.

27   Samuel Sewall. *Samuel Sewall's Diary*. Edited by Mark Van Doren. New York, 1963. This is an abridgment of the original diary of the New England Puritan magistrate and official. Covers 1675–1729.

28   William Stout. *The Autobiography of William Stout of Lancaster 1665–1752*. Edited by J. D. Marshall. Manchester, 1967. A Quaker merchant.

29   Anthony à Wood. *The Life and Times of Anthony à Wood*. Edited by Llewelyn Powys. London, 1961. Abridgment not entirely satisfactory. Covers 1632–95. Oxford antiquarian and anti-Puritan.

Notes

1　The author disagrees with approaches such as Emory Elliott's, which postulate the uniqueness of the American experience and explain changes in American emotionology as resulting solely from changes in local conditions (*Power and the Pulpit in Puritan New England* [Princeton, 1975], p. 65).

2　For a discussion of how much ideas about emotion color what people actually claim to feel, see Carol Zisowitz Stearns and Peter N. Stearns, *Anger: The Struggle for Emotional Control in America's History* (Chicago, 1986), passim.

3　For a discussion of the meaning of emotionology, see Peter N. Stearns with Carol Z. Stearns, "Emotionology: Clarifying the History of Emotions and Emotional Standards," *American Historical Review* 90, no. 4 (1985): 813–36.

4　For a good statement on the uses and limitations of diaries, see Linda A. Pollock, *Forgotten Children, Parent–Child Relations from 1500 to 1900* (Cambridge, 1983), pp. 69ff. On the particular genre of Puritan diaries, see Owen C. Watkins, *The Puritan Experience. Studies in Spiritual Autobiography* (New York, 1972).

5　For an annotated list of the diaries used, see appendix to this chapter.

6　For a discussion of the controversy, see Stearns with Stearns, "Emotionology."

7　The author does not have much sympathy with the notion of trying to quantify the diaries, which are different enough from one another to make such rigorous comparison almost impossible. An example of such a quantitative approach is Michael Barton, *Goodmen: The Character of Civil War Soldiers* (University Park, Pa., 1981).

8　Arthur Kleinman and Byron Good, "Introduction," Kleinman and Good, *Culture and Depression. Studies in the Anthropology and Cross-Cultural Psychiatry of Affect and Disorder* (Berkeley and Los Angeles, 1985), pp. 4, 30.

9　Roger Lowe, *The Diary of Roger Lowe*, ed. William Sachse (London, 1938), pp. 74–5, 19, 50, 70, 55, 46–47.

10　Ralph Josselin, *The Diary of Ralph Josselin 1616–1683*, ed. Alan MacFarlane (London, 1976), pp. 5, 10, 43, 56, 289, 20. For a similar reaction, see Oliver Heywood, *The Reverend Oliver Heywood, Autobiography, Diaries. . . .*, ed. J. Horsfall Turner (Brighouse, Eng., 1882–85), 1: 266.

11　John Dee, *Autobiographical Tracts*, ed. James Crosley (Chetham Society, 1851), pp. 78–79.

12　Anne Clifford, *The Diary of The Lady Anne Clifford*, ed. Vita Sackville-West (London, 1923), pp. 62, 69, 70, 73.

13　Elizabeth Freke, *Mrs. Elizabeth Freke Her Diary 1671 to 1714*, ed. Mary Carbery (Cork, 1913), pp. 35, 41–42, 118.

14　Lowe, *Diary*, pp. 114, 91, 56, 52. For discussion of Puritan "projection" in dealing with anger, see John Putnam Demos, *Entertaining Satan; Witchcraft and the Culture of Early New England* (Oxford, 1982), pp. 187–88, 195–97.

15　Samuel Sewall, *Samuel Sewall's Diary*, ed. Mark Van Doren (New York, 1963), pp. 199, 191.

16　Ebenezer Parkman, *The Diary of Ebenezer Parkman 1719–55*, ed. Francis G. Walett (Worcester, 1974), pp. 24–25, 45.

17　Rhys Isaac, *The Transformation of Virginia 1740–1790* (Chapel Hill, 1982), p. 119. See also Stearns and Stearns, *Anger*, chap. 2; Michael MacDonald, *Mystical Bedlam: Madness, Anxiety and Healing in Seventeenth-Century England* (Cambridge, 1981), pp. 109ff.; Robert Muchembled, *Popular Culture and Elite Culture in France 1400–1750*, trans. Lydia Cochrane (Baton Rouge, 1985), pp. 31–33, 119ff. Walter Ong sees this as typical of preliterate cultures (Walter J. Ong, *Orality and Literacy* [London, 1982], pp. 43–45).

18　Anthony à Wood, *The Life and Times of Anthony à Wood*, ed. Llewelyn Powys (London, 1961), pp. 287, 298; John Oglander, *Sir John Oglander. A Royalist's Notebook*, ed. Francis Bamford (New York, 1971), p. 87; Sewall, *Diary*, p. 207; Heywood, *Autobiography*, 1: 345.

19　Josselin, *Diary*, p. 40; Sewall, *Diary*, pp. 115–16.

20　Elias Ashmole, *The Diary and Will of Elias Ashmole*, ed. R. T. Gunther (Oxford, 1927), pp. 165–68, 30–31.

21　Wood, *Life*, p. 331; Sewall, *Diary*, pp. 220–21.

22　Heywood, *Autobiography* 2: 240ff., 294. Richard Norwood, *The Journal of Richard Norwood*, ed. Wesley Frank Craven and Walter B. Hayward (New York, 1945), p. 32.

23　Lowe, *Diary*, p. 105.

24　Lowe, *Diary*, p. 70.

25　Sewall, *Diary*, pp. 164–65, 185, 195.

26   Sewall, *Diary*, pp. 200–202, 210. Also, Heywood, *Autobiography*, 1: 333, 338; 2: 278.

27   Oglander, *Notebook*, p. 166.

28   Henry Newcome, *A Plain Discourse about Rash and Sinful Anger* . . . (Manchester, 1693).

29   Henry Newcome, *The Autobiography of Henry Newcome, MA*, ed. Richard Parkinson (Manchester, 1852), p. 296; Dudley Ryder, *The Diary of Dudley Ryder 1715–1716*, ed. William Mathews (London, 1939), pp. 53–54 and 311.

30   Lowe, *Diary*, p. 62; Parkman, *Diary*, p. 21.

31   Heywood, *Autobiography*, 1: 333. Newcome, *Autobiography*, pp. 99, 197–98, 58.

32   Ryder, *Diary*, pp. 281, 132, 38, and similarly pp. 119, 371, 38–39.

33   Lowe, *Diary*, p. 70; John Wesley, in Philip J. C. Greven, Jr., *Child-Rearing Concepts, 1628–1861* (Itasca, Ill., 1973), p. 65; Muchembled, *Popular Culture*, pp. 26ff.; Alan MacFarlane, *The Family Life of Ralph Josselin* (Cambridge, Eng., 1970), pp. 172ff.; Charles Lloyd Cohen, *God's Caress. The Psychology of Puritan Religious Experience* (New York and Oxford, 1986), pp. 204–5.

34   Lowe, *Diary*, pp. 46–47, 80.

35   Newcome, "To the reader" in *Anger; Autobiography*, pp. 144–45; Ryder, *Diary*, pp. 303–4.

36   Wood, *Life*, pp. 141–42; Freke, *Diary*, p. 57; Norwood, *Journal*, p. 47; Lowe, *Diary*, pp. 16, 28, 50. See also Stearns and Stearns, *Anger*, pp. 21ff.

37   Newcome, *Anger*, p. 42; *Autobiography*, p. 16. Witherspoon in Greven, *Child-Rearing*, pp. 90, 85; Jean-Louis Flandrin, *Families in Former Times: Kinship, Household and Sexuality*, trans. Richard Southern (Cambridge, 1979), pp. 127ff. For identification of both God and father as angry, see Paul S. Seaver, *Wallington's World. A Puritan Artisan in Seventeenth-Century London* (Stanford, 1985), p. 75.

38   Oglander, *Notebook*, p. 239; John Robinson, *Essayes* . . . (London, 1638), pp. 446–47, 494; Cohen, *God's Caress*, p. 131.

39   Newcome, *Anger*, pp. 6, 10–11, 65ff.; *Autobiography*, pp. 296–97; Ryder, *Diary*, pp. 125, 155, 60.

40   MacDonald, *Mystical Bedlam*, 126–28.

41   David Hunt, *Parents and Children in History* (New York, 1970), chap. 7.

42   Adam Eyre, "A Dyurnall," in *Yorkshire Diaries and Autobiographies in the Seventeenth and Eighteenth Centuries*, ed. James Raine (Durham, 1877), p. 67. See also Seaver, *Wallington*, p. 8.

43   Norwood, *Journal*, p. 77. For similar stress on submission and fear of pride, see Josselin, *Diary*, pp. 43, 56–57; also Seaver, *Wallington*, p. 10. For a discussion of fear as the appropriate and pervasive emotional stance of early modern people, see Muchembled, *Popular Culture*, chap. 1.

44   On legitimation of anger in other cultures, see Edward L. Schieffelin, "The Cultural Analysis of Depressive Affect: An Example from New Guinea," pp. 101–3, and Catherine Lutz, "Depression and the Translation of Emotional Worlds," pp. 63–100, in Kleinman and Good, *Culture and Depression*. For an argument that anger always implies a judgment about being in the right, see Robert C. Solomon, "The Jamesian Theory of Emotion in Anthropology," in Richard Shweder and Robert A. LeVine, *Culture Theory, Essays on Mind, Self, and Emotion* (Cambridge, Eng., 1984), p. 250.

45   Ryder, *Diary*, pp. 303–4. This is not to argue, of course, that the old view disappeared entirely. The writings of Jonathan Edwards clearly were "old-fashioned" on God's anger. The point is that an alternative view was emerging.

46   William Byrd, *William Byrd of Virginia. The London Diary (1717–1721)*, ed. Louis B. Wright and Marion Tinling (New York, 1958), p. 209; also 213, 254, 269, 276, 282, 315, 435, 437, 440.

47   Clearly, I take issue with Emory Elliott's view that this change was unique to the local situation in New England (*Power*, pp. 13–14).

48   Sewall, *Diary*, pp. 89–90, 125; Oglander, *Notebook*, p. 245; *Oxford English Dictionary*. Also, Heywood, *Autobiography*, 1: 261, 300.

49   Oglander, *Notebook*, p. 113.

50   Josselin, *Diary*, p. 5; Sewall, *Diary*, p. 216. Lowe; *Diary*, p. 68; Ryder, *Diary*, pp. 282, 294–96; Norwood, *Journal*, p. 12.

51   MacDonald, *Mystical Bedlam*, pp. 150ff. For a discussion of some other cultures which dignify sadness, see Kleinman and Good, "Introduction," p. 3.

52   Newcome, *Autobiography*, pp. 207–8; also 197, 216–17. Parkman, *Diary*, p. 23; Norwood, *Journal*, p. 64.

53   Ryder, *Diary*, pp. 141, 91, 63. John Byrom, *The Private Journal and Literary Remains of John Byrom*, ed. Richard Parkinson (Manchester, 1853–57), p. 295.

54   Joe L. Dubbert, *A Man's Place: Masculinity in Transition* (Englewood Cliffs, N.J., 1979), pp. 32–34.

55   Josselin, *Diary*, pp. 50, 54–56, 17, 32; Sewall, *Diary*, p. 124.

56   Clifford, *Diary*, p. 32; Lowe, *Diary*, p. 15; Sewall, *Diary*, pp. 155, 78, 215; Josselin, *Diary*.

57   "Cultural Analysis of Depressive Affect: An Example from New Guinea," in Kleinman and Good, *Culture and Depression*, pp. 101–33.

58   Josselin, *Diary*, pp. 51, 17; Lowe, *Diary*, p. 24; Norwood, *Journal*, p. 17; Heywood, *Autobiography*, 1: 319.

59   William Stout, *The Autobiography of William Stout of Lancaster 1665–1752*, ed. J. D. Marshall (Manchester, 1967), pp. 103–4, 141–42.

60   Norwood, *Journal*, pp. 26–27, 93–99, 104. Heywood, *Autobiography*, 2: 238.

61   Parkman, *Diary*, pp. 7–8.

62   Elliott, *Power*, pp. 197–98.

63   Ryder, *Diary*, pp. 29, 334, 229.

64   MacDonald, *Mystical Bedlam*, pp. 180ff.; Watkins, *Experience*, p. 6.

65   MacDonald, *Mystical Bedlam*, p. 140; Newcome, *Anger*, pp. 26–28. Walter Calverley, "Memorandum Book of Sir Walter Calverley, Bart.," in *Yorkshire Diaries*, pp. 139–40.

66   Lowe, *Diary*, p. 38; Newcome, *Autobiography*, p. 48; Byrd, *Diary*, pp. 375, 276.

67   Newcome, *Anger*, p. 46; Adam Martindale, *The Life of Adam Martindale*, ed. Richard Parkinson (Chetham Society, 1844), pp. 22, 25; Sereno E. Dwight, "The Works of President Edwards . . ." (1829), and John Locke "Some Thoughts Concerning Education" (1690), in Greven, *Childrearing*, 77, 41.

68   Alan MacFarlane, *Ralph Josselin*, p. 170. For another example, see Ashmole, *Diary*, pp. 103, 106, 121, 129, 138–39, and passim; Eyre, "Dyurnall," p. 68.

69   Ashmole, *Diary*, pp. 31, 49; Norwood, *Journal*, p. 41.

70   For an example, see Walter Powell, who records no emotion on the death of a wife, a new marriage, or the birth of a child (*The Diary of Walter Powell 1603–1654*, ed. Joseph Alfred Bradney [Bristol, 1907], p. 4). Ashmole, *Diary*, pp. 12–13, records no emotion on his father's death or his own marriage.

71   Ryder, *Diary*, pp. 32, 46.

72   Though Ong, in *Orality and Literacy*, would argue that degrees of literacy and literary expression cause changes in emotionality rather than the reverse.

73   For the older view, see J. Leff, "Culture and the Differentiation of Emotional States," *British Journal of Psychiatry* 123 (1973): 299–306. For a revisionist view, see Kleinman and Good, "Introduction" and "Epilogue," in *Culture and Depression*.

74   Lowe, *Diary*, pp. 532, 55; Josselin, *Diary*, passim.

75   Cohen, *God's Caress*, p. 239, chap. 8. Cohen himself admits that the experience of grace after conversion is not well documented (pp. 212–13). His discussion of John Winthrop's diary ignores the very evidence it presents of the diarist's conflict and suffering even after conversion. See also Seaver, *Wallington*, pp. 19–20.

76   Norwood, *Journal*, p. 106.

77   Robert I. Levy, *Tahitians; Mind and Experience in the Society Islands* (Chicago, 1973), p. 405.

78   Oglander, *Notebook*, pp. 215–16; Norwood, *Journal*, pp. 101–3. MacDonald, *Mystical Bedlam*, pp. 173ff.

79   Clifford Geertz, *Local Knowledge* (New York, 1983), p. 59. See also Arthur Mitzman, "The Civilizing Offensive: Mentalities, High Culture and Individual Psyches," *Journal of Social History* 20:4 (1987), pp. 663–87.

80   Keith Thomas, *Religion and the Decline of Magic* (New York, 1971); Muchembled, *Popular Culture*; Josselin, *Diary*, pp. 53, 56, 57, passim; Sewall, *Diary*, p. 124; Newcome, *Autobiography*, pp. 104, 108; Norwood, *Journal*, p. 4; Ashmole, *Diary*, pp. 8–9; Seaver, *Wallington*, p. 90.

81   This certainly is not to argue that the early diarists did not love their children deeply. The evidence strongly supports Linda Pollock's revisionist view on that question. But Pollock has ignored the question of how differently love may have expressed itself over changing centuries, and has therefore been seemingly unaware of the relative neglect that early modern parents had for the safety of their offspring. She has nowhere dealt with the frequency of accidents that happened to early modern children. (*Forgotten Children*.)

82   Thomas, *Religion and the Decline of Magic*. Stuart Clark has argued that it is theoretically impossible for early modern people to have experienced themselves as lacking control since they could not have been aware of something they never had. He also has suggested that cognitive structures and behaviors such as rituals should not be explained in terms of emotional needs unless one can offer evidence that the emotional states can be identified independently of the cognitions or behaviors ("French Historians and Early Modern Popular Culture," *Past and Present* 100 [1983]: 62–99, especially pp. 88–90). Study of these diaries proves that Clark is wrong in suggesting that early modern

people experienced no discomfort from lack of control. This essay also shows that it is indeed possible to discuss the emotionality of a culture by examining what members state about their own emotions. Clark is also wrong, then, in suggesting that "emotionalist" explanations must be ex post facto, prejudiced, "reductionist" approaches to behavior and cognition.

83   Muchembled, *Popular Culture*, pp. 39ff.

84   John Demos, "Shame and Guilt in Early New England," in [Carol Z. Stearns and Peter N. Stearns (eds.), *Emotion and Social Change: Towards a New Psychohistory* (New York, 1988)]. Elliott, *Power*, pp. 68–69; Cohen, *God's Caress*, pp. 218–20.

85   The author takes issue with Elliott's analysis of similar changes as resulting solely from generational changes in New England (*Power*, pp. 174ff.). Clearly the changes were more widespread than he realized.

86   Stearns and Stearns, *Anger*, chap. 3.

87   A traditional view of the damage caused by nineteenth-century views of emotionality is Bernard I. Murstein, *Love, Sex, and Marriage through the Ages* (New York, 1974), pp. 260–64. Also John Haller and Robin Haller, *The Physician and Sexuality in Victorian America* (New York, 1977), pp. 24–42. Toward a partial revision, stressing moral elevation through control of emotions such as anger, see Nancy Cott, *The Bonds of Womanhood: Women's Sphere in New England 1780–1833* (New Haven, 1977), pp. 64–69; Patricia Branca, *Silent Sisterhood* (Pittsburgh, 1975).

88   For an analysis of the relationships between anger and assertion, see Joseph De Rivera, *A Structural Theory of the Emotions* (New York, 1977), pp. 83ff. de Rivera further argues, as do I, that depression is an alternative to anger "when values are being challenged but anger seems unprofitable and there are reasons (such as dependency) against exercising alternatives that create distance." Depression as a contracting of the self or experience of being "pressed down" is also described by de Rivera (pp. 121–22). The distinction brings to mind a patient of mine, a young woman formerly depressed and now often angry, who told me, "when I'm angry, it's like I know I have a self."

89   Again, I take issue with Stuart Clark, "French Historians and Early Modern Culture." The assumption here, that one must always take cultures entirely at face value, seems to rest on several conceptual errors. Error one is to argue that there are no mental structures which affect a culture but of which the culture may be unaware (p. 99). This is, in effect, a statement that the unconscious does not exist, a statement with which few sensitive social scientists can be entirely comfortable. Error two is the assumption that it is somehow dignified for people to develop cognitive structures to explain their world, but undignified for them to develop structures to allay anxiety. This assumption, which runs throughout Clark's article, leads to his accusing historians such as Muchembled with a lack of respect for the past. One must point out, then, that it is Clark, not Muchembled, who is unable to accept the reality that one of man's universal activities is to try to allay anxiety. A discussion of early modern anxiety is not equivalent to a statement that early modern people are inferior or that modern people have less anxiety. Clark needs to reassess his motives in suggesting that it is proper for historians to look only at the cognitive, and not at the emotional, difficulties of our forefathers. Finally, Clark is misguided in positing a rigid distinction between historians who look at the past in terms of its own meanings and those who come as "sociologically privileged observers" (p. 95). An either/or approach can hardly aid our collective endeavor to understand human experience. We must respect other cultures on their own terms, but also, in delineating them, make them comprehensible to ourselves. There is a kind of romanticism in an approach which overstresses the "differentness" of other cultures. It is not a sign of disrespect, but rather of respect, to employ the wisdom of modern social science in an effort to understand the past. To do otherwise is to make our ancestors noble savages. Empathic and objective understanding are both useful and should not be mutually exclusive. For an argument that historians need in some sense to see beyond the past's own meanings in order to understand change, see Keith Thomas, "An Anthropology of Religion and Magic, II," *Journal of Interdisciplinary History* 6, no. 1 (Summer 1975): 102–3. For a general argument in favor of objective as well as empathic understanding, see Melford E. Spiro, "Some Reflections on Cultural Determinism and Relativism with Special Reference to Emotion and Reason," In Shweder and LeVine, *Culture Theory*, pp. 323–46.

90   For a discussion of the necessity of making a distinction between feelings and mental illness, see Kleinman and Good, "Epilogue," in *Culture and Depression*.

91   I dispute Muchembled's view that early modern people because of external anxieties were more pervasively anxious or neurotic than modern ones (*Popular Culture*, 30–31).

92   Greven, *The Protestant Temperament. Patterns of Child-Rearing, Religious Experience and the Self in Early America* (New York, 1977), pp. 74, 11, 113, 123, 28ff., 43ff.

93   Greven, *Protestant Temperament*, pp. 113, 253.

Chapter 11

Nancy Schnog

CHANGING EMOTIONS: MOODS AND THE NINETEENTH-CENTURY AMERICAN WOMAN WRITER

SOMETIMES IT MAY SEEM as if there were nothing more natural or inherent to emotional life than a mood. Moods, common knowledge tells us, are those subtle emotional influences which color perception, shape behavior, and yield sustained, if not durable, moments of happiness, sadness, nostalgia, and regret, among other feelings. Everyday experience confirms that moods are emotional states which are labile, sometimes volatile, and seemingly inexplicable in origin, while a psychological common sense about emotional life teaches us that moods always have been an inextricable part of human emotional experience. It is an open question whether or not moods, as described by contemporary usage, comprise what the historian John Demos has called a fundamental "building block" in human nature; what is more certain, however, is that moods, as a category for locating the nature of emotion, have shifted in meaning and ideological significance across cultures and centuries. The diagnostic manual of psychiatry DSM-IV defines mood as "a pervasive and sustained emotion that colors the perception of the world. Common examples of mood include depression, elation, anger, and anxiety." However, if people of all generations have felt moods, they have conceived of them, and thus interpreted their meaning, in very different ways.[1]

Historically, the term *mood* has varied in meaning and in the avenues of authority construing that meaning.[2] Through the eighteenth century, mood designated thought or emotion of a particular stripe: "mind, heart, thought, feeling" with "specific colouring" (of courage, spirit, stoutness, pride, or anger). Although early use of mood included the idea that mood changes one's state of mind, only during the nineteenth century did mood connote something more uncontrollable and less desirable than that: during the mid-1800s mood accrues the meaning of "Fits of variable or unaccountable temper; especially melancholy, gloomy, or bad-tempered fits." In the twentieth century the term *mood* entered scientific discourse as part of the classificatory systems of psychiatry: what was once thought of as "fits of variable temper" was re-imagined in the 1940s as the clinically unhealthful "mood swing." In 1987 psychiatrists further tightened the relationship between mood and pathology by re-classifying the major syndromes of depression and manic-depression as "mood disorders."[3] As this brief genealogy suggests, it is a specifically twentieth-century invention of the psychological that assumes "mood" to be a basic unit and diagnostic measure of psychological normality and abnormality.

Moreover, recent scholarship suggests that to equate moods with the vagaries of merely personal feeling is to forget that moods enter the social world as a gendered concept and a weapon of cultural politics. Moved to action by the linkage between women and moods in the premenstrual syndrome controversies of the 1970s, contemporary feminists have been among the first to analyze the politics implicit in widely accepted essentialized notions of female moodiness. Eerily reminiscent of late nineteenth-century contentions that the womb controls the female mind and disposes it toward irrationality and debility, today's diagnosticians and promoters of PMS argue that hormones control the woman and ineluctably dispose her to monthly occurrences of irritability, moodiness, and anger. Feminists responding to such theories, while never denying the possible biological basis for PMS, have become sophisticated deconstructors of the cultural messages embodied in this rhetoric of cyclic female moodiness. Anthropologist Emily Martin has shown, for example, how popular concerns with women's moods vary according to the market interests of late industrial capitalism.[4] Martin argues that when women are needed in the workforce, as in wartime, they are deemed sufficiently rational as people and as workers; on the other hand, when the workforce contracts and women's services are no longer required, as in postwar years, the culture rationalizes their exclusion with a doctrine of physical weakness and emotional volatility. For Martin the PMS controversy of the 1970s—a national debate about women's emotional nature and trustworthiness as citizens and as workers—functioned as part of what Susan Faludi has called "the backlash myth"; it was there to remind Americans that, even as women make their most significant economic and professional inroads into public life, they are, by nature, physically handicapped and emotionally unstable.[5]

If various groups can use a rhetoric of moods as a tool of social conservation, women, feminist anthropologists argue, can use moody self-expression as a vehicle of social protest. During the first wave of feminist writing on menstruation, feminists told women that the time had come to put an end to culturally entrenched negative visions of "the curse" and to celebrate the potential creativity and good stemming from this biological fact.[6] Moving beyond a politics of reversal and celebration, feminist scholars have provided compelling new readings of menstruation and its avowed symptomology. Of a piece with her writing on moods and work attitudes, Emily Martin views women's assertion of moodiness through PMS as a subversive challenge to an industrial system that places women in lower ranks of the service economy and demands of them bodily and emotional "work discipline."[7] For Martin, mood symptoms provide women with a value for intermittent shutdowns, a protest against the dehumanizing organization of labor. In a different vein, anthropologist Alma Gottlieb argues that PMS discourse actively socializes women into a two-sided view of female personality: twenty-one days a month, they feel beholden to the traditional script of sweet-tempered and altruistic femininity, yet they can use the period surrounding the menses to enact its opposite.[8] Gottlieb suggests that, from the moment adolescent girls learn about their periods, they are taught by teachers, parents, and doctors "about anticipated mood shifts from 'nice' to 'irritable,' " which are then viewed as "a natural occurrence." Far from a subversive transition in emotional demeanor, the moody PMS sufferer gives voice to anger and complaints when she knows that "those complaints will be rejected as illegitimate," while enacting a script intrinsic to Western culture's dualistic and ambivalent views of women.[9]

In this chapter I use this historically and politically constituted category of moods as a guide for exploring the meaning of the many nineteenth-century writings by American women writers that take "moods" as a central term and subject. I was cued to the importance of this topic by the title of Louisa May Alcott's early novel, *Moods* (1864), and this chapter builds on the curiosity it sparked. In a time when so many literary sentimentalists wrote novels dealing with matters of social reform, why did Alcott choose a title so resonant with emotional implications? Critics know that Alcott's *Moods* was largely autobiographical:

what might this tell us about the ways moods were shaped—or generated—by nineteenth-century social structures and tolerated as part of the course of female development? And, finally, how did nineteenth-century middle-class Americans think about moods—as good or bad, as empowering or dangerous—in a time when, as Warren Susman has argued, both male and female temperament was defined by a concept of "character" that subordinated the self to the higher moral claims of duty, self-denial, citizenship, and integrity?[10]

In this chapter I show how, in the second half of the nineteenth century, white middle-class women writers used the category of moods to stage a public conversation about their inner potential to assume roles beyond the proverbial angel in the house—in particular, those of the romantic individual and the inspired artist. Part one of this chapter focuses on mid-nineteenth-century sentimental attitudes toward women's moods and the large pre-scriptive literature that sought to control them through the social performance of female cheerfulness. Part two goes on to examine three works of women's fiction—Louisa May Alcott's *Moods* (1864), Elizabeth Stuart Phelps Ward's *Story of Avis* (1877), and Kate Chopin's *Awakening* (1899)—that challenge the domestic standard of constructed serenity through their thematization of their female protagonist's moods.[11] In contrast to scholarship in nineteenth-century American literature that posits an opposition between the genres of female sentimentality and male romanticism, this chapter studies the importance of mascu-line romantic ideologies to postbellum women writers who sought to reconfigure their literary work as aesthetically complex and their literary personae as emotionally "real."[12] The novels of Alcott, Phelps, and Chopin reveal that the transition in women's writing from sentimentality to literary realism—from the conceptual world of the "true woman" to that of the "new woman"—involved a major shift in the scripting of female emotion and espe-cially in the encoding of women's moods. Whereas mid-century women writers tended to erase moods from their female heroines in conformity with domestic principles, women writers of the late nineteenth century reclaimed them in conjunction with a masculine romantic philosophy that, for at least a century, had equated moods with individualism, creativity, and emotional depth.

The moody woman

The sentimental literature of the antebellum era—the form that, according to the historian Mary Ryan, peaked in its popularity in the 1850s—constituted moodiness as a major problem and flaw in female temperament.[13] Literary scholars have shown how sentimental novels such as Catharine Maria Sedgwick's *New-England Tale* (1822) and Susan Warner's *Wide Wide World* (1851) functioned as spiritual training narratives, teaching young women how to control intense emotion, especially anger, and how to deny self-fulfilling wishes in the service of what Anna Freud called "altruistic other-direction." A related genre of women's sentimental writing has received less attention: the stories of prenuptial and marital relations that continued women's emotional education by placing strong taboos on the acknowledgment and display of the married woman's moods. Authors of sentimental fictions and domestic advice manuals employed two literary figures as a mode of organizing the proper emotional expressions of married women. They introduced the figure of the moody woman who instructed readers to censure a whole arsenal of negative feelings (anxiousness, sadness, nervousness, and irritability) and to ward off their display through the outward demeanors of self-absorption, sulkiness, standoffishness, and coldness. Emerging in tandem with this image and helping to render it unacceptable was an alternative portrait of the habitually cheerful woman, unshakable in her pose of contentment and a symbol of perfect emotional adjustment to the roles of spouse and homemaker.

In 1833 Emma Willard, the founder of Troy Female Seminary, explained that in her era the label of moodiness was often used to stigmatize women who consorted too closely with political feminism. In *The Advancement of Female Education*, Willard commented that women's rights advocates are often accused of losing their feminine characters and "often when such women are found moody and are thought capricious it is this which is the cause of their ill-humor and dejection."[14] Early sentimental fiction writers instructed their women readers to sidestep such epithets—and the progressive politics that provoked them—by suppressing "moody" behavior and by assuming the visibly "domestic" look of cheerfulness. In senti-mental literature these messages were articulated with particular force in the writing of Elizabeth Stuart Phelps, one of the most popular early nineteenth-century women writers and the mother of the well-known postbellum writer Elizabeth Stuart Phelps Ward.[15] Like many authors of her generation, Phelps used her stories to establish middle-class standards of female deportment and home management. What makes Phelps's stories unusual, how-ever, is the explicit way in which they tie domestic practices—housekeeping, childrearing, dress, and personal cleanliness—to emotional conduct. One witnesses this extension of domestic ideology into the realm of the emotions in what is, today, Phelps's most often anthologized tale, "The Angel over the Right Shoulder: Or, The Beginning of the New Year" (1852), as well as in her lesser-known collection of stories, *The Tell-Tale: Or, Home Secrets Told by Old Travellers* (1853).[16]

The conventional happy ending of Phelps's "Angel over the Right Shoulder" provides one index of the importance the author attributed not simply to the role of divine mother-hood but to the "angelic" wife's and mother's emotional self-presentation. This story's protagonist, Mrs. James, at her husband's prodding commits herself to a long-desired course of study and, when faced with constant interruptions from her family, must ultimately come to grips with the futility of her program. Within this framework the story's main line of interest is Mrs. James's journey out of the depression caused by her daily routine of self-sacrifice and her emergence into a state of happiness with her limited domestic role. What makes this story's happy ending different from hundreds of other sentimental tales is that it literalizes and personalizes the meaning of a "happy" outcome: this story's act of closure spotlights not the positive resolution of a family problem, but the specific duty of Mrs. James to become a happy person. Thus in the closing paragraph we learn that, through the agency of a dream (recounting Mrs. James's future salvation through maternal benevolence), the protagonist leaves behind "Sad thoughts and sadder misgivings—undefined yearnings and ungratified longings" in order to approach a "*Glad* New Year" with "fresh resolution and cheerful hope, and a happy heart" (215). Phelps's triple reiteration of adjectives of glee in the penultimate sentence of her story is neither an empty cliché nor a meaningless pattern of repetition.[17] Rather, in this case Phelps's underlined and capitalized "*Glad*" and its synonyms are used to underscore the specifically emotional responsibility of the middle-class mother to maintain and express a "happy heart."

The marriage stories in Phelps's *Tell-Tale* repeat and expand on these ideas. These tales picture properly and improperly domesticated homes and associate them with their female housekeepers' either rightly or wrongly conceived notions of bodily care and emotional carriage. In these stories Phelps links her properly domesticated homes—places which feature disciplined children, arranged parlors, neat dinner tables, and well-dressed family members—to the presence of happy wives and mothers. The women in these homes fill "cheerful parlors" with "cheerful chat" (114); they are "full of affection" and "kind and genial" (104); they nurture "sweetness of character" (25) and exude "a calm and steady light" (123). Oppositionally, Phelps attaches her improperly domesticated homes—places defined by messy parlors, unruly children in shabby clothes, and disorderly family meals—to the stewardship of housekeepers who are physically unkempt and emotionally uncontrolled.

These stories identify an expansive list of emotional demeanors that are disruptive to the goal of domestic cheerfulness. At different times, the tales censure women who adopt "a distressed tone of voice" (18), wear "a doleful expression" (18), sport a carriage both "glum" and "mum" (50), fall into "the sulks" (103), act "offish" or "blue" (104), exude "chilliness" as opposed to "sunshine" (106), become "irritable and nervous" (125), or exhibit "moody ill-humour" (43) or "moody silence" (118). Altogether, the marriage stories in *The Tell-Tale* offer a veritable compendium of negative demeanors and, by extension, negative feelings not to be tolerated in middle-class women.

There is, however, one story in *The Tell-Tale* that significantly disrupts the volume's otherwise consistent perspective of disdain toward the moody woman. This tale, "The Husband of a Blue," points to a current of ambivalence within Phelps's writing on self-enforced cheerfulness—an uncertainty that has important implications for the way we ultimately understand the ideological functions of the literature of female emotional comportment. In "The Husband of a Blue," Phelps gingerly concedes that, due to variations in temper and interest, not every woman can or should assume the duties of matrimony and its related work of emotional uplift. This story records the marital history of a woman who is "blue" in two senses of the word: she is a bluestocking, an erudite woman who "cared for little but her books" (98), and blue by temperament, a woman with tendencies for the "sulks" (103). As in "The Angel over the Right Shoulder," the moral lesson this story teaches is the harm done to family life through a wife's and mother's "selfish" devotion to her own intellectual interests. Yet in a more direct fashion than the earlier story, "The Husband of a Blue" links the anti-domestic nature of its protagonist, Marion Gray, to her proclivity for changing emotions and their expression. Marion's Aunt Clara, the story's narrative voice and embodiment of true womanhood, underscores this fact in the following analysis of her niece's character:

> She [Marion] seemed to feel it her right to call upon Mr. Ashton [her husband] to accommodate himself to her hours and plans. . . . If he failed to do so, she was sufficiently offended to be moody. Did he urge her leaving her study at an inconvenient time, to receive and entertain callers, her brow was clouded; in short, whenever his wishes crossed hers, and he did not readily yield them, she fell into what must, even in a learned woman, be called the *sulks*. She was unsociable and reserved: she read almost constantly, and there was an indescribable chill and constraint about her, which sensibly affected one's spirit like going into a damp cellar. Aunt Clara saw that Marion was never *genial*, excepting when she had her own way. (103)

As this passage suggests, Marion has got her lessons in domesticity upside-down: instead of caring for and serving her husband in accordance with the tenets of true womanhood, she expects her husband to perform this role for her. Indeed, Marion's freewheeling expression of negative sentiment—the clouded brows, sulks, and chilliness mentioned here, as well as the standoffish and irritable behavior described later in the story—marks her failure in domestic rectitude as much as her ill-conceived notion of women's labor. At the end of the story the narrator establishes her negative assessment of this "moody and exacting wife" (104) with the following words: "little did Marion think . . . that, in the final summing up of the results of her life, its most important item would be the effect which her character as an *affliction* had upon the work and influence of her husband" (134).

One fact in this story, however, dramatically modifies the narrator's indictment of Marion's character: that is, the ethical dilemma that Phelps builds around the conditions of Marion's marriage. As the story opens, Marion is presented as being fully aware of and perfectly open about her indisposition to things domestic. Marion, we are informed, had "told him [her suitor] frankly, with look and voice, which spoke more even than her words, 'that she loved him, but she hated house-keeping, and that next to his society, she cared for little but her books' " (99). In the face of this confession, Ashton Gray overrides his beloved's anxieties toward marriage with a guarantee to "so adjust the cares of his new home that his wife's studies should not be broken in upon" (100). The story's ethical dilemma is established when Ashton retreats from his side of this bargain. As a husband and father, Ashton yearns for a more complete domesticity, and expects, increasingly, that Marion play her part. Carefully, then, Phelps divides the responsibility for this couple's disastrous marriage between the wife's bookishness and the husband's deceit. As Marion says in response to one of her husband's many postmarital reproofs: "I am wholly unfitted for domestic employments; and you are unhappy because I do not give them my thoughts and time. You do expect from me a degree of attention to them which you gave me to understand that you should not expect. You have deceived me in this matter" (107).

This aspect of the plot should be noted with care for two reasons. On the one hand, by pinpointing the external forces that drive Marion toward moodiness, Phelps mitigates the blame that the story otherwise places on her reputation as an "affliction." Here, in other words, Phelps seems to show an understanding that the moodiness she vilifies in women is not always of their own making. Most intriguingly, however, readers of the work of Elizabeth Stuart Phelps Ward will note that her mother's story of a broken marital compact in "The Husband of a Blue" apparently served as the prototype for her own novel of derailed female talent in *The Story of Avis*.[18] In rewriting her mother's tale, Ward rescripts its moral content and its negative vision of female moods. In the daughter's story, sympathy, not judgment, is brought to the career-oriented woman, whose individuality and creativity are equated with the positive value of her moods.

The cheerful woman

In her day Phelps was not alone in marketing the image of the ever-cheerful housewife. One of the most forceful articulations of cheerfulness as the middle-class woman's normative emotional pose can be found in Catharine Beecher and Harriet Beecher Stowe's *American Woman's Home* (1869), in a chapter entitled "The Preservation of Good Temper in the Housekeeper."[19] According to these authors, the key to family happiness lies with the temper of the housewife, with the woman who is, specifically, "gentle, sympathizing, forbearing, and cheerful" (212). Although a composite portrait of female character, the essay most often repeats the quality of cheerfulness, which thus surfaces as its dominant term. The Beecher sisters' ideal housewife maintains a "cheerful temper," possesses a "cheerful and vivifying power," sustains others through her "cheerful kindness and sympathy," and works hard to preserve a "cheerful frame of mind." If, on the one hand, the device of repetition helps Beecher and Stowe communicate their belief in the power of cheerfulness, the use of contrast aids them on the other. The authors' picture of the cheerful woman is situated against a portrait of her opposite: the woman who "jars the spirits" of her family by wearing "a sorrowful, a discontented, or an angry face" or by indulging "in the frequent use of sharp and reprehensive tones" (212). In their attempt to present cheerfulness as a singular ideal of female temperament, these writers clearly delimit the states of feeling that have the potential to disrupt it: the feelings, specified here, of sorrow, discontent, and anger.

In Beecher and Stowe's understanding of it, cheerfulness is neither a transitory state nor a static ideal of character; for them, cheerfulness amounts to a specifically female strategy of social control within middle-class family life. The Beecher sisters perceive cheerfulness as a disposition with *agency*, one that, when enacted, sheds a positive "influence" over family life.

For, as the authors contend, the sphere "illuminated by her [the mother's] smile, and sustained by her cheering kindness and sympathy," exerts "a peaceful and invigorating influence" that "everyone, without thinking of it, or knowing why it was so, experienced" (212). In order to ensure the proper expression of cheerfulness, the authors provide specific directions for its staging, instructions focused mainly on a woman's regulation of voice and face. The woman who wears "a countenance of anxiety and dissatisfaction" and indulges "in tones of anger or complaint" destroys the comfort of her family, while the mother who wears a smile and speaks in "kind and gentle tones" sheds "a cheering and vivifying power" (212) over her household. Working from a premise akin to modernday behaviorism, Stowe and Beecher suggest that the "habitual" performance of this role will facilitate a woman's successful adjustment to the stance of cheerfulness.

Antebellum guides to marriage also identified female cheerfulness as an emotional and economic asset within middle-class family life. In his advice manual *The Young Wife; Or, Duties of Women in the Marriage Relation* (1837), William A. Alcott opens his fourth chapter, "Cheerfulness," with the admonition that the young wife "owes it to her husband and to the world to be cheerful."[20] Alcott designs his chapter around family histories of failure and success. The home governed by a cheerless housewife invites disaster: children in these families grow up to be "peevish," "gloomy," "discontented," and "unhappy" (44), while their fathers head for the companionship of the "tavern-keeper" (45). Alternatively, the cheerful wife "warms his [her husband's] heart, and inspires hope" while leading her partner to "habits of industry . . . to other virtues and to happiness" (46). While many domestic writers envisioned middle-class women as providing therapeutic relief to husbands drained of energy by commercial life, Alcott imagines female cheerfulness as the specific agent of relief. As the author notes, the domestic woman performs the work of helping her husband to recuperate: "Above all . . . by the reception she gives him in the evening. When he comes home . . . after dark . . . he finds not only the lighted window and the blazing hearth, but the still more cheering light of his wife's countenance, to welcome him" (47).

Like Stowe and Beecher, Alcott instructs his female readership on the correct means of performing cheerfulness. In Alcott's conception, a woman properly sustains her husband, "Not by wise words, in the form of direct instruction—not by her sage counsels—not even by her example, alone. It is by her never-tiring cheerfulness; or at least chiefly so. . . . I need only say that her countenance always wears a smile, an unaffected one, too, when she meets him; and that her every word or action corresponds to the feelings indicated by her countenance. Everything she says or does in his presence warms his heart and inspires his hope" (47). Here the wife's role is most effectively performed not through her intellectual or rational self—the self capable of offering "instruction" or "counsels"—but through her uplifted and uplifting emotional self. This self must enlist both her "countenance" and "feelings" in her enactment of cheerfulness: the look of cheerfulness must correspond with and reflect the feeling of happiness it refers to. Even more, this performance must be "never-tiring" or perpetual: as Alcott states in a related passage, "maternal kindness" must operate "not through the medium of occasional smiles or acts of kindness but by an uninterrupted series of those looks and acts that make their impression on the heart" (44). As this passage spells it out, the proper administration of female cheerfulness depends on its saturation of a woman's whole being: it must be displayed physically, felt inwardly, and enacted permanently.

The politics of cheerfulness

The cheerful woman of nineteenth-century domestic fiction and advice manuals appears as the not too distant ancestor of the "happy housewife heroine" that Betty Friedan finds at the heart of the mass women's magazine fiction of the 1950s: a woman perfectly "happy" in her private, domestically defined role, "existing only for and through her husband and children."[21] "Staring uneasily at this image," Friedan writes, "I wonder if a few problems are not somehow better than this smiling, empty passivity. If they are happy, these young women who live the feminine mystique, then is this the end of the road? Or are the seeds of something worse than frustration inherent in this image?"[22] Friedan's questions are important for understanding why early nineteenth-century women writers not only held to but helped produce the image of the cheerful woman. Did the ideology of cheerfulness reflect an ideal, a reality, a veiled frustration, a dishonest charade, or some combination of all of the above?

At the most basic level, the literature of cheerfulness appears to have worked in tandem with and assisted the creation of the image of the "true woman." It is now a truism of women's history that the cult of domesticity constructed the white middle-class woman as pietistic, pure, submissive, and selfless: examining this construct, one wants to note that these traits locate the nature of exemplary behavior while saying little about the inner states that attach to them.[23] The writing on cheerfulness filled this gap: it helped secure women's secondary status by refusing any sustained analysis of feelings potentially threatening to the perception of women's perfect social adjustment. In this sense the cultural arbiters of cheer reveal an implicit understanding of just how easily sadness and sulkiness, anger and offishness, resentment and clouded brows can translate into "female complaints" and marital quarrels, the seedbed of potentially larger protests. Working from expression to feeling, the rhetoric of cheerfulness sought to harmonize women's outward display of cheerfulness with its emotional referent, happiness, and, in so doing, to diffuse the emotional seeds of women's personal and social discontent.

However, behind the scenes of women's idealized depictions of cheerful housewives lay a more complicated reality. As Mary Kelley has shown in a related context, the popular women writers who came of age in the 1850s faced painful psychological contradictions—what Kelley calls "a crisis of being"—as they tried to merge their private identities as mothers with their public identities as authors.[24] As a first generation of women striving for a professional literary role, writers like Phelps and Stowe widened their sphere of public activity, while never straying too far from their domestic compass; the woman writer, who won a public self through her authorship, made significant retreats from it by hiding her name through a pseudonym, by clinging to a moral and domestic rather than an artistic definition of her work, and by feeling guilt, self-doubt, and ambivalence connected with her disassociation from her traditional role. If we return to the case of Elizabeth Stuart Phelps, we can see that her career mirrored these patterns of professional development and emotional conflict: she wrote under the name H. Trusta; she understood her writing in terms of domestic instruction; and, as memorials of the author show, she experienced a "crisis of being" that was intimately connected to both her authorship and her fictional insistence on habitual maternal happiness.

In her autobiography Elizabeth Stuart Phelps Ward speaks this way of the mother she lost as an eight-year-old: "The author . . . lived before women had careers and public sympathy in them. Her nature was drawn against the grain of her times and of her circumstances: and where our feet find easy walking, hers were hedged."[25] She was "one of those rare women of the elder time whose gifts forced her out, but whose heart held her in."[26] Both Ward and her father, Austin Phelps, recorded their memories of Elizabeth Stuart Phelps, and their memoirs provide fascinating, if sometimes opposing, insights into the way Phelps managed her family, her work, and her emotions as she stepped into an early version of the role of "new woman." The daughter claims that her mother obtained "a strong and lovely symmetry" between the roles of writer and mother, but she also insists, to the contrary, that "her last book and her last baby came together and killed her."[27] In Austin Phelps's recollections, his wife emerges as a woman desperately struggling to obtain "symmetry" in a context that refused it. Austin Phelps's memoir highlights the autobiographical content of Phelps's stories of married intellectual women: it suggests that Phelps herself actively guarded against the consuming interest of her intellectual labors in order to avoid becoming like Marion Gray, and that she did so by consciously placing her home duties before her work like the reformed Mrs. James. As Austin Phelps says, "The Angel over the Right Shoulder" illustrates "the sincerity of the religious convictions which she [Elizabeth Stuart Phelps] carried into these [her own] household plans," while "The Husband of a Blue" reflects "her jealous vigilance over her own tastes, lest they should encroach on the comfort of those who were dependent upon her."[28]

Even more to the point, Austin Phelps offers the following description of the emotional struggle undergone by his wife:

> It was the "struggle of her life" to control the fickleness of her physical temperament, and rise above despondency. "Nobody knows," she would often say, "how I do struggle for it." It was her habitual fear that her family might suffer for the want of a cheerful, sunny home. This is a disclosure, however, which will surprise the majority of her friends—so vigilant was she in watching her various moods, and so successful in breathing the spirit of joy around her. Her presence in any group was almost invariably a guarantee of vivacious and genial conversation. She often concealed physical infirmity, that she might come to her little home circle with a cheerful look. (66–67)

This passage shows that, for Phelps, the cheerful woman was neither an accomplished ideal nor present reality; it was, instead, a laboriously and painfully sought-after goal, one struggled toward through vigilance, concealment, and what the literary critic Alfred Habegger has called "a methodical sort of buoyancy."[29] From the vantage point described by Austin Phelps, it appears that Elizabeth Stuart Phelps used the figure of the cheerful woman as a psychological life-line to a domestic self-image that, in her own life, was under siege. Seeking the goal of cheer through a script of vivacity and geniality (recall that Marion Gray was never "genial") seems to have enabled Phelps to invest herself in her new authorial position, while retaining an emotional bridge to a role she was, in fact, distancing herself from (at least for the two hours a day that, like Mrs. James, she permitted herself to write). Put another way, the performance of cheerfulness seems to have acted for Phelps as a solvent for the guilt produced by her dual careers as well as a strategy for negotiating the transition between domestic woman and professional writer. Although Austin Phelps frames the major struggle of his wife's life as a matter of her "physical temperament," drawing a line between his wife's constitutional weakness and the social pressures upon her, it seems likely that both the physical and the social contributed to the inner drama Phelps enacted between her "various moods" and "cheerful look."

This examination of Phelps's life enables us to see that her fictional depictions of moody women were multivalent in meaning. Biographical documents suggest that physical problems, in combination with the legacies of her upbringing, did indeed complicate Phelps's search for an evenly experienced cheerfulness. As a young woman Phelps suffered from illness, invalidism, and what appears to have been an episode of "hysteria." At the same time, Phelps was afraid of perpetuating within her own family her father's severe Calvinism and morbid attunement to death.[30] Moreover, as Phelps's first popular novel, *The Sunny Side; Or, The Country Minister's Wife* (1851), suggests, Phelps experienced her own role as the minister's wife as an exhausting performance—yet always one to be represented as "sunny"—in other-directedness. Joel Pfister has argued that "the heated-up" psychological relations of middle-class families in mid-nineteenth-century America led to literary expressions by Poe, Hawthorne, and Melville of marital aggressivity and murder.[31] In the case of Phelps, moods appear to have been the problematic emotional upshot not simply of a frail body but of social arrangements in which the minister's sermons came before the wife's fictions, in which children had to be cared for while publishers waited for more copy, in which private conscience contended with public aspirations, and in which personal troubles had to be harnessed to the demeanor of cheerfulness.

Reconsiderations and challenges

In the post-Civil War years, a number of "second-generation" middle-class women writers—writers whose careers peaked in the last three decades of the nineteenth century— used their fiction to rethink and challenge the domestic construction of female character as uniformly cheerful. At the head of this list stands Louisa May Alcott, whose 1864 novel *Moods* explored the emotional roles available to middle-class girls and women of her time. Although many of Alcott's critics regarded her book as a "divorce novel" and condemned the young author for approving of divorce, Alcott always maintained that her intent with her early novel was to study not marriage but girls' emotional preparedness for it. *Moods*, Alcott wrote, was "meant to show a life affected by *moods*, not a discussion of marriage which I knew little about, except observing that very few were happy ones."[32] In a letter to one disgruntled reader, disturbed by what he took to be the novel's endorsement of sexual attraction as the foundation for marriage, Alcott tried to set the record straight by telling him: "The design of Moods was to show the effect of a moody person's moods upon their life, & Sylvia, being a mixed and peculiar character, makes peculiar blunders & tries to remedy them in an uncommon manner."[33]

Whereas Phelps typically places her moody women within the context of marriage, Alcott focuses her point of interest on the "naturally" moody girl and her prospects for entering into a happily conceived marriage. Alcott's protagonist, the seventeen-year-old Sylvia Yule, represents a significant departure from Phelps's negatively characterized moody woman, yet a markedly ambivalent one. *Moods* deals with its avowed subject matter—the moods of girls and women—in a contradictory fashion. On the one hand, the novel strives for a positive characterization of its female protagonist by showing how her inborn moodiness fulfills a male transcendental ideal of emotional spontaneity and individualism. On the other hand, the novel imagines a dark future for the girl who carries this ideal into her marriage and adulthood. As this novel sees it, it is lovely and charming to be a moody tomboyish girl, but it is dangerous, even deadly, to enter womanhood lacking emotional stability, constancy, and self-control.

In *Moods* Alcott traces Sylvia Yule's development from transcendental girl to genteel woman and highlights, thereby, the oppositional ways that Emersonian transcendentalists and Stowian domestics construct male and female emotion. In the opening chapters Alcott establishes Sylvia Yule as the novel's emotionally tempestuous heroine and scripts her moodiness as a positive attribute by linking it to an Emersonian philosophy of emotional spontaneity. Alcott ties Sylvia's character to a masculine transcendentalism in a number of ways. She opens the novel by sending Sylvia, along with three male companions, on a boating expedition reminiscent of Henry David Thoreau's journey down the Concord and Merrimack rivers. Later, she again likens Sylvia's character to Thoreau's by presenting her as a witness to "a battle between black ants and red" and as a chronicler of nature who learns "the landscape by heart." But Alcott associates her heroine with transcendental philosophy in an even more important way: in *Moods* she takes pains to show that Sylvia's inborn moodiness fulfills Emerson's transcendental injunction to emotional self-contradiction and freedom.

In "Self-Reliance" (1841) Emerson presents his exemplary individual as the noncon-forming man who heeds the call of what Emerson refers to variously as Spontaneity, Instinct, and Whim. Describing his own creative method, Emerson proudly declares: "I shun father and mother and wife and brother when my genius calls me. I would write on the lintels of the door-post, Whim."[34] Alcott situates her protagonist within this discourse of creative individualism by introducing the reader to Sylvia Yule in a chapter that, following Emerson, is entitled "Whims." Like Jo March of Alcott's *Little Women* (1869), Sylvia Yule is a tomboy: she dresses like a "lad," befriends insects and animals, insists that she can "walk, run, and climb like any boy" (51), and manipulates events in order to get herself invited on her brother's river boat trip. Yet in this novel, Sylvia's tomboyism is defined as much by her volatile emotional life as by her physical skills. What draws the two male protagonists and every other character to Sylvia is her tumultuous emotional self, described as "whimsical and hard to please" (24), "always in extremes" (24), "many-sided" (22), "capricious" (57), and subject to "perverse fits" (17) and the performance of "wild things" (25). Drawing on a theory of inherited personality, Alcott casts Sylvia as the offspring of an unhappy marriage, a "regretful husband" and "sad wife," who conferred upon their daughter "conflicting tem-peraments, with all their aspirations, attributes, and inconsistencies" (84). In a deliberate echo of the language in Emerson's essay "Experience" (1844), the narrator tells us, "These two masters ruled her soul and body, making Sylvia an enigma to herself and her life a train of moods" (84).

As Barbara Sicherman has noted, in the 1860s tomboy characters were "not only tolerated but even admired—up to a point, the point at which they were expected to become women."[35] This is precisely the case for Sylvia Yule: when she is a seventeen-year-old "child," Sylvia's moods function positively and mark her as a female individual distinct from the conventional girls "all made on the same pattern" who "all said, did, thought, and wore about the same things" (24). Yet once she becomes an eighteen-year-old "woman" enveloped in the rituals of courtship, Alcott's moody female is doomed to unhappiness and untimely death. Similar to Emily Dickinson, who described marriage as "the soft Eclipse" of a "Girl's life,"[36] Alcott portrays Sylvia's eighteenth birthday as the dividing line between the past and future, the time when Sylvia "looked backward to the girlhood just ended, and forward to the womanhood just beginning" (28). Consequently, the sections that follow Sylvia's "fateful" river trip—fateful because it is there that she becomes entwined in a love triangle that disappoints its three participants—move her swiftly toward an unhappy fate. Enviable in youth, moods, according to Alcott, do not mix with marriage. They lead Sylvia down the path of divorce and early, death.

As was the case for Phelps, Alcott's choice of moods as the subject of her early novel reaches back to her personal life and, in particular, to contradictions she herself experienced in relation to cultural scripts of domestic and romantic emotion. Those scripts shaped Louisa's young life in unusually intimate ways: her father strictly adhered to domestic ideals of female emotional self-regulation, while her adolescent hero and close family friend, Ralph Waldo Emerson, exuberantly endorsed the exceptionalism of male emotional freedom. The Alcott family letters show that Amos Bronson Alcott, in compliance with these gendered ideals, interpreted the emotionally volatile temperaments of his wife, Abigail, and his second daughter, Louisa, as dangerous and unnatural. In his journal he characterizes these family members as "Two devils—the mother fiend and her daughter." He describes Louisa as "impulsive and moody" and calls her the "Possessed One."[37] Growing up in a family governed by Bronson's vision of a celestial home "where peace and joy, and gentleness and quiet, abide always, and from which sounds of content and voices of confiding love, alone ascend," Louisa had little option but to construe her "moody" nature as a problem of temperament, an abnormal deviation from her father's and her culture's dominant ideals of femininity.[38]

Ironically, Alcott's *Moods* appropriates Emerson's romantic rhetoric of moods as the authority through which to challenge and revise her father's (and broader culture's) demonic conception of them. Alcott links her subject directly to Emerson by opening her novel with an epigraph drawn from "Experience": "Life is a train of moods like a string of beads; and as we pass through them they prove to be many colored lenses, which paint the world their own hue, and each shows us only what lies in its own focus."[39] Written in the aftermath of the death of Emerson's young son, "Experience" uses what Stanley Cavell has called "the logic of moods" to locate a new pessimism in Emerson's thought, his strongly reduced faith in the self's power to apprehend the world objectively, and his increased sense of life as "a succession of moods or objects" where "gladly we would anchor, but the anchorage is quicksand."[40] Here it is important to note that Emerson's invocation of moods as a critique of objectivity retains a strain of the romanticism that marks his earlier essays. Moods, one must remember, give "color" to experience even as they block a synthesizing vision of it. Most important for Alcott, however, Emerson's meditation on life as a "train of moods" registers an idea of emotional flux as a natural and universal component of human experience—an idea, it appears, that spoke powerfully to the "moody" girl stigmatized by her father as "the Possessed One." In 1864, when Alcott published the first edition of *Moods*, she left the work of formulating a woman's inner life as a "train of moods" as wishful, unfinished business. Eighteen years later, she finished it. In 1882 Alcott rewrote her novel's ending and allowed her moody heroine to live.

In *The Story of Avis*, one of the first major studies of female artistic development in American women's writing, Elizabeth Stuart Phelps Ward moves the representation of women's moods further along the trajectory of creative individualism. Ward endows her artist-protagonist with a proclivity toward moods not only to signify her singularity but also to reference her potential to develop as a great "high cultural" artist of her time. In a major departure from the representational technique of her mother, Ward endows her protagonist with moods as one of her primary means of establishing Avis's artistic temperament and extraordinary nature. Whereas Alcott connects her heroine's moods to a concept of female individualism derived from transcendental philosophy, Ward links her heroine's moods to a concept of inspired artistry derived from nineteenth-century ideas of romantic genius. In *The Story of Avis* Ward scripts Avis's moods as the foundation of her anointed identity as an artist and as the source of the prophetic visions which inspire her best work.

Literary historians have shown that the writing of Johann Wolfgang von Goethe, Jean-Jacques Rousseau, and William Wordsworth, among others, bequeathed to nineteenth-century Euro-Americans romantic ideas of the artist as an elevated being more sensitive, passionate, and introspective than others, as a solitary self alienated from society, and as a person disposed to imaginative reverie and spiritual insight.[41] As Eli Zaretsky has written, "Beginning with romanticism, artists declared that art was the product less of a particular craft of discipline than of the artist's inner life."[42] When that "inner life" was characterized, it was typically imaged as tempestuous, unstable, and, in some cases, mad. Romantic poets, in particular, appear to have favored the term "mood" as a vehicle for locating this kind of extra-sensitive and emotionally fluid interiority. In his autobiographical poem *The Prelude* (1850), Wordsworth links his younger self's communion with nature to his capacity for "fleeting moods" which confer "visionary power."[43] Later in the poem Wordsworth discloses that, as a young man, he experimented with gestures of poetic temperament by indulging in "Moods melancholy, fits of spleen, that loved / A pensive sky, sad days, and piping winds" (VI, 170–75). In this regard it is of note that Emerson begins his essay "The Poet" (1844) with a poem that echoes Wordsworth's vision of the artistic power of moods. Emerson's verse epigraph speaks of "A moody child and wildly wise" who becomes the poet who communicates "musical order, and pairing rhymes."[44]

In *The Story of Avis*, Avis's moods are affiliated with these romantic meanings. Ward presents Avis—whose name derives from the Latin for bird—as more capable of transcendence than the typical woman of Harmouth by virtue of her aesthetic gifts, her physical beauty, and her visionary moods. The book opens just after Avis's return from Europe on an evening when she makes her homecoming debut at the Harmouth Poetry Club, a small-town literary affair in which male faculty readers and their female students have gathered to read Edmund Spenser's *Faerie Queen*. In order to emphasize the gifted nature of her protagonist, Ward presents Avis to the reader as the charmed subject of a tableau vivant. Surrounded by her peers, Avis cuts an imperial image by sitting in front of carmine drapery which accentuates her "solitary look," emphasizes "the aloofness in her very beauty" (7), and draws the attention of the group like a "magnet" (4). On this evening Avis's re-entry into Harmouth society is brought to completion when she agrees to exhibit her sketch of Spenser's Una, an occasion of textual importance insofar as it calls forth Avis's romantic conception of the artist's calling. When Philip Ostrander, in a foreboding of Avis's later subjection to him, says that her sketch of Una reveals "Truth . . . subject to Love, omnipotently subject" (10), Avis responds with the following denial: "I am not responsible for Spenser's theology . . . and an artist has such gloriously lawless moods! Why should I trouble myself to think about Una every day? I had a pretty girl to draw so I drew her. But I put the lion in, so people shouldn't make a mistake" (10).

In speaking of the artist as one who possesses "such gloriously lawless moods," Ward places her heroine within a specifically Wordsworthian and, more broadly, romantic interpretation of the artist's interiority. This is not surprising, as Ward herself was an avid reader of Wordsworth and tied her intellectual awakening at the age of sixteen to her father's readings of De Quincey and Wordsworth, which "opened for me, as distinctly as if I had never heard of it before, the world of letters as a Paradise from which no flaming sword could ever exile me."[45] Like the opium eater and poet portrayed by these writers, Avis's creativity is tied to the romantic trope of intense inner experience; her "fertile moods" serve as the occasion for prophetic vision. For example, the night before Avis is to exhibit her first American portrait, one of Ostrander, she lies sleepless, "seeing the souls of unwrought pictures, like disembodied spirits, sweep by, vision upon vision, electrotyped upon the darkness with the substance of wine or opium fantasies; an experience which chanced to her only in her most fertile moods" (61). A far cry from her mother's view of moods as afflicting, Ward endows Avis with moods as the extrasensory power which stirs "the souls" of pictures from the artist's unconscious. In a related scene, Avis's mood provides the impetus for her discovery of the idea of her sole masterpiece, a painting of the Sphinx. This scene opens with Avis locking herself in her room, trying to block out the voices of college boys singing Civil War songs, while her own civil war takes place over her wish to find the inner resources to work and live as an artist. On this night, "Avis shut and locked the door of her bare, old-fashioned room, looking about it with a kind of triumphant rebellion. These four walls shut out the world from the refined license of her mood. She wanted nothing of it,— the great unholy world, in which seers struggled and sinned for their visions. Let them go fighting and erring on" (79).

In this scene Avis courts the "refined license of her mood" not by partaking in "opium fantasies" but by doing something related to it (and unprecedented in nineteenth-century middle-class women's fiction): she *elects* to imbibe a "cautious dose" of "*liqueur*" (80). Avis nurtures her feelings of moody rebelliousness by drinking French wine and laying down to experience "a self-articulate hour" (88) of drunken revery. It is in this state of mind that a parade of portrait subjects appears to Avis—an earthen vase, a mid-ocean wave, a medley of faces grown old with toil—and, finally, the mystery of womanhood as embodied in the Sphinx. Through this experiment with a mind-altering substance, Avis attempts to empower her own artist-psyche by claiming the traditionally male privileges of "high stimulant, rough virtues, strong vices, all the great peril and power of exuberant, exposed life" (79). Through this scene Ward suggests that to be an artist is not simply to be a highly skilled painter, but also to harbor a particular kind of "inner life"—one marked by potent and prophetic moods. As the narrator says after Avis's night of intoxication, "there had been nothing unprecedented in the character of these fantasies, excepting in their number and variety. Her [Avis's] creative moods were always those of tense vision, amounting to optical illusion, failing of it only where the element of deception begins" (83).

It is important to acknowledge, however, that, for all the inner power assigned to Avis through her "fertile" and "creative" moods, and for all the distance this encoding marks from the moral position of her mother, Ward's scripting of this emotionally "deep" female protagonist does nothing to save her from a fate akin to Marion Gray's and Sylvia Yule's. Similar to her predecessors', Avis's careers, both artistic and marital, end in failure. In Ward's novel romantic identity is thus divorced from social empowerment: there is never a suggestion that Avis's visionary moods will help her navigate her way out of a situation of unforeseen marital demands and domestic entrapment. When, in 1899, Kate Chopin brought the theme of the moody woman to life again in the character of Edna Pontellier, the aspiring artist-protagonist of *The Awakening*, she mapped more carefully than Ward the liabilities of this romantic inscription of female moods. In *The Awakening* Chopin shows how readily romantic tropes of interiority can slide into a disabling form of emotional self-absorption, at the same time inviting pejorative labels of female irrationality and emotional disorder.

One finds all the signs in Chopin's novel that Edna's character should be interpreted within an idiom of emergent romantic individualism: Edna seeks liberation from her bourgeois marriage, rebels against convention, prefers solitude to sociability, longs for an impossible fusion with men and nature, and identifies herself with the artistic worlds of music and painting. Read in relation to the literary traditions outlined above, Edna Pontellier's propensity for moods figures as one more convention through which Chopin marks her protagonist's capacity for romantic subjectivity. The overt romanticism of the book's lyrical refrain—"The voice of the sea is seductive; never ceasing, whispering, clamoring, murmuring, inviting the soul to wander for a spell in abysses of solitude; to lose itself in mazes of inward contemplation" (57)—finds a psychological correlative in the book's description of Edna's susceptibility to moods—feelings that also lose the protagonist in "mazes of inward contemplation." This discourse of the emotions surfaces early in the text in a scene that depicts one summer's night of marital discord between the Pontelliers and that recounts in some detail Edna's response to it. The reader's introduction to Edna's emotional character reads this way: "An indescribable oppression, which seemed to generate in some unfamiliar part of her consciousness, filled her whole being with vague anguish. It was like a shadow, like a mist passing over her soul's summer day. It was strange and unfamiliar; it was a mood. She did not sit there inwardly upbraiding her husband, lamenting at the Fate, which had directed her footsteps to the path which they had taken. She was just having a good cry all to herself. The mosquitos made merry over her. . . . The little stinging imps succeeded in dispelling a mood which might have held her there in the darkness half the night longer" (49).

Here, as in *The Story of Avis*, the female protagonist's potential to experience complex and deep emotion is translated into a rhetoric of mood saturated with romantic overtones: Edna's mood emerges from some hidden and "unfamiliar" part of her consciousness and possesses an intensity that is overwhelming and enchanting. Yet in a departure from her precursor, Chopin also suggests how romantic conventions of mood can steep the self in paralyzing forms of self-preoccupation and emotional self-mystification. The description above begins to point to such meanings by having Edna construe her "indescribable oppression" in a register of the emotions provided by romanticism; that is, as a set of overpowering feelings that are inwardly generated, undefinable, and spellbinding. The novel's omniscient narration suggests, however, that to define the self's emotions this way is to separate them from a specific causality—in this case from the anger and spousal resentment that inspired Edna's "mood" in the first place—and to estrange them from those origins. Indeed, Edna's mood becomes knowable to her precisely because it is constituted by "vague anguish" and *not* by the affective processes of "inwardly upbraiding her husband" and "lamenting" at "Fate." Thus this first account of Edna's discovery of her mood points subtly to the ways in which a romantic vocabulary of interiority can foster a belief in privatized, generalized, and ultimately enigmatic forms of psychological suffering. Divorced from a social context and concrete origins, Edna's mood indeed functions like the novel's "voice of the sea": it "invites the soul to wander for a spell in abysses of solitude."

Later sections of the novel reveal that, once ensconced in the explanatory mechanism of mood, Edna can process only the outcomes but never the causes of her feelings. In Chopin's novel, in other words, mood describes a condition of emotional confusion that Edna is unable to move beyond. During Edna's period of apprenticeship to her art she wavers between "the days when she was very happy without knowing why . . . happy to be alive and breathing" and "the days when she was unhappy, she did not know why—when it did not seem worthwhile to be glad or sorry, to be alive or dead" (109).[46] In a similar vein the narrator speaks of the many periods when "Edna stayed indoors and nursed a mood with which she was becoming too familiar for her own comfort and peace of mind. It was not despair; but it seemed to her as if life were passing by, leaving its promise broken and unfulfilled" (127). Through such descriptions Chopin exhibits the limits of a discourse of mood as romantic agony: the terminology of mood enables Edna to comprehend her situation in terms of some sketchy apprehension of romantic desire and longing, but it stalls her ability to search for these feelings' concrete origins and social meanings.

The discourse of moods in *The Awakening* brings with it another variety of disablement: Edna's romantic enactment of female selfhood is construed by the men around her as a sign not of emergent individualism, but of innate female weakness. Alcée Arobin, Edna's high-society lover, harnesses Edna's moods to his self-interest by using them in the service of his love-making. As the narrator says, Alcée makes himself attractive to Edna by displaying "good-humored subservience," "tacit adoration," and by remaining "ready at all times to submit to her moods, which were as often kind as they were cold" (133). When Léonce Pontellier becomes concerned that his wife is "growing a little unbalanced mentally," he procures the advice of the family physician, Dr. Mandelet, who offers the following diagnosis of Edna's condition: "Woman, my dear friend, is a very peculiar and delicate organism—a sensitive and highly organized woman, such as I know Mrs. Pontellier to be, is especially peculiar. . . . Most women are moody and whimsical. This is some whim of your wife, due to some cause or causes which you and I needn't try to fathom" (119). In the thought of Dr. Mandelet, women's moods should not be taken too seriously, nor should their "causes" be plumbed, because they are an innate characteristic and evanescent expression of, it is implied, the inferior sex. Thus it is with perspicacity and irony that Chopin uncovers the fundamental likeness between the book's romantic and patriarchal readings of Edna's moods: Edna's reverential attention to her feelings and the doctor's dismissive stance toward them share common ground in their disregard of and disinterest in their socially specific origins.

Conclusion

In conclusion, I want to return to my earlier question about the title of Louisa May Alcott's novel and summarize my response to the set of interests Alcott and other women writers explored through their discussions of mood. Alcott, it seems, chose the title *Moods* because she sensed that culturally created ideas about emotion played a key role in underwriting and naturalizing gendered social roles and their accompanying modes of interiority. In taking on moods as her subject, Alcott tried to revise a tradition of domestic emotional ideals by injecting it with a powerful does of American romantic ideology, notably Ralph Waldo Emerson's. If middle-class women were going to be freed from the prescriptive mandates of smiles and cheer, they had to learn first, Alcott's novel suggests, that their "whims" contained signifying purposes that transcended the evangelical and moral interpretations of antebellum domestic writers. What this chapter has shown is that Alcott was far from alone in her efforts.

In the post-Civil War period middle-class women writers, who, in many cases, were themselves choosing literary lives over maternal careers, moved to rescript the habitually smiling face of domestic emotion by reaching out to romantic ideas of artistic selfhood that had been in circulation for nearly a century. To continue Mary Kelley's observation about women's transforming professional identities, when middle-class women writers sought to reinvent themselves as individuals and artists and to put behind them the legacy of the woman writer as domestic moralist or professional hack, they gravitated toward romantic concepts of genius that posited a "deep" inner life and one, more often than not, traversed by vacillating and "fertile" moods. In their time Ward and Chopin were criticized for portraying these emotional tendencies in their heroines. One contemporary reviewer of *The Story of Avis* called the book "morbid through and through" and added, "the author represents unhealthy and abnormal moods of mind and emotions as being normal and typical."[47] *The Awakening* called forth similar diatribes: it was referred to as a "picture of soul-dissection" that was "morbid" and "unhealthily introspective."[48] For many twentieth-century critics influenced by post-Freudian concepts of inner conflict and sexual desire, it is precisely these features of the texts—the characters' various "moods of mind and emotions"—that qualify them for reconsideration as important if not unforgettable works of women's psychological realism.

In this chapter I have tried to show how the emotional "deepening" of the female subject in mid- to late nineteenth-century women's writing arose not from writers' unprecedented insights into universal conflicts in human nature nor from a changing social climate that, in the post-Civil War era, suddenly enabled women writers to talk about them. Rather this chapter argues that, in a time when middle-class women writers sought to move their representations of female interior life beyond sentimentality, they did so by drawing on romantic literary conventions that had supplied Anglo-American male writers with a language of emotional power, spontaneity, and depth for nearly a century. The white middle-class woman writer who wanted to represent the female self as an artistically inspired and emotionally profound individual took hold of a pre-Freudian idiom—a romantic language of "moods"—as a means of expressing these previously unrecognized potentials.

Notes

1   See *Diagnostic and Statistical Manual of Mental Disorders, Fourth Edition* (Washington, D.C.: American Psychiatric Association, 1994), 768.

2   For historical usage of the term *mood*, I draw on the *Oxford English Dictionary*.

3   See *Diagnostic and Statistical Manual of Mental Disorders, Third Edition—Revised* (Washington, D.C.:

American Psychiatric Association, 1987). Here the category once called "affective disorders" is re-classified as "mood disorders." The label "affective disorders" came to be seen as an inadequate term for mental illnesses which involve "prolonged" changes in emotional states, such as major depression and bipolar disorder. I want to thank Marc Riess for sharing with me his knowledge of psychiatric methods of classification.

4   See Martin, *The Woman in the Body: A Cultural Analysis of Reproduction* (Boston: Beacon Press, 1987), 113–38.

5   The term is from Faludi's wide-ranging discussion of the cultural politics of gender in *Backlash: The Undeclared War Against American Women* (New York: Doubleday, 1991).

6   Some of this politics of reversal is exhibited in Janice Delaney, Mary Jane Lupton, and Emily Toth, *The Curse: A Cultural History of Menstruation* (Urbana: University of Illinois Press, 1976).

7   Martin, *Woman in the Body*, 113–38.

8   Gottlieb, "American Premenstrual Syndrome: A Mute Voice," *Anthropology Today* 4 (1988): 10–13. For another interesting discussion of the cultural symbolism and political uses of women's moods, see Carol Tavris, *The Mismeasure of Women* (New York: Simon and Schuster, 1992).

9   Gottlieb, "American Premenstrual Syndrome," 13.

10 See Susman, *Culture as History: The Transformation of American Society in the Twentieth Century* (New York: Pantheon, 1984), 271–85.

11 The chapter uses the following editions of these texts: Louisa May Alcott, *Moods*, ed. Sarah Elbert (New Brunswick, N.J.: Rutgers University Press, 1991); Elizabeth Stuart Phelps, *The Story of Avis*, ed. Carol Farley Kessler (New Brunswick, N.J.: Rutgers University Press, 1985); Kate Chopin, *The Awakening*, ed. Sandra M. Gilbert (New York: Penguin Books, 1983). All subsequent references to these editions will appear parenthetically in the text.

12 For two important examples, see Jane Tompkins, *Sensational Designs: The Cultural Work of American Fiction, 1790–1860* (New York: Oxford University Press, 1985), and the introduction in *Provisions: A Reader from Nineteenth-Century American Women*, ed. Judith Fetterley (Bloomington: Indiana University Press, 1985).

13 See Ryan, *The Empire of the Mother: American Writing about Domesticity, 1830–1869* (New York: Harrington Park Press, 1985).

14 As quoted by Anne Firor Scott in "The Ever Widening Circle: The Diffusion of Feminist Values from the Troy Female Seminary," *History of Education Quarterly* (Spring 1979): 21.

15 For the sake of clarity, the mother (1815–1852) will be referred to as Elizabeth Stuart Phelps, and the daughter (1844–1911) will be referred to as Elizabeth Stuart Phelps Ward.

16 Elizabeth Stuart Phelps (pseudonym H. Trusta), "The Angel over the Right Shoulder: Or, The Beginning of the New Year," reprinted in Fetterley, *Provisions*, 203–15; and Phelps, *The Tell-Tale: Or, Home Secrets Told By Old Travellers* (Boston: Phillips, Sampson, and Company, 1853). Further references to these editions will be cited parenthetically in the text.

17 Divergent interpretations of the "real" ending of this story can be found in Carol Holly, "Shaming the Self in 'The Angel over the Right Shoulder,'" *American Literature* 60 (March 1988): 42–60, and in Fetterley, *Provisions*, 203–09.

18 Carol Farley Kessler makes a similar claim in her essay "A Literary Legacy: Elizabeth Stuart Phelps, Mother and Daughter," *Frontiers* 5 (1981): 28–33. Whereas Kessler reads Marion Gray as a woman motivated "by a passion for creative activity," I argue that she is presented as a student and intellectual, a bluestocking. The elder Phelps was still far from defining the creative woman in artistic terms; this shift would be tested in the writing of her daughter.

19 See Catharine Beecher and Harriet Beecher Stowe, *American Women's Home: Or, Principles of Domestic Science* (Hartford, Conn.: Stowe-Day Foundation, 1987). Further references to this edition appear parenthetically in the text.

20 See "Cheerfulness," in William A. Alcott, *The Young Wife; Or, Duties of Women in the Marriage Relation* (Boston: George W. Light, 1837), 4. Subsequent references to this edition appear parenthetically in the text.

21 See Betty Friedan, *The Feminine Mystique* (New York: Bantam Doubleday, 1983), 47.

22 Ibid., 64.

23 There is still much to be discovered about the emotional prescriptions connected to the ideology of "true womanhood." On middle-class women and grief, see Karen Halttunen, *Confidence Men and Painted Women: A Study of Middle-Class Culture in America, 1830–1870* (New Haven: Yale University Press, 1982); on love, see Karen Lystra, *Searching the Heart: Women, Men, and Romantic Love in Nineteenth-Century America* (New York: Oxford University Press, 1989); on emotion and gender

roles, see Peter N. Stearns, "Girls, Boys, and Emotions: Redefinitions and Historical Change," *Journal of American History* 80 (June 1993): 36–73.

24   For a densely documented portrayal of the lives and writing of mid-nineteenth-century women, see Kelley, *Private Woman, Public Stage: Literary Domesticity in Nineteenth-Century America* (New York: Oxford University Press, 1984).

25   See Elizabeth Stuart Phelps Ward, *Chapters from a Life* (Boston: Houghton Mifflin, 1896), 12–13.

26   Ibid., 13.

27   Ibid., 12, 14.

28   See Austin Phelps, *A Memorial of the Author*, in Elizabeth Stuart Phelps [H. Trusta], *The Last Leaf from Sunny Side* (Boston: Phillips, Sampson, 1853), 66. Further references to this work appear parenthetically in the text.

29   For a suggestive discussion of Elizabeth Stuart Phelps Ward's literary identifications with her mother, see Alfred Habegger, *Gender, Fantasy, and Realism in American Literature* (New York: Columbia University Press, 1982), 51.

30   Information about Phelps's life must be gleaned from Austin Phelps, *A Memorial of the Author*, and Elizabeth Stuart Phelps Ward, *Chapters from a Life*. There is some discussion of the Phelps family, albeit not wholly flattering, in Ann Douglas, *The Feminization of American Culture* (New York: Avon, 1977).

31   See Pfister, *The Production of Personal Life: Class, Gender, and the Psychological in Hawthorne's Fiction* (Stanford: Stanford University Press, 1991).

32   *The Journals of Louisa May Alcott*, ed. Madeleine Stern (Boston: Little, Brown, 1989), 147.

33   *The Selected Letters of Louisa May Alcott*, ed. Joel Myerson, Daniel Shealy, and Madeleine Stern (Boston: Little, Brown, 1987), 110.

34   See Emerson, *Selected Essays*, ed. Larzer Ziff (New York: Penguin Books, 1982), 179.

35   See Barbara Sicherman, "Reading *Little Women*: The Many Lives of a Text," in *U.S. History as Women's History: New Feminist Essays*, ed. Linda Kerber, Alice Kessler-Harris, and Kathryn Kish Sklar (Chapel Hill: University of North Carolina Press, 1995), 255.

36   See Emily Dickinson, *Final Harvest*, ed. Thomas H. Johnson (Boston: Little, Brown, 1961), 22.

37   Amos Bronson Alcott, *Journals*, ed. Odell Shepard (Boston: Little, Brown, 1938), 173. See entries for Mar. 16, 1846, and Feb. 7, 1847. Whether Louisa's mother, Abigail Alcott, derived her sense of mother-daughter likeness from her husband's or her own observations, she implicated herself as the source of Louisa's uneven temper, tying it to a depression she suffered when Louisa was *in utero*: "I was suffering," Abigail writes in her diary, "under one of those periods of mental depression which women are subject to during pregnancy, and I had been unusually so with Louisa—which accounts to me for many of her peculiarities and moods of mind, rather uncommon for a child of her age." Amos Bronson Alcott, *Journals*, 145. See entry for July 26, 1842.

38   As quoted in Karen Halttunen, "The Domestic Drama of Louisa May Alcott," *Feminist Studies* 10 (Summer 1984): 235. An excellent study of the emotional designs of Alcott's *Little Women* can be found in Judith Fetterley, "*Little Women*: Alcott's Civil War," *Feminist Studies* 5 (Summer 1979). Fetterley provides a related analysis of Alcott's *Behind a Mask* in "Impersonating 'Little Women': The Radicalism of Alcott's *Behind a Mask*," *Women's Studies* 10 (1983): 1–14.

39   Emerson, *Selected Essays*, 288–89.

40   Ibid., 292. For philosophical studies which examine Emerson's use of a discourse of moods see Stanley Cavell, *The Senses of Walden* (San Francisco: North Point Press, 1981): 123–60, and Anthony J. Cascardi, "The Logic of Moods: An Essay on Emerson and Rousseau," *Studies in Romanticism* 24 (Summer 1985): 223–37.

41   Helpful discussions of nineteenth-century conceptions of the artist can be found in Maurice Beebe, *Ivory Towers and Sacred Founts* (New York: New York University Press, 1964), and Raymond Williams, *Culture and Society, 1780–1950* (Harmondsworth, England: Penguin, 1963). On women, genius, and artistry, see Christine Battersby, *Gender and Genius: Towards a Feminist Aesthetics* (Bloomington: Indiana University Press, 1989).

42   Zaretsky, *Capitalism, the Family, and Personal Life* (New York: Harper & Row, 1976), 59.

43   See Wordsworth, *The Prelude: A Parallel Text*, ed. J. C. Maxwell (New Haven: Yale University Press, 1981). Subsequent references to this edition (the 1850 version of Wordsworth's poem) appear parenthetically in the text. For the relevant passage, see book II, lines 303–13.

44   Emerson, *Selected Essays*, 259.

45   See Ward, *Chapters from a Life*, 64. In the same passage Ward credits Elizabeth Barrett Browning with the power of having "revealed to me my own nature" (64).

46 The narrator directs the reader's interpretation of this emotional reportage with the additional remark that "It was during such a mood [as the latter] that Edna hunted up [her friend] Mademoiselle Reisz" (109).

47 "New Books," *Philadelphia Inquirer* (Oct. 31, 1877), in Ward, *Story of Avis*, ed. Kessler, 273.

48 See contemporary reviews in Chopin, *The Awakening*, ed. Margaret Culley (New York: Norton, 1976), 145–53.

Chapter 12

Carolyn Kay Steedman

STORIES

T**HIS [CHAPTER] IS ABOUT LIVES** lived out on the borderlands, lives for which the central interpretative devices of the culture don't quite work. It has a childhood at its centre – my childhood, a personal past – and it is about the disruption of that fifties childhood by the one my mother had lived out before me, and the stories she told about it. Now, the narrative of both these childhoods can be elaborated by the marginal and secret stories that other working-class girls and women from a recent historical past have to tell.

This [chapter], then, is about interpretations, about the places where we rework what has already happened to give current events meaning. It is about the stories we make for ourselves, and the social specificity of our understanding of those stories. The childhood dreams recounted in this book, the fantasies, the particular and remembered events of a South London fifties childhood do not, by themselves, constitute its point. We all return to memories and dreams like this, again and again; the story we tell of our own life is reshaped around them. But the point doesn't lie there, back in the past, back in the lost time at which they happened; the only point lies in interpretation. The past is re-used through the agency of social information, and that interpretation of it can only be made with what people know of a social world and their place within it. It matters then, whether one reshapes past time, re-uses the ordinary exigencies and crises of all childhoods whilst looking down from the curtainless windows of a terraced house like my mother did, or sees at that moment the long view stretching away from the big house in some richer and more detailed landscape. All children experience a first loss, a first exclusion; lives shape themselves around this sense of being cut off and denied. The health visitor repeated the exclusion in the disdainful language of class, told my mother exactly what it was she stood outside. It is [my proposition] that that specificity of place and politics has to be reckoned with in making an account of anybody's life, and their use of their own past.

My mother's longing shaped my own childhood. From a Lancashire mill town and a working-class twenties childhood she came away wanting: fine clothes, glamour, money; to be what she wasn't. However that longing was produced in her distant childhood, what she actually wanted were real things, real entities, things she materially lacked, things that a culture and a social system withheld from her. The story she told was about this wanting, and it remained a resolutely social story. When the world didn't deliver the goods, she held the world to blame. In this way, the story she told was a form of political analysis, that allows a political interpretation to be made of her life.

Personal interpretations of past time – the stories that people tell themselves in order to explain how they got to the place they currently inhabit – are often in deep and ambiguous conflict with the official interpretative devices of a culture. This [story] is organized around a conflict like this, taking as a starting point the structures of class analysis and schools of cultural criticism that cannot deal with everything there is to say about my mother's life. My mother was a single parent for most of her adulthood, who had children, but who also, in a quite particular way, didn't want them. She was a woman who finds no place in the iconography of working-class motherhood that Jeremy Seabrook presents in *Working Class Childhood*, and who is not to be found in Richard Hoggart's landscape. She ran a working-class household far away from the traditional communities of class, in exile and isolation, and in which a man was not a master, nor even there very much. Surrounded as a child by the articulated politics of class-consciousness, she became a working-class Conservative, the only political form that allowed her to reveal the politics of envy.

Many of these ambiguities raise central questions about gender as well as class, and the development of gender in particular social and class circumstances. So the usefulness of the biographical and autobiographical lies in the challenge [they] may offer to much of our conventional understanding of childhood, working-class childhood, and little-girlhood. In particular, [they] challenge the tradition of cultural criticism in this country, which has celebrated a kind of psychological simplicity in the lives lived out in Hoggart's endless streets of little houses. It can help reverse a central question within feminism and psychoanalysis, about the reproduction of the desire to mother in little girls, and replace it with a consideration of women who, by refusing to mother, have refused to reproduce themselves or the circumstances of their exile. The personal past that this [chapter] deals with can also serve to raise the question of what happens to theories of patriarchy in households where a father's position is not confirmed by the social world outside the front door. And the story of two lives that follows points finally to a consideration of what people – particularly working-class children of the recent past – come to understand of themselves when all they possess is their labour, and what becomes of the notion of class-consciousness when it is seen as a structure of feeling that can be learned in childhood, with one of its components a proper envy, the desire of people for the things of the earth. Class and gender, and their articulations, are the bits and pieces from which psychological selfhood is made.

*

I grew up in the 1950s, the place and time now located as the first scene of Labour's failure to grasp the political consciousness of its constituency and its eschewal of socialism in favour of welfare philanthropism.[1] But the left had failed with my mother long before the 1950s. A working-class Conservative from a traditional Labour background, she shaped my childhood by the stories she carried from her own, and from an earlier family history. They were stories designed to show me the terrible unfairness of things, the subterranean culture of longing for that which one can never have. These stories can be used now to show my mother's dogged search, using what politics came to hand, for a public form to embody such longing.

Her envy, her sense of the unfairness of things, could not be directly translated into political understanding, and certainly could not be used by the left to shape an articulated politics of class. What follows offers no account of that particular political failure. It is rather an attempt to use that failure, which has been delineated by historians writing from quite different perspectives and for quite different purposes, as a device that may help to explain a particular childhood, and out of that childhood explain an individual life lived in historical time. This is not to say that this [chapter] involves a search for a past, or for what really happened.[2] It is about how people use the past to tell the stories of their life. So the evidence presented here is of a different order from the biographical; it is about the experience of my own childhood, and the way in which my mother re-asserted, reversed and restructured her own within mine.

Envy as a political motive has always been condemned: a fierce morality pervades what little writing there is on the subject. Fiercely moral as well, the tradition of cultural criticism in this country has, by ignoring feelings like these, given us the map of an upright and decent country. Out of this tradition has come Jeremy Seabrook's *Working Class Childhood* and its nostalgia for a time when people who were 'united against cruel material privations . . . discovered the possibilities of the human consolations they could offer each other', and its celebration of the upbringing that produced the psychic structure of 'the old working class'.[3] I take a defiant pleasure in the way that my mother's story can be used to subvert this account. Born into 'the old working class', she wanted: a New Look skirt, a timbered country cottage, to marry a prince.

The very devices that are intended to give expression to childhoods like mine and my mother's actually deny their expression. The problem with most childhoods lived out in households maintained by social class III (manual), IV and V parents is that they simply are not bad enough to be worthy of attention. The literary form that allows presentation of working-class childhood, the working-class autobiography, reveals its mainspring in the title of books like *Born to Struggle; Poverty, Hardship, But Happiness; Growing Up Poor in East London; Coronation Cups and Jam Jars* – and I am deeply aware of the ambiguities that attach to the childhood I recount. Not only was it not very bad, or only bad in a way that working-class autobiography doesn't deal in, but also a particular set of emotional and psychological circumstances ensured that at the time, and for many years after it was over and I had escaped, I thought of it as *ordinary*, a period of relative material ease, just like everybody else's childhood.

I read female working-class autobiography obsessively when I was in my twenties and early thirties (a reading that involved much repetition: it's a small corpus), and whilst I wept over Catherine Cookson's *Our Kate* I felt a simultaneous distance from the Edwardian child who fetched beer bare-footed for an alcoholic mother, the Kate of the title (I have to make it very clear that my childhood was really *not* like that). But it bore a relationship to a personal reality that I did not yet know about: what I now see in the book is its fine delineation of the feeling of being on the outside, outside the law; for Catherine Cookson was illegitimate.[4]

In 1928, when Kathleen Woodward, who had grown up in not-too-bad Peckham, South London, wrote *Jipping Street*, she set her childhood in Bermondsey, in a place of abject and abandoned poverty, 'practically off the map, derelict', and in this manner found a way, within an established literary form, of expressing a complexity of feeling about her personal past that the form itself did not allow.[5]

The tradition of cultural criticism that has employed working-class lives, and their rare expression in literature, had made solid and concrete the absence of psychological individuality – of subjectivity – that Kathleen Woodward struggled against in *Jipping Street*. 'In poor societies,' writes Jeremy Seabrook in *Working Class Childhood*

> where survival is more important than elaboration of relationships, the kind of ferocious personal struggles that lock people together in our own more leisured society are less known.[6]

But by making this distinction, the very testimony to the continuing reverberation of pain and loss, absence and desire in childhood, which is made manifest in the words of 'the old working-class' people that make up much of *Working Class Childhood*, is actually denied.

It would not be possible, in fact, to write a book called 'Middle Class Childhood' (this in spite of the fact that the shelves groan with psychoanalytic, developmental and literary accounts of such childhoods) and get the same kind of response from readers. It's a faintly titillating title, carrying the promise that some kind of pathology is about to be investigated. What is more, in *Working Class Childhood* the discussion of childhood and what our society has done to the idea of childhood becomes the vehicle for an anguished rejection of post-War materialism, the metaphor for all that has gone wrong with the old politics of class and the stance of the labour movement towards the desires that capitalism has inculcated in those who are seen as the passive poor. An analysis like this denies its subjects a particular story, a personal history, except when that story illustrates a general thesis; and it denies the child, and the child who continues to live in the adult it becomes, both an unconscious life, and a particular and developing consciousness of the meanings presented by the social world.

Twenty years before *Working Class Childhood* was written, Richard Hoggart explored a similar passivity of emotional life in working-class communities, what in *The Uses of Literacy* he revealingly called 'Landscape with Figures: A Setting' – a place where in his own memories of the 1920s and 1930s and in his description of similar communities of the 1950s, most people lacked 'any feeling that some change can, or indeed ought to be made in the general pattern of life'.[7] All of Seabrook's corpus deals in the same way with what he sees as 'the falling into decay of a life once believed by those who shared it to be the only admissible form that life could take'.[8] I want to open the door of one of the terraced houses, in a mill town in the 1920s, show Seabrook my mother and her longing, make him see the child of my imagination sitting by an empty grate, reading a tale that tells her a goose-girl can marry a king.

Heaviness of time lies on the pages of *The Uses of Literacy*. The streets are all the same; nothing changes. Writing about the structure of a child's life, Seabrook notes that as recently as thirty years ago (that is, in the 1950s, the time of my own childhood) the week was measured out by each day's function – wash-day, market-day, the day for ironing – and the day itself timed by 'cradling and comforting' ritual.[9] This extraordinary attribution of sameness and the acceptance of sameness to generations of lives arises from several sources. First of all, delineation of emotional and psychological selfhood has been made by and through the testimony of people in a central relationship to the dominant culture, that is to say by and through people who are not working class. This is an obvious point, but it measures out an immensely complicated and contradictory area of historical development that has scarcely yet been investigated. Superficially, it might be said that historians, failing to find evidence of most people's emotional or psycho-sexual existence, have simply assumed that there can't have been much there to find. Such an assumption ignores the structuring of late nineteenth- and early twentieth-century psychology and psychoanalysis, and the way in which the lived experience of the majority of people in a class society has been pathologized and marginalized. When the sons of the working class, who have made their earlier escape from this landscape of psychological simplicity, put so much effort into accepting and celebrating it, into delineating a background of uniformity and passivity, in which pain, loss, love, anxiety and desire are washed over with a patina of stolid emotional sameness, then something important, and odd, and possibly promising of startling revelation, is actually going on. [It is a] refusal of a complicated psychology to those living in conditions of material distress [. . .]

The attribution of psychological simplicity to working-class people also derives from the positioning of mental life within Marxism:

> Mental life flows from material conditions. Social being is determined above all by class position – location within the realm of production. Consciousness and politics, all mental conceptions spring from material forces and the relations of production and so reflect these class origins.

This description is Sally Alexander's summary of Marx's 'Preface to a Contribution to the Critique of Political Economy', and of his thesis, expressed here and elsewhere, that 'the mode of production of material life conditions the general process of social, political and mental life'.[10] The attribution of simplicity to the mental life of working people is not, of course, made either in the original, nor in this particular critique of it. But like any theory developed in a social world, the notion of consciousness as located within the realm of production draws on the reality of that world. It is in the 'Preface' itself that Marx mentions his move to London in the 1850s as offering among other advantages 'a convenient vantage point for the observation of bourgeois society', and which indeed he did observe, and live within, in the novels he and his family read, in family theatricals, in dinner-table talk: a mental life apparently much richer than that of the subjects of his theories. Lacking such possessions of culture, working-class people have come to be seen, within the field of cultural criticism, as bearing the elemental simplicity of class-consciousness and little more.

Technically, class-consciousness has not been conceived of as *psychological* consciousness. It has been separated from 'the empirically given, and from the psychologically describable and explicable ideas that men form about their situation in life', and has been seen rather as a possible set of reactions people might have to discovering the implications of the position they occupy within the realm of production.[11] Theoretical propositions apart though, in the everyday world, the term *is* used in its psychological sense, is generally and casually used to describe what people have 'thought, felt and wanted at any moment in history and from any point in the class structure'.[12] Working-class autobiography and people's history have been developed as forms that allow the individual and collective expression of these thoughts, feelings and desires about class societies and the effect of class structures on individuals and communities. But as forms of analysis and writing, people's history and working-class autobiography are relatively innocent of psychological theory, and there has been little space within them to discuss the *development* of class-consciousness (as opposed to its expression), nor for understanding of it as a *learned* position, learned in childhood, and often through the exigencies of difficult and lonely lives.

Children present a particular problem here, for whilst some women may learn the official dimensions of class-consciousness by virtue of their entry into the labour market and by adopting forms of struggle and understanding evolved by men,[13] children, who are not located directly within the realm of production, still reach understandings of social position, exclusion and difference. At all levels, class-consciousness must be learned in some way, and we need a model of such a process to explain the social and psychological development of working-class children (indeed, of all children).

When the mental life of working-class women is entered into the realm of production, and their narrative is allowed to disrupt the monolithic story of wage-labour and capital and when childhood and childhood learning are reckoned with, then what makes the old story unsatisfactory is not so much its granite-like *plot*, built around exploiter and exploited, capital and proletariat, but rather its *timing*: the precise how and why of the development of class-consciousness. But if we do allow an unconscious life to working-class children, then we can perhaps see the first loss, the earliest exclusion (known most familiarly to us as the oedipal crisis) brought forward later, and articulated through an adult experience of class and class relations.

An adult experience of class does not in any case, as Sally Alexander has pointed out, 'produce a shared and even consciousness', even if it is fully registered and articulated.[14] This uneven and problematic consciousness (which my mother's life and political conviction represents so clearly) is one of the subjects of this [chapter]. A perception of childhood experience and understanding used as the lineaments of adult political analysis, may also help us see under the language and conflicts of class, historically much older articulations – the subjective and political expressions of radicalism – which may still serve to give a voice to people who know that they do not have what they want, who know that they have been cut off from the earth in some way.[15]

The attribution of psychological sameness to the figures in the working-class landscape has been made by men, for whom the transitions of class are at once more ritualized than they are for women, and much harder to make. Hoggart's description of the plight of the 'scholarship boy' of the thirties and forties, and the particular anxiety afflicting those in the working class

> who have been pulled one stage away from their original culture and have not
> the intellectual equipment which would then cause them to move on to join the
> 'declassed' professionals and experts[16]

makes nostalgic reading now in a post-War situation where a whole generation of escapees occupies professional positions that allow them to speak of their working-class origins with authority, to use them, in Seabrook's words 'as a kind of accomplishment'.[17] By the 1950s the division of the educational establishment that produced Hoggart's description were much altered and I, a grammar-school girl of the 1960s, was sent to university with a reasonably full equipment of culture and a relative degree of intellectual self-awareness. Jeremy Seabrook, some eight years older than me and at Cambridge in the late fifties, sat with his fellow travelers from working-class backgrounds 'telling each other escape stories, in which we were all picaresque heroes of our own lives'.[18]

But at the University of Sussex in 1965, there were no other women to talk to like this, at least there were none that I met (though as proletarianism was fashionable at the time, there were several men with romantic and slightly untruthful tales to tell). And should I have met a woman like me (there must have been some: we were all children of the Robbins generation), we could not have talked of escape except within a literary framework that we had learned from the working-class novels of the early sixties (some of which, like *Room at the Top*, were set books on certain courses); and that framework was itself ignorant of the material stepping-stones of our escape: clothes, shoes, make-up. We could not be heroines of the conventional narratives of escape. Women are, in the sense that Hoggart and Seabrook present in their pictures of transition, without class, because the cut and fall of a skirt and good leather shoes can take you across the river and to the other side: the fairy-tales tell you that goose-girls may marry kings.

The fixed townscapes of Northampton and Leeds that Hoggart and Seabrook have described show endless streets of houses, where mothers who don't go out to work order the domestic day, where men are masters, and children, when they grow older, express gratitude for the harsh discipline meted out to them. The first task is to particularize this profoundly a-historical landscape (and so [I] detail a mother who was a working woman and a single parent, and a father who wasn't a patriarch). And once the landscape is detailed and historicized in this way, the urgent need becomes to find a way of theorizing the result of such difference and particularity, not in order to find a description that can be universally applied (the point is *not* to say that all working-class childhoods are the same, nor that experience of them produces unique psychic structures) but so that the people in exile, the inhabitants of the long streets, may start to use the autobiographical 'I', and tell the stories of their life.

*

There are other interpretative devices for my mother which, like working-class auto-biographies of childhood, make her no easier to see. Nearly everything that has been written on the subject of mothering (except the literature of pathology, of battering and violence) assumes the desire to mother; and there are feminisms now that ask me to return Persephone-like to my own mother, and find new histories of my strength. When I first came across Kathleen Woodward's *Jipping Street*, I read it with the shocked astonishment of one who had never seen what she knows written down before. Kathleen Woodward's mother of the 1890s was the one I knew: mothers were those who told you how hard it was to have you, how long they were in labour with you ('twenty hours with you', my mother frequently reminded me) and who told you to accept the impossible contradiction of being both desired and a burden; and not to complain.[19] This ungiving endurance is admired by working-class boys who grow up to write about their mother's flinty courage. But the daughter's silence on the matter is a measure of the price you pay for survival. I don't think the baggage will ever lighten, for me or my sister. We were born, and had no choice in the matter; but we were burdens, expensive, never grateful enough. There was nothing we could do to pay back the debt of our existence. 'Never have children dear,' she said; 'they ruin your life.' Shock moves swiftly across the faces of women to whom I tell this story. But it is *ordinary* not to want your children, I silently assert; normal to find them a nuisance.

I read the collection *Fathers: Reflections by Daughters*, or Ann Oakley's *Taking It Like a Woman*[20] and feel the painful and familiar sense of exclusion from these autobiographies of middle-class little-girlhood and womanhood, envy of those who belong, who can, like Ann Oakley, use the outlines of conventional romantic fiction to tell a life story. And women like this, friends, say: but it was like that for me too, my childhood was like yours; my father was like that, my mother didn't want me. What they cannot bear, I think, is that there exists a poverty and marginality of experience to which they have no access, structures of feeling that they have not lived within (and would not want to live within: for these are the structures of deprivation). They are caught then in a terrible exclusion, an exclusion from the experience of others that measures out their own central relationship to the culture. The myths tell their story, the fairy-tales show the topography of the houses they once inhabited. The psychoanalytic drama, which uses the spatial and temporal structures of all these old tales, permits the entry of such women to the drama itself. Indeed, the psychoanalytic drama was constructed to describe that of middle-class women (and as drama it does of course describe all such a woman's exclusions, as well as her relationship to those exclusions, with her absence and all she lacks lying at the very heart of the theory). The woman whose drama psychoanalytic case-study describes in this way never does stand to one side, and watch, and know she doesn't belong.

What follows is largely concerned with how two girl children, growing up in different historical periods, got to be the women they became. The sense of exclusion, of being cut off from what others enjoy, was a dominant sense of both childhoods, but expressed and used differently in two different historical settings. This detailing of social context to psycho-logical development reveals not only difference, but also certain continuities of experience in working-class childhood. For instance, many recent accounts of psychological develop-ment and the development of gender, treat our current social situation as astonishingly new and strange:

> On the social/historical level . . . we are living in a period in which mothers are increasingly living alone with their children, offering opportunities for new psychic patterns to emerge. Single mothers are forced to make themselves subject to their children; they are forced to invent new symbolic roles . . . The child cannot position the mother as object to the father's law, since in single parent households her desire sets things in motion.[21]

But the evidence of some nineteenth- and twentieth-century children [. . .] shows that in their own reckoning their households were often those of a single female parent, sometimes because of the passivity of a father's presence, sometimes because of his physical absence. Recent feminisms have often, as Jane Gallop points out in *The Daughter's Seduction*, endowed men with 'the sort of unified phallic sovereignty that characterises an absolute monarch, and which little resembles actual power in our social, economic structure'.[22] We need a reading of history that reveals fathers mattering in a different way from the way they matter in the corpus of traditional psychoanalysis, the novels that depict the same familial settings and in the bourgeois households of the fairy-tales.

A father like mine dictated each day's existence; our lives would have been quite different had he not been there. But he didn't *matter*, and his singular unimportance needs explaining. His not mattering has an effect like this: I don't quite believe in male power; somehow the iron of patriarchy didn't enter into my soul. I accept the idea of male power intellectually, of course (and I will eat my words the day I am raped, or the knife is slipped between my ribs; though I know that will not be the case: in the dreams it is a woman who holds the knife, and only a woman can kill).

Fixing my father, and my mother's mothering, in time and politics can help show the creation of gender in particular households and in particular familial situations at the same time as it demonstrates the position of men and the social reality represented by them in particular households. We need historical accounts of such relationships, not just a longing that they might be different.[23] Above all, perhaps, we need a sense of people's complexity of relationship to the historical situations they inherit. In *Family and Kinship in East London*, the authors found that over half the married women they interviewed had seen their mothers within the preceding twenty-four hours, and that 80 per cent had seen them within the previous week. Young and Willmott assumed that the daughters wanted to do this, and interpreted four visits a week on average as an expression of attachment and devotion.[24] There exists a letter that I wrote to a friend one vacation from Sussex, either in 1966 or in 1967, in which I described my sitting in the evenings with my mother, refusing to go out, holding tight to my guilt and duty, knowing that I *was* her, and that I must keep her company; and we were certainly not Demeter and Persephone to each other, nor ever could be, but two women caught by a web of sexual and psychological relationships in the front room of a council house, the South London streets stretching away outside like the railway lines that brought us and our history to that desperate and silent scene in front of the flickering television screen.

Raymond Williams has written about the difficulty of linking past and present in writing about working-class life, and the result of this difficulty in novels that either show the past to be a regional zone of experience in which the narrator cancels her present from the situation she is describing, or which are solely about the experience of flight. Writing like this, comments Williams, has lacked 'any sense of the continuity of working class life, which does not cease just because the individual [the writer] moves out of it, but which also itself changes internally'.[25]

This kind of cancellation of a writer's present from the past may take place because novels – stories – work by a process of temporal revelation: they move forward in time in order to demonstrate a state of affairs. The novel that works in this way employs contingency, that is, it works towards the revelation of something not quite certain, but *there*, nevertheless, waiting to be shown by the story,[26] and the story gets told without revealing the shaping force of the writer's current situation.

The highlighting not just of [this] subject matter [. . .] but also of the possibilities of written form it involves, is important, because the construction of the account [. . .] has something to say about the question that Raymond Williams has raised, and which is largely to do with the writing of stories that aren't central to a dominant culture. My mother cut herself off from the old working class by the process of migration, by retreat from the North to a southern country with my father, hiding secrets in South London's long streets. But she carried with her her childhood, as I have carried mine along the lines of embourgeoisement and state education. In order to outline these childhoods and the uses we put them to, the structure of psychoanalytic case-study – the narrative form that Freud is described as inventing – is used in this [chapter].[27] The written case-study allows the writer to enter the present into the past, allows the dream, the wish or the fantasy of the past to shape current time, and treats them as evidence in their own right. In this way, the narrative form of case-study shows what went into its writing, shows the bits and pieces from which it is made up, in the way that history refuses to do, and that fiction can't.[28] Case-study presents the ebb and flow of memory, the structure of dreams, the stories that people tell to explain themselves to others. [. . .]

But something else has to be done with these bits and pieces, with all the tales that are told, in order to take them beyond the point of anecdote and into history. To begin to construct history, the writer has to do two things, make two movements through time. First of all, we need to search backwards from the vantage point of the present in order to appraise things in the past and attribute meaning to them. When events and entities in the past have been given their meaning in this way, then we can trace forward what we have already traced backwards, and make a history.[29] When a history is finally written, events are explained by putting them in causal order and establishing causal connections between them. But [. . .] this [chapter] does not make a history (even though a great deal of historical material is presented). For a start, I simply do not know enough about many of the incidents described to explain the connections between them. I am unable to perform an act of historical explanation in this way.

This tension between the stories told to me as a child, the diffuse and timeless structure of the case-study with which they are presented, and the compulsions of historical explanation, is no mere rhetorical device. There is a real problem, a real tension here that I cannot resolve (my inability to resolve it is part of the story). [The stories told] aren't stories in their own right: they exist in tension with other more central ones. In the same way, the processes of working-class autobiography, of people's history and of the working-class novel cannot show a proper and valid culture existing in its own right, underneath the official forms, waiting for revelation. Accounts of working-class life are told by tension and ambiguity, out on the borderlands. The story – my mother's story, a hundred thousand others – cannot be absorbed into the central one: it is both its disruption and its essential counterpoint: this is a drama of *class*.

But visions change, once any story is told; ways of seeing are altered. The point of a story is to present itself momentarily as complete, so that it can be said: it does for now, it will do; it is an account that will last a while. Its point is briefly to make an audience connive in the telling, so that they might say: yes, that's how it was; or, that's how it could have been. So now, the words written down, the world is suddenly full of women waiting, as in Ann Oakley's extraordinary delineation of

the curiously impressive image of women as always waiting for someone or something, in shopping queues, in antenatal clinics, in bed, for men to come home, at the school gates, by the playground swing, for birth or the growing up of children, in hope of love or freedom or re-employment, waiting for the future to liberate or burden them and the past to catch up with them.[30]

The other side of waiting is wanting. The faces of the women in the queues are the faces of unfulfilled desire; if we look, there are many women driven mad in this way, as my mother was. This is a sad and secret story, but it isn't just hers alone.

*

What historically conscious readers may do with this [chapter] is read it as a Lancashire story, see here evidence of a political culture of 1890–1930 carried from the Northwest, to shape another childhood in another place and time. They will perhaps read it as part of an existing history, seeing here a culture shaped by working women, and their consciousness of themselves as workers. They may see the indefatigable capacity for work that has been described in many other places, the terrifying ability to *get by*, to cope, against all odds. Some historically conscious readers may even find here the irony that this specific social and cultural experience imparted to its women: 'No one gives you anything,' said my mother, as if reading the part of 'our mam' handed to her by the tradition of working-class auto-biography. 'If you want things, you have to go out and work for them.' But out of that tradition I can make the dislocation that the irony actually permits, and say: 'If no one will write my story, then I shall have to go out and write it myself.'

The point of being a Lancashire weaver's daughter, as my mother was, is that it is *classy*: what my mother knew was that if you were going to be working class, then you might as well be the best that's going, and for women, Lancashire and weaving provided that elegance, that edge of difference and distinction. I'm sure that she told the titled women whose hands she did when she became a manicurist in the 1960s where it was she came from, proud, defiant: look at me. (Beatrix Campbell has made what I think is a similar point about the classiness of being a miner, for working-class men.)[31]

This is a [chapter] about stories and [. . .] about *things* (objects, entities, relationships, people), and the way in which we talk and write about them: about the difficulties of metaphor. Above all, it is about people wanting those things, and the structures of political thought that have labelled this wanting as wrong. [. . .]

Notes

1   Gareth Stedman-Jones, 'Why is the Labour Party in a Mess?' in *Languages of Class: Studies in English Working Class History, 1832–1982*, Cambridge University Press, Cambridge, 1983, pp. 239–56. Beatrix Campbell surveys critiques of the 1950s in *Wigan Pier Revisited*, Virago, 1984, pp. 217–34. See also James Hinton, *Labour and Socialism: A History of the British Labour Movement, 1867–1974*, Wheatsheaf, Brighton, 1983, pp. 182–7.

2   'What actually happened is less important than what is felt to have happened. Is that right?' says Ronald Fraser to his analyst, and his analyst agrees. Ronald Fraser, *In Search of a Past*, Verso, 1984, p. 95.

3   Jeremy Seabrook, *Working Class Childhood*, Gollancz, 1982, pp. 23–7, 33.

4   Catherine Cookson, *Our Kate*, Macdonald, 1969.

5   Kathleen Woodward, *Jipping Street* (1928), Virago, 1983.

6   Seabrook, op. cit., p. 140.

7   Richard Hoggart, *The Uses of Literacy*, Penguin, 1959, p. 91.

8   Jeremy Seabrook, *The Unprivileged* (1967), Penguin, 1973, Foreword.

9   ibid., pp. 202–3.

10   Sally Alexander, 'Women, Class and Sexual Difference', *History Workshop Journal*, 17 (1984), pp. 125–49. Karl Marx, 'Preface to "A Contribution to the Critique of Political Economy" ' (1859), *Early Writings*, The Pelican Marx Library, Penguin, 1975, pp. 424–8.

11   George Lukas, *History and' Class Consciousness*, Merlin Press, 1968, pp. 46–82, especially pp. 50–5. See also Eric Hobsbawm, 'Notes on Class Consciousness', in *Worlds of Labour*, Weidenfeld and Nicolson, 1984, pp. 15–32.

12   Lukas, op. cit., p. 51.

13   Pauline Hunt, *Gender and Class Consciousness*, Macmillan, 1980, pp. 171–9. A direct and simple learning isn't posited here; but it is the workplace and an existing backdrop of trade-union organization that provides for the expression of women's class consciousness.

14   Alexander, op. cit., p. 131.

15   Carolyn Steedman, 'Exclusions', in *Landscape for a Good Woman: A Story of Two Lives*, Rutgers University Press, New Brunswick NJ, 1987, pp. 119–121; and Gareth Stedman-Jones, 'Rethinking Chartism' in Stedman-Jones, op. cit., pp. 90–178.

16   Hoggart, op. cit., p. 293.

17   Jeremy Seabrook, *What Went Wrong?*, Gollancz, 1978, pp. 260–61.

18   ibid., p. 262.

19   To be told how difficult it was to give birth to you is an extremely common experience for all little girls, and as John and Elizabeth Newson point out in *Seven Years Old in the Home Environment*, Allen & Unwin, 1976, pp. 186–7, chaperonage, and the consequent amount of time girls spend in adult company, is likely to make such topics of conversation accessible to them. But the punishment and the warning involved in telling girl children about the difficulties their birth presented to their mother is rarely written about. But see Carolyn Steedman, *The Tidy House: Little Girls Writing*, Virago, 1982, pp. 34–5, 145–7.

20   Ursula Owen (ed.), *Fathers: Reflections by Daughters*, Virago, 1983. Ann Oakley, *Taking It Like a Woman*, Cape, 1984.

21   E. Ann Kaplan, 'Is the Gaze Male?', in Ann Snitow *et al.* (eds), *Desire: The Politics of Female Sexuality*, Virago, 1984, p. 335.

22   Jane Gallop, *Feminism and Psychoanalysis: The Daughter's Seduction*, Macmillan, 1982, p. xv.

23   For recent arguments concerning the necessity of historicization, see Jane Lewis, 'The Debate on Sex and Class', *New Left Review*, 149 (1985), pp. 108–20.

24   Michael Young and Peter Willmott, *Family and Kinship in East London*, Penguin, 1962, pp. 44–61.

25   Raymond Williams, *Politics and Letters*, NLB/Verso, 1979, pp. 271–2. See also Seabrook, *What Went Wrong?*, p. 261, where the same process is described: a working-class life, ossified by time, enacted in 'symbolic institutional ways, by those who teach in poor schools, or who write novels and memoirs about a way of life which they have not directly experienced since childhood'.

26   Seymour Chatman, *Story and Discourse: Narrative Structure in Fiction and Film*, Cornell University Press, 1978, pp. 45–8.

27   See Steven Marcus, 'Freud and Dora: Story, History, Case-History', in *Representations*, Random House, New York, 1976, pp. 247–310 for the argument that Freud invented a new narrative form in his writing of the 'Dora' case. See also Carolyn Steedman, 'Histories', in *Landscape for a Good Woman: A Story of Two Lives*, Rutgers University Press, New Brunswick NJ,1987, pp. 130–34.

28   For a brief discussion of the way in which historical writing masks the processes that brought it into being, see Timothy Ashplant, 'The New Social Function of Cinema', *Journal of the British Film Institute, 79/80* (1981), pp. 107–9, and Hayden White, 'The Value of Narrativity in the Representation of Reality', *Critical Inquiry*, 7:1 (1980), pp. 5–27.

29   Paul Ricoeur, *Time and Narrative*, University of Chicago Press, Chicago, 1984, pp. 118, 157.

30   Ann Oakley, *From Here to Maternity: Becoming a Mother*, Penguin, 1981, p. 11.

31   Campbell, op. cit., pp. 97–115.

Bibliography

Alexander, Sally, 'Women, Class and Sexual Difference', *History Workshop Journal*, 17 (1984), pp. 125–49

Ashplant, Timothy, 'The New Social Function of Cinema', *Journal of the British Film Institute*, 79/80 (1981), pp. 107–9

Berger, John, *About Looking*, Writers & Readers, 1980.

Campbell, Beatrix, *Wigan Pier Revisited*, Virago, 1984

Chatman, Seymour, *Story and Discourse: Narrative Structure in Fiction and Film*, Cornell University Press, New York, 1978

Cookson, Catherine, *Our Kate*, Macdonald, 1969

Fraser, Ronald, *In Search of a Past*, Verso, 1984

Freud, Sigmund, 'Fragment of an Analysis of a Case of Hysteria ("Dora")', (1905) The Pelican Freud Library, vol. 8, *Case Histories I*, Penguin, 1977, pp. 27–164

—— 'Family Romances' (1908), *Standard Edition of the Collected Works*, vol. 9, Hogarth Press, 1959, pp. 234–41

—— 'Some Character Types Met With in Psychoanalytic Work' (1916), *Standard Edition of the Collected Works*, vol. 14, Hogarth Press, 1957

—— 'From the History of an Infantile Neurosis (the "Wolf Man")' (1918), The Pelican Freud Library, vol. 9, *Case Histories II*, Penguin, 1979, pp. 287–90

Gallop, Jane, *Feminism and Psychoanalysis: The Daughter's Seduction*, Macmillan, 1982

Hinton, James, *Labour and Socialism: A History of the British Labour Movement, 1867–1974*, Wheatsheaf, 1983

Hobsbawm, Eric, *Worlds of Labour*, Weidenfeld & Nicolson, 1984

Hoggart, Richard, *The Uses of Literacy*, Penguin, 1959

Hunt, Pauline, *Gender and Class Consciousness*, Macmillan, 1980

Kaplan, E. Ann, 'Is the Gaze Male?', in Ann Snitow *et al.* (eds), *Desire: The Politics of Female Sexuality*, Virago, 1984

Lewis, Jane, 'The Debate on Sex and Class', *New Left Review*, 149 (1985), pp. 108–20

Lukas, George, *History and Class Consciousness*, Merlin Press, 1968

Marcus, Steven, 'Freud and Dora: Story, History, Case-History', in *Representations: Essays on Literature and Society*, Random House, New York, 1976, pp. 247–310

Marx, Karl, 'Preface to "A Contribution to the Critique of Political Economy" ' (1859), *Early Writings*, Pelican Marx Library, Penguin, 1975, pp. 424–8

Newson, John and Elizabeth, *Seven Years Old in the Home Environment*, Allen & Unwin, 1976

Oakley, Ann, *From Here to Maternity: Becoming a Mother*, Penguin, 1981

—— *Taking It Like a Woman*, Cape, 1984

Owen, Ursula, (ed.), *Fathers: Reflections by Daughters*, Virago, 1983

Ricoeur, Paul, *Time and Narrative*, University of Chicago Press, Chicago, 1984

Seabrook, Jeremy, *City Close-Up*, Penguin, 1973

—— *The Unprivileged* (1967), Penguin, 1973

—— *What Went Wrong?*, Gollancz, 1978

—— *Working Class Childhood*, Gollancz, 1982

Stedman-Jones, Gareth, *Languages of Class: Studies in English Working Class History, 1832–1982*, Cambridge University Press, Cambridge, 1983

Steedman, Carolyn, *The Tidy House: Little Girls Writing*, Virago, 1982

—— *Landscape for a Good Woman: A Story of Two Lives*, Rutgers University Press, New Brunswick NJ, 1987

White, Hayden, 'The Value of Narrativity in the Representation of Reality', *Critical Inquiry*, 7:1 (1980), pp. 5–27

Williams, Raymond, *Politics and Letters*, NLB/Verso, 1979

Woodward, Kathleen, *Jipping Street* (1928), Virago, 1983

Young, Michael, and Willmott, Peter, *Family and Kinship in East London*, Penguin, 1962

PART 2

Considering culture

Introduction

ADOPTING DIVERSE PERSPECTIVES, topics and methodologies, the chapters in Part 2 of this reader illustrate core aspects of a cultural emotion studies. In focusing on emotions, they offer new understandings of key themes taken up by cultural studies such as nation, the public sphere, popular culture, subjectivity, social identity, discourse and power relations. Together, they demonstrate what emotions 'do' and how they contribute to knowledge production.

The broad intellectual/political project of cultural studies has emphasised the significance of radical contextuality in investigating social phenomena. To this end, the majority of essays in Part 2 examine specific emotions, including fear, hate, care, shame and grief. All chapters conduct their explorations in relation to specific historical and cultural circumstances ranging from globalisation and contemporary definitions of citizenship and nationhood in Britain, the United States of America and Australia, to the encounter between the West and Arab Muslim perspectives, and the aftereffects of 11 September 2001 (9/11). The chapters also consider the impact of emotions on the everyday lives and practices of people, particularly in terms of discourse, subject construction, and theatrical, cinematic and televisual representation.

Cultural studies' commitment to strategic political intervention is evidenced in the degree to which all the chapters analyse emotions in relation to challenging inequities based on, and constituting, gender, race, ethnicity, class, sexuality and nationality. With the exception of nationality, we have not framed the sections in Part 2 on the basis of identity categories. However, it is important to note that issues of social identity permeate the chapters. Due to the long-standing historical association between women and emotion, feminist studies, of necessity, began to engage with emotions. As a result, gender is a pivotal component in a number of chapters (Probyn, Gobert, L. Williams, Pribram, Mernissi). Many of the essays deal explicitly with the intersection of emotion and race or ethnicity (Appadurai, Ahmed, Harding, Dyson, Probyn, Mernissi, Butler) and, in the process, establish that race, ethnicity and class are inseparable. Additional chapters explore the ways in which sexuality can be productive in better understanding the operations of emotionality (Berlant, Probyn).

As relational phenomena, emotions need to be considered not as properties of the individual but as cultural practices that help give social formations their meanings and power. The chapters in Part 2 examine some of the ways that emotions are part of the reproduction of social structures and institutions, performing vital functions in the organization of social, political, economic and ideological practices. Emotions are reciprocally constituting cultural and individual phenomena that matter in understanding the meanings of power relations in everyday life. It is the interactivity of emotions with subjectivity, identity, meaning production and social formations that renders a cultural approach to emotions significant.

Confounding nationhood

Within cultural studies, considerable attention has focused on challenging 'the closed borders of the nation-state' by theorising national identities as complex, changing, and fragmented entities (Gilroy 1997: 340). From an essentialist perspective, national identity has been understood as a unified sameness, bringing with it a sense of safety and security which is threatened by difference (Gilroy 1997: 313). In contrast, cultural studies scholars have argued that nation, nationhood and national identity do not occur naturally but, rather, are historical and cultural formations which provide socially and culturally constructed forms of collective organisation and identification (Barker 2008: 252). Further, practices of cultural representation are crucial to the reproduction of national identity, attempting to unify 'deep internal divisions and differences' (Hall 1992: 297). Such divisions exist when concepts of nationality intersect with other identity categories, especially as nations become increasingly pluralised.

Nation and national unity are constructed through narratives which represent the traditions and meanings of nationhood through stories, symbols and rituals (Bhabha 1990). Nation-building practices often involve the idea of 'a foundational myth of collective origin' and link national identity with 'a pure, original people or "folk" tradition' in order to establish a collective commonality founded in sameness (Barker 2008: 253).

The chapters included in 'Confounding nationhood' use emotion as a critical concept with which to generate new understandings of the reproduction of national identities and racism. All three essays are concerned with the contingency and fragmentation of the concept, 'the nation' and the ways national identities are produced through emotion, specifically fear and hate. They each explore the operation of emotions in constituting boundaries – inside/outside, inclusion/exclusion – and notions of 'the other' as a source of fear and insecurity. Arjun Appadurai argues that there are dual pressures facing contemporary nation-states: the external demands of globalisation and the internal forces of cultural minorities. Using a range of examples but concentrating most on India, he argues that fear, resulting from both pressures, has led to increased ethnic violence. Sara Ahmed and Jennifer Harding focus on the pressure from within, examining hate and fear among racial groups in the UK. Ahmed considers white hate groups who adhere to the idea of Britain as a 'white' nation and, in doing so, construct non-whites into 'hated bodies'. Harding takes up the perspective of refugees in London, exploring how they are 'identified' – made into identities – in contrast to how they might identify themselves.

In 'Fear of small numbers', Appadurai asks why there is so much fear of and rage about national minorities across the globe, whether they are constituted by race, ethnicity or religion, and despite their small numbers and relative weakness in political and military terms. In order to tackle this question, he introduces three competing categories: national identity, cultural majorities and cultural minorities. He argues that fear of cultural minorities is the result of the changing relationship between cultural majorities and national identity in an era of globalisation and human rights for minorities. The desire is intensifying for cultural majorities to be linked to the idea of the nation in a relationship based on exclusive equivalency. The existence of even a small minority within the national imaginary is seen as an intolerable deficit in the purity of the national whole. In an era of globalisation, migration and increasing hybridity, in which national identity progressively faces the threat of decline, minorities excite fear and rage precisely because they make the majority feel like a majority rather than 'a whole and uncontested ethnos' (chapter 14: 237).

Drawing on a range of international examples, but focusing in some detail on the Hindu majority and Muslim minority in India, Appadurai argues that it is precisely the smallness of the gap between national totality, majority dominance and minority presence that produces the anxiety of incompleteness, creating the fear and frustration that drives those forms of degradation and ethnic violence that shock us most. For majorities obsessed with the singularity, completeness and purity of the national whole, minorities are a constant reminder of its failure or impossibility.

However, Appadurai reminds us, even if historically present in a specific national context, fear and hatred must be mobilised and remobilised through 'the discourses of crisis and the practices of violence' (245). His work references the historical dominance and power of nationhood and national identity but, under the dual pressures from without and within in changing circumstances, he also reveals their intense fragility. Appadurai's chapter shows us how reconceptualising politics and theory through the prism of emotions enables us to engage with both familiar and new problems in altered terms.

In her chapter, 'The organisation of hate', Ahmed discusses race in relation to threats to an imagined nation and identifies racism as a politics of hatred. She considers how hate works to 'secure collectives' and 'align some subjects with some others and against other others', that is, how identities are brought into being through hate (251).

Drawing on elements of Marxist and psychoanalytical theory, she puts forward a model of hate as an 'affective economy', which involves the idea that emotions 'do not positively inhabit *anybody* or *anything*, meaning that "the subject" is simply one nodal point in the economy, rather than its origin or destination' (254). Ahmed argues that hate is not contained in an individual subject, body, object or sign. Rather, hate circulates among them, producing the effects that it does through their interactions. In other words, hate is involved in the very negotiation of boundaries between selves and other, and in the distinctions between communities. Ahmed's contention that emotion is neither fixed nor located inside the individual subject provides an understanding of the fluidity and contingency of collective identities such as nationality.

Recalling Grossberg's work on affective investment (chapter 3), Ahmed points out that '[a]ttending to the politics of hate allows us to address the question of how subjects and others become *invested*' in cultural norms that establish the bodies and subjectivities of certain social collectives in specific and, in this instance, hateful ways (chapter 14: 261). She argues that emotions like hate are a means by which both individual subjects and entire communities within a nation are established but, additionally, such emotions are also the instruments that 'unmake' the world of the other through affective pain.

In 'Emotional subjects: language and power in refugee narratives', Harding discusses connections between emotion, subjectivity and power relations in oral history narratives collected as part of a project documenting the contributions of refugees to the history, culture and economy of London. She considers the role of fear in constituting refugee identities and framing public responses to immigrant strangers, as well as efforts to link more 'positive' emotions to refugees and, thereby, include them in the heritage of the city.

She examines how the use of 'emotion words' in discourse on refugees and asylum seekers works to define and constrain them, simplifying, universalising and marginalising the value of their experiences. Analysing interview transcripts, she delineates how 'emotion talk' has participated in the production of specific subjectivities, collective identities and power relations.

'Emotion talk', as part of discourse on asylum, indicates how refugee subjects *ought* to feel about themselves and how disadvantaged other minorities feel about them, working to secure collective identities and trace boundaries between some groups of subjects and, in Ahmed's terms, other others. In particular, Harding discusses how fear works to define and limit refugees and vulnerable others, while being perceived as disempowering by refugee subjects themselves. In contrast, refugees seek to define themselves in the terminology of anger, rage and passionate political commitments to social justice. This essay contributes to an understanding of how emotions work to define the boundaries that constitute unequal relations and subordinated identities.

Transforming the public

The notion of a public sphere, defined in relation to and dependent on a private sphere, has a long history in Western social and political thought, dating from ancient Greek and Roman society, where it was understood to be a realm of free association between free citizens in which citizens discussed 'issues of common interest' (Thompson 1995: 120). The domestic sphere, regarded as the realm of physical reproduction, enabled the citizen to move from the private world of the mundane and natural to the public world of culture and achievement (Habermas cited in Slater 1998: 138–139). While the public sphere depended on the private sphere, the latter was considered to have little intrinsic value.

Modernity transformed some of these relations in ways that are pertinent for a cultural emotion studies. The ancient world located all economic activity in the private household, carried out by women and slaves. Modernity, in contrast, divides economic activity between a public world of work, production and enterprise, and a private world of domestic life and reproduction, usually understood in terms of a gendered division of labour. Modernity also saw the 'bourgeois idealization' of the private sphere, made up of family and affective ties, as a 'haven' from the public world, along with the development of the ideal of romantic love and the notion that 'the central human relationship was an entirely private relation of love between two people', detached from social and public considerations (inconceivable in the premodern world) (Slater 1998: 146).

A further meaning of the public/private distinction has been made between general and particular interests. In late modernity, the public has come to be understood as 'the part of life that is shared, visible, and accountable'. Public life is governed by 'common norms, rules, and values' (Slater 1998: 150). The public is the realm that is controlled by the state but the state also constantly encroaches on the private. The private has been understood as that part of social life, which is 'most intimate, inward, and concerned with private identity'. The private retains the aura of being 'the space for the exercise of free-will in an increasingly public world' (ibid.).

Cultural studies practitioners have been engaged in debate about the nature, pertinence and limitations of a 'public sphere'. They have variously responded to Habermas' conceptualisation of the public sphere as 'a space for debate based on conversational equality', that is, a space emerging in bourgeois society, that 'mediates between civil society and the state', where 'the public organises itself' and where 'public opinion is formed' (Barker 2008: 455). The importance of this conceptualisation is that it has focused attention on areas outside of formal political life. However, it is problematic because it is an idealised construct that assumes a unified public. An alternative conceptualisation highlights multiple public spheres organised around communities defined by race, gender, sexuality, class and religion that are sometimes overlapping, sometimes separate (Smith 2001).

The three chapters included in 'Transforming the public' all examine the role of emotion in public discourse, considering how attention to emotion transforms conceptualisations of what 'the public' is or might become. Yet all three offer strikingly different perspectives and outcomes. Lauren Berlant and Michael Eric Dyson take up diverse aspects of the relationship between the state and its citizenry in the USA. Elspeth Probyn considers the relationship between various communities of citizens in Australia. Each author foregrounds how emotional analysis sheds light on shifting and contested notions of the public, in an era in which the reliance on a clear-cut public/private divide has destabilised, becoming provisional and problematic.

In the 'Intimate public sphere', Berlant discusses citizenship in the USA as always in process, 'continually being produced out of a political, rhetorical, and economic struggle over who will count as "the people" and how social membership will be measured and valued' (chapter 16: 292). Her work is influenced by Nietzsche's theory of *ressentiment* which describes a 'cultural ethos and politics of reproach, rancor, moralism, and guilt' (Brown 1995: 26), and by Wendy Brown's contention that argument for state and legal protections based on the subordination of identity categories 'entrenches the injury–identity connection it [overtly] denounces', leading to a politics of victimisation, powerlessness and *ressentiment* (Brown 1995: 21).

Berlant is most concerned with the development of what she calls the intimate public sphere, which entails 'collapsing the political and the personal' (chapter 16: 280) so that suffering and individual trauma have come to define and limit contemporary meanings of citizenship in the USA. She argues that this new intimate public is the result of conservative ideology, beginning with and following the Reagan years. The right has been so successful, Berlant argues, that there is now 'no public sphere' in the USA, 'no context of communication and debate that makes ordinary citizens feel that they have a common public culture' (281). Instead, contemporary American citizenship is defined by the sentimental, family orientated acts and values of private individuals, as well as in the public rhetoric of trauma, pain and suffering.

Berlant's concern is that in privatising citizenship and, thereby, displacing an earlier version of the public sphere and legitimate political discussion, the ability to recognise and debate forms of power, hierarchy and inequity are also displaced. Citizenship is rendered 'a category of feeling irrelevant to practices of hegemony or sociality in everyday life' (286), in which the national public forum is no longer an appropriate or even possible site of struggle over racial, sexual, economic and other inequalities.

In contrast to Berlant, Dyson finds considerable merit in taking up a 'private' concept such as caring or empathy, deploying it in a public context and, thereby, redefining its social and political meanings and value. He turns his attention to the disastrous US government response on behalf of its citizens, particularly its African-American citizens, in the wake of Hurricane Katrina in 2005. Focusing on rapper Kanye West's nationally televised and subsequently much-debated comment that 'George Bush doesn't care about black people', Dyson reframes it as a question: what does it mean to say that George W. Bush, as a public figure in his capacity as head of state, cares or fails to care about black people?

In reaction to West's comments, one of those who defended George W. Bush was his father, the former president: 'I know this president and I know he does care . . . that's what's in his heart.' However, Dyson points out that the issue is 'a claim not about Bush's personal life, but rather his professional life' (305). Resorting to what resides in someone's heart has become the standard defence for public figures accused of speech or behaviour that is racially offensive. Indeed, it is an essentialist claim, appealing to the notion of deep, authentic emotional truth. Instead, Dyson argues, we must pay attention to distinctions such as those between personal caring, moral caring and political caring.

'Structures of care' and 'sentiments of empathy' must also be understood as functions of public policies and practices (304). As such, it is a legitimate claim, an assessable statement, and a political necessity to speak about 'an uncaring Bush regime' (307). Deploying public concepts of care and empathy becomes another means of holding public officials accountable for the success or failure of a government in its responsibilities to its citizenry.

While Berlant and Dyson examine the relationship between a state and its citizens, Probyn considers the public in terms of the relationship between divergent, subordinated communities within a society and how they might interrelate productively. In 'Shaming theory, thinking dis-connections: feminism and reconciliation', she reflects on the Reconciliation initiative in Australia between Aboriginal peoples and white Australians. Probyn's interest is in utilising the concept of shame on the part of feminists, gays and lesbians to acknowledge disconnections as well as connections with Aboriginal peoples. Thinking in terms of connections, of the links between forms of otherness, is the more comfortable position. Shame, however, allows for the possibility of acknowledging disconnections, of coming to terms with the reality of the racist past and its ongoing present.

Thinking connections is about knowing; thinking disconnections is about acknowledging ignorance. 'Reconciliation must be for whites a challenge to *learn*, and not to *know*' (315; italics in original). For Probyn, it is shame that makes such learning possible. Shame marks the uneasiness of the shifting line between ignorance and knowledge: shame at knowing about past atrocities or shame at the carefully constructed edifice of public ignorance and denial. 'Being ashamed is painful, and an easy way out is to disengage from the affect, to distance oneself from the object of shame' (316).

Yet, Probyn argues, there is value in remaining on the shifting, painful line of shame. Although normally viewed as a negative emotion, Probyn is drawn to the possibility of utilising shame's intensity towards constructing conditions of dignity for specific publics on the part of other publics. She uses the concept of shame, and the humility that comes with it, as a politically productive way of relating to others. Shame's incorporation into social and political domains enables this emotion to become a means of recognising differences as well as commonalities between identity groups, of acknowledging one's own ignorance and of indicating respect for indigenous peoples.

Popular arts

Popular culture, including arts and the media, has played a central role in cultural studies since its inception. One of the founding strategies of cultural studies was to counteract the overvalorisation of 'high art' (for instance, F. R. Leavis and *The Great Tradition*) and the dismissal of most forms of mass or popular culture. For many members of the Frankfurt School, for example, mass art and entertainment were viewed largely as a means of duping the masses. An early cultural studies counterargument was put forward by Stuart Hall and Paddy Whannel in *The Popular Arts* (1964). Hall and Whannel made the case for a hybrid form that negotiated between high art and mass culture. They labelled this intermediary category popular art, and initiated arguments explaining why it was both valuable and necessary to give it critical attention.

Developed further under the multifaceted concept of representation, popular media and arts have been pivotal to many cultural studies projects, for instance, its work on ideology. Popular culture has proven itself to be crucial ground for 'getting at' ideological configurations that explain the ideas and values of specific communities of viewers and, indeed, help construct their very subjectivities and identities. Representation is used in the dual sense of both *reflecting* and *affecting* the ways culturally situated audiences construct, understand and act in the worlds they inhabit.

Oddly, though, representational studies has paid relatively little attention to the ways emotions are represented in popular media and popular arts. Yet, such texts are particularly fertile sources for exploring the diverse, changing and contested meanings of emotions. Emotions have always been fundamental to how popular culture 'works' – that is, how it creates its impacts and meanings. Indeed, popular culture's complex, intricate deployments of emotion are arguably a primary means by which it remains 'popular'. As Grossberg notes, 'a large part of the struggle over popular culture concerns the ability of certain practices to have such [affective] effects' (1992: 79). Cultural theorists have moved towards the analysis of popular culture precisely because it has mass emotional appeal and resonance. As such, it matters. Political positions can be claimed, shaped or resisted through instances of felt popular culture.

The three chapters in 'Popular arts' investigate the intersection of emotion with theatre, film and television. In 'Dramatic catharsis, Freudian hysteria and the "Private theatre" of Anna O.', Darren Gobert links Freudian theory on psychoanalytic catharsis to contemporaneous theatrical theory of catharsis as purgation. He examines Aristotle's notion of theatrical *katharsis* and the philosopher's ambiguous and variously interpreted explanation of it: 'tragedy is defined by its ability to induce emotional *katharsis* through the incitement of pity and fear' (chapter 19: 321). The concept of catharsis as emotional purgation gained acceptance following an 1880 publication by theatrical and classics scholar, Jacob Bernays. Gobert argues that Bernays' interpretation becomes possible because of a more general cultural understanding of emotions as medically 'pathological' and 'pathogenic' and, therefore, requiring discharge, reflecting 'prevalent late-nineteenth century European ideas about the emotions and their association with irrationality' (324).

The same set of widely held assumptions about emotions that enables Bernays' reinterpretation of Aristotelian *katharsis* underlies Breuer's and Freud's development of the medical therapy of psychoanalysis. Emotions 'serve as a safety valve through which people discharge unconscious drives' (325). The failure to successfully discharge them results in psychic and physical illnesses such as hysteria, necessitating psychoanalysis' cathartic method of treatment. Gobert's point is that many of the suppositions concerning emotion in the late nineteenth and early twentieth centuries that have been attributed to Freud, and which live on in our present-day understandings, were 'more diffusely co-authored by his cultural context' (330). Gobert locates Breuer and Freud in their particular era, demonstrating the inherent instability and the cultural-historical specificity of varying concepts of emotion.

Turning to Breuer's and Freud's first and most famous hysteric, Anna O. (Bertha Pappenheim), Gobert describes psychoanalysis' cathartic method as a kind of narrative medicine. It is therapy as memory retrieval and release or, as Pappenheim coins it, the 'talking cure' (327). Repressed emotions are extracted from the unconscious by being spoken or 'staged'. Gobert indicates 'how a new set of assumptions about emotions makes possible a set of emotional experiences and expressions' (329). A new understanding of emotion rendered Bertha Pappenheim's illness both possible and intelligible, and enabled the construction of Breuer's and Freud's narrative of Anna O.

Linda Williams, in her chapter 'Melodrama revised', analyses how both emotion and action have served as integral aspects of Hollywood narrative film from its early days to the present. Yet, the role of emotion has been largely overlooked or dismissed as sentimentality aimed primarily at audiences of women. In contrast, action became linked to realism and 'supposedly masculine cultural values' (341); it is the latter which much of film studies has understood as the dominant form of popular cinema. But 'strong emotions that can move audiences to tears are not the special province of women', nor are they absent from films associated first or foremost with male audiences (339–340).

To make her argument, Williams reconsiders the category of melodrama not as a specific group of genres such as the woman's or family film but as a larger mode of narrativity that encompasses both emotion and action. This melodramatic mode, which includes the 'masculine' action genres of westerns, gangster films and cop films, constitutes 'the typical form of American popular narrative' (341). She elaborates the ways in which this extensive range of popular films and genres are characterised by the dialectic of pathos and action that seeks the dramatic revelation of moral virtue, innocence and justice.

The misclassification of melodrama as a sentimental, feminised form of excess has resulted in disregarding one of the most crucial aspects and fundamental appeals of popular film: 'its capacity to generate emotion in audiences' (337). Williams suggests that it is time to return to an understanding of moving pictures in both senses of the term: as movement in action and as the ability to move us emotionally.

In 'Cold comfort: emotion, television detection dramas, and *Cold Case*', Deidre Pribram considers a prevalent contemporary television category of programming – the police or detective drama – and investigates the way emotions and generic formulas interact to create its meanings. Utilising Raymond Williams' concept, structure of feeling, as the 'omissions and consequences' of the stated ideals of an era, Pribram examines representations of loss and consolation, which have played a central emotional role in the detective genre.

Yet, the detection genres have long been viewed as rational, masculine narrative forms that seek to circumscribe emotional discourses. Pribram argues that the series, *Cold Case*, in developing a structure based on two timeframes – past and present – foregrounds the victims of murder as dramatic and emotional personalities in more complex ways than is the generic norm. By focusing on the emotional repercussions of loss, *Cold Case* pushes at the boundaries of the generic formula and, in doing so, reveals much about both the ideological patterns and limitations of the genre.

The detection genres rely on a causal link between 'case solved', 'justice served' and 'comfort provided'. In accentuating the emotional impact of human loss, at times *Cold Case* unravels the generic chain of causality, failing to provide emotional reassurance or consolation. In Williams' terms, case solved and justice served become the stated ideals while the inability to provide reassurance or comfort are their omissions and consequences. Interweaving emotion analysis with the more established textual techniques of generic and ideological analysis allows us to more productively explore how narrative structures, like the police or detective drama, participate in the role of generating shared or contested cultural meanings.

Affecting subjects

Subjectivity has been a central area of investigation in cultural studies since the early 1990s, questioning the nature of the subject and of cultural identities (nationality, gender, sexuality, race and ethnicity). Cultural studies has become concerned with 'how we come to be the sorts of people we are' – that is, 'how we are produced as subjects' and 'how we identify with (or emotionally invest in) descriptions of ourselves as certain sorts of people' (Barker 2008: 11).

Cultural studies practitioners, along with others in the social sciences and humanities, have rejected the humanist/Enlightenment concept of the individual as a 'fully centred, unified individual, endowed with the capacities of reason, consciousness and action' (Hall 1992: 275). This humanist subject possesses a fixed inner core or identity, ontologically prior to his/her social existence. In contrast, the non-humanist subject is variously understood as decentred, contested, contingent, fractured, incomplete, and produced historically, discursively and relationally.

Hall suggests that 'a series of ruptures in the discourses of modern knowledge' – including Marxism, psychoanalysis, linguistic theory, the work of Foucault and feminism – have contributed to understandings of the late modern subject as fractured and decentred (1992: 285). The work of Marx and, later, Althusser, displaced the notion that there is 'a universal essence of Man', which is an attribute of each individual, and contributed to an understanding of the subject as historically specific, fractured and 'formed in ideology' (Hall 1992; Barker 2008: 221). Psychoanalysis and Freud's 'discovery' of the unconscious, further interpreted by Lacan, challenged the notion of the self as whole and unified, focusing instead on the development of self in relation to others and on the fundamental incompleteness of identity (Hall 1992). The work of structural linguist Ferdinand de Saussure led to a foregrounding of the role of language in constructing identities and realities. Language is seen not as a means of reflecting independent thoughts, essences and realities, but as a social system that pre-exists, and constitutes, the social world (ibid.). The significance of Foucault's work lies in its radical historicisation of the subject, its focus on modern disciplinary power, and its account of the subject 'as an effect' of discourse (Hall 2000: 23; Hall 1992). Feminism, as a theoretical critique and social movement, has undermined distinctions between public and private, inside and outside, and replaced the singularity and sameness implied by 'Mankind' with 'the question of sexual difference' (Hall 1992: 290).

To this rich heritage must also be added Judith Butler's performative theory of language and the subject (Butler 1990, 1992, 1993). Butler moves beyond Foucault's early analyses of subjectivity as a discursive production, which brings subjects into existence by providing subject positions from which they may speak, but has little to say about why individuals take up some subject positions and not others. Performativity is understood 'not as the act by which a subject brings into being what she/he names, but, rather, as the reiterative power of discourse to produce the phenomena that it regulates and constrains' (Butler 1993: 2). And, significantly, Butler's concept of gender performativity involves 'a linking of this process of "assuming" a sex with the question of *identification*, and with the discursive means by which the heterosexual imperatives enables certain sexed identifications and forecloses and/or disavows other identifications' (Butler 1993: 3).

These theoretical approaches present different, and sometimes conflicting, positions but all tend to present a decentred fragmented human subject and a contested notion of the individual. Subjectivity and identity, then, are seen not as fixed but rather as historically and culturally contingent, coming into existence and cohering through discourse in the narratives of self we construct and in those that are constructed for us.

The three chapters included in 'Affecting subjects' consider the role of emotions in producing subjectivities, identities and power differentials. They each examine the ways in which emotions are not individual but social and relational and, as such, involved in producing the boundary constituting self and others. The emotions experienced by a subject reveal something about relations with others and about cultural differences. As Butler suggests, when we speak of the subject we are not always speaking about the individual, since we are fundamentally social, involved in relations with others and constituted in 'cultural norms that precede and exceed us' (chapter 24: 399).

In 'Scheherazade goes West: different cultures, different harems', Fatima Mernissi uses emotion as an investigative tool to remind us of the boundaries and differences between cultures. Relating her experiences while on a book tour for *Dreams of Trespass: Tales of a Harem Girlhood*, Mernissi undertakes a comparative analysis of Eastern and Western conceptualisations of 'the harem'. In the West she finds that male fantasies about the harem centre on passive, obedient women who are always sexually available, evidenced in representations of them as idle, indoors and in 'embarrassingly vulnerable nudity' (372). Additionally, for Western men 'intellectual exchange with women is an obstacle to erotic pleasure' (369). In contrast, in the Eastern harem women are depicted as 'self-assertive, strong-minded, uncontrollable, and mobile' and 'cerebral confrontation with women is necessary to achieve orgasm' for men (372, 369).

To consider the ways in which cultures manage emotions differently in order to structure their erotic responses, Mernissi turns to the example of the late seventeenth- and early eighteenth-century French painter Ingres, noted for his portraits of harem women or odalisques. Focusing most specifically on jealousy, Mernissi asks why Madame Ingres (his first wife, Madeleine) was not offended, as a Muslim woman would have been, when Ingres began introducing odalisques into his paintings shortly after they were married and continued to paint them over many years. In describing this as Ingres' 'emotional problem' and insulting to his wife, Mernissi indicates that, from a Muslim perspective, there exists no similarly clear-cut distinction between professional and personal lives, as in the West (371).

Mernissi problematises the relationship between 'work' or 'art' versus the 'privacy' of marriage. For her, his paintings are part of his relationship with his wife and, as such, are troublesome. Mernissi's essay helps make Western customs and assumptions feel 'strange' – particularly in their reliance on a trouble-free public/private divide. She also indicates the ways that representations of the harem say less about a specific reality than about the subjectivities of the men who imagine them and about the women who are constructed by those imaginations. Mernissi's work demonstrates the epistemological possibilities of using emotion as an analytical tool to explore culturally differentiated subjectivities and to challenge racist and sexist assumptions.

In 'Malediction', Denise Riley explores how vindictive words and 'spoken injury' operate (chapter 23: 375). She considers different explanations for why injury may continue to be felt acutely for decades after an initial verbal attack. While the hurt is experienced as embedded within the subject, with a ferocious innerness, despite having come from outside as part of another's rage, she argues that, finally, it cannot be explained as either a linguistic or a psychic phenomenon. She frames her argument by posing the following questions: Is the felt hurt the product of the force of verbal assault – the full strength of another's rage? Or do malignant words resonate within their target because of the subject's vulnerability based on an earlier, perhaps deeply buried psychic wound? Does the hurt come from inside or outside? Do I speak (from the inside outwards) or am I spoken (from the outside inwards)?

Riley's essay is concerned with how malignant words, and the emotions they communicate and evoke, operate across a boundary between self and other, inside and outside, surface and depth. She denies these distinctions, refusing the 'synthetic alternatives' of either a psychic or a linguistic explanation (375). Instead, Riley contends that 'the deepest intimacy joins the supposedly linguistic to the supposedly psychic', in which neither is separable or to be subsumed one under the other (375, 384).

Emphasising the basic sociality of language, Riley notes that 'the cruel word' calls us into social being, 'if of a deathly kind' (381). Whether through expressions of hate or expressions of love, the linguistic interpellations by which we are 'accidentally spoken' are also always affective (385). Riley's work is of relevance to a cultural emotion studies because it considers the role of language and affect in subjectivity while refusing dualisms such as self/other, psychic/linguistic, inside/outside.

Judith Butler, in 'Violence, mourning, politics', searches for the possibility of political community in vulnerability, loss and grief, based on the kinds of subjectivities these emotions construct and reveal about ourselves. She argues that, in grief, one is undone by another, indicating how the relationality of subjectivity is at the core of grief. Butler points out that the loss of another has transformative effects on the one that has lost, since in the losing something is revealed about ourselves and how we are delineated through our ties to others. It is our ties to others that constitute who we are: 'I have lost "you" only to find that "I" have gone missing as well' (chapter 24: 388).

Butler suggests that what is lost is the 'relationality that is composed neither exclusively of myself nor you, but is to be conceived as *the tie* by which those terms are differentiated and related' (388; italics in original). That is, the self is made simultaneously distinct and inseparable from the other in the process of mourning. Grief is not something one 'has' but, rather, is a mode of relationality. We are both constituted and dispossessed by our relations. While Biddle argued that shame is an emotion that works to distinguish self from other, Butler analyses grief in terms of the ways it undermines that very distinction.

Butler goes on to make the case that grief is not privatising and depoliticising, as people tend to think. On the contrary, it may furnish a sense of community by bringing to the fore relational ties 'that have implications for theorising fundamental dependency and ethical responsibility' (388). She contends that because we are fundamentally social, responsibility and ethics cannot be thought apart from relational ties. Using the example of the transformation in American national identity that might have occurred, but did not, following the losses and changed international relations of 9/11, she continues to see the potentialities of grief as a resource for politics. The difficulty is that some lives remain more vulnerable and more grievable than others, ignoring the reality that, in the context of global violence, loss has made a tenuous 'we' out of all of us.

Bibliography

Barker, C. (2008) *Cultural Studies. Theory and Practice.* 3rd Edition. London: Sage.

Bhabha, H. (1990) *Nation and Narration.* London and New York: Routledge.

Brown, W. (1995) *States of Injury: Power and Freedom in Late Modernity.* Princeton, NJ: Princeton University Press.

Butler, J. (1990) *Gender Trouble: Feminism and the Subversion of Identity.* New York and London: Routledge.

—— (1992) 'Contingent Foundations: Feminism and the Question of "Postmodernism" ', in

J. Butler and J. Scott (eds) *Feminists Theorize the Political*. New York and London: Routledge.

—— (1993) *Bodies That Matter: On the Discursive Limits of 'Sex'*. New York and London: Routledge.

Gilroy, P. (1997) 'Diaspora and the Detours of Identity', in K. Woodward (ed.) *Identity and Difference*. Thousand Oaks, CA, and London: Sage/Open University.

Grossberg, L. (1992) *Bringing It All Back Home: Essays on Cultural Studies*. Durham, NC: Duke University Press.

Hall, S. (1992) 'The Question of Cultural Identity' in S. Hall, D. Held and T. McGrew (eds) *Modernity and its Futures*. Cambridge: Polity Press.

—— (2000) 'Who Needs "Identity"?', in P. du Gay, J. Evans and P. Redman (eds) *Identity: A Reader*. London/Thousand Oaks/New Delhi: Sage.

Hall, S. and Whannel, P. (1964) *The Popular Arts*. London: Hutchinson Educational.

Leavis, F. R. (1948) *The Great Tradition*. London: Chatto and Windus.

Mernissi, F. (1994) *Dreams of Trespass: Tales of Harem Girlhood*. Reading, MA: Addison-Wesley.

Slater, D. (1998) 'Public/private', in C. Jenks (ed.) *Core Sociological Dichotomies*. London/Thousand Oaks/New Delhi: Sage.

Smith, P. (2001) *Cultural Theory*. Oxford: Blackwell.

Thompson, J. (1995) *The Media and Modernity: A Social Theory of the Media*. Cambridge: Polity Press.

V CONFOUNDING NATIONHOOD

Chapter 13

Arjun Appadurai

FEAR OF SMALL NUMBERS

THERE IS A BASIC PUZZLE surrounding rage about minorities in a globalizing world. The puzzle is about why the relatively small numbers that give the word minority its most simple meaning and usually imply political and military weakness do not prevent minorities from being objects of fear and of rage. Why kill, torture, or ghettoize the weak? This may be a relevant question for ethnic violence against small groups at any time in history (Hinton 2002). Here, I seek to engage this puzzle with special reference to the era of globalization, especially from the late 1980s until the present.

Fear of the weak

The comparative historical question does not, in any case, apply to all of human history, since minorities and majorities are recent historical inventions, essentially tied up with ideas about nations, populations, representation, and enumeration which are no more than a few centuries old. They are also today *universal* ideas, since the techniques of counting, classification, and political participation that underlie the ideas of majority and minority are everywhere associated with the modern nation-state.

The idea of a majority is not prior to or independent from that of a minority, especially in the discourses of modern politics. Majorities are as much the product of enumeration and political nomination as are minorities. Indeed, majorities need minorities in order to exist, even more than the reverse.

Hence, the first step toward addressing why the weak, in so many ethnonationalist settings, are feared, is to go back to the "we/they" question in elementary sociological theory. In this theory, the creation of collective others, or them's, is a requirement, through the dynamics of stereotyping and identity contrast, for helping to set boundaries and mark off the dynamics of the we. This aspect of the theory of the scapegoat, the stereotype, and the other grows out of that brand of symbolic interactionism that was made explicit in the works of Cooley and Mead, but it is also entirely central to the core of Freud's understanding of group dynamics, including his classic essay on the narcissism of minor differences (which I discuss later in the chapter).

In this sociological tradition, the understanding of the process of we-making is limited, since it is seen as a mechanical by-product of the process by which theys are created. The process requires simple contrasts and sharp boundaries which help to consolidate "we" identities. The making of we's, of collective selves, is given short shrift in this tradition, since it is regarded as sociologically natural and unrequiring of deeper thought. Mainstream sociological theory, especially in regard to group formation, does explore the role of conflict (as in the tradition of Simmel) or of religion (in the tradition of Durkheim) or of antagonistic interest (as in the tradition of Marx) in the building of collective identities. But even though these traditions do cast some light on the formation of we identities as a partially independent process, without reference to the we/they dialectic, they do not tend to be deeply reflective about the formation of what I have elsewhere called "predatory identities" (2000a).

Predatory identities

I define as predatory those identities whose social construction and mobilization require the extinction of other, proximate social categories, defined as threats to the very existence of some group, defined as a we. Predatory identities emerge, periodically, out of pairs of identities, sometimes sets that are larger than two, which have long histories of close contact, mixture, and some degree of mutual stereotyping. Occasional violence may or may not be parts of these histories, but some degree of contrastive identification is always involved. One of these pairs or sets of identities often turns predatory by mobilizing an understanding of itself as a threatened majority. This kind of mobilization is the key step in turning a benign social identity into a predatory identity.

The formation of an ethnos into a modern nation often provides the basis for the emergence of predatory identities, identities that claim to require the extinction of another collectivity for their own survival. Predatory identities are almost always majoritarian identities. That is, they are based on claims about, and on behalf of, a threatened majority. In fact, in many instances, they are claims about cultural majorities that seek to be exclusively or exhaustively linked with the identity of the nation. Sometimes these claims are made in terms of religious majorities, such as Hindus, Christians, or Jews, and at other times in terms of linguistic, racial, or other sorts of majorities, such as Germans, Indians, or Serbs. The discourse of these mobilized majorities often has within it the idea that it could be itself turned into a minority unless another minority disappears, and for this reason, predatory groups often use pseudo-demographic arguments about rising birthrates among their targeted minority enemies. Thus, predatory identities arise in those circumstances in which majorities and minorities can plausibly be seen as being in danger of trading places. This inner reciprocity is a central feature of this analysis and will be revisited below in this chapter.

Predatory identities emerge in the tension between majority identities and national identities. Identities may be described as "majoritarian" not simply when they are invoked by objectively larger groups in a national polity but when they strive to close the gap between the majority and the purity of the national whole. This is a key point about the conditions under which identities turn predatory. Majority identities that successfully mobilize [. . .] the *anxiety of incompleteness* about their sovereignty can turn predatory. Incompleteness, in this sense, is not only about effective control or practical sovereignty but more importantly about purity and its relationship to identity.

[Elsewhere] I [have] referred to Mary Douglas's contributions to the subject of purity and categorical identity (Appadurai 2006, ch. 3). Her insights can be extended to note that predatory identities, especially when they are associated with majoritarianism, thrive in the gap between the sense of numerical majority and the fantasy of national purity and wholeness. Predatory identities, in other words, are products of situations in which the idea of a national peoplehood is successfully reduced to the principle of ethnic singularity, so that the existence of even the smallest minority within national boundaries is seen as an intolerable deficit in the purity of the national whole. In such circumstances, the very idea of being a majority is a frustration, since it implies some sort of ethnic diffusion of the national peoplehood. Minorities, being a reminder of this small but frustrating deficit, thus unleash the urge to purify. This is one basic element of an answer to the question: why can small numbers excite rage? Small numbers represent a tiny obstacle between majority and totality or total purity. In a sense, the smaller the number and the weaker the minority, the deeper the rage about its capacity to make a majority feel like a mere majority rather than like a whole and uncontested ethnos.

The most remarked twentieth century example of this sense of frustrated purity is, of course, the mobilization of "Germanness" as a predatory identity by the Nazis, directed especially but not exclusively against the Jews. Many scholars have forcefully argued that especially for the assimilated Jewish members of the German bourgeoisie, it was possible, even well into the period of Nazi power, to believe that they were Jewish in an entirely secondary sense and that they were in every important regard fully German. Conversely, it is possible to argue that far from being a successful mobilization of a continuous, unchanging, nationally coded feature of the German people, anti-Semitism had to be regularly mobilized and reawakened through powerful campaigns of racial and political propaganda, through which Jews could be seen as non-Germans and anti-Germans. The special contribution of Nazis to the complex traditions of European anti-Semitism has been identified by some important scholars to be the infusion of scientific racism and its accompanying eugenic and demographic ideas to earlier forms of religious and social stereotyping.

Even Daniel Goldhagen (1996), who otherwise creates a remarkably racialized picture of the identities of "ordinary Germans," concedes that the Nazis made critical new contributions to the definition and mobilization of Germanness as the identity of a threatened majority, threatened especially by the racial cancer (also a Nazi trope) of the Jews. Whatever the status of Goldhagen's arguments about what he called "eliminationist anti-Semitism" and its mobilization among the vast majority of ordinary Germans, the major weakness of the book is its refusal to recognize its own massive evidence, not so much of a deep, primordial, and hardwired form of anti-Semitism among all Germans, successfully captured by the Nazis for the project of eliminating all Jews from the face of the earth, but of the extraordinary amount of energy that was required to turn many German nationals into instruments of the Final Solution.

The huge apparatus of Nazi media and spectacle, the tireless circulation of racialized propaganda and officially circulated rumors, and the self-fulfilling performances (in which degraded Jewish populations were seen as evidence of the subhuman qualities of Jews) were a remarkable feat of active ideological and political engineering. Even in themselves they could be seen as evidence of the effort required to build a successful national consensus in favor of the campaign against Jews as a central platform of the Third Reich. One could also argue that the engagement of civilians of various kinds in police battalions, death camps, and forced marches, which were part of the machinery of the Final Solution, were themselves among the massive political performatives through which Jews were successfully rendered subhuman and those Germans who were directly involved were drawn, by violent action, into the consensus about Jews as national filth.

There is a great deal more that could be said about Nazi anti-Semitism and the larger national project of National Socialism. For the purposes of this argument, the main point is that once the project of Germanness became defined in ethno-racial terms and the logic of purity came into play, a variety of minorities became sites of rage about incomplete purity: homosexuals, the aged and infirm, Gypsies, and, above all, Jews. Jews were painted in Nazi propaganda as representing various kinds of social, political, and economic threats, but they were above all seen as a cancer, as a problem for the purity of German-Aryan blood, for the almost perfect project of a nationally pure and untainted ethnos. German identity, as mobilized by the Nazis, required the complete elimination of Jews from the German social body, and since the German project was a project of world dominion, it required their elimination worldwide.

The Nazi project of eliminating many minorities from the earth also casts light on another aspect of the way predatory identities are mobilized. In this case, perhaps for the first time in the history of humanity, two contradictory impulses were mobilized in the project of genocide. The first was the mechanical, technological, and bureaucratic side of the project, captured in Hannah Arendt's memorable phrase about "the banality of evil" (Arendt 1963). The second, however, is the degradation, abuse, and horrifyingly intimate violence that was wreaked by German soldiers, conscripts, camp guards, militias, and ordinary citizens at every level and in every site of the Final Solution. This is the contradictory intimacy generated by predatory identities. One way to understand this contradiction is that reducing target populations to subhuman states facilitates the work of large-scale murder by creating distance between killers and killed and by providing a self-fulfilling proof of the ideological argument that the victims are subhuman, vermin, insects, scum, garbage, and yet a cancerous part of the valued national body.

Yet there is more to the degradation that frequently accompanies large-scale genocidal violence. I would suggest that it is precisely the smallness of the gap between national totality and minority presence that produces the anxiety of incompleteness and creates the frustration and rage that drives those forms of degradation that shock us most, from Nazi Germany to Rwanda, from Kosovo to Mumbai. Again we must review some arguments about the narcissism of small differences, which I do later in the chapter.

The Nazi example might appear to be an extreme case that has little in common with such recent liberal majoritarianisms as those of India, Pakistan, Britain, or Germany (among others), all of which are more open to social difference than the Nazis were. The Hindutva ideology in India, for example, the "sons of the soil" ideology in Malaysia, or various ideologies of citizenship in Europe might be seen as liberal majoritarianisms, that is, as majoritarianisms which seek to be inclusive. Are these majoritarianisms fundamentally different from the more "totalitarian" ones that the Nazis installed in Germany in the 1930s and 1940s? My suggestion is that all majoritarianisms have in them the seeds of genocide, since they are invariably connected with ideas about the singularity and completeness of the national ethnos.

The difficult question is to assess how and under what conditions liberal majoritarianisms might turn illiberal and potentially genocidal. When does the fact of incomplete national purity become susceptible to translation and mobilization in the service of building a predatory identity? There are two ways of answering this question without entering into an elaborate empiricist study of causes, conditions, and comparisons. One is to suggest that liberal thought has a fundamental ambivalence about the legitimacy of collectivities as political actors and, as a result, is always open to the manipulation of arguments about quality disguised as arguments about quantity. This approach is explored below in this chapter.

The second is a more generally historical and tentative answer to the question of when the condition of incomplete purity propels an argument for genocide. The historical ingredients for this transformation or tipping point appear to include the following: the capture of the state by parties or other groups that have placed their political bets on some sort of racialized nationalist ideology; the availability of census tools and techniques that encourage enumerated communities to become norms for the idea of community itself; a felt lack of fit between political borders and community migrations and populations, yielding a new alertness to politically abandoned ethnic kin or to ethnic strangers claiming to be one's kinsmen; and a successful campaign of fear, directed at numerical majorities, which convinces them that they are at risk of destruction by minorities, who know how to use the law (and the entire apparatus of liberal-democratic politics), to advance their special ends. To these factors, globalization adds its specific energies, which are discussed at the end of this chapter. This set of factors is not intended to be exhaustive or predictive. It is intended to suggest that the Nazi project may have been extraordinary in its consistency and the reach of its genocidal imagination. But as an ideology of majoritarianism turned predatory, it does not allow us to imagine that liberalism is immune from the conditions that produce majoritarian genocide. India in the past two decades is a prime case of the latter possibility.

The Nazi case certainly invites us to see how predatory identities are formed and to recognize that the reflexive theory of the other, in which scapegoats (often minorities) are viewed as a functional requirement for the building up of feelings of we-ness, is both mechanical and partial. The mobilization of feelings of we-ness, especially in the strong form that I have here called predatory, depends on the tension between ideas of the sacred wholeness of the national demos and the statistical idea of a majority. Majoritarianism thrives where majorities become seized of the fantasy of national purity, in that zone where quantity meets — but does not completely define — quality. This issue opens up another dimension of the problem of small numbers, which is the link between number, quantity, and political voice.

Number in the liberal imagination

Numbers have an ambivalent place in liberal social theory, and the relationship between numbers and categories is today at the heart of some central tensions between liberal social theory and democratic norms. The issue of majorities in the modern nation-state allows us to examine these tensions in a productive manner. From a certain point of view, the critical number, for liberal social theory, is the number one, which is the numerical sign of the individual. Insofar as the individual is at the normative heart of liberalism and is shared ground even among competing liberalisms, the number "one" is the smallest important number for liberalism. As the smallest integer, the number "one" has a number of properties of interest to mathematicians, but for liberal social theory, it is in some sense the only important number, other than zero. The number zero is almost as important because it is the key to converting integers into numbers in the hundreds, the thousands, the millions, and so on. In other words, zero is the numerical key to the idea of the masses, which is one of the categories around which liberal and democratic thought part ways. Lenin is quoted as having said: "Politics is where the masses are, not where there are thousands but where there are millions, that is where serious politics begins" (Merton and Sills 2001).

Much liberal thought imagines large groups as aggregations of individuals (that is, of infinite combinations of the number one). A significant part of the utilitarian tradition in liberal thought, from Bentham to Rawls, tries to imagine collective life as organized around forms of aggregate decision making which privilege the individual or a number of persons no larger than one. In this way, liberal thought, both in terms of theories of representation, of the collective good, and of social science, imagines aggregations of individuals as constituted by the addition of large sets of the number one. Put another way, the appearance of collectivities, in the central traditions of liberal thought, is a matter of the aggregation of singular interests and agents seeking solutions to the fact that they are forced to interact with one another. This is, of course, only a way of restating the standard characterizations of market models in neoclassical economics and of the images of collective life that lie behind them. In this sense, liberal thought imagines collectivities to be social forms whose logics, motives, and dynamism can always be inferred from some method for understanding the aggregation of interested individuals.

For liberal thought, from its very beginnings, the problem about democracy is the possibility that it could encourage the political legitimacy of large numbers. The sharp contrast between the people and the masses is constituted in liberal thought around what happens to the number "one" when many zeros are added to it. The idea of the masses (as in Ortega y Gasset's classic book, *The Revolt of the Masses*) is associated in liberal thought with large numbers that have lost the rationalities embedded in the individual, in the number one. Thus, the masses are always seen as the product and the basis of fascism and totalitarianism, both because of the sense of their being composed of nonindividuals (or individuals who had lost their mental capabilities to exercise their own rational interests) and of the sense of a collectivity orchestrated by forces outside itself, such as a state, a dictator, or a myth which was not produced by the deliberative interaction between individuals. The quotation from Lenin captures precisely what liberal thought fears about large numbers. It is because of this potential affinity between large numbers and the birth of the masses that much liberal thought has rightly been characterized by a fear of large numbers. This much seems intuitively clear. But where then does the fear of *small* numbers come in?

Except for the number one, which is a special case, small numbers are troubling to liberal social thought for a variety of reasons. First, small numbers are associated with oligopolies, elites, and tyrannies. They suggest the possibility of what today is called "elite capture" of resources, privileges, and the very capacity to mediate. Small numbers are also a worry because they raise the specter of conspiracy, of the cell, the spy, the traitor, the dissident, or the revolutionary. Small numbers introduce the intrusion of the private into the public sphere, and with it the associated dangers of nepotism, collusion, subversion, and deception. They harbor the potential for secrecy and privacy, both anathema to the ideas of publicity and transparency that are vital to liberal ideas of rational communication and open deliberation.

More broadly, small numbers always carry the possibility of what in the liberal vernacular of the United States are called "special interests" and thus pose threats to some idea of the "general interest," which is believed to be best served when individuals deliberate or negotiate as individuals with *all other individuals* in the polity, through some legible mechanism of representation.

Minorities are the only powerful instance of small numbers which excite sympathy rather than distrust in the liberal imagination, and that is because they incarnate that numerical smallness of which the prime case is the number one, the individual. So once liberal thought becomes intimately connected to electoral democracy and to deliberative procedures in legislation, the idea of the minority acquires a powerful valence (as with the great regard shown for minority opinions in the U.S. Supreme Court). In fact, the idea of a minority is in its political genealogy not an ethical or cultural idea but a procedural one, having to do with dissenting opinions in deliberative or legislative contexts in a democratic framework. Thus, in the history of liberal thought, the positive interest in minorities and their opinions has much to do with dissent and little to do with difference. This distinction is an important contributor to the contemporary fear of minorities and requires careful examination.

Dissent and difference in contemporary polities

The initial positive value attached to minorities in Western liberal thought is fundamentally procedural. It has to do with the valuation of rational debate, of the right to dissent, of the value of dissent as a sign of the larger value of free speech and opinion, and of the freedom to express dissenting opinions on matters of public moment without fear of retribution. The U.S. Constitution is perhaps the best place to examine the centrality of dissent to the very idea of freedom. But if we are not careful, we are likely to reverse the course of history and place a relatively recent development, what we may call *substantive* dissent (for example, the right to express even morally monstrous opinions, the right to criticize the policies of the state, or the right to question the religious opinions of the majority) from what we may call *procedural* dissent, which is the original context for the positive value placed on minorities, and especially on minority opinion. The key word here is opinion, for procedural minorities are not cultural or social minorities, they are temporary minorities, minorities solely by and of opinion. Social and cultural minorities, what we may call substantive minorities, are permanent minorities, minorities that have become social and not just procedural.

If we look at the history of Western laws and ideas pertaining to minorities, they take on their full liberal force largely after the birth of the United Nations and in the various conventions pertaining to human rights that are produced after the birth of the United Nations. Of course, there are various piecemeal ideas about the protection of minorities before the formation of the United Nations, but it is only in the second half of the twentieth century, as the idea of human rights became the major currency for negotiating international agreements about the elementary entitlements of all humanity, that substantive social minorities became critical foci of constitutional and political concern in many democracies throughout the world. The rights of minorities, seen under the larger rubric of human rights, acquired a remarkably wide credibility during this period, and, in different national settings, became the basis for major juridical and constitutional struggles over citizenship, justice, political participation, and equality.

This process, in which social and cultural minorities became universally seen as bearers of real or potential rights, conceals a poorly theorized, even unanticipated, transfer of normative value from procedural minorities and temporary minorities to substantive minorities, which often became permanent social and cultural collectivities.

This unintended displacement of the liberal concern with protecting the opinions of procedural minorities (such as minorities on courts, councils, parliaments, and other deliberative bodies) onto the rights of permanent cultural minorities is an important source of the current, deep ambivalence about minorities in democracies of all varieties. The many debates about multiculturalism in the United States and Europe, about subordinate nationalities in various parts of the ex-Soviet Union, about secularism in India, about "sons-of-the-soil" in many countries in Asia, about "autochthony" in many regions of Africa, and about the rights of "indigenous people" throughout Latin America and in places as far apart as New Zealand, Canada, Australia, and Hawaii are different in important ways. But they have in common a concern about the rights of cultural minorities in relation to national states and various cultural majorities, and they always involve struggles over cultural rights as they relate to national citizenship and issues of belonging. In many cases, these struggles have been directly related to the emergence of predatory ethnic identities and of successful efforts to mobilize majorities in projects of ethnic cleansing or ethnocide. These conflicts accelerated during the 1980s and 1990s, during which many nation-states had to simultaneously negotiate two pressures: the pressure to open up their markets to foreign investment, commodities, and images and the pressure to manage the capacity of their own cultural minorities to use the globalized language of human rights to argue for their own claims for cultural dignity and recognition. This dual pressure was a distinctive feature of the 1990s and produced a crisis in many countries for the sense of national boundaries, national sovereignty, and the purity of the national ethnos, and it is directly responsible for the growth of majoritarian racisms in societies as diverse as Sweden and Indonesia as well as Romania, Rwanda, and India.

Muslims in India: appeasement and purity

The case of India is instructive in regard to the argument about substantive and procedural minorities that I have been developing. The Indian nation-state was formed in 1947 through a political partition that also produced Pakistan as a new nation-state, formed as a political haven for the Muslims who lived in Britain's Indian Empire. There is a huge and contentious scholarship surrounding the story of Partition, the politics that led to it, and the bizarre geographies it produced (with East and West Pakistan flanking an independent India from 1947 to 1973 when East Pakistan succeeded in seceding from West Pakistan, giving birth to Bangladesh, a new nation on India's eastern borders). I will not take up this politics here, except to note that it produced a permanent state of war between India and Pakistan; spawned the apparently unsolvable crisis of Kashmir; created an alibi for the identification of India's Muslim citizens with its major cross-border enemy, Pakistan; and laid the groundwork for India's current crisis of secularism.

The story of this crisis is also too complex to be told here. What is noteworthy is that as Hinduism and its political mobilizers evolved a cultural politics in the course of the nineteenth and twentieth centuries, the birth of Pakistan created a new link between the Hindu sense of we-ness, the constitutional concern about the rights of minorities, and the rise of a major Hindu political coalition to power in the 1990s. This coalition, of political parties and various affiliated social movements (sometimes called the Sangh Parivar), is virtually coterminous with India's exposure to the pressures of globalization, and it has been bracketed by two of the most horrendous attacks against Muslims in India since the massacres of the Partition: the destruction of the Babri Masjid, a Muslim mosque in North India in 1992, preceded and followed by a wave of genocidal riots against Muslim populations throughout India, and the murderous pogrom against Muslims in the state of Gujarat in 2002. The decade that is bracketed by these events also witnessed the national consolidation of a large body of Indian public opinion, including those of its educated and once-liberal middle classes, against the inclusive, pluralist, and secularist ideals of the Indian constitution and of Nehru, India's first, most charismatic, prime minister. In its place, the coalition of grassroots movements and political parties, led by the Indian People's Party (the Bharatiya Janata Party or BJP), succeeded in creating a deep link between the memory of Hindu humiliations by the pre-British Muslim rulers of India, the dubious patriotism of India's Muslim citizens, the known wish of Pakistan to destroy India militarily, and the growth in militant actions by Muslim terrorists connected with anti-Indian aspirations in the contested state of Kashmir.

Much scholarly and journalistic attention has been paid to this remarkable story in which the world's largest democracy, born with a constitution that pays remarkable attention to religious inclusion, secular tolerance for religious difference, and a general concern with protecting the "weaker sections" of society, could, within forty years of its birth, have turned into an aggressively Hinduized polity, which repeatedly and systematically sought to identify India with Hindus and patriotism with Hindutva (Hindu-ness). This Indian development casts a particular light on the fear of minorities that is worth examining in some detail.

My argument needs to recognize, at this stage, a major interruption from the world of political events. Since the first draft of this paper was written in October 2003 and revised in August 2004, a momentous and unexpected electoral event occurred in India. The Hindu right-wing coalition, led by the BJP, was resoundingly defeated in the recent general elections, and a new coalition, led by the Congress Party of the Nehrus, is back in power. This extraordinary democratic revolution, not the first in the history of independent India, has shocked even the canniest political pundits (not unlike the fall of the Soviet Union in 1989). Though the significance of this major change is still being digested by the experts, there is general agreement among most analysts that the defeat of the BJP coalition expressed two messages. One was that the Indian electorate (both rural and urban) was fed up with the message of Hindutva and did not see it as any substitute for plans and policies concerning the economy and everyday politics at the local level. The second was that the bottom half of the Indian electorate (both rural and urban) was also fed up with seeing the benefits of globalization being consumed by a small group in the ongoing circus of state corruption and elite consumption, with few tangible benefits for themselves. In other words, callous globalization and cynical anti-Muslim mobilization were no longer viable platforms for a national coalition. So we have another novel moment in Indian politics, where the Congress and its allies steer a difficult course between economic justice and global markets and between localized and caste-based politics and a larger, postethnic and pluralist politics.

But it remains crucial to ask why many of India's political parties, a significant part of its population, and a shocking number of cosmopolitan, liberal intellectuals turned to the Hindutva message in the period between 1985 and 2004, a historical period which covers a third of India's history as an independent nation. And the question is not simply historical or academic. The forces of Hindu majoritarianism have not simply disappeared, and its methods, values, and techniques are still very much alive in the Indian polity. We are in a moment of respite, and in order to ensure that the Hinduization of Indian politics remains history, we need to think through this period with as much care as we can summon.

The rise of the Hindu Right as India's major and majoritarian political coalition and its capture of mainstream national opinion largely in the 1980s, after decades of being a fragmented and marginal set of political movements, was connected to four major developments that relate to the issue of numbers and minorities. Each of these developments has something instructive to say about other nations and locations elsewhere in the world.

The first development had to do with minorities that are linked to global movements, identities, and networks. Muslims in India have always been subject to the charge of being more loyal to the wider Muslim world than to India, and their alleged sentimental links to Pakistan (often strenuously repudiated by Indian Muslims) have always been read in the context of the resources and political aspirations of global Islam. In India in the 1980s, the Hindu Right took a special interest in the flow of resources from the Muslim Middle East to religious and educational institutions in India, arguing that this sort of subsidy of Indian Muslims needed to be monitored and restricted and that it justified a controversial policy of reconversions undertaken by the Hindu Right, especially among poorer rural and tribal populations, alleged to have been duped into conversion by the forces of global Islam. Such reconversions were also instituted with Indian Christian communities and remain a major platform for the grassroots violence and political strategy of the Hindu Right today. In its early manifestations in the 1980s, this battle of conversions was underwritten by the invocation of the size, power, and influence of global Islamic interests and forces, which were seen as the Trojans hidden within the relatively small number of Muslims in Indian communities. Thus, to put the matter crudely, the relatively small numbers of Muslims in India were seen as a mask for the large numbers of Muslims around the world. Today, this picture of militant, transnational Islam has become virtually naturalized in the discourse of Islamic terrorism, especially in the wake of 9/11.

In the Indian case, this picture of Indian Muslims as instruments (and objects) of global Islamic movements (usually portrayed as violent, antinational, and anti-Hindu) was supported by the ongoing commitment of Indian Muslims to going on the Haj (a specially sacred pilgrimage to Mecca, seen as a desirable action at least once in the life of any devout Muslim) and by the growing traffic between Indian workers (of all kinds and classes) and the oil-rich sheikdoms of the Middle East, especially Saudi Arabia, Dubai, Kuwait, and Bahrain, starting in the 1980s. Among these migrants to the Persian Gulf was a significant number of Indian Muslims, though there is little sign that this was anything other than an economic option for them. Nevertheless, the traffic between India and the Gulf was the site of a great deal of moral and political anxiety which expressed itself in such bureaucratic innovations as the creation of the office of "The Protector of Immigrants," a government agency designed to ensure that Indian workers were not being exported to the Gulf for immoral or fraudulent reasons. In a related moral drama, there was a great deal of attention paid to the growing practice of marriages arranged between richer (and often older) Arab men from the Gulf and Muslim women (often very young) from poor families in impoverished Muslim communities in cities such as Hyderabad, Lucknow, and Agra. This picture of Muslim male depravity and polygamy, targeting the already exploited community of Muslim women, was circulated in the popular press and in such commercial films as *Baazaar*, which were calculated to excite the worst stereotypes of this marriage market. It is highly likely that these commercial and popular images of the abuse of poor Indian Muslim women by decadent Arab men and money lay behind the celebrated legal controversy surrounding a Muslim woman called Shah Bano, who sued her husband for support after he divorced and abandoned her, in accordance with Muslim personal law (one subset of the specialized body of law applicable to many aspects of family and civil life for different religious communities in India) (Das 1990).

The Shah Bano case, which was one of the most publicized legal dramas in India after independence, pitted the state against the judiciary, Hindus against Muslims, feminists against each other, secularists against traditionalists. It also created a deep and harmful opposition between the interests of women and those of minorities (since Shah Bano's appeal was against the customary family laws of her own community). The case showed every sign of rocking the stability of the regime of Rajiv Gandhi, the then prime minister of India, who represented the Nehruvian tradition of secularism and even-handedness toward all religious communities. The Hindu Right, led by the then rising BJP, exploited the Shah Bano case mercilessly, painting themselves as the true protectors of the abused Muslim woman and of women's rights generally, while using the public interest in the case to disseminate vicious messages about the authoritarian power of the Muslim community over its women and the generalized sexual immorality and irresponsibility of Muslim males. The case was eventually resolved through a series of legal and political compromises, but it created a major public doubt about the benefits of secularism and laid some of the grounds for the bizarre idea that the Hindu Right was a more responsible protector of Muslim women's rights than anybody else. It also laid the foundations for a debate, unresolved right up to the present, about the desirability of a Uniform Civil Code (UCC), which is now seen as problematic by most political parties and progressive women's groups but is actively supported by the Hindu Right, for which it is a major vehicle for Hinduizing the personal law of all minority communities.

The Shah Bano case points up the ways in which issues surrounding minorities, in a complex multireligious democracy like India, can become flash points for fundamental debates about gender, equality, legality, the boundaries of state power, and the ability of religious communities to police themselves. The point here is that small numbers can unsettle big issues, especially in countries like India, where the rights of minorities are directly connected to larger arguments about the role of the state, the limits of religion, and the nature of civil rights as matters of legitimate cultural difference.[1] In a very different context, India's long history of actions and litigations concerning affirmative or remedial action, in the context of the scheduled castes, produced the national convulsions over the 1980 report of the Mandal Commission, which sought to give teeth to a policy of job reservations for castes considered to have been historically the victims of discrimination. The Hindu Right recognized the tension between the rise of the lower castes, signaled by the Mandal Report, and was active in its efforts to take advantage of the rage of the Hindu upper castes, who saw themselves as threatened anew by the political aspirations of their poorer fellow Hindus. Many scholars have pointed out that the Hindu Right, throughout the 1980s, mobilized the politics of the Masjid (the Mosque) against those of Mandal (the intra-Hindu battle over reserved jobs for lower castes). It has also been noted that the effort to create a unified Hindu caste front, in the face of the caste battles unleashed by the Mandal Report, made the Muslim minority a perfect "other" in the production of a mobilized Hindu major-ity. Most important for the issue of numbers, Amrita Basu, a distinguished student of the politics of communal violence in North India, has observed that the idea of a Hindu majority actually hides the numerical minority of upper caste, landed Hindu castes who have much more to fear from the rise of the lower castes than they have to fear from Muslims in their own localities (Basu 1994). When we place this concern against the general politicization and mass mobilization of the lower castes in public politics throughout India, arguably the single greatest transformation in the political landscape of India over the past half century (Jaffrelot 2003), we can see that the fear of small numbers is further inflected by the Hindu minority which actually has the most to gain from the cultural fiction of a Hindu majority.

The Hindu majority is a double fiction in contemporary India, first because the category "Hindu" is unthinkable in contemporary politics apart from its birth in colonial ethnograph-ies and census categories and second because the deep divisions between upper and lower castes, always a feature of life in agrarian India, has grown into one of the most important fissures in the politics of North India in the past two decades. Thus, the Hindu majority is demonstrably a project, not a fact, and like all racialized categories and all predatory identities, it requires mobilization through the discourses of crisis and the practices of violence. The existence of minorities, such as Muslims, is an important aspect of these crises and practices, but the relation is not one of simple contrast and stereotyping, as I proposed earlier.

The relationship between Hindu caste politics and the anti-Muslim propaganda of the Hindu Right, especially since the 1980s, is also tied up with a major feature of Indian electoral politics since Indian independence, which is captured in the discourse of the vote bank. Indian elections are frequently seen, especially at the rural, local level, as turning substantially on the power of this or that party or candidate to capture a whole set of votes from a particular caste or religious community, which is bought off through its elites, and constitutes a vote bank. Bringing together the associations of an elite-manipulated, collectiv-ized vote and of a vote bought corruptly, the image of the vote bank, which is freely used by all Indian politicians against one another, captures the deep history of links between the census and British colonial ideas of community and electorate, notoriously institutionalized in the separate electorates created early in the twentieth century for Hindus and Muslims in local elections under colonial rule. These enumerated communities (Kaviraj 1992) remain a major nightmare for liberal thought in India, because they catch both the liberal abhorrence of mass politics and its special corruptions and of the negative drag of ascription and kinship in a modernizing democracy. Today, the importance of vote banks has been somewhat undercut by the growing power of independent grassroots movements which resist whole-sale manipulation by politicians and by the cynicism with which politicians themselves make and break alliances and affiliations. Still, the Hindu Right never lost an opportunity to raise the specter of the Muslim vote bank, often accusing its major competitor, the now victorious Congress Party, of pandering to Muslims in an effort to capture the Muslim vote bank in local elections and, by implication, in state and national elections. The amazing defeat of the BJP in the 2004 general elections showed that this particular bogey was not enough to buy the loyalty of the largely rural Indian electorate.

This point brings us to the final feature of the fear of minorities in India, which has wider implications. The Hindu Right, especially through its dominant political parties, has consistently accused the Congress (the party historically associated with Nehruvian secular-ism, pluralism, and active tolerance of Muslims as a cultural minority) of appeasement in its dealings with Muslims demands, complaints, and claims on the state. The discourse of appeasement is fascinating, because it is deeply linked to the slippage I earlier discussed between the sense of being a majority and the frustration of incomplete identification with the undivided ethnos of the polity. When the Hindu Right baits secular parties and move-ments with the charge of "appeasing" Muslims, it implies both a certain opportunism and cowardice on the part of the secularists and simultaneously (as with the Nazis and Munich) creates an image of the slippery slope which leads from the fear of giving in to this or that local demand of Muslim communities to giving in wholesale in the militarized, now nuclear-ized battle with Pakistan, which is the large-scale backdrop of all militant Hindu propaganda in India. The discourse of appeasement is the link between minority claims within national boundaries and the struggle with enemy states across the border, in this case Pakistan. Thus, appeasement is another discursive device that allows the small numbers of Indian Muslims to be swollen and impregnated with the threat of Pakistan and, beyond that, of the militant multitudes of the world of global Islam. In the period immediately following the 9/11 attacks, as I have argued above in this chapter, these connections were revived and reimag-ined through the global invocation of Islamic terrorism. I turn now, by way of conclusion, to the figure of the suicide bomber, born in the struggles between Tamils and Sinhalas in Sri Lanka in the 1970s, and the relationship of this solitary figure to issues of number, minority, and terror.

How small are small numbers? Minorities, diasporas, and terror

The suicide bomber, whether in Israel, Sri Lanka, New York, Iraq, or London, is the darkest possible version of the liberal value placed on the individual, the number "one." The suicide bomber today is the ideal type of the terrorist, since in this figure several nightmares are condensed. He or she, first of all, completely closes the boundary between the body and the weapon of terror. Whether by strapping bombs to his or her body or by otherwise disguising explosives in his or her body, suicide bomber is an explosive body that promises to distribute its own bloody fragments and mix them in with the bloody parts of the civilian populations it is intended to decimate. Thus, not only does the suicide bomber elude detection, he or she also produces a horrible mixture of blood and body between enemies, thus violating not only the soil of the nation but the very bodies of the victims, infecting them with the blood of the martyr. Second, the suicide bomber is a revolting version of the idea of the martyr, highly valued in Christianity and Islam, for instead of being a passive martyr, he or she is an active, dangerous, exploding martyr, a murderous martyr. Third, the suicide bomber, as with the brainwashed agent in *The Manchurian Candidate*, is invariably portrayed as being in some paranormal state of conviction, ecstasy, and purpose, often built up through quasi-religious techniques such as isolation, indoctrination, and drug-induced hallucination, on the eve of the suicidal attack. This image is the very antithesis of the liberal individual acting in her interest, for the idea of a willingly exploded body does not fit easily into most models of rational choice. Fourth, imagined as an automaton, the suicide bomber, while a terrifying example of the individual, the number "one," is in fact always seen as an instance of the crazed mob or mass, the victim of propaganda and extrarational conviction, a perfect example of the mindless regimentation of the masses and of the dangerous unpredictability of the mob.

In all these regards, the suicide bomber is the pure and most abstract form of the terrorist. In this sense, the suicide bomber also captures some of the central fears surrounding terror. As a figure that has to get close to the place of attack by appearing to be a normal citizen, the suicide bomber takes to the extreme the problem of uncertainty which I have discussed earlier. In one suicide bombing in Israel, a suicide bomber disguised himself as a rabbi, thus subverting the very heart of the visible moral order of Israeli Jewish society. Likewise, the suicide bomber thrives in the spaces of civilian life, thus producing a form of permanent emergency that also requires a new approach to the problem of civilians and civil life in the age of globalized terrorism. This brings us to a final feature of the problem of small numbers in an era of globalized networks of terror, such as those that became a full part of public consciousness after 9/11.

Small numbers and global networks

The events of 9/11 are now sufficiently behind us that we can begin to sift through the xenophobia, sentimentality, and shock that the attacks produced to ponder the more persistent images that remain from that event, now to be seen via the dark glass of the war on Iraq. Osama bin Laden is almost certainly alive, the Taliban are regrouping in Afghanistan and Pakistan, various warlords keep Afghanistan in a profound state of dependency on foreign money, arms, and soldiers, and there is a fierce insurgency against American forces in Iraq. The Iraqis, subdued initially by shock and awe, seem to hate Americans as much as they did Saddam Hussein, and the weapons of mass destruction seem to be alibis for the weapons of mass construction, largely in the hands of Bechtel and Halliburton. In both Afghanistan and Iraq, most especially in Iraq, the United States appears to be experimenting with a new political form, which may be called "long-distance democracy," a strange form of imperial federalism, where Iraq is treated as the fifty-second American state, operating under the jurisdiction of the National Guard and various other Federal forces from Washington in order to handle a disaster (produced in this instance by the decapitation of Saddam's regime).

The problem of numbers, minorities, and terror is alive and well in Iraq, along with the question of whether an Iraqi "people" can be produced out of the chaotic megapolitics of Shias, Kurds, and other large minorities. On one hand, the U.S. administration in Iraq faces the bewildering problem of minorities, such as the Shias, who are in absolute numerical terms very large and well connected to the ruling regime of Iran, or of the Kurds, who span the borders of Iran, Iraq, and Turkey and constitute a huge minority. As the United States completes its nonexit, having rushed in teams of experts to build an Iraqi constitution overnight (just as they did in Afghanistan), there is a deep conceptual logjam involving large numerical minorities, the insistence among most Iraqis that the new polity has to be "Islamic," and the sense that a real democracy cannot be Islamic, except in the thinnest sense. Struggles over the nature of such basic ideas as constitutionalism, election, democracy, and representation go on in Iraq in the shadow of tank battles and full-scale warfare in places like Najaf and Falluja.

Two points about the ongoing Iraq debacle are relevant to the problem of small numbers and the fear of minorities. One is that even after ending the career of a truly murderous despot, likely feared and hated by many Iraqis, the U.S. military is still dogged by the fear of small numbers, those small groups of militia, civilians, and others who conduct sneak attacks on the U.S. forces and sometimes take suicidal risks to inflict damage and kill U.S. soldiers. Fully embedded as they are within the civilian population, finding these "terrorists" is a nightmarish task of divination for U.S. forces that counted on total Iraqi surrender after one evil individual — Saddam Hussein — had been toppled from power. Thus the United States, as an occupying power in Iraq, faces the fear that the small numbers who are continuing to torment and kill its soldiers are true representatives of the Iraqi people, who were originally scripted to greet the Americans as liberators and unfold the spectacle of a civil society underneath the carcass of the dictator.

Iraq also represents the more abstract challenge of producing a national people from what seem to be only large ethnic or religious minorities. In both Iraq and Afghanistan, the United States found itself between a rock and hard place as it embarked on the project of building long-distance democracies: either they must allow these countries to constitute themselves as Islamic republics, thus recognizing that the only way to create peoples is by placing the very religion they most fear at the heart of the definition of the nation, or they must find ways to assemble coalitions of numerically large minorities, thus conceding that civil society in Iraq and in many places like Iraq has to be built over a long period of time, and that all there is to work with are minorities. But these are minorities with global connections and large populations associated with them. In facing this difficult set of choices, after starting a war that refuses to end, the United States has to engage with issues of minority, uncertainty, terror, and ethnic violence that plague many societies in the era of globalization. There are indications that some Iraqis may already be engaged in what has been called ethnic dry-cleaning in preparation for more brutal ethnic cleansing. If that scenario comes to pass, we will need, more than ever, to find new ways of negotiating the distance between the small numbers that provoke rage in the world's mobilized majorities, whose large numbers Lenin presciently saw as marking the beginnings of what he considered "serious politics."

Globalization, numbers, difference

I now return to two important themes: one is the issue of minor differences and the other is the special link between globalization and the growing rage against minorities. In my view, these themes are not unrelated. Michael Ignatieff (1998) is perhaps the most articulate analyst to invoke Freud's famous essay on "the narcissism of minor differences" in order to deepen our sense of the ethnic battles of the 1990s, especially in Eastern Europe. Mostly informed by his deep knowledge of that region, Ignatieff uses Freud's insight about the psychodynamics of narcissism to cast light on why groups like the Serbs and the Croats should come to invest so much in mutual hatred, given the complex interweaving of their histories, languages, and identities over many centuries. This is a fruitful observation that can be extended and deepened by reference to some of the arguments developed here.

In particular, I suggested that it was the small gap between majority status and complete or total national ethnic purity that could be the source of the extreme rage against targeted ethnic others. This suggestion — what I earlier glossed as the anxiety of incompleteness — allows us a further basis for extending Freud's insight into complex, large-scale, public forms of violence, since it allows us to see how narcissistic wounds, at the level of public ideologies about group identity, can be turned outward and become incitements to the formation of what I have called "predatory identities." The underlying dynamic here is the inner reciprocity between the categories of majority and minority. As abstractions produced by census techniques and liberal proceduralism, majorities can always be mobilized to think that they are in danger of becoming *minor* (culturally or numerically) and to fear that minorities, conversely, can easily become *major* (through brute accelerated reproduction or subtler legal or political means). These linked fears are a peculiarly modern product of the inner reciprocity of these categories, which also sets the conditions for the fear that they might morph into one another.

And this is also where globalization comes in. In a variety of ways, globalization intensifies the possibility of this volatile morphing, so that the naturalness that all group identities seek and assume is perennially threatened by the abstract affinity of the very categories of majority and minority. Global migrations across and within national boundaries constantly unsettle the glue that attaches persons to ideologies of soil and territory. The global flow of mass-mediated, sometimes commoditized, images of self and other create a growing archive of hybridities that unsettle the hard lines at the edges of large-scale identities. Modern states frequently manipulate and alter the nature of the categories through which they conduct their censuses and the statistical means through which they enumerate the populations within these groups. The global spread of improvised ideologies of constitutionalism, with elements drawn from the United States, France, and England, provokes new globalized debates about ethnicity, minority, and electoral legitimacy, as we see today in Iraq. Finally, the multiple, rapid, and largely invisible ways in which large-scale funds move through official interstate channels, quasi-legal commercial channels, and completely illicit channels tied up with networks like Al-Qaeda are intimately tied up with globalized institutions for money laundering, electronic transfers, new forms of cross-border accounting, and law, all of which constitute that form of finance capital which virtually defines the era of globalization. These rapid, often invisible, and frequently illicit movements of money across national boundaries are widely, and rightly, seen as creating the means for today's minority to become tomorrow's majority. Each of these factors can contribute to the exacerbation of social uncertainty [. . .] and thus create the conditions for crossing the line from majoritarian anxiety to full-scale predation, even to genocide.

Thus, the fear of small numbers is intimately tied up with the tensions produced for liberal social theory and its institutions by the forces of globalization. Minorities in a globalizing world are a constant reminder of the incompleteness of national purity. And when the conditions — notably those surrounding social uncertainty — within any particular national polity are ripe for this incompleteness to be mobilized as a volatile deficit, the rage of genocide can be produced, especially in those liberal polities where the idea of minority has, in some way, come to be a shared political value affecting all numbers, large and small.

Note

1   I owe this important point to Faisal Devji, who made it in the context of a lecture on the partition of British India at Yale University in fall 2003.

Bibliography

Appadurai, Arjun. 2000. "The Grounds of the Nation-State: Identity, Violence and Territory." In *Nationalism and Internationalism in the Post-Cold War Era*. Ed. Kjell Goldmann, Ulf Hannerz, and Charles Westin. London: Routledge.

—— 2006. *Fear of Small Numbers: An Essay on the Geography of Anger*. Durham, NC: Duke University Press.

Arendt, Hannah. 1963. *Eichmann in Jerusalem: A Report on the Banality of Evil*. New York: Viking Press.

Basu, Amrita. 1994. "When Local Riots Are Not Merely Local: Bringing the State Back In, Bijnor 1988–92." *Economic and Political Weekly*, 2605–21.

Cooley, Charles Horton. 1964. *Human Nature and the Social Order*. Introduction by Philip Rieff. Foreword by Herbert Mead. New York: Schocken Books.

Das, Veena. 1990. *Mirrors of Violence: Communities, Riots and Survivors in South Asia*. Delhi: Oxford University Press.

Devji, Faisal. 2005. *Landscapes of the Jihad: Militancy, Morality and Modernity*. Ithaca: Cornell University Press.

Douglas, Mary. 1966. *Purity and Danger: An Analysis of Concepts of Purity and Taboo*. London: Routledge and Kegan Paul.

Goldhagen, Daniel. 1996. *Hitler's Willing Executioners: Ordinary Germans and the Holocaust*. New York: Knopf.

Hinton, Alexander Laban, ed. 2002. *Annihilating Difference: The Anthropology of Genocide*. Berkeley: University of California Press.

Ignatieff, Michael. 1998. *The Warriors Honor: Ethnic War and the Modern Conscience*. New York: Henry Holt.

Jaffrelot, Christophe. 2003. *India's Silent Revolution: The Rise of the Lower Castes in North India*. New York: Columbia University Press.

Kaviraj, Sudipta. 1992. "The Imaginary Institution of India." In *Subaltern Studies*, vol. 7. Ed. Partha Chatterjee and Gyanendra Pandey. Delhi: Oxford University Press.

Merton, Robert King, and David L. Sills, eds. 2001. *Social Science Quotations: Who Said What, When, and Where*. New Brunswick, N.J.: Transaction Publishers.

Ortega y Gasset, José. 1957. *The Revolt of the Masses*. New York: Norton.

Simmel, Georg. 1950. "The Stranger." In *The Sociology of Georg Simmel*. Trans. and ed. Kurt H. Wolff. Glencoe, Ill.: Free Press.

Chapter 14

Sara Ahmed

THE ORGANISATION OF HATE

The depths of Love are rooted and very deep in a real White Nationalist's soul and spirit, no form of 'hate' could even begin to compare. At least not a hate motivated by ungrounded reasoning. It is not hate that makes the average White man look upon a mixed racial couple with a scowl on his face and loathing in his hear [sic]. It is not hate that makes the White housewife throw down the daily jewspaper in repulsion and anger after reading of yet another child-molester or rapist sentenced by corrupt courts to a couple short years in prison or on parole. It is not hate that makes the White workingman curse about the latest boatload of aliens dumped on our shores to be given job preference over the White citizens who built this land. It is not hate that brings rage into the heart of a White Christian farmer when he reads of billions loaned or given away as 'aid' to foreigners when he can't get the smallest break from an unmerciful government to save his failing farm. No, it is not hate. It is Love.

(The Aryan Nations' Website)[1]

HOW DO EMOTIONS such as hate work to secure collectives through the way in which they read the bodies of others? How does hate work to align some subjects with some others and against other others? In this chapter, I consider the role of hate in shaping bodies and worlds through the way hate generates its object as a defence against injury. We can see such defensive uses of hate within fascist discourse. It is a common theme within so-called hate groups to declare themselves as organisations of love on their web sites. This apparent reversal (we do and say this because we love, not because we hate) does an enormous amount of work, as a form of justification and persuasion. In the instance above, it is the imagined subject of both party and nation (the White nationalist, the average White man, the White housewife, the White workingman, the White Citizen and the White Christian farmer) who is hated, and who is threatened and victimised by the law and polity. Hate is not simply present as the emotion that explains the story (it is not a question of hate being *at its root*), but as that which is affected by the story, and as that which enables the story to be affective.

Such narratives work by generating a subject that is endangered by imagined others whose proximity threatens not only to take something away from the subject (jobs, security, wealth), but to take the place of the subject. The presence of this other is imagined as a threat to the object of love. This narrative involves a rewriting of history, in which the labour of others (migrants, slaves) is concealed in a fantasy that it is the white subject who 'built this land'.[2] The white subjects claim the place of hosts ('our shores'), at the same time as they claim the position of the victim, as the ones who are damaged by an 'unmerciful government'. The narrative hence suggests that it is love for the nation that makes the white Aryans feel hate towards others who, in 'taking away' the nation, are taking away their history, as well as their future.

We might note that this emotional reading of others as hateful aligns the imagined subject with rights and the imagined nation with ground. This alignment is affected by the representation of the rights of the subject and the grounds of the nation as under threat, as 'failing'. *It is the emotional reading of hate that works to stick or to bind the imagined subjects and the white nation together.* The average white man feels 'fear and loathing'; the White housewife, 'repulsion and anger'; the White workingman 'curses'; the White Christian farmer, feels 'rage'. The passion of these negative attachments to others is redefined simultaneously as a positive attachment to the imagined subjects brought together through the capitalisation of the signifier, 'White'. It is the love of White, or those that are recognisable as White, which supposedly explains this shared 'communal' visceral response of hate. *Because we love, we hate, and this hate is what brings us together.*

This narrative, I would suggest, is far from extraordinary. Indeed, it reveals the production of the ordinary. The ordinary is here fantastic. The ordinary white subject is a fantasy that comes into being through the mobilisation of hate as a passionate attachment closely tied to love. The emotion of hate works to animate the ordinary subject, to bring that fantasy to life, precisely by constituting the ordinary as in crisis, and the ordinary person as the *real victim*. The ordinary becomes that which is *already* under threat by the imagined others whose proximity becomes a crime against person as well as place. [. . .] The ordinary or normative subject is reproduced as the injured party; the one that is 'hurt' or even damaged by the 'invasion' of others. The bodies of others are hence transformed into 'the hated' through a discourse of pain. They are assumed to 'cause' injury to the ordinary white subject such that their proximity is read as the origin of bad feeling. Indeed, it is implied that the white subject's good feelings (love) have been 'taken' away by the abuse of such feelings by others.

So who is hated in such a narrative of injury? Clearly, hate is *distributed* across various figures (in this case, the mixed racial couple, the child-molester, the rapist, aliens and foreigners). These figures come to embody the threat of loss: lost jobs, lost money, lost land. They signify the danger of impurity, or the mixing or taking of blood. They threaten to violate the pure bodies; such bodies can only be imagined as pure by the perpetual restaging of this fantasy of violation. Note the work that is being done through this metonymic slide: mixed race couplings and immigration become readable as (like) forms of rape or molestation; an invasion of the body of the nation, evoked here as the vulnerable and damaged bodies of the white woman and child. The slide between figures constructs a relation of resemblance between the figures. What makes them 'alike' may be their 'unlikeness' from 'us'. Within the narrative, hate cannot be found in one figure, but works to create the outline of different figures or objects of hate, a creation that crucially aligns the figures together, and constitutes them as a 'common threat'. Importantly, then, hate does not *reside* in a given subject or object. Hate is economic; it circulates between signifiers in relationships of difference and displacement. To understand such affective economies of hate, I will consider the way in which 'signs' of hate work, and their relation to bodies. My examples will refer specifically to racism as a politics of hatred, and will include an analysis of hate crime as a legal response to racism.

Affective economies

If hate involves a series of displacements that do not reside positively in a sign or figure, then hate does not originate within an individual psyche; it does not reside positively in consciousness. As such, hate operates at an unconscious level, or resists consciousness understood as plenitude, or what we might call 'positive residence'. My reliance on 'the unconscious' here signals my debt to psychoanalytical understandings of the subject. It is hence important that I clarify how my argument will exercise a concept of the unconscious. In his paper on the unconscious, Freud introduces the notion of unconscious emotions, where by an affective impulse is perceived but misconstrued, and which becomes attached to another idea (Freud 1964a: 177). What is repressed from consciousness is not the feeling as such, but the idea to which the feeling may have been first (but provisionally) connected. Psychoanalysis allows us to see that emotions such as hate involve a process of movement or association, *whereby 'feelings' take us across different levels of signification, not all of which can be admitted in the present.* This is what I call the 'rippling' effect of emotions; they move sideways (through 'sticky' associations between signs, figures and objects) as well as forwards and backwards (repression always leaves its trace in the present – hence 'what sticks' is bound up with the 'absent presence' of historicity). In the Aryan Nations' quote, we can see how hate slides sideways between figures, as well as backwards, by reopening past associations, which allows some bodies to be read as being the cause of 'our hate'.

Indeed, insofar as psychoanalysis is a theory of the subject as lacking in the present, it offers a theory of emotion as economy, *as involving relationships of difference and displacement without positive value.* That is, emotions work as a form of capital: affect does not reside positively in the sign or commodity, but is produced as an effect of its circulation. I am using 'the economic' to suggest that objects of emotions circulate or are distributed across a social as well as psychic field, borrowing from the Marxian critique of the logic of capital. In *Capital*, Marx discusses how the movement of commodities and money, in the formula (M-C-M: money to commodity to money), creates surplus value. That is, through circulation and exchange 'M' acquires more value (Marx 1976: 248). Or, as he puts it: 'The value originally advanced, therefore, not only remains intact while in circulation, but increases its magnitude, adds to itself a surplus-value or is valorised. *And this movement converts it into capital*' (Marx 1976: 252, emphasis mine). I am identifying a similar logic: the movement between signs or objects converts into affect. Marx does link value with affect through the figures of the capitalist and the miser. He says: 'This boundless drive for enrichment, this passionate chase after value, is common to the capitalist and the miser' (Marx 1976: 254). Here passion drives the accumulation of capital: the capitalist is not interested in the use-value of commodities, but the 'appropriation of ever more wealth' (Marx 1976: 254). What I am offering is a theory of passion not as the drive to accumulate (whether it be value, power or meaning), but as that which is accumulated over time. Affect does not reside in an object or sign, but is an effect of the circulation between objects and signs (= the accumulation of affective value). Signs increase in affective value as an effect of the movement between signs: the more signs circulate, the more affective they become.

Of course, this argument does not respect the important Marxian distinction between use value and exchange value and hence relies on a limited analogy. In some ways, my approach has more in common with a psychoanalytic emphasis on difference and displacement as the form or language of the unconscious, described [earlier]. Where my approach involves a departure from psychoanalysis is in my refusal to identify this economy as a psychic one (although neither is it *not* a psychic one), that is, to return these relationships of difference and displacement to the signifier of 'the subject'. This 'return' is not only clear in

Freud's work, but also in Lacan's positing of 'the subject' as the proper scene of absence and loss (see Ahmed 1998: 97–8). In contrast, my model of hate as an affective economy suggests that emotions do not positively inhabit *anybody* or *anything*, meaning that 'the subject' is simply one nodal point in the economy, rather than its origin and destination. This is extremely important: it suggests that the sideways and backwards movement of emotions such as hate is not contained within the contours of a subject. The unconscious is hence not the unconscious of a subject, but the failure of presence – or the failure to be present – that constitutes the relationality of subject, objects, signs and others. Given this, affective economies are social and material, as well as psychic. Indeed, if the movement of affect is crucial to the very differentiation between 'in here' and 'out there', then the psychic and the social cannot be installed as proper objects. Instead, I examine how materialisation involves a process of intensification.

More specifically, it is the circulation of hate between figures that works to materialise the very 'surface' of collective bodies. We can take as an example the speeches on asylum seekers by one of the previous leaders of the Conservative Party in the UK, William Hague. Between April and June 2000, other speeches were in circulation that became 'stuck' or 'attached' to the 'asylum seekers' speech partly through temporal proximity, but also through the repetition with a difference, of some *sticky words* and language. In the case of the asylum speeches, Hague's narrative is somewhat predictable. Words like 'flood' and 'swamped' are used, which create associations between asylum and the loss of control and hence work by mobilising fear, or the anxiety of being overwhelmed by the actual or potential proximity of others. These words were repeated in 2003 by the current British Home Secretary David Blunkett, who used 'swamped' to describe the effect on others that children of asylum seekers would have if they were taught in local schools. When criticised, he replaced the word 'swamped' with 'overwhelmed'. The assumption here is that 'over-whelmed' resolves the implication of 'swamped', but as we can see, the word still evokes the sensation of being overtaken or taken over by others. The word constructs the nation as if it were a subject, as one who 'could not cope' with the presence of others. Such words generate effects: they create impressions of others as those who have invaded the space of the nation, threatening its existence.

In the earlier speech, Hague differentiates between those others who are welcome and those who are not by differentiating between genuine and bogus asylum seekers. Partly, this enables the national subject to imagine its generosity in welcoming some others. The nation is hospitable as it allows those genuine ones to stay. And yet at the same time, it constructs some others as already hateful (as bogus) in order to define the limits or the *conditions* of this hospitality. The construction of the bogus asylum seeker as a figure of hate also involves a narrative of uncertainty and crisis, but an uncertainty and crisis that *makes that figure do more work*. How can we tell the difference between a bogus and a genuine asylum seeker? It is always possible that we may not be able to tell, and that the bogus may pass their way into our community. Such a possibility commands us (our right, our will) to keep looking, and justifies our intrusion into the bodies of others.

Indeed, the possibility that we may not be able to tell the difference swiftly converts into the possibility that *any* of those incoming bodies may be bogus. In advance of their arrival, they are read as the cause of an injury to the national body. The figure of the bogus asylum seeker evokes the figure of the 'bogey man', as a figure that stalks the nation and haunts its capacity to secure its borders. The 'bogey man' could be anywhere and anyone; a ghost-like figure in the present, who gives us nightmares about the future, as an anticipation of a future injury. We see 'him' again and again. Such figures of hate circulate, and indeed accumulate their affective value, precisely insofar as they do not have a fixed referent. So the figure of the bogus asylum seeker is detached from particular bodies: any incoming bodies *could be* bogus, such that their 'endless' arrival is anticipated as the scene of 'our injury'.[3] The impossibility of reducing hate to a particular body allows hate to circulate in an economic sense, working to differentiate some others from other others, a differentiation that is never 'over', as it awaits others who have not yet arrived. Such a discourse of 'waiting for the bogus' is what justifies the repetition of violence against the bodies of others in the name of protecting the nation.

Hague's speech also generated certain effects through its temporal proximity to another speech about Tony Martin, a man sentenced to life imprisonment for murdering a 16-year-old boy who had attempted, along with one other person, to burgle his house. One sentence of Hague's circulates powerfully. He stated following the sentencing of Martin (but without reference to the Martin case) that the law is 'more interested in the rights of criminals than the rights of people who are burgled'. *Such a sentence evokes a history that is not declared* (this is how attachment can operate as a form of speech, as resistance to literalisation). The undeclared history sticks, and it positions Martin as the victim rather than the criminal, as a person who was burgled, rather than a person who killed. The victim of the murder is now the criminal; the crime that did not happen because of the murder (the burglary) takes the place of the murder as the true crime, and as the real injustice.

The implicit argument that killing in defence of your home makes you a victim acquired more force when Tony Martin was released in August 2003. Tabloids described Tony Martin as an 'ordinary farmer' whose home was ruined during his prison sentence (McGurran and Johnston 2003: 4). The headline on the front page of the *Daily Mirror* sums it up: 'He killed to protect his house . . . but now the memories are too much' (*Daily Mirror*, 9 August 2003). The tragedy of the story is not the death of 'a teenage burglar' but Tony Martin's loss of his home: 'This isn't a home any more. It's a shell' (McGurran and Johnston 2003: 4). The 'shell', an empty and barren place, becomes a sign of the injustice of Martin's prison sentence. The moral of the story becomes: those who defend their property must be defended by the law. In other words, the reversal of the victim/criminal relationship is an implicit and unarticulated defence of the right to kill those who unlawfully enter one's property.

The coincidence of William Hague's words: 'The law is more interested in the rights of criminals than the rights of people who are burgled' in connection with asylum seekers was also affective. The detachment of that sentence allows the two cases to get stuck together, burglary and asylum, which now both become matters of the right to defence. More specifically, the figure of the asylum seeker is aligned with the figure of the burglar. The alignment does important work: it suggests that the asylum seeker is 'stealing' something from the nation. The 'characteristics' of one figure get displaced or transferred onto the other. Or we could say that it is through the association between the figures that they acquire 'a life of their own', as if they contain an affective quality. The burglar becomes a foreigner, and the asylum seeker becomes a criminal. At the same time, the body of the murderer (who is renamed as the victim) becomes the body of the nation; the one whose property and well-being is under threat by the proximity of the other. The sticking together of these speeches produces the following claim: the nation, like Tony Martin, has the right to expel asylum seekers (whatever the means), who as burglars are trying to steal something from the nation, otherwise the nation itself will become 'the shell'. The moral of the story becomes: if we let them in, they will turn the nation 'into a shell', and take the land on which 'we have worked'.

Such a defensive narrative is not explicitly articulated, but rather works through the 'movement' between figures. The circulation does its work: it produces a differentiation between 'us' and 'them', whereby 'they' are constituted as the cause of 'our' feeling of hate. Indeed, we can see how attachment involves a sliding between pain and hate: there is a perceived injury in which the proximity of others (burglars/bogus asylum seekers) is felt as the violence of negation against both the body of the individual (the farmer) and the body of the nation. Bodies surface by 'feeling' the presence of others as the cause of injury or as a form of intrusion. The signs of hate surface by evoking a sense of threat and risk, but one that cannot be simply located or found. This difficulty of location is what makes hate work the way that it does; it is not the impossibility of hate as such, but the mode of its operation, whereby it surfaces in a world made up of other bodies. It is the failure of hate to be located in a given object or figure, which allows it to generate the effects that it does.

Hated bodies

In this section, I examine how hate works on and through bodies. How does hate involve the spatial reorganisation of bodies through the very gestures of moving away from others that are felt to be the 'cause' of our hate? We need to reflect firstly on the experience of hate. Hate is an intense emotion; it involves a feeling of 'againstness' that is always, in the phenomenological sense, intentional. Hate is always hatred of something or somebody, although that something or somebody does not necessarily pre-exist the emotion. It is possible, of course, to hate an individual person because of what they have done or what they are like. This would be a hate brought about by the particularity of engagement, and one that makes it possible to say, 'I hate you' to a face that is familiar, and to turn away, trembling. It is this kind of hate that is described by Baird and Rosenbaum when they talk of 'seeth[ing] with passion against another human being' (Baird and Rosenbaum 1992: 9). And yet, classically, Aristotle differentiated anger from hatred in that 'anger is customarily felt towards individuals only, whereas hatred may be felt toward whole classes of people' (cited in Allport 1992: 31). Hate may respond to the particular, but it tends to do so by aligning the particular with the general; 'I hate you because you are this or that', where the 'this' or 'that' evokes a group that the individual comes to *stand for* or stand in *for*. Hatred may also work as a form of investment; it endows a particular other with meaning or power by locating them as a member of a group, which is then imagined as a form of positive residence (that is, as residing positively in the body of the individual).

As an investment, hate involves the negotiation of an intimate relationship between a subject and an imagined other, as another that cannot be relegated to the outside. Indeed, a psychoanalytical model used to explain hatred is projection. Here, the self projects all that is undesirable onto another, while concealing any traces of that projection, so that the other comes to appear as a being with a life of its own (see Laplanche and Pontalis 1988: 352). We also have the Kleinian model of projective identification, which is described by Ian Craib as 'a more profound form of projection . . . I behave in such a way as to lead the other person to experience that quality in themselves' (cited in Bird and Clarke 1999: 332). However, this model of projection or projective identification is limited to the extent that it repeats the commonly held assumption that hate moves from inside to outside (pushing what is undesir- able out), even if it undermines the objectivity of this distinction. In other words, it takes for granted the existence of negative feelings within the subject, which then become 'the origin' of hatred for others. Whilst there is of course a certain truth within this insistence (bad feelings are crucial to modes of subject formation), negative feelings 'within' might also be effects. The very distinction between inside and outside might be affected by hate. Rather than assuming that hate involves pushing what is undesirable within the self onto others, we could ask: *Why is it that hate feels like it comes from inside and is directed towards others who have an independent existence?*

To consider hatred as a form of intimacy is to show how hatred is ambivalent; it is an investment in an object (of hate) whereby the object becomes part of the life of the subject even though (or perhaps because) its threat is perceived as coming from outside. Hate then cannot be opposed to love. In other words, the subject becomes attached to the other through hatred, as an attachment that returns the subject to itself. Certainly, within psychological theories of prejudice, hate is seen as tied up with love. Or, to put it more precisely, love is understood as the pre-condition of hate. Gorden W. Allport in his classic account *The Nature of Prejudice* suggests that the 'symbiosis and a loving relation always precede hate. There can, in fact, be no hatred until there has been long-continued frustration and disappointment' (Allport 1979: 215). Allport draws on Ian Suttie's *The Origins of Love and Hate*, which argues that hatred 'owes all its meaning to a demand for love' (Suttie 1963: 37), and is bound up with the anxiety of the discovery of the not-self (Suttie 1963: 40). Freud, of course, considers the intimacy of love and hate as affectations for objects throughout the corpus of his work. In *Beyond the Pleasure Principle*, the love for the mother is 'expressed' through a hostile game with a mother-substitute: in the child's game *'fort da'*, the child sends an object away, and then pulls it back. The game is partly read as an attempt to convert the passivity of love, in the face of the loved other's departure, with hostile aggression, as if to say 'All right, then, go away!' (Freud 1964c: 16). If the demand for love is the demand for presence, and frustration is the consequence of the necessary failure of that demand, then hate and love are intimately tied together, in the intensity of the negotiation between presence and absence.

It would be problematic to derive all forms of hate from the psycho-dynamics of the child's relation to its first love, the mother. Such a derivation would be a clear instance of the psychologisation of emotions, in which different emotions are always referred back to a primal scene. And yet from the Freudian model, we can begin to grasp the complexity of attachments to objects, and the ways in which such attachments are *sustained* through the conversion of positive to negative feeling. As David Holbrook suggests in *The Masks of Hate*: 'Indifference would manifest our lack of need for the object. Where there is hate there is obviously an *excessive need* for the object' (Holbrook 1972: 36). In other words, hate is opposed to indifference: in hate, the object makes a difference, but cannot satisfy the subject, whose need goes beyond it. However, it is not that the object itself is needed, or that the object is simply determinant. The subject may need the destructive relation to that object: one may be attached to the attachment of hate. Christopher Bollas (1995) differentiates between hate that is destructive, and 'loving hate', which seeks to conserve the object. There is a relation between destructive attachments and conservation: *for the destructive relation to the object to be maintained the object itself must be conserved in some form.* So hate transforms this or that other into an object whose expulsion or incorporation is needed, an expulsion or incorporation that requires the conservation of the object itself in order to be sustained. Such an argument does not presume that one must have first loved an object to hate it (the conversion of hate to love is possible but not necessary), but it does suggest that hate sustains the object through its mode of attachment, in a way that has a similar dynamic to love, but with a different orientation. As Mikkel Borch-Jacobsen puts it, 'Hate wants *to get its hands on* the other; it wants to touch even when it wants to destroy' (Borch-Jacobsen 1993: 10).

Hate is involved in the very negotiation of boundaries between selves and others, and between communities, where 'others' are brought into the sphere of my or our existence as a threat. This other, who may stand for or stand by other others, *presses* against me, threatening my existence. The proximity of the other's touch is felt as a negation. Hate involves a turning away from others that is lived as a turning towards the self. We can now see why stories of hate are *already* translated into stories of love. Of course, it is not that hate is involved in any demarcation between me and not-me, but that some demarcations come into existence through hate, which is felt as coming from within and moving outwards towards others. If hate is felt as belonging to me but caused by an other, then the others (however imaginary) are required for the very continuation of the life of the 'I' or the 'we'. To this extent, boundary formations are bound up with anxiety not as a sensation that comes organically from within a subject or group, but as the effect of this ongoing constitution of the 'apartness' of a subject or group.

However, it would be insufficient to posit the story of the 'I' and 'we' as parallel or homologous. Rather, what is at stake in the intensity of hate as a negative attachment to others is how hate creates the 'I' and the 'we' as utterable simultaneously in a moment of alignment. At one level, we can see that an 'I' that declares itself as hating an other (and who might or might not act in accordance with the declaration) comes into existence by also declaring its love for that which is threatened by this imagined other (the nation, the community and so on). But at another level, we need to investigate the 'we' as the effect of the attachment itself; such a subject becomes not only attached to a 'we', but the 'we' is what is affected by the attachment the subject has to itself and to its loved others. Hence in hating another, this subject is also loving itself; hate structures the emotional life of narcissism as a fantastic investment in the continuation of the image of the self in the faces that together make up the 'we'. The attachment to others becomes divided as negative and positive (hate and love) precisely through imaging the faces of the community made up of other 'me's', of others that are loved *as if they were me*.

When Freud suggests in *Group Psychology* (1922) and *The Ego and the Id* (1964b) that we identify with those we love he went some way toward addressing this relationship between ego formation and community. The ego is established by imitating the lost object of love; it is based on a principle of a likeness or resemblance or of *becoming alike*. [. . .] However, I would argue that love does not pre-exist identification (just as hate does not pre-exist dis-identification); so it is not a question of identifying with those we love and dis-identifying with those we hate. Rather, it is through forms of identification that align this subject with this other, that the *character* of the loved is produced as 'likeness' in the first place. Thinking of identification as a form of alignment (to bring into line with ourselves – the subject as 'bringing into line') also shows us how identifications involve dis-identification or an active 'giving up' of other possible identifications (see Butler 1997b). That is, by aligning myself with some others, I am aligning myself against other others. Such a 'giving up' may also produce the character of the hated as 'unlikeness'. What is at stake in the emotional intensities of love and hate, then, is the production of the effect of likeness and unlikeness as characteristics that are assumed to belong to the bodies of individuals. This separation of others into bodies that *can be* loved and hated is part of the work of emotion; it does not pre-exist emotion as its ground – 'I love or hate them *because* they are like me, or not like me.' The effects of the circulation of objects of hate are hence retrospectively evoked as the origin of hate ('I hate them *because* they are unlike us'). So hate works by providing 'evidence' of the very antagonism it affects; we cite the work that it is doing in producing the characteristics of likeness and unlikeness when we show the reasons for its existence. In seeing the other as 'being' hateful, the subject is filled up with hate, which becomes a sign of the 'truth' of the reading.

I have suggested that emotions, which respond to the proximity of others, do not respond the way that they do because of the inherent characteristics of others: we do not respond with love or hate because others are loveable or hateful. It is through affective encounters that objects and others are perceived as having attributes, which 'gives' the subject an identity that is apart from others (for example, as the real victim or as the threatened nation). How does this attribution work on and through bodies? Let's take the following quote from Black feminist Audre Lorde, about her encounter with a white woman on a train:

The AA subway train to Harlem. I clutch my mother's sleeve, her arms full of shopping bags, christmas-heavy. The wet smell of winter clothes, the train's lurching. My mother spots an almost seat, pushes my little snow-suited body down. On one side of me a man reading a paper. On the other, a woman in a fur hat staring at me. Her mouth twitches as she stares and then her gaze drops down, pulling mine with it. Her leather-gloved hand plucks at the line where my new blue snowpants and her sleek fur coat meet. She jerks her coat closer to her. I look. I do not see whatever terrible thing she is seeing on the seat between us — probably a roach. But she has communicated her horror to me. It must be something very bad from the way she's looking, so I pull my snowsuit closer to me away from it, too. When I look up the woman is still staring at me, her nose holes and eyes huge. And suddenly I realise there is nothing crawling up the seat between us; it is me she doesn't want her coat to touch. The fur brushes past my face as she stands with a shudder and holds on to a strap in the speeding train. Born and bred a New York City child, I quickly slide over to make room for my mother to sit down. No word has been spoken. I'm afraid to say anything to my mother because I don't know what I've done. I look at the sides of my snowpants secretly. Is there something on them? Something's going on here I do not understand, but I will never forget it. Her eyes. The flared nostrils. The hate.

(Lorde 1984: 147–8)

In this encounter Audre Lorde ends with 'The hate', as an emotion that seems detached from bodies, surrounding the scene with its violence. And yet, the word 'hate' works by working on the surfaces of bodies. This bodily encounter, while ending with 'The hate', also ends with the reconstitution of bodily space. The bodies that come together, that almost touch and co-mingle, slide away from each other, becoming relived in their apartness. The particular bodies that move apart allow the redefinition of social as well as bodily integrity. The emotion of 'hate' aligns the particular white body with the bodily form of the community – the emotion functions to substantiate the threat of invasion and contamination in the body of a particular other, who comes to stand for and stand in for, a group of others. In other words, the hate encounter aligns, not only the 'I' with the 'we' (the white body, the white nation), but the 'you' with the 'them' (the black body, black people).

Does Audre's narrative of the encounter involve her self-designation as the hated; does she hate herself? Certainly, her perception of the cause of the woman's bodily gestures is a misperception that creates an object. The object – the roach – comes to stand for, or stand in for, the cause of 'the hate'. The roach crawls up between them; the roach, as the carrier of dirt, divides the two bodies, forcing them to move apart. Audre pulls her snowsuit, 'away from it too'. But the 'it' that divides them is not the roach. Audre comes to realise that, 'it is me she doesn't want her coat to touch'. What the woman's clothes must not touch is not a roach that crawls between them, but Audre herself. Audre becomes the 'it' that stands between the possibility of their clothes touching. She becomes the roach – the impossible and phobic object – that threatens to crawl from one to the other: 'I don't know what I've done. I look at the sides of my snowpants secretly. Is there something on them?' Hate slides between different signs and objects whose existence is bound up with the negation of its travel. Audre becomes the roach that is then imagined as the cause of the hate. The association between the roach and her body works powerfully. Her body becomes an object of hate through 'taking on' the qualities already attached to the roach: dirty, contaminating, evil. The transformation of *this* or *that* other into an object of hate is over-determined. It is not simply that any body is hated: particular histories of association are reopened in each encounter, such that some bodies are already encountered as more hateful than other bodies. Histories are bound up with emotions precisely insofar as it is a question of *what sticks*, of what connections are lived as the most intense or intimate, as being closer to the skin.

Importantly, then, the alignment of some bodies with some others and against others take place in the *physicality of movement*; bodies are dis-organised and re-organised as they face others who are already recognised as 'the hated'. So the white woman loses her seat to keep the black child at a distance, in the 'speeding' movements of the train. The organisation of social and bodily space creates a border that is transformed into an object, as an effect of this intensification of feeling. The white woman's refusal to touch the black child does not simply *stand for* the expulsion of blackness from white social space, but *actually re-forms that social space through re-forming the apartness of the white body*. The re-forming of bodily and social space involves a process of *making the skin crawl*; the threat posed by the bodies of others to bodily and social integrity is registered on the skin. Or, to be more precise, the skin comes to be felt as a border through the violence of the impression of one surface upon another. In this way, hate creates the surfaces of bodies through the way in which bodies are aligned with and against other bodies. How we feel about others is what aligns us with a collective, which paradoxically 'takes shape' only as an effect of such alignments. It is through how others impress upon us that the skin of the collective begins to take shape.

Hate crime

Hate involves the surfacing of bodies through how we encounter others in intimate and public spaces. The politics of racial hatred involves attributing racial others with meaning, a process we can describe as 'the making of unlikeness'. Hatred is a negative attachment to an other that one wishes to expel, an attachment that is sustained through the expulsion of the other from bodily and social proximity. In this section, I want to bring the arguments of the previous two sections together. That is, I will explore how affective economies of hate, where hate circulates in signs that are detached from particular bodies, affect the way bodies take shape. In particular, I will consider how the movement between signs of hate affects the bodies of those who become the objects of hatred.

In order to explore the connection between the language of hate and the surfacing of bodies, I will examine the politics of hate crime. Hate crimes typically are defined when the crime is committed *because of* an individual's group identity (defined in terms of race, religion, sexuality):

> If a person . . . intentionally selects the person against whom the crime . . . is committed or selects the property which is damaged or otherwise affected by the crime . . . *because* of the race, religion, color, disability, sexual orientation, national origin or ancestry of that person or the owner or occupant of the property, the penalties for the underlying crime are increased [*Wisconsin* v. *Mitchell*.].
>
> (Jacobs and Potter 1998: 3, emphasis added)

What is at stake in hate crime is the *perception* of a group in the body of an individual. However, the way in which it is perception that is at stake is concealed by the word 'because' in hate crime legislation, which implies that group identity is already in place, and that it works only as a cause, rather than also being an effect of the crime.[4] The fact that hate crime involves a perception of a group in the body of the individual does not make the violence any less real or 'directed'; this perception has material effects insofar as it is enacted through violence. That is, hate crime works as a form of violence against groups *through* violence against the bodies of individuals. Violence against others may be one way in which the other's identity is fixed or sealed; the other is *forced* to embody a particular identity by and for the perpetrator of the crime, and that force involves harm or injury.

The legal response to hate crime is one way of dealing with the injustice of violence against minority groups.[5] I suggest that 'hate crime' may be useful as a technology of redress because it can make explicit the role of hate as an intense and negative attachment to others in the politics of racism, as well as other forms of structural violence. As Zillah Eisenstein argues, attending to hate allows us to show how racism involves psychic and bodily investments (Eisenstein 1994: 5–22). For some, this is the risk of hate crime legislation: it can attribute power to psychology, or transform power into psychology. David Theo Goldberg, for example, argues that the use of hate turns racist expression into a psychological disposition (Goldberg 1995: 269). AnnJanette Rosga argues that the use of hate crime as a category has 'a susceptibility to individualised models of oppression through its mobilisation of personal, psychological notions of prejudice and hatred' (Rosga 1999: 149). These critiques are useful, and they remind us of the importance of understanding emotions not as psychological dispositions, but as investments in social norms. Attending to the politics of hate allows us to address the question of how subjects and others become *invested* in norms such that their demise would be felt as a kind of living death. While we need to take care to avoid psychologising power and inequality, we also need to avoid reifying structures and institutions. To consider the investments we have in structures is precisely to attend to how they become meaningful – or indeed, are felt as natural – through the emotional work of labour, work that takes time, and that takes place in time. So 'hate crime' as a category can show us that violence against others involves forms of power that are visceral and bodily, as well as social and structural.

But if hate is part of the production of the ordinary, rather than simply about 'extremists' (perhaps we should say that 'extremes' are part of the production of the ordinary), then we need to ask if it makes any sense to talk about hate as a crime. While it might be important to challenge the narrative which sees hate as something extremists do (which saves the 'ordinary nation', or 'ordinary subjects', from any responsibility for its violence), it is equally important to see that there are different ways in which hate operates. In other words, particular acts (including physical violence directed towards others, as well as name calling and abusive language) do not necessarily *follow* from the uneven effects of hate. Of course, not all subjects hate in the same way. We can demarcate certain actions as wrong and unjustifiable. Such actions can be seen as the responsibility of individuals or groups who commit them. Undermining the distinction between hate and hate crime in the non-opposition between the ordinary and criminal does not mean an emptying out of responsibility for the effects of hate crime.

The terms of my argument about the usefulness of hate crime as a category also suggest its limits: hate crime does not refer to a discrete set of enactments that stand apart from the uneven effects that hate already has in organising the surfaces of the world (though neither does it simply follow from them, as I have suggested). The limits of hate crime then may partly be the limits of the law that seeks to designate the criminal as an ontological category. Insofar as hate enacts the negation that is perceived to characterise the existence of a social group, then we can link hate to injustice, an injustice that is, of course, irreducible to the law, at the same time as it has a relation to it (see Derrida 1992). If hate is always directed to others as a way of *sealing* their fate, then hate may be *about* the effect it has on others. Given this, the introduction of hate crime as a category should be used as a way of making visible the effects of hate, by *listening to the affective life of injustice*, rather than establishing the truth of law.

We can return to Audre Lorde's example. We can ask: How is the black body re-formed in the encounter? What happens to those bodies that are encountered as objects of hate, as having the characteristic of 'unlikeness'? In my earlier reading, I emphasised the effect of the encounter on the white body that becomes lived as apart. What I failed to ask was the role of hate, as a social encounter between others, on the bodies of those who are designated as hated. It is this failure that I take as symptomatic of a tendency to think of hate and hate crime from the point of view of those who hate rather than those who are hated. The destruction of the bodies of the hated is, of course, what is often sought in hate crime itself. To allow such bodies to disappear in our own analysis would be to repeat the crime rather than to redress its injustice.

In the case of Audre's story, Audre's gestures mimic the white woman's. Her gaze is 'pulled down', following the gaze of the white woman. This pulling down of the gaze and the transformation of the black body into an object of its own gaze seems crucial. The hated body becomes hated, not just for the one who hates, but for the one who is hated. This 'taking on' of the white gaze is central to Frantz Fanon's argument in *Black Skin, White Masks*, where he describes how the black body is 'sealed into that crushing objecthood' (Fanon 1986: 109). When Audre's gaze is pulled down with the white woman's, she feels 'afraid'. She comes to recognise herself as the object of the woman's hate: she is 'hailed', in Althusser's (1971) sense, as the hated. The 'doing' of hate is not simply 'done' in the moment of its articulation. A chain of effects (which are at once affects) are in circulation. The circulation of objects of hate is not free. In this instance, bodies that are attributed as being hateful – as the origin of feelings of hate – are (temporarily) sealed in their skins. Such bodies assume the *character of the negative*. That transformation of this body into the body of the hated, in other words, leads to the enclosure or sealing of the other's body within a figure of hate. The white woman who moves away from Audre moves on, of course. *Some bodies move precisely by sealing others as objects of hate.*

Our task may then be to reflect on how it feels to be an object. Mari J. Matsuda's work emphasises the effects of hate on the bodies of the victims. She writes:

> The negative effects of hate messages are real and immediate for the victims. Victims of vicious hate propaganda experience physiological symptoms and emotional distress ranging from fear in the gut to rapid pulse rate and difficulty in breathing, nightmares, post-traumatic stress disorder, hypertension, psychosis and suicide.
>
> (Matsuda 1993: 24)

The enactment of hate through verbal or physical violence, Matsuda suggests 'hits right at the emotional place where we feel the most pain' (Matsuda 1993: 25). Such lived experiences of pain can be understood as part of the work of hate, or as part of what hate *is doing*. Hate has effects on the bodies of those who are made into its objects; such bodies are affected by the hate that is directed towards them by others. Hate is not simply a means by which the identity of the subject and community is established (through alignment); hate also works to unmake the world of the other through pain (see Scarry 1985). Or hate crimes seek to *crush* the other in what Patricia Williams has called 'spirit murder' (cited in Matsuda 1993: 24).

If the effect of hate crime is affect, and an affect which is visceral and bodily, as Matsuda's work has emphasised, then *the body of the victim is read as testimony*, as a means by which the truth of hate crime is established in law. This poses a particular problem for the incitement to hatred laws as they relate to hate speech. The effects must be seen as fully determined by the crime, a determination that, in a strict sense, is very difficult to establish, without evidence that can be described as bruised skin or other traces of bodily violence. So critics such as Ray Jureidini have mentioned the 'subjectivity' of hate speech laws as a problem: 'Some people are offended by ethnic jokes and name-calling as a problem, some are not' (Jureidini 2000: 13). If the affect and effects of hate speech are not fully determined, then to what extent can 'harm' become evidence for the injustice of hate speech? To what extent can listening to the victim's story become a means of delivering justice?

We can consider here the important critiques made by Wendy Brown (1995) and Lauren Berlant (2000) of 'wound culture', which fetishises the wound as proof of identity. Wound culture takes the injury of the individual as the grounds not only for an appeal (for compensation or redress), but as an identity claim, such that 'reaction' against the injury forms the very basis of politics, understood as the conflation of truth and injustice (Brown 1995· 73) What must follow from such critiques should not be a refusal to listen to histories of pain as part of the histories of injustice, whereby pain is understood as *the bodily life of such histories*. The fetishising of the wound can only take place by concealing these histories; the greater injustice would be to repeat that fetishisation by forgetting the processes of being wounded by others. I am suggesting the *importance of listening to the affects and effects of hate and hate crime* as a way of calling into question, rather than assuming, the relationship between violence and identity. To say these affects and effects are not fully determined, and that they do not congeal into an identity, is not to suggest that the affects and effects don't matter, and that they are not a form of injustice, even if they cannot function in a narrow sense as evidence or an identity claim. Indeed, to treat such testimonies of injury as evidence would perform its own injustice: the language and bodies of hate don't operate on the terrain of truth, they operate to make and unmake worlds, made up of other bodies. Listening to the affects of hate crime must involve recognising that the affects are not always determined: we cannot assume we know in advance what it feels like to be the object of hate. For some, hate enactments may involve pain; for others, rage. So if the pain of others is the 'intention' of hate crime, then hate crime is not always guaranteed to succeed. We have to have open ears to hear the affects of hate.

But what does the failure of hate as an action against others to determine fully its effects mean for politics? In *Excitable Speech* (1997a) Judith Butler considers the impossibility of deciding in advance the meaning of hate speech for hate crime. She suggests that any signifier can be mobilised in different ways and in new contexts, so that even signs we assume stand for hate (and can only stand for hate), can operate otherwise, such as the burning cross (Butler 1997a: 19). Butler hence criticises the work of Matsuda, amongst others, which she suggests assume that hate resides in particular signs and that the effects of such signs are already determined in advance of their circulation. I am in agreement with Butler. As I have argued in this chapter, hate is economic, and it does not reside positively in a sign or body. But Butler overlooks the relationship between affect and effect that is crucial to Matsuda's own work. Following Matsuda, we need to relate the question of the effect of hate speech with *affect*, which includes the question of how others have been affected by hate speech. Following Butler, we might recognise that the affects are not determined in advance. But if they are not determined in advance, then how do they come to be determined? We need to ask: How do certain signs of hate produce affective responses? Or why are some signs of hate repeated? Is it because such signs are over-determined; is it because they keep open a history which is already open insofar as it is affective?

The fact that some signs are repeated is precisely *not* because the signs themselves contain hate, but because they are effects of histories that have stayed open. Words like 'Nigger' or 'Paki' for example tend to stick; they hail the other precisely by bringing another into a history whereby such names assign the other with meaning in an economy of difference. Such words and signs *tend to stick*, which does not mean they cannot operate otherwise. Rather, they cannot simply be liberated from the history of this use as violence or insult, even if they cannot be reduced to that history. Another way of putting this is to say that some words stick because they become attached *through* particular affects. So, for example, someone will hurl racial insults (the white woman who retreats from Audre may mutter under her breath to a compliant witness, 'nigger' and 'roach': an insult that is directed against an other, but mediated by a third party), precisely because they are affective, although it is not always guaranteed that the other will be 'impressed upon' or hurt in a way that follows from the history of insults. It is the affective nature of hate speech that allows us to understand that whether such speech works or fails to work is not really the important question. Rather, the important question is: *What effects do such encounters have on the bodies of others who become transformed into objects of hate?*

This question can only be asked if we consider how hate works as an affective economy; hate does not reside positively in signs, but circulates or moves between signs and bodies. The circulation of signs of hate involves movement and fixity; some bodies move precisely by sealing others as objects of hate. Tracking the history of hate involves reading the surfaces of bodies, as well as listening to those who have been shaped by this history.

Notes

1   http://www.nidlink.com/~aryanvic/index-E.html Accessed 4 January 2002.

2   Thanks to David Eng for this point.

3   For the British National Party, this argument that 'any' body could be bogus gets translated into 'all' are bogus: 'We will abolish the "positive discrimination" schemes that have made white Britons second-class citizens. We will also clamp down on the flood of "asylum seekers", all of whom are either bogus or can find refuge much nearer their home countries.' See the British National Party website, http://www.bnp.org.uk/policies.html#immigration Accessed 30 July 2003.

4   There are some difficulties around cause and effect here. I would argue with Rosga (1999) that hate crime legislation does tend to reify social groups, by assuming that groups are sealed entities that hate is then directed towards. At the same time, I would question the work of critics such as Jacobs and Potter (1998), who in arguing against the efficacy of the category 'hate crime' suggest that the legislation itself is creating the divisions that the crime is supposed to be a result of. They hence imply that such divisions would not exist if they were not introduced and then exacerbated through hate crime legislation. I cannot go along with this. Rather, I would argue that hate crimes (which I define as forms of violence directed towards others that are perceived to be members of a social group, whereby the violence is 'directed' towards the group) work to effect divisions partly by enforcing others into an identity through violence. This does not mean that others are not aligned with an identity (= identification) before the violence. In other words, the enactment of hate through violence does not 'invent' social groups out of nothing. Rather, such enactments function as a form of enforcement; hate crimes may work by sealing a particular other into an identity that is *already* affective. The distinction between cause and effect is hence not useful: hate both affects, and is affected by, the sealing of others into group identities. This is why some bodies and not others become the object of hate crimes: hate ties the particular with the group only by reopening a past history of violence and exclusion that allows us to recognise the bodies of some others *as out of place* (see Ahmed 2000: 38–54). Of course, the relevant laws within the UK – the 'incitement to racial hatred' in Part III (ss. 17–29) of the Public Order Act 1986 – are about hate speech rather than hate crime defined in the terms above. Here, racial hatred is not described as the origin of crime, but as the effect (there is criminal liability if a person uses or publishes words or commits acts that are theatening, abusive or insulting, and which are likely to 'stir up' racial hatred). Hence hate speech laws tend to criminalise hate as effect, and hate crime laws to criminalise hate as origin; both of them fail to recognise the role played by hate *in an economy of affects and effects.*

5   In a very interesting article, Muneer Ahmad examines the use of the language of 'hate crime' after September 11, analysing the discourses around the murder of five men. He suggests that 'the hate crime killings before September 11 were viewed as crimes of moral depravity, while the hate killings since September 11 have been understood as crimes of passion' (Ahmad 2002: 108). This shift

occurs, he suggests, because the 'hate' that was directed against 'others' was shared by the vast majority of Americans; in other words, the crimes become 'crimes of passion' insofar as a collective anger against the attacks gets displaced into an anger towards racial others. Thanks to David Eng for directing me to Ahmad's article.

References

Ahmad, M. (2002), 'Homeland Insecurities: Racial Violence the Day after September 11', *Social Text* 72, 20 (3): 101–15.

Ahmed, S. (1998), *Differences that Matter: Feminist Theory and Postmodernism*, Cambridge: Cambridge University Press.

—— (2000), *Strange Encounters: Embodied Others in Post-Coloniality*, London: Routledge.

—— (2004), *The Cultural Politics of Emotion*, New York: Routledge.

Allport, G. W. (1979), *The Nature of Prejudice*, Reading, MA: Addison-Wesley Publishing Company.

—— (1992), 'The Nature of Hatred' in R. M. Baird and S. E. Rosenbaum (eds), *Bigotry, Prejudice and Hatred: Definitions, Causes and Solutions*, Buffalo, NY: Prometheus Books.

Althusser, L. (1971), *Lenin and Philosophy*, trans. B. Brewster, New York: Monthly Review Press.

Baird, R. M. and Rosenbaum, S. E. (1992), 'Introduction' in R. M. Baird and S. E. Rosenbaum (eds), *Bigotry, Prejudice and Hatred: Definitions, Causes and Solutions*, Buffalo, NY: Prometheus Books.

Berlant, L. (2000), 'The Subject of True Feeling: Pain, Privacy and Politics' in S. Ahmed, J. Kilby, C. Lury, M. McNeil and B. Skeggs (eds), *Transformations: Thinking Through Feminism*, London: Routledge.

Bird, J. and Clarke, S. (1999), 'Racism, Hatred, and Discrimination Through the Lens of Projective Identification', *Journal for the Psychoanalysis of Culture and Society* 4 (2): 332–5.

Bollas, C. (1995), 'Loving Hate', *Annual of Psychoanalysis* 12 (13): 221–37.

Borch-Jacobsen, M. (1993), *The Emotional Tie: Psychoanalysis, Mimesis, and Affect*, Stanford: Stanford University Press.

Brown, W. (1995), *States of Injury: Power and Freedom in Late Modernity*, Princeton: Princeton University Press.

Butler, J. (1997a), *Excitable Speech: A Politics of the Performative*, New York: Routledge.

—— (1997b), *The Psychic Life of Power: Theories in Subjection*, Stanford: Stanford University Press.

Derrida, J. (1992), 'Force of Law: The "Mystical Foundation of Authority"' in D. Cornell, M. Rosenfeld and D. G. Carlson (eds), *Deconstruction and the Possibility of Justice*, New York: Routledge.

Eisenstein, Z. (1994), 'Writing Hatred on the Body', *New Political Scientist* 30/31: 5–22.

Fanon, F. (1986), *Black Skin, White Masks*, trans. C. L. Markmann, London: Pluto Press.

Freud, S. (1922), *Group Psychology and the Analysis of the Ego*, trans. J. Strachey, London: The International Psycho-Analytical Press.

—— (1964a), 'The Unconscious', *The Standard Edition of the Complete Psychological Works of Sigmund Freud*, vol. 14, trans. J. Strachey, London: The Hogarth Press.

—— (1964b), 'The Ego and the Id', *The Standard Edition of the Complete Psychological Works of Sigmund Freud*, vol. 19, trans. J. Strachey, London: The Hogarth Press.

—— (1964c), 'Beyond the Pleasure Principle', *The Standard Edition of the Complete Psychological Works of Sigmund Freud*, vol. 18, trans. J. Strachey, London: The Hogarth Press.

Goldberg, D. T. (1995), 'Afterword: Hate, or Power?' in R. K. Whillock and D. Slayden (eds), *Hate Speech*, Thousand Oaks, CA: Sage.

Holbrook, D. (1972), *The Masks of Hate: The Problem of False Solutions in the Culture of an Acquisitive Society*, Oxford: Pergamon Press.

Jacobs, J. B. and Potter, K. (1998), *Hate Crimes: Criminal Law and Identity Politics*, New York: Oxford University Press.

Jureidini, R. (2000), 'Origins and Initial Outcomes of the Racial Hatred Act 1995', *People and Place*: http://elecpress.monash.edu.au/pnp/pnpv5nl/jureidin.htm

Laplanche, J. and Pontalis, J.-B. (1988), *The Language of Psycho-Analysis*, trans. D. Nicholson-Smith, London: Karnac Books.

Lorde, A. (1984), *Sister Outsider: Essays and Speeches*, Trumansburg, NY: The Crossing Press.

McGurran, A. and Johnston, J. (2003), 'The Homecoming: It's too Painful: Martin's Sad Return to Farm', *Daily Mirror*, 9 August: 4–5.

Marx, K. (1976), *Capital: A Critique of Political Economy*, vol. 1, trans. B. Fowkes, Harmondsworth: Penguin Books.

Matsuda, M. J. (1993), 'Public Response to Racist Speech: Considering the Victim's Story' in M. J. Matsuda, C. R. Lawrence and R. Delgads, *Words That Wound: Critical Race Theory, Assaultive Speech, and the First Amendment*, Boulder: Westview Press.

Rosga, A. (1999), 'Policing the State', *The Georgetown Journal of Gender and the Law* 1: 145–71.

Suttie, I. D. (1963), *The Origins of Love and Hate*, Harmondsworth: Penguin Books.

Chapter 15

Jennifer Harding

EMOTIONAL SUBJECTS: LANGUAGE AND POWER IN REFUGEE NARRATIVES

Introduction

EMOTIONS ARE HIGHLY intangible and generally exceed our capacities to represent them through language and gesture. Yet, they are effective, intense and powerful communicative practices. Whilst recognising that feelings are not/cannot be always put into words, I examine specific instances where emotions are spoken of and subjects are produced as 'emotional' as part of dominant discourses and the reproduction of unequal power relations.

I discuss connections between emotion, subjectivity and power relations in oral history narratives collected as part of a recent project documenting the lives of refugees in London. I consider how the use of 'emotion words' in discourse on refugees/asylum seekers works to define and position them and to simplify, universalise and limit their experiences. I examine how individual refugees, reflecting on their lives, constitute themselves and others through emotion language, with reference to feeling rules. In short, I consider how 'emotion talk' has participated in the production of specific subjectivities, social realities, and power relations. I endeavour to contextualise and historicise emotion talk.

To be clear, I am not viewing emotions as properties of individuals. Rather, I regard them as fluid inter-subjective processes, which are simultaneously part of the constitution of individuals and collectives, and the relations between them, and of social structures, institutions, patterns of organization, and power relations (Harding and Pribram 2004; Ahmed 2004). Emotions are inevitably part of cultural politics and my interest lies in investigating, not what they are, but what emotions *do* (Ahmed 2004; Harding and Pribram Introduction to this volume). I am concerned with how emotions are spoken about and ascribed to individuals and collectives, and the implications of this.

I am interested in how emotion talk and the production of emotional subjects as a distinctive social practice may form an effective and productive part of certain discourses. In this instance, I am concerned with discourses and counter discourses, which focus on the 'problem' of asylum. I am using 'discourse', in Foucault's sense of the term, to refer to historically and culturally located practices, which not only represent but also constitute social phenomena – including the subjects and objects of discourse, social institutions, practices, and relationships, and power/knowledge (Foucault 1979, 1986). Discourse may be said to produce specific emotions and subjects who are or are not 'emotional' and, in this process, their relations with other subjects (Lupton 1998). Emotion can be seen as part of the ongoing discursive production of subjects and power relations.

Discourse on asylum in Britain – including the policies, institutions and technologies designed to manage immigration – has changed significantly over the last fifty years (Schuster and Solomos 1999; Bloch and Levy 1999). In the last decade, the number of individuals seeking asylum has increased and asylum has been become a prominent issue, fiercely debated in public by politicians, policy makers and journalists and closely linked to the contemporary concerns about social inclusion/cohesion and national identity (Lewis 2005). Talk about fear, anxiety and anger features in this discourse as part of the definition and management of different groups of subjects.

Emotion talk can be seen as a powerful communicative practice – a contemporary 'technology of self' (Foucault 1985) and a 'language of personhood' (Rose 2000). Talk about emotion can be seen as a practice whereby individuals come to focus attention on themselves, their relations to themselves and to others, and to recognise and understand themselves as (certain sorts of) subjects at a specific historical moment (Foucault 1985). Emotion talk – including practices directed at emotion management – can be seen to work *as specific languages of personhood* to shape different forms of self-recognition and locate subjects in particular 'regimes of the person' (Rose 2000). Here, I am concerned with how 'emotion talk' constitutes and delimits the specific forms of personhood – the 'capacities and attributes for social existence as particular sorts of persons' – available to human subjects *as refugees* or, for that matter, *as any other sort of subject* (du Gay 2000, 279) and what individuals and collectives do about this. I explore this through discussion of a project specifically conceived and designed to counter negative and hostile feelings about refugees represented in various mass media.

Here, I consider how discourse on asylum – whether rendering it problematic or challenging its problematisation – creates variously positioned emotional subjects. I examine how emotional elements in these discourses frame refugees' accounts of their experience and how refugees use emotion language to position themselves as part of collectives, and construct and contest subjectivities and social realities.

Emotion and epistemology

The Refugee Communities History Project (RCHP) was an oral history project, which aimed to make an intervention in cultural politics and empower refugee communities by enabling them to produce alternative narratives of their lived experience. It set out to document the contributions made by refugee communities to recent history of London and to promote diversity and inclusiveness within the city.

Between 2004 and 2006, the RCHP collected, archived and disseminated 164 life story interviews with refugees who came to Britain in the period since 1951 (Day, Harding and Mullen 2008). The project was initiated and managed by the Evelyn Oldfield Unit, a refugee-led organisation, which provides support for refugee community organisations (RCOs), in partnership with the Museum of London, London Metropolitan University and fifteen refugee community organisations.[1] I worked on this project between 1999 and 2007 as a member of the project steering group (involved in project design, planning, and fund raising) and as one of the project partners responsible for training fieldworkers.

The RCHP was conceived in response to media hostility towards refugees, and as a way of engendering public understanding and empathy with the experiences, views and concerns of refugees as articulated by refugees themselves. It aimed to highlight the contributions made by refugees to the history, culture and economy of London (where they make up 5% of the population) through their work in business, healthcare, education, other service industries, community and voluntary sectors, and the arts (GLA 2001). The project deliberately adopted a broad definition of 'contribution' to include not only the high profile activities of those prominent in the arts, business, education, politics, and also the less visible, but vitally important, activities of those who work in the service industries, voluntary sector, or care for others including their families.

A fieldworker was employed at each of the fifteen participating refugee community organisations and trained to conduct oral history interviews with a diverse range of individuals within their own communities,[2] including refugee men and women of different ages, different religious and political affiliations and ethnicities. Fieldworkers helped to disseminate the material collected via production and exhibition of different artefacts in local community exhibitions and in a high profile exhibition at the Museum of London.[3]

Although public debate articulated through the media tends to conflate 'immigrant', 'refugee' and 'asylum seeker', there are clearly important distinctions between these subject positions. Interviewees remarked that immigrants choose to leave their native country and to seek a better life in another, whereas asylum seekers and refugees are forced to flee, knowing that they may never be able to return to, their homeland. In pragmatic terms, the project recognised the recent historical emergence in the UK of a distinction in legal status and entitlements (to work and welfare benefits) between 'asylum seekers' who wait (often for several years) for Home Office decisions on their cases, and those whose claims and status as 'refugees' had been officially recognised as legitimate. The project steering committee decided that 'refugees', rather than 'asylum seekers' would be interviewed. The main reasons for this were, first, that those granted legal status were thought more likely to feel comfortable about participating in the project and, second, they were likely to have spent more time in London and have more to relate about this experience.

For the purposes of this project, the definition of 'refugee' was based on that of the 1951 United Nations Convention relating to the Status of Refugees and the 1967 United Nations Protocol relating to the Status of Refugees. Those interviewed had claimed asylum under the terms of the 1951 UN Convention and 1967 Protocol and, as a result, had been granted: a) refugee status; or b) indefinite leave to remain; or c) exceptional leave to remain; or d) humanitarian protection. Use of these official and legal definitions was problematic, since they may have been inconsistently applied by individual bureaucrats and subject to varying interpretations in different historical, political and policy climates.

I explore emotion, power and subjectivity through analysis of a sample of transcribed oral history interviews produced as part of the RCHP. Interviewing can be seen as a process whereby narrators are located within particular 'regimes of the person'. The interviews, designed to elicit spoken autobiographical narratives, created speaking positions for interviewees as articulate, reflective, and ready to relate thoughts and feelings about their lived experience to an audience, in order to counteract publicly articulated negative views about refugees. Interviewers were directed to elicit accounts of what narrators did and what they felt *as refugees*, as part of a politics of community empowerment and an alternative production of power/knowledge. In other words, a significant aspect of the project's agenda was to challenge that discourse, couched in emotional terms, which contributed to subordination and marginalisation of refugees as a generic social grouping. The implication of this was, perhaps, that enlightened subjects among the host community would be less fearful and anxious, and enlightened refugee subjects would feel proud and empowered.

Emotion is generally understood to be a crucial element in knowledge production in oral history as the researcher is assumed to naturally and necessarily take up an empathetic position in relation to the subject/narrator and identify with his/her pain and suffering (Hamilton 2008). Oral history has been 'linked to grassroots and progressive politics, with the democratic impulse to 'give voice' to historical subjects marginalised, oppressed or forgotten by traditional documentary history' (Hamilton 2008). This assumption underpinned the RCHP and shaped the expectations of participants. Hamilton, however, warns of the limitations of alternative claims to power/knowledge, based on emotional engagement. She argues that it is important to distinguish between empathy and solidarity in oral history, as it cannot be assumed that 'hitherto silenced voices will challenge dominant discourses in a progressive way' (Hamilton 2008).

The production of autobiographical spoken narrative in interview can be seen as a process through which subjectivity is negotiated and performed. Narrators may take up, refuse or refashion speaking positions offered by the research agenda and questions posed. Also, what is said in interview is not simply a narrator's report on a reality (events and experiences) outside of the interview, but the result of a collaboration between narrator and audience who negotiate and co-create spoken narratives (Harding 2006).[4] This creative work on the past and self necessarily draws on the repertoire of discourses available to subjects at the time. That is, ontological narratives are shaped by the social world, firstly, through the audiences which each individual encounters and, secondly, through the 'cultural discourses which frame and provide structure for the narrative' (Elliot 2005, 127). They may also provide a means – through the linking of self-narratives to collective narratives – of identifying with 'imagined communities' based on 'class, gender, race, ethnicity and nation' (Jacobs, 2002, 273). In short, the interview is a site for the production, rather than transmission, of knowledge and meaning (Elliot 2005, 24). Interview transcripts can be treated as texts, documenting enactment of subjectivity and self-interpretation in relation to others at specific historical moments. They can be analysed for how subjects respond to and appear to be compelled and constrained by specific discourses, and also how they endeavour to resist and create alternative understandings and subjectivities.

The historical context of the project was one in which critics writing about asylum discourse and project participants identified recent withdrawal of sympathy and growing climate of hostility toward asylum seekers and refugees in media and policy debate. Critics, in turn, have employed emotion language to make intelligible a politics of fear and inequality. Next, I examine the production and subordination of refugee and non-refugee emotional subjects in writing about discourse on asylum.

Talk about asylum

Empathy and compassion, along with fairness, have been considered key elements constituting British national identity. In contemporary Britain, Lewis (2005) argues that there is much support for the *idea* of asylum and the principal that Britain should protect and offer refuge to those who need it. However, anxiety about the implications of immigration for social and economic resources, and national identity and security, has been attributed to some sections of the host community. More recently, fears about immigration have escalated and become entangled with the issues of race relations, foreign policy and terrorism in the public imagination (ICAR 2005).

Critics reviewing public discourse on asylum and immigration point out that the number of people seeking asylum in the UK has risen since 1997. During the subsequent decade, immigration and asylum have been the focus of extensive political and policy debate and media coverage, and, consequently, have come to dominate the public imagination (Lewis

2005, 20). The prevailing tone of political, media and public discourses on asylum has been negative, foregrounding the problems of asylum and immigration, and advocating restrictionist policy responses (Lewis 2005; ICAR 2005). The politics of asylum have shifted the focus away from causes of forced migration to the volume and implications of asylum for British economy and society and abuse of the asylum system (Lewis 2005). This perspective and the resultant policy measures[5] have been widely represented in the media, which has also depicted the asylum system as 'out of control' (Lewis 2005, 20). Government has sought to demonstrate control via legislation, which in turn has tended to emphasise the problematic and potentially overwhelming nature of asylum seekers (Article 19; ICAR 2005; Lewis 2005). The effects of this discourse have been to render asylum seeking problematic and constitute asylum seekers as a collective which threatens vulnerable other subjects with physical violence, competition for jobs, social housing and health services and loss of (British) values and identity. This discourse produces asylum seekers as a source of public anxiety, fear and anger (Lewis 2005, 1).

One effect of media and policy debate on asylum, and the 'languages of personhood' (Rose 2000) which have taken shape through this, has been the definition of strangers, who may be asylum seekers, refugees or immigrants, as both threatening and deceitful. Such discourse has conflated these different subject positions to that of the single figure of the abject 'asylum seeker', which is then used to refer to all non-white and white eastern European migrants (Lewis 2005). The term 'bogus asylum seeker' is commonly used to denote false claims of persecution and endangerment, masking a real desire for economic security, which is seen as dishonest, criminal and materially depriving vulnerable 'native' others. 'Bogus' has become the default adjective attached to 'asylum seekers' as it is widely assumed that the majority of asylum seekers are not actually in fear of persecution (Lewis 2005). In emotional terms, the 'bogus asylum seeker' has abused trust and engendered fear. Fear is a 'hijacked' emotion word ascribed to members of the host community, which defines and locates them as likely victims of harassment or crime, economic deprivation and cultural and social change as a result of immigration and asylum in relation to threatening migrant 'others'. At the same time, and less well heard, fear is also deployed to describe and constitute the social realities and subjectivities of asylum seekers living with the daily threat of harassment and attack.[6]

Talk about fear defines and distinguishes a number of vulnerable and subordinated collectives – young, old, lower social class *and also* refugees and asylum seekers – but makes the greatest distinction between 'us' and 'them', the host community and immigrant strangers, rendering the latter problematic, marginal, threatening and the legitimate focus of fear, anger and hate. Talk about fear marks out immigrants as a source of threat to identity and existence – 'abject' in Kristeva's sense of the term and, therefore, needing to be repelled (1982) – and entrenches them in a position of oppressed marginality.

Tolerance and compassion, attributed to some groups and not others, works to distinguish more privileged, liberal, enlightened groups. Compassion, it is implied, is 'done' by and defines those who have better jobs and education. Lack of tolerance of asylum seekers is attributed to disadvantaged groups who perceive themselves to be in competition for resources and services and, whilst based on 'perceived rather than actual impacts', this is connected with the reality of social vulnerability and politics of inequality and injustice (Lewis 2005, 49).[7]

Vocabularies of emotion work as a means of distinction, defining boundaries and relationships between those who fear and those who threaten, those who tolerate and those who do not, and investing in social norms and moral meanings, which enforce hegemonic power relations. Emotion words, then, play a significant part in defining and explaining social problems and making visible different positions of social inclusion/exclusion. And, emotion words work 'to secure collectives' by aligning 'some subjects with others and against other others' (Ahmed 2004, 42).

Discourse, and counter discourses, on asylum produce emotional subjects as part of the definition and subordination of vulnerable collectives, including both UK and other 'others'. Through specific emotional vocabularies individuals are located in specific 'regimes of the person' and their capacities for social existence defined and limited. Such emotional vocabularies frame the constitution of subjectivity through spoken autobiography by helping to shape the discursive terrain on and through which refugees may represent themselves. I now discuss examples of spoken narratives from the RCHP.

Framing the RCHP in emotional terms

The Refugee Communities History Project (RCHP) was not designed to investigate emotion, power or subjectivity and was led by a 'community empowerment', rather than academic, agenda. However, I suggest that vocabularies of emotion were crucial to the project on a number of levels. The project aimed to challenge negative emotions – fear, hate and lack of trust – towards refugees articulated in public discourse and, in attempting this, created alternative understandings of, and subject positions for, refugees as grateful, deserving and reciprocating.

The project design – through selection of interview subjects – emphasised the 'authenticity' and positive contributions of refugee subjects, in contrast to negative public images of refugees as bogus and 'a threat to national security'. Interviews contributed to this by enshrining fear as a foundational emotion, both as a cause or root of *becoming a refugee* and as a negative response among host communities. The question posed by many of the interviewers at the very start of each interview – 'Can you tell me a little about the circumstances which brought you here'? – elicited an account of persecution and fear. In other words, interviewees 'explained' and justified *why* they had sought asylum. In this way, the 'authenticity' of the refugee subject was established *in relation to fear* at the outset, as someone with a 'well-founded fear of being persecuted', and who is outside the country of his/her nationality and is unable, or owing to such fear, is unwilling to return to it (Article 1, 1951 UN Convention). This line of questioning helped to produce refugee subjectivity as brought into being through talk about fear and the refugee subject as deserving of help, by virtue of being a 'genuine' victim of persecution. Fear was part of a vocabulary through which individuals constituted and recognised themselves *as certain sorts of subjects* and understood their relations to others. Fear, in this context, was discussed in relation to specific historically, geographically and politically located conflicts and violence.

A strong focus on contribution, in the project agenda and in individual interviews, created the idea of the successful or 'good' refugee as someone who gives something back (Gabriel and Harding 2009). However, this was identified in different ways. Some interviewees described success in mainstream society through conventional achievements as evidenced by high status and/or well-paid occupations, or gaining UK qualifications. Other interviewees described sacrifices – such as low paid work, more than one job, working long hours as well as caring for the family – made in order to support their children's 'success' in conventional terms. Some described working in the areas of paid/unpaid refugee sector work. Many expressed a sense of empathy for and obligation to work for vulnerable communities as part of reciprocating the support they had received on arrival in London (Gabriel and Harding 2009). A majority of those interviewed emphasised the importance of the collective over the individual, associated with a passionate commitment to social justice and/or community and/or family.

The project aimed to document how refugees 'make good', through coming to terms with fear, loss and displacement and becoming productive citizens. A 'making good narrative', then, involved the creation of a range of emotional subject positions and active management of emotion. Whilst a focus on emotion talk represents only one of many possible ways of reading RCHP interview transcripts, I argue that it provides an important way of exploring how unequal power relations can be subtly reproduced through vocabularies of emotion and emotion management in productive as well as constraining ways.

Next, I discuss eight transcribed interviews with three men and five women[8] who all came to the UK between 1974 and 1976 as political refugees from Chile following the military *coup*, which brought Pinochet to power. Whilst they articulate many concerns in common with other interviewees, they express distinct concerns connected with the historical, cultural and political context of their arrival in the UK. They have all had thirty years of living in exile in which to reflect, and have had the opportunity to return to Chile but unlike many others have not resettled there. Furthermore, they described arriving in the UK in the mid-1970s to (comparatively) sympathetic local environments, which they contrasted with recent negative media representations and hostile reception of refugees. A focus on this group of eight enables some historicisation of the production of subjects *as refugees* in and through emotion words and elaboration of the meanings of specific emotions.

Emotional subjects

Spoken narratives were elicited by questions about leaving Chile, arrival and reception in the UK, settling (finding work, accommodation, social networks), and return to Chile. These questions enabled a specific narrative to emerge – showing how refugees were deserving, grateful and useful citizens – and helped to create subjectivities based on productivity (in economic, social, cultural and political terms).

The narratives created through the project employed distinctive emotion vocabularies in constituting subjectivity and inter-subjectivity. First, interviewees spoke of the fear that made them flee their country of origin. Second, they described a sense of relief and gratitude at escaping persecution and the hope of returning to Chile once the crisis had blown over. Third, they spoke of their deep sense of sadness and grief at the loss of the lives they had planned and the family and friends left behind. Interviewees spontaneously discussed the meanings of 'refugee' as a subject position using emotion words and their capacities for becoming a 'good refugee' in terms of emotion management.

Interviewees were asked about their experiences of, and feelings about, arrival in the UK. Talk about arrival evoked a sense of threshold and prompted comparisons between the UK and Chile. It produced subjectivities and social realities constituted in terms of mixed emotions. Most spoke of a sense of gratitude and relief at escaping persecution and being given refuge. Some described feelings of pain, shock and loss. On arriving in winter, aged 42, K described his shock at the sheer physical, social and emotional strangeness as he encountered a 'monochromic landscape' and 'reserved culture'. N, a single mother in her thirties when she arrived in the UK, described pain at being separated from her homeland: 'my roots are in the air'. She said that nothing could make up for the loss of life she had – career, status, family – and the life she wanted: 'you planned your life, you had a project' (N). She lost status when she came to London and her qualifications, unrecognised, effectively 'meant nothing'.

Whilst some described instances of hostility, all described experiencing kindness and sympathy. All contrasted the circumstances of their reception in 1976 with those of refugees in 2006, thereby highlighting historical differences in public discourses, government policy and contemporary 'structures of feeling'.[9] All had visas and official refugee status and entitlement to benefits prior to arrival in the UK. They described active support for Chilean refugees from the Labour government, Labour Party, trade unions, voluntary organisations, local Chilean solidarity groups and others on the political left. Interviewees describe being looked after, some staying with English families when they first arrived, being helped to negotiate health, housing and education services by volunteer advocates and receiving grants to continue studying. They said that they were welcomed in contrast to asylum seekers today, who come to 'fortress Europe' (O) and have 'traumatic experiences' of the immigration system (V).

Despite their own more positive experiences, keen awareness of negative discourse on asylum in 2006 inevitably provided a frame of reference for Chilean interviewees, as they constituted themselves as subjects deserving of help, through talk about fear (of persecution) and gratitude (for safety). Through their narratives they established themselves once more as subjects who were worthy of compassion, and wanted to repay their 'debt' by becoming productive citizens.

Being a 'genuine' refugee appeared to entail occupying a subject position as dejected and in need of support. For some the very term 'refugee' communicated emotional dependence and subordination, a subject position, which they both recognised (as pertaining to others) and refused (for themselves). For example, when the interviewer asked V how she felt when she knew she had a visa to Britain, venturing that her response might be relief, she refused this and any expression of gratitude and said 'I thought "very decent of them" ' . . . 'but I've always been political' and 'I happen to believe in the right to international protection'. In other words, she chose to make the political point that international protection was a right, thereby positioning herself as a politically conscious subject within an international community.

> V: . . . one of the very important things I have to tell you is that [pause] and it was a shock to me actually. One of the English women at the airport told me that I didn't look like a refugee. What she meant by that is that a) I was very strong, b) I was a happy person, yeah? And c) I was arrogant, in terms of my standing and how I saw the world you know? I didn't see it as if Britain was doing me a favour for putting me up. Not at all. I was very aware that this was a right to be asserted somewhere, and it is a right, you know, that it was . . . So, I wasn't you know, your, your typical refugee, as it were. You know kind of broken down and all that sort of stuff . . . What I had was rage – I was very, very angry. You know and yeah. Very, very angry and stroppy . . .

Emotion words figured strongly in this narrative as the interviewee both described and rejected the emotional positioning to which refugees are typically ushered and, instead, strongly asserted an alternative emotional position in anger and rage which was at the same time a position of legitimacy and entitlement. In this way, she resists subordination and marginalisation and recognising herself as a certain sort of subject – broken down and miserable – enacted through dominant emotion discourse on what genuine and deserving refugees *are*. She resists expectations about what she ought to feel in this context. In this instance, relief and gratitude are characterised as demeaning and disempowering, anger and rage as empowering (emotion) practices.

On several other occasions the interviewee returned to the fact that she did not *look like* a refugee, and refused to recognise herself *as a subject* in what she identified as the 'pitiful' figure of refugee, stereotyped as physically and emotionally crushed. Instead, she asserted positive aspects of being a refugee, in which she could recognise herself – being political, organising support for those in jail and starving. She spoke of her obsession with fighting for social justice and again said that 'rage kept me alive and kept me healthy and kept me strong'. She distanced herself from what she saw as a disempowered position – this time, that of being overwhelmed and incapacitated by 'sadness and loss' – even though she acknowledged that this might be a significant part of other refugees' experience. Again, she used vocabularies of emotion – anger and rage – to contest subject positions and social realities typically constituted for refugees based on (what she sees as) negative disempowering emotions, and to create a different empowered sense of self and relations to others.

The constraints and limitations of the discursive construction of refugees, using specific vocabularies of emotion, as thoroughly dejected and pitiable is echoed in the narratives of other interviewees, who preferred the term 'exile' to 'refugee'.

> N: I don't like the word refugee, you know, I have my reservation with the word refugee, because I feel refugee is a word that possessed you, it lives you make it, and as a victim, terrible victim without–, just a bundle of clothes with you and although I recognise there are people who . . . who are . . . who fit this image, I–, I have never feel a refugee in that sense. I feel more . . . an exile, yeah? It would be wrong for me to feel a refugee in the other sense, that I am absolutely dispossess and I have nothing. Yes I have nothing when I came to this country, but I have my knowledge, you see, and I think that makes a lot of difference.[10]

For N, her education and profession as a university teacher meant that she had resources to organise and make a new life. She said that people do not like to say that they are refugees because they are ashamed of what it means to be a refugee (in this context, utterly dependent on strangers for everything), demonstrating, perhaps, how emotional meanings help to constitute refugee subjectivity and that emotion as communicative practice performs a hegemonic function in constituting subjects as refugees and delimiting their capacities for social existence.

Refugees' subjectivities and social realities are limited by feelings they are expected and permitted to express in relation to their pasts and their new lives in the present. To start with, individuals have to demonstrate that they are genuine refugees deserving of compassion and asylum and, as such, dejected and dependent. Then they must transform themselves into good refugees, by making a life in London as economically independent productive subjects. They are expected to transform themselves in emotional terms and exercise a degree of emotion management.

Emotion management

Inquiry by interviewers about employment, accommodation, making friends, political and cultural activities was driven by a desire to counter negative emotion talk constituting refugees as a threat to the economy and national identity. Interviewers asked for a chronological description of all paid and unpaid work, designed to bring into being the normatively regulated productive refugee subject, who has managed to find work despite not being allowed to practice his/her profession immediately, or at all, as a counter response to public discourse on refugees as unproductive and a drain on resources. This subject had to some extent managed their feelings and moved beyond an overwhelming and incapacitating sense of dislocation.

Those who had arrived in London in their early twenties tended to describe receiving support for further study and successful professional careers. In this sense, their narratives produced a stereotypical story of refugee who despite displacement and trauma, got over this, worked hard, made good and was successful and, to some extent, happy. D exemplified this position and saw herself as one of the lucky ones. Having escaped prison and death, her only hope was to survive. She was very grateful to have a second chance at life. She described joy at being reunited with her husband, studying for a PhD, getting to the top of her profession in the public sector, having children and buying her own home.

V, who was also in her twenties when she arrived in the UK, again strongly resisted the terms of reference implicit in the questions and project and speaking positions offered. She refused to produce a chronological list of jobs when asked but did respond to questions about the work that she had found most meaningful. She vehemently challenged the emotion positions, constituted through the project agenda, for refugees as good and productive subjects who 'came out shining in spite of a bleeding heart' and 'made good against the odds'. She adamantly refused to give a traditional 'success story', which conformed to established feeling rules, and emphasised an alternative subjectivity through her ongoing passionate political commitment to social justice.

Older refugees, who had been in their thirties or forties when they arrived in the UK in the 1970s, reported more enduring effects of loss and grief and difficulty in establishing themselves in their previous professions. In a sense, they had not managed emotion and had not 'made it' in conventional professions. However, through their narratives, they elaborated a way of living, a set of practices, embodying alternative passionate commitments to family, community, and principles of social justice. These individuals were productive in an unpaid capacity, working to support and for a more just society. Their narratives invested 'care' and 'tolerance' with deep collective political significance and defined a passionate commitment to politics and collective good.

For example, O had been a university teacher and social worker in Chile, but started work cleaning houses and working in a kitchen – often doing several jobs at the same time – once she arrived as a refugee in the UK. She began studying for a degree but was unable to complete her course because of her commitment to working as an interpreter and translator for the Chilean Solidarity Campaign (which involved touring cities in the UK), and to caring and providing for her family as a single parent. Whilst she felt 'very depressed' at not finishing her degree, her passionate commitment to her family and supporting the struggle in Chile were a duty and priority. She also described a sense of outrage and anger, shared with others, at what was happening in Chile: 'What had happened to us was really outrageous and we wanted the world to know' (O).

N had not been able to work as an academic in the UK. She joined a voluntary organisation and became part of a support group for people who had survived torture and, with other Chileans, began a support, advice and information service for refugees to help them settle and find work. After ten years of living in the UK, her life was changed for the better when she got a job at a refugee organisation 'teaching people how to look for a job and go and do things and understanding the labour market' (N). She described training refugees to be employable by teaching them to understand cultural codes and cultural difference, about ways of being friendly, or not, using humour and, generally, 'fitting in' at work. Managing workplace relations specifically involves managing one's own emotions and reading the emotions of others: 'For example, for me was very difficult, one of the more difficult things to learn, was not to show emotion' (N).

N indicates how being emotional, or not being emotional, constitutes collective identity, cultural difference and workplace culture. She said that what she appreciated about British culture was tolerance of difference, respect for other people, kindness and compassion: 'English people are distant – they treat you very nicely and are tolerant – but they leave you alone' (N). These characteristics may also be a source of social exclusion in the workplace, because people may not be direct and say what they mean and you may not understand what is expected of you. In particular, she stated that workplace culture in the UK is one in which individuals are expected to take initiative, whereas this is alien to people from more authoritarian societies. N also spoke of needing to teach refugees how to write a *curriculum vitae*, which highlights their achievements, since 'for us this was the most difficult part to learn to sell ourselves to an employer, try to persuade employers that we were the right person' (N). In her culture, this would be seen as unacceptably arrogant. In this way, N discusses cultural difference, workplace culture and social inclusion/exclusion in terms of emotion management.

All those interviewed said they had felt very sad to leave Chile and hoped to return after a year or so. None expected to stay in the UK for thirty years, and most described their feelings at the time as 'just passing through', saying that they always 'kept suitcases behind the door'. During this long period, they developed careers, made friends, had children, and put down some roots, but did not feel fully at home in London. However, they all mentioned they appreciated the diversity and vibrancy of multicultural London and felt that it 'included' them. A sense of displacement and the historical circumstances of their forced migration did constitute them as a politically engaged collective. Most described a heightened sense of passion about community and politics when Pinochet was detained in London in 1998 and they met daily to demonstrate with other Chilean families. V took this point further when she said that 'as a political animal and activist' she could make her home anywhere. She always found a place in different political communities in London and was able to feel a sense of place rather than displacement, continuity rather than discontinuity.

Emotion and empowerment

Analysis of narrative created through the Refugee Communities History Project demonstrates how 'emotion talk' may participate in the constitution of subjectivities, social realities and relations of power in a specific historical and cultural context.

Emotion talk was a crucial device of meaning production and central to the project's goals. Emotion figured in the motivation for and design of the project, which aimed to use ontological narratives and a range of media and communication devices to challenge public discourse articulating hostile feelings and negative attitudes towards refugees. Such public discourse has used emotion words to simplify, universalise and limit the experiences and capacities for social existence of refugees. 'Emotion talk', as part of discourse on asylum, indicates how refugee subjects ought to feel about themselves and how disadvantaged others feel about them, working to secure collective identities and trace boundaries between some groups of subjects and others.

The project had counter hegemonic 'emotional work' to do by substituting empathy for fear in public discourse, and highlighting similarities as well as differences, among refugee and non-refugee communities. It aimed to enable refugees to represent themselves, and the rich diversity and productivity of their lives, through autobiographical narratives, thereby engendering pride in the past and hope for a more inclusive future among a broader community of refugees. That is, an implicit, if not explicit, aim was to produce and align collectives in relation to/ through alternative, more positive, emotion positions.

Underlying this endeavour, was a commitment to the idea that knowledge produced might lead to empowerment of refugee communities through the emotional engagement – that is, empathy – with narrators of an audience in the present (interview) and imagined future (exhibition, broadcast, publication). Whilst much oral history work seeks to empower non-hegemonic groups through its methodology, this is necessarily incomplete and often problematic (Harding 2002; Harding and Gabriel 2004). It is beyond the scope of this discussion to consider the extent of 'enlightenment' and 'empowerment' in this project. However, it is apparent from analysis of interview transcripts that interviewees endeavoured to distance themselves from what they saw as the disempowering connotations of 'refugee' and refigure their identities and experiences through alternative relations of power/knowledge.

Narrators were directed by interviewers towards establishing their authenticity as refugees in relation to talk about fear of persecution. However, they refused to recognise themselves only and permanently through this emotion, which positioned them as dejected and dependent, and, therefore, disempowered. They acknowledged fear as constituting them as refugees, individually and collectively, but claimed to inhabit this only as a temporary subject position. In speaking about their lived existence in London, they created subjectivities through different (emotion) terms. They articulated an ethics of existence and sense of themselves as passionately committed to social justice, community, and helping others. Through these narratives they challenged the forms of personhood, and limited capacities for social existence, attributed to refugees as either threatening or fearful or productive only by virtue of high status or well-paid professions. They elaborated an everyday practice, or way of living, that focused less on individualism and individual attainment and more on collective political action. For some, rage and anger, as alternative emotion positions, were empowering and provided motivations for resistance and collective political activism.

In the narratives discussed here, emotions provided a vocabulary for constituting and reconstituting subjectivity and inter-subjectivity, relations to self and to others. This, I suggest, has made intelligible aspects of the reproduction of contemporary power relations and possibilities for challenge and intervention.

Notes

1   Partners in the Refugee Communities History Project included Afghan Association of London, African Community Health and Research Organisation, with the Lwo Cultural Group, Bosnian Resource Information Centre Kosovar Support, Chinese Information and Advice Centre, Council for Assisting Refugee Academics, Eritrean Education and Publication Trust, Ethiopian Community in Britain, Haringey Somali Community and Cultural Association, Imece Turkish Speaking Women's Group, Iraqi Community Association, Kurdish Association, Latin American Association, Latin American Women's Rights Service, with Latin American Disabled People's Project and Latin American Elderly People's Project, Roma Support Group, Tamil Relief Centre. The project was funded by the Heritage Lottery Fund, City Parochial Foundation and Trust for London.

2   In all but two instances the fieldworkers came from the communities in which they worked, increasing the likelihood that interviewees could be interviewed in their mother tongue.

3   *Belonging: Voices of London's Refugees*, Museum of London, Oct 2006–Feb 2007.

4   The individual attempting to relate life experiences in the form of a story, must reflect on those experiences, select the salient aspects, and order them into a coherent whole. She/he also indicates how the listener should understand their meaning and significance, and how she/he should respond (Elliot 2005).

5   The government has introduced legislation on asylum and immigration at a phenomenal rate (ICAR 2005), including 'legislation aimed at limiting the numbers of asylum seekers by speeding up the process, limiting abuse of the system and increasing removals'; 'substantial changes in the welfare arrangements for asylum seekers with the creation of the National Asylum Support Service (NASS) and the dispersal policy' (Lewis 2005, 1).

6   In March 2001, Channel 4 screened 'Bloody Foreigners', a documentary that graphically illustrated the victimisation of dispersed asylum seekers in Liverpool. Research and monitoring suggest that daily levels of harassment of asylum seekers are significant in many areas. However, it is mainly the

most violent attacks and high-profile campaigns that receive media coverage and public attention and the absence of systematic data collection means that aggregate data on harassment of asylum seekers and refugees is not readily available (ICAR 2005).

7   Lewis suggests feelings about asylum seekers are likely to be influenced by social class, education, local issues and the extent to which individuals feel vulnerable to economic competition as well as level of contact with immigrant communities (Lewis, 2005).

8   Of this group, four of the eight were in their early twenties, three in their early thirties and one over forty. Three came alone, three with partners, and two women came as single parents with dependent children.

9   For discussion of this term, see Harding and Pribram 2004.

10   This is a verbatim transcription of a section of interview.

Bibliography

Ahmed, S. 2004. *The Cultural Politics of Emotion*. Edinburgh: Edinburgh University Press.

Bloch, A. and Levy, C. (eds). 1999. *Refugees, Citizenship and Social Policy in Europe*. London: Macmillan Press Ltd.

Day, A., Harding, J., and Mullen, J. 2008. 'Refugee Stories: The Refugee Communities History Project, Partnership and collaboration' in Skartveit, H-L. and Goodnow, K. (eds), *Museums and Refugees: New Media, Play and Participation*. Paris: UNESCO.

Du Gay, P. 2000. 'Introduction' in P. du Gay, J. Evans and P. Redman (eds), *Identity: A Reader*. London: Sage and The Open University, pp. 1–5.

Elliot, J. 2005. *Using Narrative in Social Research. Qualitative and Quantitative Approaches*. London: Sage.

Foucault, M. 1979. *Discipline and Punish. The Birth of the Prison*. New York: Vintage Books.

—— 1985. *The Use of Pleasure. The History of Sexuality. Volume Two*. Harmondsworth, Middlesex: Penguin Books.

—— 1986. *The Archaeology of Knowledge*. London: Tavistock.

Gabriel, J. and Harding, J. 2009. 'On Being a "Good" Refugee' in G. Bhattacharyya (ed.), *Ethnicities and Values in a Changing World*. Aldershot: Ashgate Publishing Ltd. Forthcoming.

Greater London Authority, 2001. *Refugees and Asylum Seekers in London: A GLA Perspective*. London: GLA.

Hamilton, C. 2008. 'On Being a 'Good' Interviewer: Empathy, Ethics and the Politics of Oral History', *Oral History*, 36/2, pp. 35–43.

Harding, J. 2002. 'Talking about Homelessness: A Teaching and Research Initiative in East London', *Teaching in Higher Education*, Vol. 7, No. 1, pp. 81–95.

—— 2006. 'Questioning the Subject in Biographical Interviewing', *Sociological Research Online*, Vol. 11, No. 3.

Harding, J. and Gabriel, J. 2004. 'Communities in the Making: Pedagogic Explorations Using Oral History', *International Studies in the Sociology of Education*, Vol. 14, No. 3, pp. 185–201.

Harding J. and Pribram, E. D. 2004. 'Losing Our Cool? Following Williams and Grossberg on Emotions', *Cultural Studies*. Vol. 18, No. 6. pp. 863–883.

Information Centre about Asylum and Refugees. 2005. *Key Issues*. http://www.icar.org.uk/?lid=5019

Jacobs, R. 2002. 'Civil Society and Crisis: Culture, Discourse, and the Rodney King Beating' in L. Spillman (ed.), *Cultural Sociology*. Oxford: Blackwell Publishers, pp. 272–286.

Kristeva, J. 1982. *Powers of Horror. An Essay on Abjection*. New York: Columbia University Press.

Lewis, M. 2005. *Asylum. Understanding Public Attitudes*. ippr. http://www.ippr.org.uk/publicationsandreports/publication.asp?id=294

Lupton, D. 1998. *The Emotional Self. A Sociocultural Exploration*. Sage: London.

Rose, N. 2000. 'Identity, Genealogy, History' in P. du Gay, J. Evans and P. Redman (eds), *Identity: A Reader*. London: Sage and The Open University, pp. 313–326.

Schuster, L. and Solomos, J. 1999. 'The Politics of Refugee and Asylum Policies in Britain: Historical Patterns and Contemporary Realities' in A. Bloch and C. Levy (eds), *Refugees, Citizenship and Social Policy in Europe*. London: Macmillan Press Ltd, pp. 51–75.

VI TRANSFORMING THE PUBLIC

Chapter 16

Lauren Berlant

THE INTIMATE PUBLIC SPHERE

SOMETHING STRANGE has happened to citizenship. During the rise of the Reaganite right, a familial politics of the national future came to define the urgencies of the present. Now everywhere in the United States intimate things flash in people's faces: pornography, abortion, sexuality, and reproduction; marriage, personal morality, and family values. These issues do not arise as private concerns: they are key to debates about what "America" stands for, and are deemed vital to defining how citizens should act. In the process of collapsing the political and the personal into a world of public intimacy, a nation made for adult citizens has been replaced by one imagined for fetuses and children.[1] How did these changes come to be, and why?

The story can be told many ways. During this period, a cartoon version of a crisis in U.S. citizenship has become established as a standard truth. In the cartoon version of the shaken nation, a citizen is defined as a person traumatized by some aspect of life in the United States. Portraits and stories of citizen-victims — pathological, poignant, heroic, and grotesque — now permeate the political public sphere, putting on display a mass experience of economic insecurity, racial discord, class conflict, and sexual unease.

This coupling of suffering and citizenship is so startling and so moving because it reveals about national power both its impersonality and its intimacy. The experience of social hierarchy is intensely individuating, yet it also makes people public and generic: it turns them into *kinds* of people who are both attached to and underdescribed by the identities that organize them. This paradox of partial legibility is behind much of the political and personal anger that arises in scenes of misrecognition in everyday life — at work, on the street, at home, under the law, and even in aesthetic experience. Yet the public rhetoric of citizen trauma has become so pervasive and competitive in the United States that it obscures basic differences among modes of identity, hierarchy, and violence. Mass national pain threatens to turn into banality, a crumbling archive of dead signs and tired plots.

This exhaustion of cultural struggle over the material and symbolic conditions of U.S. citizenship is a desired effect of conservative cultural politics, whose aim is to dilute the oppositional discourses of the historically stereotyped citizens — people of color, women, gays, and lesbians. Against these groups are pitted the complaints not of stereotyped peoples burdened by a national history but icons who have only recently lost the protections of their national iconicity – politicians who are said to have lost their "zone of privacy"; ordinary citizens who are said to feel that they have lost access to the American Dream; white and male and heterosexual people of all classes who are said to sense that they have lost the respect of their culture, and with it the freedom to feel unmarked.[2]

Indeed, today many formerly iconic citizens who used to feel undefensive and unfettered feel truly exposed and vulnerable. They feel anxious about their value to themselves, their families, their publics, and their nation. They sense that they now have *identities*, when it used to be just other people who had them.[3] These new feelings provoke many reactions. One response is to desire that the nation recommit itself to the liberal promise of a conflict-free and integrated world. Another is to forge a scandal, a scandal of ex-privilege: this can include rage at the stereotyped peoples who have appeared to change the political rules of social membership, and, with it, a desperate desire to return to an order of things deemed normal, an order of what was felt to be a general everyday intimacy that was sometimes called "the American way of life." To effect either restoration of the imagined nation, the American ex-icon denigrates the political present tense and incites nostalgia for the national world of its iconicity, setting up that lost world as a utopian horizon of political aspiration.

These narratives of traumatized identity have dramatically reshaped the dominant account of U.S. citizenship. They also show that politics by caricature can have profound effects: on the ways people perceive their own social value and the social value of "Others"; on the ways they live daily life and see their futures; and on mainstream political discourse, which exploits the national identity crises it foments to claim a popular mandate for radical shifts in norms of ideology and political practice.[4]

[This chapter] attends to the ways in which these rhetorics of a traumatized core national identity have come to describe, and thereby to make, something real. It tracks the triumph of the Reaganite view that the intimacy of citizenship is something scarce and sacred, private and proper, and only for members of families. It focuses on the ways conservative ideology has convinced a citizenry that the core context of politics should be the sphere of private life. In so doing, it develops a different story about what has happened to citizenship in both the law and daily life during the last few decades. The privatization of citizenship has involved manipulating an intricate set of relations between economic, racial, and sexual processes.

Here is another way of telling the story. My first axiom is that there is no public sphere in the contemporary United States, no context of communication and debate that makes ordinary citizens feel that they have a common public culture, or influence on a state that holds itself accountable to their opinions, critical or otherwise. By "ordinary citizens" I mean ones without wealth and structural access to brokers of power. The antiwar, antiracist, and feminist agitations of the sixties denounced the hollow promises of the political pseudo-public sphere; then, a reactionary response grew dominant, which claimed that, in valuing national criticism over patriotic identification, and difference over assimilation, sixties radicals had damaged and abandoned the core of U.S. society.

A conservative coalition formed whose aim was the privatization of U.S. citizenship. One part of its project involved rerouting the critical energies of the emerging political sphere into the sentimental spaces of an amorphous opinion culture, characterized by strong patriotic identification mixed with feelings of practical political powerlessness. A number of different forces and themes converged to bring about this end: the antifederal but patriotic nationalism of Reagan Republicanism, which sought to shrink the state while intensifying identification with the utopian symbolic "nation"; a rhetorical shift from a state-based and thus political identification with nationality to a culture-based concept of the nation as a site of integrated social membership; the expansion of a mass-mediated space of opinion formation that positions citizens as isolated spectators to the publicity that claims to represent them; the marketing of nostalgic images of a normal, familial America that would define the utopian context for citizen aspiration. Much of this agenda continues beyond the Reagan years, as Clintonite liberalism strives to find a middle ground on the right.

This set of successful transformations has reinvigorated the idea of the American Dream. It would be all too easy to ridicule the Dream, and to dismiss it as the motivating false consciousness of national/capitalist culture. But the fantasy of the American Dream is an important one to learn from. A popular form of political optimism, it fuses private fortune with that of the nation: it promises that if you invest your energies in work and family-making, the nation will secure the broader social and economic conditions in which your labor can gain value and your life can be lived with dignity. It is a story that addresses the fear of being stuck or reduced to a type, a redemptive story pinning its hope on class mobility. Yet this promise is voiced in the language of unconflicted personhood: to be American, in this view, would be to inhabit a secure space liberated from identities and structures that seem to constrain what a person can do in history. For this paradoxical feeling to persist, such that a citizen of the Dream can feel firmly placed in a zone of protected value while on the move in an arc of social mobility, the vulnerability of personal existence to the instability of capitalism and the concretely unequal forms and norms of national life must be suppressed, minimized, or made to seem exceptional, not general to the population. This sets the stage for a national people imagining itself national only insofar as it feels unmarked by the effects of these national contradictions.

The fear of being saturated and scarred by the complexities of the present and thereby barred from living the "Dream" has recently produced a kind of vicious yet sentimental cultural politics, a politics brimming over with images and faces of normal and abnormal America. In the patriotically-permeated pseudopublic sphere of the present tense, national politics does not involve starting with a view of the nation as a space of struggle violently separated by racial, sexual, and economic inequalities that cut across every imaginable kind of social location. Instead, the dominant idea marketed by patriotic traditionalists is of a core nation whose survival depends on personal acts and identities performed in the intimate domains of the quotidian.

It is in this sense that the political public sphere has become an intimate public sphere. The intimate public of the U.S. present tense is radically different from the "intimate sphere" of modernity described by Jürgen Habermas. Habermas portrays the intimate sphere of the European eighteenth century as a domestic space where persons produced the sense of their own private uniqueness, a sense of self which became a sense of citizenship only when it was abstracted and alienated in the nondomestic public sphere of liberal capitalist culture. In contrast, the intimate public sphere of the U.S. present tense renders citizenship as a condition of social membership produced by personal acts and values, especially acts originating in or directed toward the family sphere. No longer valuing personhood as something directed toward public life, contemporary nationalist ideology recognizes a public good only in a particularly constricted nation of simultaneously lived private worlds.[5]

This vision of a privatized, intimate core of national culture rings dramatic changes on the concept of the body politic, which is rarely valued as a *public*.[6] In the new nostalgia-based fantasy nation of the "American way of life," the residential enclave where "the family" lives usurps the modernist promise of the culturally vital, multiethnic city; in the new, utopian America, mass-mediated political identifications can only be rooted in traditional notions of home, family, and community. Meanwhile, the notion of a public life, from the profession of politician to non-family-based forms of political activism, has been made to seem ridiculous and even dangerous to the nation. Downsizing citizenship to a mode of voluntarism and privacy has radically changed the ways national identity is imagined, experienced, and governed in political and mass-media public spheres and in everyday life.

[This chapter] asks why it is, and how it has come to be, that a certain cluster of demonic and idealized images and narratives about sex and citizenship has come to obsess the official national public sphere. It asks why the most hopeful national pictures of "life" circulating in the public sphere are not of adults in everyday life, in public, or in politics, but rather of the most vulnerable minor or virtual citizens – fetuses, children, real and imaginary immigrants – persons that, paradoxically, cannot yet act as citizens. It asks why acts that are not civic acts, like sex, are having to bear the burden of defining proper citizenship. It asks why a conservative politics that maintains the sacredness of privacy, the virtue of the free market, and the immorality of state overregulation contradicts everything it believes when it comes to issues of intimacy. It asks why the pursuit of some less abstracted and more corporeal forms of "happiness" – through sex and through multicultural and sexual identity politics – has come to exemplify dangerous and irresponsible citizenship for some and utopian practice for others.[7] Meanwhile, it also asks to what degree liberals and the left have absorbed the conservative world view, relinquishing the fight against structural inequality for a more labile and optimistic culturalist perspective.

[I] track [various] controversial guiding image[s] of U.S. citizenship through the process of [their] privatization; and highlight some pilgrimages to Washington, the capital space which stands in for the nation, acting as its local form. These secular pilgrimages measure the intimate distances between the nation and some of the people who seek to be miraculated by its promise. We will see that in the reactionary culture of imperiled privilege, the nation's value is figured not on behalf of an actually existing and laboring adult, but of a future American, both incipient and pre-historical: especially invested with this hope are the American fetus and the American child. What constitutes their national supericonicity is an image of an American, perhaps the last living American, not yet bruised by history: not yet caught up in the processes of secularization and sexualization; not yet caught in the confusing and exciting identity exchanges made possible by mass consumption and ethnic, racial, and sexual mixing; not yet tainted by money or war. This national icon is still tacitly white, and it still contains the blueprint for the reproductive form that assures the family and the nation its future history. This national icon is still innocent of knowledge, agency, and accountability and thus has ethical claims on the adult political agents who write laws, make culture, administer resources, control things.

But most important, the fetal/infantile person is a *stand-in* for a complicated and contradictory set of anxieties and desires about national identity. Condensed into the image/hieroglyph of the innocent or incipient American, these anxieties and desires are about whose citizenship – whose subjectivity, whose forms of intimacy and interest, whose bodies and identifications, whose heroic narratives – will direct America's future. But the abstract image of the future generated by the national culture machine also stands for a crisis in the present: what gets consolidated now as the future modal citizen provides an alibi or an inspiration for the moralized political rhetorics of the present and for reactionary legislative and juridical practice.

These questions – of sex and citizenship, of minor and full citizens, and of mass national culture – have long been concerns regarding the United States (from Tocqueville's suspicion of democracy's infantilizing effects to the infantilized masculinity of the cold war).[8] But the national nervous system has become especially animated by the right-wing cultural agenda of the Reagan revolution.[9] One effect of this revolution has been to stigmatize these long-standing anxieties as "victim politics," a phrase that deliberately suppresses the complexity, ambivalence, and incoherence of social antagonism in the everyday life of contemporary citizenship.

The right-wing cultural agenda of the Reagan revolution [. . .] is my name for the public discourse around citizenship and morality that a complex bloc of activists has engendered during roughly the last two decades.[10] I have suggested that it bases its affirmative rhetoric on a nationalist politics of intimacy, which it contrasts to threatening practices of nonfamilial sexuality and, by implication, other forms of racial and economic alterity. The Reagan revolution not only has suffused "the personal" with political meanings well beyond those imagined in the "sexual revolution" of the 1960s, but it has had three other important consequences. First, it has helped to create some extremely limiting frames for thinking about what properly constitutes the practice of U.S. citizenship. One famous example of this process is Peggy Noonan and George Bush's image of the American people as "a thousand points of light."[11] This brightly lit portrait of a civic army of sanctified philanthropists was meant to replace an image of the United States as a Great Society with a state-funded social safety net. It sought to substitute intentional individual goodwill for the nation-state's commitment to fostering democracy within capitalism. Practical citizenship is here figured as something available to good people with good money. Now the Christian Coalition and the Republican Party are promoting legislation to put this fantasy into institutional practice by, among other things, advocating the transfer of federal entitlement programs for the "deserving poor" to private, voluntary, "faith-based" organizations.[12]

In addition, following the Reaganite tendency to fetishize both the offensive example and the patriotic norm, the increasingly monopolistic mass media act as a national culture industry whose mission is to micro-manage how any controversial event or person changes the meaning of being "American." The constant polling used by this media apparatus, which includes the solicitation of testimony on talk radio and television, along with telephone interviews, has paradoxically enabled the standards and rhetorics of citizenship to become so privatized and subjective that even privileged people can seem legitimately to claim "outsider," if not "minority," status.[13] With political ideas about the nation sacrificed to the development of feelings about it, nationality has become a zone of trauma that demands political therapy.

The third consequence of the Reaganite cultural revolution involves the way intimacy rhetoric has been employed to manage the economic crisis that separates the wealthy few from everyone else in the contemporary United States. By defining the United States as a place where normal intimacy is considered the foundation of the citizen's happiness, the right has attempted to control the ways questions of economic survival are seen as matters of citizenship. This use of intimacy is extremely complicated. First, it helps displace from sustained public scrutiny the relation between congealed corporate wealth and the shifting conditions of labor; second, it becomes a rhetorical means by which the causes of U.S. income inequality and job instability in all sectors of the economy can be personalized, rephrased in terms of individuals' capacity to respond flexibly to the new "opportunities" presented to them within an increasingly volatile global economy; third, it enables the hegemonic state-business class to promote a virulent competition between the native-born and immigrant poor. Even when economic issues are explicitly joined to institutions of intimacy — as in the current emphasis on family-oriented state entitlements for the middle classes — the "economic" foregrounds personal acts of saving and consumption over what happens in the workplace and the boardroom.[14]

As discussions of the politics of sex and bodily identity in the United States have become so fascinating and politically absorbing, a concern with the outrages of American class relations has been made to seem trite and unsexy. It is my view that a critical engagement with what ought to constitute the social privileges and obligations of citizenship must be reorganized around these questions — of national capitalism, metropolitan and rural poverty, environmental disintegration, racist thinking and ordinary concrete practice, and other banalities of national evil. Questions of intimacy, sexuality, reproduction, and the family are properly interrelated with these questions of identity, inequality, and national existence. No doubt these issues and institutions of intimacy will continue to be central to the disposition of national life, but as separate entities they should no longer overorganize the terms of public discussion about power, ethics, and the nation.

The materialist litany that the previous paragraph just begins to recite has been made to seem orthodox, boring, facile, or an occasion for paralyzed mourning.[15] Numerous efforts have been devoted to neutralizing these issues, all of which aim to separate out consideration of the economic conditions of citizenship from questions of culture and subjectivity. It almost goes without saying that the wealth of the wealthy classes in the United States is protected by this divisive rhetoric. The suggestion that capitalism is always on the brink of failing – as the current rhetoric of downsizing and scarcity would claim – terrorizes many workers into feeling competitive with each other and into overvalorizing individual will, as though personal willpower alone would be enough to make "market democracy" deliver on its "promise." Likewise, the utopia of a color-blind and gender-consensual society has been used as an alibi to make cases of egregious inequality seem like exceptions to a national standard, rather than a structural condition. In addition, the political alliance between business culture and the Christian right enables legitimate political dissent and outrage to be recast as immorality and even blasphemy.[16] Finally, the use of intimacy as a distraction from critical engagement with a general matrix of ordinary hard hierarchy actually impairs discussions of intimacy itself, in its broader social contexts.

The hegemonic achievement of Reaganite conservatism is also evident in its effects on its adversaries on the left. For example, a growing number of scholars and activists who speak from identity movements celebrate the ways U.S. subalterns develop tactics for survival from within capitalist culture: forms of activity like gay marriage, critically-motivated acts of commodity consumption, and identity-based economic investment zones are said to make marginalized social groups more central, more legitimate and powerful in capitalist society. Yet for all the importance of survival tactics, a politics that advocates the subaltern appropriation of normative forms of the good life makes a kind of (often tacit) peace with exploitation and normativity, as well as with the other less happy and frequently less visible aspects of capitalist culture outlined above.[17]

In addition, many radical social theorists see the political deployment of intimacy crises as merely ornamental or a distraction from "real" politics. They have become alienated by the intensities of the sex and identity wars, which seem to be disconnected from more important and public questions of equity, justice, and violence in political life in general.[18] But they have been misdirected by a false distinction between the merely personal and the profoundly structural.[19] These forms of sociality too often appear to be in separate worlds of analysis and commitment, with catastrophic political consequences for critical engagement with the material conditions of citizenship.[20] It is [my] purpose to challenge both the terms of the Reaganite revolution and the ways it has been opposed. Above all, it is to interfere with the intimate image of the national body that has, like a sunspot, both illuminated and blinded the world of mass politics and national fantasy in the contemporary United States.

"I hate your archive": on methodology and national culture

Americans experience themselves as national through public sphere accounts of what is important about them: this is why the manufacture of public opinion is crucial both for producing citizens and seeing how citizens are produced.[21] Yet people are not saturated by their identity as citizens, even during political campaigns, at baseball games, or listening to talk radio. Unless the terms of their normality or membership are being actively challenged, many people claim that their national identity is an extremely minor or null modality of their everyday experience of who they are. Being American or national feels inconsequential to their ordinary survival and makes no difference when they are thinking about what it is in their intimate lives that sustains them.

I am not trying to argue that citizenship is *really* the central category for people who imagine themselves primarily propped up by other identifications and axes of hope for the future. Nor am I claiming that the sum of the texts I engage equals the meaning of being American. Quite the contrary. Practices of citizenship involve both public-sphere narratives and concrete experiences of quotidian life that do not cohere or harmonize. Yet the rhetoric of citizenship does provide important definitional frames for the ways people see themselves as *public*, when they do.

At the moment, an incessant public struggle over the meaning of being a citizen of the United States encounters a widespread sense that the nation-state is an autonomous device that has little to do with the needs of ordinary people. The reactionary right's hegemonic project has been to say that it is closing this gap. Yet it is also the case that the abstracting of the U.S. state from its citizens has become more acute during the era of Reaganism. The anti-political politics of contemporary conservative culture has many paradoxical effects on citizen subjectivity, among which is the angry fading of public political agency aspirations. Nowhere is this paradox more starkly evident than in the recent proliferation of hyperpatriotic but antifederal militia-style activity.

The patriotic intensity of the Reaganite right works against identification with government itself, especially in its federal incarnation. It makes citizenship into a category of feeling irrelevant to practices of hegemony or sociality in everyday life. We might call this antipolitical politics "national sentimentality": it is sentimental because it is a politics that abjures politics, made on behalf of a private life protected from the harsh realities of power.[22] The sense that this discussion is considered *not* to be about citizenship, that it is about using power only to create the conditions of true intimacy, has been one of the great advertising coups of the conservative campaign to turn the nation into a privatized state of feeling.

I have deliberately used the language of advertising to describe the means by which the contemporary conservative or traditional conception of national life has been advanced. Advertising makes explicit the routes by which persons might individually and collectively give a name to their desire. It does not tell the truth about desires that already exist, although it does not merely invent desires for people. But advertising helps bring to consciousness a will to happiness that transcends any particular advertisement or commodity, but which becomes authorized by them. The official public-sphere campaign to demonize radical justice movements and to make only particular kinds of national life iconic has deployed the very strategies of linking happiness to desire that advertising uses, so that politicians can say that all who hold a certain sustaining set of wishes hold the same intimate feelings about how they should be reflected in national life, whether or not people actually do make these linkages in any conscious, consistent, or coherent way. The right-wing national culture industry thus forges the very name of political desire; at this moment, the absorption of these wishes into the brand names "American Dream" and "American Way of Life" has virtually taken on the form of common sense. [. . .] Paradoxically, once they become banal, they are at their most powerful: no longer inciting big feelings and deep rages, these claims about the world seem hardwired into what is taken for granted in collective national life.[23]

In the spring of 1994, I delivered a lecture [. . .]. Afterward, a colleague said, "I really admired your thinking, but – I hate your archive." I loved this moment (I knew an anecdote was forming), but I had to know more. Was this an aggressive disciplinary question, implicitly asking me to return to the more canonical or literary texts on which I had honed my professional reading and analytic skills? Did he think it was cheating, somehow, to read closely texts that are not obviously conceptually challenging? In response to these queries he assented generally, but he also wanted me to speak more explicitly in the traditional languages and narratives of critical theory, and in particular to make explicit the ways Foucault, Benjamin, and Gramsci have enabled my understanding of national culture. (He was right about that, but apparently hadn't heard the ways other work — say, that of Eve Sedgwick, Hortense Spillers, Fredric Jameson, Michael Warner, and Judith Butler — has also made this analysis possible. But this miscue over my archive raises other questions about the politics of academic theory.)[24] This exchange also helped me to clarify the professional juncture at which I and others in cultural studies stand at the present moment:[25] because humanists traditionally get value by being intimate with the classics (literary and theoretical), those who think through popular materials and waste thought on objects that were not made for it threaten to degrade the value of intellectual life in general and the value of the humanities in particular.

In the previous paragraphs I demonstrate why a different strategy of reading can be productive for the analysis of contemporary American life. One does not find the materials of the patriotic public sphere theorizing citizenship in either beautiful or coherent ways. These materials frequently use the silliest, most banal and erratic logic imaginable to describe important things, like what constitutes intimate relations, political personhood, and national life. I am conducting a counterpolitics of the silly object by focusing on some instances of it and by developing a mode of criticism and conceptualization that reads the waste materials of everyday communication in the national public sphere as pivotal documents in the construction, experience, and rhetoric of quotidian citizenship in the United States.[26] The very improvisatory ephemerality of the archive makes it worth *reading*. Its very popularity, its effects on the law and on everyday life, makes it important. Its very ordinariness requires an intensified critical engagement with what had been merely undramatically explicit.

There might, of course, be other reasons why people might hate my archive. A reader might feel that [it] is not evenhanded and that it is stacked in order to be politically correct, while others have suggested that it is far too sympathetic to the kinds of utopian wishes for unconflicted normality expressed by both liberals and conservatives. One colleague asked me: "Why bother reading middlebrow nonsense like *Time* magazine and reactionary dogma like the *Contract with America*, when you could be theorizing and promoting the world-building activities evident in the pamphlets, zines, polemics, and literatures of radical or subaltern publics?" I do track both formal and informal subaltern resistance, [. . .] but I am more interested in looking at the moments of oppressive optimism in normal national culture: to see what kinds of domination are being imagined as forms of social good; what kinds of utopian desires are being tapped and translated into conservative worldviews; what means are being used to suppress the negative fallout of affirmative culture; what it might take to make linked kinds of knowledge, power, and experience no longer seem separate. I read these mainstream documents and discourses of the nation not as white noise but as powerful language, not as "mere" fiction or fantasy but as violence and desire that have material effects.

Someone might also hate my archive because it is so resolutely *national*. Increasingly, radical scholars have been demanding the end of an American Studies that places the United States and the nation form in general at the center of the history of the present tense.[27] Transnational capital and global media produce subjects and publics that are no longer organized around the politics of representation within the confines of a single state, and states increasingly ally with transnational capital in organizing processes of production that transect their borders. In addition, the combination of migration and new technologies of travel and interpersonal communication have so changed and challenged the ways national life operates that the notion of a modal person who is a citizen with one pure national affiliation and loyalty to only the place she or he currently lives markedly underdescribes the experiences and political struggles of persons across the globe.

But this does not mean that states are not still powerful political agents, or that the ideology of nationhood has become enervated, the faint howling of an archaic dream of democratic legitimation. Indeed, it is precisely under transnational conditions that the nation becomes a more intense object of concern and struggle. This is why [I] focus on the story the official national culture industry tells in the contemporary United States, a story that instates an intimate public sphere as a site of mediation in which citizens can both feel their linkage to one another through the nation and negotiate their relation to the transnational. In this way the nation form retains its centrality to definitions and possibilities of political agency. Borrowing its aura from romantic or domestic privacy, this sentimental version of the nation provides a scene in which fragments of identity are held to become whole. Part of the aim of soliciting intensified identification with the idealized nation is a highly contested project of shrinking the state and breaking down its function as a "utopia of social labor."[28] The simultaneous contraction of the state and expansion of the nation produces an incoherent set of boundary-drawing panics about the profound economic and cultural effects of transnational capitalism and immigration. Tracking the American Dream machine, for all its banality and parochialism, must thus be part of the project of describing the specificity of politics and subjectivity in a present tense that is at once national and transnational.

I try saying something different about these national objects through experimental or unusual kinds of storytelling, for I feel that I can best show how the national present has been constructed through radical recontextualization.[29] This kind of writing does not aspire merely to comment on or contextualize its object; it brings new objects into being via the textual performance. I want to make the hegemonic national icon/stereotype and the narratives that maintain the political culture they operate in look unfamiliar and uninevitable, while also shifting the ways mass politics, critical practice, identity, embodiment, and intimate political feelings can be imagined and mobilized.

This project of frame-breaking through overreading the discursive scene of the contemporary nation was first inspired by the following passage from Harriet Jacobs's *Incidents in the Life of a Slave Girl* (1861). Jacobs tells the story to show how slaves maintained optimism about political and personal freedom despite massive evidence to the contrary. Some slaves even clung to the idea of a United States that would, if it could, purify itself of its most unjust institution. Jacobs's friend reports that another slave, a literate one, has read in the newspaper some exciting news: on learning that the president tolerated a nation that trafficked in slavery, "the queen of 'Merica . . . didn't believe it, and went to Washington city to see the President about it. They quarrelled; she drew her sword upon him, and swore that he should help her to make them all free." This prompts Jacobs to observe:

> That poor ignorant woman thought that America was governed by a Queen, to whom the President was subordinate. I wish the President was subordinate to Queen Justice.[30]

Jacobs shows that a great deal of language and logic circulating through the national public sphere is absurd, ignorant, and extremely consequential to the ways people understand and act within what they perceive to be the possibilities of their lives. She takes seriously this failed communication about the nation not only to show how dominated people find ways to sustain their hopefulness in a cruel world, but also to show how the kinds of invention, innovation, and improvisation her illiterate interlocutor practiced with only partial knowledge could be used radically, for the reimagination of collective political life within the nation.

The drastic redefinition of American personhood during the Reagan era has been established as common sense by being marketed as merely descriptive of what already exists, even while controversy has long been raging around its contours. This compels me to write [. . .] an iconoclastic national counterfantasy, one meant to make you pause long enough to consider how, if you are a U.S. citizen or live in the United States, the ephemera of patriotic conservative orthodoxy have become central to your public definition.

On heterosexuality [. . .]

In the quasi-queer film *Boys on the Side* (dir. Herbert Ross, 1995), a heterosexual man who is speaking to a lesbian about his longing for a woman they both desire says, "I think hetero-sexuality's going to make a comeback." His joke would be an ironic throwaway line were it not for the film's commitment to associating heterosexuality with "life" and lesbian desire with the virtue of abstinence and the tragedy of death by AIDS. (This takes some doing, since the AIDS transmitted in the film originates in a heterosexual one-night stand, but no matter.) The defining sexual event of the generation currently coming to national power in the United States was the sexual revolution, with its accompanying shift in the availability of birth control/abortion: this was a revolution, largely, in heterosexuality. While gay- and lesbian-rights movements were contemporary with the sexual revolution, the revolution that dominated the public-sphere discussion of sex and feminism was not mainly concerned with nonheterosexual forms of identity or behavior. In contrast, for the current generations entering into sexuality, the defining issue is AIDS and other forms of disease and death. The transformation in national sexual culture from thinking about sexuality in terms of lives already in progress to imagining sexuality in the shadow of deaths to be avoided registers a shift in the contours of national personhood that is widely experienced, but little narrated. This is a revolution that has forced a generation of sexual subjects to become conscious of a much larger variety of life practices, and to see that these constitute a field of choices and identifications ordinary people make.

No one coming into sexuality in contemporary America can avoid thinking about gay, lesbian, bisexual, transsexual, transgendered, or other categories of sexuality. Some might share with their parents a nostalgia for a time when sex practice seemed to flow naturally from the life-building hopes children are taught to have for the stable reproductive family and for wedding presents. These are the people for whom the desire for heterosexual-ity to make a "comeback" actually makes some sense. To them, a "comeback" would mean that you would not have to think about sexual preference; it would mean that only the rare and unfortunate people who have the nondominant sexuality would have to imagine it, and then keep it to themselves.

Many of us, however, experience the world as permeated by the practices and narratives of what Michael Warner has called heteronormative culture – a public culture, juridical, economic, and aesthetic, organized for the promotion of a world-saturating heterosexuality.[31] The phenomenal forms of heteronormative culture will vary as people locate themselves differently in racial, class, gender, regional, or religious contexts, contexts which mark the experience of sexualization with specific traumatic/liberatory intensity. But nowhere in the United States has heterosexuality gone into a decline or "left" in a way that makes the idea of a comeback even remotely plausible. It has been and remains culturally dominant. There is a vast culture industry constantly generating text and law on behalf of hetero-sexuality's preservation and extension into resistant or unincorporated domains of identifi-cation and fantasy. Take, for example, *The Crying Game* (dir. Neil Jordan, 1992), with its offer of a celibate same-sex couple in heterosexual drag as the fantasy solution to the problem of sexual and postcolonial violence. Or take sex education, which has again become controversial now that its tendency is to speak of things not conjugally heterosexual, like different sexual preferences and nonreproductive sexual practices. According to the cultural agenda of the radical right, sex education, when it happens at all, should be a great terrorist device for breaking in straight sexual subjects who fancy each other but don't have sex, as in *The Crying Game:* if not, it will be seen simply as an immoral mechanism for promoting sex.

Yet it is a sexual and political fact that heterosexual life no longer seems the only mentionable one in the United States. This is what continues to fuel a state of sexual emergency, through homophobic and racist policies in the state and federal system, along with various forms of defensiveness, rage, and nostalgia among ordinary citizens who liked it better when their sexuality could be assumed to be general for the population as a whole. Heterosexuality has never "left": it has had to become newly explicit, and people have had to become aware of the institutions, narratives, pedagogies, and social practices that support it.

The false history of ex-privileged heterosexuality – the story that it went out of fashion – tells us something important about how nationality and sexuality meet up in the official public sphere. Identity is marketed in national capitalism as a property. It is something you can purchase, or purchase a relation to. Or it is something you already own that you can express: *my* masculinity, *my* queerness, for example (this is why bisexuality has not made it fully into the sexual star system: it is hard to *express* bisexuality). Michel Foucault and scholars like Judith Butler and Jonathan Ned Katz have shown how sexuality is the modern form of self-intelligibility: I am my identity; my identity is fundamentally sexual; and my practices reflect that (and if they don't, they require submission to sexual science, self-help, or other kinds of law).[32] The account of the total correspondence between acts and identities that marked the controversy over gays in the military manifested the juridical understanding of sexuality: my perverse act expresses my perverse identity; the state has a compelling interest in protecting the family by repressing my perversion; hence, no gays in the military; and hence, no privacy protection for any non-reproductive sexual practice or identity. Insofar as the politics and the medical crisis brought into collective awareness by AIDS has made it impossible to draw an absolute public boundary between U.S. citizens and gay people, and as that increasing consciousness makes people aware of and more interested in gay, lesbian, and queer culture, it has also helped broaden the conservative rage against non-heteronormative forms of sexual activity and identity, which include all kinds of nonreproductive heterosexual activity, and sex and childbirth outside marriage.

But identity need not be simply a caption for an image of an unchanging concrete self. It is also a theory of the future, of history. This leads to the second way sexuality has met up with national fantasy. I have described the first way in the regulation of "perversion" on behalf of a heterofamilial citizenship norm. The second is in the way the generational form of the family has provided a logic of the national future. When the modal form of the citizen is called into question, when it is no longer a straight, white, reproductively inclined heterosexual but rather might be anything, any jumble of things, the logic of the national future comes into crisis.

This crisis of the national future, stimulated by sexual politics, comes at a time when America feels unsure about its value in a number of domains: in world military politics, in global economics, in ecological practice, and in the claim that the nation has a commitment to sustaining justice, democracy, and the American Dream when there seems to be less money and reliable work to go around. Along with sex-radical politics and feminism, multiculturalism and transnational capitalism and the widening social inequities that have accompanied it have called the national narrative into question. *What will the American future look like?* Suddenly no narrative seems to flow naturally from the identity people thought was their national birthright: of course, that birthright was partly protected because it was tacit. But let us think for a minute about this birthright, its corporeal norms, and the future it purported to produce.

Here is a brief story about the history of birthright citizenship in the United States, beginning with a familiar kind of long view. In the eighteenth century, the United States came into being via a democratic revolution against a geographically distant monarchial authority and an economically aggressive colonial marginality. The fantasy of a national democracy was based on principles of abstract personhood (all persons shall be formally equivalent) and its rational representation in a centralized state and federal system. The constitutional American "person" was a white male property owner: more than that, though, was unenumerated in the law.

These abstract principles of democratic nationality have always been hypocritical.[33] From the beginning, entire populations of persons were excluded from the national promise which, because it was a promise, was held out paradoxically: falsely, as a democratic reality, and legitimately, as a promise, the promise that the democratic citizenship form makes to people caught in history. The populations who were and are managed by the discipline of the promise – women, African Americans, Native Americans, immigrants, homosexuals – have long experienced simultaneously the wish to be full citizens and the violence of their partial citizenship. Of course, the rules of citizenship constantly change, both in the law and in the public sense of how persons ought to be treated, protected, and encouraged to act. But it is not false to say that over the long term some of us have been American enough to provide labor but not American enough to be sustained by the fullest resources of democratic national privilege.

During the twentieth century, however, changes in the economy and in the juridical and everyday life politics of identity have forced the birthright assumptions of U.S. nationality into a vulnerable explicitness, and this very explicitness is making the patriots of the ex-tacit nation very unhappy. In response, a virulent form of revitalized national heterosexuality has been invented, a form that is complexly white and middle class. [. . .] I do not mean to be coming out against [heterosexuality]. I simply do not see why the nation has to have an official sexuality, especially one that authorizes the norm of a violent gentility; that narrows the field of legitimate political action; that supports the amputation of personal complexity into categories of simple identity; that uses cruel and mundane strategies both to promote shame for non-normative populations and to deny them state, federal, and juridical supports because they are deemed morally incompetent to their own citizenship. This is the heterosexuality I repudiate.[34]

Feminist politics has long authorized my dedication to producing new contexts for understanding the politics, economics, and everyday practices of intimacy; its conjuncture with queer and materialist theory and activism is the context for this project. Queer/feminist activity in and outside the academy has enticed its participants to develop new names, analytics, contexts, and institutions for politics, practices, and subjectivities. It has broadened the notion of what sexuality is beyond the public/private divide, and has challenged a notion of gender that can overorganize how to understand machineries of domination, a notion that has tended to push questions of sexuality, race, class, and ethnicity to an ever-receding horizon of what "we" feminists promise to understand "later." This kind of commitment to conjunctural practice has also challenged the forms and styles of writing, research, and representation that typically buttress professional credentials, pushing me to work rigorously beyond my expertise in ways that feel at once risky and absolutely necessary. [. . .]

[This] is not a redemptive text that maps or draws what kind of utopia a revitalized citizenship form or a post-heteronormative nation would be. In this sense it is not the opposite of the Christian Coalition's *Contract*. Confronting the unpredictable effects of changes in longstanding habits of political subjectivity – how relations among the state, the law, economics, and intimacy are imagined, for example – is a necessary precondition for thinking past the scene of normativity that pervades the contemporary United States. At the same time, to create new contexts that are something other than slightly less bad versions of what exists requires committing to two kinds of work: discerning places where counter-hegemonic alliances might be produced, and taking on the discomforts and risks even to "privilege" (with a small *p*) entailed by that commitment. The tactic is to begin to enumerate some of these forms of risk and optimism while tracking the divisive and wishful forms of the American Way of Life, with its particularly constricted dream of vanquishing economic, cultural, and sexual unpleasantness. In this spirit [I do] a diva turn on citizenship, attempting to transform it from a dead (entirely abstract) category of analysis into a live social scene that exudes sparks, has practical consequences, forces better ways of thinking about nationality, culture, politics, and personhood.

I have suggested that citizenship is a status whose definitions are always in process. It is continually being produced out of a political, rhetorical, and economic struggle over who will count as "the people" and how social membership will be measured and valued. It must, then, be seen as more than a patriotic category. [C]itizenship provides an index for appraising domestic national life, and for witnessing the processes of valorization that make different populations differently legitimate socially and under the law. The pilgrimage to Washington D.C. that links different citizenship scenes depicts both real and conceptual distances that occupants of the United States have felt the need to traverse: not always because they want to usurp the space of national mastery, but sometimes because they seek to capture, even fleetingly, a feeling of genuine membership in the United States. In reformulating citizenship as a vital space on which diverse political demands can be made, [I] seek also to remind that despite all appearances the conservative engagement with sex is also a comprehensive politics of citizenship, one that has had practical, theoretical, and extraordinarily intimate public consequences.

Notes

1   In 1996, both the Republican and Democratic presidential nominating conventions were organized around the patriotic image of a nation made of and for children. The image of the citizen-child took its authority and intensity not from the moralizing hostility of Republican "family values" rhetoric that marked the previous election, but from the optimistic liberalism about privatization issued by Hillary Rodham Clinton. Clinton's book *It Takes a Village* argues in chapters such as "Children Are Citizens Too" that the most powerful motive for an expanded context of social justice in the United States is the world adults will bring into being for their children. In 1996, the Republicans argued that it takes a "family," not a "village," to raise a child; the Democrats responded by claiming that raising nontraumatized citizens requires the beneficent service of a much more broadly defined population of trusted guardians that includes families, communities, teachers, childcare workers, police, social service agencies, and so on. Despite their differences, each of these positions locates the nation's virtue and value in its intimate zones, in personal acts of pedagogy and sustenance. For more serious and complicated engagements with these issues on a local, national, and global scale, see Stephens, *Children and the Politics of Culture*.

2   Much has been written about the psychological, sociological, and economic consequences for U.S.

"white males" who see subaltern-rights movements as having put in place unjust obstacles to their achievement and social value. (According to one article, in the seven months after the November 1994 elections, fourteen hundred news columns used the phrase "angry white men" to describe the bloc of voters who voted the Republicans into office [*Detroit News* 30 May 1995: A9].) My guess is that the population identified this way is actually much more diverse in membership. Many people of color and women identify with the world of desire for accumulation and self-extension attributed, here, to "white men." In addition, the *USA Today* article that initiated this postelection conclusion actually specified the "AWM" as a male, working-class, high-school graduate: as usual in analyses of national politics, class motives are subordinated to the corporealized identity form.

For commentaries that employ the concept of the angry white male citizen, see E.J. Dionne, "A Fashionable Stereotype That Explains Very Little," *International Herald Tribune* 4 May 1995; Dumm, *united states*; Ehrenreich, *The Snarling Citizen*; Faludi, *Backlash*; Richard Goldstein, "Save the Males," *Village Voice* 7 March 1995: 21–29; J. Hoberman, "Victim Victorious," *Village Voice* 7 March 1995: 31–33; Jeffords, *Hard Bodies*; Pfeil, *White Guys*; Pollitt, *Reasonable Creatures*, 31–41, 115–23; Paul Rockwell, "These Angry White Men Say Yes to the Concept," *San Francisco Herald Examiner* 19 June 1995: A15; James Toedtmann, "Poll Warns of Angry Women Voters," *Newsday* 6 October 1995: A64.

3   On this point, see Cindy Patton's brilliant analysis, "Refiguring Social Space."

4   [C]artoons have a long and hallowed place in the production of critical discourse in the U.S. public sphere. But political cartoons have used the body to represent, *in extremis*, the distorting tendencies of power and identity that political culture engenders. At this moment, I am arguing, extreme images of personhood count as modal citizenship in the identity politics contexts of the United States, which seems to be ravaged by a farce-style moral and civil war between icons and hyphenated stereotypes. As Congresswoman Patricia Schroeder (Democrat of Colorado) opines about the real-politik context in which she operates, "Many progressives think you have to have big reports with lots of analysis and details. And I'm saying we need to have the equivalent of verbal cartoons to show what these people [the currently vigorous Christian/conservative right-wing alliance in the U.S. Congress] are doing. When I called Reagan the 'Teflon President,' people got it. What good is a 900 page report if the people never read it?" *Ms.* 6, no. 8 (March/April 1996): 24.

5   Habermas, *The Structural Transformation of the Public Sphere*, 27–37, 43–51, 151–75, and 231–50.

6   My argument that the Reaganite right has attempted to privatize citizenship by reframing it as an intimate form of social membership might seem to suggest that the dominant nation now uncannily repeats the conservative politico-familial mood of the U.S. postwar period. There are some important confluences too, especially in the continuing and paradoxical public-sphere worry that commodity culture both fulfills people and has potentially immoral effects on individuals, family life, and the nation generally. But contemporary work on sex, gender, race, and citizenship generally argues that while the early cold war era placed the white, middle-class family at the core of postwar national consumer and political culture, the family sphere was not considered the moral, ethical, and political *horizon* of national or political interest. There are many reasons for this dissimilarity. One has to do with the particular ways familialism played in the externalization of the communist/totalitarian threat to the United States during the cold war. This process produced the normative "American" family as a site of symbolic/ideological vulnerability that both symbolized the danger the nation faced and emphasized the difference between families and the tutelary state, which had a knowledge/power apparatus that could, if strong enough, protect ordinary citizens. Furthermore, challenges to state racism during this period of the welfare state's expansion put pressure on *public* institutions in the United States to catch up to citizen desire for more equivalence between democratic ideals and national/capitalist practices. In contrast, as the cold war waned and both the state and the industrial sector contracted, the intimacy wars have escalated, producing citizens whose proper horizon of national interest is said to be the family and its radiating zones of practice. See Corber, *In the Name of National Security*; Rogin, *Ronald Reagan, the Movie*; Dolan, *Allegories of America: Narratives, Metaphysics, Politics*; Myerowitz, *Not June Cleaver*; May, *Homeward Bound*; Omi and Winant, *Racial Formation in the United States*. For a prophetically longer view of the emergence of intimacy as the index of normativity in the United States, see Sennett, *The Fall of Public Man*.

7   For an aligned project of understanding the ambiguous impulses at play in the contemporary United States, involving identity, nationality, commodity identification, and public-sphere intimacy forms, see Gilroy, " 'After the Love Has Gone.' "

8   Tocqueville, *Democracy in America*; see also Rogin, *Ronald Reagan, the Movie*.

9   I take the logic of the nervous system as an image of the social machinery of politics and subjectivity from Taussig, *The Nervous System*.

10   On the popular contexts of right-wing culture in the everyday of the nation see Diamond, *Roads to
Dominion*; and Grossberg, *We Gotta Get Out of This Place*.

11   President Bush used the phrase (penned by speechwriter Peggy Noonan) "a thousand points of light"
to describe the new, defederalized, post-welfare-state nation both in his speech accepting the
presidential nomination and in his inaugural speech five months later. See the *New York Times*
19 August 1988: A14, and 21 January 1989: A10.

12   See Gillespie and Schellhass, *Contract with America*; Moore, *Restoring the Dream*; Christian Coalition,
Contract with the American Family.

13   Much has been written about the ways media conglomerates are advancing the U.S. public sphere's
atrophy. See especially the special issue of *The Nation* titled "The National Entertainment State,"
vol. 262, no. 22: 3 June 1996. For earlier and fuller analyses of the material, as opposed to psychic,
subordination of the citizen to private "public" media interests in a complicated collusion with the
security sector of the federal government, see Schiller, *Information and the Crisis Economy* and *Culture,
Inc*; and Mowlana, Gerbner, and Schiller, *Triumph of the Image: The Media's War in the Persian Gulf – A
Global Perspective*.

14   One recent exception to this general conservative tendency to use a highly moralized intimacy
rhetoric as a distraction from the discussion of citizenship's material contexts is the populism of
Patrick Buchanan, a perennial national presidential candidate and pundit who simultaneously wields
morality rhetoric and taps into workers' rage at the amoral abandon with which corporate downsizing has been taking place. But the protectionist policy Buchanan offers as the solution to the problem
of globalization is all tied up with a nationalist intimacy rhetoric that demonizes foreignness and
nonnormative difference in general, promoting a linkage among all sorts of phobias – xenophobia
and homophobia in particular.

15   In particular the influential work of Chantal Mouffe, from which I have learned much, presumes the
inefficacy of class rhetorics for the progressive revitalization of citizenship discourse. Mouffe chooses
an antiessentialist form of identity politics, which focuses on the contingencies of identity, and its
potential for alliance building, in her reconstruction of citizenship. However, the unassimilability of
class discourse to identity politics could just as easily be the *model* for what a conjunctural alliance
politics might look like: Mouffe's exclusion of the economic (and class experience) from the realm
of cultural politics seems a critical flaw in her imagination of new social movements. See Mouffe,
"Preface, Democratic Politics Today" and "Democratic Citizenship and the Political Community,"
in *Dimensions of Radical Democracy*, 1–14, 225–39.

16   For example, the nonprofit organization Focus on the Family, headed by the radio and print
journalist and minister, Dr. James C. Dobson, lobbies for family values in everyday life and the
national public sphere with sacred verve and rational clarity. See his magazines *Focus on the Family* and
Citizen, the latter of which gives encouragement, explanation, argument, and tactical maps for being
effective in the political public sphere. See also note 12.

17   For texts that imagine a mutual transformation of subaltern and capitalist culture see, for example,
The Black Public Sphere, ed. The Black Public Sphere Collective (Chicago: University of Chicago
Press, 1995), especially Austin, " 'A Nation of Thieves': Consumption, Commerce, and the Black
Public Sphere," 229–52; D'Emilio, "Capitalism and Gay Identity"; Griggers, "Lesbian Bodies in the
Age of (Post) mechanical Reproduction"; Sedgwick, *Epistemology of the Closet*. Queer theory in
particular has generally occupied the scene of tactical subversion rather than anticapitalist radicalism:
for critical analyses of this tendency, see Hennessey, "Queer Visibility in Commodity Culture";
Lauren Berlant and Michael Warner, "Sex in Public" (*GLQ*). For a critique of the capitalist optimism
of cultural studies in general, see Berland, "Angels Dancing."

18   This includes most liberal and materialist social theory, and would require an interminable note.

19   To break down analytic distinctions between political, economic, and cultural domains of experience
and analysis has long been a project of a certain strain of Marxist cultural theory. In my own
development, the promise and challenge of *Social Text* I (winter 1979) remains vital. See especially
Jameson, "Reification and Utopia in Mass Culture"; and John Brenkman, "Mass Media: From
Collective Experience to the Culture of Privatization," 94–109. See also Jameson, "Five Theses on
Actually Existing Marxism."

20   For an analytic that engages the ways the dominant media of the contemporary U.S. public sphere
produce national knowledge via a series of discrete, unrelated events (thus frustrating the formation
of a critical culture) see Hansen, foreword, in *Public Sphere and Experience*. Taken as a whole, Negt and

Kluge's work on fantasy, experience, and political life is central to [my] thinking. See especially chapter 1, "The Public Sphere as the Organization of Collective Experience," 1–53.

21   Again, this note would be interminable. One might begin with Habermas, "On the Concept of Public Opinion," in *The Structural Transformation of the Public Sphere*, 236–50; Herman and Chomsky, *Manufacturing Consent*; Heath, "Representing Television"; and Schwoch, White, and Reilly, *Media Knowledge*.

22   Since its inception as a kind of radical thought around abolition in the U.S. mid-nineteenth century, national sentimentality has been a project of privileged white citizens dedicated to reframing citizenship. In the nineteenth century this involved replacing citizenship's original status as a property- or identity-based condition of political legitimacy with a notion of citizenship as a private and personal formation based on subjective relations of identification and similarity. In the nineteenth century, national sentimentality was a terribly flawed vehicle for inducing a more racially and economically equitable mass national democracy: in the late twentieth century, the reverse is the case. See Samuels, *The Culture of Sentiment*. See also Mohanty, "Cartographies of Struggle."

23   For theoretical accounts of banality, violence, and national life, see Baudrillard, *In the Shadow of the Silent Majorities* and "From the System to the Destiny of Objects"; Mbembe, "Prosaics of Servitude and Authoritarian Civilities"; Mbembe and Roitman, "Figures of the Subject in Times of Crisis"; Morris, "Banality in Cultural Studies."

24   I often encounter people who think that "real" theory is philosophy while queer theory involves moralizing identity performances dressed up as thinking. This position strikes me as anti-intellectual and, need I say it, sexually anxious. In 1986 I heard a talk by Julia Lesage that argued for using citation not only to mark the range of a text's knowledge but also as a device for building alliances. [. . .]

25   At the time of this writing a backlash against cultural studies is emerging in the humanities and humanistic social sciences. Some important concerns are expressed in this resistance: about the risks of cultural or historical anachronism and comparison; about the status of scholarship that seems at times motivated by an unselfconscious presentism and/or a smug moralism that is legitimated as "politics"; about the analytic status of critical writing that uses autobiography or other forms of generic syncretism; and about nonrigorous engagements with a mass culture that is all too available for reading. Many progressive scholars join traditional ones in this debate, agreeing that politicized work on culture should still follow certain established notions of evidence, argument, archival work, tone of voice, and theoretical and historical rigor.

But it is certainly hasty and may be in bad faith to identify cultural studies generally as anecdotal, posturing, and easy to do. It is merely defensive to assume that its sites of challenge and its critical experimentality inherently produce work that is lacking in consequential knowledge and serious concepts. Those of us who work with theory have all seen people use the strategy of generalizing about the value of a threatening kind of thinking by distorting and amplifying weak sentences or underdeveloped concepts in particular cases: for example, one colleague uses the phrase "another essay about Madonna's nipples" to inveigh against cultural studies. But this kind of cheap shot, and the more subtle ones, must be countered, and for a number of reasons. The backlash against cultural studies is frequently a euphemism for discomfort with work on contemporary culture around race, sexuality, class, and gender. It is sometimes a way of talking about the fear of losing what little standing intellectual work has gained through its studied irrelevance (and superiority) to capitalist culture. It expresses a fear of popular culture and popularized criticism. At the same time it can express a kind of antielitism made in defense of narrow notions of what proper intellectual objects and intellectual postures should be. On the left it frequently expresses a fear that critical metatheory will lose its standing as the ground of politics and *real* thinking. I am not saying that work in cultural studies is always what I wish it were: but as the attacks on it cloak so many kinds of worthy and unworthy aggression and anxiety it behooves us to try to say what they are and to fight the unworthy ones in their real terms. It goes without saying that this list of counterinsurgent motives can and should be augmented.

26   For an aligned view about the place of irony and archival creativity in critical studies of nationality, see John Caughie, "Playing at Being American."

27   See, for example, Appadurai, *Modernity at Large*; Dominelli, *Women Across Continents*; Ginsburg and Rapp, *Conceiving the New World Order*; Grewal and Kaplan, *Scattered Hegemonies*; Kaplan and Pease, *Cultures of U.S. Imperialism*; Rouse, "Thinking through Transnationalism"; Schneider and Brian Wallis, *Global Television*; Shohat and Stam, *Unthinking Eurocentrism*; Spivak, "The Politics of Translation," and "Acting Bits/Identity Talk."

28 Habermas laments the exhaustion of the utopia of labor and privatization of society both in contemporary European and U.S. public spheres in "The New Obscurity: The Crisis of the Welfare
State and the Exhaustion of Utopian Energies," in Habermas, *The New Conservatism*, 48–70.
29 On radical recontextualization as critical method and a condition of historical possibility see Spivak,
Outside in the Teaching Machine and Bhabha, "The Commitment to Theory."
30 Jacobs, *Incidents in the Life of a Slave Girl*, 45.
31 Warner, introduction, *Fear of a Queer Planet*.
32 The literature on "identity" is, again, very large: some examples from it include Foucault, *The History
of Sexuality*, v. 1–3; Butler, *Gender Trouble*; Katz, *The Invention of Heterosexuality*; Danielsen and Engle,
After Identity, especially essays by Halley ("The Politics of the Closet") and Coombe ("The Properties
of Culture and the Politics of Possessing Identity"); Rouse, "Questions of Identity"; and Spivak,
Outside in the Teaching Machine. For an essay that opens new comparative ways of thinking about
identity as property in the self, see Petchesky, "The Body as Property."
33 The bibliography on the historical relation between U.S. citizenship and corporealized quasi nationality or subnationality is substantial. I summarize it in *The Anatomy of National Fantasy*, 11–17,
222–23. For an important politico-philosophical engagement with the means by which a culture of
democratic rights hypocritically produces a turbulent politics of race, gender, and ethnicity, see
Balibar, *Masses, Classes, Ideas*.
34 Elshtain argues strenuously against the current U.S. drive to consign "shameful" identities to the
private or to use shame to draw the boundary between full and incompetent citizenship, a desire
she sees as making democracy impossible. See *Democracy on Trial*, especially chapter 2, "The Politics
of Displacement," 37–63.

Bibliography

Appadurai, Arjun. *Modernity at Large: Cultural Dimensions of Globalization*. Minneapolis: U of Minnesota
P, 1996.
Austin, Regina. " 'A Nation of Thieves': Consumption, Commerce, and the Black Public Sphere."
The Black Public Sphere. Ed. the Black Public Sphere Collective. Chicago: U of Chicago P, 1995.
229–52.
Balibar, Etienne. *Masses, Classes, Ideas: Studies on Politics and Philosophy after Marx*. New York: Routledge,
1994.
Baudrillard, Jean. "From the System to the Destiny of Objects." *The Ecstasy of Communication*. Trans.
Bernard and Caroline Schutze. Ed. Slyvère Lotringer. New York: Semiotexte, 1987. 77–96.
—— . *In the Shadow of the Silent Majorities . . . Or the End of the Social and Other Essays*. Trans. Paul Foss,
Paul Patton, and John Johnston. New York: Semiotexte, 1983.
Benjamin, Walter. "A Short History of Photography." *Classic Essays on Photography*. Ed. Alan Trachtenberg.
1931. New Haven: Leete's Island, 1980. 202–3.
—— . "Theses on the Philosophy of History." *Illuminations*. Trans. Harry Zohn. New York: Schocken,
1969. 253–64.
Berland, Jody. "Angels Dancing: Cultural Technologies and the Production of Space." *Cultural
Studies*. Ed. Lawrence Grossberg, Cary Nelson, and Paula Treichler. New York: Routledge,
1992. 39–55.
Berlant, Lauren. *The Anatomy of National Fantasy: Hawthorne, Utopia, and Everyday Life*. Chicago: U of
Chicago P, 1991.
—— . *The Queen of America Goes to Washington City*. Durham, NC: Duke UP, 1997.
Bhabha, Homi K. "The Commitment to Theory," in Homi K. Bhabha, *The Location of Culture*. New
York: Routledge, 1994. 19–39.
Butler, Judith. *Bodies That Matter*. New York: Routledge, 1993.
—— . *Gender Trouble: Feminism and the Subversion of Identity*. New York: Routledge, 1990.
Caughie, John. "Playing at Being American." *Logics of Television: Essays in Cultural Criticism*. Ed. Patricia
Mellencamp. Bloomington: Indiana UP, 1990. 44–58.
Christian Coalition. *Contract with the American Family: A Bold Plan by the Christian Coalition to Strengthen
the Family and Restore Common-Sense Values*. Nashville: Moorings, 1995.
Clinton, Hillary Rodham. *It Takes a Village: And Other Lessons Children Teach Us*. New York: Simon, 1996.
Coombe, Rosemary J. "The Properties of Culture and the Politics of Possessing Identity: Native Claims

in the Cultural Appropriation Controversy." *After Identity*. Ed. Dan Danielsen and Karen Engle. New York: Routledge, 1995. 251–70.

Corber, Robert J. *In the Name of National Security: Hitchcock, Homophobia, and the Political Construction of Gender in Postwar America*. Durham: Duke UP, 1993.

Danielsen, Dan, and Karen Engle. *After Identity: A Reader in Law and Culture*. New York: Routledge, 1995.

D'Emilio, John. "Capitalism and Gay Identity." *Powers of Desire: The Politics of Sexuality*. Ed. Ann Snitow, Christine Stansell, and Sharon Thompson. New York: Monthly Review, 1983. 100–113.

Diamond, Sara. *Roads to Dominion: Right-Wing Movements and Political Power in the United States*. New York: Guilford, 1995.

Dolan, Frederick M. *Allegories of America: Narratives, Metaphysics, Politics*. Ithaca: Cornell UP, 1994.

Dominelli, Lena. *Women Across Continents: Feminist Comparative Social Policy*. New York: Harvester, 1991.

Dumm, Thomas L. *united states*. Ithaca: Cornell UP, 1994.

Ehrenreich, Barbara. *The Snarling Citizen*. New York: Farrar, 1995.

Elshtain, Jean Bethke. *Democracy on Trial*. New York: Basic, 1995.

Faludi, Susan. *Backlash: The Undeclared War against American Women*. New York: Crown, 1991.

Foucault, Michel. "Governmentality." *The Foucault Effect: Studies in Governmentality*. Ed. Graham Burchell, Colin Gordon, and Peter Miller. Chicago: U of Chicago P, 1991. 87–104.

——. *The History of Sexuality*. Vols. 1–3. Trans. Robert Hurley. New York: Pantheon, 1978, 1985, 1986.

Gillespie, Ed, and Bob Schellhass, eds. *Contract with America: The Bold Plan by Rep. Newt Gingrich, Rep. Dick Armey, and the House Republicans to Change the Nation*. New York: Times, 1994.

Gilroy, Paul. " 'After the Love Has Gone': Bio-Politics and Etho-Poetics in the Black Public Sphere." *The Black Public Sphere*. Ed. the Black Public Sphere Collective. Chicago: U of Chicago P, 1995. 53–80.

Ginsburg, Faye D., and Rayna Rapp, eds. *Conceiving the New World Order: The Global Politics of Reproduction*. Berkeley: U of California P, 1995.

Grewal, Inderpal, and Caren Kaplan. *Scattered Hegemonies*. Minneapolis: U of Minnesota P, 1994.

Griggers, Cathy. "Lesbian Bodies in the Age of (Post)mechanical Reproduction." *Fear of a Queer Planet: Queer Politics and Social Theory*. Ed. Michael Warner. Minnesota: U of Minnesota P, 1993. 78–192.

Grossberg, Lawrence. *We Gotta Get Out of This Place: Popular Conservatism and Postmodern Culture*. New York: Routledge, 1992.

Habermas, Jürgen. *The New Conservatism: Cultural Criticism and the Historians' Debate*. Trans. Shierry Weber Nicholsen. Cambridge: MIT P, 1989.

——. *The Structural Transformation of the Public Sphere: An Inquiry into a Category of Bourgeois Society*. Trans. Thomas Burger. Cambridge: MIT P, 1989.

Halley, Janet E. "The Politics of the Closet: Legal Articulation of Sexual Orientation Identity." *After Identity: A Reader in Law and Culture*. Ed. Dan Danielsen and Karen Engle. New York: Routledge, 1995. 24–38.

Hansen, Miriam. Foreword. *The Public Sphere and Experience: Toward an Analysis of the Bourgeois and Proletarian Public Sphere*. Ed. Oskar Negt and Alexander Kluge. Trans. Peter Labanyi, Jamie Owen Daniel, and Assenka Oksiloff. Minneapolis: U of Minnesota P, 1993. ix–xli.

Heath, Stephen. "Representing Television." *Logics of Television: Essays in Cultural Criticism*. Ed. Patricia Mellencamp. Bloomington: Indiana UP, 1990. 276–302.

Hennessy, Rosemary. "Queer Visibility in Commodity Culture." *Social Postmodernism*. Ed. Linda Nicholson and Steven Seidman. Cambridge: Cambridge UP, 1995. 142–83.

Herman, Edward S., and Noam Chomsky. *Manufacturing Consent: The Political Economy of the Mass Media*. New York: Pantheon, 1988.

Hoberman, J. "Victim Victorious." *Village Voice* 7 March 1995: 31–33.

Jacobs, Harriet. *Incidents in the Life of a Slave Girl: Written by Herself*. Ed. Jean Fagan Yellin. (Orig. ed. Lydia Maria Child.) Cambridge: Harvard UP, 1987.

Jameson, Fredric. "Five Theses on Actually Existing Marxism." *Monthly Review* 47, no. 11 (April 1996): 1–10.

——. "Reification and Utopia in Mass Culture." *Social Text* 1 (winter 1979): 130–48.

Jeffords, Susan. *Hard Bodies: Hollywood Masculinity in the Reagan Era*. Bloomington: Indiana UP, 1994.

Kaplan, Amy, and Donald Pease. *Cultures of U.S. Imperialism*. Durham: Duke UP, 1993.

Katz, Jonathan Ned. *The Invention of Heterosexuality*. New York: Dutton, 1995.

Mann, Denise. "The Spectacularization of Everyday Life: Recycling Hollywood Stars and Fans in Early Television Variety Shows." *Star Texts: Image and Performance in Film and Television*. Ed. Jeremy G. Butler. Detroit: Wayne State UP, 1991. 333–60.

——— . "Body Narratives, Body Boundaries." *Cultural Studies*. Ed. Lawarence Grossberg, Cary Nelson, and Paula A. Treichler. New York: Routledge, 1992. 409–23.

May, Elaine Tyler. *Homeward Bound: American Families in the Cold War Era*. New York: Basic, 1988.

Mbembe, Achille. "Prosaics of Servitude and Authoritarian Civilities." *Public Culture* 5 (fall 1992): 123–48.

Mbembe, Achille, and Janet Roitman. "Figures of the Subject in Times of Crisis." *Public Culture* 7, no. 2 (winter 1995): 323–52.

Mohanty, Chandra Talpade. "Cartographies of Struggle: Third World Women and the Politics of Feminism." *Third World Women and the Politics of Feminism*. Ed. Chandra Talpade Mohanty, Ann Russo, and Lourdes Torres. Bloomington: Indiana UP, 1991. 1–47.

Moore, Stephen, ed. *Restoring the Dream: The Bold New Plan by House Republicans*. New York: Times, 1995.

Morris, Meaghan. "Banality in Cultural Studies." *Logics of Television: Essays in Cultural Criticism*. Ed. Patricia Mellencamp. Bloomington: Indiana UP, 1990. 14–43.

Mouffe, Chantal. Preface, "Democratic Politics Today"; and "Democratic Citizenship and the Political Community." *Dimensions of Radical Democracy: Pluralism, Citizenship, Community*. New York: Verso, 1992. 1–14, 225–39.

Mowlana, Hamid, George Gerbner, and Herbert I. Schiller. *Triumph of the Image: The Media's War in the Persian Gulf – A Global Perspective*. Boulder: Westview, 1992.

Myerowitz, Joanne, ed. *Not June Cleaver: Women and Gender in Postwar America, 1945–1960*. Philadelphia: Temple UP, 1994.

Negt, Oskar, and Alexander Kluge. *Public Sphere and Experience: Toward an Analysis of the Bourgeois and Proletarian Public Sphere*. Foreword by Miriam Hansen. Trans. Peter Labanyi, Jamie Owen Daniel, and Assenka Oksiloff. Minneapolis: U of Minnesota P, 1993.

Omi, Michael, and Howard Winant. *Racial Formation in the United States: From the 1960s to the 1990s*. 2nd ed. New York: Routledge, 1994.

Patton, Cindy. "Refiguring Social Space." *Social Postmodernism: Beyond Identity Politics*. Ed. Linda Nicholson and Steven Seidman. New York: Cambridge UP, 1995. 216–49.

Petchesky, Rosalind P. "The Body as Property: A Feminist Re-vision." *Conceiving the New World Order: The Global Politics of Reproduction*. Ed. Faye D. Ginsburg and Rayna Rapp. Berkeley: U of California P, 1995. 387–406.

Pfeil, Fred. *White Guys: Studies in Postmodern Domination and Difference*. New York: Verso, 1995.

Pollitt, Katha. *Reasonable Creatures: Essays on Women and Feminism*. New York: Vintage, 1995.

Rogin, Michael Paul. *Ronald Reagan, the Movie: And Other Episodes in Political Demonology*. Berkeley: U of California P, 1987.

Rouse, Roger. "Questions of Identity: Personhood and Collectivity in Transnational Migration to the United States." *Critique of Anthropology* 15, no. 4 (1995): 353–80.

——— . "Thinking through Transnationalism: Notes on the Cultural Politics of Class Relations in the Contemporary United States." *Public Culture* 7, no. 2 (winter 1995): 353–402.

Samuels, Shirley, ed. *The Culture of Sentiment: Race, Gender, and Sentimentality in Nineteenth-Century America*. New York: Oxford UP, 1992.

Schiller, Herbert I. *Information and the Crisis Economy*. Norwood, NJ: Ablex, 1984.

Schneider, Cynthia, and Brian Wallis, eds. *Global Television*. Cambridge: MIT P, 1988.

Schwoch, James, Mimi White, and Susan Reilly. *Media Knowledge: Readings in Popular Culture, Pedagogy, and Critical Citizenship*. Albany: SUNY P, 1992.

Sedgwick, Eve Kosofsky. *Epistemology of the Closet*. Berkeley: U of California P, 1990.

——— . "A Poem Is Being Written." *Tendencies*. Durham: Duke UP, 1993. 177–214.

Sennett, Richard. *The Fall of Public Man*. New York: Norton, 1976.

Shohat, Ella, and Robert Stam. *Unthinking Eurocentrism: Multiculturalism and the Media*. London: Routledge, 1994.

Spillers, Hortense. "Mama's Baby, Papa's Maybe: An American Grammar Book." *Diacritics* 17, no. 2 (summer 1987): 65–81.

——— . "Notes on an Alternative Model – Neither/Nor." *The Difference Within: Feminism and Critical Theory*. Ed. Elizabeth Meese and Alice Parker. Philadelphia: Benjamins, 1989. 165–87.

Spivak, Gayatri Chakravorty. "Acting Bits/Identity Talk." *Critical Inquiry* 18 (summer 1992): 770–803.

——— . "Can the Subaltern Speak?" *Marxism and the Interpretation of Culture.* Ed. Cary Nelson and Lawrence Grossberg. Urbana: U of Illinois P, 1988. 271–313.

——— . "The Politics of Translation." *Destabilizing Theory: Contemporary Feminist Debates.* Ed. Michèle Barrett and Anne Phillips. Cambridge, MA: Polity, 1992. 177–200.

——— . *Outside in the Teaching Machine.* New York: Routledge, 1993.

Stephens, Sharon, ed. *Children and the Politics of Culture: Risks, Rights and Reconstructions.* Princeton: Princeton UP, 1995.

Taussig, Michael. *The Nervous System.* New York: Routledge, 1992.

Tocqueville, Alexis de. *Democracy in America.* Vol. 1. Trans. Henry Reeve. Ed. Philips Bradley. New York: Vintage, 1945.

Warner, Michael. Introduction. *Fear of a Queer Planet.* Minneapolis: U of Minnesota P, 1993. vii–xxxi.

——— . "The Mass Public and the Mass Subject." *Habermas and the Public Sphere.* Ed. Craig Calhoun. Cambridge: MIT P, 1992. 377–401.

Chapter 17

Michael Eric Dyson

DOES GEORGE W. BUSH CARE ABOUT BLACK PEOPLE?

Bush has not shown that he cares for civil rights or cares for the interests of black people.

Jesse Jackson, civil rights leader and Katrina volunteer

My cousin hollered, "You're shot." I got up and tried to jump over the tree stumps in the street, and as soon as I got in mid-air another blast hit me in my back. And I fell on the ground again. Somehow, it was a miracle, I got up again, and I began to run. I heard [the white guys] saying, "Nigger, you gotta run." I ran around a corner and I saw this black guy sitting on the porch, and I said "Man, help me." And he said, "Come on," but he was in the house with some white people. When I went to the back of the house, this white lady said "I can't help you. You gotta get out of here." So I ran away from their house. And I ran up to this truck with two white guys, and I said, "Please, please, please help me." I felt like I was going to die. And the older white guy said, "Get away from my truck. We can't help you. We're liable to shoot you ourselves." And they pulled off and called me a nigger. It's like [white people] were using the opportunity to do something they've been waiting to do. And I'm thinking about racism and all that's running in my head. I'm like, "I can't believe this." After everything we've gone through, and everything I've been through, I would have never imagined this happening to me.

Darnell Herrington, Katrina survivor

WHEN PRESIDENT BUSH and the federal government tragically failed to respond in a timely and life-saving manner to the disaster on the Gulf Coast, they made themselves vulnerable to the charge that race was the obvious reason for their delay. And that charge was vigorously pursued—in media and entertainment camps, in black and poor communities across the nation, by many of the nation's distinguished intellectuals and political critics, and, indeed, by observers around the world.[1] Many claimed that had there been mostly white people trapped by Katrina's vengeance, the government would have gotten into town a lot quicker. "If it was a bunch of white people on roofs in the Hamptons," actor Colin Farrell colorfully stated on television's *Access Hollywood*, "I don't have any f****** doubt there would have been every single helicopter, every plane, every single means that the government has to help these people."[2]

Perhaps social commentator and humorist Nancy Giles captured the feelings of many when she more diplomatically, but with no less outrage, framed the issue on CBS's *Sunday Morning*:

> After meeting with Louisiana officials last week, Rev. Jesse Jackson said, "Many black people feel that their race, their property conditions and their voting patterns have been a factor in the response." He continued, "I'm not saying that myself." Then I'll say it: If the majority of the hardest hit victims of Hurricane Katrina in New Orleans were white people, they would not have gone for days without food and water, forcing many to steal for mere survival. Their bodies would not have been left to float in putrid water. . . . We've repeatedly given tax cuts to the wealthiest and left our most vulnerable American citizens to basically fend for themselves. . . . The President has put himself at risk by visiting the troops in Iraq, but didn't venture anywhere near the Superdome or the convention center, where thousands of victims, mostly black and poor, needed to see that he gave a damn.[3]

Would Bush and the federal government have moved faster to secure the lives of the hurricane victims if they had been white? The question must be partnered with a second one that permits us to tally a few of the myriad injuries of the racial contract that has bound American citizens together: did the largely black and poor citizens in the Gulf Coast get left behind because they were black and poor?

It is clear that President Bush and officials of the federal government, like the rest of us, have been shaped by racial forces that have continually changed our society since its founding. The tragic reign of slavery for 250 years, the colossal efforts of the government and the legal system to extend white supremacy through Jim Crow law, and the monumental effort of black folk to resist these forces while redefining black identity have formed the rhythms, relations, and rules of race. The rhythms of race have largely to do with customs and cultural practices that feed on differences between racial groups. The relations of race have mostly to do with the conditions that foster or frustrate interactions between racial groups. The rules of race have to do with norms and behavior that reflect or resist formal barriers to social equality.

The rhythms, relations, and rules of race have both defined the forces against which progress must be made and provided a measure of the progress achieved. They help us understand that even when fundamental changes in law and practice occur—say, the Fourteenth Amendment, the *Brown v. Board of Education* Supreme Court decision, or the Civil Rights Act of 1964—there is the matter of racial vision and imagination to consider. They help us see that racial terror has bled through the boundaries of law as surely as harmful racial customs and beliefs persist in the deep pockets of a formally changed society.

This framework must be kept in mind as we answer the question of whether race played a role in how the federal government responded to Katrina's victims. But as I've made clear, the question shouldn't be whether race played a role, but what role it played. How can race possibly be quarantined from a consideration of Katrina when it so thoroughly pervades our culture—the choices we make, the laws we adopt and discard, and the social practices that are polluted by its pestering ubiquity? Of course race colored the response to Katrina, although it may not mean that explicit racial prejudice fueled the decision to leave poor black folk defenseless before the fury of nature.

After all, one need not have conscious or intentional racist beliefs to act out a script written long before specific actors come on the political stage to play. We take our cues from different parts of the culture that have vastly opposed ways of viewing the same racial event. Our conscious decisions are drawn from the reservoir of beliefs, attitudes, and dispositions that form our group's collective racial unconscious. When we gear up for response to a particular event, when we dissect or process a specific item of information, we pull from these resources, which have shaped our understanding of what can and should be done. The collective racial unconscious, and the rhythms, relations, and rules of race, together constitute the framework for making decisions, even those that apparently have nothing to do with race. Thus, one can reasonably say that race was the farthest thing from one's mind even as its subtle propositions lure one forward into territory invisibly bounded by racial criteria. And one can scrupulously proclaim, and mean it, that race does not affect one's calculus of desert, of how resources should be shared, while appealing to ancient racial understandings that shape just who is seen as meriting a particular sort of treatment.

It should also be clear that although one may not have racial intent, one's actions may nonetheless have racial consequence. In discussing the charge that racism was at the heart of the response to Hurricane Katrina, Senator Barack Obama said, "I've said publicly that I do not subscribe to the notion that the painfully slow response of FEMA [the Federal Emergency Management Agency] and the Department of Homeland Security was racially-based. The ineptitude was color-blind."[4] Obama went on to say that "I see no evidence of active malice, but I see a continuation of passive indifference on the part of our government towards the least of these."[5] However, one may agree with Obama that there was no racial intent, no "active malice," in the response to Katrina, and yet hold the view that there were nonetheless racial consequences that flowed from the "passive indifference" of the government to poor blacks. Active malice and passive indifference are but flip sides of the same racial coin, different modalities of racial menace that flare according to the contexts and purposes at hand. In a sense, if one conceives of racism as a cell phone, then active malice is the ring tone at its highest volume, while passive indifference is the ring tone on vibrate. In either case, whether loudly or silently, the consequence is the same: a call is transmitted, a racial meaning is communicated.

When it comes to the federal government's response to the victims of Hurricane Katrina, the specific elements at play must be examined. There were poor blacks, mostly from Louisiana, drowning in twenty-five-foot floods, stranded in their homes, or crammed into makeshift shelters, awaiting help from a Texas-bred president and an Oklahoma-born head of FEMA. At its core, this was a Southern racial narrative being performed before a national and global audience. If Southern whites have been relatively demonized within the realms of whiteness—when compared to their Northern peers, they are viewed as slower, less liberal, more bigoted, and thoroughly "country"—then Southern blacks are even more the victims of social stigma from every quarter of the culture, including Northern and Southern whites, and even among other blacks outside the region.

Southern blacks, especially poor ones, are viewed as the worst possible combination of troubled elements—region, race, and class—that on their own make life difficult enough. They are stereotyped as being backward, belligerently opposed to enlightenment, and tethered to self-defeating cultural habits that undermine their upward thrust from a life of penury and ignorance. Their woes are considered so entrenched that they cannot be overcome by social programs or political intervention. Not even a change of geography is seen as completely successful; when transposed to Northern terrain, poor Southern blacks are believed to be victims of a time warp of anachronistic values that work against absorption into the middle class and instead drive them to carve enclaves of urban horror from their rural roots.

When they were not being painted in unflattering terms on the canvas of social history, the lives of poor Southern blacks have stirred the colorful fantasies of whites across their native region and beyond. The exotic Southern black supposedly had more soul, was closer to nature as a semiliterate savage, could sing and dance well, was more innately spiritual, was oblivious to the caste system that kept her in poverty, and, hence, was happy to be the white Southerner's slave, servant, or entertainer. The art created by poor blacks was rarely recognized by whites unless it confirmed crude stereotypes of black sensual longing and intellectual emptiness. The complex and demanding creations of poor blacks, whether sophisticated blues lyrics or visual art of high quality, was either dismissed, ignored, or, at best, seen as exceptional to the inferior work of other black artists. In fact, white culture was burdened by bigoted beliefs in the inherent inferiority of black humanity, intelligence, and culture. Such beliefs die hard. Even when the customs that ushered them into prominence fade, those Southern whites who inherit from their ancestors and predecessors the rhythms, rules, and relations of race—and the collective racial unconscious—find it difficult to defeat or betray their racial orientation to the world.

To be sure, caricatures of black identity have been swept away in many white Southern quarters and replaced with far more sophisticated and nuanced ideas about black folk. But such progress runs hard into another wall constructed out of racial history: the structural inequities that support the inferior social position of poor blacks. While one may point to enlightened ideas about black folk as proof of racial progressivism, the persistence of, and investment in, complicated legacies of social inequality by the very whites who wear their racial bona fides on their sleeves are equally confusing and troubling.

For instance, Bill Clinton, who garnered wide black political support, and continues to enjoy wide black affection, is as enlightened a Southern white man as has come into politics. He intuitively sways to the rhythms of black life; he stands on the transformed racial relations that the civil rights movement inaugurated; and he helped to forge a modest defense of affirmative action, a significant racial rule. Despite his racial charisma, or perhaps because of it, he was able to do considerable damage to black interests, especially those of poor blacks, by signing a crime bill that viciously targeted them, and a welfare reform bill that heaped stigma, but no help, on the backs of the vulnerable.

If George Bush lacks Clinton's racial charisma, he also lacks Clinton's grasp of the need to play the racial game at a high, if ultimately manipulative, level. Clinton proved every bit a victim of the collective racial unconscious of his Southern white heritage, except the lesson he learned was that one must survive by appearing to support black interests while exploiting them. Thus, Clinton forged political survival in a racial climate still suspicious of black intelligence and humanity by signaling support for the white mainstream through his embrace of conservative policies that hurt the black poor. Clinton criticized Bush for his leadership in the federal government's response to Katrina, noting the disproportionate burden borne by the black poor.[6] Yet, because some of Clinton's presidential decisions hurt poor blacks, neoliberal neglect is sometimes just as large a factor in their suffering as conservative assault. It may have been Bush's hands stretching forth to rebuke the interests of poor blacks in Katrina's aftermath, but the misery of the black poor has been indelibly marked by Clinton's fingerprints.

Still, Bush's racial approach does not benefit black folk. Not only does Bush lack Clinton's mix of advantages and deficits, but he lacks as well the instincts and policies that might push, or play to, racial progress in our epoch. His racial etiquette has been shaped in an ethos of hard conservative forces that fought racial progress when it was unfolding and roadblocks its path today. Not only is Bush devoid of the devout, if devious, racial grammar deployed by Clinton. He lacks as well a suitable language of political empathy and moral suasion that resonates with the rhythms of black culture—or an appreciation for the structural and institutional matters that might revive poor black life.

It is safe to say that race played a major role in the failure of the federal government—especially for Bush and FEMA head Michael Brown—to respond in a timely manner to the poor black folk of Louisiana because black grief and pain have been ignored throughout the nation's history. Bush and Brown simply updated the practice. Southern black suffering in particular has been overlooked by Southern whites—those in power and ordinary citizens as well. In discussing the profound differences between white and black Southern historical memory, historian W. Fitzhugh Brundage captures how whites ignored black success and suffering, while blacks sought to overcome the segregated conscience of white society to emphasize a unified national memory and purpose.

> Southern white historical memory exalted white civilization, legitimated white power, and virtually excluded any admission of meaningful black agency in the region's past. White accounts seemed to insulate blacks from history. There was, in white history, no acknowledgment of true suffering or real accomplishments among blacks. They were without personal ancestry, their lives were small, and there was a great void in their past. And if southern whites grudgingly acknowledged the restoration of the union, they still embraced a willfully sectional historical identity. This jealous defense of sectional honor that was at the heart of the white southern memory had no parallel in black memory. Rather, most southern blacks, in rhapsodically nationalist terms, imagined a biracial America in which they would assume their place as equal and full citizens. To the same extent that white southerners insisted on their sectional identity, southern African Americans exalted their national ties. Likewise, blacks recounted a past in which black participation figured decisively in all of the nation's defining moments.[7]

The black poor of the Delta lacked social standing, racial status, and the apparent and unconscious identifiers that might evoke a dramatic empathy in Bush and Brown. Had these factors been present, it might have spurred Bush and Brown to identify *with* the black poor, indeed, see themselves *as* the black poor. Since their agency and angst had been minimized in the Southern historical memory, the black poor simply didn't register as large, or count as much, as they might have had they been white. If they had been white, a history of identification—supported by structures of care, sentiments of empathy, and an elevated racial standing—would have immediately kicked in. That might have boosted considerably their chances of survival because the federal government, including Bush and Brown, would have seen their kind, perhaps their kin, and hence themselves, floating in a flood of death in the Delta.

The undeniable incompetence of the federal disaster relief infrastructure still might have hampered the chances of even white folk surviving Katrina. But their relatively higher social and racial standing might have prompted a quicker attempt to respond, and thus to work out the problems. It also might have made Bush and Brown more adventurous, more daring, more willing to suspend rules, more determined to accept help from whatever quarters it came (they turned down offers of help from several countries), and more open to deferring procedural correctness in the interest of saving lives. The irony is that poor blacks were pained by their erasure from the historical record—both in the past and with Katrina—because, as Ignatieff argues, they uphold, and expect in return, the social contract. And, as Brundage writes, they are fully invested in a democratic and multiracial accounting of the nation's history.

Ignatieff's and Brundage's arguments about race and memory and political obligation can help to decipher Kanye West's controversial television appearance in which he charged

President Bush with indifference to the plight of the black poor. On September 2, 2005, the rapper appeared on an NBC telethon in support of the American Red Cross disaster relief efforts in the Gulf Coast. After Harry Connick, Jr., played piano as he longingly achingly sang "Do You Know What It Means to Miss New Orleans?" accompanied by Wynton Marsalis's crisp but mournful trumpet wails, the cameras turned to comedian Mike Myers and West. Both of them were to read from a script. Myers was faithful to the task. "With the breach of three levees protecting New Orleans," Myers said in clipped speech that was nearly perfunctory, "the landscape of the city was changed dramatically, tragically and perhaps irreversibly. There is now over 25 feet of water where there was once city streets and thriving neighborhoods."[8] Myers half-turned to the obviously nervous West, who cleared his throat before he spoke.

"I hate the way they portray us in the media," West intoned. "If you see a black family, it says, 'They're looting.' You see a white family, it says, 'They're looking for food.' And, you know, it's been five days [waiting for the government to arrive] because most of the people are black. And even for me to complain about it, I would be a hypocrite because I've tried to turn away from the TV because it's too hard to watch. I've even been shopping before even giving a donation. So now I'm calling my business manager right now to see what is the biggest amount I can give. And just to imagine if I was down there, and those are my people down there. So anybody out there that wants to do anything that we can help—with the way America is set up to help the poor, the black people, the less well-off, as slow as possible. I mean, the Red Cross is doing everything they can. We already realize a lot of people that could help are at war right now, fighting another way. And they've given them permission to go down and shoot us!"[9]

West's nervy chiding of the federal government froze Myers's face in disbelief and small panic. But he soldiered on and stuck to the script, rushing his words as if he wanted to quickly as possible banish the anxious feelings that fluttered in his eyes. "And subtle, but in many ways even more profoundly devastating, is the lasting damage to the survivors' will to rebuild and remain in the area. The destruction of the spirit of the people of Southern Louisiana and Mississippi may end up being the most tragic loss of all." Once again, Myers turned to West, this time with a bit of trepidation creasing his brow. West let out his final off-script pronouncement with as sure a statement as he had made during his brief and amiable diatribe. "George Bush doesn't care about black people."[10] With that, just as Myers mouthed the beginning of his plea for viewers to phone in—"Please call . . ."—someone in the NBC control room, working with a seven-second delay aimed at blocking profanity, finally understood West's tack and ordered the camera to turn unceremoniously away from the duo and cut to comedian Chris Tucker, who picked up his cue and tried to roll past West's punches.

Kanye West simply made Ignatieff's and Brundage's arguments into a polemic. West was suggesting that the government had callously broken its compact with its poor black citizens, and that it had forgotten them because it had not taken their pain to heart. West's claim that "George Bush doesn't care about black people" was a claim not about Bush's personal life, but rather his professional life. Bush's wife and father understandably jumped to his defense. "I think all of those remarks were disgusting," Laura Bush said in an interview with American Urban Radio Networks. "I mean I am the person who lives with him. I know what he is like, and I know what he thinks, and I know he cares about people."[11] On CNN's *Larry King Live* talk show, former president George H.W. Bush defended his son against the "particularly vicious comment that the president didn't care, was insensitive on ethnicity. . . . Insensitive about race. Now that one hurt because I know this president and I know he does care . . . that's what's in his heart."[12]

Unlike Bush's wife and father, West was not referring to the president's personal sentiments about black people, which he probably had no way of knowing. Neither was West addressing Bush's personal concern for black people. West was speaking of George Bush as the face of the government. In fact, our understanding of West's comments depends on our making distinctions in three categories. First, one must address the question of *personae*—is one referring to a *private* persona that is, relatively speaking, autonomous and independent, or is one referring to a *public* persona that is representational and functional? Second, one must address the question of *identities*—is one referring to an *individual* identity that primarily concerns one's self, an *institutional* identity that is concerned with one's role in relation to a particular institution, or a *social* identity that is concerned with one's role in society? Third, one must address the question of *care*—is one speaking of *personal* care, an area of interest limited to, or rooted in, one's own life; *moral* care, an area of interest shaped by consideration of ethical effects on self and others; or *political* care, an area of interest shaped by the consideration of political concern and consequences in society?

With these distinctions in mind, it is clear that when West declared that Bush doesn't care about black people, he was referring to Bush's public persona, not his private one, since what was at stake was his function as a representative public figure; that he was referring to Bush's institutional and social identities, as the face of the federal government and in his role as president of the United States; and that he was speaking of Bush's political care in his role as chief symbol of the nation's political organization. West was thus calling into question—and in my opinion rightly so—the apparent lack of political concern by a public figure whose duty it is to direct the resources of the nation to those areas that cry out for address. When West claimed that Bush doesn't care about black people, it was a critical judgment about the failure of the government, which George Bush represents, to take care of, in a timely fashion, those citizens under his watch. When Bush conceded that the response of the government was "unacceptable"—and when he later took full responsibility for the failure of the government to adequately do its job—he was partially acknowledging the legitimacy of West's criticism. In the political realm, care is measured, in part, by the satisfaction of legitimate claims with effective action that fulfills the duties and obligations of one's office.

Perhaps one of the reasons President Bush cares so little about the black poor is that he has not found political favor among them, or, for that matter, among most blacks. Poor blacks are neither economically stable nor vote rich; they matter very little in the president's political philosophy. In 2000, Bush got 8 percent of the black vote; in 2004, he got 11 percent, extending a trend begun in the 1930s of blacks voting heavily Democratic. Of course, black freedom struggles, especially the civil rights movement, destroyed, then reshaped, the Democratic Party in the South, driving whites into the party of Richard Nixon, and later Ronald Reagan. Over time, the racist Southern Democrats of the Jim Crow era gave way to the liberal Democrats of the civil rights era. As a result, Republicans have largely spurned the black vote for the last forty years and courted conservative white constituencies that were hostile to black interests and people.[13] This may help explain why Bush didn't rush to Democratic-dominated territory in Louisiana nearly as quickly as he did to Republican-friendly ground in Mississippi after Katrina struck. As critic Jacob Weisberg says, "it's a demonstrable matter of fact that Bush doesn't care much about black votes," and that, "in the end, [it] may amount to the same thing" as not caring about black people.[14]

Weisberg argues that because "they don't see blacks as a current or potential constituency, Bush and his fellow Republicans do not respond out of the instinct of self-interest when dealing with their concerns." Rendering assistance to low-income blacks is a "matter of charity to them, not necessity."[15] Their condescending attitude is magnified in New Orleans, "which is 67 percent black and largely irrelevant to GOP political ambitions." Only at election time are cities in swing states with large black populations important to Republicans—and in the immediate past, to Bush and his aides. Since Louisiana's paltry nine electoral votes are not presently up for grabs in an election cycle, the state doesn't show up much on the conservative political radar. "If Bush and Rove didn't experience the spontaneous political reflex to help New Orleans," Weisberg writes, "it may be because they don't think of New Orleans as a place that helps them."[16] Weisberg detects the president's lack of political care for black folk in his delayed and lackluster response to Katrina, while Hurricanes Charley and Frances, which affected the Republican stronghold of Florida, prompted the president and the federal government to greater urgency and generosity.

> Had the residents of New Orleans been white Republicans in a state that mattered politically, instead of poor blacks in a city that didn't, Bush's response surely would have been different. Compare what happened when hurricanes Charley and Frances hit Florida in 2004. Though the damage from those storms was negligible in relation to Katrina's, the reaction from the White House was instinctive, rapid, and generous to the point of profligacy. Bush visited hurricane victims four times in six weeks and delivered relief checks personally. Michael Brown of FEMA, now widely regarded as an incompetent political hack, was so responsive that local officials praised the agency's performance. The kind of constituency politics that results in a big life-preserver for whites in Florida and a tiny one for blacks in Louisiana may not be racist by design or intent. But the inevitable result is clear racial discrimination.[17]

Bush's claim that race played no role in the recovery efforts betrayed a simplistic understanding of how a complex force like race operates in the culture. "My attitude is this: The storm didn't discriminate and neither will the recovery effort," Bush said. "When those Coast Guard choppers . . . were pulling people off roofs, they didn't check the color of a person's skin. They wanted to save lives."[18] Katrina's fury may have been race neutral, but not its effect: 80 percent of New Orleans's minority households lived in the flooded area, while the same was true for only 54 percent of the city's white population. The average household income of those in the flooded area trailed those who lived on New Orleans's higher ground by $17,000.[19] Concentrated poverty rendered poor blacks much more vulnerable to the effects of natural disaster. Before Katrina, these blacks had been hit by hurricanes of social and economic devastation. Such a fact never seems to register with the president. Nor does it prod him into deep reflection about the unintended, but certainly foreseen, racial consequences of catastrophe and mayhem.

The proof of Bush's lack of political care for blacks before Katrina is equally distressing: under his presidency black poverty has increased, black unemployment has risen, and affirmative action has been viciously assaulted. The Bush administration has disseminated what the Government Accountability Office called "covert propaganda" by paying conservative black commentator Armstrong Williams to say good things about educational policies that hurt black folk.[20] By giving tax breaks to the wealthy, and by freezing the minimum wage at $5.15 an hour, Bush has undermined the fragile prospects of the working poor and the black working class. By seeking to cut the food stamp budget by $1.1 billion over the next decade, Bush will douse even further the fortunes of the black poor.

Nearly forty years ago, Muhammad Ali's single line captured the reason for his conscientious objection to the Vietnam War while summing up millions of black people's feelings—"Ain't no Viet Cong ever called me 'nigger.' "[21] Now, Kanye West's simple sentence brilliantly condensed an analysis that millions of other blacks have made about an uncaring Bush regime. As a public figure who is the ultimate representative of the American government, George Bush doesn't care about black people—no matter how many black folks like Condoleezza Rice (who defended the president against West's charge as well) he puts in vaunted places.[22] He may have promoted some blacks, but as for the rest of us, he has left us far behind. Bush's slow response to black suffering by wind and water was but a symptom of a larger, equally dangerous political neglect.

Indeed, what Katrina's gale forces have uncovered, yet again, is the strong disagreement between blacks and whites over the role that race plays in who gets what and when in our society—and what group most often gets left out, and behind, in the social contract. Polls taken immediately after Katrina prove the racial divide. A CNN/USA Today/Gallup poll found that 60 percent of blacks believed that race caused the government's delay in rescuing folk, leaving many of them to starve or drown, while only 12 percent of whites agreed.[23] The racial divide was similar when taking class into consideration: 63 percent of blacks blamed poverty for the slow rescue, while 21 percent of whites held that view. Until many white and well-off folk feel the full force of black pain, and open their eyes to see racial and class suffering, that divide will only widen. And the black poor will continue to be left behind long after Katrina recovery efforts are over.

Notes

1   For instance, in an interview with me in October 2005, Reverend Jesse Jackson supported Kanye West's views while expanding on them. "Well, Bush has not shown that he cares for civil rights or cares for the interest of black people. And there are several outstanding examples. Bush put a wreath at Dr. King's gravesite one day and the next day sent Olson [the solicitor general] to the Supreme Court to kill affirmative action. Like today Rosa Parks is lying in repose in the Rotunda. So he . . . nominates an extreme right-wing states' rights judge to the Supreme Court, who is against everything Ms. Parks stood for. Another example is the U.N. Commission on Racism in South Africa. He wouldn't send Colin Powell. He put a man [in] the attorney general's office, John Ashcroft, who was very hostile to civil rights. He has refused to meet with civil rights leadership for four years. So his administration has been quite hostile to the civil rights struggle, period. Women, labor, African Americans—[all have been] locked out."

2   Access Hollywood, September 5, 2005.

3   Sunday Morning, September 4, 2005.

4   Barack Obama, "Statement of Senator Barack Obama on Hurricane Relief Efforts," September 6, 2005, http://obama.senate.gov/statement/050906-statement_of_senator_barack_obama_on_-hurricane_katrina_relief_efforts.

5   Ibid.

6   Philip Shenon, "Clinton Levels Sharp Criticism at the President's Relief Effort," The New York Times, September 19, 2005, p. A21.

7   W. Fitzhugh Brundage, The Southern Past: A Clash of Race and Memory (Cambridge, Mass.: The Belknap Press of Harvard University Press, 2005), pp. 99–100.

8   "A Concert for Hurricane Relief," NBC, September 2, 2005.

9   Ibid.

10   Ibid.

11   "First Lady: Charges that Racism Slowed Aid 'Disgusting,' " CNN.com, September 9, 2005, http://www.cnn.com/2005/POLITICS/09/08/katrina.laura bush.

12   "Interview with George H.W. Bush, Barbara Bush," Larry King Live, CNN, September 5, 2005.

13   Jacob Weisberg, "An Imperfect Storm: How Race Shaped Bush's Response to Katrina," Slate, September 7, 2005, http://www.slate.com/id/2125812/?nav=navoa.

14   Ibid.

15   Ibid.

16   Ibid.

17   Ibid.

18   Susan Page and Mario Puente, "Poll Shows Racial Divide on Storm Response," USA TODAY, September 13, 2005.

19   Alan Berube and Bruce Katz, "Katrina's Window: Confronting Concentrated Poverty Across

America," Brookings Institution, October 2005, http://www.brookings.edu/metro/pubs/20051012_concentratedpoverty.htm.

20   Robert Pear, "Buying of News by Bush's Aides Is Ruled Illegal," *The New York Times*, October 1, 2005.

21   Bruce Weber, "CRITIC'S NOTEBOOK: Power, Pitfalls and 'The Great White Hope'; A Washington Company Revisits a Shining Moment from a Decidedly Different Era," *The New York Times*, September 14, 2000, p. E1.

22   Dave Goldiner, "Who Is to Blame? Terror War Crippled FEMA, Say Experts," *New York Daily News*, September 5, 2005. p. 7.

23   "Reaction to Katrina Split on Racial Lines," CNN.com, September 13, 2005, http://www.cnn.com/2005/12/katrina.race.poll/index.html.

Chapter 18

Elspeth Probyn

SHAMING THEORY, THINKING DIS-CONNECTIONS: FEMINISM AND RECONCILIATION[1]

OF LATE I seemed to have misplaced an assurance about the self-evident nature of feminism's connection to political and social injustice. This is probably due to a range of factors, but the splintering of feminism and the nature of the insiderist arguments about its direction are undoubtedly germane. To generalise, this has produced a welter of books and articles aimed at criticising and redressing feminism's direction, and a climate akin to Stuart Hall's description of current postcolonial theory: 'a certain nostalgia run[ning] through some of these arguments for a return to a clear-cut politics of binary opposi- tions . . . between goodies and baddies' (1996: 243). As feminism becomes consolidated in university departments of women's studies, or gender studies, increasingly those of us located within these institutions are called upon as professional feminists or queers, pre- sumed to be qualified as commentators on a wide range of questions. In turn, this raises the vexing question of what it means to reply 'as a feminist'. Of course, the problem of who speaks for whom, and the injunction not to represent all women in the name of an implicitly white feminism, has now been on the agenda for quite some time. But it may also be that 'responses' to this challenge have produced hesitancy, timidity and sometimes solipsism as individuals learn only to speak in their own name. There is also the question of what constitutes something that needs to be responded to. The speed with which 'local' events are now broadcast worldwide has been amply commented on in the name of postmodernist celebration or nihilism. There is then an overwhelming array of events to which one could respond.

If my topic here is the question of how to make feminist theory meet up with the present, it is obviously connected with the issue of how feminists respond to events. My use of 'event' needs some clarification. There is of course the straightforward sense of an event as something noteworthy. But even this common-sense understanding raises questions about what, and to whom, an event might be constituted as important. In turn, this catches at the more elaborate sense that Gilles Deleuze gives to events as a mode of designating the relations of past, present and future. We might say that he thus rescues 'event' from being thought of as monumental, of history as composed of a narration that connects cairn-like structures of the past. In his discussion of a rhizomatic analytics, Deleuze describes 'lived events' as multiplicities of 'historical determinations, concepts, individuals, groups, social formations', all of which coexist 'on a single page, the same sheet' (1993: 32). 'Event' in this way therefore compels us to think about the conjugation of forces: individuals, concepts and theories that at any time enfold the past within the present, constraining or enabling action.

While there is a long history behind the term, I want to think about Reconciliation as an event in order to capture how it was mobilised in 1997. 'Reconciliation' is an initiative first raised by the Hawke Labor government in Australia and actively continued by Paul Keating only to be considerably stonewalled by the present Prime Minister, John Howard, and his Coalition government. Perhaps most crucially, analysing Reconciliation as event breaks with the idea that there would be/can be an inevitable progress in terms of racialised relations between white and black Australians: that the injuries to Aboriginals were part of a 'history' that we were all finished with. With the election of a conservative government, it became clear that such a teleology was not possible. Moreover, as an event, the reappearance of Reconciliation profoundly disturbed the past and present, as well as the identity of actors involved. Indeed, the reproduction of Reconciliation as an event reminds us that all individuals are actors within the interplay of history, racism, concepts and ideas. It also enjoins ideas, theories and bodies in quite visceral ways: for instance, my own individual paralysis was fed by a feeling that the theories that I deal in were not up to the occasion. The question of 'how to respond' was fused at the level of the individual. What could I as a feminist do? What could I as a new Australian possibly say in regard to the question of racism and resentment that was shaking the 'tolerant' and 'lucky' country? As many may know from experience, such questions are guaranteed to make the self and others squirm – at best they evince defeatism, at worst, a paranoid delusion of individual control in the face of systemic inequities.

Thankfully I was jolted out of this morass by attending the Australian Reconciliation Convention. This was a gathering of thousands of white and black Australians held in late May 1997 in Melbourne, in order to set the grounds for further local and national action in terms of furthering Reconciliation. As an important drawing in of the past, its timing coincided with the thirtieth anniversary of the referendum that was to 'bring about basic human rights for Australia's indigenous peoples' (*Convention Program*). Organised by the Aboriginal Reconciliation Council headed by Patrick Dodson, this was an event in commonsensical terms. But beyond being merely noteworthy, it also rearranged assumptions about the past and about what was possible in the present. As part of a wider process, the Reconciliation Convention was a nodal point that brought together nearly two thousand whites and blacks, leaders and ordinary individuals. From the space of many painful and some proud memories, the Convention was to galvanise the delegates and the rest of Australia into further and future action. It took place, however, at a time when the Australian nation was, as it continues to be, fractured by competing accounts of the past and where there was little political vision of the future.[2] It marked the present as a moment of vastly diverging lines. A moment of conflict when a previously unspeakable level of racism is tolerated and fanned by the inaction of the government, when many of the achievements of reconciliation are being ripped apart as the government moves to close down the legal openings and the affective optimism in regard to Aboriginal land rights brought about by the Mabo and Wik rulings.[3] In brief, these rulings finally recognised native entitlement to land based on indigenous inhabitation of country before white invasion. The Convention also coincided with the completion of *Bringing Them Home* (1997), the report of the National Inquiry into the Separation of Aboriginal and Torres Strait Islander Children from Their Families. This inquiry took evidence from 535 Indigenous people about their experiences of the government policies that forcibly removed thousands of indigenous children from their families. Commonly called the Stolen Generations, in the careful words of the inquiry, the laws, practices and policies that continued into the 1970s were dedicated to the removal and the genocidal eradication of the indigenous people of Australia. The Stolen Generations is part of and now most spectacularly represents a long history of both governmental policy and white academic actions (especially on the part of anthropology) that the noted Aboriginal scholar Marcia Langton has summed as: 'imagine an Australia in which no "full-bloods" survived because they [anthropologists] observed the "miscegenation" on the last frontiers and projected its effects into the future' (1993: 198).

More than anything, the forced removal of children who then suffered emotional, economic, physical and sexual abuse by their white 'guardians' has complicated white Australians' relation to the past. This past is structured by the founding colonial and legal myth of *terra nullius*, the conceit of an empty land awaiting the explorer. There is a specific structure of knowledge and ignorance that is the uninhabited ground, the *terra nullius*, of racism and with which reconciliation for whites must first and foremost contend. In speaking about reconciliation I am addressing the singularity of the Australian situation although there may be links to other sites. For instance, the phenomenon of nations apologising is emerging elsewhere: the Canadian government to the peoples of the First Nations, Japan to the 'comfort women', the UK to the Irish about the famine, maybe even the US to its African-American citizens for slavery, and, of course, the vital processes ongoing in South Africa. While these events are inspiring, I will dwell here on the specificities of Australian Reconciliation, both because Australia is where I now live and because I think that generalised models wreak considerable epistemological and political damage. If I argue strongly that feminist engagements must be specific, I would also state that my immigration to Australia entails a responsibility to engage with the structures of white privilege that enabled my relatively easy move.

In simplistic terms, and enabled by the particular spatial myth of the empty land, Australian history could be told as a straight line leading from point zero through to civilisation. But as the evidence accumulates about the shameful nature of the past, the only ones to have a clear line are those who subscribe to a denial of what Prime Minister Howard calls 'the black arm band' version of history. This infamous phrase of Howard's was directed at any critical rethinking of white Australia's past. While the relationship of those in the present to past actions is a complicated one, as Carlos Ginzburg succinctly puts it, if none of our actions can alter the past, we must remember that, 'human actions can deeply affect the *memory* of the past by distorting its traces, by putting them into oblivion, by utterly destroying them' (1994: 118). A recent editorial cartoon in the *Sydney Morning Herald* by Leunig succinctly summarises what happens when the traces of history are destroyed. In an eerily deserted landscape that recalls the image of *terra nullius*, he has depicted the Independent MP Pauline Hanson's racist party, 'One Nation', as an empty ark being filled with bundles of different affects: fear, anger, impotence, paranoia, resentment, in short all the affective baggage of *ressentiment*.[4]

If, as Anne McClintock has argued (1992), the linearity of the concept of post-colonialism is a liability in theoretical terms, in real terms it is also far from straightforward as the present twists hopes for the future. In the Deleuzian sense of the present as event, it 'is what gives a new and unexpected direction to a continuous line' (Boundas 1997: 24). While we may 'know' the past, and project knowledge onto the future, in important ways we cannot know the present. For Deleuze, events 'deterritorialize the present and point towards a different future' (Patton 1996: 14). The question of direction also poses formidable challenges to critical thought. This is a moment when the present rises up, taps you on the shoulder, and says, 'well, what can your theories make of this?' In response to the present, I want to consider a feminist and queer engagement with Reconciliation and the expressions of shame that have heralded its public reception amongst many whites. I do so because, while the exigency of Reconciliation is clear, the links between feminists, queers and Reconciliation may be somewhat hazy even given good intentions on the part of individuals. One of the many lessons I learned at the Reconciliation Convention is that the near-automatic response on the part of feminists to analyse the gender- and sex-related elements of any social situation may need to be reconsidered. Or at least, the type of reaction on the part of some feminists to critique 'patriarchal' relations, or that of some gays and lesbians to focus on the lack of queer visibility, in this context seems rather small minded. Another thing I learned was that white theorists will need to put aside the type of ego attachment that comes with developing 'clever' solutions to present problems. The fact that there is no one solution to Reconciliation, that the present is ongoing, meets up with Stuart Hall's argument that being 'driven by a Promethean desire for the theoretically correct position – a desire to out-theorise everyone else' is not only wrong headed politically and morally, but is also bad theory (1996: 249). If, that is, we want our theories to be up to the demands of the present.

Taking from Wendy Brown's question of whether we can 'develop a feminist politics without *ressentiment?* . . . Could we learn to contest domination with the strength of an alternative vision of collective life, rather than through moral reproach?' (1995: 47), I want to map some of the elements that might inform this engagement with Reconciliation. While, as I stated at the outset, the present produces a sense that one must *do something* as opposed to *doing theory*, I emphasise that this is a response from the point of contemporary theory. Yet I hope to show that yoking theory to Reconciliation is not to get me off the hook, rather it is to sink the hook deeply within my thinking.

Against a tendency to generalise about feminism, I should specify that my point of departure is a theoretical position at the intersection of feminism and queer. This intersection has been dominated by attention to the body and to sexual practices, and arguments about the performative aspect of all identity categories. These are theories that are informed by queer experiences, and I want to build on and question the particular queer relation to shame. I want to wager that theories of bodily affect – including foremost that of shame – may be of some use as whites of the Australian nation respond in emotional terms to the fact that they/we have to come to terms with the full historical and present reality of sharing the land with its original custodians.

Elsewhere, and along with others, I have argued that as theorists we are imbricated in what we seek to study. In trying to reroute a tendency towards a solipsist attention to the self, I have also argued that 'the body' or 'desire' are not ends in themselves but rather should be put to work as hyphens connecting practices and ideas (Probyn 1996). The model I took was informed by the work of Foucault and Deleuze, in particular their argument about the relation between theoretical work and politics, figured in the image of a relay race: 'Practice is an ensemble of relays from one theoretical point to another, and theory, a relay between one practice and another' (Foucault 1977: 206). This prefigures yet coincides with the arguments of several feminists who critically integrate the relations of race and gender. In many ways what people like Vron Ware (1996) and Catherine Hall (1996) and others are attempting is a lot tougher than what Foucault and Deleuze were doing in that 1972 interview. For a start, Foucault and Deleuze did not overtly, at least, deal with the concept of difference and the facts of ethnic and sexual inequalities. Nor did they have to contend with the ways in which, as Ware says, 'in recent years the concept of difference [has been] used almost ritualistically to evoke discourses of "race" (and sometimes gender)'. As she puts it, this evocation often occludes actual discussion of racism, and she suggests that 'examination of the way whiteness ("race") intersects with gender and sexuality can shift what can sometimes amount to an obsession with difference toward the less fashionable concept of radical connectedness' (1996: 144–145). In a similar move, Hall critiques white feminist historians for being slow to respond to the black feminist critique which has insisted on the interconnections between the power relations of 'race' and gender' and calls for a model of analysis that can grasp 'the raced and gendered ways in which inter-connections and inter-dependencies have been played out' (1996: 70, 76).

Whilst I am in full agreement with the substance of these critiques, I believe that we need to pay attention to the dis-connections as well as to the connections; or rather that thinking in terms of connection requires consideration of conceptual and material limits that serve as moments of disconnection. In general terms, this necessitates uncoupling feminist and queer theories from gender, the body and sexuality as their privileged objects of study. This is to move away from forms of analysis directed at 'the body' or at 'sexuality', towards those that, while they may be moved by the body and sexual desire, end up at different places. For me, this follows from Deleuze's comment that 'as soon as a theory is enmeshed in a particular point, we realise that it will never possess the slightest practical importance unless it can erupt in a totally different area' (Foucault 1980: 208). In simple terms, the challenge I take from this is one of redirecting queer and feminist theories so that they erupt within the arena of reconciliation. This is not the disparate application of queer; rather it implies a reconfiguration of the field in which the arguments emerge or erupt – like a potato plant rhizomatically breaking up the ground in which it finds itself. This cannot be some sort of superficial queering predicated on insiderist knowingness; it means confronting deep ignorance about what reconciliation can be, ignorance of the grounds that may allow for eventual connection and coexistence between black and white. Reconciliation is therefore placed at that intersection of ignorance and knowingness that has marked white relations with the indigenous people, laid onto a map of national identity that for much of its official 209 years of occupation was based on an abyss of ignorance: the empty land waiting to be filled with white knowledge, the 'knowingness' on the part of whites about Aboriginal people and culture fuelled by ignorance, the emergent 'clever country'. The point is, as Eve Sedgwick argues, 'to pluralize and specify' that ignorance: to acknowledge a 'plethora of ignorances, and . . . begin to ask questions about the labor, erotics, and economics of their human production and distribution' (1993: 25).

At another level, this also means derailing the feminist impulse to connect up 'ritual-istically' or automatically the questions of race, gender, sexuality, class, etc. Perhaps ironic-ally, the move to reconciliation must first contend with the reconnaissance (which in the French connotes a grateful recognition) of difference and singularity: the pause of silence heard in dis-connection. This entails an argument against the types of connections that rou-tinely and automatically link together quite disparate groups on the basis of what we think we know in the name of Otherness. This is to think about connections and dis-connections made without a ground of ressentiment, without the positing of a knowing ground of common suffering, exclusion and oppression.

A sense of that temptation to connect queers and indigenous people can be heard in a poem by Paula Gunn Allen called 'Some like Indians Endure' (1988), parts of which I will now quote.

> i have it in mind that
> dykes are indians
>
> . . .
>
> indian is an idea
> some people have
> of themselves
> dyke is an idea some women
> have of themselves

the place where we live now
is idea
because whiteman took
all the rest
. . .
so dykes
are like indians
because everyone is related
to everyone
in pain
in terror
in guilt
in blood
in shame
in disappearance
that never quite manages
to be disappeared
we never go away
even if we're always
leaving

(1988: 9–13)

In the face of the shame, guilt and remorse that white lesbians may individually feel in regard to the treatment of the indigenous people of Australia as well as those of the Americas and elsewhere, this poem allows for a sense of connection and 'knowingness' that I want to argue is premature. That is, and with the crucial caveat, if it is a white dyke reading and listening to it. That Paula Gunn Allen, a Laguna Pueblo/Sioux and a professor of Native American studies, proffers this connection between Indians and dykes is one thing, and is a testimony to her intellectual and political generosity. It would, however, be a travesty of that generosity if white queers were to take advantage of it to celebrate connections instead of responding to it as a challenge to build and interrogate the grounds for possible connections. Against the plundering of knowledge that takes place under the rubric of cultural appropriation displayed in both commercial ventures but also in a type of white feminist lesbian assimilation of a generalised indigenous spirituality in the name of 'the goddess', Reconciliation must be for whites a challenge to *learn*, and not to *know*. It will be the site of connection only when whites have fully realised the extent of the violent historical and material limits that render impossible any easy cohabitation under the label of 'Other'. At the present moment, shame marks that impossibility.

All this is a rather long lead in to the image of shame that motivates this chapter. As most of the indigenous Australians and some of the whites stood courageously and honourably with their backs to Howard at the Reconciliation Convention in Melbourne,[5] I sat with my head in my hands in shame. Whilst my shame was in part caused by the spectacle of the white politicians at the Convention, it was also informed by the immediacy of my ignorance, at being unable to place historic figures, incapable of pronouncing Aboriginal names and nations. I was also ashamed at the jabs of knowledge that intruded, imported into this situation: questions like whether there was room for me as a recent white migrant, for those who identify neither as black nor white; I wondered whether a 'People's Movement' based on the civil rights models of the 1960s was possible in these postmodern times. In turn, these questions caused my ears to burn, ashamed at the pettiness.

In the subsequent coverage in the predominantly white press, shame is everywhere.

Pronouncements of shame on the part of 'ordinary Australians' can be heard in letters to the editor, call-in shows, and literally on the street, as well as from extraordinary ones like the 'lipstick queen', Poppy King, who would not now accept her 1995 Australian of the Year award because she is 'ashamed to say today that I am Australian' (*Courier Mail* 28 June 1997), and the ex-pat Germaine Greer who told an audience in London that 'she would not return to Australia until Aboriginal sovereignty was recognised' (which to many in Australia came as a bit of a relief) (*Sun Herald* 8 June 1997). While it may be heartening that shame seems to be displacing guilt, nonetheless this shame seems to mark the uneasiness of the shifting line between ignorance and knowledge. We experience shame at now knowing the past atrocities, shame at the carefully constructed and preserved edifice of ignorance. Or is it shame at the 'open secret' of Australia's past? At being caught out? Is it the blurring of inside/outside, public/private as this 'new' knowledge based in ignorance is screened in the international scene, prompting the Minster of Aboriginal Affairs, John Herron, to squirm: 'I hate Australians going overseas and dumping on our country' (*Sun Herald* 8 June 1997).

If this has all the markings of a painful coming-out scene as interlocutors stammer and blush at the telling of the 'open secret', it also marks the difficulty that many white Australians have in coming to terms with the gap between knowledge and ignorance. This often plays out in rather tortuous attempts to find the right analogy. In response to the report on the Stolen Generations even respected writers like Bob Ellis twist and turn trying to find ways to link up white and black realities which are posed as worlds apart. With analogies to the lynchings in the American South of the 1930s, to white 'victims of pederastic abuse', and to 'losing a pet dog and never seeing it again', Ellis tries to get his readership to *imagine* the wrongs done to Aboriginals. He ends his column with these lines: 'And I am, today, ashamed to be Australian. How about you?' (*Sydney Morning Herald* 30 May 1997).

While the reasons for shame are clear, and the reports in the media on the Stolen Generations have been crucial in lifting Howard's gag-order on the past, it is still unclear what confessions of shame are going to produce in the present. Like the shame engendered in straights confronted by the gayness of an acquaintance, the structure here is of oscillation between knowing and ignorance: a type of 'you're kidding?/well I knew all along'. Between knowing and ignorance, what I am afraid of is that we are seeing a generalised model of shame emerging, that the shame of *now* knowing precludes investigation of wide areas of ignorance that remain. As we might attest, being ashamed is painful, and an easy way out is to disengage from the affect, to distance oneself from the object of shame, to fall back on established knowledge now shifted to another site. In this case, one way out of the present shameful conundrum is to construct Reconciliation as about two massive and knowable blocks: whites and blacks, and worse, that the whites are doing something for blacks. Here shame either obscures relations of power, or as a free-floating sentiment can all too easily dissipate the presumably sincere feelings of its speakers.

But what exactly is shame? A dictionary defines it as: distress or humiliation caused by consciousness of one's guilt, dishonour or folly; the capacity for feeling this; the state of disgrace or discredit. It is interesting to note that the train of thought here maps out what may be happening to shame within the Australian public sphere. Thus following the particular events of the Reconciliation Convention and the report on the Stolen Generations, what we have are statements attesting to distress, and/or to the feelings of distress caused by distress at the knowledge of horrific actions. Performances of this were exemplified in the display of emotion in Parliament by the Leader of the Opposition, Kim Beasley, when he spoke about the report on the Stolen Generations, and in the subsequent reactions to it, many of which intimated that Beasley should be ashamed of his demonstration of shame. Beasley is a large man ('big Kim'), prompting one letter writer to the *Sydney Morning Herald* to state, 'That a man of his proportions could stand there and choke on his words was appalling' (4 June 1997), to which another replied more in anger at the 'fat-ist' nature of the remark than at the issue of the Stolen Generations.

If this type of exchange shows up some of the unproductive connections inaugurated by shame, it also displays the dynamics of knowing and ignorance. Faced with shame, the choice is made to ignore the import of its cause in favour of a knowing attack on Beasley's person. As the work of Silvan Tomkins (1995) on affect and shame makes clear, shame is a bodily affect, and moreover it is profoundly interpersonal, or produced within proximity to others. Tomkins defines shame as an 'affect of indignity, of defeat, of transgression, and of alienation' (1995: 133). These are all terms that attest to that feeling when one blunders in and across lines of demarcation, of knowledge, that blushing sense of being caught out on a lie. It is also crucial to note, as Jennifer Biddle (1997) does in her important article, that the cultural structure of shame varies widely, and that Tomkins is writing out of and about a white European attitude. For Tomkins shame is to be seen in the simple acts of hanging one's head, lowering one's eyes. These acts must take place within physical proximity to others: they are both an indication of interest foiled and at the limits of possible communication. While there must be a prior interest and knowledge of the person in order for shame to occur, shame is 'a specific inhibitor of continuing interest and enjoyment'. An example he uses is the moment when 'one started to smile but found one was smiling at a stranger' (1995: 134). And here we might think about that particular feeling of shame when you've misread signals of interest from a woman who turns out to be fatally straight. In fact, the increasingly popular performance of queer codes by those who would never actually have sex with the same sex is a rich area for the production of shame – again the specific modalities are played along lines of knowing (the codes) and ignorance and disavowal ('you didn't really think that I was?').

While Tomkins details a myriad of small acts that result in and from shame, what is more telling is his remark that any philosophy or psychology which does not 'confront the problem of human suffering is seriously incomplete', and that 'the nature of the experience of shame guarantees a perpetual sensitivity to any violation of the dignity of man' (1995: 136). The trick then is how to direct the intensity of shame towards constructing conditions for dignity. As Sedgwick writes, the 'psychological operations of shame, denial, projection around "ignorance" produce pulsations of wild energies' (1993: 25). With Adam Frank, she argues that shame can also open the way to rethinking the connections that are and are not possible amongst different people and groups. They hazard that 'perhaps . . . [shame] can be a switch point for the individuation of imaging systems, of consciousness, of bodies, of theories, of selves, an individuation that decides not necessarily an identity but a figuration, distinction, or mark of punctuation' (Sedgwick and Frank 1995: 22). Thinking about shame as a local and embodied expression whose meanings are many but are also always finite, limited by its specific manifestation, they argue, may enable 'a political vision of difference that might resist both binary homogenization and infinitizing trivialization' (15).

I want to end by returning to the event/present of Reconciliation. Against a model of ritualistic connection, one point of departure may be in rethinking shame in its differently inhabited, corporeal and historical manifestations. What white gays, lesbians, feminists and queers might bring to this project is precisely a detailed examination of how shame works at a bodily level to open and close lines of connection: shame as a switching point re-routing the dynamics of knowing and ignorance. Unlike empathy, shame does not permit any automatic sharing of commonality: it is that which poses deep limits to communication. Shame can be made to insist on the specific nature of the acts that caused it; it can be made to mark the awesome materiality of its own condition of possibility. It stakes out the moments of possible reconciliation without losing sight of the conditions which have produced their specific feeling and modality. The possibilities of connection are many, but they are also always circumscribed by the finite materiality that shame marks. And it is this marking that is constitutive of localised action, of reconciliation performed in local realities that brings the past into the present. Shame thus can be used to initiate what Sedgwick calls 'a fight not against originary ignorance, nor for originary ignorance, but against the killing pretence that a culture does not know what it does' (1993: 51).

To return briefly to the question of feminists responding to the present, in the image of the relay race, a queer and feminist theory and practice of Reconciliation is to be found in the marking out of the possible connections, as well as respect for the moments of dis-connection. Shame here marks the point when the lines of knowing and ignorance become scrambled and self-consciously entwined. Inspired by a philosophy of coexistence, this is to enrich the idea of a relay of ideas and practices, to see our actions and ideas as coexisting without colonising. It is, I think, of tantamount importance that those whites who have been and are bodily moved by the affect of shame now turn our attentions to the present. In such a way, it may be possible to redirect the flow of shame on the part of the Australian public before it becomes stagnant, strangled in guilt, or squashed by the baggage of *ressentiment* that Leunig depicts as boarding the grim ark of 'One Nation', marooned in an empty land. We need to remember that looking downwards is also a traditional Aboriginal sign of respect for the land.[6] The bodily gesture of shame expressed by whites in the hanging of the head may yet be retrained as an attitude of respect for the indigenous people of Australia, a starting point in Reconciliation.

Notes

1   This chapter constitutes a very initial response to a situation that is deeply historical, and more complex than I am able to adequately convey. For a history of white involvement in promoting progressive politics in regard to Aboriginal issues, see Reynolds (1998). I want to thank the students of the Department of Women's Studies who organised an initial Reconciliation meeting, and the members of the Koori Centre and the Indigenous Studies Unit at the University of Sydney for responding so generously. My thanks in particular to Wendy Brady and Janet Mooney, and to the organisers of the *Transformations* conference, for their comments on earlier drafts of this chapter, I thank Gretchen Poiner, Rosemary Pringle and the *Transformations* collective.

2   This is not to belittle the many efforts both theoretical and practical that are ongoing in rethinking the past, present and future of Australia. Aboriginal scholars and historians have been instrumental in forging new relations and conceptions of the past and the present (Goodall 1996). In terms of bringing history to the present, the collaboration of Marcia Langton and Henry Reynolds on the ABC television series *Frontier*, was crucial (see Reynolds 1996). In terms of responding to the present in more strictly academic terms, Australian philosophers have endeavoured to rework the reach of certain concepts. See, for instance, Paul Patton's (1997) use of Deleuze as a way of offering new lines of thinking in regard to the ramifications of the Mabo and Wik decisions. In terms of grass roots movements, the recently formed group Australians for Native Title is instrumental in bringing national and international attention to land rights, and in other areas, groups like the Anti Violence Project in conjunction with Aboriginal groups formulated a powerful anti-homophobia and violence campaign called 'Black + White + Pink'.

3   For a very interesting rethinking of what follows from the Mabo and Wik rulings, see the special issue of *Law, Text, Culture* entitled 'In the Wake of Terra Nullius' (1998).

4   Hanson was expelled from the Liberal party for her racist comments during the 1995 election campaign. She consequently won the seat of Ipswich in Queensland as an independent MP. She is a notable case of seething white *ressentiment* against the so-called advantages of a number of very different groups: Asians, Aboriginals, multinational corporations, and queers. This very diverse grouping both confirms and complicates Nancy Fraser's recent argument that an 'approach aimed at redressing injustices of distribution can end up creating injustices of recognition' (1997: 25). For an interesting discussion about whether sexual discrimination can be seen in the same terms as

racial or gendered injustice, see the exchange between Fraser and Judith Butler (Fraser 1998; Butler 1998).

5   Within many Aboriginal communities this is a recognised sign of not wishing to continue the conversation; it is of course a visceral way of marking dis-connection with the speaker.

6   With thanks to Anthony McKnight's contribution to the Reconciliation meeting at the Koori Centre, which raised the central differences between white and Aboriginal physical attitudes to the land.

References

Aboriginal Reconciliation Council (1997) *Convention Program*, Melbourne.

Allen, P.G. (1988) 'Some Like Indians Endure', in W. Roscoe (ed.) *Living the Spirit: A Gay American Indian Anthology*, New York: St Martin's Press.

Biddle, J. (1997) 'Shame', *Australian Feminist Studies* 12, 26: 227–239.

Boundas, C. (1997) 'Deleuze on Time and Memory', *Antithesis* 2, 2:11–29.

Bringing Them Home (1997) Report of the National Inquiry into the Separation of Aboriginal and Torres Strait Islander Children from Their Families, Canberra: Human Rights and Equal Opportunity Commission, Commonwealth of Australia.

Brown, W. (1995) *States of Injury: Power and Freedom in Late Modernity*, Princeton, N.J.: Princeton University Press.

Butler, J. (1998) 'Merely Cultural', *New Left Review* 277: 33–44.

Deleuze, G. (1993) 'Rhizomes Versus Trees', in C. Boundas (ed.) *The Deleuze Reader*, New York: Columbia University Press.

Foucault, M. and Deleuze, G. (1980) 'Entretien: les intellectuels et le pouvoir', *L'Arc* 49: 3–10.

Foucault, M. (with G. Deleuze) (1997) 'Intellectuals and Power', in D.F. Bouchard (ed.) *Language, Counter-memory, Practice*, trans. D.F. Bouchard and S. Simon, Ithaca, N.Y.: Cornell University Press.

Fraser, N. (1997) *Justice Interruptus: Critical Reflections on the 'Postsocialist' Condition*, London and New York: Routledge.

—— (1998) 'Heterosexism, Misrecognition and Capitalism: A Response to Judith Butler', *New Left Review* 228: 140–150.

Ginzburg, C. (1994) 'Killing a Chinese Mandarin: The Moral Implications of Distance', *New Left Review* 208: 107–120.

Goodall, H. (1996) *Invasion to Embassy: Land in Aboriginal Politics in New South Wales, 1770–1972*, Sydney: Allen and Unwin, in association with Black Books.

Hall, C. (1996) 'Histories, Empires and the Post-Colonial Moment', in I. Chambers and L. Curti (eds) *The Post-Colonial Question: Common Skies, Divided Horizons*, New York and London: Routledge.

Hall, S. (1996) 'When Was "The Post-Colonial"? Thinking at the Limit', in I. Chambers and L. Curti (eds) *The Post-Colonial Question: Common Skies, Divided Horizons*, New York and London: Routledge.

Langton, M. (1993) 'Rum, Seduction and Death: "Aboriginality" and Alcohol', *Oceania* 63: 195–206.

Law, Text, Culture (1998) 'In the Wake of Terra Nullius' 4, 1 (special issue).

McClintock, Anne. (1992) 'The Myth of Progress: Pitfalls of the Term Post-Colonialism', *Social Text* 31: 32.

Patton, P. (1996) 'Introduction', in P. Patton (ed.) *Deleuze: A Critical Reader*, Oxford: Blackwell.

—— (1997) 'Justice and Difference: The Mabo Case', in P. Patton and D. Austin-Brooks (eds) *Transformations in Australian Society*, University of Sydney: Research Institute for Humanities and Social Sciences Publications.

Probyn, E. (1996) *Outside Belongings*, New York and London: Routledge.

Reynolds, H. (1996) *Frontier: Aborigines, Settlers and Land*, Sydney: Allen and Unwin.

—— (1998) *This Whispering in Our Hearts*, Sydney: Allen and Unwin.

Sedgwick, E. Kosofsky (1993) *Tendencies*, Durham, N.C.: Duke University Press.

Sedgwick, E. Kosofsky and Frank, A. (1995) 'Shame in the Cybernetic Fold: Reading Silvan Tomkins', in E. Sedgwick and A. Frank (eds) *Shame and Its Sisters: A Silvan Tomkins Reader*, Durham, N.C.: Duke University Press.

Tomkins, S. (1995) 'Shame–Humiliation and Contempt–Disgust', in E. Sedgwick and A. Frank (eds) *Shame and Its Sisters: A Silvan Tomkins Reader*, Durham, N.C.: Duke University Press.

Ware, V. (1996) 'Defining Forces: "Race", Gender and Memories of Empire' in I. Chambers and L. Curti (eds) *The Post-Colonial Question: Common Skies, Divided Horizons*, New York and London: Routledge.

Chapter 19

R. Darren Gobert

DRAMATIC CATHARSIS, FREUDIAN HYSTERIA AND THE 'PRIVATE THEATRE' OF ANNA O.[1]

STAGE ACTING REQUIRES that actors make manifest what is initially immaterial, physically embodying characters that are incorporeal, existing only on the page. Indeed, the immateriality is doubled, since it is more accurate to say that actors physically embody their own imaginative conceptions of the characters they are charged to represent. These conceptions, of course, centrally include the emotions experienced by the characters: cast in the role, every actor conceives of Creon's anger or Phaedra's love differently, since he or she conceives of anger or love differently. These conceptions may not be, and indeed are usually not, consciously examined; they inhere in – and have been naturalized by – the cultural location of the actor in question. Thus, the material representations to which these conceptions give rise emanate from and reflect broader cultural understandings. The history of 'emotion' on stage therefore illuminates shifts in the history of 'emotions' more generally.

One thread of this stage history that has been of particular interest to me concerns interpretations of Aristotle's *katharsis*[2] clause in *Poetics* (1449b) – in which he claimed that tragedy is defined by its ability to induce emotional *katharsis* through the incitement of pity and fear[3] – since this claim has proven so vital to how actors and playwrights conceive of stage emotion (and, indeed, of emotion in general). While the question of what *katharsis* means (and, relatedly, how to translate the classical Greek word κάθαρσις) has been declared solved at various points in the histories of theatre and dramatic theory, the solutions are inevitably prone to debunking at later moments: the views of and translations by Aristotle's earliest Italian Renaissance commentators receded as they were supplanted by others in a process that has continued uninterruptedly in Aristotelian commentary until the present day. Both solutions and debunkings are signposts, directing our attention to the axiomatic assumptions that undergird them. Commentators in different historical moments have not had the same thing in mind when they have written of the 'emotions' in general and 'pity' and 'fear' in particular, although they usually appear to have been unaware that their presuppositions were historically constituted: after all, the impulse to historicize at all is of very recent vintage. Examining these signposts helps us better to understand the landscape, the genealogy, of 'emotion' as a historical concept. I here consider one particular moment of this genealogy: the emergence, after the 1880 publication of classicist Jacob Bernays's *Zwei Abhandlungen über die aristotelische Theorie des Drama* [*Two Essays on the Aristotelian Theory of Drama*], of the notion of *katharsis* as a 'purgation' on the part of the theatrical spectator.

Bernays's medical view of *katharsis* emerges as dominant in Western scholarship. I argue, only and precisely because of its consonance with the simultaneously developing discourse of medical psychology and in particular psychoanalysis: Bernays's theory is directly supported by the model of emotion offered by his niece's husband, Sigmund Freud. In other words, if Bernays's theory came to be regarded as the 'solution' to the problem of Aristotelian *katharsis*, it did so because of assumptions – articulated by psychoanalysis but products of their culture more generally – that legitimated its cultural authority. These assumptions comprise a particularly spatialized understanding of emotion, one embodied by the Freudian hysteric whose contemplation leads Freud to his earliest theorizing of affect. Here, I read the paradigmatic hysteric – Josef Breuer's patient 'Anna O.' – in order to demonstrate the relationship between her particular somatic performance of emotion and the immaterial concepts that this performance embodies. Connecting Freud's 'hysteria' and Bernays's 'purgation', I historicize one key moment in the conceptual history of the emotions.

Bernays on *katharsis*

Even the most careful theatre historian may forget that knowing precisely what Aristotle himself 'meant' when he spoke of dramatic *katharsis* is an impossibility, perhaps especially because *katharsis* concerns emotions. We cannot adequately access either Aristotle's culture or the symbols (even its language is dead) with which his culture constructed emotions and disseminated emotional meanings; and the available evidence in Aristotle's corpus is too self-contradictory: Aristotle cross-refers his discussion of emotion in Book 8 of the *Politics* to the *Poetics*; in turn, Book 19 of the *Poetics* makes explicit reference to the 'rhetorical' emotions that he theorizes in some depth in Book 2 of the *Rhetoric*. Yet the seemingly protocognitivist understanding of emotions in the *Rhetoric* is irreconcilable with the discussion in the *Politics*, which considers emotions as noncognitive physiological perturbations.[4] That Aristotle also theorized the emotions in *Nichomachean Ethics*,[5] *On the Soul*,[6] *Parts of Animals* and *Movement of Animals*[7] complicates rather than clarifies matters.

In coming to terms with the elliptical *katharsis* clause in the *Poetics*, we have restricted and contradictory data. We know from Book 4 that all men take pleasure in imitative representations and that this emotion derives from the enjoyment of learning; this capacity, Aristotle claims is inherent to man. We know from Books 6, 7, and 14 that the means to stir emotion in the spectator or auditor resides in the play's plot — although the play's spectacle does stir emotions to a lesser extent. We know from Book 13 that we feel pity for someone who does not merit his misfortune, and fear for the unfortunate who are like ourselves. And most famously, we know from Book 6 that the goal of tragedy is to effect, by means of the emotions of pity and fear, *katharsis* — although how Aristotle means to use the term,[8] and whether the object of this *katharsis* is meant to be emotions more generally or 'pity and fear' specifically,[9] would both seem to be philologically unverifiable.

Theatre and classics students today are likely to be taught that the term *katharsis* best translates as 'clarification'; this translation of the word entered the Liddell-Scott-Jones *Greek-English Lexicon* for the first time in 1940, and the theory that this was Aristotle's intended sense had become by the late 1980s the majoritarian view, due to the influence of Stephen Halliwell's *Aristotle's Poetics* and Martha Nussbaum's *The Fragility of Goodness* (both

1986) and, as I argue elsewhere, the ascent of cognitivism in philosophical and psychological discourse (see Gobert 2006).[10] Older views of *katharsis*, such as 'purification', are similarly historically traceable; as with 'clarification', if they became naturalized as 'what Aristotle meant', the process was facilitated by the concurrent naturalization of a specific understanding of emotion.

Such is the case with the notion of *katharsis* as 'purgation'. This translation of the Greek word, unlike 'clarification', goes back to Aristotle's early Renaissance interpreters: Minturno, for one, used the idea of a medical purgation of illness to understand Aristotelian *katharsis* as early as the mid-sixteenth century, in his 1559 *De Poetica* and 1564 *Arte Poetica*. In the latter text, Minturno writes that '[a]s a physician eradicates, by means of poisonous medicine, the perfervid poison of disease which affects the body, so tragedy purges the mind of its impetuous perturbations by the force of these emotions beautifully expressed in verse' (Spingarn 1924, 80). But such a narrowly medical view of *katharsis* failed to gain cultural traction in the sixteenth century, since there was no basis in science to understand how theatre could be conceived as, to quote the French classicist André Dacier, 'truly a medicine'.[11]

The sense of *katharsis* as 'purgation' that an earlier generation of Aristotle readers was likely taught has a comparatively recent historical emergence: Bernays's 1857 treatise *Grundzüge der verlorenen Abhandlung des Aristoteles über die Wirkung der Tragödie* [*Foundations of Aristotle's Treatise on the Effect of Tragedy*]. The question is: How did Bernays's theory became so popular in only a few decades as to be considered 'standard', in the words of one scholar, and to have 'almost universal assent', in the words of another? (Sparshott 1983, 15; Barnes 1979, viii). Bernays writes that Aristotle is 'explained' if we 'understand' *katharsis* in its medical sense (1979, 159). *Katharsis* can only be thus understood, however, in an historical context that views unpurged emotions as a medical problem with physiological consequences, in a culture with appropriately resonant assumptions about emotion. Bernays's 1857 publication was well regarded by fellow philologists, but it did not have such resonance, as suggested by Bernays's defensive forestalling of his detractors: 'Let no one primly wrinkle his nose and talk of a degradation of aesthetics to the rank of medicine' (1979, 159). However, when he republished the treatise as *Zwei Abhandlungen über die aristotelische Theorie des Drama* in 1880, he was read and discussed outside academic circles. Indeed, the book and its central concept achieved something like popular success, especially in Vienna.[12] Evidence of this success is provided by Bernays's contemporary Willhelm Wetz, who grumbled in 1897: 'Bernays could have supplied us with ten times more insight into tragedy than his research on . . . catharsis . . . actually does: [but] who doubts that, in contrast to his hundred admirers, he would have found only one?'[13]

Wetz's point is that Bernays's popularity reflected a trendy fascination not with dramatic theory or with Aristotle but rather with medical psychology, the discourse that was then revolutionizing cultural understandings of the emotions and, therefore, the emotions themselves. For example, between the two Bernays publications (that is, between 1857 and 1880) August Ambroise Liébeault's *Du Sommeil et des états analogues* [*Induced Sleep and Analogous States*] (1866) and Daniel Hack Tuke's *Influence of the Mind upon the Body* (1872) had both become influential, hypnosis had been resuscitated as a medical practice and psychological healing had come to be associated with neurology clinics instead of asylums in Western European practice.[14] It is in this context – the medicalization of human psychology that in the late-nineteenth century took 'lively ferment', to quote Stanley Jackson (1999, 7) – that Bernays's success must be located.

Bernays situates his analysis of the *katharsis* clause in the *Poetics* against the more specific usage of the term in the *Politics*, in which Aristotle had stated that music confers many benefits on its listeners, among them 'cathartic purposes'. These, he says in an unkept promise, will be treated 'more fully in [his] work on *Poetics*' (1981, 473). Since Aristotle himself connects the

Politics to the *Poetics*, Bernays augments one brief discussion with another. Aristotle's remarks in the *Politics* figure musical *katharsis* as a means of alleviating excitement:

> Any feeling which comes strongly to some souls exists in all others to a greater or less degree – pity and fear, for example, but also excitement. This is a kind of agitation by which some people are liable to be possessed; it may arise out of religious melodies, and in this case it is observable that when they have been listening to melodies that have an orgiastic effect on the soul they are restored as if they had undergone a [*katharsis*]. Those who are given to feeling pity or fear or any other emotion must be affected in precisely this way, and so must other people too, to the extent that some such emotion comes upon each. To them all inevitably comes a sort of pleasant [*katharsis*] and relief.[15] (1981, 473–74)

In light of Aristotle's emphasis on orgiastic 'feeling', which Bernays views as pathogenic, Bernays argues that it is wrong-headed to assume, as commentators since the Renaissance frequently had, that the goal of *katharsis* is principally, or even consequently, moral: 'Aristotle's primary example of catharsis, which is drawn from the Greek experience of ecstasy, is pathological; and it is that which leads him to consider the possibility of a similar cathartic treatment for all other emotions' (1979, 158). Thus, the problem of *katharsis* in the *Poetics* should be approached from the same standpoint that Aristotle adopts in the *Politics*, which, as Bernays succinctly puts it, is 'a *pathological* standpoint' (1979, 158).

Bernays assumes that emotions are 'pathological' and 'pathogenic' for Aristotle, noting that Aristotle's paradigm in the *Politics* derives from the 'realm of psychopathology' (1979, 158). His failure to historicize this understanding provides a case in point about the very phenomenon that I interrogate: Bernays's unexamined, naturalized assumption is generally symptomatic of prevalent late-nineteenth century European ideas about the emotions and their association with irrationality.[16] Since Bernays assumes that the emotions to be relieved by music or tragedy are pathological, it follows that their *katharsis* should be constituted by their removal from the organism. This removal brings healing in the same way that a doctor's care brings healing: 'ecstasy turns to calm', Bernays writes, 'as sickness turns to health through medical treatment . . . Thus the puzzling piece of *emotional* pathology is explained: we can make sense of it if we compare it with a pathological *bodily* reaction' (1979, 159). The negative, 'orgiastic effect on the soul' (Aristotle 1981, 474) that Aristotle finds in men possessed by ecstasy can be relieved by carefully administering these same effects, by means of intoxicating melodies, so that the effects can swell, diminish and eventually pass, leaving the sufferer in an improved state. This homeopathic model of musical *katharsis* Bernays applies to the *Poetics*, which, he claims, intends to theorize tragedy as a means of therapeutically inducing, through scenes of suffering, the emotions of pity and fear with sufficient force that pity and fear in the spectators' systems will be expelled: '*katharsis* is a term transferred from the physical to the emotional sphere, and used of the sort of treatment of an oppressed person which seeks not to alter or to subjugate the oppressive element but to arouse it and to draw it out, and thus to achieve some sort of relief for the oppressed' (Bernays 1979, 160).

Psychoanalytic emotion

The purgation theory of *katharsis* emerges as dominant in the era that it does precisely because of its consonance with the model of emotion provided by the concurrently developing discourse of medical psychology, a discourse whose dominant voice would be provided by Freud. There is a symmetry, in other words, between purgative *katharsis* and Freudian psychoanalysis as 'the first instrument for the scientific examination of the human mind', in James Strachey's phrase (1957, xvi). Indeed, there is a very clear symmetry: in theorizing psychotherapeutic 'catharsis' in his 1895 *Studien über Hysterie*, written with Josef Breuer. Freud never recognizes a debt to the *Poetics*, but he seems to have cribbed substantially from his wife's uncle's treatise on Aristotle.[17] His recurrent references to plays by Goethe, Schiller and Shakespeare may reflect significantly more than the doctor's celebrated fondness for literature (Breuer and Freud 1957, 87, 192, 206, 229, 245 n.2, 250). Tragedy is never displaced from the heart of the theory of catharsis, even in medical practice – an explanation, perhaps, for Pedro Laín Entralgo's suggestive claim that in addressing the emotions '[t]he psychotherapist . . . turns out Aristotelian rhetoric without knowing it' (1970, 181).

Tragic – or, at any rate, traumatic – events are central to Freud's earliest theoretical work on the nature and structure of emotion. This work takes place alongside his development with Breuer of the 'cathartic method', although Freud's most explicit formulations of emotion occur in his later writings,[18] after he had repudiated his mentor. Freud writes in his *Introductory Lectures on Psycho-Analysis* that emotions or affects are comprised of physiological changes together with the subject's registering of these changes in feeling: '[a]n affect includes in the first place particular motor innervations or discharges and secondly certain feelings; the latter are of two kinds – perceptions of the motor actions that have occurred and the direct feelings of pleasure and unpleasure which, as we say, give the affect its keynote' (1963, 395). Freud continues his definition by explaining: 'But I do not think that with this enumeration we have arrived at the essence of an affect. We seem to see deeper in the case of some affects and to recognize that the core which holds the combination we have described together is the repetition of some particular significant experience. This experience could only be a very early impression of a very general nature' (1963, 395–96). Freud thus locates the cause – the core, the essence – of the emotional response not in the context of the perceiver's immediate experience (say, witnessing a sad event) but in an earlier, unconscious experience, in a forgotten, even inherited, memory. (While Freud tends to focus on repressed memories from an individual's experience, he presumes that certain memories precede birth, a presumption that, Strachey notes, is possibly based on Charles Darwin's explanation of the emotions as evolutionary relics [Freud 1963, 396 n.1]. For example, Freud mentions Darwin's account of tail-wagging in dogs as an analogue for emotional reactions like screaming in his narrative of Emmy von N. [Breuer and Freud 1957, 91].) Elsewhere, in *Inhibitions, Symptoms, and Anxiety*, Freud reiterates this model by describing emotional states as having 'become incorporated in the mind as precipitates of primaeval traumatic experiences, and when a similar situation occurs they are revived' (1959, 93). Therefore, as William Lyons summarizes well in his important book *Emotion*, '[t]he actual emotion is a resurrection of the original traumatic emotional state triggered by some present event which stirs that memory' (1980, 26).

Emotions in the Freudian view are unavoidable, as many of them stem from traumas inherited or inevitable, like the primal scene. Secondly, emotions are healthy, since they serve as a safety valve through which people discharge unconscious drives. The failure to perform this discharge emotionally – a performance that Freud and Breuer term 'abreaction' – is in fact psychically and, therefore, physically unhealthy and potentially calamitous: failure to abreact causes neurosis, a particularly acute form of which is hysteria. Freud theorizes the structure of emotion inductively in light of his theory of hysteria, hence his formulation in the *Introductory Lectures* that 'an affective state would be constructed in the same way as a hysterical attack and, like it, would be the precipitate of a reminiscence' (1963, 396). Neurotic people whose blocks prevent abreaction will suffer from potentially severe physical symptoms; these symptoms can be alleviated only by removing the block and purging the emotion through the cathartic method. Psychoanalytic catharsis, therefore, aims to purge specific emotions that are impeding the psychic life of the analysand because of their failure to leave the unconscious; such emotions are said to be 'inadmissible to consciousness' or *bewusstseinsunfähig* (Breuer and Freud 1957, 225).

Despite Strachey's plaint that the term 'leaves much to be desired' because of its ambiguity (Breuer and Freud 1957, 225 n.1), the multivalency is richly productive: constructed out of *Bewusstsein* ('consciousness') and *unfähig* ('unable' or 'incompetent'), the coinage recalls its analogue *hoffähig* ('admissible to Court'). Breuer's neologism thus stresses both the imperial nature of consciousness, which determines admissibility, and the incapacity of the emotion, which lacks competence; it also makes clear the spatial terms in which he and Freud conceive of the emotions. In neurosis the inadmissible/incompetent emotion remains – like the originating memory in which it is tied up – in a repressed state, and in its failure to be abreacted properly, the emotion is made manifest only in strange symptoms of physical illness, bodily manifestations of suppressed memory. The analyst's task is to read the symbols of suppressed memory (which occur in the case studies primarily as bodily perturbations) and help ease the memory into consciousness.

Anna O.

The first of Breuer and Freud's hysterics, Anna O. (Bertha Pappenheim[19]), fell sick in Vienna in 1880, the same year that Bernays re-published his commentary on Aristotle. A 'markedly intelligent' young woman of twenty-one, possessed of 'great poetic and imaginative gifts' and guided by a 'powerful intellect' and 'sharp and critical common sense' (Breuer and Freud 1957, 21), Anna O. suffers symptoms that include diplopia (seeing double), a severe squint, hallucinations, episodic muscular paralyses, somnambulism and a strange aphasia that eventually culminates – shortly after her father's unfortunately timed death in April 1881 – in a complete inability to speak or understand her native language, German (Breuer and Freud 1957, 22–25).

Most strikingly, Anna O. comes during the time of her illness to suffer from the condition that figures in the *Studies on Hysteria* as the paradigmatic hysterical symptom: the dissociation that Breuer and Freud call 'splitting' or, using French, '*double conscience*', wherein the sufferer experiences two different ontological states or states of consciousness, one 'normal' and the other 'hallucinatory' – a '*condition seconde*'. (The term *condition seconde* is borrowed from the clinical work of Jean-Marie Charcot, a French neurologist to whose work on hysteria Breuer and Freud are indebted; as Jackson notes, Charcot is another important contributor to, and product of, the medicalization of psychology in the 1880s [1999, 84–85, 250–55].) The two states exist side by side, an ontological analogue for Anna O.'s diplopia: 'being double' in addition to 'seeing double'. Of her double consciousness, Breuer notes that 'though her two states were thus sharply separated, not only did the secondary state intrude into the first one, but – and this was at all events frequently true, and even when she was in a very bad condition – a clear-sighted and calm observer sat, as she put it, in a corner of her brain and looked on at all the mad business' (1957, 46). This dissociative state, Breuer tells us, is structurally similar and possibly causally related to her lifelong tendency to day-dream: in both cases, Anna O. indulges in what she calls, instructively, her 'private theatre' (1957, 41).

In spite of her intelligence and remarkable capacity for self-insight, Anna O. is ignorant both of the precipitating event of her bodily perturbations and the causal connection between them, since the traumatic event that has occasioned the blocked emotion is similarly repressed from consciousness. As Breuer and Freud put it, 'the nature of the trauma exclude[s] a reaction' (1957, 10). The physical symptoms of hysteria are the emergent effects of the forgotten memory, which 'acts like a foreign body which long after its entry must continue to be regarded as an agent that is still at work' (Breuer and Freud 1957, 6). In this sense, hysterical trauma is unlike our universal, unconscious primal experiences described in the *Introductory Lectures*, which are also repressed but whose generated emotions are allowed to be expressed. Catharsis thus involves not the purging of an inherited affect-source but rather the purging of a block incurred in lived experience.

Since the psychoanalytic model of emotion links all emotion to memory, it is unsurprising that psychoanalytic catharsis yokes cathartic purgation to remembering. Once the memory has been retrieved and the emotion thereby abreacted, the illness ceases. As Breuer and Freud note, 'each individual hysterical symptom immediately and permanently disappeared when we had succeeded in bringing clearly to light the memory of the event by which it was provoked and in arousing its accompanying affect, and when the patient had described that event in the greatest possible detail and had put the affect into words' (1957, 6). The necessity of putting the 'affect into words' highlights two important features of Breuer and Freud's cathartic method. First, since the unearthing of the trauma happens through the questioning of a trained physician, the analysand is compelled to explore his or her[20] unconscious memories through language – a compulsion that Jacques Lacan would later seize upon in his revision of Freud, which denies the possibility of experience outside language.[21] In Breuer's succinct formulation, '[t]elling things is a relief' (1957, 211). This formulation lies at the foundation of the psychoanalytic method, which emerges out of his visits with Anna O.:

> The stories were always sad and some of them very charming . . . As a rule their starting-point or central situation was of a girl anxiously sitting by a sick-bed. But she also built up her stories on quite other topics. – A few moments after she had finished her narrative, she would wake up, obviously calmed down . . . If for any reason she was unable to tell me the story during her evening hypnosis she failed to calm down afterwards, and on the following day she had to tell me <u>two</u> stories in order for this to happen. (Breuer and Freud 1957, 29)

Thus, psychoanalytic catharsis is the 'talking cure', a term of Anna O.'s own that Breuer and Freud retained (Breuer and Freud 1957, 30).[22]

It is therefore telling that, in Anna O.'s case, the deterioration of her health can be directly mapped onto her faltering ability to communicate: word retrieval problems soon lead to an inability to conjugate verbs ('she used only infinitives', Breuer notes [1957, 25]) and a disregard for articles. At her worst she is virtually unintelligible, 'almost completely deprived of words . . . put[ting] them together laboriously out of four or five languages' (Breuer and Freud 1957, 25). Eventually, she loses even her ability to understand German, which leaves her unable to communicate with her nurse; strangely, she regains expressive and receptive language skills in English, so that among her caregivers Breuer alone can communicate with her.

Conversely, in recovery Anna O. regains her linguistic abilities and can continue her talking cure. But in her seemingly endless capacity for producing 'imaginative products' lies Breuer's strongest evidence of her illness (1957, 30). Anna's inability to end her stories testifies to her emotional block: she cannot have closure, either narratively or emotionally. Just as *katharsis* in Aristotle's *Poetics* is linked to the unravelling of the action, and thus *katharsis* effects (and is an effect of) the plot's dénouement, the cathartic method brings resolution to the pathogenic emotion by purging or exhausting it through language. Thus, there is a connection between well-abreacted trauma and well-plotted narrative, a connection usefully underscored by Breuer's assertion that Goethe dealt with distressing affects by discharging them in literary creation (1957, 206–07). Freud would similarly point out in *The Interpretation of Dreams* (reliably or not) that *Hamlet* was written 'immediately after' the death of Shakespeare's father, under the 'immediate impact of his bereavement' (1958, 265).

In order to help her achieve creative closure, then, Breuer guides Anna O. as she mines her history for forgotten traumas; in accordance with the etiology of hysteria, he reads the manifest, mnemic symbols of her hysteria and prompts her to give voice to latent narratives. For example, Anna's hydrophobia (which prevents her from drinking water even during the particularly hot summer of 1880) is connected to a memory of seeing a little dog drink out of a glass – a 'disgusting' sight that her politeness initially prevented her from expressing and which she unwittingly forced into unconsciousness, to her later detriment (Breuer and Freud 1957, 34). But once she remembers and narrates the event under hypnosis, the disgust is released along with the memory, and 'thereupon the . . . [hydrophobia] vanished, never to return' (Breuer and Freud 1957, 35).

Since 'every sense-perception calls back into consciousness any other sense-perception that appeared originally at the same time', Breuer traces strands of her hysteria back to their originating traumas and cures Anna O. one symptom at a time (1957, 208). His goal is to arrive at the most important causal factor (1957, 35). In Anna O.'s case, Breuer notes in his chronicle of her treatment that she once had a 'waking dream' in which she

> saw a black snake coming towards the sick man [her father, before his death] from the wall to bite him. . . . She tried to keep the snake off, but it was as though she was paralysed. Her right arm, over the back of the chair, had gone to sleep and had become anaesthetic and paretic; and when she looked at it the fingers turned into little snakes with death's heads . . . When the snake vanished, in her terror she tried to pray. But language failed her: she could find no tongue in which to speak, till at last she thought of some children's verses in English and then found herself able to think and pray in that language. (1957, 38–39)

This episode, particularly rich in mnemic symbols, typifies the patient's hysteria: in the private theatre of her waking dream – experiencing what Breuer and Freud elsewhere describe as 'the hallucinatory reproduction of a memory' (1957, 14) – she suffers physiological symptoms (a hallucination and paralysis) that signify an emotional block, which is in turn reflected in compromised language skills. On the last day of her cathartic method, Breuer re-stages this scene by 're-arranging the room so as to resemble her father's sickroom' (1957, 40). In it, Anna is able to 'reproduc[e] the terrifying hallucination . . . which constituted the root of her whole illness. During the original scene she had only been able to think and pray in English; but immediately after its reproduction she was able to speak German. She was moreover free from the innumerable disturbances which she had previously exhibited' (Breuer and Freud 1957, 40). Thus, the most serious plot-strand of her narratively complex hysteria is resolved: its originating emotional moment at her father's bedside is revisited, and the attendant blocked emotions are released in (and their release is signalled by) their unproblematic narration in German. Anna O. thereafter leaves Vienna and eventually 'regain[s] her mental balance entirely' and 'enjoy[s] complete health' (Breuer and Freud 1957, 41).[23]

As Breuer describes them, Anna O.'s aphasic incapacity to create language and, even more strikingly, her subsequent inability to end her stories highlight neurotic hysteria's resemblance to a dramaturgical problem; her story thus again adumbrates the *Studies'* debt to Aristotle's *Poetics*, which links emotional *katharsis* to plotting. One of Breuer's verbs, *tragieren* ('to play tragically' or 'to tragedize'), clearly evokes the theatrical nature of medical catharsis; Breuer assumes that Anna O.'s emotional experiences and narration are shaped by concerns of aesthetics, narrative structure or genre.[24] Indeed, Breuer's devotion to Aristotelian closure – Book 7 of the *Poetics* stresses the completeness of the plot and its organically connected beginning, middle, and end (Aristotle 1989, 15–16) – may partially explain if not excuse the tidiness of Anna O.'s chapter in the *Studies*: the heroine of Breuer's narrative leaves Vienna to enjoy perfect health after her abreactive closing monologue, while Bertha Pappenheim needed to be institutionalized after Breuer's treatment (Jones 1953, 225; Borch-Jacobsen 1996, 21).

Moreover, that Anna O.'s recovery is enabled by Breuer's *mise en scène* – he mimetically reproduces the scene of her father's sickroom – highlights the important relationship in which his and Freud's cathartic method situates spectacle and sufferer, as well as the crucially gendered relationship between patient and analyst, which has been helpfully high-lighted by feminist critics.[25] Breuer exploits Anna O.'s *condition seconde* – her capacity for 'being double' – by positioning her both as an actor and as a spectator to a show with which she is made imaginatively to engage. He thus facilitates the abreaction of her repressed emotion in catharsis. Later Freud would usefully mobilize this insight to explain the function of all tragedy: in 'Psychopathic Characters on the Stage', he argues that tragic plots are limited only by the 'neurotic instability of the public' (1953, 310). Echoing Aristotle, who assesses potential dramatic actions in the *Poetics* by applying the test of probability, Freud suggests that the best plots will resonate with the probable emotional blocks of audiences (1953, 308). Staging these plots, the stage director acts as an analyst, alleviating repression and thereby bringing pleasure. Freud therefore answers a vexing paradox in the *Poetics* – why audiences experience pleasure by witnessing fearful or pitiable events – with a gloss on Aristotle. Clearly recapitulating his wife's uncle's understanding of *katharsis*, Freud writes: 'If, as has been assumed since the time of Aristotle, the purpose of drama is to arouse 'terror and pity' and so 'to purge the emotions', we can describe that purpose in rather more detail by saying that it is a question of opening up sources of pleasure or enjoyment in our emotional life' (1953, 305).

Theorizing the emotions

That Anna O. fell ill in December of 1880, just after Bernays's *Zwei Abhandlungen* was published, is a coincidence worth reiterating: Juan Dalma (1963) has also delineated the connection between Anna's 'cure' and the interest in catharsis spurred by Bernays's 1880 publication, a connection that Ellenberger supplements by intimating that Anna was herself familiar with Bernays's book (1970, 484; see also Sulloway 1979, 56–57). Pappenheim's biographer, Melinda Given Guttman, concurs (2001, 62). In his *Remembering Anna O.*, Mikkel Borch-Jacobsen surmises that Pappenheim may have faked her symptoms accordingly (1996, 85–86) and argues that Breuer described them selectively and creatively when he was reconstructing her case from his 1882 clinical notes for the 1895 *Studies* (1996, 52–61).

However, whether Pappenheim had read Bernays is finally irrelevant. In delineating this convergence, in demonstrating that Freud's cathartic method was deeply rooted in Aristotelian notions, in arguing that Freud fertilizes the cultural environment that allows Bernays's 'purgation' model to take root, I do not seek to 'debunk' Bernays, Breuer, or this or that idea of Freud's. Rather, I seek to demonstrate how a new set of assumptions about emotions makes possible a set of emotional experiences and expressions. A certain under-standing of emotions undergoes historical ascent in such a way as to make a certain reading of Aristotelian *katharsis* both possible and intelligible. But so too does this understanding of emotion make Anna O.'s illness possible and intelligible. Like a stage actor, Anna O. unwittingly expresses in her emotional behaviour many of her culture's unexamined presumptions about emotions. To locate a moment of intelligibility, and to mark it as different from another, serves to throw into relief the inherent instability, transhistorically, of 'emotion' as a concept.

All feeling persons, like actors on a stage, reveal their presumptions about emotion in every emotional expression. Moreover, as agents of culture we play a role in the naturalizing of our culture's suppositions about emotion. The suppositions of 1880 or 1895 Vienna – many of them now attributed to Freud but more diffusely co-authored by his cultural context – have subsequently become naturalized in our cultural discourse: for example, the notion that the essence of emotions resides in the unconscious or in forgotten memories from early childhood experience, the relationship between emotional health and language that underlines all narrative medicine or the notion that we should not 'bottle up' our emotions. (Incidentally, for Freud the 'pleasure' of theatre resides precisely in its help in this regard: 'the prime factor', he wrote, 'is unquestionably the process of getting rid of one's own emotions by 'blowing off steam' [austoben]; and the consequent enjoyment corresponds . . . to the relief produced by a thorough discharge' [1953, 305].[26]) One can see such ideas recapitulated and reinforced in our culture's representations: in our theatre, on our television shows, in our therapists' offices, in our everyday language and experience.

These ideas, however, currently sit uneasily with newer cognitivist ideas: to cite my central example, the psychoanalytic understanding of emotion is difficult to reconcile with the now-standard reading of emotional *katharsis* as 'clarification'. The case of Freudian hysteria and Aristotelian purgation is offered, then, for its metatheoretical implications, since the case can only be seen clearly with hindsight, now that its axiomatic assumptions have begun to be historicized. To insist on the historicizing of commonsense ideas is merely to spot a danger when we are talking about the emotions, merely to highlight the difficulty of defining exactly what we are presupposing when we say this or that about 'emotional states' – and the difficulty, even impossibility, of not taking for granted our own precepts, those that inform our own emotional expressions. After all, if Bernays's critical machinery is inevitably limited by its cultural location, so too is ours. As Stanley Fish has articulated, critical analysis requires not only the 'demotion' of the cultural norms under scrutiny, but also an unexamined allegiance to new norms that will enable such analytic scrutiny. Fish makes an important – ultimately Hegelian – point, which we ignore at our peril: relativism is 'not a position one can occupy . . . because no one can achieve the distance from his own beliefs and assumptions which would result in their being no more authoritative *for him* than the beliefs and assumptions held by others' (1999, 53).

Kenneth Bennett has criticized the ahistorical tendency of Aristotelian commentary, in which the *katharsis* question 'has become a window through which the critic can complacently view his own critical machinery at work' (1981, 207–08). A more profitable way of making his claim would be to acknowledge that any critical machinery brought to illuminate the problem must inevitably be limited by its cultural location. We can nonetheless marry our theorizing about emotion, first, to an awareness of the impossibility of historicizing the present moment and, second (and therefore), to what Paul Ricoeur calls a hermeneutics of suspicion. I invoke Ricoeur purposefully: like his, my interpretive approach also presumes that texts (in my case, performances) are themselves heuristic, providing a mode of learning reality. Like all cultural artefacts, they are always materially expressive (like the actor's embodiment of Creon's anger) and also mimetic – whether consciously or not, they are imitative of previous expressions, previous conceptions. In this sense, the complicated nexus of relationships from which an actor's emotion derives – between immaterial conceptions (page) and physical manifestation (stage) – suggests the equally complicated nexus of relationships from which 'real-life' emotion derives.

For this reason, an apparent slippage in my argument is meant to be theoretically productive: my conflation of the public stage and the 'private theatre' and of actors and Anna O., herself a literary representation not coextensive with Bertha Pappenheim. Like Breuer and Freud, who cite the 'mental process' of Lady Macbeth as evidence for their theory of neurosis (1957, 245 n.2), I finally presume that 'real-life' performances of emotions are not different in kind but deeply interrelated with 'staged' performances of emotion: indeed, it is richly suggestive that the once-aphasic Anna O. teaches herself to write again 'copying the alphabet from her edition of Shakespeare' (Breuer and Freud 1957, 26). I similarly presume that Breuer's narration of Anna O.'s case is no less significant than Pappenheim's illness for the historian of emotions, who seeks to understand 'emotion' in 1880 or 1895 by looking at its representation. Pappenheim's emotions and Breuer's narration of them are both performative; both materially express the conceptions of the performer in question and his or her cultural context. Therefore, both Pappenheim's hysteria and Breuer's narrative are artefacts, signs, to be read – and to be historicized. In both cases, an agent or actor – both words, tellingly, share the root, *agere*, to do – manifests or embodies understandings.

In theorizing the emotions, we have as evidence to be read only such signs: emotional expressions, products of culture, whether words or tears. A hermeneutics of suspicion recognizes that the meaning of any such text is concealed. If this concealment is largely unwitting on the part of the text's author, it is partly because of the ahistoricity of the present that I described earlier. The various historical understandings of *katharsis*, and especially Bernays's now-displaced theory of 'purgation', provide crucial object lessons in this ahistoricity for theorists of the emotions. This is not to suggest, of course, that the task's theoretical impossibility means that we must abandon hope of making stable claims about the emotions. After all, the word 'emotions' (like 'affects', 'feelings', 'passions') is itself a laden cultural product, and we nonetheless adhere to a necessary fiction that the word can neutrally signify a class of responses, of phenomena across cultures, that bear a family resemblance to one another. But as Clifford Geertz puts it in *Interpretation of Cultures*, we need to aim not at 'discovering the Continent of Meaning and mapping out its bodiless landscape'; rather, we should restrict ourselves to 'guessing at meanings, assessing the guesses, and drawing explanatory conclusions from the better guesses' (1973, 20).

I view emotions as emergent products of culture: constructed in and by social contexts, neither transhistorical nor transcultural. This is not to suggest that there are no important biological factors involved in emotion. However, since both our understanding and experience of emotions are inexorably shaped by culture in general and discourse in particular, it becomes impossible to separate physiological factors from the linguistic tools we use to understand and express those factors: we are returned, perpetually, to the heuristic function of our own experiences, or own representations. Therefore, I follow the work of recent cultural anthropology[27] in imagining that emotions cannot be ontologically prior to the cultural beliefs that give rise to them and the cultural behaviours – such as crying or acting – that express them. To presume there are culturally specific emotions that are constituted within and by particular cultures helps to undermine the universalist and essentialist views that have dominated so much of the concept's history, steering attention to the more profitable notion that emotions are, in the words of Michelle Rosaldo, *'embodied* thoughts' expressed in the behaviour of cultural agents (1984, 143; her emphasis). Such a presumption helps us to understand the role played by an agent's cultural context: to see more clearly why Bertha Pappenheim's emotional performance may have unfolded as it did, and why Anna O.'s emotional performance unfolds as it does in Breuer's narration. Importantly, however, the presumption also implicates each of us as theorists of emotion, who reflect and shape our cultural understandings with each word that we write. After all, the views of emotion that predominate in any given moment require and are constituted by their cultural recapitulations.

Notes

1   For ease of reading, I have quoted English-language translations of all foreign texts. However, each quotation was scrutinized against the original; where appropriate or necessary, or where no published translation exists, this original is included. Uncredited translations are my own. I gratefully acknowledge Ross Arthur for his aid with classical Greek texts and Nemanja Protic and Katie Fry for their research assistance.

       These remarks were first delivered at the *Emotional Geographies* conference at Queen's University, Kingston, in May 2006.

2   A note about usage: like other critics, I use '*katharsis*' in its strictly Aristotelian sense and 'catharsis' in its more general senses, including that theorized by Freud and Josef Breuer.

3   In G.M.A. Grube's translation: 'Tragedy, then, is the imitation of a good action, which is complete and of a certain length, by means of language made pleasing for each part separately; it relies in its various elements not on narrative but on acting; through pity and fear it achieves the purgation (catharsis) of such emotions' (Aristotle 1989, 12).

4   On the recurrent claim that the *Rhetoric* betrays a cognitivist understanding of emotion in general and pity and fear in particular, see, for example, Fortenbaugh 1979, Lyons 1980 (33–35), and chapter six of Halliwell 1986. Belfiore 1992 dissents, seeing the account in the *Rhetoric* as internally self-contradictory, since it marries physiological and wholly cognitive elements (184, 187).

5   Aristotle has cause to theorize particular emotions and feelings at various points in the *Ethics*; on 'fear' in particular, see 1976, 127–30.

6   Aristotle spends much of Book I of *On the Soul* discussing the composition of emotion, which, he says – in a distinction that is keenly relevant here – is both 'matter' and 'form': 'the natural philosopher and the dialectician would give a different definition of each of the affections, for instance in answer to the question "What is anger?" For the dialectician will say that it is a desire for revenge or something like that, while the natural philosopher will say that it is a boiling of the blood and hot stuff about the heart. And one of these will be expounding the matter, the other the form and rationale' (1986, 129).

7   Aristotle's explicit physiological explanations of animal emotions in the *Parts of Animals* shed light on human emotional reactions; see, for example, 1984b, 1013. In *Movement of Animals*, he similarly explains the relationship between emotional responses and physiology. See, for example, 1984b, 1092–93.

8   White 1984 catalogues all instances of the Greek word *katharsis* and its derivatives in classical literature; Aristotle's entries total 156 (110–23). The extended discussion of the word and its cognates in Moulinier 1952 is still widely cited. Belfiore 1992 more narrowly surveys Aristotle's usage of the word (291–336); her total is 161 (292).

9   The debate over whether 'pity and fear' effects either the *katharsis* of 'these emotions' or 'such emotions' begins with the earliest Renaissance commentators and is without end. (Some influential commentators have gone further afield: Else 1957 famously offers 'those painful or fatal acts', for example [221] and Golden 1962 offers 'such incidents' [58].)

10   The first theory of Aristotelian *katharsis* as clarification appears in Golden 1962, although it is adumbrated earlier in the century (see Haupt 1915). For Halliwell's most succinct articulation, see 1986, 200–201; for Nussbaum's, see 1986, 391.

11   'la Tragedie est donc une veritable medecine, qui purge les passions . . . Mais c'est une medecine agreable, qui ne fait son effet que par le plaisir' (spelling original; Dacier 1692, 83).

12   See for example, Swales (1998, 28) who notes the 'surge of interest' in catharsis, which became a 'very fashionable topic of discussion among the fin-de-siècle Viennese *haute bourgeoisie*.' Ellenberger (1970, 484) also notes the 'widespread interest' that followed, calling catharsis 'the current topic of conversation in Viennese salons.' Sulloway (1979, 56–57) notes that 'In Vienna, as elsewhere, this whole subject . . . assumed for a time the proportions of a craze.'

13   'J. Bernays hätte uns in selbständiger Forschung zehnmal mehr Aufschlüsse über das Wesen des Tragischen verschaffen dürfen, als seine Deutung des Katharsisprocesses uns thatsächlich lieferte:

wer zweifelt daran, daß er für hundert Bewunderer seiner meisterhaften Katharsisabhandlung im andern Falle höchstens einen gefunden hätte?' (Wetz 1897, 30).

14   On the discourse and practices of medical psychology in the 1880s, see Jackson 1999, especially chapters one and six. Jackson's examples are drawn from France, Austria, Germany, England, Holland, and Switzerland.

15   T. A. Sinclair's translation, which I quote, renders Aristotle's two usages of the word 'katharsis' as 'curative and purifying treatment' and 'purgation'.

16   For this insight, I am grateful to Mick Smith.

17   Bernays died in 1881, after Freud's engagement to Martha but before their wedding. Freud and Breuer's debt to Bernays has gone largely unrecognized by critics: for exceptions see Swales (1998, 28), Mitchell-Boyask (1994, 28–29) and Jean Bollack (1998, 54). There is surprisingly little discussion of the relationship between the two men, which Hirschmüller (1989, 157) characterizes as 'special'. He also speculates on Breuer's familiarity with Bernays's work, reminding us of the coincidence that Bernays died during Anna O.'s treatment, and of the many obituaries that popularly circulated at the time (Hirschmüller 1989, 156–57).

18   Hence Breuer's note in the *Studies* that '[n]o attempt will be made here to formulate either a psychology or a physiology of the affects' (1957, 201). Freud's clearest articulations of the structure of emotion can be found in the 'Anxiety' chapter of his *Introductory Lectures on Psycho-Analysis*; while many elements of psychoanalysis had by then radically evolved, Freud's conception of an affect had not.

19   Pappenheim would later become as famous for her pioneering feminism and social work as she is infamous for being the first 'hysteric'. Melinda Given Guttman's biography *The Enigma of Anna O.* (2001) is the most extensive.

20   Usually 'her', of course – in keeping with an association between woman and emotion that has been particularly pronounced in the West since the seventeenth century. While the name 'hysteria' (from the Greek word for womb) etymologically ties the disorder to woman (Veith 1965, ix), the possibility of male hysteria does arise incidentally in the nearly 4,000-year history of the disease. A cultural history is provided by Ilza Veith's *Hysteria: The History of a Disease*.

21   Lacan logically extends Freud by noting that language structures all human existence and experience. It is thus misguided to assume that any analysand can have an experience (after his or her infant 'mirror stage') that exists outside of language, or exclusively in the realm of biology, as Freud and Breuer assume. Hence Lacan's dictum that the unconscious is structured like a language: 'l'inconscient est structuré *comme* une langage. Je dis *comme* pour ne pas dire, j'y reviens toujours, que l'inconscient est structuré *par* un langage' (1975, 46–47).

22   Indeed, Anna O.'s coinage 'talking cure' – as well as her insistence on 'chimney-sweeping' (Breuer and Freud 1957, 30) by telling stories to relieve herself – led to Ernest Jones's declaration that she was 'the real discoverer of the cathartic method' (1953, 223 n. *b*).

23   Freud would later summarize elements of Anna O.'s story in his *Five Lectures on Psycho-Analysis*, in which he describes her traumatic emotions as 'unusual somatic innervations' and 'physical symptoms of the case' (1957, 18). In this telling, Freud radically de-emphasizes Breuer's role in the process – he has Anna O. 'reproduc[ing] . . . scenes' unaided – which reflects the breakdown of his and Breuer's relationship. Details of Freud's later representations of Breuer's relationship with Anna O. are provided by Forrester and Cameron 1999.

24   Breuer: 'Da sie, diese Dinge [her hallucinations] durchlebend, sie theilweise sprechend tragirte, kannte die Umgebung meist den Inhalt dieser Hallucinationen' (1895, 20). ['Since she acted these things through as though she was experiencing them and in part put them into words, the people around her became aware to a great extent of the content of these hallucinations' (1957, 27).]

25   See, to cite only one example, Guttman, who remarks of Jean-Marie Charcot that he 'turned his clinic into a theatrical spectacle. Charcot did not allow his "hysterics" to speak, nor did he listen to them. To him the "hysteric" was an actress who, under Charcot's direction, played the role of "woman", a creature of frailty and despair, who permitted man to be the strong protector and the superb lion' (2001, 76).

26   In theorizing theatre in 'Psychopathic Characters', Freud here revisits a term (*austoben*) that Breuer had used to describe emotional discharge in the *Studies*: 'Mental pain discharges it [excitation] in difficult breathing and in an act of secretion: in sobs and tears. It is a matter of everyday experience that such reactions reduce excitement and allay it. As we have already remarked ordinary language expresses this in such phrases as "to cry oneself out", "to blow off steam", etc. What is being got rid of is nothing else than the increased cerebral excitation' (Breuer and Freud 1957, 201–02).

27   This work is much indebted to Geertz's methodology: for example, work on Utku Eskimos (Briggs 1970) or among the Ilongot of the Philippines (Rosaldo 1980). Studies more narrowly focused on culturally specific emotions include (most significantly) Catherine Lutz, whose work on the emotional life of the Ifaluk is seminal: see Lutz 1988 and Lutz 1995.

References

Aristotle (1976), *Ethics* [*Nichomachean Ethics*], trans. J. A. K. Thomson (New York: Penguin).

—— (1981), *Politics*, trans. T. A. Sinclair, Revised Edition (New York: Penguin).

—— (1984a), *Movement of Animals*, trans. A. S. L. Farquharson, in Jonathan Barnes (ed.), *The Complete Works of Aristotle*, i (Princeton: Princeton UP), 1087–98.

—— (1984b), *Parts of Animals*, trans. W. Ogle, in Jonathan Barnes (ed.), *The Complete Works of Aristotle*, i (Princeton: Princeton UP), 994–1086.

—— (1986), *De Anima (On the Soul)*, trans. Hugh Lawson-Tancred (New York: Penguin).

—— (1989 [1958]), *Poetics: On Poetry and Style*, trans. G. M. A. Grube (Indianapolis: Hackett).

—— (1991), *The Art of Rhetoric*, trans. Hugh Lawson-Tancred (New York: Penguin).

Barnes, Jonathan et al. (eds.) (1979), *Articles on Aristotle*, iv (London: Duckworth).

Belfiore, Elizabeth S. (1992), *Tragic Pleasures: Aristotle on Plot and Emotion* (Princeton: Princeton UP).

Bennett, Kenneth (1981), 'The Purging of Catharsis', *British Journal of Aesthetics* 21:3, 204–13.

Bernays, Jacob (1857), *Grundzüge der verlorenen Abhandlung des Aristoteles über die Wirkung der Tragödie* (Breslau).

—— (1880), *Zwei Abhandlungen über die aristotelische Theorie des Drama* (Berlin).

—— (1979), 'Aristotle on the Effect of Tragedy', trans. Jennifer and Jonathan Barnes, in Barnes et al. (eds.), *Articles on Aristotle*, iv (London: Duckworth), 154–65.

Bollack, Jean (1998), *Jacob Bernays: Un Homme entre deux mondes* (Paris: PU du Septentrion).

Borch-Jacobsen, Mikkel (1996), *Remembering Anna O.*, trans. Kirby Olson (New York: Routledge).

Breuer, Joseph and Freud, Sigmund (1895), *Studien über Hysterie* (Leipzig).

—— (1957), *Studies on Hysteria*, trans. and ed. James Strachey (New York: Basic).

Briggs, Jean L. (1970), *Never in Anger: Portrait of an Eskimo Family* (Cambridge: Harvard UP).

Dacier, André (1692), *La poétique d'Aristote traduite en françois, avec des remarques* (Paris: C. Barbin).

Dalma, Juan (1963), 'La Catarsis en Aristoteles, Bernays y Freud', *Revista de Psiquiatría y Psicología Medica* 4, 253–69.

Ellenberger, Henri F. (1970), *The Discovery of the Unconscious* (New York: Basic).

Else, Gerald F. (1957), *Aristotle's Poetics: The Argument* (Cambridge: Harvard UP).

Fish, Stanley (1999), 'Is There a Text in this Class?', in H. Aram Vesser (ed.), *The Stanley Fish Reader* (Oxford: Blackwell), 38–54.

Forrester, John and Laura Cameron (1999), ' "Cure With A Defect": A Previously Unpublished Letter by Freud Concerning "Anna O." ', *International Journal of Psychoanalysis* 80, Part 5, 929–42.

Fortenbaugh, William W. (1979), 'Aristotle's *Rhetoric* on Emotions' in Jonathan Barnes et al (eds.), *Articles on Aristotle*, iv (London: Duckworth), 133–53.

Freud, Sigmund (1953), 'Psychopathic Characters on the Stage', trans. James Strachey, in James Strachey et al. (eds.), *The Standard Edition of the Complete Psychological Works*, vii (London: Hogarth), 305–10.

—— (1957), *Five Lectures on Psycho-Analysis*, trans. James Strachey, in James Strachey et al. (eds.), *The Standard Edition of the Complete Psychological Works*, xi (London: Hogarth), 3–58.

—— (1958), *The Interpretation of Dreams*, trans. James Strachey, in James Strachey et al. (eds.), *The Standard Edition of the Complete Psychological Works*, iv–v (London: Hogarth).

—— (1959), *Inhibitions, Symptoms, and Anxiety*, trans. James Strachey, in James Strachey et al. (eds.), *The Standard Edition of the Complete Psychological Works*, xx (London: Hogarth), 77–178.

—— (1963), *Introductory Lectures on Psycho-Analysis: Part III (General Theory of the Neuroses)*, trans. James Strachey, in James Strachey et al. (eds.), *The Standard Edition of the Complete Psychological Works*, xvi (London: Hogarth), 243–463.

Geertz, Clifford (1973), *The Interpretation of Cultures* (New York: Basic).

Gobert, R. Darren (2006), 'Cognitive Catharsis in *The Caucasian Chalk Circle*', *Modern Drama* 49:1, 12–41.

Golden, Leon (1962) 'Catharsis', *TAPA* 93, 51–59.

—— (1973) 'The Purgation Theory of Catharsis', *Journal of Aesthetics and Art Criticism* 31, 473–91.

Guttman, Melinda Given (2001), *The Enigma of Anna O.: A Biography of Bertha Pappenheim* (London: Moyer Bell).

Halliwell, Stephen (1986), *Aristotle's Poetics* (Chapel Hill: U of North Carolina P).

Haupt, Stephan Odon (1915), *Wirkt die Tragödie auf das Gemüt oder den Verstand oder die Moralität der Zuschauer?* (Berlin: Leonard Simion).

Hirschmüller, Albrecht (1989) *The Life and Work of Josef Breuer: Physiology and Psychoanalysis* (New York: New York University Press).

Jackson, Stanley W. (1999), *Care of the Psyche: A History of Psychological Healing* (New Haven: Yale UP).

Jones, Ernest (1953), *The Life and Work of Sigmund Freud*, i (New York: Basic).

Lacan, Jacques (1975), *Le Séminaire: Livre XX*, Jacques-Alain Miller (ed.), (Paris: Seuil).

Laín Entralgo, Pedro (1970), *The Therapy of the Word in Classical Antiquity*, trans. and eds. L. J. Rather and John M. Sharp (New Haven: Yale UP).

Liddell, Henry George et al., (eds.) (1940), *A Greek-English Lexicon*, 9th Edition (Oxford: Clarendon).

Liébeault, August Ambroise (1866), *Du Sommeil et des états analogues* (Paris).

Lutz, Catherine (1988), *Unnatural Emotions: Everyday Sentiments on a Micronesian Atoll and Their Challenge to Western Theory* (Chicago: U of Chicago P).

—— (1995), 'Need, Nurturance, and the Emotions on a Pacific Atoll', in Joel Marks and Roger T. Ames (eds.), *Emotions in Asian Thought: A Dialogue in Comparative Philosophy* (Albany: SUNY P), 235–52.

Lyons, William (1980), *Emotion* (Cambridge: Cambridge UP).

Minturno, Antonio Sebastiano (1559), *De Poetica . . . libri sex* (Venice).

—— (1564), *L'Arte Poetica* (Venice).

Mitchell-Boyask, Robin N. (1994), 'Freud's Reading of Classical Literature and Classical Philology', in Sander L. Gilman et al. (eds.), *Reading Freud's Reading* (New York: New York UP), 23–46.

Moulinier, Louis (1952), *Le Pur et l'impur dans la pensée des Grecs* (Paris: Klincksieck).

Nussbaum, Martha C. (1986), *The Fragility of Goodness* (Cambridge: Cambridge UP).

Rosaldo, Michelle Z. (1980), *Knowledge and Passion: Ilongot Notions of Self and Social Life* (New York: Cambridge).

—— (1984), 'Toward an Anthropology of Self and Feeling', in Richard A. Shweder and Robert A. LeVine (eds.), *Culture Theory: Essays on Mind, Self, and Emotion* (New York: Cambridge UP), 137–57.

Sparshott, Francis (1983), 'The Riddle of *Katharsis*', in Eleanor Cook et al. (eds.), *Centre and Labyrinth: Essays in Honour of Northrop Frye* (Toronto: U of Toronto P), 14–37.

Spingarn, J. E. (1924), *A History of Literary Criticism in the Renaissance* (New York: Columbia UP).

Strachey, James (1957), 'Introduction', in Josef Breuer and Sigmund Freud, *Studies on Hysteria* (New York: Basic), ix–xxviii.

Sulloway, Frank J. (1979), *Freud, Biologist of the Mind* (New York: Basic).

Swales, Peter J. (1998), 'Freud's Master Hysteric', in Frederick C. Crews (ed.), *Unauthorized Freud: Doubters Confront a Legend* (New York: Viking), 22–33.

Tuke, Daniel Hack (1872), *Influence of the Mind upon the Body* (London).

Veith, Ilza (1965), *Hysteria: The History of a Disease* (Chicago: U of Chicago P).

Wetz, Willhelm (1897), *Shakespeare vom Standpunkte der vergleichenden Literaturgeschichte* (Hamburg).

White, Daniel R. (1984) 'A Sourcebook on the Catharsis Controversy', Diss. Florida State U.

Chapter 20

Linda Williams

MELODRAMA REVISED

MELODRAMA is the fundamental mode of popular American moving pictures. It is not a specific genre like the western or horror film; it is not a "deviation" of the classical realist narrative; it cannot be located primarily in woman's films, "weepies," or family melodramas—though it includes them. Rather, melodrama is a peculiarly democratic and American form that seeks dramatic revelation of moral and emotional truths through a dialectic of pathos and action. It is the foundation of the classical Hollywood movie.

American melodrama originates in the well-known theatrics and spectacles of the nineteenth-century stage, which many critics and historians have viewed as antithetical to cinematic realism. I will argue, however, that supposedly realist cinematic *effects*—whether of setting, action, acting or narrative motivation—most often operate in the service of melodramatic *affects*. We should not be fooled, then, by the superficial realism of popular American movies, by the use of real city streets for chases, or by the introduction of more complex psychological motivations for victims and villains. If emotional and moral registers are sounded, if a work invites us to feel sympathy for the virtues of beset victims, if the narrative trajectory is ultimately more concerned with a retrieval and staging of innocence than with the psychological causes of motives and action, then the operative mode is melodrama. In cinema the mode of melodrama defines a broad category of moving pictures that move us to pathos for protagonists beset by forces more powerful than they and who are perceived as victims. Since the rise of American melodrama on the mid-nineteenth-century stage, a relatively feminized victimhood has been identified with virtue and innocence. At least since Uncle Tom and Little Eva, the suffering victims of popular American stage and screen have been the protagonists endowed with the most moral authority.

In the present essay I set out the terms of a revised theory of a melodramatic mode—rather than the more familiar notion of the melodramatic genre—that seems crucial to any further consideration of popular American moving pictures. An initial survey of the status and place of melodrama in film studies serves as an explanation for the neglect of this basic mode.

The place of melodrama in film studies

In her insightful introduction to a volume of essays on melodrama, *Home Is Where the Heart Is: Studies in Melodrama and the Woman's Film*, Christine Gledhill tells us that film studies has conceived melodrama in "predominately pejorative terms."[1] From the turn of the century to the sixties, melodrama was the "anti-value for a critical field in which tragedy and realism became cornerstones of 'high' cultural value, needing protection from mass, 'melodramatic' entertainment" (5). Popular cinema was validated only as it seemed to diverge from melodramatic origins in works of humanist realism.

Gledhill notes that the rise of genre criticism in the sixties did little to recover the reputation of melodrama, partly because genre criticism was marked by defensiveness and partly because it focused on discrete genres whose iconography was recognizable at a glance. In the few places where melodrama was seen to have a visible generic existence—in the family melodrama and the woman's film—melodrama could offer neither the thematic and evolutionary coherence exhibited by, say, the western, nor sufficient cultural prestige to appeal to the cognoscenti—condemned as it was by association with a mass and, above all, "female audience" (6).

The two major strikes against melodrama were thus the related "excesses" of emotional manipulativeness and association with femininity. These qualities only began to be taken seriously when excess could be deemed ironic and thus subversive of the coherence of mainstream cinema. Thus, as Gledhill notes, melodrama was "redeemed" as a genre in film studies in the early seventies through a reading of the ironic melodramatic excesses located especially in the work of Douglas Sirk. "Through discovery of Sirk, a genre came into view" (7).

Sirk's gloriously overblown melodramas of the fifties—*Magnificent Obsession* (1954), *All That Heaven Allows* (1956), *Written on the Wind* (1957), *Imitation of Life* (1959)—were enthusiastically defended by seventies film critics and theorists, along with a range of other films by Nicholas Ray, Vincente Minnelli, and Elia Kazan, as scathing critiques of the family and of a repressed and perverse fifties normalcy. In 1972 Thomas Elsaesser's essay "Tales of Sound and Fury" made important links between Hollywood cinema and the heritage of European melodramatic forms. As Gledhill notes, the essay transcended its own formalist approach, suggesting that American cinema begins and rests within a melodramatic tradition.[2]

Unfortunately, however, the issue of the formative influence of melodrama was not pursued by Elsaesser or others. Gledhill insightfully points out that "to have pursued Elsaesser's line of investigation would have meant rethinking, rather than dismissing, the 'great tradition' of humanist realism. . . . In particular it would have meant rethinking both realism and the nineteenth-century novel in their relationship with melodrama" (8).

Film studies established a rigid polarity: on the one hand, a bourgeois, classical realist, acritical "norm," and on the other hand, an antirealist, melodramatic, critical "excess." In this way melodrama could never be investigated as a basic element of popular cinema, but only as an oppositional excess. More importantly, this so-excessive-as-to-be-ironic model rendered taboo the most crucial element of the study of melodrama: its capacity to generate emotion in audiences.

Critics of fifties family melodrama delighted in the way the repressed emotions of characters seemed to be "siphoned off" onto the vivid colors and mute gestures and general hysteria of the mise-en-scène, but they were strangely silent about the emotional reactions of audiences to all this hysteria induced by the mise-en-scène. It was almost as if there were a "bad" melodrama of manipulated, naively felt, feminine emotions and a "good" melodrama of ironical hysterical excess thought to be immune to the more pathetic emotions.[3]

As a way of surveying feminist film critics' approach-avoidance to affective response in the study of the melodramatic woman's film, I would like to summarize a debate that took place originally between E. Ann Kaplan and myself over a hypothetical female viewer's response to the melodramatic woman's film, *Stella Dallas* (King Vidor, 1937). My concern here is not to reanimate old arguments, but rather to restate what, in a veiled and coded way, this debate now seems to have really been about: women's attraction-repulsion to the pathos of virtuous suffering.

King Vidor's *Stella Dallas*, starring Barbara Stanwyck as the ambitious working-class woman whose daughter becomes her life, is an excruciatingly pathetic maternal melodrama of mother-daughter possession and loss. In 1984 I published an article entitled " 'Something Else Besides a Mother': *Stella Dallas* and the Maternal Melodrama" in *Cinema Journal*.[4] Uncomfortable with the "gaze is male" formulation of much feminist film theory of the time, which saw all mainstream cinema structured by male desire and a masculine subject position,[5] as well as with the exceptional, ironic status of what was then valued in Sirkian melodrama, I was interested in the construction of feminine viewing positions in more straightforwardly sentimental woman's films. In particular, I disagreed with E. Ann Kaplan's previously published reading of the film, which saw a female viewer who identified with Stella, the film's suffering mother protagonist, as acceding to the necessity for her sacrifice. Kaplan argued that the female spectator was rendered as passive and pathetic as Stella herself by the end of the film.[6]

Without abandoning the basic paradigm of a centered and unifying, distanced cinematic "gaze," I nevertheless borrowed concepts from Peter Brooks's study of late-eighteenth- and nineteenth-century stage melodrama to argue that *Stella Dallas* belonged to a melodramatic mode distinct from classical realism in its emphasis on the domestic sphere of powerless women and children protagonists whose only possible agency derives from the virtue of their suffering. "What happens," I asked, "when a mother and daughter, who are so closely identified that the usual distinctions between subject and object do not apply, take one another as their primary objects of desire?" And "what happens when the significant viewer of such a drama is also a woman?"[7]

My answer ran counter to Kaplan's and borrowed from an earlier essay by Christine Gledhill in which she noted that "there are spaces in which women, out of their socially constructed differences as women, can and do resist."[8] Maternal melodramas, I argued, not only address female audiences about issues of primary concern to women, but these melodramas have inscribed in them "reading positions" based upon the different ways women take on their identities under patriarchy—reading positions that result from the social fact of female mothering.[9]

At the pathos-filled end of the film, the viewer sees Stella looking through a picture window at her daughter, who is marrying into an upper-class milieu to which Stella herself will never belong. Outside the window in the rain, self-exiled from the ideal world within, Stella, the mother who gives up the one thing in the world dear to her, is nevertheless triumphant in her tears. Is the female viewer so identified with Stella's triumphant tears, I asked, that she has no ability to criticize or resist the patriarchal value system that makes her presence in her daughter's newly acquired social milieu excessive?

Because the end of the film so insistently frames the issue of female spectatorship—placing Stella like a movie spectator outside the window gazing at the daughter who is now lost to her—*Stella Dallas* seemed a crucial film. Kaplan argued that a female viewer was positioned by the film, like Stella herself, as powerless witness of a scene that excluded her. I argued that although this final scene functions to efface Stella, the female spectator does not necessarily acquiesce in the necessity of this sacrifice, nor does she identify solely with the effaced Stella at this final moment.

I argued, in other words, that there was room for some negotiation in a female viewing position that was animated by the contradiction of identifying both as a woman and a mother.[10] The crux of my argument, however, rested upon a fairly complex reinterpretation of psychoanalytic concepts of fetishistic disavowal. I claimed that the female spectator is as capable of experiencing the contradiction between knowledge and belief in an image as any healthily neurotic male viewer. However, in arguing that women spectators could be voyeurs and fetishists too, though with a difference, I unfortunately recuperated the monolithic gaze paradigm of spectatorship that I had wanted to escape. What seemed to be at issue was the question of spectatorial unity: could a female spectator be divided in her reactions to a work that was not ironically parodying the powerful maternal emotions of pride in the success of the child and, simultaneously, sorrow in loss? I answered, against Kaplan, that such division was possible, but the way I cast the division, as Brechtian distanciation and critique, avoided the more crucial and obvious question of spectatorial emotion in melodrama.

The quintessentially feminine emotion of pathos was viewed as a key agent of women's oppression by feminists in the early and mid-eighties. Anger was viewed by feminism as a liberating emotion, pathos as enslaving.[11] Viewer identification with pathetic suffering seemed only to invoke the dangerous specter of masochism, which seemed antithetical to a woman's quest to break out of patriarchal power and control. The entirely negative specter of masochism loomed large in Mary Ann Doane's brilliant 1987 study of the woman's film, The Desire to Desire. To Doane the excessive pathos of the woman's film always threatened to overwhelm the female spectator in a dangerously close masochistic "over-identification" with the victimized woman.[12] With the marked exception of Gledhill, none of the feminist critics to join directly or indirectly in this debate could conceive of a female spectator moved by the wedding spectacle on the other side of the window as anything but manipulated.[13] The only way I could retrieve what I sensed to be the importance of melodrama was to argue that such moving images also made us angry, that women were not their dupes; we were critical too. I wrote: "It is a terrible underestimation of the female viewer to presume that she is wholly seduced by a naive belief in these masochistic images. . . . For unlike tragedy, melodrama does not reconcile its audience to an inevitable suffering. Rather than raging against a fate that the audience has learned to accept, the female hero often accepts a fate that the audience at least partially questions."[14]

Though I still agree with this today, I am struck by the unwillingness to recognize the importance of melodramatic pathos—of being moved by a moving picture. Both drawn to and repelled by the spectacle of virtuous and pathetic suffering, feminist critics were torn: we wanted to properly condemn the abjection of suffering womanhood, yet in the almost loving detail of our growing analyses of melodramatic subgenres—medical discourse, gothic melodrama, romance melodrama, maternal melodrama—it was clear that something more than condemnation was taking place. An opposition to female suffering was certainly an important goal of feminism, but in the process of distinguishing our "properly" feminist distance from melodrama's emotions, we failed to confront the importance of pathos itself and the fact that a surprising power lay in identifying with victimhood.[15]

It was not simply that feminist critics who offered analyses of woman's films were divided over the effects of pathos on audiences; we were convinced that pathos was, in itself, an excess of feeling that threatened to overwhelm the emerging liberated woman. With the great advantage of hindsight, I would say that the entire Stella Dallas debate was over what it meant for a woman viewer to cry at the end of the film. Did the emotion swallow us up, or did we have room within it to think? Could we, in other words, think both with and through our bodies in our spectating capacities as witnesses to abjection? And wasn't this whole debate carried out as if men never cried at the movies?[16] The persistent error in all this early work on melodramatic woman's films was the idea that these were exceptional texts, both as melodramas and as melodramas with a specific address to women viewers. Strong emotions that can move audiences to tears are not the special province of women, but of a melo-dramatic "feminization" that, as Ann Douglas long ago noted, has been a persistent feature of American popular culture at least since the mid-nineteenth century.[17] If the sad-ending maternal melodrama with its pathos centered on the lost connection to the mother seemed the quintessential example of all melodrama, then the thing to do would be to explore this pathos in relation to a range of other popular films rather than to bracket it as melo-dramatic excess. Instead, we perpetuated the notion that melodrama was a minority genre in which the excessive and archaic nineteenth-century emotions of women anachronistically flourished.

Once again it was Christine Gledhill who saw that the real problem in our thinking about the exceptional nature of melodrama was inextricable from prevalent theories of the classical realist text. Melodrama needs to be understood, Gledhill argued, as an aesthetic and epistemological mode distinct from (if related to) realism, having different purposes, and deploying different strategies, modes of address, forms of engagement and identification.[18] Borrowing from Peter Brooks's study of the nineteenth-century novel's inheritance from the melodramatic stage, Gledhill argued that melodrama emerged as a response to an implicit gap in bourgeois epistemology.[19] Where realism ignores these contradictions in its con-fidence in the causal explanations of the human sciences, modernism seeks obsessively to expose them. Melodrama, however, takes a different approach: "it both insists on the realities of life in bourgeois democracy—the material parameters of lived experience, individual personality, the fundamental psychic relations of family life—and, in an implicit recognition of the limitations of the conventions of representation . . . proceeds to insist on, force into an aesthetic presence, desires for identity, value, and fullness of signification beyond the powers of language to supply."[20] As a result, melodrama is structured upon the "dual recognition" of how things are and how they should be. In melodrama there is a moral, wish-fulfilling impulse towards the achievement of justice that gives American popu-lar culture its strength and appeal as the powerless yet virtuous seek to return to the "innocence" of their origins.

In thus turning to melodrama—not as a genre exceptional to a classical realist norm, but as a more pervasive mode with its own rhetoric and aesthetic—Gledhill embraces melodrama's central feature of pathos and "solves" the problem of its apparent monopathy. She argues that if a melodramatic character appeals to our sympathy, it is because pathos involves us in assessing suffering in terms of our privileged knowledge of its nature and causes. Pathos is thus "intensified by the misrecognition of a sympathetic protagonist because the audience has privileged knowledge of the 'true' situation."[21] Gledhill shows, for example, how scene after scene of *Stella Dallas* permits the viewer to see a character misconstruing the meaning of an act or gesture. These scenes work, she argues, because the audience is outside a particular point of view but participating in it with a privileged knowledge of the total constellation. Pathos in the spectator is thus never merely a matter of losing oneself in "over-identification." It is never a matter of simply mimicking the emotion of the protagonist, but, rather, a complex negotiation between emotions and between emotion and thought.

The understanding of melodrama has been impeded by the failure to acknowledge the complex tensions between different emotions as well as the relation of thought to emotion. The overly simplistic notion of the "monopathy" of melodramatic characters—the idea that each character in melodrama sounds a single emotional note that is in turn simply mimicked by the viewer—has impeded the serious study of how complexly we can be "moved." Certainly Stella, smiling through her tears, is the very embodiment of internally conflicted and complex emotions. If pathos is crucial to melodrama, it is always in tension with other emotions and, as I hope to show in the following, is in a constant dynamic relation with that other primary staple of American popular movies: action—the spectacular rescues, chases, and fights that augment, prolong, and conclude pathos.

The question to put to *Stella Dallas*, and by extension to the "subgenre" of the woman's film, and finally to the pervasive melodramatic mode of American cinema, is thus not whether it is complicit with or resistant to dominant, patriarchal ideology.[22] All American melodrama is produced, and operates within, dominant patriarchal, western, capitalist discourses and ideologies. However, these discourses and ideologies are frequently contradictory and constantly in flux. Popular American movies have been popular because of their ability to seem to resolve basic contradictions at a mythic level—whether conflicts between garden and civilization typical of the western, or between love and ambition typical of the biopic, the family melodrama, and the gangster film.[23]

The most fruitful approach to melodrama would thus not be to argue over the progressive or regressive nature of particular texts for particular viewers—whether women, gays, lesbians, African Americans, Native Americans, Italian Americans, Jewish Americans, and so on. Rather, we should do as Gledhill suggests and has magnificently begun to do herself: pick up the threads of a general study of melodrama as a broadly important cultural form inherited from the nineteenth-century stage, in tension with and transformed by realism and the more realistic techniques of cinema, yet best understood *as melodrama*, not failed tragedy or inadequate realism.

Melodrama should be viewed, then, not as an excess or an aberration but in many ways as the typical form of American popular narrative in literature, stage, film, and television. It is the best example of American culture's (often hypocritical) notion of itself as the locus of innocence and virtue. If we want to confront the centrality of melodrama to American moving-image culture, we must first turn to the most basic forms of melodrama, and not only to a subghetto of woman's films, to seek out the dominant features of an American melodramatic mode. For if melodrama was misclassified as a sentimental genre for women, it is partly because other melodramatic genres such as the western and gangster films, which received early legitimacy in film study, had already been constructed, as Christine Gledhill notes, in relation to supposedly masculine cultural values.[24]

Because this pat division between a presumably realist sphere of masculine action and a presumably melodramatic sphere of feminine emotion was not challenged, narrative cinema as a whole has been theorized as a realist, inherently masculine, medium whose "classical" features are supposedly anathema to its melodramatic infancy and childhood.[25] Whereas silent cinema has always been recognized as melodrama at some level, the "essential" art and language of cinema has not. Rather, melodrama has been viewed either as that which cinema has grown up out of or that to which it sometimes regresses.

However, as both Steve Neale and Christine Gledhill note, exhibition categories continued to assert the melodramatic base of most genres well into the sound era. The names of these categories are themselves revealing: western melodrama, crime melodrama, sex melodrama, backwoods melodrama, romantic melodrama, and so on.[26] A glance through the *AFI Catalog of Features, 1921–1930*, reveals an even more remarkable proliferation of categories of melodrama: stunt melodrama, society melodrama, mystery melodrama, rural melodrama, action melodrama, crook melodrama, underworld melodrama, and even comedy melodrama, as well as just plain melodrama. Though one might attribute this proliferation of types of melodrama to the predominance of the silent era in this period, a look at a more recent AFI volume—that covering 1961–1970—shows that many of these categories have persisted at least in the eyes of archivists and catalogists. In fact, in addition to nine of the preceding categories, this period even lists a new one, science fiction melodrama.[27] What is striking in these examples is the way the noun *melodrama* functions as a basic mode of storytelling. The term indicates a form of exciting, sensational, and, above all, moving story that can be further differentiated by specifications of setting or milieu (such as *society melodrama*) or genre (such as *western melodrama*). It is this basic sense of melodrama as a modality of narrative with a high quotient of pathos and action to which we need to attend if we are to confront the most fundamental appeal of movies.

The melodramatic mode: excess or norm?

Perhaps the most important single work contributing to the rehabilitation of the term *melodrama* as a cultural form has been Peter Brook's *The Melodramatic Imagination: Balzac, Henry James, Melodrama, and the Mode of Excess*. Brooks offers a valuable appreciation of the historical origins of the nineteenth-century melodramatic project. This appreciation is still the best grounding for an understanding of its carryover into twentieth-century mass culture. Brooks's real project was not to study melodrama per se but to understand the melodramatic elements informing the fiction of Honoré de Balzac and Henry James. In the process, however, he sought out the roots of the melodramatic imagination in the French popular theater and offered important reasons for its rise and persistence.

Brooks's greatest advantage in this project may have been his ignorance of film theory and criticism. Unlike film critics who have seen melodrama as an anachronism to be overcome or subverted, Brooks takes it seriously as a quintessentially modern (though not modernist) form arising out of a particular historical conjuncture: the postrevolutionary, post-Enlightenment, postsacred world where traditional imperatives of truth and morality had been violently questioned and yet in which there was still a need to forge some semblance of truth and morality.[28]

Brooks's central thesis is that, in the absence of a moral and social order linked to the sacred, and in the presence of a reduced private and domestic sphere that has increasingly become the entire realm of personal significance, a theatrical form of sensation developed that carried the burden of expressing what Brooks calls the " 'moral occult,' the domain of operative spiritual values which is both indicated within and masked by the surface of reality"(5). This quest for a hidden moral legibility is crucial to all melodrama.

The theatrical function of melodrama's big sensation scenes was to be able to put forth a moral truth in gesture and to picture what could not be fully spoken in words. Brooks shows that the rise of melodrama was linked to the ban on speech in unlicensed French theaters. Usually, the unspeakable truth revealed in the sensation scene is the revelation of who is the true villain, who the innocent victim. The revelation occurs as a spectacular, moving sensation—that is, it is felt as sensation and not simply registered as ratiocination in the cause-effect logic of narrative—because it shifts to a different register of signification, often bypassing language altogether. Music, gesture, pantomime, and, I would add, most forms of sustained physical action performed without dialogue, are the most familiar elements of these sensational effects.

Brooks points to Guilbert de Pixérécourt's 1818 melodrama *La Fille de l'exilé*, in which a sixteen-year-old Siberian girl travels to Moscow to seek pardon from the czar for her exiled father. On the way she falls into the hands of Ivan, her father's persecutor, himself now threatened by ferocious Tartars. The girl saves Ivan in a big sensation scene by holding the cross of her virtuous dead mother over his head. The Tartars shrink back under the power of this holy sign. But the sensation does not end there. Ivan tells the Tartars that the poor girl who protects him is actually the devoted daughter of the man he once persecuted: "Ah! such generosity overwhelms me! I lack the words to express . . . All I can do is admire you and bow my head before you." In a "spontaneous movement" the Tartars form a semicircle around the girl and fall on their knees, astonished at her goodness. The sensation so grandiosely orchestrated here is that of the recognition of virtue by the less virtuous (24–25). Melodramatic denouement is typically some version of this public or private recognition of virtue prolonged in the frozen tableau whose picture speaks more powerfully than words. Each play is not only the drama of a moral dilemma but also the drama of a moral sentiment—usually of a wronged innocence—seeking to say its name but unable, in a postsacred universe, to speak directly (43). Despite the fact that Brooks's study works hard to give melodrama its due rather than to treat it as failed tragedy or as realism manqué, his subtitle, *The Mode of Excess*, indicates that he too views melodrama as a mode in excess of a more classical norm. Instead of tracing the importance of theatrical melodrama in popular culture where it has most powerfully moved audiences, Brooks traces its influence on the "higher art" bourgeois novel, first in Honoré de Balzac, then in the subtle, unspoken revelations of guilt and innocence so crucial to the novels of Henry James. His real interest is thus in how melodrama is subtly embedded in the canon of the nineteenth-century realist novel.

We have already seen how Christine Gledhill solves the problem of Brooks's opposition between realism and melodrama by arguing that melodrama is always grounded in what, for its day, is a strong element of realism: "Taking its stand in the material world of everyday reality and lived experience, and acknowledging the limitations of the conventions of language and representation, it proceeds to force into aesthetic presence identity, value and plenitude of meaning."[29] In other words, Gledhill shows that melodrama is grounded in the conflicts and troubles of everyday, contemporary reality. It seizes upon the social problems of this reality—problems such as illegitimacy, slavery, racism, labor struggles, class division, disease, nuclear annihilation, even the Holocaust. All the afflictions and injustices of the modern, post-Enlightenment world are dramatized in melodrama. Part of the excitement of the form is the genuine turmoil and timeliness of the issues it takes up and the popular debate it can generate when it dramatizes a new controversy or issue. Such was the case when the controversy surrounding the humanity of slaves arrived on the scene in popular melodrama in 1852. Such was the case more recently as homophobia, persecution of the Irish by the British, and persecution of the Jews by the Germans came on the scene in three of the most noted films in the competition for the 1993 Academy Awards: *Philadelphia* (Jonathan Demme), *In the Name of the Father* (Jim Sheridan), and *Schindler's List* (Steven Spielberg).

Where melodrama differs from realism is in its will to force the status quo to yield signs of moral legibility within the limits of the "ideologically permissible."[30] Anyone who has ever taught Greek tragedy to college students knows the difficulty of explaining the concept of tragic fate to them. Try as one might to explain that Oedipus or Agamemnon are not actually punished for wrongdoing when they meet their fates, American students imbued with the popular values of melodrama cannot help but see these fates as punishment for antidemocratic, "over-weening" pride. Thus Americans read Greek tragedy melodramatically.

The British, to some extent, and the French, to a greater extent, have long traditions of classical tragedy that lead them to believe that the "norms" of literature and theater are antithetical to melodrama. Americans, however, have a different set of norms. Whether we look at the novelistic romances of Hawthorne, Stowe, or Twain, the popular theater of Belasco, Aiken, Daly, or Boucicault, the silent films of Griffith, DeMille, or Borzage, or the sound films of Ford, Coppola, or Spielberg, the most common thread running among them is not merely a lack of realism or an "excess" of sentiment, but the combined function of realism, sentiment, spectacle, and action in effecting the recognition of a hidden or misunderstood virtue. Hawthorne's Hester Prynne, Stowe's Uncle Tom, Twain's Jim and Huck, Ford's searcher, and Spielberg's E.T., Elliot, and Schindler all share the common function of revealing moral good in a world where virtue has become hard to read.

Let us consider for a moment two highly melodramatic scenes in two of the Oscar-winning films mentioned previously: the moment in *Philadelphia* when Andrew

Becket (Tom Hanks) bares his torso to the jury to reveal the marks of skin lesions on his AIDS-stricken body, and the moment toward the end of *Schindler's List* when Schindler (Liam Neeson) emotionally breaks down to reveal his regret at not having rescued more Jews. Both moments are pathetic; both reveal their heroes in instants of weakness and vulnerability that become emblematic of their moral goodness, and both are moments when other people recognize and bear witness to a goodness that is inextricably linked to suffering. The fragile, disease-wracked body of the gay man "on trial," the powerful body of Schindler cowed and speechless in this singular moment of weakness before the Jews he has rescued, share the mute pathos inherent to melodrama.

Both scenes can also easily be criticized as false to a realist representation of the characters. Hanks is portrayed, against gay stereotype, as far too untheatrical a character to find emotional satisfaction in revealing his body in this way; Schindler is portrayed as a man who would never stop to reflect upon the moral good or bad of what he has done—this, indeed, is the genius of Thomas Keneally's novel, based on highly distanced, factual reportage. There is no such moment of moral self-reflection and recognition in Keneally's novel. Yet the theatrical displays of virtue constitute the key emotional highlights of both films and, though false to realism, are melodramatically viable.

Much of the derision of melodrama in American popular culture derives from the sense that such emotional displays of virtue necessarily cheapen a more pure and absolute (and also sternly masculine) morality. Ann Douglas's study of nineteenth-century American culture traces the long process by which a rigorous Calvinist morality was supplanted by what she views as a cheaply sentimental "feminization" of American culture carried out by ministers and lady novelists. Using Little Eva's death in Harriet Beecher Stowe's *Uncle Tom's Cabin* as her own melodramatic point of departure, Douglas argues that a wholesale debasement of American culture took place in the idealization of feminine qualities of piety, virtue, and passive suffering.

Douglas opposes a popular literature of "excessive" feminine sentimentalism to a high canonical literature—Melville, Thoreau, Whitman—which was masculine and active but never popular. Her study of the feminization of nineteenth-century American culture is an explanation of how a masculine "high" culture was supplanted by a feminine "low" culture. Douglas blames the increased anti-intellectualism and consumerism of American culture, as well as the ensuing backlash of popular culture masculinization, on a facile cultural feminism.[31] Rather than blame the excesses of feminization, however, we need to investigate the reasons for its popularity: the search for moral legibility in an American context in which the old Calvinist moral certainty was waning. Mass culture melodrama in novels, plays, and later in film and television has been the most important cultural form to fill that void. The end of Calvinist morality thus functions much like the end of the sacred in Brooks's model. In a country with a much less established tradition of high art and letters than Europe, it is not surprising that melodrama filled this void so thoroughly. Another way of putting this would be to say that whereas England had Dickens, and France had Hugo—both popular melodramatists who were also in a sense "great" writers—America had Stowe and later a host of melodramatic filmmakers: Griffith, Ford, Vidor, Coppola, Demme, Spielberg, and so on.

We are diverted, therefore, from the significance of melodrama if we pay too much attention to what has been condemned as its excessive emotionality and theatricality. Theatrical acting and Manichaean polarities are not the essence of this form. They are the means to something more important: the achievement of a felt good, the merger—perhaps even the compromise—of morality and feeling.

Recent critics have attempted to recuperate emotionality and sensationalism from the status of excess. Tom Gunning has rehabilitated the term *attraction* in order to address the emotional and sensational side of cinema spectatorship. Gunning borrows the term from

Sergei Eisenstein's celebration of spectacles with particularly strong "sensual or psychological impact" and the ability to aggressively grab and move spectators.[32] The acknowledgment of the existence of a "cinema of attractions" different from the linear narrative of the "classical" realist text has fruitfully called attention to the spectacle side of cinematic visual pleasures in early cinema.

However, when the term simply posits the existence of an ideological "other"—whether spectacle or spectator—who "escapes" the dominant ideology of the classical, it remains implicated in the putative dominance of the "classical." Janet Staiger argues convincingly that the notion of a war between working class attraction or sensation on the one hand and bourgeois cause-effect narrative with a bourgeois constituency on the other is an over-simplification. Staiger deftly negotiates between those historians who have placed too large a claim on the otherness of cinematic attractions vis-à-vis the classical narrative and those who, like her former collaborators David Bordwell and Kristen Thompson, have argued that "narrative continuity and clarity are the only means of pleasure [audiences] seek during an evening at the theater or movies."[33] Demolishing claims that even the quite primitive 1903 Edwin S. Porter version of *Uncle Tom's Cabin* was a pure spectacle of unreadable cause-effect—since all classes of audience knew the story that lay behind the tableau and since even the tableaux were arranged in a cross-cut manner—Staiger claims that the film "interlaces spectacle with a tight crisscrossing of two subplots for a final, *if melodramatic*, climax. Narrativity and visual spectacle existed as available sites of affective response for all spectators of various classes" (emphasis mine).[34] Staiger offers an important corrective to the concept of a purely linear cause-effect narrative, noting that narrativity and visual spectacle work together to produce affective response. However, as with Brooks and Gunning, the notion of excess still lurks in the telling "if melodramatic" in the preceding quotation, as if *Uncle Tom's Cabin* could ever not be melodramatic. We must study melodrama as melodrama, not as a form that wants to be something else.

Another critic to address the vexed question of the classic versus the melodramatic is Rick Altman. Against Bordwell, Thompson, and Staiger's notion of the dominance of the classical Hollywood cinema, Altman argues that melodrama is more deeply "embedded" within even our most hallowed notion of the classic text than has been realized.[35] For example, he argues that the notion of the "classic" in the "classical Hollywood cinema" is a linear chain of psychologically based causes leading from an initial question or problem to a final, well-motivated solution. According to Bordwell, Thompson, and Staiger, this classical paradigm of narrative logic in which events are subordinated to personal causes of psychologically defined individual characters became the standardized mode of production for the feature film.[36]

Ephemeral spectacle, showmanship, and moments of "artistic motivation," in which audiences admire the show rather than get caught up in the cause-effect linear progress toward narrative resolution, are treated as exceptional moments of what Russian formalist critics call "laying bare the device." Such moments of "flagrant" display are for Bordwell, Thompson, and Staiger of *The Classical Hollywood Cinema* exceptional, and regressive, throwbacks to vaudeville, melodrama, and other spectacle-centered entertainments, though sometimes they are quasi-legitimized by genre.[37] For Bordwell et al. it is the nineteenth-century well-made play that is the major theatrical influence on classical narrative.

The notion that the classical Hollywood narrative subordinates spectacle, emotion, and attraction to the logic of personal causality and cause and effect assumes that the "action" privileged by the form is not spectacular. However, we have only to look at what's playing at the local multiplex to realize that the familiar Hollywood feature of prolonged climactic action is, and I would argue has always been, a melodramatic spectacle (and Gunning's notion of attraction) no matter how goal-driven or embedded within narrative it may be.

Nothing is more sensational in American cinema than the infinite varieties of rescues, accidents, chases, and fights. These "masculine" action-centered multiple climaxes may be scrupulously motivated or wildly implausible depending on the film. However, though usually faithful to the laws of motion and gravity, this realism of action should not fool us into thinking that the dominant mode of such films is realism. Nor should the virility of action itself fool us into thinking that it is not melodramatic.

Altman argues that film scholars have not attended to the popular theater as the original source of these spectacles. He rightly chides film historians and scholars for skipping over such works in their rush to link the emerging film to the realist novel. He also points out that this repression of popular theater has the effect of denying Hollywood cinema its fundamental connection to popular melodramatic tradition. "Unmotivated events, rhythmic montage, highlighted parallelism, overlong spectacles—these are the excesses in the classical narrative system that alert us to the existence of a competing logic, a second voice."[38] To Altman, these excesses give evidence of an "embedded melodramatic mode that subtends classical narrative from *Clarissa* to *Casablanca*." He warns that we should recognize the possibility that such excesses may themselves be organized as a system.[39] I would argue further that if we are to understand melodrama as a system, then we would do well to eliminate the term *excess* from attempts to describe this systematicity. For like Brooks, Altman too easily cedes to the dominance of the classical, realist model with melodrama as its excess. In this model, melodrama remains an archaic throwback rather than, as in Gledhill's model, a fully developed third alternative to both realist and modernist narrative.

Film study needs an even bolder statement: not that melodrama is a submerged, or embedded, tendency within realist narrative—which it certainly can be—but that it has more often itself been the dominant form of popular moving-image narrative. The supposed excess is much more often the mainstream, though it is often not acknowledged as such because melodrama consistently decks itself out in the trappings of realism and the modern (and now, the postmodern). What Altman refers to as the dialectic of the melodramatic mode of narrative in American popular culture is nothing less than the process whereby melodrama sheds its old-fashioned values, acting styles, and ideologies to gain what Gledhill calls the "imprimateur of 'realism' " while it still delivers the melodramatic experience.[40]

Thus the basic vernacular of American moving pictures consists of a story that generates sympathy for a hero who is also a victim and that leads to a climax that permits the audience, and usually other characters, to recognize that character's moral value. This climax revealing the moral good of the victim can tend in one of two directions: either it can consist of a paroxysm of pathos (as in the woman's film or family melodrama variants) or it can take that paroxysm and channel it into the more virile and action-centered variants of rescue, chase, and fight (as in the western and all the action genres).

Much more often melodrama combines pathos and action. *Philadelphia* and *Schindler's List* combine both through the device of splitting the more active hero function (in the person of Schindler and the black, originally homophobic, lawyer played by Denzel Washington) from that of the more passive, suffering victims (Andrew Becket and the none-too-individualized Jews). The important point, however, is that action-centered melodrama is never without pathos, and pathos-centered melodrama is never without at least some action.

But virtuous sufferer and active hero can also be combined in the same person. Stella Dallas throws herself quite actively into the self-sacrificial task of alienating her daughter's affections. She also physically pushes through the crowd in order to effect the ultimate sacrifice of seeing but not participating in her daughter's wedding. Rambo—to cite a stereotypically masculine, action-oriented example—suffers multiple indignities and pathetically suffers in ways that elicit audience empathy before he begins his prolonged rescue-revenge.

Big "sensation" scenes, whether of prolonged "feminine" pathos or prolonged "masculine" action, or mixtures of both, do not interrupt the logical cause-effect progress of a narrative toward conclusion. More often, it is these spectacles of pathos and action that are served by the narrative. As American melodrama developed from stage to screen, and from silence to sound, it frequently instituted more realistic causations and techniques for the display of both pathos and action, but it never ceased to serve the primary ends of displaying both.

To study the relation between pathos and action is to see that there is no pure isolation of pathos in woman's films nor of action in the male action genres. If, as Peter Brooks argues, melodrama is most centrally about moral legibility and the assigning of guilt and innocence in a postsacred, post-Enlightenment world where moral and religious certainties have been erased, then pathos and action are the two most important means to the achievement of moral legibility.

An early model in silent cinema for this pathos, self-sacrificing side of melodrama is Griffith's *Broken Blossoms* (1919), where the Chinese victim-hero proves his virtue by not taking sexual advantage of the waif he befriends. His attempt to save her from the clutches of her brutal father comes too late, however, and in the pathos-filled ending, in which a virtuous heroine in need of rescue does not get saved in the nick of time, he can only lay out her body and join her in death. This pathos side of melodrama continues in a range of sad-ending melodramas: in most woman's films, in many family melodramas, in sad musicals in which song and dance do not save the day—*Applause* (1929), *Hallelujah* (1929), *A Star is Born* (1954, 1976)—and in "social problem" films without optimistic endings, such as *I Am a Fugitive from a Chain Gang* (1932) or *You Only Live Once* (1937). It also continues in biopics such as *Silkwood* (1983) or *Malcolm X* (1992). In these films, victim-heroes, following in the footsteps of the nineteenth-century melodrama's Uncle Tom and Little Eva, achieve recognition of their virtue through the more passive "deeds" of suffering or self-sacrifice.

The action side of the melodramatic mode finds its silent cinema prototype in Griffith's *The Birth of a Nation* (1915) and *Way Down East* (1920). It is continued in most of the male action genres—westerns, gangster films, war films, cop films, and Clint Eastwood films—as well as happy musicals and social problem films in which more active hero-victims either solve problems through action, as in *Salt of the Earth* (1953) and *Norma Rae* (1979), or are themselves rescued from some fix. In these films the suffering of the victim-hero is important for the establishment of moral legitimacy, but suffering is less extended and ultimately gives way to action. Similarly the recognition of virtue is at least partially achieved through the performance of deeds. Here pathos mixes with other emotions: suspense, fear, anxiety, anger, laughter, and so on, experienced in the rescues, chases, gunfights, fistfights, and spaceship fights of the various action genres.

Obviously there is also a powerful gender and racial component to these two poles of melodrama: the "Yellow man" in *Broken Blossoms*, like his prototype Uncle Tom, is highly feminized and relegated to passive forms of action. Women and minorities traditionally suffer the most and act the least in melodrama. Yet there are notable exceptions. Eliza, the mulatta slave who, unlike Tom in *Uncle Tom's Cabin*, escapes across the ice floes of the Ohio river, is masculinized via action just as Tom is feminized through passive suffering.

Critics and historians of moving images have often been blind to the forest of melodrama because of their attention to the trees of genre. For example, the *Rambo* films were very quickly assimilated into the specific genre of the Vietnam films but have not been much considered as the male action melodramas they so clearly are.[41] Yet a quick look at the first two films in the series, *First Blood* (1982) and *Rambo: First Blood Part II* (1985), can help us to see the much more important influence of the mode of melodrama as a means of "solving" problems of moral legitimacy.

In the first film John Rambo (Sylvester Stallone), a traumatized Vietnam vet, goes on a rampage in a small northwestern town where he has come to find a buddy from the war. The film ends on a spectacular display of pathos as Rambo breaks down and cries in the arms of his former commander. Weeping over a multitude of losses—the loss of the war, the loss of buddies, the loss of innocence—Rambo is presented entirely as a victim of a government that would not let him win. *Rambo: First Blood Part II*, the more wildly popular sequel to this film, rechannels this pathos into action as Rambo is given his chance to "win this time." But even the virile action-orientation of the sequel is premised upon our continued perception of Rambo as a virtuous victim whose only motive is a melodramatic desire to return to the innocence of an unproblematic love of country and the simple demand for that love's return: "for our country to love us as much as we love it."

Thus even the sequel works hard to establish the pathos of Rambo's victim status; it begins with Rambo suffering silently on a chain gang. *Rambo* has been justly derided as representing the height of American bad conscience—even false consciousness—about the Vietnam War. But if we want to criticize *Rambo*, or for that matter the rash of films from *The Green Berets* and *The Deer Hunter* to *Platoon* and *Casualties of War* lined up on both sides of the Vietnam fiasco, we do well to see that what makes them tick is precisely their ability to address the moral dilemma of bad conscience, to reconfigure victims and villains. What makes them tick is thus not simply their action-adventure exploits but the activation of such exploits within a melodramatic mode struggling to "solve" the overwhelming moral burden of having been the "bad guys" in a lost war. The greater the historical burden of guilt, the more pathetically and the more actively the melodrama works to recognize and regain a lost innocence.

In its own way, *Schindler's List* represents a more respectable and serious but no less melodramatic example of the impulse to regain a lost innocence vis-à-vis the guilt of the Holocaust. The venal Schindler ultimately relieves the rest of us—Americans and Germans alike—of the historical burden of guilt, not because he was the exceptional man who acted when others did not, but because he was so much the ordinary, materialistic businessman. Schindler's rescue of over a thousand Jews also rescues the potential moral good of all ordinary people who played along with the Nazis.

This may sound as if I am equating melodrama with the most egregious false consciousness. In one sense I am. Melodrama is by definition the retrieval of an absolute innocence and good in which most thinking people do not put much faith. However, what we think and what we feel at the "movies" are often two very different things. We go to the movies not to think but to be moved. In a postsacred world, melodrama represents one of the most significant, and deeply symptomatic, ways we negotiate moral feeling.

Steven Spielberg and George Cosmatos (*Rambo*'s director) make us "feel good" about the Holocaust and Vietnam by rewriting the primary scenario of destruction and devastation with the historically quite fanciful (even if one of them is true) rescues of helpless victims (Jews in *Schindler's List;* MIAs in *Rambo*). But even if no rescue is possible, as in the case of Spike Lee's *Malcolm X*, which strictly observes the facts of Malcolm's assassination, the film is recognizably melodramatic in its recognition of innocence. What counts in melodrama is the feeling of righteousness, achieved through the sufferings of the innocent. This, ultimately, is why the movie's Schindler must finally break character and suffer for the insufficiencies of his actions. Suffering gives him the moral recognition that melodrama—not realism—requires. Without it, Schindler is merely heroic.

Westerns, war films, and Holocaust films, no less than woman's films, family melodramas, and biopics, participate, along with any drama whose outcome is the recognition of virtue, in the melodramatic mode of American film. Film criticism may do well to shift from the often myopic approach to the superficial coherence of given genres and toward the deeper coherence of melodrama.

Notes

1   Christine Gledhill, "The Melodramatic Field: An Investigation," in *Home Is Where the Heart Is: Studies in Melodrama and the Woman's Film*, ed. Gledhill (London: BFI, 1987), 5.

2   Thomas Elsaesser, "Tales of Sound and Fury: Observations on the Family Melodrama," *Monogram 4* (1975): 1–15. Reprinted in Gledhill, *Home*, and in Marcia Landy, ed. *Imitations of Life: A Reader on Film and Television Melodrama* (Detroit: Wayne State University Press, 1991).

3   See, for example, Geoffrey Nowell-Smith, "Minnelli and Melodrama," *Screen* 18, no. 2 (summer 1977): 113–18. Reprinted in Gledhill, *Home*, and in Landy, *Imitations*. Christine Gledhill comments on this division by noting the effective creation of two audiences of melodrama, "one which is implicated, identifies and weeps, and one which, seeing through such involvement, distances itself. The fact that . . . the first is likely to be female and the other male was not remarked on" (Gledhill, "The Melodramatic Field," 12).

4   Linda Williams, " 'Something Else Besides a Mother': *Stella Dallas* and the Maternal Melodrama," *Cinema Journal* 24, no. 1 (fall 1984): 2–27. Reprinted in Gledhill, *Home*, and in Landy, *Imitations*.

5   See Laura Mulvey, "Visual Pleasure and Narrative Cinema," *Screen* 16, no. 2 (autumn 1975): 6–18. Reprinted in Mulvey, *Visual and Other Pleasures* (Bloomington: Indiana University Press, 1989). See also Mary Ann Doane, *The Desire to Desire: The Woman's Film of the 1940s* (Bloomington: Indiana University Press, 1987); E. Ann Kaplan, *Woman and Film: Both Sides of the Camera* (New York: Methuen, 1983).

6   Williams, "Something Else," 5.

7   Ibid.

8   Gledhill, "Recent Developments in Feminist Film Criticism," *Quarterly Review of Film Studies 3*, no. 4 (1978). Revised and reprinted in Mary Ann Doane, Patricia Mellencamp, and Linda Williams, eds., *Re-Vision: Essays in Feminist Film Criticism* (Frederick, Md.: University Publications of America, 1984), 42.

9   Williams, "Something Else," 5.

10   Christine Gledhill has fruitfully used the term *negotiation* to describe the way audiences do not conform to the supposedly rigidly prescribed viewing positions described in feminist "gaze theory." "Pleasurable Negotiations," in *Female Spectators: Looking at Film and Television*, ed. E. Deidre Pribram (New York: Verso, 1988).

11   Later, the investigation of masochistic pleasures in looking would prove a fertile, if perhaps overly reactive, alternative to the lock-step of the sadistic-voyeuristic male-gaze paradigm. See Gaylin Studlar, *In the Realm of Pleasure: Von Sternberg, Dietrich and the Masochistic Aesthetic* (Urbana: University of Illinois Press, 1988); see also Kaja Silverman, ed., *Male Subjectivity at the Margins* (New York: Routledge, 1992) and Carol J. Clover, *Men, Women, and Chainsaws* (Princeton: Princeton University Press, 1992).

12   Doane, *The Desire to Desire*.

13   Those who joined the debate include Patrice Petro and Caryl Flinn, "Dialogue," *Cinema Journal 25*, no. 1 (fall 1985); Jackie Byers, *All That Hollywood Allows: Re-Reading Gender in 1950s Melodrama* (Chapel Hill: University of North Carolina Press, 1991), 166–209.

14   Williams, "Something Else," 22.

15   This paradoxical power of the victim seems one of the great unexamined moral forces of American culture and one that is inextricable from our highly litigious legal system. To suffer innocently, to be the victim of an abusive power, is to gain moral authority, to become a kind of hero, no matter how pathetic, from Uncle Tom to Rodney King, from the helpless and unfriended victim of the nineteenth-century melodrama to Erik and Lyle Menendez.

16   This assumption that men don't cry, and are not even invited to cry by contemporary melodrama, seems particularly specious given the increasing number of film and television narratives focused on male victim-heroes. Even when these victim-heroes are encased in fantastically muscular "hard bodies," even when the narrative empowers them to fight and win (as in the *Rambo* and *Die Hard* series), the bulk of these films pivot upon melodramatic moments of masculine pathos usually ignored by critics who emphasize the action and violence. And when the victim-hero doesn't win, the pathos of his suffering seems perfectly capable of engendering what Thomas Schatz (in private conversation) has termed a good "guy cry." See, for example, films as diverse as *A River Runs through It* (Robert Redford, 1992) and *Philadelphia* (Jonathan Demme, 1993).

17   See Ann Douglas, *The Feminization of American Culture* (New York: Avon, 1977).

18   Christine Gledhill, "Dialogue," *Cinema Journal* 25, no. 4 (summer 1986): 44–48.

19   Peter Brooks, *The Melodramatic Imagination: Balzac, Henry James, Melodrama, and the Mode of Excess* (New Haven: Yale University Press, 1976).

20   Gledhill, "The Melodramatic Field," 45.

21   Ibid., 45–46.

22   This is the question E. Ann Kaplan has subsequently put to the form of the maternal melodrama. Kaplan argues that there are two basic kinds of maternal melodramas: those that are "complicit" and those that are "resistant" to dominant patriarchal capitalist ideology. *Motherhood and Representation: The Mother in Popular Culture and Melodrama* (London: Routledge, 1992), 12–16, 76–179. I argue that such typologies are beside the point because so many ideologies are in conflict and flux within the general parameters of a dominant patriarchal culture.

23   Robert Ray, for example, has noted this mythic dimension of the "classic Hollywood cinema," citing it as one of the important elements of what Truffaut once called "a certain tendency of the Hollywood cinema" and relating it to the tradition of American exceptionalism. However, Ray may too quickly subsume this mythic-resolution-seeking nature of popular films to the subordination of style to story, of affects and effects to narrative, typical of the model of the bourgeois realist text derived from the novel. I am arguing that the "certain tendency of the Hollywood cinema" is at least as importantly melodramatic as it is realistic. *A Certain Tendency of the Hollywood Cinema* (New Jersey: Princeton University Press, 1985), 32–33, 56–57.

24   Gledhill writes, "In Hollywood, realism came to be associated with the masculine sphere of action and violence." "The Melodramatic Field," 35.

25   This pat division between melodrama and realism has been especially the case in "gaze theory"—the theory that dominant cinema is organized for the power and pleasure of a masculine spectator-subject—but it has also been evident in formalist and cognitivist paradigms as well.

26   Gledhill, "The Melodramatic Field," 35. Steve Neale, "Melo Talk: On the Meaning and Use of the Term 'Melodrama' in the American Trade Press," *Velvet Light Trap* (fall 1993): 66–89.

27   My colleague Rhona Berenstein, citing publicity from *Mad Love* (1935) and *Trader Horn* (1931), adds the categories horror melodrama and jungle melodrama respectively.

28   Brooks, *The Melodramatic Imagination*, 15.

29   Gledhill, "The Melodramatic Field," 38.

30   Ibid., 38.

31   Douglas, *The Feminization*.

32   See Sergei Eisenstein, "Montage of Attractions," trans. Daniel Gerould, *The Drama Review* 18 (March 1974): 78–79. And see Tom Gunning, "The Cinema of Attraction," *Wide Angle* 8, no. 3/4 (1986); Gunning, "An Aesthetics of Astonishment: Early Film and the (In)Credulous Spectator," *Art and Text* 34 (spring 1989): 114–133, reprinted in Williams, ed., *Viewing Positions: Ways of Seeing Film* (New Brunswick, N.J.: Rutgers University Press, 1994).

33   Janet Staiger, *Interpreting Films: Studies in the Historical Reception of American Cinema* (Princeton: Princeton University Press, 1992), 118.

34   Ibid., 118.

35   Rick Altman, "Dickens, Griffith, and Film Theory Today," *South Atlantic Quarterly* 88, no. 2 (1989): 331. Reprinted in Jane Gaines, ed. *Classical Hollywood Narrative* (Durham: Duke University Press, 1992), 331.

36   David Bordwell, Janet Staiger, Kristen Thompson, *The Classical Hollywood Cinema: Film Style and Mode of Production to 1960* (New York: Columbia University Press, 1985).

37   Ibid., 21–22.

38   Altman, "Dickens, Griffith, and Film Theory Today," 346.

39   Ibid., 347.

40   Christine Gledhill, "Between Melodrama and Realism," 137.

41   Susan Jeffords, *The Remasculinization of America: Gender and the Vietnam War* (Bloomington: Indiana University Press, 1989), 128. See also Jeffords's *Hard Bodies: Hollywood Masculinity in the Reagan Era* (New Brunswick: Rutgers University Press, 1994).

Chapter 21

E. Deidre Pribram

COLD COMFORT: EMOTION, TELEVISION DETECTION DRAMAS, AND *COLD CASE*

Equilibrium of comfort

TO SPEAK ABOUT emotions is to attempt to address a notoriously challenging and vast category of cultural existence, akin to undertaking an analysis of "the body" or "reason." But as contemporary work in cultural studies and poststructuralism has shown, undertaking explorations of the body and reason are extremely pressing and productive areas of critical inquiry. Culturalist approaches to emotions, however, have only recently begun to emerge as a distinct area of investigation. A useful entry point into the complexities of emotion as a sociocultural category is Raymond Williams' concept, *structure of feeling*.

Williams developed the notion of structure of feeling to describe the emotional relations of a specific time period and cultural location. He understood structure of feeling as an articulation most readily accessible in the literature of a period, both high art and popular fiction, but which indicated a more general cultural "possession" or presence (chapter 1: 44). Describing structure of feeling as the "felt sense of the quality of life at a particular place and time," he was pointing to occurrences that are culturally shared or widely felt, not solely individual emotional responses (36). The emphasis on "felt" is important; Williams was describing something "of feeling much more than of thought – a pattern of impulses, restraints, tones" (44). In place of the "official consciousness of an epoch – codified in its doctrines and legislation," he was attempting to bring into historical and theoretical discourse the experiential results of living within a specific social and cultural context (44).

Williams drew a distinction between the knowledge which can be derived from an era's institutions and social structures versus an understanding of its emotional relations (41). That is, structure of feeling attempts to account for the emotional repercussions, usually unacknowledged, of what it means to live in a particular time and place. In *The Long Revolution*, originally published in 1961, Williams goes to significant lengths to distinguish "structure of feeling" from "social character," a distinction he upholds a number of years later, in 1979, when commenting on the earlier work (46). In Williams' analysis, social character is "the abstract of a dominant group" (38), representing "the official or received thought of a time" (46). Social character refers to the prescribed ideas and values of a social group at a specific historical moment. In contrast, structure of feeling deals "not only with the public ideals but with their omissions and consequences, as lived," that is, experiences that exist beyond or in addition to the articulated beliefs and values of a specific society or social group (39). The concept is necessary, Williams felt, because the stated public ideals overlook as much as they pinpoint. One interpretation of structure of feeling, then, has to do with that which is overlooked or disregarded.

In Williams' estimation, what is disregarded has to do largely with the ways public ideals are experienced or felt by people, how they are "lived." He describes such disregarded lived experiences as omissions when they are unacknowledged, unaccounted for, or otherwise rendered invisible. He calls them consequences because they are the repercussions, the *affects*, of what it means to live out the beliefs and values of one's era. They are, in other words, "real" – experienced, felt – whether they are adequately acknowledged by a society or not. The development of the notion of structure of feeling makes possible the identification of such lived omissions and consequences which are myriad, complex, and dispersed across the social landscape. Their identification, in turn, holds out the prospect of making some sense of these largely unacknowledged or inadequately explained aspects of existence.

Taking the cue from Williams, we can turn to the television detective drama to consider the "public ideals" that they promote and, more to the point here, the structures of feeling that might exist side by side with that "official or received thought." Following Williams' arguments, the stated ideals of an era are necessarily accompanied by their own "omissions and consequences, as lived." Such omissions and consequences, as the counterpart of the public ideals of an epoch, help signal a contemporary structure of feeling. The representation of stated ideals requires the constraint of associated structures of feeling which, otherwise, might threaten the validity of the received thought. And although such structures of feeling may not be overtly apparent, their traces, their omissions and consequences, remain detectable.

More specifically, I want to argue that the police drama, *Cold Case*, one of the five detective programs currently airing in the U.S. under the imprimatur of executive producer Jerry Bruckheimer, introduces "emotional content" into the generic mix. The structure of feeling that it makes apparent focuses on the issue of loss, most notably the consequences of the loss of life, a theme common to most police dramas. However, *Cold Case*, in introducing the emotional repercussions of such losses, concurrently makes clear the inadequacy of discourses of "justice," including the detection genre, in either explaining or containing those emotional losses. In doing so, it strains at the boundaries of its own genre, unsettling an equilibrium of comfort normally established in the detective drama through the circumscribing of emotion.

Signatures and styles

Executive producer Jerry Bruckheimer's remarkably successful run of detective shows includes *CSI: Crime Scene Investigation; CSI: Miami; CSI: New York; Without a Trace*; and *Cold Case*. In a television landscape crowded with police and legal dramas, in order to succeed, each show must develop its own "brand," its signature preoccupations and stylistic approach. Each additional entry into the field is pressured to play on, and perhaps expand, some variation of the well-known but still highly competitive television detection genre.

CSI: Crime Scene Investigation, the flagship show of the Bruckheimer collection, promotes the virtues of science, technology, reason, logic, and precision – "the evidence doesn't lie." In contrast, *Cold Case* delves more deeply into the world of emotions, an attribute not lost on viewers or critics. "*Cold Case* is rare among procedural detective dramas for examining not just the evidence, but also the emotional fallout of unsolved mysteries" (Roush, 67). The concern here is what does such "emotional fallout" point to or tell us? If we trace the show's emotional tendencies, what do they suggest about the place of emotion in popular representation?

Cold Case's signature technique of characters aging before our eyes or suddenly shedding their years speaks to the pathos of age, mutability, and loss. Set in Philadelphia, *Cold Case*'s distinguishing visual style is the transformation of characters from who they were "then" to whom they are now. Over the course of an episode, we see individual characters swing, almost effortlessly, over time, moving from past to present, aging and becoming younger again. This visual approach is accomplished through precisely choreographed cinematography and editing, and the careful match-casting of "before and after" versions of individual characters. The actors selected, in addition to other requirements, must be believable as older and younger renditions of each other. While past and present variations on a character must resemble each other, they also clearly are intended to differ. The older incarnation is meant to demonstrate the effects – the ravages – of time and events on that individual's person and life.

If *Cold Case*'s stylistic approach focuses on the pathos of aging, and the investigation of mutability in life, *CSI: Crime Scene Investigation*'s signature visual technique revolves around the striking fast motion effects shots that delve into flesh, tunneling past the victim's organs, bones, and muscles in order to determine what caused his or her death. *CSI* takes us on a very literal "internal journey" into character. The *body* is emphasized, the physical human remains laid out on a slab, ready to be autopsied and probed, each component closely inspected and minutely tested, in an effort to force to the surface bits and pieces of evidence.

In place of *CSI*'s emphasis on the science and technology of crime-solving – the reassuring certainty and solidity of a *body* of evidence – *Cold Case* stresses stories about human transformation over time. In the words of series' creator, Meredith Stiehm, the show treats "time as a character" (qtd. in Levin, 2E). How *Cold Case* plays on a familiar genre to attain its emotion-centric variation, and what light this sheds on the concept of structure of feeling, is the focus of this particular police genre investigation.

Incarnations

In an episode titled "Volunteers," set in 1969 and 2004, the series' first season, we open in the past on a young white woman (Maggie Grace), wearing a skirt, cardigan and pearls, and walking along a deserted street.[1] A beat-up yellow station wagon pulls up next to her, and a young white woman (Amber Nicole Benson) and a young black man (Garland Whitt) get out. They are dressed in hippie-identified clothing of the era: she in striped bell bottoms, a fringed poncho, and a peace symbol on a leather strap around her neck; he in bell-bottom jeans, a white cotton Madras shirt, and wooden love beads. The two arrivals grab the young woman, blindfold her, and place her in the backseat of the car, in what appears to be a kidnapping in progress. We see close-ups of money changing hands between the abducted woman and the African-American man. The scene is interrupted repeatedly by a change to still shots in black and white as somebody – another person surreptitiously present – takes photos of the events we are witnessing. We abruptly dissolve to the hippie twosome, lying next to each other on the ground, dead, blood visibly oozing from the young man's head.

Cut to 2004: two skeletons are found in the concrete foundations of a recently-razed building. Some remnants of clothing are found with them, including a necklace in the shape of a peace sign suspended on a leather strap. The two victims are identified as Julia Hoffman, 22, and Gerard Gary, 23, who disappeared together in June of 1969.

As the show cuts back and forth between scenes from 2004 and 1969, the show's lead detective, Lilly Rush (Kathryn Morris), and her partner, Scotty Valens (Danny Pino), interview people from Julia's and Gerard's past. It transpires that the two were involved in a then illegal activity – helping women obtain safe abortions. Julia and Gerard were co-workers, not lovers, as the detectives initially assumed; volunteers in an underground organization named Jane, a group that existed in actuality, from 1967 to 1973, until abortion was legalized (Rosen, 54).

The detectives learn that FBI files exist on the organization Jane. Included in those files are several months of photos of Gerard and Julia, tracking them in their illegal, volunteer work. The photos were taken by an unnamed FBI informant – the source of the black and white still images at the show's opening – up to and concluding with the day Gerard and Julia escort Renee, the scared, 17 year old woman, with whom we first see the volunteers on the day the two disappear.

In the course of their investigation, one of the people the detectives interview is Adam Clarke (Chris Sarandon, Riley Schmidt), now a successful motivational author and speaker. In 1969, he was Julia's boyfriend, as well as a high-profile leader of the anti-war movement. He has told the detectives he explained away Julia's sudden disappearance at the time by assuming she ran away to Canada with Gerard. Ultimately, though, they realize that Adam Clarke, motivational speaker and previous anti-war leader, is both FBI informant and murderer. Discovered by Julia and Gerard as he takes their photos surreptitiously on the day of Renee's abortion, he is exposed as the informant. If – when – they tell others, Adam's credibility and leadership position in the movement would disappear. As Lilly puts it, "Adam Clarke, 60s babe magnet, star of the anti-war movement – and FBI informant." Instead, Gerard and Julia disappear.

When Lilly and Scotty take Adam into custody in 2004, he describes Julia and Gerard as "heroic." Quietly and anonymously, they were helping women, putting themselves at risk of discovery and arrest for what they believed in, while Adam took public and high-profile credit for the cause he was privately betraying. We feel the anger of injustice because Adam's actions sprang from hypocrisy and self-preservation, not heroism. He turns FBI informant after he is arrested for drugs, rather than face a prison sentence. He kills Julia and Gerard rather than lose his public position and place in history. "I was a leader in the revolution. We were living like it meant something. I loved that life. Couldn't stand to give it up."

The episode arouses our anger over politics and ethics. Concurrently, it also points to the injustices of *time*. For the greatest, the most galling injustice the show visually and viscerally depicts is that Adam is given the opportunity to age, while Julia and Gerard do not. We see Adam both in his early 20s and mid-to-late 50s. We see other characters from 1969 make a similar physical transition over time. But Julia and Gerard are forever frozen at 22 and 23. No later versions of them exist. What is lost – stolen from them – is the opportunity to age. Lilly observes that, "Adam gets 35 years to have a life till his luck runs out." The 35 years in which Adam gets "to have a life" are in addition to the 22 and 23 years of Julia's and Gerard's existences, more time than either of the victims had in their entirety.

Coda

Cold Case episodes come to a close by following a recurring coda. Typically, they start with a shot of the newly-uncovered murderer being handcuffed and taken away. But this sequence – the arrest of the guilty party, normally the finale in the detective show genre –

marks, in *Cold Case*, only the beginning of the end. Once the suspect is taken into custody, a choreographed sequence ensues, set to music of the era,[2] involving final glimpses of the various people affected by that week's murder – family members, friends, past lovers – in both their older and younger guises. Usually the coda ends with a final exchange of looks between Lilly and the murder victim, who suddenly appears reincarnated in the present, apparently only visible to Lilly.

The reincarnated individuals are often portrayed smiling as if to suggest that despite their murders they are at peace, and they are at peace, in part, because they are satisfied with the result of Lilly's investigation, satisfied that justice in their case has finally been realized. The coda and the final exchange of looks between victims and detective are meant to offer us something of a "happy ending." By resolving their cases and establishing their previously unknown fates, Lilly and her colleagues have rendered a service to the victims.

The coda replaces the gunplay, chase sequence, or other culminating action of the traditional police drama. *Cold Case*'s climactic "action" takes the form of emotional denouement. The 1969 episode elaborates even further on the usual coda by utilizing the black and white still photos taken by Adam over three months and discovered in the FBI files. In this episode, Julia and Gerard appear to Lilly, not in the final shots of the coda but near its beginning, just after Lilly guides an arrested Adam into the back of the police car. Lilly glances up and, across the street, sees Gerard and Julia in their 1969 personas, suddenly visible to Lilly in 2004.

Julia and Gerard look towards Lilly, both smiling, Gerard's arm around Julia's shoulder. This visual dissolves to black and white images of Gerard and Julia helping unidentified women. The coda continues with various *Cold Case* detectives passing the still photos on to people Julia and Gerard were close to or positively affected in the past. Finally it ends with Lilly putting the case files back in storage, no longer needed as the case is now solved. But before she does so, Lilly saves one of the photos of Gerard and Julia for herself, a suggestion that this somehow keeps Gerard and Julia alive, that they've affected her too, that what they did is not forgotten.

The inclusion of the black and white still photos prolongs this episode's coda to a complex exchange between Julia and Gerard, and all of the other characters – those from their past lives and those from the detective squad – with whom they have interacted. The effect of this expanded coda is to reinforce Gerard's and Julia's political commitment and to reaffirm how many other lives they have touched for the better.

In recreating scenes from the past, and by having dead victims reincarnate in the present, *Cold Case* manages to keep its victims at the dramatic forefront to a greater degree than most shows in the genre. Rather than being featured primarily as cadavers whose physical circumstances in coming to be that way hold the potential solution to the mystery, *Cold Case* attempts to deal more directly with the victims as living personalities. *CSI*'s emphasis on the body is replaced, in *Cold Case*, by a greater focus on the circumstances of the characters' lived existences: their activities and their relationships. This proves to be both a source of the series' distinction from its competitors and its "problem" as exemplar of the crime genre.

The *Cold Case* "problem"

Narrative concerns in detective dramas are generally based upon a tradition of socially-sanctioned discourses of justice: the preservation of established law and order. The hero/detective is a representative of the institutions of juridical protection; his/her function is to instate and reinstate "justice," by acting on behalf of victims of crime and as agents for society at large.

Toby Miller notes that recent years have seen "a proliferation of police, detective and crime drama with endless variations and reworkings of a basic formula in which society is protected and the status quo maintained by the forces of law and order" (19). Within the framework of this classic formula, "detection has meant the identification and defeat of wrongdoers, by applying reason to explain events that are irregular and socially undesirable" (18).

Miller's emphasis on the proliferation of police and detective programs and the prominence they place on the reinstatement of law and order is echoed by Elayne Rapping. Rapping argues that an array of social issues, once located in other public or community venues, increasingly have been "criminalized" in order to bring them within the jurisdiction of legal discourses (136). This has been paralleled by an expansion in television police and legal shows, both fiction and documentary, accompanied by a broadening in the narrative/ ideological terrain taken to be their purview. The result is the tendency to view "virtually everything in public and private life as a matter of crime and punishment" (264). According to Miller, then, the representation of discourses of law and order is a common and unabated generic pattern. Further, following Rapping, mediated juridical discourses can be linked to a dominant, and growing, cultural paradigm.

Susanna Lee points out that "[t]he detective series genre has always represented both the desire for reassurance and the simultaneous sense of the impossibility of that reassurance" (81). The habitual re-imposition of social order is a double-edged, uneasy narrative foundation because it can only ever be temporary. Social equilibrium and the accompanying reassurance it provides must always be reinstated because it is always threatened, in both narrative and cultural terms. Such reassurance can not be sought – or promised – once and for all. This would account, in part, for the genre's proliferation: renewal and repetition are fundamental to its terms of existence. Although the attempt to reassure always contains its own impossibility, the genre is defined on the premise and promise of its continual – and in Rapping's terms, expanding – attempts at reassertion. Such momentary or imaginary respites, in the face of ongoing perceived threats, equate successful resolution with provisional comfort, to be performed again and again in subsequent cases.

In the traditional detective series formula, in order to provide such comfort, "solving the crime" and "bringing to justice" are conventionally interchangeable concepts and terms. The dramatic and emotional satisfaction of the case being solved rests precisely in the criminal being held culpable for the crime, and in the knowledge that the injustice committed against the (usually innocent) victim is being redressed. Of course, following Lee, the equivalency of "case solved" and "justice served," while a staple of generic expectation, is simultaneously part of generic fantasy. Ideologically reassuring to audiences, it provides us with the detective genre version of a happy ending, an ending which only succeeds if it is constantly reenacted.

The "problem" for *Cold Case* is that in reincarnating murder victims, in re-embodying them by visualizing the past in the present in order to keep their stories and their characters at the forefront, we also are reminded persistently of their *absence*. Like Julia and Gerard, they reappear in the coda, smiling as if to suggest that they are satisfied with the results of Lilly's investigation, satisfied that in their cases justice has finally been realized. But the impression we are left with most forcefully is of their nonexistence. The most visually compelling effect of the *Cold Case* "brand" is to reaffirm that the victims are indeed frozen in the past, that they do not have incarnations in the present.

While all of the other characters from their era, including the murderer, have two versions, played by two actors, the victims have only one – outdated, past tense. In the highly competitive conditions for police, crime, and detective dramas in today's televisual market-place, *Cold Case* has developed its own signature variation of a well-known generic formula. The issue of mutability for the characters who age over time creates a nostalgic longing, a certain poignant sadness that the series can play on. However, the narrative dilemma for the program resides in the characters who do not age.

The show's visual techniques make manifest the loss of these characters' present days, what would have been their futures. Ultimately, the most striking effect of the dead victims' appearances in the present-day is not to affirm the restitution of justice in their cases but to give us visual proof that they are lost, condemned to a life never lived. This is a level of injustice that cannot be redressed by the detective genre or by the discourses of justice the detective genre relies upon. Often, we are not left with the feeling of justice served. Instead, what we cannot erase about the final glimpses of the victims is the sense of loss, of waste, that their lives stopped where they did, while other lives – those of their family and friends, the killers', Lilly's, and ours – continue.

The resolution of a *Cold Case* episode is then, at best, a bittersweet moment, a moment more bitter with the loss of the victim's future than sweet with the notion of justice served through the better-late-than-never capture of the perpetrator. In other words, the "problem" with the *Cold Case* formula is that while the case is invariably solved on a weekly basis, the series tends to decouple the generic connection between the resolution of the case and the reassuring re-imposition of justice. It dislocates the familiar equivalency of "case solved" and "justice served."

In Williams' terms, the equivalency of case solved and justice served are the stated ideals of our era. However, experiential omissions and consequences are the inevitable counterpart of those public ideas. The motif of loss is not, of course, new to the detective drama: such shows are generally constructed around the loss of life. Of the five Bruckheimer detective series, for instance, four usually feature a weekly murder to be solved.[3] Loss of life, loss of safety and security, are staples of the detection genres. How to endure and potentially rectify the personal toll of such losses is one of the forms of reassurance we desire from the genre.

The significant difference with *Cold Case* lies in the way it forefronts the omissions and consequences of such loss. Whether intended by the series' producers or not, one of the effects of the show's signature formula is that the emotional repercussions connected to loss tend to outweigh the reassurances of stability and the continuity of public ideals, in Williams' terms. Rather than stressing the efficacy of the policies and practices of generic justice in ameliorating social ills, in providing comfort to the victims and their loved ones, *Cold Case* lingers amid the weightiness of the losses themselves. The structure of feeling that it isolates describes the "felt sense" of the anxiety and despair that cannot be comforted by notions of justice served.

Television detectives frequently point out that what they do is for the sake of victims and their loved ones. It is also a staple of police shows to have victims of crime or their surviving representatives thank detectives for their work; gratitude and relief are extended, thereby positioning the legal process as a healing process. And so, Horatio Cane (David Caruso) on *CSI: Miami* insists that one of his team members continue the painstaking process of developing and analyzing forensic evidence although, due to other circumstances, they already know the case cannot be brought to trial. Horatio refuses to explain his reasons for continuing the investigation to his highly frustrated lab technician who sees the additional work as a waste of time and resources. Instead, Horatio *shows* his younger assistant his motives when he uses the forensic evidence from the investigation to explain to a victim's family members what precisely happened to their loved one, positioning the facticity of evidence as a source of comfort. On *CSI: New York*, when the friend of a just-murdered young woman wonders aloud what she should tell the victim's family, Mac Taylor (Gary Sinise), suggests she let the family know that they – New York's CSI team – are doing everything they can to find those responsible for the crime, the most consoling words he knows.

In a 1998 article on British detective dramas, Charlotte Brunsdon pinpoints a "structure of anxiety" in certain programs of the mid-1980s to mid-1990s. The structure of anxiety which she identifies as a common thread linking several police dramas of the era is formulated around sociopolitical concerns. Specifically, she finds these shows are "socially expressive" (242) in their concern with contemporary issues such as: who can police? (which segments of society have the right to serve as forces of justice); and who is accountable for policing practices? (including or especially acts of excess or misconduct).

My concern, like Brunsdon's, focuses on a structure of anxiety evident in certain detective dramas. However, I am attempting to pinpoint a structure of anxiety of an entirely different origin. In place of the sociopolitical events she identifies, my interest lies in the socioemotional implications of crime, and the inefficacy of policing forces and notions of justice in redressing those anxieties. These are two different approaches to narrative interpretation; however, one need not preclude the other. Specific instances of the detective drama are capable of, and do, encompass the social in both its political and emotional manifestations.

Cold Case is the only Bruckheimer detective drama with a female lead, but given the emotional terrain that I'm arguing the show emphasizes, the departure from a male-headed ensemble cast isn't surprising. Long-standing cultural associations between women and emotion make a female lead investigator not only plausible, but likely, for the series' subject matter.[4] The question I am primarily concerned with here is what occurs when emotional knowledges and experiences are "allowed in" to a genre which traditionally has been thought to circumscribe such discourses, as in the example of *CSI* with its emphasis on science, rationality, and facticity? However, the emotion question is not neatly separable from gender concerns in that, historically, the vast majority of lead and supporting detectives in detection dramas have been male, and the application of reason to explain events, in Miller's words, has been coded as masculine. Moreover, detection dramas as masculine genres have been presumed to bracket out emotional discourses.

In an article on the British detective series, *Cracker*, Glen Creeber argues that the lead character, Fitz, is a compelling incorporation of the traditional "old sleuth" and the "new man." As old sleuth, Fitz fits the "masculine archetype" of the hard-boiled detective, one component of which is his professional unemotional quality (171). He is "rugged, quick-witted and the embodiment of cool masculine power . . . relying almost wholly on reason to understand and decode the world around him" (171, 173). In his considerable professional skills, if not in his more disastrous personal life, Fitz is a controlled individual, driven by reason, not emotionality.

Similarly, Jason Mittel describes the 1950s series, *Dragnet*, as an ideologically conservative but seminal text in the establishment of the police drama that would follow in subsequent decades (124, 127). Among its specific techniques, the flat and monotone acting style filtered out "most emotional nuances and dramatic pauses," prioritizing "*systemic* over *emotional* realism" (137; italics in original). Here, emotional detachment is equated with the successful operation of the criminal justice system in a binary structuration in which chaos, crime, and emotions are located, together, outside the realm of reason, justice, and correct police procedure. Lead detective, Joe Friday is "detached, objective, reliable" with "no visible flaws, biases, or even emotions," again equating elements like flaws and biases with emotions (141, 140).

That the masculine attributes of detective genres bracket emotions is a debatable but fairly widespread contention. It is at least accurate to say that traditional detection genres deal *uncomfortably* with emotions, which is not, of course, equivalent to their absence. However, to the extent that masculine detective dramas circumscribe emotional discourses, what then occurs when a show like *Cold Case*, an exemplar of the genre, re-inserts emotional content explicitly into the generic mix? What are the implications for the genre and for the study of emotion?

Cold comfort

"Revenge," an episode set in 1998 and 2005, tells the story of a 9 year old boy, Kyle Bream (Cayden Boyd).[5] We first see Kyle at the mall, shopping for back-to-school clothes with his parents, Tina and Ken Bream (Bridgid Brannagh, Brent Sexton). Some banter is exchanged among the family about Kyle's desire to look good in order to impress a particular girl who will be in his in-coming class.

His father, Ken, picks out several shirts Kyle likes, although his mother complains that they're expensive at "twenty-five bucks a pop." But to her son's delight, she agrees to let him get at least one. Kyle asks to go to the dressing room on his own to try on the shirts. In keeping with the series' opening formula, this is the last time the Breams see their son alive. Kyle has been kidnapped and sold to a pedophile. One month later, Kyle's body washes up on shore at a local harbor, the boy having drowned.

"Revenge" is a graphic episode. It is not sexually graphic: we are told about, not shown, any acts of sexual molestation. Nor is the episode graphic in terms of violence; Kyle drowns off-camera. It is, however, emotionally graphic. The episode dwells on this 9 year old boy's feelings of terror, abandonment, and despair during the time he is held captive, in the month between his disappearance and the discovery of his body.

Manipulated by his pedophile captor, Rudy Tanner (Vincent Angell), Kyle comes to believe that his parents have purposefully abandoned him. They have not come to get him because he is too expensive, demanding things like back-to-school shirts at "twenty-five dollars a pop." In other words, in Kyle's mind and heart, the kidnapping and his new "home" with Rudy are his own fault. Psychologically and emotionally manipulated by his captor – not too difficult to accomplish with a scared and depressed 9 year old boy – Kyle is led to believe he himself is responsible for the turn of events in his life.

Worse, Kyle begins to feel that he owes allegiance, obedience, and gratitude to his new guardian/molester for taking him in – "rescuing" him – when even his own parents no longer wanted him. Kyle's state of mind, his deepening despair and increasing dependence on Rudy, are developed over five difficult to watch scenes, culminating in Kyle's growing acceptance of Rudy's caresses and the new "home" he is being offered.

We may well be better prepared to look at blood and guts – the *body* of evidence – than to be faced with the emotionally horrific, such as the terror of an abducted, sexually molested child, in the weeks, days, and final hours before his death. In this regard, Kyle's story turns on a cruel irony. In the few minutes before his death, Kyle learns, through a newspaper account, that his parents have not abandoned him, but instead have been diligently and anxiously searching for him.

But Kyle's moment of happiness and hope is fleeting. He is shown the newspaper account by Rudy's then 13 year old son and previous sexual molestation victim, Archie (Andrew Michaelson, Jesse Head). Jealous of his father's ardent attention towards Kyle, and diminished interest in his own no-longer-boyish self, Archie uses the newspaper account to lure Kyle to his death.

Archie entices Kyle into the cold, deep water by reassuring him that his parents are waiting for him just across the harbor, knowing full well that Kyle cannot possibly survive the swim. Drawn by the false hope of being reunited with his parents, Kyle, against his own fears and better judgment, sets off into the water.

The mystery to be solved in the "Revenge" episode of *Cold Case* is to determine who is responsible for Kyle Bream's death. However, en route to solving the week's primary mystery, the detectives manage to settle another cold case. A few months after Kyle's body is discovered in 1998, Rudy Tanner, his pedophile captor, is found shot to death. Positioned as something of a subplot to the main mystery of Kyle's death, the discovery of Rudy's killer is more dramatically affecting than the revelation that Archie, himself a victim of sexual molestation as a child, is Kyle's murderer.

Following Kyle's death, his parents, Tina and Ken, track down their son's abductor/buyer through a child pornography site Rudy is running. The site includes sexual images of Kyle, as well as other young boys. When the Breams locate Rudy, it is, as Tina explains, "time to make things right." Ken finds Rudy and shoots him. The problem is, as Tina further explains, "It didn't help, though [relieve the pain. Kyle's] still gone." Here, neither legal justice (Archie's arrest) nor personal justice (Rudy's death) – "revenge" in the episode's terms – eases the pain or provides relief.

Nor is there any sense of relief in the show's customary coda. In this episode, Lilly stands at the harbor where Kyle's body was found. Kyle suddenly reappears, walking towards Lilly, his somber face filling the frame. We cut to a shot of Lilly smiling slightly at him, then back to a wide shot of a still-unsmiling Kyle as he turns around, walking back along the pier. His image dissolves into thin air, into the past, before he reaches the water. The sequence ends on a shot of Lilly turning and walking away in the other direction.

There is no happy ending here, no sense of satisfaction for a job well done. In its place, we are left with something akin to an acknowledgment of overwhelming powerlessness in the ability to protect those most deserving of protection. Instead of concluding with comfort, relief, or a sense of victory, the outcome is discomfort as we are forced to acknowledge the futility of "justice," whether legal or personal, as remedy for some of the most painful events in life.

Apparently intended to offset this effect, the episode doesn't end here, but returns to a parallel subplot that has been woven throughout the episode. It concerns Lieutenant John Stillman (John Finn) and his now-adult daughter Janie (Melinda Page Hamilton), a new mother herself. Eighteen years previously, Janie was raped by an acquaintance. Scared and ashamed at the time, she refused to press charges or otherwise let her father pursue the matter, leaving the Lieutenant powerless to do anything. Now, years later, the rapist reappears in her neighborhood, working as a bartender at a local restaurant she frequents. When the Lieutenant learns of this, he goes to the restaurant and threatens the rapist, forcing him to quit his job and disappear from his daughter's neighborhood.

The final scene of "Revenge," following the exchange of looks between Lilly and Kyle, takes place at the baptism of the Lieutenant's grandchild. The Lieutenant holds his infant grandson while his daughter stands next to him, smiling. The episode ends here, on the suggestion that, if many years after the fact and perhaps only in half-measure, the Lieutenant has managed to protect his daughter after all.

Bracketing emotion

In her article on the long-running series, *Law and Order*, Susanna Lee argues that the program frequently acknowledges the policing and legal systems' inefficacy in providing reasonable standards of juridical order, particularly in the wake of events such as September 11, 2001. Instead of reassuring us of the competency with which they carry out their social and ideological functions, the detectives and district attorneys of *Law and Order* offer us *psychic reassurance*.

> Before, the position of strength to which one returned was the triumph of good over bad, detective over criminal, social order over social chaos. Now, I argue the resolution presented by the crime drama is psychic rather than conceptual or social. On screen in *Law and Order* is a fiction of human rather than social response to trauma – a microcosmic mise-en-scène of personal resistance to trauma and violence. (88)

In this view, the central concern of the series has shifted from reassuring us about the re-imposition of a social and moral equilibrium to concentrating on providing a model of personal ("human") psychic and emotional equilibrium.

The position of strength of the *Law and Order* characters resides in their emotional "detachment and evenness," their "steadiness of tone" and impassive qualities in the face of the relentless violence and disorder that they encounter (83). Their hallmark is their ability to return to the scenes of the crime, week after week, without demoralization or defeat. In this argument, it is precisely their stoicism in keeping violence and disorder from affecting the commitment with which they perform their jobs that signals the characters' professionalism. The audience relates to the *Law and Order* characters via the wish that, faced with similar circumstances, we will be able to respond with comparable composure. The characters represent models of behavior for the audience who, when confronted with the specter of violence themselves, hopes that "the actual experience . . . could really be the same as watching it on television," at least as it is portrayed by the *Law and Order* professionals (87).

It may well be an overstatement to suggest that a series such as *Law and Order* has given up the ghost of social and "conceptual" faith in the juridical system. However, more to the point here is that the mission of the detective drama remains one of providing reassurance, albeit in this argument, a reassurance that has shifted from offering up ideological and moral solutions for social ills to ways of coping with them psychically. If we cannot hold back the forces that threaten social stability, then at least we can confront them with equanimity and professionalism.

Although Lee's account does provide a rare exploration of the emotional aspects of police and legal dramas, her analysis raises several issues. First, widely-felt psychic disturbances have cultural and ideological origins and meanings. They are modes of social, as well as personal, organization, determined in and through specific cultural contexts. Lee's investigation does not explain how such psychic trauma originates and flourishes, nor does it consider the reasons such trauma takes on its particular manifestations as, I believe, the notion of structures of feeling begins to do. Psychic and "human" considerations need not be opposed to or preclude social and conceptual factors. Instead, analyzing the cultural and ideological aspects of emotional manifestations holds out the potential for a richer, more productive understanding of "the personal."

Second, it is difficult to see how Lee's explanation of *Law and Order*'s emotional empathy through distanciation as a contemporary technique of dealing with new-found forms of violence and trauma, takes us much beyond older generic modes and models. Here, I refer to the emotional detachment and stoicism that exemplifies traditional generic masculine and rational codes of behavior, both contemporary (*Cracker*) and historical (*Dragnet*), as outlined earlier by Creeber and Mittel. It would be as reasonable to suggest, in the face of arguably altering cultural conditions, that what the characters in *Law and Order* represent is generic *continuity* through their calm, efficient professionalism.

Third, Lee's argument is based on the idea that the genre remains predicated on a successful resolution of reassurance. Although the terms of the resolution have shifted, from reassurances about the security of social circumstances to our capability in personally coping with threatening and painful social conditions, the genre is still predicated on an outcome that provides some measure of comfort. However, what then occurs in the instance of *Cold Case*, a series that I argue is often unable to provide a resolution that either comforts or reassures, given the specific ways it has developed the genre's traditions? In *Cold Case*, we see an instance in which the detection genre faces increasing difficulty in offering up the fantasy of reassurance, either social/ideological or psychic.

I am arguing that analyzing *Cold Case* in terms of how it represents emotion causes us to re-evaluate the efficacy of the genre's professional codes and practices, including its detectives' demeanors of empathetic professionalism. Following such an interpretation, the show is as likely to foreground how little comfort or amelioration its characters can provide, either systemically or emotionally. As 9 year old Kyle's mother recognized, when it was "time to make things right," neither revenge nor legal justice provide relief. There is no exchange of smiles in the coda between detective and reincarnated victim in Kyle's case – only the inadequate consolation of a job technically, professionally, well done.

In "Violence, Mourning, Politics," Judith Butler suggests that there is something to be gained from lingering in the company of grief and dwelling with loss.

> When grieving is something to be feared, our fears can give rise to the impulse to resolve it quickly, to banish it in the name of an action invested with the power to restore the loss or return the world to a former order, or to reinvigorate a fantasy that the world formerly was orderly. (chapter 24: 392)

In detection dramas, the impulse to action takes the form of solving the case, apprehending the perpetrator, and holding him or her culpable for the crime. This set of interrelated actions is meant to restore the loss suffered and return the world to its assumed former order, thereby providing reassurance. In this scenario, detectives are invested with the narrative power to comfort because their actions are understood to banish the grief that accompanies loss and the fears associated with social instability.

However, as Butler reminds us, the notion that the world formerly – or ever – was an orderly place is a fantasy. The narrative fantasies of the detection genre and the discourses of justice the genre relies upon are predicated, not upon dwelling with loss, but on excising it as entirely and expeditiously as possible.

Conclusion

One of the traditional functions of the detective genre has been to uphold and reaffirm the public ideal of "justice," the ability of concepts of law and order to contain and subdue other levels of existence, such as disturbing emotions around personal loss and sorrow. A troubling aspect of social reality like emotionality, with which we are often poorly equipped to deal, becomes "resolved" by other discourses, in the instance of the police procedural, by the capture and punishment of undesirable social elements and the reinstatement of social equilibrium. Through this process, troubling emotions are meant to dissipate.

Yet, in many instances of the genre, attempts are made to excise emotions from the text because they exceed the ideological safeguards of concepts such as the redemptive, equalizing power of juridical discourses. This suggests a contradiction within the genre, betraying uncertainty about how to manage the emotional terrain it is designed to evoke. To what degree and in which ways can grief and anger be aired in order for the narrative to fulfill its generic purpose of calming those emotions and reclaiming a former imagined order? Conversely, to what extent should emotions surrounding loss be circumscribed – or in wishful terms, banished – to avoid difficulty in realigning them with ideological concepts of comfort achieved through justice served?

The ways emotions are represented in popular narrative forms is a potentially rich area of analysis that, surprisingly, has received little attention in film and television studies, despite the fact that emotion is a core element to the processes of storytelling. In cases in which characters are depicted or interpreted as relying "almost wholly on reason" and emotional detachment, we might start by asking how, precisely, do such texts circumscribe emotion and, in order to achieve that end, what attendant issues must be minimized, overlooked, or completely negated?

As we have seen in the example of *Cold Case*, not all instances of the genre bracket emotion. However, in bringing emotions to the fore, the series risks making apparent certain structures of feeling that it is often one of the common practices of its genre to keep submerged. One of the traditional functions of the law and order genres, in Raymond Williams' terms, is their representation of the "public ideal" that prevailing notions of justice offer a social equilibrium between crime and its victims, that the legal system is the hero that can comfort and console. The stated ideal is that "justice" avenges loss: it makes otherwise senseless loss somehow bearable and, in the process, it realigns people and events, returning social forces to the comfort of equilibrium.

However, analysis based on the textual representation of specific emotions offers an alternate interpretation in which we see that contemporary generic discourses of law and order often are inadequate in the face of the acute emotional loss and sorrow depicted. Analysis of the representation of emotion is a site of opportunity where it becomes possible to view discourses of justice, and the generic narratives based on those discourses, as deficient in explaining or redressing the omissions and consequences we live.

Notes

1   "Volunteers" first aired on March 7, 2004. The episode was written by Jan Oxenberg and directed by Allison Anders.
2   The series routinely employs period music in an evocative manner. The codas are usually visually enacted against an appropriate background song. In the 1969 episode, the coda unfolds to *Get Together* by The Youngbloods ("C'mon people now, smile on your brother").
3   *Without a Trace* is somewhat different. Based on the FBI's missing persons unit, the cases are more often than not lost and found, although the threat of loss of life remains.
4   As if self-consciously aware of this, the show's producers initially depicted Lilly Rush as largely hopeless in her own emotional personal and social life, living alone with a number of disfigured cats, yet brilliant at understanding the emotional and psychological motivations of witnesses and perpetrators in her professional life. Additionally, the program surrounds her with male colleagues who are unusually emotionally responsive, for instance, her partner Scotty spent the first season displaying great compassion for his schizophrenic girlfriend.
5   "Revenge" first aired on March 13, 2005, in *Cold Case*'s second season. It was written by Dan Dworkin and Jay Beattie, and directed by David Von Ancken.

References

Brunsdon, Charlotte. "Structure of Anxiety: Recent British Television Crime Fiction," *Screen* 39.3 (1998): 223–243.
Creeber, Glen. "Old Sleuth or New Man? Investigations into Rape, Murder and Masculinity in *Cracker*," *Continuum: Journal of Media and Cultural Studies*, 16.2 (2002): 169–183.

Lee, Susanna. " 'These Are Our Stories': Trauma, Form, and the Screen Phenomenon of *Law and Order*," *Discourse* 25.1/2 (2004): 81–97.

Levin, Gary. "*Cold Case* Goes Further Back in Time to Solve Crime," *USA Today*, 27 Aug. 2004: 2E.

Miller, Toby. "The Action Series" and "The Police Series," in *The Television Genre Book*, ed. Glen Creeber, London: BFI, 2001.

Mittell, Jason. *Genre and Television: From Cop Shows to Cartoons in American Culture*, New York: Routledge, 2004.

Rapping, Elayne. *Law and Justice as Seen on TV*, New York: New York University Press, 2003.

Rosen, Ruth. *The World Split Open: How the Modern Women's Movement Changed America*, New York: Penguin, 2001.

Roush, Matt. "Hits & Misses," *TV Guide*, 24–30 Oct. 2004: 67.

VIII AFFECTING SUBJECTS

Chapter 22

Fatima Mernissi

SCHEHERAZADE GOES WEST: DIFFERENT CULTURES, DIFFERENT HAREMS

I NEVER REALIZED until my book tour [for *Dreams of Trespass: Tales of a Harem Girlhood*[1]] that a smile can betray so much of one's inner feelings. Arabs, like many Westerners, think it is the eyes that give one away. "The eye is the wide gateway to the soul," wrote Ibn Hazm, an expert on love, "the scrutinizer of its secrets, conveying its most private thoughts."[2] Growing up, I was taught that a woman should lower her gaze, so that men could never know her thoughts. The so-called modesty of Arab women is in fact a war tactic. But the smile, I discovered during my book tour, can give one away as easily as the eye—and in many different ways. Not all of those journalists' smiles were alike. Each, according to nationality, expressed a different mixture of feelings.

We can break the West into two camps as far as smiles are concerned: the Americans and the Europeans. The American men, upon hearing the word "harem," smiled with unadulterated and straightforward embarrassment. Whatever the word means for Americans hinges on something linked to shame. The Europeans, in contrast, responded with smiles that varied from polite reserve in the North to merry exuberance in the South, with subtleties fluctuating according to the distance of the journalists' origin from the Mediterranean. French, Spanish, and Italian men had a flirtatious, amused light in their eyes. Scandinavians and Germans, with the exception of the Danes, had astonishment in theirs—astonishment tinged with shock. "Were you really born in a harem?" they would ask, looking intently at me with a mixture of apprehension and puzzlement.

My book starts with the sentence: "I was born in a harem," and that short sentence seemed to contain some mysterious problem, because everyone, without exception, started his interview by asking, like a magic formula, "So, were you really born in a harem?" The intensity of the look accompanying the inquiry signaled that my interviewer did not want me to evade the question—as if there were some shameful secret involved. Yet for me, not only is the word "harem" a synonym for the family as an institution, but it would also never occur to me to associate it with something jovial. After all, the very origin of the Arabic word "haram," from which the word "harem" is derived, literally refers to sin, the dangerous frontier where sacred law and pleasure collide. *Haram* is what the religious law forbids; the opposite is *halal*, that which is permissible. But evidently, when crossing the frontier to the West, the Arabic word "harem" lost its dangerous edge. Why else would Westerners associate it with euphoria, with the absence of constraints? In their harem, sex is anxiety-free. [. . .]

That is when I decided to reverse roles by interviewing the male journalists who were interviewing me. "Why are you smiling?" I would ask softly when yet another one exhibited signs of excitement. "What is amusing about the harem?" This two-way exchange turned my ex-interviewers into helpful informants who soon taught me that we were not talking about the same thing: Westerners had their harem and I had mine, and the two had nothing in common.

Apparently, the Westerner's harem was an orgiastic feast where men benefited from a true miracle: receiving sexual pleasure without resistance or trouble from the women they had reduced to slaves. In Muslim harems, men expect their enslaved women to fight back ferociously and abort their schemes for pleasure. The Westerners also referred primarily to pictorial images of harems, such as those seen in paintings or films, while I visualized actual palaces—harems built of high walls and real stones by powerful men such as caliphs, sultans, and rich merchants. My harem was associated with a historical reality. Theirs was associated with artistic images created by famous painters such as Ingres, Matisse, Delacroix, or Picasso—who reduced women to odalisques (a Turkish word for a female slave)—or by talented Hollywood moviemakers, who portrayed harem women as scantily clad belly-dancers happy to serve their captors. Some journalists also mentioned operas like Verdi's *Aida* or ballets like Diaghilev's *Scheherazade*. But whatever image they referred to, the journalists always described the harem as a voluptuous wonderland drenched with heavy sex provided by vulnerable nude women who were happy to be locked up.

This is indeed a miracle, I thought as I listened to the Westerners' descriptions. Muslim male artists are much more realistic when it comes to envisioning the harem as a source of erotic bliss. Even in their fantasies, as expressed in miniature paintings or in legends and literature, Muslim men expect women to be highly aware of the inequality inherent in the harem system and therefore unlikely to enthusiastically satisfy their captors' desires.

Many of the Muslim courts employed artists who illustrated art books with miniature paintings. The paintings were not hung on walls, or exhibited in museums, but were kept as a private luxury, to be enjoyed only by the rich and the powerful, who could contemplate them whenever they liked. Contrary to what many Westerners believe, Islam has a rich tradition of secular painting, in spite of its ban on images. It is only in religious rituals that the use of pictorial representation is totally prohibited. From the eighth century onward, Muslim dynasties invested consistently in secular painting. The Umayyad princes decorated their pleasure house of Qusayr 'Amra (in what is now the Transjordan desert, near the Dead Sea) with huge frescoes, while the sixteenth-century Safavid dynasty of Persia raised the art of miniature painting to its highest peak. Most of the miniatures illustrated legends and love poems, and were thus an opportunity for both writers and painters to express their fantasies about women, love, passion—and the risks involved therein.

In both miniatures and literature, Muslim men represent women as active participants, while Westerners such as Matisse, Ingres, and Picasso show them as nude and passive. Muslim painters imagine harem women as riding fast horses, armed with bows and arrows, and dressed in heavy coats. Muslim men portray harem women as uncontrollable sexual partners. But Westerners, I have come to realize, see the harem as a peaceful pleasure-garden where omnipotent men reign supreme over obedient women. While Muslim men describe themselves as insecure in their harems, real or imagined, Westerners describe themselves as self-assured heroes with no fears of women. The tragic dimension so present in Muslim harems—fear of women and male self-doubt—is missing in the Western harem.

The most talkative of the male journalists I met during my book tour were the Mediterranean Europeans. They would define the harem, with sly laughter full of malice, as "a wonderful place where beautiful women are sexually available." Many sophisticated Frenchmen, on the other hand, associated the harem with paintings depicting brothels, like those by Henri de Toulouse-Lautrec (*Au Salon de la rue des Moulins*, 1894) and Edgar Degas (*The Client*, 1879). Most of the Scandinavians just blushed and smiled at the mere mention of the "forbidden" word, letting me infer that politeness and good manners require that some embarrassing subjects best be avoided. The exception to this rule were the Danes, who behaved more like their French and Spanish colleagues by bursting into merry laughter at first, and then, when slightly encouraged, going into great detail about the luxurious embroidered silks that the harem women wear, their long and uncombed hair, and their supine, patiently waiting positions.

Many American journalists described the harem women as Hollywood-inspired dancing slaves. One even started whistling the song that Elvis Presley, dressed as an Arab, performed when he invaded a harem to rescue a sequestered beauty in *Harum Scarum* (1965).[3] [. . .] Jim, a Paris-based American journalist who earns his living by writing about films, taught me a Hollywood expression regarding sexy Oriental movies that I had never heard before: "t and s." The letter "t" stands for "tits" and the letter "s" for "sand."[4] As we were talking, the Disney version of *Aladdin*, which appeared in 1992 shortly after the Gulf War ended, came up, and another journalist hummed the opening song of the movie.[5]

Other Americans remembered the 1917 and 1918 Twentieth Century Fox screen versions of *Aladdin and His Lamp* and *Ali Baba and the Forty Thieves*, or the 1920 *Kismet*, while the multiple versions of *The Thief of Baghdad* seemed to be a cultural landmark of sorts in Western men's psyche. Some quoted the 1924 Douglas Fairbanks version, others the 1940 version, and still others, the 1961 French-Italian version starring Steve Reeves. The 1978 television version, where the caliph of Baghdad was none other than Peter Ustinov, was also mentioned. And an elderly journalist quoted *The Sheik* (1921) with Rudolph Valentino while smiling and caressing an imaginary mustache.

When I envision a harem, I think of a densely populated place where everyone is always watching everyone else. In Muslim harems, even married men and women have great difficulty finding a private place in which to caress each other. As for the married women in the harem, sexual gratification is impossible since they must share their men with hundreds of frustrated "colleagues." So when you think calmly about what a harem is, pornographic bliss is a totally unrealistic expectation. Even if a man kills himself at the task and stuffs himself full with aphrodisiacs, which were an important component of the harem culture, court chronicles reveal that even the most entranced of lovers could outdo himself only sometimes, and then only with that single woman he adored, for as long as his flame kept burning. Meanwhile, the other wives and concubines had to live with their frustrations. So how, I wondered, did Western men create their images of an idyllic, lustful harem?

In Western images of harems, women have no wings, no horses, and no arrows. These Western harems, unlike Muslim ones, are not about terrible sex-wars during which women resist, disturb men's schemes, and sometimes become masters, confusing caliphs and emperors alike. One of the women most often portrayed in Muslim miniatures—be they Persian, Turkish, or Mughal—is Zuleikha, from the biblical legend of Joseph, as narrated in Sura 12 (Verse 12) of the Koran under the title "Yusuf." The story unfolds in Egypt, where Zuleikha, a mature woman married to a powerful man, Putiphar, falls madly in love with the handsome Yusuf when her husband brings him home, expecting her to adopt him as a son. The miniatures show her as an aggressive female sexually harassing the pious Yusuf, who miraculously resists her seductive moves, thus maintaining law and order. The miniatures echo the tragic potentiality of adultery, especially when initiated by a sexually frustrated married woman. However, although the Koran narrates the main events of the legend, Muslim artists do not refer, strangely enough, to the sacred text as the source of their inspiration. Instead, they claim the two giant Persian poets, Firdawsi and Jami, who both wrote a "Yusuf and Zuleikha" epic, the first around A.D. 1010, and the second around 1483.[6] And, although the sacred and profane sources have strikingly different endings, both share one single feature: Zuleikha's capacity to neutralize law and instate chaos.[7]

But to get back to the texts. Although I myself cannot, unfortunately, read either Firdawsi or Jami in the original, being illiterate in Persian, I am always bewitched whenever I read Sura 12 of the Koran, so powerful is its poetry. Sura 12 describes Yusuf as a handsome young man who is a victim of sexual harassment: "And she, in whose house he was, asked of him an evil act. She bolted the doors and said: Come. He said: I seek refuge in Allah!" (Sura 12:23).[8] The Arabic expression used in the verse, "rawadathu 'an Nafsih," is quite explicit: It literally means that she harassed him sexually.

The Sura of Yusuf starts with suspense, in which the reader is invited to help solve a riddle: Who attacked whom? Was it Zuleikha who physically assaulted the pious Yusuf, whose shirt was torn to pieces (12:26), or was it Yusuf who attacked Zuleikha? No wonder the legend is so obsessively reproduced by Muslim artists—its topic is not so much adultery as its probability. Men can make marriage laws and declare them sacred, but there is always a possibility that women will not feel bound by them. And it is this small chance that women might not obey and thereby destabilize the male order that is so striking a component of Muslim culture in both historical reality and fantasy.

As one might expect, Zuleikha, the adulteress, is denied the privilege of having her name in the Koran; she is referred to only as "she." There is also a sect, the extremist "Ajarida," that refuses to admit that the Sura of Yusuf is part of the Koran. According to Shahrastani, a Persian writer of the twelfth century, the Ajarida claim that "A love story cannot be part of the Koran."[9] This might sound logical, if love is considered to be a threat to the established order, but it is the logic of extremism, not of Islam. And this distinction is crucial if we are to understand what is going on in the Muslim world today. Yes, there are Muslim extremists who kill women in the streets of Afghanistan and Algeria, but it is because they are extremists, not because they are Muslim. These same extremists also kill male journalists who insist on expressing different opinions and introducing pluralism into the political dynamic. Islam, both as a legal and a cultural system, is imbued with the idea that the feminine is an uncontrollable power—and therefore the unknowable "other." All the passionate if not hysterical debates about women's rights taking place today in Muslim parliaments from Indonesia to Dakar are in actuality debates about pluralism. These debates relentlessly focus on women because women represent the stranger within the Umma, the Muslim community. It is no wonder that the first decision of Imam Khomeini, who paradoxically declared Iran a republic in 1979, was to ask women to veil. Elections, yes. Pluralism, no. The Imam knew what he was doing. He knew that an unveiled woman forces the Imam to face the fact that the Umma, the community of believers, is not homogeneous.

In Islamic societies, politicians can manipulate almost everything. But thus far, no fundamentalist leader has been able to convince his supporters to renounce Islam's central virtue—the principle of strict equality between human beings, regardless of sex, race, or creed. Women, like Christians or Jews, are considered to be the equal of men in Islam, even though they are granted a minority status that restricts their legal rights and denies them access to the decision-making process. Women in most Islamic nations can participate in their countries' respective decision-making bodies, but only indirectly. Women have a legal status similar to the *dhimmi* ("protected") status of religious minorities and are represented in parliament by a *wali* or *wakil*. Since the *wali* or *wakil* (literally, "representative") is necessarily a Muslim male, women and minorities are condemned to invisibility to keep the fiction of homogeneity alive.

To understand the dynamics in the Muslim world today, one has to remember that no one contests the principle of equality, which is considered to be a divine precept. What is debated is whether *Shari'a*, the law inspired by the Koran, can or cannot be changed. The debate is therefore reduced to "who" made the law. If it is men who made it, then the text can be reinterpreted; reform is possible. But extremists who oppose the democratization of the laws claim that *Shari'a* is as divine as the Koran and therefore unchangeable. The scandalous trial of the Egyptian Abu Zeid, an expert in the historicity of the Koran, who was sentenced as a heretic by a fundamentalist judge in an Egyptian court in August 1996, is but one such dramatization of this clash between the pro-democracy Ijtihad camp (*Shari'a* can be reformed because it is man-made) and the extremists who oppose it.

Once again, women are the focus of this debate because sexual inequality is rooted in *Shari'a*, but even the most fervent extremists never argue that women are inferior, and Muslim women are raised with a strong sense of equality. [. . .]

One can easily predict that women will stir even more violent debates in the decade to come, as globalization forces both Muslim states and their citizens to redefine themselves and create new cultural identities, rooted more in economics than in religion. The fear of the feminine represents the threat from within; the debate about globalization, the threat from without; and both discussions will necessarily be focused on women. Femininity is the emotional locus of all kinds of disruptive forces, in both the real world and in fantasy. And, to get back to my book tour, it is this apparent absence of the feminine as a threat in the Western harem that fascinated me. [. . .]

[Journalist] Jacques [Dupont] highlighted with the humor and self-mockery that is so unique to Parisians something that is frightening to admit in serious conversation today: What attracts him to a woman, at least at the level of fantasy, is the absence of intellectual exchange. Through his comments, he clarified for me the second distinctive feature of the Western harem: Intellectual exchange with women is an obstacle to erotic pleasure. Yet in real or imagined Muslim harems, cerebral confrontation with women is necessary to achieve orgasm. Could it be that things are so different in the West? I wondered. Could it be that cultures manage emotions differently when it comes to structuring erotic responses? I was so baffled by these strange discoveries that I started with the basics: searching through dictionaries in both cultures, checking elementary words such as "odalisque," "desire," "beauty," "attraction," "sexual pleasure," and so on, and listening carefully to what the Western men had to say.

How did Monsieur Ingres manage to have a real Christian wife, whom he married in front of a priest, and at the same time officially paint and sell nude odalisques? Did his wife get jealous when he gazed for hours at the buttocks and thighs of *La Grande Odalisque*? As an Arab woman, I would have been watching him very carefully, just as the *jarya* had watched Harun Ar-Rachid in his harem, where jealousies flared and burned many lives. Was Monsieur Ingres in love with his wife or was theirs an unromantic *mariage de raison*, an arranged marriage? Was he a wildly passionate man, so hot and sexy that Madame Ingres could not cope with his lustful cravings and so accepted the fact that he painted nude images to calm himself? This could be an explanation for the presence of the mysterious Turkish odalisques in a republican French household. It is similar to the explanation frequently given in my hometown of Fez, whenever a middle-aged wife looks for a young bride to help her satisfy her husband's virile demands. Or, at least, those virile demands are often the *official* explanation provided. The real reason is usually economic: In a country where polygamy is enforced by men as sacred law, the aging wife volunteers to find her husband a second bride in order to be able to stick around. The wife swallows her pride and controls her jealousy as she tries to create a new role for herself—that of the removed, but dignified, asexual, menopausal first wife. Without the security of a salary or second income, to express jealousy when your aging husband is ogling younger women is to risk embarking on a penniless future.

Jealousy is so demeaning, as we all know. When I am jealous, it is the only time I can understand how easy it would be to become a criminal. Often, the Muslim woman who chooses to swallow her jealousy turns to religion as a substitute and creates for herself a spiritual life by regularly attending the mosque and religious celebrations. This, after all, is the "Orient," where injustice against women is still camouflaged as sacred law. But when a modern Muslim woman has a salary, like myself, the jealous fights that rage in Muslim kingdoms are similar to those that rage in the republics. Many of my male university colleagues complain about jealous wives and girlfriends who slice their car tires so badly that the gentlemen think twice before upsetting them again. And Madame Ingres was freed from the priests and their manipulations thanks to the French Revolution, wasn't she? Did she really enjoy witnessing her beloved husband dreaming so openly about exotic rivals? Did Monsieur and Madame Ingres have a stormy marriage? Did she scream at him to stop him from painting odalisques? Or shove him down onto her couch and ravish him? I would have buried the damn brushes or given them away to needy painters. How do the French deal with emotions? Does the French Declaration of the Rights of Man and Citizen say anything at all about jealousy?

Ingres was nine years old in 1789, the year in which the French people established "Liberté, Égalité, Fraternité" as the foundation of the Republic of France. And Ingres was a true son of the ideals of the French Revolution: Born in modest circumstances, he then rose up the social ladder effortlessly, his talent recognized, honored, and splendidly rewarded. But if the Republic changed social conditions and paved the way for children of humble origins to shine professionally and thrive economically, nothing of the sort was guaranteed in the more shadowy fields of romance and emotional fulfillment.

Ingres's public life unfolds like a magnificent advertisement for the French Republic. But the Revolution did not seem to have made the successful young man any bolder emotionally. He was not able to take the initiative in choosing his own wife, but instead fell back on the traditional arranged marriage. He got engaged twice to young women who attracted him, but for whatever reason, both engagements were broken off.

For me, as an Arab woman extremely preoccupied with human rights, Ingres's life is fascinating. Although he was a liberated Western man fed on democratic ideas, he couldn't choose his own wife and fantasized about slave women as the epitome of beauty. What kind of revolution, I wonder, do we need to make men dream of self-assertive independent women as the epitome of beauty?

The 1789 French Declaration of the Rights of Man and Citizen was a landmark in the history of mankind. In it, subordination of women was rejected as a sign of despotism. Despotism and slavery were both condemned as shameful characteristics of uncivilized Asian nations. "The servitude of women," wrote Montesquieu in The Spirit of Laws, "is very much in conformity with the genius of despotic government, which likes to abuse everything. Thus in Asia, domestic servitude and despotic government have been seen to go hand in hand in every age."[10] The writings of Montesquieu, who was born in 1689 and died in 1755, twenty-five years before the birth of Ingres, inspired the French people. And the monstrous Asian despotism that Montesquieu so roundly condemned when defining his cherished democracy was none other than that of the Turkish Ottoman empire.[11] Therefore, one would expect that a painter who celebrated odalisques, or Turkish slaves, as ideal beauties in the early days of the French Republic would have been rejected as an uncivilized savage. But this was not so; not only was Ingres's career successful, but his paintings of odalisques were bought by some of the most influential political figures of his century. [. . .]

[O]n the fourth of December, 1813, Ingres and Madeleine Chapelle wed. Although not much is known about Ingres's domestic life, one thing appears to be certain: He and Madeleine had a monogamous marriage. However, only a year after their wedding, Ingres introduced a slave woman into his emotional life—his famous *Grande Odalisque*. But citizen Madeleine Ingres did not scream and protest as a Muslim woman would. In my native Fez medina, women staged huge uproars when their husbands married a second wife, holding funeral-like protests, during which their friends and relatives wailed along with them in the harem courtyards. The fact that polygamy is institutionalized by male law does not make it emotionally acceptable to women. Many queens, as historians have written, suffocated or choked their husbands when they discovered their plans to acquire a second wife, or when the rival actually arrived in the home. Still other historical records show that it was often the women who were the victims of jealousy. "A seventeenth-century document in the Topkapi Palace archives," writes Alev Lytle Croutier in her book, *Harem*, "speaks of the rivalry between Sultana Gülnush and the odalisque Gülbeyaz—(Rose-white), which led to a tragic end. Sultan Mehmed IV had been deeply enamored of Gülnush . . . but after Gülbeyaz entered his harem, his affections began to shift. Gülnush, still in love with the sultan, became madly jealous. One day, as Gülbeyaz was sitting on a rock and watching the sea, Gülnush quietly pushed her off the cliff and drowned the young odalisque."[12]

It was 1814 and Ingres had just turned thirty-four. Unlike Madeleine, his French wife, who could walk and talk, and probably had many domestic chores to attend to, *La Grande Odalisque* was created to do nothing but lie around and look beautiful. In effect, by spending months painting a beautiful woman, Ingres was declaring daily to his wife that she was ugly! Or, at least, that is what a Muslim woman would conclude. How men's and women's emotions unfold in a French harem like the one created by Ingres is incomprehensible to me. What was Ingres's emotional problem? Was he afraid to invest too much emotionally in his wife? The emotional landscape is definitely one of the keys to understanding cultural differences between East and West, I realized. Clearly, I could learn much about my own emotional problems if I could understand why Madeleine Ingres was not jealous. [. . .]

When moved, Ingres expressed his emotions—especially tenderness. He did not hesitate, for example, to write a letter to Madeleine saying how much he missed her presence during the ceremony when Charles X awarded him the Légion d'Honneur in 1824. "When my name was pronounced in the midst of the cheers," he went on, "my poor legs and my face must have given away the state of extreme vulnerability I felt when I had to cover the distance separating me from the king to receive the *Croix* (cross) he gracefully bestowed on me. . . ."[13] Ingres also confessed to Madeleine that he had cried; "You would have cried too if you were there, just like I am still doing while writing to you about it." Ingres was then forty-five and, unlike those men who grow more narcissistic with success, he seems to have mellowed and grown appreciative of the tenderness and emotion he felt toward Madeleine. During this period, he once advised a husband, posing for him for a portrait, to look at his wife so "that his eyes soften."[14] Ingres's fascination with women's emotions, and his attempts to capture their fleeting moods and changing fashions, also contributed to his portraits' appeal.

So it was no wonder that Ingres was devastated when Madeleine, his confidante for more than thirty-five years, died in 1849. Then nearly sixty-nine, he felt so lonely that he decided to remarry three years later. Again he asked friends, this time the Marcottes, to help him arrange his new marriage, and on the 15th of April, 1852, he wed Delphine Ramel. At age forty-two, the new bride was almost thirty years younger than him—a point he often reminded her of—and belonged to a comfortable middle-class family. Before their marriage, she had lived with her father, a mortgage administrator in Versailles.

This second marriage seems to have been as happy as the first. Wrote Ingres to a friend in 1854: "I see nobody or rarely a few friends who have the kindness to admire my present life. My excellent wife is adjusting very well to this way of living. She creates solitude for me and embellishes it almost every evening with two sonatas by the divine Haydn which she interprets very well and with true feeling. Sometimes I accompany her."[15]

Yet, in the midst of this conjugal bliss, Ingres began to paint *The Turkish Bath*, one of his most diabolically voluptuous harems, filled with nude women. The year was 1859, and this time, with the younger Delphine at his side, he seems to have been more emboldened than before as far as his harem fantasies were concerned. Instead of introducing one single odalisque into his monogamous marriage, as he had with Madeleine, he now introduced more than twenty Turkish women, only one of whom looked like Delphine. [. . .]

All the harem women that Ingres fantasized about and painted nonstop for fifty years were idle, helplessly passive, and always pictured indoors, reclining on sofas in an embarrassingly vulnerable nudity. Yet this fantasy of passive harem women does not exist in the Orient!

Ironically, in the Orient—land of harems, polygamy, and veils—Muslim men have always fantasized, in both literature and painting, about self-assertive, strong-minded, uncontrollable, and mobile women. The Arabs fantasized about Scheherazade of *The Thousand and One Nights*; the Persians painted adventurous princesses like Shirin, who hunted wild animals across continents on horseback; and the Mughals, or Turco-Mongols, from central Asia, gave the Muslim world wonderful erotic paintings filled with strong, independent-looking women and fragile, insecure-looking men. [. . .]

Notes

1   Mernissi, Fatima. *Dreams of Trespass: Tales of a Harem Girlhood*. Reading, MA: Addison-Wesley, 1994.

2   Ibn Hazm, *The Ring of the Dove: A Treatise on the Art and Practice of Arab Love*, English translation by A. J. Arberry (London: Luzac & Company, LTD, 1953), p. 34. For the purist who wants to read the Arab original, and it is worth it since the translation is regarded as blasphemous, see *Tawq al Hamama: Fi al-Alfa wa l-Ullaf*, Faroq Saʾd, ed. (Beirut: Manchourat Maktabat al Hayat, 1972), p. 70.

3   To learn more about this song, read Ella Shohat, "Gender and Culture of Empire: Toward a Feminist Ethnography of the Cinema," in *Visions of the East: Orientalism in Films*, Matthew Bernstein and Gaylyn Studlar, eds. (Rutgers, N.J.: Rutgers University Press, 1997), p. 48.

4   For more information on "t" and "s," see ibid., p. 11.

5   I later learned, reading Matthew Bernstein's introduction to *Visions of the East*, that this song was the object of great controversy between the Disney Company and the American Arab Antidiscrimination Committee. The Committee attacked Disney for racist stereotyping and won the case. Disney was forced to change the lyrics that went, "I come from a land, a faraway place, where they cut off your ear, if they don't like your face." See Bernstein, op. cit., p. 17, note 20.

6   Sir Thomas Arnold, *Painting in Islam: A Study of Pictorial Art in Muslim Culture* (New York: Dover Publications, 1965), p. 106.

7   In the sacred sources, be they the Bible or the Koran, Zuleikha is depicted as a loser since Yusuf defeats her adulterous scheme by resisting her seductive moves. But the Persian poets give a happier ending to their "Zuleikha and Yusuf" stories. In their version, the prophet Yusuf, after rejecting Zuleikha in his youth, meets her again later, but hardly recognizes her, as she has grown old, ugly, sick, and destitute. Then, miraculously, he restores her beauty and health—a scene often depicted in miniatures. "The poets carried the story far beyond the point reached in the Book of Genesis or in the Quran," explains Sir Thomas Arnold in *Painting in Islam*. "Potiphar dies and Zulaykha is reduced to a state of abject poverty, and with hair turned white through sorrow, and eyes blinded by continual weeping, she dwells in a hut of reeds by the roadside, and her only solace in her misery is listening to the sound of Joseph's cavalcade as from time to time it rides past." One day, Joseph recognizes Zuleikha and "He then prays to God on her behalf, and her sight and her beauty are restored to her." Ibid., p. 108.

8   Quotation from *The Meaning of the Glorious Koran*, translated by Mohammed Marmaduke Pickthall (New York: Mentor Books, n.d.), p. 177.

9   In Arabic, "wa qalu: la yajuz an takuna qiçata l'ichqi mina l'qur'an" ("And they said: It is impossible that a love story can be part of the Koran"). From Shahrastani, *Al Milal wa-Nihal* (Beirut: dar Ça'b, 1986), vol. 1, p. 128. The author died in the year 547 of the Hijira (twelfth century). A good translation of this book is the French one by Claude Vadet, *Les Dissidences en Islam* (Paris: Geuthner, 1984). The Ajaridite position on Joseph is on page 236.

10 Montesquieu, *The Spirit of Laws* (*De l'Esprit Des Lois*), translated and edited by Anne M. Cohler, Basia Carolyn Miller, and Harold Samuel Stone (Cambridge: Cambridge University Press, 1989), p. 270.

11 See Alain Grosrichard's introductory chapter to his book *The Sultan's Court: European Fantasies of the East* (New York: Verso, 1997).

12 Alev Lytle Croutier, *Harem* (New York: Abbeville Press, 1998), pp. 34–35.

13 H. Lapauze, "Le Roman d'Amour de Mr Ingres," Paris, 1910, pp. 282–287, quoted by Pierre Angrand, *Monsieur Ingres et son Epoque* (Lausanne–Paris: Bibliothèque des Arts, 1967), footnote number 2, p. 48.

14 The portrait was that of Cavé. In Pierre Angrand, *La Vie de Mr Ingres*, p. 211, footnote number 2.

15 Letter to Pauline Guibert, dated 6 September 1854, quoted in Angrand, p. 247.

Chapter 23

Denise Riley

MALEDICTION

THE WORST WORDS REVIVIFY themselves within us, vampirically. Injurious speech echoes relentlessly, years after the occasion of its utterance, in the mind of the one at whom it was aimed: the bad word, splinterlike, pierces to lodge. In its violently emotional materiality, the word is indeed made flesh and dwells amongst us – often long outstaying its welcome. Old word-scars embody a "knowing it by heart," as if phrases had been hurled like darts into that thickly pulsating organ. But their resonances are not amorous. Where amnesia would help us, we can't forget.

This sonorous and indwelling aspect of vindictive words might help to characterize how, say, racist speech works on and in its targets. But wouldn't such a speculation risk simply advocating a systematic cultivation of deafness on the part of those liable to get hurt – or worse, be a criticism of their linguistic vulnerability; "They just shouldn't be so linguistically sensitive"? There's much to be said, certainly, in favor of studiously practicing indifference. But the old playground chant of "sticks and stones may break my bones, but words can never hurt me" was always notoriously untrue. The success of a tactics of indifference to harsh speech will also depend on the vicissitudes of those words' fate in the world, and that lies beyond my control. I change too. The thing upon which malevolent accusation falls, I am still malleable, while the words themselves will undergo their own alterations in time, and so their import for me will weaken or intensify accordingly. On occasion the impact of violent speech may even be recuperable through its own incantation; the repetition of abusive language may be occasionally saved through the irony of iteration, which may drain the venom out of the original insult, and neutralize it by displaying its idiocy.[1] Yet angry interpellation's very failure to always work as intended (since at particular historical moments, I may be able to parody, to weaken by adopting, to corrode its aim) is also exactly what, at other times, works for it. In any event, interpellation operates with a deep indifference as to where the side of the good may lie. And we can't realistically build an optimistic theory of the eventual recuperability of linguistic harm. For here there's no guaranteed rational progress – nor, though, any inescapable irrationality. Repetition will breed its own confident mishearing,[2] but its volatile alterations lean neither toward automatic amelioration nor inevitable worsening.

This observation, though, leaves us with the still largely uninvestigated forensics of spoken injury. Pragmatic studies of swearing certainly exist, but swear words as such are not the topic I have in mind. Nor is "righteous" anger. My preoccupation here is far darker, and restricted to the extreme: some sustained hostility of unremitting verbal violence, like the linguistic voodoo which can induce the fading away of its target, a phenomenon which can't be dismissed as an archaism. The curse does work. Verbal attacks, in the moment they happen, resemble stoning. Then isn't it too labored to ask how they do damage: isn't the answer plain, that they hurt just as stones hurt? At the instant of their impact, so they do. Yet the peculiarity of violent words, as distinct from lumps of rock, is their power to resonate within their target for decades after the occasion on which they were weapons. Perhaps an urge to privacy about being so maliciously named may perpetuate the words' remorseless afterlife: I keep what I was told I was to myself, out of reserve, shame, a wish not to seem mawkish and other not-too-creditable reasons; yet even if I manage to relinquish my fatal stance of nursing my injury, it may well refuse to let go of me. Why, though, should even the most irrational of verbal onslaughts lodge in us as if it were the voice of justice; and why should it stubbornly resist ejection, and defy its own fading? For an accusation to inhere, must its human target already be burdened with her own prehistory of vulnerability, her psychic susceptibility; must it even depend on her anticipating readiness to accept, even embrace, the accusation that also horrifies her? Maybe, then, there's some fatal attraction from the aggression uttered in the present toward earlier-established reverberations within us – so that to grasp its lure, we would have to leave a linguistic account to turn instead to a prelinguistic psychic account. Yet here the standard contrast between the linguistic and the psychic, in which we are usually forced to plump for either the unconscious or language, is especially unhelpful. There's nothing beyond interpellation, if by that *beyond* is meant a plunge into an ether of the psyche as soon as we topple off the ledge of the historical and linguistic. For refusing these thoroughly synthetic alternatives needn't commit us to a belief in an instantaneous, ahistorical impact of the bad word – or to assume some primal word of injury which laid us open subsequently to verbal assault, as if the chronology of harm must always unfold in a straight line of descent.

The impact of violence in the present may indeed revive far older associations in its target. An accusation will always fall onto some kind of linguistic soil, be it fertile or poor; and here a well-prepared loam is no doubt commoner than a thin veneer on bare rock. Should we, though, necessarily call such a variation in anger's reception its "psychic" dimension, in a tone which implies a clear separation from the domain of words? There has, undoubtedly, to be something very strong at work to explain why we can't readily shake off some outworn verbal injury. The nature of this strong thing, though, might better be envisaged as a seepage or bleeding between the usual categorizations; it need not be allocated wholesale to an unconscious considered as lying beyond the verbal, or else to a sphere of language considered as narrowly functional.[3] For the deepest intimacy joins the supposedly linguistic to the supposedly psychic; these realms, distinct by discursive convention, are scarcely separable. Then instead of this distinction, an idea of affective words as they indwell might be more useful – and this is a broadly linguistic conception not contrasted to, or opposed to, the psychic. So, for instance, my amateur philology may be a quiet vengeance: my fury may be, precisely, an intense, untiring, scrupulous contemplation of those old words of malediction which have stuck under the skin.

The tendency of malignant speech is to ingrow like a toenail, embedding itself in its hearer until it's no longer felt to come "from the outside." The significance of its original emanation from another's hostility becomes lost to the recipient as a tinnitus of remembered attack buzzes in her inner ear.[4] The hard word reverberates – so much so that it holds the appeal of false etymology (it's easy to assume that to *reverberate* derives from characteristically self-repeating verbal actions, whereas it meant striking or beating back). That it reverberates, rather than echoes, places it well beyond the possibilities of ironic recuperation that Echo offers; reverberation will only resound, to its own limit. And rancorous phrases, matted in a wordy undergrowth, appear to be "on the inside" as one fights them down while they perpetually spring up again. This is where it's crucial to recall that the accusations originally came from the outside, and the rage they echo was another's rage. But this half-consolation of the realist's recourse to history is not enough. We also need to dedramatize the words as they continue their whirring, and to sedate their bitter resonances in the inner ear's present time. For however does anyone withstand this common experience of being etched and scored with harsh names? One art of survival, I'll suggest, is to concede that "yes, this person really wanted me dead then"; yet in the same breath to see that the hostile wish is not identical with the excessive hostility of the lingering word, which has its own slow-burning temporality. The accuser's personal rage has a different duration from the reson-ances of the recalled inner word: to be able to separate and apportion these two will help. We'd need to try out some art of seeing the denouncer as separate from the denunciation, while also at its mercy himself. Is there some stoical language practice to counter the property of accusation to continue its corrosive work, even though the accuser may have died years ago? How this might be attempted is ventured in the following discussion, where no kindly strategy of humanizing and forgiving the pronouncer of the bad word or of grasp-ing the special susceptibility of its human target is suggested, but a cooler tactic of enhancing the objectification of the word itself. It's the very thinglike nature of the bad word which may, in fact, enable its target to find release from its insistent reverb.

Accusation often lodges in the accused

There was until recently in Paris, on rue Pavée in the quatrième, a decrepit-looking language school which displayed in its window, in English (on a dusty cloth banner, in fifties-style white on red lettering) this injunction: "Don't let the English language beat you – Master it before it masters you." A curious exhortation to have been chosen as a motto by any language school – since for the native speaker the onrush of language is unstoppable, yet the exhortation is also irrelevant for the nonnative, who's never subject to joyous capture by a language not her first.

But what certainly threatens any comforting notion of our mastering language is the gripping power of predatory speech, which needs our best defensive efforts in the face of its threatened mastery of us. It's true enough, though, that not only imperious accusation is apt to indwell. So can lyric, gorgeous fragments, psalms and hymns; beautiful speech also comes to settle in its listeners. There's an unholy coincidence between beauty and cruelty in their verbal mannerisms; citation, reiteration, echo, quotation may work benignly, or as a poetics of abusive diction. If graceful speech is memorable, by what devices do violently ugly and lovely language both inhere; what does the internal strumming of metrical quotation have in common with the compulsions of aggressive speech? Yet perhaps the happily resonant indwelling of lyric may be explained in ways also fitting the unhappy experience of being mastered by hard words far better forgotten. Evidently there exists what we could call "linguistic love," a love sparked and sustained by the appeal of another's spoken or written words – that is, by something in the loved person which is also not of her and which lies largely beyond her control – her language. But if there is a linguistic love which is drawn outward to listen, there's also linguistic hatred, felt by its object as drawn inward. A kind of "extimacy" prevails in both cases. Imagined speech hollows can resemble a linguistic nursing home, in which old fragments of once-voiced accusation or endearment may resent-fully or soulfully lodge. Where verbal recurrences are distressed, they are carried as scabs, encrustations, calcification, cuts. If inner speech can sing, it can also tirelessly whisper, mutter, contemplate under its breath to itself, and obsessively reproach itself. It can angrily fondle those names it had once been called. If there's a habitual (if not inevitable) closeness between accusation and interpellation, there's also an echolalic, echoic aspect to interpellation itself. Persecutory interpellation's shadow falls well beyond the instant of its articulation. There are ghosts of the word which always haunt any present moment of enunciation, rendering that present already murmurous and thickly populated. Perhaps "the psyche" *is* recalled voices as spirit voices manifesting themselves clothed in the flesh of words, and hallucinated accusation may underscore some factually heard accusation. There is in effect a verbal form of post-traumatic stress disorder, marked by unstoppable aural flashbacks. Here anamnesia, unforgetting, is a linguistic curse of a disability. We hear much about the therapeutics of retrieved memory. The inability to *forget*, too, has been classified as a neurological illness.[5]

If language spills to flood everywhere, if it has no describable "beyond," such a broadly true claim can't tell us exactly how it operates on its near side and why its apparent innerness is so ferocious. The reach of a malevolent word's reverberation is incalculable; it may buzz in the head of its hearer in a way that far exceeds any impact that its utterer had in mind. Yet its impress may be weak. Or it may feed melodramas of an apparent addiction to domestic-as-linguistic violence: imagine someone who habitually ends up in a position of pleading with those deaf to all her appeals to act humanely, when it was long clear that they would not do so, yet at those dark moments it seemed to her that her whole possibility of existence was at stake in extracting a humane word from them, although in the past this had always proved impossible. She compulsively redesigns a scenario in which her question "Am I a bad person?" can be asked and answered in its own unhappy terms; for she cannot get her ancient interrogation taken seriously by someone who's not already her opponent; anyone else would rephrase her question, returning it to her to demonstrate its hopelessness. Only she can undo it. Meanwhile if she persists in posing it as it stands, it will only receive an affirmative answer. Then must the force of "the psychic" be isolated here, if the unrelenting person to whom she presents her hopeless appeal is always rediscovered with a terrible reliability, if some damaging interlocutor conveniently appears and reappears for her – while she, the impassioned questioner, labors as if to discover grounds for believing, despite her own sound memories of actual events, that such cruelty could not really have happened?

To continue in this (fatally exhilarating) vein of psychologizing speculation – the capacity of lacerating accusation to indwell may be such that while its target is fearful that it may be true, she's also fearful that it may *not* be true, which would force the abandonment of her whole story. As if in order to "justify" the decades of unhappiness that it has caused her, she almost needs the accusation to be correct – as much as in the same breath, she vehemently repudiates it. Perhaps she would rather take the blame on herself for the harm of the past, because it has already and irretrievably been visited upon her, than to admit it had happened arbitrarily, in that she was then (as a child) truly helpless, an accidental object lying in the path of the assault. Perhaps the need for the accusation to be true, as well as to be simultaneously fought against, is in part her wish to have some rationale, and hence less of frightening contingency as the only explanation for the damage. Perhaps her pleadings for exoneration are also pleadings to have some logic underlying the blame laid bare, so that at last she can grasp and understand it. Hence her tendency to ask repeatedly, "But then why am I, as you tell me I am, an evil person?" There is an anxiety of interpellation, in which its subject ponders incessantly to herself "Am I that name; am I really one of those?" Her query, while it interrogates the harsh attribution, stays under its rigid impress. She needs to find those to whom she can address it and have it taken seriously, despite its capacity to provoke their irritation; this is why recalcitrantly obdurate people will always prove her "best" (that is, least malleable) addressees. She is reluctant to be emancipated from her distressing situation, only because that rescue would makes retrospective nonsense out of a wrong that she was forced to live out as if it had a rationale. Her attachment to the apparent truth inherent in her damnation (even while she nervously denies it) is that in order to make sense of the misery it has caused, she must know it to have been deserved. To have that mimesis of logic taken away from her in retrospect, to be shorn of its "necessity" in the name of her own emancipation is hard – despite the fact that she also profoundly disbelieved in it. For a long time she has struggled intently to convey intelligibility to the damage in the moment that she underwent it, as if there had to be a truth in it. This is a difficult point, and I'm not hinting at any masochistic notion of hers that her pain is deserved, is her own fault – but am simply describing her wish for there to have been some necessity to it, in order to justify it in retrospect.

These last two paragraphs have mimicked a train of speculation as to why, for some purely imaginary heroine of pathos, another's bitter words might have come to be entertained gravely by her. Yet if we're inquiring what exists already that chimes within its target in order for lacerating interpellation to work, the pathology of that accusation itself might accompany our habitual attention to the weaknesses of the accused. An air of reason makes its fatal appearance whenever accusation insistently claims that it is speaking a purely rational cause and effect in its sentence "You are this bad thing, because I say so." The fantasy of formulaic interpellation is that it's only addressing the target which stands before it, whereas its own temporality is badly askew.[6] Then the distorting work of repeated echo may happen for the hearer too: "I've heard this accusation before, so it must hold some truth." Compelled to seek out any logic in the charges against her, she may desperately try to impose some sequence upon what is badly skewed. Perhaps her will to unearth some reason within cruelty will mean that she won't ever detect and register anything intelligible in whatever benign utterances might later come her way. But now we have slipped straight back onto the terrain of speculative psychology again. Next we might try turning it, not onto the target, but onto the utterer of the bad word.

Accusers themselves are forcibly spoken

It is the cruel gift of the malignant word to linger and echo as if fully detached from its original occasion, whose authoritative hostility I might by now, having recognized it as such, have dethroned. For the word itself still retains its reverberating autonomy, despite my potential overthrow of its speaker. This fact may offer one answer to the suspicion that accusation can retain me in its clutches only because I am especially emotionally pliable in the face of the authority of the Other. The word, instead, may be the real Other. The Other may be cut down to size as words, and dedramatized to lowercase.

A difficulty with theories of the capitalized Other is that they shortcircuit the complexity of influences, suggesting a narrowed dialectic, since they function as descriptions of a fantasied mastery which operates within and on the singular figure of the self. But my "I" also always emerges from somewhere else, before the congealing of the Other, and across some history of linguistic exchanges prior to my mastery of words.[7] I am the residue of echoes which precede my cohering and imbue my present being with a shadowiness. These aural shadows may be dispelled, but they may thicken and assume deeper powers of obscurantism. This uncertainty also troubles my accuser equally – perhaps worse. Which is not to deny that there is domination; but we could remember that the big Other of theorized fantasy is also mapped onto the mundane lowercase other in the daily world, those ordinary human others who are also produced by the script of rage, driven along by its theatrical autopilot. The accuser, too, is spoken.

Wittgenstein, a nervously driven questioner himself, brooded over the psychology of compulsive philosophical doubt: "Why should anyone want to ask this question?"[8] The same musing could be turned toward the accuser as a phenomenon: "Why ever should anyone want to speak with this violence?" But there's another thought which sidelines such an interrogation of my accuser's motives: the reflection that he is dispossessed of his own words in advance. The rhetoric of rage speaks him mechanically and remorselessly. However much the accuser feels himself to triumph in the moment of his pronouncement, he is prey to echo. For, as Wallace Stevens neatly observed of the cavernous grandeur of inner oratory, "When the mind is like a hall in which thought is like a voice speaking, the voice is always that of someone else."[9] The orator of violence is merely an instrument of dictation by tics and reflexes. There's nothing gratifyingly original about the language of attack, in which old speech plays through the accuser; it's the one who speaks the damage who becomes its sounding board. (I'm not inching toward a sneaking sympathy for the utterer of hate: that he himself is not remotely in possession of his language does nothing whatsoever to soften his words as they streak through him to crash onto their target.) Rage speaks monotonously. The righteousness of wrathful diction's vocabulary sorely restricts it, the tirade marked by that lack of reflection which alone lets the raging speaker run on and on. Once any awareness of his repetitiousness creeps over him, rather than feel vindicated by the tradition which is driving him, he's more likely to feel embarrassed enough to stop. His fury may be exaggerated by his helplessness at being mastered by his own language (whether or not he gives this description to his subjugation). For the language of anger is so dictatorial that it won't allow him to enjoy any conviction that he's voicing his own authenticity. Meanwhile, my very existence as the butt of his accusation is maddening to him, since under his onslaught, I'm apparently nothing for myself any longer but am turned into a mere thing-bearer of his passion. This is almost irrespective of my own passivity or my retaliation; it's because his utterance has, in its tenor, thrown me down. For the rage speaker, I can have no life left in me, or rather none of that combative life that he needs to secure his own continuing linguistic existence for himself. Attacked, I'm rendered discursively limp, but no real relief can be afforded to my adversary by what he has produced as my rag doll quiescence. The more intense the anger, the less the sense of any agency its utterer possesses, until eventually he feels himself to be the "true victim" in the affair. Hence that common combination of rage with self-pity: a lachrymose wrath. In the light of all this, the injunction to "get in touch with your anger" is hardly the therapeutically liberating practice its proposers assume. Instead, the following variant on the Parisian language school's exhortation, cited earlier, that we should master language before it masters us – "master the language of anger before it masters you" – would prove more emancipating.

But what about being the bad speaker myself? There's an experience that could be described as a linguistic occasion, of being poised somewhere halfway between "language speaks me" and "I speak language." It is the flashing across the mind of words which fly into the head as if they somehow must be said. A clump of phrases shape their own occasion, which swells toward articulation. But I can stop their translation into speech; when maxims are actually uttered aloud, then something else has already given these wordy impulses a currency and licensed their entry into a world of ordered fantasy. This "something else" runs close to the question of somewhere else. Where is the place where language works? A doubtful contrast of inner and outer haunts the puzzle of whether I speak (from the inside outward) or whether I am spoken (from the outside in). This old tension between speaking language and being spoken by it still stretches uncertainly; neither the topography of language's extrusion from the speaker's mouth like ectoplasm, nor its companion, the topography of linguistic entry from the outside, seems an apt resolution. The latter offers a vision of penetration through the ear, like that persuasive Byzantine myth of the annunciation and conception, in which a falling star has shot the ear of the patient Virgin Mary. Some-times, in an attempt to resolve such puzzles of the place of speech, its polarities get folded together so that the conventionally outer traverses the conventionally inner. Here, for instance: "This passion of the signifier now becomes a new dimension of the human condi-tion in that it is not only man who speaks, but that in man and through man it speaks, that his nature is woven by effects in which is to be found the structure of language, of which he becomes the material, and that therefore there resounds in him, beyond what could be conceived of by a psychology of ideas, the relation of speech."[10] How does such a resonance work in respect of bad words? If words themselves can neatly exemplify the concept of extimacy, in that they are good candidates to be that trace of externality, the foreign body lodged at the very heart of psychic life, nevertheless our impression of an unalloyed inward-ness in the case of inner speech is still acute. Despite the attractions of conceiving language as lying out there and lunging in from the outside to speak the speaker, we still sense that we fish up our inner words, or dredge them up. But in the case of recalled damaging speech, it's less like a trawling expedition to plumb some depth, but more of its rising up unbidden, kraken-like, to overwhelm and speak us. Yet at the same time we can also understand this unconscious to come from the outside, in the shape of the common and thoroughly external unconscious of unglamorous language. This mutates into what we experience as our pro-foundly inner speech. Or as Volosinov (who by the word *ideological* appears to mean the whole world of signs and gestures)[11] tautly formulated it: "Psychic experience is something inner that becomes outer, and the ideological sign, something outer that becomes inner. The psyche enjoys extraterritorial status in the organism. It is a social entity that penetrates inside the organism of the individual person."[12] These shards of imported sociality as bad words remain as impersonal traces in me, in the way that swearing is impersonal; I have not thought them up, they are derivations, clichéd fragments of unoriginality which have lodged in my skull. Usually my verbal memory isn't bland or kindly, or even discreet in its recall. Linguistic shrapnel can lie embedded for years, yet still, as old British soldiers from the First World War reportedly used to say, "give me gyp in damp weather." Still, language is not exactly speaking me at these points – for, unlike the swear word that escapes me when I hammer my thumb, I retain some capacity to not utter it. A single speech event doesn't work in isolation, but darts into the waiting thickness of my inner speech to settle into its dense receptivity. It may become a furious dialogue where I'll plead with some imagined inward other; its script grows heavy with his antagonism, which it preserves in me. My subsequent distress is rehearsed intently and silently under my breath, in a darker version of Volosinov's more benevolent persuasion: "Therefore the semiotic material of the psyche is preeminently the word – inner speech. Inner speech, it is true, is intertwined with a mass of other motor reactions having semiotic value. But all the same, it is the word that constitutes the foundation, the skeleton of inner life. Were it to be deprived of the word, the psyche would shrink to an extreme degree: deprived of all other expressive activities, it would die out altogether."[13]

My swollen (because word-stuffed) psyche can, however, assume the most unbecoming shapes. Some graceless prose of the world has got me in its grip, and my word-susceptible faculty is seized and filled up by it. It's a neurolinguistic circus, this wild leaping to my tongue of banally correct responses, bad puns, retold jokes to bore my children, and undiscerning quotes. To this list could be added many other kinds of stock formulas, in the shape of racist utterance, idle sexism, and other readymades. Inner language is not composed of graceful musing, but of disgracefully indiscriminate repetition, running on automatic pilot. Nevertheless, even if such reflections mean that I'm displaced as an original thinker,

I'm not quite evacuated. Even if my tawdry inner language is thinking me (although *thought* is too dignified a term for such gurglings), there's many a slip between inner thought and lip. It's certainly speaking in me; but I can subdue it before it fully speaks me, I can edit or inhibit the invading words. I am an enforced linguistic collaborator, but only insofar as a long parade of verbal possibilities marches across my horizons. Thought is made in the mouth, but it can also be halted before it passes the lips. And if it isn't, this is hardly an expression of my spontaneity, but rather of my consent to language's orders. Uttering bad words entails an especial passivity of allowing myself to be spoken by automated verbiage, by an "it is speaking in me." If I don't moderate my bad words, my supposedly authentic expression of my feeling consists merely in my obedience to the rising of what is ready made to the tongue. I'm not literally compelled to speak my love, my despair, or my cynicism. Uttered aggression happens when something in me has licensed the articulation of my linguistic impulses into more than flickers. An expression flashes over me and it will have its way, but only if I don't throw it out. That's the extent of the action of my linguistic will; it is no powerful author of its own speech. It comes puffing up in the wake of the inner linguistic event to deal with its violence, to assent to it or demur, or to ascribe some given sentiment or abrogate to myself that standard echoing opinion. What it takes for me, apropos being or not being a bad speaker myself, is not to be a beautiful soul with the hem of my skirts drawn aside from the mud of linguistic harm, but to elect whether to broadcast or to repress the inward yet still thoroughly worldly chattering of imported speech that fills me.

The word as thing

Gripped by visions of exuberance swelling into parsimony, Hegel wrote: "Speech and work are outer expressions in which the individual no longer keeps and possesses himself within himself, but lets the inner get completely outside of him, leaving it at the mercy of something other than himself. For that reason we can say with equal truth that these expressions express the inner too much, as that they do so too little . . ."[14] Such a reflection seems to lean toward an antiexpressivist stance, in which a notion of language's natural "expressivity" becomes terribly misleading, either because my utterance is too immediately saturated with me, or is too radically separated from me and is under the sway of whatever carries my words away and out of the range of my intentions. It would be bad naming in particular, through its overblown immediacy, which "does not therefore provide the expression which is sought"[15] and lacks that finally productive self-alienation which pertains (at least in the spasmodically softer focus of the "Hegelian" view) to language proper. In this, Language or Word is Spirit. And if in addition we hold the word to be also historical and material, then the cruel word must also call us into social being, if of a deathly kind. As for the possibility of our resisting it, the language hangs there, supremely indifferent as to whether it is resisted or not. What's more critical for what we could roughly call the Hegelian word view is that to ignore language's sociality would go violently against the way of language in the world. Sociality, of course, is not sociability. On the aspect of making people up, one post-Hegelian has claimed,

> What I seek in speech is the response of the other. What constitutes me as subject is my question. In order to be recognised by the other, I utter what was only in view of what will be. In order to find him, I call him by a name that he must assume or refuse in order to reply to me. . . . But if I call the person to whom I am speaking by whatever name I choose to give him, I intimate to him the subjective function that he will take on again in order to reply to me, even if it is to repudiate this function.[16]

In this manner, Lacan continues to emphasize, I install him as a subject.

Yet we might demur here, in respect of malediction. For hatred aims not at any animated exchange with a respondent, but at that person's annihilation. My defense against serious verbal onslaught, then, could well adopt an analogous tactic of impersonality, and espouse a principled *non*engagement with the proffered scenario of (hostile) recognition. I'll ignore the utterer, the better to dissect the utterance. To isolate the word as thing, to inspect it and refuse it, demands a confident capacity to act unnaturally toward language, which normally functions as an energetic means of exchange. Bad words' peculiarly seductive distraction incites me to slip toward self-scrutiny, because another's angry interpellation so readily slides into becoming my own self-interpellation, where a thousand inducements to self-description, self-subjectification, and self-diagnosis are anyway waiting eagerly at its service.[17] But if I simply act "naturally" toward these lures of the bad word, by treating it as any token of exchange and recognition between speakers, I'll be thrown down by it. Then how may I shield myself from its furious resonances? If I don't want to stay petrified by it, then instead I have to petrify it—and in the literal sense. That is, I'll assert its stony character.

Verbal aggression may seem, at first, to be only formally language, and scarcely that at all. It resembles a stone hurled without reflection, which the furious thrower has snatched up just because it lay to hand. The target can't deflect the blow, but will be spared its aftereffects because she realizes the impersonal quality of the thing. The word considered as stone will shock but not break her. The denunciation hurts on impact but later it weakens, as its target sees there is only an accidental link between what was hurled and the will to hurl. She realizes that the bad word is not properly "expressive" of the speaker's impulse to aggressive speech (it cannot be, since "there is always at once too much as too little"[18]) while the impulse needs to be understood in itself and independently of its instrument. So if I decide to embrace this defensive strategy, I can inform the malignant word that it's not really a word by the strenuous artifice of detaching it from the person who pronounced it (dispatching him, for the time being, to wander stripped of his tongue in the idiosyncratic shades of his own psychology). This is my opening gambit. Next I'll turn to contemplate the malevolent word, now separated from its speaker, and quivering furiously like an abandoned dart lost to the guiding authority of the hand that threw it. Now I have to aim at its death, in the same way that, as a spoken accusation, it had aimed at my death. I can kill it only by artificially abstracting it from the realm of language altogether (although I realize perfectly well that human utterance always bristles with such weapons). I have to let it go indifferently, as a thing to which I myself have become as indifferent as the bad word itself had really been, all along, to me. The *accuser* was not indifferent, then. But the afterlife of malignant speech is vigorously spectral, quite independent of its emission at the instant of rage. The bad word flaps in its vampire's afterlife in the breast of its target, who can try to quell it, but "cannot go the length of being altogether done with it to the point of annihilation: in other words, he only *works* on it."[19] The spoken savagery hovers there still. However can its target "work" on it? Stripping the speaker away from the word brings it into a loneliness, into its prominent isolation from the occasion of its utterance. This act of detaching it returns it to its impersonal communality, and into the dictionary of latent harm, while wrenching it away from its respectably bland and democratic-sounding claim to share in language's supposed intersubjectivity. And as suggested, I can also turn the phenomenology of cruel speaking against my accuser to characterize him as not having been the master, let alone the origin, of his own sadism, but of having been played like a pipe, swayed like a hapless reed. The words that rushed to his tongue were always an ersatz rhetoric. The diction of hatred long precedes its speakers. Meanwhile, I can also recognize his distance from me, his indifference – an indifference which, by now, is not only a spent feeling only coolly attentive to me, but of a psychology which has long since returned to itself, and now wanders about the world intent on its fresh preoccupations, far out of the range of my unhappy surveillance.

But may not my commentary have dealt in too cavalier or too sunnily optimistic a fashion with the hurtful word's curious duration? I've been implying that the intention to hurt can be treated by its target as almost irrelevant, and that there's an impersonality in hate speech which can be harnessed for protective and quasi-therapeutic purposes. But the injured person may well feel that the aggressive speech was heavy with a plan to hurt her and was calculatedly aimed at the gaps in her armor; how, then, could her conviction of this deliberate intent to cause pain be at all eased by the thesis that bad words also enthrall, in all senses, their own speaker? To which reasonable objection I'd reply that my speculations are indeed an exercise in mounting a defense, and they do sideline this question of recognizing a pointed intention to destroy. But they also usefully detach the fact of an intent to hurt from any assumption that the angry speaker controls the repercussions of his words; for the targeted person might well assume his invincibility and so run the risk of crediting the violent speaker with more than he really possesses. What's more, following the Stoic principle of discerning what's up to you, or what lies within your proper sphere of concern, you'd do far better to return the other to the vagaries of his own passion, rather than pursue him or her in your imagination with interrogations about motives: "Leave another's wrongdoing where it lies."[20]

Yet there's still a further turn in the work that has to be done. Love's work pales in comparison with Hate's work, in the sense of the legacy of being hated, which condemns its recipients to an iniquitous toil of elucidation.[21] Having returned the bad word to its waiting niche in the stout dictionary of unkindness, I'll need not only to return the speaker to the accident of himself, but I have to attempt a further labor of emancipation for myself. I must recognize his indifference to my present tormented memories of his old utterances, and return him to an absolute indifference in which I abandon him, even in my speculations. I, too, need to "have done with the thing altogether."[22] But to succeed in having done with it demands a prior and ferocious dwelling on it, which first unsparingly remembers the reverberating word as word — yet only in order to restore its truly impersonal quality, to return it to the generality of utterance from whence it came, and to acknowledge its superb and sublimely indifferent capacity to take me or leave me. That is, I'll get rid of understanding myself as "the suffering person." And I shall manage to give up that unhappy and unproductive self-designation only at the same stroke in which I can fully grasp the impersonality of the bad word. This I'll come to do as a consequence of registering its cruelty, letting it sink completely into me — that is, by going straight through the route of the profoundly personal. Only then, through entering its peculiar blackness unprotected, can I sever the word from its speaker in order to imaginatively return him to his true contingency and to his present cheerily amnesiac indifference to my continuing lacerations by his verbal attack, the occasion of which has doubtless long since escaped his mind.

By this stage, I've gradually and waveringly relinquished what's standardly taken to be a Hegelian concept of language, because it would have been too optimistic, since too tranquilly intersubjective, for the task at hand. Now instead, some of Hegel's own and less sunny descriptions of language as a "stain," a "contagion," and the ground of "a universal infection" of selves may receive their testing ground on the territory of damaging words.[23] (Admittedly, there are pleasant kinds of stains, and perhaps even happy contagions; but Hegel's scattered metaphor of infection is harder to recuperate.) Let's follow its logic. To enable my release, my initial infection by the bad word with virulent fear and the most relentless self-doubt is necessary. A mild anxiety won't suffice. My entire self-conception must have tottered. "If it has not experienced absolute fear, but only some lesser dread, the negative being has remained for it something external, its substance has not been infected by it through and through."[24] With this apparently paradoxical association of language with infection, we're dealing, in short, with the true sociability of language – as contagion, as a mouth disease. To recover, as I must, from accusation's damaging impact on me, I can't effectively stand lonely proof against it, but instead have to admit something that so far I have been reluctant to consider: that, *exactly as my injury*, it enjoys a fully languagelike status. Now, in this moment, I have abandoned all my earlier humanist strategy of seeing the bad word as a hurled stone and therefore not as true language. Instead I've begun to understand that the bad word is an indifferently speaking stone. In sum, that harsh language evinces a sheer indifference both to me and also to my accuser, an ultimately sociable impersonality, and a sadism, that (uninterested in me though it is) has worked successfully on me while it also suffers its own corrosion and decay.

But if instead I overlook all these characteristics of language, and meditate solely "psychologically," I'll examine only my own idiosyncratically undefended subjecthood by discovering some prior susceptibility within my depths, an early wound which is the key to my constant vulnerability – as if therein I could unearth some meaning to my haunting by the word and free myself. The trouble with this speculation is that the linguistic structure of my childhood verbal wounding was and is exactly the same as that which vexes me now; when I was two years old, there was no "purely psychic" naming for me even then, but an interpellation which, always linguistic, was thereby always affective. Infancy's learning to speak is also entangled in parental emotions – the hostility, anxiety, lucidity, mildness. But this evident fact only reinforces my persuasion that the linguistic and the psychic are neither separable, nor to be subsumed one under another. If there is now the same scenario, an original injury which I relive, its endless reanimation in me is not surprising, given the paucity of my capacities for self-protection then. That is, there's not a chronology of depth of my early (psychic) injury which precedes, founds, and accounts for some later and categorically different (linguistic) vulnerability – other than that vital history of my childish and necessary dependence on others' affective words.

All of these considerations which might help to deflate lacerating speech – considerations of the vatic nature of the language itself, and the transient emotion of its speaker driven by the rhetoric he deploys – might be equally applied to a recollected "I love you." The erratic love-speaker claims to have meant his declarations *then*, but now he has changed his feelings and disavows everything. And he protects himself from the charge of fickleness by avowing the innocent contingency of his declaration, rather in the way that to protect oneself from the hate speaker, one considers how the bite of his words might be eased through a recognition of their awful contingency. If we compare the aftermath of hearing "I love you" with the aftermath of hearing "I hate you," in both instances the hearer may fight to sever the utterance from its vanished utterer. With the former declaration, the struggle is to find compensation in the teeth of impermanence (those words were definitely said to me, so at least I can be sure that once I was loved even though their speaker has gone). And with the latter, to find protection from the risk of permanence (those words were directed at me, but it wasn't especially me who was hated, I just accidentally got in that speaker's way).

The stoic's route to consolation, however, can't follow this path of detecting necessity in the instance of her being loved, but contingency in the case of her being hated. She is more prone to regard both love speech and hate speech alike as workings of that language which (to return to our Parisian language school's slogan) we've not the faintest hope of mastering before it masters us. Nonetheless, we can still elect to suffer our subjugation moodily and darkly, or we can treat it more lightly and indifferently, as a by-product of the disinterested machinations of language. To espouse such a notion of linguistic impartiality in this way is, I think, the sounder course. I could be more effectively freed from damaging words by first confronting and then conceding my own sheer contingency as a linguistic subject. I am a walker in language. It's only through my meanders and slow detours, perhaps across many decades, toward recognizing language's powerful impersonality – which is always operating despite and within its air of a communicative "intersubjectivity" – that I can "become myself." Yet I become myself only by way of fully accepting my own impersonality, too – as someone who is herself accidentally spoken, not only by violent language, but by any language whatsoever – and who, by means of her own relieved recognition of this very contingency, is in significant part released from the powers of the secretive and unspeakable workings of linguistic harm.

Notes

1   See chapter 5 of my *The Words of Selves: Identification, Solidarity, Irony* (Stanford, Calif.: Stanford University Press, 2000).

2   Joan Scott, writing about history's phantasms, notes that "retrospective identifications, after all, are imagined repetitions and repetitions of imagined resemblances." "Fantasy Echo: History and the Construction of Identity," *Critical Inquiry* (winter 2001): 284–304 (quote, 287).

3   Riley, *The Words of Selves*, 84–89. For an introduction to the history of pragmatics, which does differently consider the forcefulness of language, see B. Nehrlich and D. Clarke, *Language, Action, Context: The Early History of Pragmatics in Europe and America, 1780–1930* (Amsterdam: John Benjamins, 1996).

4   The phenomenon of "audiation" and inner replaying is implicitly discussed in my chapter "A Voice without a Mouth," in *The Force of Language*, by Jean-Jacques Lecercle and Denise Riley (London: Palgrave Macmillan, 2004). (Audiation is the silent and private "running through the head" of music.)

5   This can be found, for instance, in some psychiatric classifications used in South America.

6   As Joan Scott writes, "the fantasy also implies a story about a sequential relationship for prohibition, fulfillment, and punishment (having broken the law that prohibits incest, the child is being beaten)." Scott, "Fantasy Echo," 290.

7   Jean Laplanche has remarked on the "message" which always comes to me from another, as an impingement on me of the other's unconscious, formative for my own, and has raised the question of how to take account of that constitutive alterity. "Confronted with this enigmatic message, a message compromised by any number of unconscious resurgences, the child translates it as best as he can, with the language at his disposal." Jean Laplanche, *Essays on Otherness*, ed. John Fletcher (New York: Routledge, 1998), 158–59.

8   A burden of his sustained discussion of pain and skepticism about its reporting, in his *Philosophical Investigations*, trans. G. E. M. Anscombe (Oxford: Basil Blackwell, 1963).

9   From "Adagia," in *Wallace Stevens: Collected Poetry and Prose*, ed. Frank Kermode and Joan Richardson (New York: Library of America, 1997), 907.

10   Jacques Lacan, "The Signification of the Phallus," in *Ecrits: A Selection*, trans. Alan Sheridan (London: Routledge, 2001), 315.

11   The Russian word *ideologiya* has, like *ideology*, debated meanings. As one glossary on Bakhtin's terms, by Graham Roberts, asserts, "The Russian *ideologiya* is less politically coloured than the English word 'ideology.' In other words, it is not necessarily a consciously held political belief system; rather it can refer in a more general sense to the way in which members of a given social group view the world. It is in this broader sense that Bakhtin uses the term. For Bakhtin, any utterance is shot through with 'ideologiya,' any speaker is automatically an ideologue." *The Bakhtin Reader*, ed. Pam Morris (London: Edward Arnold, 1994), 249.

12   V. N. Volosinov, *Marxism and the Philosophy of Language*, trans. from the 1930 edition by Ladislav Matejka and I. R. Titunik (New York and London: Seminar Press, 1973), 39.

13   Volosinov, *Marxism and the Philosophy of Language*, 29.

14   G. W. F. Hegel, *Phenomenology of Spirit*, trans. A. V. Miller (Oxford: Oxford University Press, 1977), 187.

15   Hegel, *Phenomenology of Spirit*, 188.

16   Jacques Lacan, "The Signification of the Phallus," 86–87.

17   ". . . through all the techniques of moral and human sciences that go to make up a knowledge of the subject." Gilles Deleuze, *Foucault*, trans. Sean Hand (London: Athlone Press, 1999), 103.

18   Hegel, *Phenomenology of Spirit*, 308.

19   Hegel, *Phenomenology of Spirit*, 116.

20   Marcus Aurelius, maxim 20, book 9, *Meditations*, trans. Maxwell Staniforth (London: Penguin Books, 1964), 142. See also, again in the spirit of Epictetus, his "That men of a certain type should behave as they do is inevitable. To wish it otherwise were to wish the fig tree would not yield its juice." Book 4, maxim 6, 65.

21   A recall of the title *Love's Work*, Gillian Rose (London: Chatto and Windus, 1995).

22   Hegel, *Phenomenology of Spirit*, 116.

23   "Just as the individual self-consciousness is immediately present in language, so it is also immediately present as a universal infection; the complete separation into independent selves is at the same time the fluidity and universally communicated unity of the many selves; language is the soul existing as soul." Ibid., 430.

24   Ibid., 119.

Chapter 24

Judith Butler

VIOLENCE, MOURNING, POLITICS

I **PROPOSE TO CONSIDER** a dimension of political life that has to do with our exposure to violence and our complicity in it, with our vulnerability to loss and the task of mourning that follows, and with finding a basis for community in these conditions. We cannot precisely "argue against" these dimensions of human vulnerability, inasmuch as they function, in effect, as the limits of the arguable, even perhaps as the fecundity of the inarguable. It is not that my thesis survives any argument against it: surely there are various ways of regarding corporeal vulnerability and the task of mourning, and various ways of figuring these conditions within the sphere of politics. But if the opposition is to vulnerability and the task of mourning itself, regardless of its formulation, then it is probably best not to regard this opposition primarily as an "argument." Indeed, if there were no opposition to this thesis, then there would be no reason to write this essay. And, if the opposition to this thesis were not consequential, there would be no political reason for reimagining the possibility of community on the basis of vulnerability and loss.

Perhaps, then, it should come as no surprise that I propose to start, and to end, with the question of the human (as if there were any other way for us to start or end!). We start here not because there is a human condition that is universally shared—this is surely not yet the case. The question that preoccupies me in the light of recent global violence is, Who counts as human? Whose lives count as lives? And, finally, What *makes for a grievable life*? Despite our differences in location and history, my guess is that it is possible to appeal to a "we," for all of us have some notion of what it is to have lost somebody. Loss has made a tenuous "we" of us all. And if we have lost, then it follows that we have had, that we have desired and loved, that we have struggled to find the conditions for our desire. We have all lost in recent decades from AIDS, but there are other losses that afflict us, from illness and from global conflict; and there is the fact as well that women and minorities, including sexual minorities, are, as a community, subjected to violence, exposed to its possibility, if not its realization. This means that each of us is constituted politically in part by virtue of the social vulnerability of our bodies—as a site of desire and physical vulnerability, as a site of a publicity at once assertive and exposed. Loss and vulnerability seem to follow from our being socially constituted bodies, attached to others, at risk of losing those attachments, exposed to others, at risk of violence by virtue of that exposure.

I am not sure I know when mourning is successful, or when one has fully mourned another human being. Freud changed his mind on this subject: he suggested that successful mourning meant being able to exchange one object for another;[1] he later claimed that incorporation, originally associated with melancholia, was essential to the task of mourning.[2] Freud's early hope that an attachment might be withdrawn and then given anew implied a certain interchangeability of objects as a sign of hopefulness, as if the prospect of entering life anew made use of a kind of promiscuity of libidinal aim.[3] That might be true, but I do not think that successful grieving implies that one has forgotten another person or that something else has come along to take its place, as if full substitutability were something for which we might strive.

Perhaps, rather, one mourns when one accepts that by the loss one undergoes one will be changed, possibly for ever. Perhaps mourning has to do with agreeing to undergo a transformation (perhaps one should say *submitting* to a transformation) the full result of which one cannot know in advance. There is losing, as we know, but there is also the transformative effect of loss, and this latter cannot be charted or planned. One can try to choose it, but it may be that this experience of transformation deconstitutes choice at some level. I do not think, for instance, that one can invoke the Protestant ethic when it comes to loss. One cannot say, "Oh, I'll go through loss this way, and that will be the result, and I'll apply myself to the task, and I'll endeavor to achieve the resolution of grief that is before me." I think one is hit by waves, and that one starts out the day with an aim, a project, a plan, and finds oneself foiled. One finds oneself fallen. One is exhausted but does not know why. Something is larger than one's own deliberate plan, one's own project, one's own knowing and choosing.

Something takes hold of you: where does it come from? What sense does it make? What claims us at such moments, such that we are not the masters of ourselves? To what are we tied? And by what are we seized? Freud reminded us that when we lose someone, we do not always know what it is *in* that person that has been lost.[4] So when one loses, one is also faced with something enigmatic: something is hiding in the loss, something is lost within the recesses of loss. If mourning involves knowing what one has lost (and melancholia originally meant, to a certain extent, not knowing), then mourning would be maintained by its enigmatic dimension, by the experience of not knowing incited by losing what we cannot fully fathom.

When we lose certain people, or when we are dispossessed from a place, or a community, we may simply feel that we are undergoing something temporary, that mourning will be over and some restoration of prior order will be achieved. But maybe when we undergo what we do, something about who we are is revealed, something that delineates the ties we have to others, that shows us that these ties constitute what we are, ties or bonds that compose us. It is not as if an "I" exists independently over here and then simply loses a "you" over there, especially if the attachment to "you" is part of what composes who "I" am. If I lose you, under these conditions, then I not only mourn the loss, but I become inscrutable to myself. Who "am" I, without you? When we lose some of these ties by which we are constituted, we do not know who we are or what to do. On one level, I think I have lost "you" only to discover that "I" have gone missing as well. At another level, perhaps what I have lost "in" you, that for which I have no ready vocabulary, is a relationality that is composed neither exclusively of myself nor you, but is to be conceived as *the tie* by which those terms are differentiated and related.

Many people think that grief is privatizing, that it returns us to a solitary situation and is, in that sense, depoliticizing. But I think it furnishes a sense of political community of a complex order, and it does this first of all by bringing to the fore the relational ties that have implications for theorizing fundamental dependency and ethical responsibility. If my fate is not originally or finally separable from yours, then the "we" is traversed by a relationality that we cannot easily argue against; or, rather, we can argue against it, but we would be denying something fundamental about the social conditions of our very formation.

A consequential grammatical quandary follows. In the effort to explain these relations, I might be said to "have" them, but what does "having" imply? I might sit back and try to enumerate them to you. I might explain what this friendship means, what that lover meant or means to me. I would be constituting myself in such an instance as a detached narrator of my relations. Dramatizing my detachment, I might perhaps only be showing that the form of attachment I am demonstrating is trying to minimize its own relationality, is invoking it as an option, as something that does not touch on the question of what sustains me fundamentally.

What grief displays, in contrast, is the thrall in which our relations with others hold us, in ways that we cannot always recount or explain, in ways that often interrupt the self-conscious account of ourselves we might try to provide, in ways that challenge the very notion of ourselves as autonomous and in control. I might try to tell a story here about what I am feeling, but it would have to be a story in which the very "I" who seeks to tell the story is stopped in the midst of the telling; the very "I" is called into question by its relation to the Other, a relation that does not precisely reduce me to speechlessness, but does nevertheless clutter my speech with signs of its undoing. I tell a story about the relations I choose, only to expose, somewhere along the way, the way I am gripped and undone by these very relations. My narrative falters, as it must.

Let's face it. We're undone by each other. And if we're not, we're missing something.

This seems so clearly the case with grief, but it can be so only because it was already the case with desire. One does not always stay intact. One may want to, or manage to for a while, but despite one's best efforts, one is undone, in the face of the other, by the touch, by the scent, by the feel, by the prospect of the touch, by the memory of the feel. And so, when we speak about "my sexuality" or "my gender," as we do and as we must, we nevertheless mean something complicated that is partially concealed by our usage. As a mode of relation, neither gender nor sexuality is precisely a possession, but, rather, is a mode of being dispossessed, a way of being *for* another or *by virtue of* another. It won't even do to say that I am promoting a relational view of the self over an autonomous one or trying to redescribe autonomy in terms of relationality. Despite my affinity for the term relationality, we may need other language to approach the issue that concerns us, a way of thinking about how we are not only constituted by our relations but also dispossessed by them as well.

We tend to narrate the history of the feminist and lesbian/gay movement, for instance, in such a way that ecstasy figured prominently in the sixties and seventies and midway through the eighties. But maybe ecstasy is more persistent than that; maybe it is with us all along. To be ec-static means, literally, to be outside oneself, and thus can have several meanings: to be transported beyond oneself by a passion, but also to be *beside oneself* with rage or grief. I think that if I can still address a "we," or include myself within its terms, I am speaking to those of us who are living in certain ways *beside ourselves*, whether in sexual passion, or emotional grief, or political rage.

I am arguing, if I am "arguing" at all, that we have an interesting political predicament; most of the time when we hear about "rights," we understand them as pertaining to individuals. When we argue for protection against discrimination, we argue as a group or a class. And in that language and in that context, we have to present ourselves as bounded beings—distinct, recognizable, delineated, subjects before the law, a community defined by some shared features. Indeed, we must be able to use that language to secure legal protections and entitlements. But perhaps we make a mistake if we take the definitions of who we are, legally, to be adequate descriptions of what we are about. Although this language may well establish our legitimacy within a legal framework ensconced in liberal versions of human ontology, it does not do justice to passion and grief and rage, all of which tear us from ourselves, bind us to others, transport us, undo us, implicate us in lives that are not our own, irreversibly, if not fatally.

It is not easy to understand how a political community is wrought from such ties. One speaks, and one speaks for another, to another, and yet there is no way to collapse the distinction between the Other and oneself. When we say "we" we do nothing more than designate this very problematic. We do not solve it. And perhaps it is, and ought to be, insoluble. This disposition of ourselves outside ourselves seems to follow from bodily life, from its vulnerability and its exposure.

At the same time, essential to so many political movements is the claim of bodily integrity and self-determination. It is important to claim that our bodies are in a sense *our own* and that we are entitled to claim rights of autonomy over our bodies. This assertion is as true for lesbian and gay rights claims to sexual freedom as it is for transsexual and transgender claims to self-determination, as it is to intersex claims to be free of coerced medical and psychiatric interventions. It is as true for all claims to be free from racist attacks, physical and verbal, as it is for feminism's claim to reproductive freedom, and as it surely is for those whose bodies labor under duress, economic and political, under conditions of colonization and occupation. It is difficult, if not impossible, to make these claims without recourse to autonomy. I am not suggesting that we cease to make these claims. We have to, we must. I also do not wish to imply that we have to make these claims reluctantly or strategically. Defined within the broadest possible compass, they are part of any normative aspiration of a movement that seeks to maximize the protection and the freedoms of sexual and gender minorities, of women, and of racial and ethnic minorities, especially as they cut across all the other categories.

But is there another normative aspiration that we must also seek to articulate and to defend? Is there a way in which the place of the body, and the way in which it disposes us outside ourselves or sets us beside ourselves, opens up another kind of normative aspiration within the field of politics?

The body implies mortality, vulnerability, agency: the skin and the flesh expose us to the gaze of others, but also to touch, and to violence, and bodies put us at risk of becoming the agency and instrument of all these as well. Although we struggle for rights over our own bodies, the very bodies for which we struggle are not quite ever only our own. The body has its invariably public dimension. Constituted as a social phenomenon in the public sphere, my body is and is not mine. Given over from the start to the world of others, it bears their imprint, is formed within the crucible of social life; only later, and with some uncertainty, do I lay claim to my body as my own, if, in fact, I ever do. Indeed, if I deny that prior to the formation of my "will," my body related me to others whom I did not choose to have in proximity to myself, if I build a notion of "autonomy" on the basis of the denial of this sphere of a primary and unwilled physical proximity with others, then am I denying the social conditions of my embodiment in the name of autonomy?

At one level, this situation is literally familiar: there is bound to be some experience of humiliation for adults, who think that they are exercising judgment in matters of love, to reflect upon the fact that, as infants and young children, they loved their parents or other primary others in absolute and uncritical ways—and that something of that pattern lives on in their adult relationships. I may wish to reconstitute my "self" as if it were there all along, a tacit ego with acumen from the start; but to do so would be to deny the various forms of rapture and subjection that formed the condition of my emergence as an individuated being and that continue to haunt my adult sense of self with whatever anxiety and longing I may now feel. Individuation is an accomplishment, not a presupposition, and certainly no guarantee.

Is there a reason to apprehend and affirm this condition of my formation within the sphere of politics, a sphere monopolized by adults? If I am struggling for autonomy, do I not need to be struggling for something else as well, a conception of myself as invariably in community, impressed upon by others, impinging upon them as well, and in ways that are not fully in my control or clearly predictable?

Is there a way that we might struggle for autonomy in many spheres, yet also consider the demands that are imposed upon us by living in a world of beings who are, by definition, physically dependent on one another, physically vulnerable to one another? Is this not another way of imagining community, one in which we are alike only in having this condition separately and so having in common a condition that cannot be thought without difference? This way of imagining community affirms relationality not only as a descriptive or historical fact of our formation, but also as an ongoing normative dimension of our social and political lives, one in which we are compelled to take stock of our interdependence. According to this latter view, it would become incumbent on us to consider the place of violence in any such relation, for violence is, always, an exploitation of that primary tie, that primary way in which we are, as bodies, outside ourselves and for one another.

We are something other than "autonomous" in such a condition, but that does not mean that we are merged or without boundaries. It does mean, however, that when we think about who we "are" and seek to represent ourselves, we cannot represent ourselves as merely bounded beings, for the primary others who are past for me not only live on in the fiber of the boundary that contains me (one meaning of "incorporation"), but they also haunt the way I am, as it were, periodically undone and open to becoming unbounded.

Let us return to the issue of grief, to the moments in which one undergoes something outside one's control and finds that one is beside oneself, not at one with oneself. Perhaps we can say that grief contains the possibility of apprehending a mode of dispossession that is fundamental to who I am. This possibility does not dispute the fact of my autonomy, but it does qualify that claim through recourse to the fundamental sociality of embodied life, the ways in which we are, from the start and by virtue of being a bodily being, already given over, beyond ourselves, implicated in lives that are not our own. If I do not always know what seizes me on such occasions, and if I do not always know what it is *in* another person that I have lost, it may be that this sphere of dispossession is precisely the one that exposes my unknowingness, the unconscious imprint of my primary sociality. Can this insight lead to a normative reorientation for politics? Can this situation of mourning—one that is so dramatic for those in social movements who have undergone innumerable losses—supply a perspective by which to begin to apprehend the contemporary global situation?

Mourning, fear, anxiety, rage. In the United States, we have been surrounded with violence, having perpetrated it and perpetrating it still, having suffered it, living in fear of it, planning more of it, if not an open future of infinite war in the name of a "war on terrorism." Violence is surely a touch of the worst order, a way a primary human vulnerability to other humans is exposed in its most terrifying way, a way in which we are given over, without control, to the will of another, a way in which life itself can be expunged by the willful action of another. To the extent that we commit violence, we are acting on another, putting the other at risk, causing the other damage, threatening to expunge the other. In a way, we all live with this particular vulnerability, a vulnerability to the other that is part of bodily life, a vulnerability to a sudden address from elsewhere that we cannot preempt. This vulnerability, however, becomes highly exacerbated under certain social and political conditions, especially those in which violence is a way of life and the means to secure self-defense are limited.

Mindfulness of this vulnerability can become the basis of claims for non-military political solutions, just as denial of this vulnerability through a fantasy of mastery (an institutionalized fantasy of mastery) can fuel the instruments of war. We cannot, however, will away this vulnerability. We must attend to it, even abide by it, as we begin to think about what politics might be implied by staying with the thought of corporeal vulnerability itself, a situation in which we can be vanquished or lose others. Is there something to be learned about the geopolitical distribution of corporeal vulnerability from our own brief and devastating exposure to this condition?

I think, for instance, that we have seen, are seeing, various ways of dealing with vulnerability and grief, so that, for instance, William Safire citing Milton writes we must "banish melancholy,"[5] as if the repudiation of melancholy ever did anything other than fortify its affective structure under another name, since melancholy is already the repudiation of mourning; so that, for instance, President Bush announced on September 21 that we have finished grieving and that *now* it is time for resolute action to take the place of grief.[6] When grieving is something to be feared, our fears can give rise to the impulse to resolve it quickly, to banish it in the name of an action invested with the power to restore the loss or return the world to a former order, or to reinvigorate a fantasy that the world formerly was orderly.

Is there something to be gained from grieving, from tarrying with grief, from remaining exposed to its unbearability and not endeavoring to seek a resolution for grief through violence? Is there something to be gained in the political domain by maintaining grief as part of the framework within which we think our international ties? If we stay with the sense of loss, are we left feeling only passive and powerless, as some might fear? Or are we, rather, returned to a sense of human vulnerability, to our collective responsibility for the physical lives of one another? Could the experience of a dislocation of First World safety not condition the insight into the radically inequitable ways that corporeal vulnerability is distributed globally? To foreclose that vulnerability, to banish it, to make ourselves secure at the expense of every other human consideration is to eradicate one of the most important resources from which we must take our bearings and find our way.

To grieve, and to make grief itself into a resource for politics, is not to be resigned to inaction, but it may be understood as the slow process by which we develop a point of identification with suffering itself. The disorientation of grief—"Who have I become?" or, indeed, "What is left of me?" "What is it in the Other that I have lost?"—posits the "I" in the mode of unknowingness.

But this can be a point of departure for a new understanding if the narcissistic pre-occupation of melancholia can be moved into a consideration of the vulnerability of others. Then we might critically evaluate and oppose the conditions under which certain human lives are more vulnerable than others, and thus certain human lives are more grievable than others. From where might a principle emerge by which we vow to protect others from the kinds of violence we have suffered, if not from an apprehension of a common human vulner-ability? I do not mean to deny that vulnerability is differentiated, that it is allocated differen-tially across the globe. I do not even mean to presume upon a common notion of the human, although to speak in its "name" is already (and perhaps only) to fathom its possibility.

I am referring to violence, vulnerability, and mourning, but there is a more general conception of the human with which I am trying to work here, one in which we are, from the start, given over to the other, one in which we are, from the start, even prior to individuation itself and, by virtue of bodily requirements, given over to some set of primary others: this conception means that we are vulnerable to those we are too young to know and to judge and, hence, vulnerable to violence; but also vulnerable to another range of touch, a range that includes the eradication of our being at the one end, and the physical support for our lives at the other.

Although I am insisting on referring to a common human vulnerability, one that emerges with life itself, I also insist that we cannot recover the source of this vulnerability: it precedes the formation of "I." This is a condition, a condition of being laid bare from the start and with which we cannot argue. I mean, we can argue with it, but we are perhaps foolish, if not dangerous, when we do. I do not mean to suggest that the necessary support for a newborn is always there. Clearly, it is not, and for some this primary scene is a scene of abandonment or violence or starvation, that theirs are bodies given over to nothing, or to brutality, or to no sustenance.

We cannot understand vulnerability as a deprivation, however, unless we understand the need that is thwarted. Such infants still must be apprehended as given over, as given over to no one or to some insufficient support, or to an abandonment. It would be difficult, if not impossible, to understand how humans suffer from oppression without seeing how this primary condition is exploited and exploitable, thwarted and denied. The condition of primary vulnerability, of being given over to the touch of the other, even if there is no other there, and no support for our lives, signifies a primary helplessness and need, one to which any society must attend. Lives are supported and maintained differently, and there are radically different ways in which human physical vulnerability is distributed across the globe. Certain lives will be highly protected, and the abrogation of their claims to sanctity will be sufficient to mobilize the forces of war. Other lives will not find such fast and furious support and will not even qualify as "grievable."

A hierarchy of grief could no doubt be enumerated. We have seen it already, in the genre of the obituary, where lives are quickly tidied up and summarized, humanized, usually married, or on the way to be, heterosexual, happy, monogamous. But this is just a sign of another differential relation to life, since we seldom, if ever, hear the names of the thousands of Palestinians who have died by the Israeli military with United States support, or any number of Afghan people, children and adults. Do they have names and faces, personal histories, family, favorite hobbies, slogans by which they live? What defense against the apprehension of loss is at work in the blithe way in which we accept deaths caused by military means with a shrug or with self-righteousness or with clear vindictiveness? To what extent have Arab peoples, predominantly practitioners of Islam, fallen outside the "human" as it has been naturalized in its "Western" mold by the contemporary workings of humanism? What are the cultural contours of the human at work here? How do our cultural frames for thinking the human set limits on the kinds of losses we can avow as loss? After all, if someone is lost, and that person is not someone, then what and where is the loss, and how does mourning take place?

This last is surely a question that lesbian, gay, and bi-studies have asked in relation to violence against sexual minorities; that transgendered people have asked as they are singled out for harassment and sometimes murder; that intersexed people have asked, whose formative years are so often marked by unwanted violence against their bodies in the name of a normative notion of the human, a normative notion of what the body of a human must be. This question is no doubt, as well, the basis of a profound affinity between movements centering on gender and sexuality and efforts to counter the normative human morphologies and capacities that condemn or efface those who are physically challenged. It must also be part of the affinity with anti-racist struggles, given the racial differential that undergirds the culturally viable notions of the human, ones that we see acted out in dramatic and terrifying ways in the global arena at the present time.

I am referring not only to humans not regarded as humans, and thus to a restrictive conception of the human that is based upon their exclusion. It is not a matter of a simple entry of the excluded into an established ontology, but an insurrection at the level of ontology, a critical opening up of the questions, What is real? Whose lives are real? How might reality be remade? Those who are unreal have, in a sense, already suffered the violence of derealization. What, then, is the relation between violence and those lives considered as "unreal"? Does violence effect that unreality? Does violence take place on the condition of that unreality?

If violence is done against those who are unreal, then, from the perspective of violence, it fails to injure or negate those lives since those lives are already negated. But they have a strange way of remaining animated and so must be negated again (and again). They cannot be mourned because they are always already lost or, rather, never "were," and they must be killed, since they seem to live on, stubbornly, in this state of deadness. Violence renews itself in the face of the apparent inexhaustibility of its object. The derealization of the "Other" means that it is neither alive nor dead, but interminably spectral. The infinite paranoia that imagines the war against terrorism as a war without end will be one that justifies itself endlessly in relation to the spectral infinity of its enemy, regardless of whether or not there are established grounds to suspect the continuing operation of terror cells with violent aims.

How do we understand this derealization? It is one thing to argue that first, on the level of discourse, certain lives are not considered lives at all, they cannot be humanized, that they fit no dominant frame for the human, and that their dehumanization occurs first, at this level, and that this level then gives rise to a physical violence that in some sense delivers the message of dehumanization that is already at work in the culture. It is another thing to say that discourse itself effects violence through omission. If 200,000 Iraqi children were killed during the Gulf War and its aftermath,[7] do we have an image, a frame for any of those lives, singly or collectively? Is there a story we might find about those deaths in the media? Are there names attached to those children?

There are no obituaries for the war casualties that the United States inflicts, and there cannot be. If there were to be an obituary, there would have had to have been a life, a life worth noting, a life worth valuing and preserving, a life that qualifies for recognition. Although we might argue that it would be impractical to write obituaries for all those people, or for all people, I think we have to ask, again and again, how the obituary functions as the instrument by which grievability is publicly distributed. It is the means by which a life becomes, or fails to become, a publicly grievable life, an icon for national self-recognition, the means by which a life becomes noteworthy. As a result, we have to consider the obituary as an act of nation-building. The matter is not a simple one, for, if a life is not grievable, it is not quite a life; it does not qualify as a life and is not worth a note. It is already the unburied, if not the unburiable.

It is not simply, then, that there is a "discourse" of dehumanization that produces these effects, but rather that there is a limit to discourse that establishes the limits of human intelligibility. It is not just that a death is poorly marked, but that it is unmarkable. Such a death vanishes, not into explicit discourse, but in the ellipses by which public discourse proceeds. The queer lives that vanished on September 11 were not publicly welcomed into the idea of national identity built in the obituary pages, and their closest relations were only belatedly and selectively (the marital norm holding sway once again) made eligible for benefits. But this should come as no surprise, when we think about how few deaths from AIDS were publicly grievable losses, and how, for instance, the extensive deaths now taking place in Africa are also, in the media, for the most part unmarkable and ungrievable.

A Palestinian citizen of the United States recently submitted to the *San Francisco Chronicle* obituaries for two Palestinian families who had been killed by Israeli troops, only to be told that the obituaries could not be accepted without proof of death.[8] The staff of the *Chronicle* said that statements "in memoriam" could, however, be accepted, and so the obituaries were rewritten and resubmitted in the form of memorials. These memorials were then rejected, with the explanation that the newspaper did not wish to offend anyone. We have to wonder under what conditions public grieving constitutes an "offense" against the public itself, constituting an intolerable eruption within the terms of what is speakable in public? What might be "offensive" about the public avowal of sorrow and loss, such that memorials would function as offensive speech? Is it that we should not proclaim in public these deaths, for fear of offending those who ally themselves with the Israeli state or military? Is it that these deaths are not considered to be real deaths, and that these lives are not grievable, because they are Palestinians, or because they are victims of war? What is the relation between the violence by which these ungrievable lives were lost and the prohibition on their public grievability? Are the violence and the prohibition both permutations of the same violence? Does the prohibition on discourse relate to the dehumanization of the deaths—and the lives?

Dehumanization's relation to discourse is complex. It would be too simple to claim that violence simply implements what is already happening in discourse, such that a discourse on dehumanization produces treatment, including torture and murder, structured by the discourse. Here the dehumanization emerges at the limits of discursive life, limits established through prohibition and foreclosure. There is less a dehumanizing discourse at work here than a refusal of discourse that produces dehumanization as a result. Violence against those who are already not quite living, that is, living in a state of suspension between life and death, leaves a mark that is no mark. There will be no public act of grieving (said Creon in *Antigone*). If there is a "discourse," it is a silent and melancholic one in which there have been no lives, and no losses; there has been no common bodily condition, no vulnerability that serves as the basis for an apprehension of our commonality; and there has been no sundering of that commonality. None of this takes place on the order of the event. None of this takes place. In the silence of the newspaper, there was no event, no loss, and this failure of recognition is mandated through an identification with those who identify with the perpetrators of that violence.

This is made all the more apparent in United States journalism, in which, with some notable exceptions, one might have expected a public exposure and investigation of the bombing of civilian targets, the loss of lives in Afghanistan, the decimation of communities, infrastructures, religious centers. To the extent that journalists have accepted the charge to be part of the war effort itself, reporting itself has become a speech act in the service of the military operations. Indeed, after the brutal and terrible murder of the *Wall Street Journal*'s Daniel Pearl, several journalists started to write about themselves as working on the "front lines" of the war. Indeed, Daniel Pearl, "Danny" Pearl, is so familiar to me: he could be my brother or my cousin; he is so easily humanized; he fits the frame, his name has my father's name in it. His last name contains my Yiddish name.

But those lives in Afghanistan, or other United States targets, who were also snuffed out brutally and without recourse to any protection, will they ever be as human as Daniel Pearl? Will the names of the Palestinians stated in that memorial submitted to the *San Francisco Chronicle* ever be brought into public view? (Will we feel compelled to learn how to say these names and to remember them?) I do not say this to espouse a cynicism. I am in favor of the public obituary but mindful of who has access to it, and which deaths can be fairly mourned there. We should surely continue to grieve for Daniel Pearl, even though he is so much more easily humanized for most United States citizens than the nameless Afghans obliterated by United States and European violence. But we have to consider how the norm governing who will be a grievable human is circumscribed and produced in these acts of permissible and celebrated public grieving, how they sometimes operate in tandem with a prohibition on the public grieving of others' lives, and how this differential allocation of grief serves the derealizing aims of military violence. What follows as well from prohibitions on avowing grief in public is an effective mandate in favor of a generalized melancholia (and a derealization of loss) when it comes to considering *as dead* those the United States or its allies have killed.

Finally, it seems important to consider that the prohibition on certain forms of public grieving itself constitutes the public sphere on the basis of such a prohibition. The public will be created on the condition that certain images do not appear in the media, certain names of the dead are not utterable, certain losses are not avowed as losses, and violence is derealized and diffused. Such prohibitions not only shore up a nationalism based on its military aims and practices, but they also suppress any internal dissent that would expose the concrete, human effects of its violence.

Similarly, the extensive reporting of the final moments of the lost lives in the World Trade Center are compelling and important stories. They fascinate, and they produce an intense identification by arousing feelings of fear and sorrow. One cannot help but wonder, however, what humanizing effect these narratives have. By this I do not mean simply that they humanize the lives that were lost along with those that narrowly escaped, but that they stage the scene and provide the narrative means by which "the human" in its grievability is established. We cannot find in the public media, apart from some reports posted on the internet and circulated mainly through email contacts, the narratives of Arab lives killed elsewhere by brutal means. In this sense, we have to ask about the conditions under which a grievable life is established and maintained, and through what logic of exclusion, what practice of effacement and denominalization.

Mourning Daniel Pearl presents no problem for me or for my family of origin. His is a familiar name, a familiar face, a story about education that I understand and share; his wife's education makes her language familiar, even moving, to me, a proximity of what is similar.[9] In relation to him, I am not disturbed by the proximity of the unfamiliar, the proximity of difference that makes me work to forge new ties of identification and to reimagine what it is to belong to a human community in which common epistemological and cultural grounds cannot always be assumed. His story takes me home and tempts me to stay there. But at what cost do I establish the familiar as the criterion by which a human life is grievable?

Most Americans have probably experienced something like the loss of their First World-ism as a result of the events of September 11 and its aftermath. What kind of loss is this? It is the loss of the prerogative, only and always, to be the one who transgresses the sovereign boundaries of other states, but never to be in the position of having one's own boundaries transgressed. The United States was supposed to be the place that could not be attacked, where life was safe from violence initiated from abroad, where the only violence we knew was the kind that we inflicted on ourselves. The violence that we inflict on others is only—and always—selectively brought into public view. We now see that the national border was more permeable than we thought. Our general response is anxiety, rage; a radical desire for security, a shoring-up of the borders against what is perceived as alien; a heightened surveillance of Arab peoples and anyone who looks vaguely Arab in the dominant racial imaginary, anyone who looks like someone you once knew who was of Arab descent, or who you thought was—often citizens, it turns out, often Sikhs, often Hindus, even some-times Israelis, especially Sephardim, often Arab-Americans, recent arrivals or those who have been in the US for decades.

Various terror alerts that go out over the media authorize and heighten racial hysteria in which fear is directed anywhere and nowhere, in which individuals are asked to be on guard but not told what to be on guard against; so everyone is free to imagine and identify the source of terror.

The result is that an amorphous racism abounds, rationalized by the claim of "self-defense." A generalized panic works in tandem with the shoring-up of the sovereign state and the suspension of civil liberties. Indeed, when the alert goes out, every member of the population is asked to become a "foot soldier" in Bush's army. The loss of First World presumption is the loss of a certain horizon of experience, a certain sense of the world itself as a national entitlement.

I condemn on several ethical bases the violence done against the United States and do not see it as "just punishment" for prior sins. At the same time, I consider our recent trauma to be an opportunity for a reconsideration of United States hubris and the importance of establishing more radically egalitarian international ties. Doing this involves a certain "loss" for the country as a whole: the notion of the world itself as a sovereign entitlement of the United States must be given up, lost, and mourned, as narcissistic and grandiose fantasies must be lost and mourned. From the subsequent experience of loss and fragility, however, the possibility of making different kinds of ties emerges. Such mourning might (or could) effect a transformation in our sense of international ties that would crucially rearticulate the possibility of democratic political culture here and elsewhere.

Unfortunately, the opposite reaction seems to be the case. The US asserts its own sovereignty precisely at a moment in which the sovereignty of the nation is bespeaking its own weakness, if not its growing status as an anachronism. It requires international support, but it insists on leading the way. It breaks its international contracts, and then asks whether other countries are with America or against it. It expresses its willingness to act consistently with the Geneva Convention, but it refuses to be bound to that accord, as is stipulated by its signatory status. On the contrary, the US decides whether it will act consistently with the doctrine, which parts of the doctrine apply, and will interpret that doctrine unilaterally. Indeed, in the very moment in which it claims to act consistently with the doctrine, as it does when it justifies its treatment of the Guantanamo Bay prisoners as "humane," it decides unilaterally what will count as humane, and openly defies the stipulated definition of humane treatment that the Geneva Convention states in print. It bombs unilaterally, it says that it is time for Saddam Hussein to be removed, it decides when and where to install democracy, for whom, by means dramatically anti-democratic, and without compunction.

Nations are not the same as individual psyches, but both can be described as "subjects," albeit of different orders. When the United States acts, it establishes a conception of what it means to act as an American, establishes a norm by which that subject might be known. In recent months, a subject has been instated at the national level, a sovereign and extra-legal subject, a violent and self-centered subject; its actions constitute the building of a subject that seeks to restore and maintain its mastery through the systematic destruction of its multilateral relations, its ties to the international community. It shores itself up, seeks to reconstitute its imagined wholeness, but only at the price of denying its own vulnerability, its dependency, its exposure, where it exploits those very features in others, thereby making those features "other to" itself.

That this foreclosure of alterity takes place in the name of "feminism" is surely something to worry about. The sudden feminist conversion on the part of the Bush administration, which retroactively transformed the liberation of women into a rationale for its military actions against Afghanistan, is a sign of the extent to which feminism, as a trope, is deployed in the service of restoring the presumption of First World impermeability. Once again we see the spectacle of "white men, seeking to save brown women from brown men," as Gayatri Chakravorty Spivak once described the culturally imperialist exploitation of feminism.[10] Feminism itself becomes, under these circumstances, unequivocally identified with the imposition of values on cultural contexts willfully unknown. It would surely be a mistake to gauge the progress of feminism by its success as a colonial project. It seems more crucial than ever to disengage feminism from its First World presumption and to use the resources of feminist theory, and activism, to rethink the meaning of the tie, the bond, the alliance, the relation, as they are imagined and lived in the horizon of a counterimperialist egalitarianism.

Feminism surely could provide all kinds of responses to the following questions: How does a collective deal, finally, with its vulnerability to violence? At what price, and at whose expense, does it gain a purchase on "security," and in what ways has a chain of violence formed in which the aggression the United States has wrought returns to it in different forms? Can we think of the history of violence here without exonerating those who engage it against the United States in the present? Can we provide a knowledgeable explanation of events that is not confused with a moral exoneration of violence? What has happened to the value of critique as a democratic value? Under what conditions is critique itself censored, as if any reflexive criticism can only and always be construed as weakness and fallibility?

Negotiating a sudden and unprecedented vulnerability—what are the options? What are the long-term strategies? Women know this question well, have known it in nearly all times, and nothing about the triumph of colonial powers has made our exposure to this kind of violence any less clear. There is the possibility of appearing impermeable, of repudiating vulnerability itself. Nothing about being socially constituted as women restrains us from simply becoming violent ourselves. And then there is the other age-old option, the possibility of wishing for death or becoming dead, as a vain effort to preempt or deflect the next blow. But perhaps there is some other way to live such that one becomes neither affectively dead nor mimetically violent, a way out of the circle of violence altogether. This possibility has to do with demanding a world in which bodily vulnerability is protected without therefore being eradicated and with insisting on the line that must be walked between the two.

By insisting on a "common" corporeal vulnerability, I may seem to be positing a new basis for humanism. That might be true, but I am prone to consider this differently. A vulnerability must be perceived and recognized in order to come into play in an ethical encounter, and there is no guarantee that this will happen. Not only is there always the possibility that a vulnerability will not be recognized and that it will be constituted as the "unrecognizable," but when a vulnerability is recognized, that recognition has the power to change the meaning and structure of the vulnerability itself. In this sense, if vulnerability is one precondition for humanization, and humanization takes place differently through variable norms of recognition, then it follows that vulnerability is fundamentally dependent on existing norms of recognition if it is to be attributed to any human subject.

So when we say that every infant is surely vulnerable, that is clearly true; but it is true, in part, precisely because our utterance enacts the very recognition of vulnerability and so shows the importance of recognition itself for sustaining vulnerability. We perform the recognition by making the claim, and that is surely a very good ethical reason to make the claim. We make the claim, however, precisely because it is not taken for granted, precisely because it is not, in every instance, honored. Vulnerability takes on another meaning at the moment it is recognized, and recognition wields the power to reconstitute vulnerability. We cannot posit this vulnerability prior to recognition without performing the very thesis that we oppose (our positing is itself a form of recognition and so manifests the constitutive power of the discourse). This framework, by which norms of recognition are essential to the constitution of vulnerability as a precondition of the "human," is important precisely for this reason, namely, that we need and want those norms to be in place, that we struggle for their establishment, and that we value their continuing and expanded operation.

Consider that the struggle for recognition in the Hegelian sense requires that each partner in the exchange recognize not only that the other needs and deserves recognition, but also that each, in a different way, is compelled by the same need, the same requirement. This means that we are not separate identities in the struggle for recognition but are already involved in a reciprocal exchange, an exchange that dislocates us from our positions, our subject-positions, and allows us to see that community itself requires the recognition that we are all, in different ways, striving for recognition.

When we recognize another, or when we ask for recognition for ourselves, we are not asking for an Other to see us as we are, as we already are, as we have always been, as we were constituted prior to the encounter itself. Instead, in the asking, in the petition, we have already become something new, since we are constituted by virtue of the address, a need and desire for the Other that takes place in language in the broadest sense, one without which we could not be. To ask for recognition, or to offer it, is precisely not to ask for recognition for what one already is. It is to solicit a becoming, to instigate a transformation, to petition the future always in relation to the Other. It is also to stake one's own being, and one's own persistence in one's own being, in the struggle for recognition. This is perhaps a version of Hegel that I am offering, but it is also a departure, since I will not discover myself as the same as the "you" on which I depend in order to be.

I have moved in this essay perhaps too blithely among speculations on the body as the site of a common human vulnerability, even as I have insisted that this vulnerability is always articulated differently, that it cannot be properly thought of outside a differentiated field of power and, specifically, the differential operation of norms of recognition. At the same time, however, I would probably still insist that speculations on the formation of the subject are crucial to understanding the basis of non-violent responses to injury and, perhaps most important, to a theory of collective responsibility. I realize that it is not possible to set up easy analogies between the formation of the individual and the formation, say, of state-centered political cultures, and I caution against the use of individual psychopathology to diagnose or even simply to read the kinds of violent formations in which state- and non-state-centered forms of power engage. But when we are speaking about the "subject" we are not always speaking about an individual: we are speaking about a model for agency and intelligibility, one that is very often based on notions of sovereign power. At the most intimate levels, we are social; we are comported toward a "you"; we are outside ourselves, constituted in cultural norms that precede and exceed us, given over to a set of cultural norms and a field of power that condition us fundamentally.

The task is doubtless to think through this primary impressionability and vulnerability with a theory of power and recognition. To do this would no doubt be one way a politically informed psychoanalytic feminism could proceed. The "I" who cannot come into being without a "you" is also fundamentally dependent on a set of norms of recognition that originated neither with the "I" nor with the "you." What is prematurely, or belatedly, called the "I" is, at the outset, enthralled, even if it is to a violence, an abandonment, a mechanism; doubtless it seems better at that point to be enthralled with what is impoverished or abusive than not to be enthralled at all and so to lose the condition of one's being and becoming. The bind of radically inadequate care consists of this, namely, that attachment is crucial to survival and that, when attachment takes place, it does so in relation to persons and institutional conditions that may well be violent, impoverishing, and inadequate. If an infant fails to attach, it is threatened with death, but, under some conditions, even if it does attach, it is threatened with non-survival from another direction. So the question of primary support for primary vulnerability is an ethical one for the infant and for the child. But there are broader ethical consequences from this situation, ones that pertain not only to the adult world but to the sphere of politics and its implicit ethical dimension.

I find that my very formation implicates the other in me, that my own foreignness to myself is, paradoxically, the source of my ethical connection with others. I am not fully known to myself, because part of what I am is the enigmatic traces of others. In this sense, I cannot know myself perfectly or know my "difference" from others in an irreducible way. This unknowingness may seem, from a given perspective, a problem for ethics and politics.

Don't I need to know myself in order to act responsibly in social relations? Surely, to a certain extent, yes. But is there an ethical valence to my unknowingness? I am wounded, and I find that the wound itself testifies to the fact that I am impressionable, given over to the Other in ways that I cannot fully predict or control. I cannot think the question of responsibility alone, in isolation from the Other; if I do, I have taken myself out of the relational bind that frames the problem of responsibility from the start.

If I understand myself on the model of the human, and if the kinds of public grieving that are available to me make clear the norms by which the "human" is constituted for me, then it would seem that I am as much constituted by those I do grieve for as by those whose deaths I disavow, whose nameless and faceless deaths form the melancholic background for my social world, if not my First Worldism. Antigone, risking death herself by burying her brother against the edict of Creon, exemplified the political risks in defying the ban against public grief during times of increased sovereign power and hegemonic national unity.[11] What are the cultural barriers against which we struggle when we try to find out about the losses that we are asked not to mourn, when we attempt to name, and so to bring under the rubric of the "human," those whom the United States and its allies have killed? Similarly, the cultural barriers that feminism must negotiate have to take place with reference to the operation of power and the persistence of vulnerability.

A feminist opposition to militarism emerges from many sources, many cultural venues, in any number of idioms; it does not have to—and, finally, cannot—speak in a single political idiom, and no grand settling of epistemological accounts has to be required. This seems to be the theoretical commitment, for instance, of the organization Women in Black.[12] A desideratum comes from Chandra Mohanty's important essay "Under Western Eyes," in which she maintains that notions of progress within feminism cannot be equated with assimilation to so-called Western notions of agency and political mobilization.[13] There she argues that the comparative framework in which First World feminists develop their critique of the conditions of oppression for Third World women on the basis of universal claims not only misreads the agency of Third World feminists, but also falsely produces a homogeneous conception of who they are and what they want. In her view, that framework also reproduces the First World as the site of authentic feminist agency and does so by producing a monolithic Third World against which to understand itself. Finally, she argues that the imposition of versions of agency onto Third World contexts, and focusing on the ostensible lack of agency signified by the veil or the burka, not only misunderstands the various cultural meanings that the burka might carry for women who wear it, but also denies the very idioms of agency that are relevant for such women.[14] Mohanty's critique is thorough and right—and it was written more than a decade ago. It seems to me now that the possibility of international coalition has to be rethought on the basis of this critique and others. Such a coalition would have to be modeled on new modes of cultural translation and would be different from appreciating this or that position or asking for recognition in ways that assume that we are all fixed and frozen in our various locations and "subject-positions."

We could have several engaged intellectual debates going on at the same time and find ourselves joined in the fight against violence, without having to agree on many epistemological issues. We could disagree on the status and character of modernity and yet find ourselves joined in asserting and defending the rights of indigenous women to health care, reproductive technology, decent wages, physical protection, cultural rights, freedom of assembly. If you saw me on such a protest line, would you wonder how a postmodernist was able to muster the necessary "agency" to get there today? I doubt it. You would assume that I had walked or taken the subway! By the same token, various routes lead us into politics, various stories bring us onto the street, various kinds of reasoning and belief. We do not need to ground ourselves in a single model of communication, a single model of reason, a single notion of the subject before we are able to act. Indeed, an international coalition of feminist activists and thinkers—a coalition that affirms the thinking of activists and the activism of thinkers and refuses to put them into distinctive categories that deny the actual complexity of the lives in question—will have to accept the array of sometimes incommensurable epistemological and political beliefs and modes and means of agency that bring us into activism.

There will be differences among women, for instance, on what the role of reason is in contemporary politics. Spivak insists that it is not *reason* that politicizes the tribal women of India suffering exploitation by capitalist firms, but a set of values and a sense of the sacred that come through religion.[15] And Adriana Cavarero claims that it is not because we are reasoning beings that we are connected to one another, but, rather, because we are *exposed* to one another, requiring a recognition that does not substitute the recognizer for the recognized.[16] Do we want to say that it is our status as "subjects" that binds us all together even though, for many of us, the "subject" is multiple or fractured? And does the insistence on the subject as a precondition of political agency not erase the more fundamental modes of dependency that do bind us and out of which emerge our thinking and affiliation, the basis of our vulnerability, affiliation, and collective resistance?

What allows us to encounter one another? What are the conditions of possibility for an international feminist coalition? My sense is that to answer these questions, we cannot look to the nature of "man," or the a priori conditions of language, or the timeless conditions of communication. We have to consider the demands of cultural translation that we assume to be part of an ethical responsibility (over and above the explicit prohibitions against thinking the Other under the sign of the "human") as we try to think the global dilemmas that women face. It is not possible to impose a language of politics developed within First World contexts on women who are facing the threat of imperialist economic exploitation and cultural obliteration. On the other hand, we would be wrong to think that the First World is *here* and the Third World is *there*, that a second world is *somewhere else*, that a subaltern subtends these divisions. These topographies have shifted, and what was once thought of as a border, that which delimits and bounds, is a highly populated site, if not the very definition of the nation, confounding identity in what may well become a very auspicious direction.

For if I am confounded by you, then you are already of me, and I am nowhere without you. I cannot muster the "we" except by finding the way in which I am tied to "you," by trying to translate but finding that my own language must break up and yield if I am to know you. You are what I gain through this disorientation and loss. This is how the human comes into being, again and again, as that which we have yet to know.

Notes

1   Sigmund Freud, *Mourning and Melancholia* (1917) Standard Edition, 14: pp. 243–58, London: Hogarth Press, 1957.

2   Sigmund Freud, *The Ego and the Id* (1923) Standard Edition, 19: pp. 12–66, London: Hogarth Press, 1961.

3   Sigmund Freud, *Mourning and Melancholia*.

4   Ibid.

5   William Safire, "All Is Not Changed", *New York Times*, September 27, 2001, p. A:21.

6   "A Nation Challenged; President Bush's Address on Terrorism before a Joint Meeting of Congress," *New York Times*, September 21, 2001, p. B:4.

7   Richard Garfield, "Morbidity and Mortality among Iraqi Children from 1990 through 1998: Assessing the Impact of the Gulf War and Economic Sanctions," in *Fourth Freedom Forum*, March, 2002. See www.fourthfreedom.org/php/p-index.php?hinc=garf.hinc.

8   The memorials read as follows: "In loving memory of Kamla Abu Sa'id, 42, and her daughter, Amna

Abu-Sa'id, 13, both Palestinians from the El Bureij refugee camps. Kamla and her daughter were killed May 26, 2002 by Israeli troops, while working on a farm in the Gaza Strip. In loving memory of Ahmed Abu Seer, 7, a Palestinian child, he was killed in his home with bullets. Ahmed died of fatal shrapnel wounds to his heart and lung. Ahmed was a second-grader at Al-Sidaak elementary school in Nablus, he will be missed by all who knew him. In loving memory of Fatime Ibrahim Zakarna, 30, and her two children, Bassem, 4, and Suhair, 3 all Palestinian. Mother and children were killed May 6, 2002 by Israeli soldiers while picking grape leaves in a field in the Kabatiya village. They leave behind Mohammed Yussef Zukarneh, husband and father, and Yasmine, daughter and age 6." These memorials were submitted by the San Francisco chapter of Arab-American Christians for Peace. The *Chronicle* refused to run the memorials, even though these deaths were covered by, and verified by, the Israeli Press (private email).

9   Daniel Pearl's wife Marianne's statement in Felicity Barringer and Douglas Jehl, "US Says Video Shows Captors Killed Reporter," *New York Times*, February 22, 2002, p. A:1.

10   Gayatri Chakravorti Spivak, *A Critique of Postcolonial Reason: Toward a History of the Vanishing Present*, Cambridge, Mass.: Harvard University Press, 1999, p. 303.

11   See Judith Butler, *Antigone's Claim: Kinship Between Life and Death*, New York: Columbia University Press, 2000.

12   Joan W. Scott, "Feminist Reverberations," unpublished paper presented at Twelfth Berkshire Conference on the History of Women, June 2002, University of Connecticut at Storrs.

13   Chandra Mohanty, "Under Western Eyes: Feminist Scholarship and Colonial Discourses," in *Third World Women and the Politics of Feminism*, ed. Chandra Mohanty, Ann Russo and Lourdes Torres, Indianapolis: Indiana University Press, 1991, pp. 61–88.

14   See also Lila Abu-Lughod, "Do Muslim Women Really Need Saving?" paper presented at symposium "Responding to War," Columbia University, February 1, 2002; and "Interview with Nermeen Shaikh," *Asia Source*, March 20, 2002, http://www.asiasource.org/news/special_reports/lila.cfm. Lila Abu-Lughod, ed., *Remaking Women: Feminism and Modernity in the Middle East*, Princeton, NJ: Princeton University Press, 1998.

15   Mahasweta Devi, *Imaginary Maps: Three Stories*, trans. and intro. Gayatri Chakravorty Spivak, New York and London: Routledge, 1995, p. 199.

16   Adriana Cavarero, *Relating Narratives: Storytelling and Selfhood*, trans. P. Kottman, New York: Routledge, 2000.

Index